Modern Tibetan Literature

and Social Change

Modern Tibetan Literature and Social Change

EDITED BY LAURAN R. HARTLEY

AND

PATRICIA SCHIAFFINI-VEDANI

FOREWORD BY MATTHEW T. KAPSTEIN

DUKE UNIVERSITY PRESS

DURHAM AND LONDON

2008

© 2008 Duke University Press
All rights reserved.
Printed in the United States of
America on acid-free paper ⊖
Designed by Amy Ruth Buchanan
Typeset in Quadraat by Tseng
Information Systems, Inc.
Library of Congress Cataloging-
in-Publication Data appear on the
last printed page of this book.

Contents

PART TWO: *Negotiating Modernities*

Foreword

During the winter of 1974–75, spent in a village not far from the border between Nepal and Tibet, the radio station that we received most clearly was the Chinese Tibetan-language transmission from Lhasa. The Sherpa household whose hospitality I enjoyed listened regularly to this broadcast during their simple evening supper, and like the local cuisine it varied little from day to day. As a condiment served alongside the potatoes, throughout that winter the broadcast treated us to a daily harangue about the evils of Confucius, Soviet revisionism, and American imperialism, with the "thieving Dalai Lama clique" thrown in for good measure. Though Tibet was just a few kilometers distant, it seemed part of an alternate universe, a black hole that would remain forever beyond reach.

Couterpoised to that inaccessible wasteland, the Tibetan refugee communities of South Asia were preoccupied above all with their survival and that of the civilization whose sole remaining custodians they felt themselves to be. Under these circumstances, the conservation of tradition took precedence over novel creation. Literary Tibetan was one of several areas in which this disposition was particularly pronounced, and with the exception of those newspapers and journals that adopted a modern, colloquial register for reporting current affairs, Tibetan writers in exile generally favored strict adherence to the classical language. Those of us engaged in the study of Tibetan civilization also saw our primary duty in the documentation of the past. Exiled Tibetans and foreign scholars in a sense thus collaborated in constructing a Tibet of memory, a Tibet that still spoke in the language of the ancient masters, revered figures such as the yogi-poet Milarepa, or the theologian Tsongkhapa. If in *The Man without Qualities* Robert Musil imagined how Saint Thomas Aquinas might emerge from the centuries into the turbulence of early-twentieth-century Vienna, in the Tibetan exile his *Gedankenexperiment* became a reality.

A mere half-decade after my sojourn among the Sherpa, as China and with it Tibet was leaving the Cultural Revolution behind, the simple bifurcation of Tibet-in-exile as a cultural repository versus "Chinese Tibet" as a cultural dead-zone began to come undone. Not only did a number of Tibetans in China eagerly embrace the prospects for revival that Deng Xiaoping's reforms permitted, but it emerged too that despite harsh repression during the Cultural Revolution years, substantial cultural resources, material and human, had survived. Indeed, even some of those who grew up during the worst of times had managed to acquire the rudiments of a Tibetan literary education. Members of this new generation, however, if educated at all, were generally educated in Chinese, and owing to this background not only were exposed to elements of Chinese literature, including classics like *The Water Margin* and modern authors like Lu Xun, but also had some familiarity with writings of Dickens, Stendahl, and Pushkin in Chinese translation. Inevitably they began to interrogate just what Tibetan literature had been in the past, and what shape it might take at present. Their theoretical reflections and creative experiments pressed at the limits of Tibetan literature in terms of both its forms and the conventions governing appropriate content. Whereas verse modeled on the refined and difficult principles of classical Sanskrit poetics had formerly dominated literary composition, its strictures were abandoned in free verse that offered a fresh, modern voice to young poets. Though the mystical trajectory of a life oriented toward Buddhist sainthood had traditionally been the preeminent subject matter of Tibetan writing, teen pregnancy and student days at the Qinghai Nationalities Institute could now figure among preferred topics. In short, just what might count as the "literary" for contemporary Tibetans became contested terrain, with all the excitement and challenge that cultural contestation can arouse. Within the newly revealed literary horizons that were now being explored, it became possible even to ask whether work written in Chinese, but by Tibetans and concerning Tibetan issues, could be counted as properly *Tibetan* literature.

The ideals of the Tibetan refugee community, seeking to conserve "authentic Tibetan culture" in a virtual state of suspended animation, also began to strain at the seams. Increasingly, memoirs and narratives came to be written in the "modern literary Tibetan" that had been formerly reserved for journalism, while for some authors English became the favored medium. In the sphere of literature, at least, the opposition of Tibet-in-exile and Tibet-in-China was now crosscut by a second division bissecting both realms: on the one hand, there were those for whom the revival and maintenance of classical literary traditions were the paramount concerns, while on the other there was the challenge of forging an original and contemporary Tibetan voice, whether in Tibet itself or abroad. The resumption of circulation between Tibetans living in India and those in China further contributed to the creative tension that was beginning to be felt, as Tibetans encountered compatriots whom they found at once familiar and foreign, and whose linguistic and literary values were not by any means consonant in all respects.

The growing complexity of the Tibetan literary world during the 1980s and since has been mirrored by important changes in the scholarship on Tibetan literature. Not only did conditions for producing Tibetan literature change radically, but so too did the conditions for its study. As it became possible to conduct research in Tibetan communities in China, younger European and American scholars began to learn Chinese as a language of Tibetological research, less frequently gravitating to Sanskrit and Indological studies, and they often pursued their investigations among Tibetans engaged in contemporary matters of concern, rather than focus on the reception of ancient traditions. At the same time, the monopoly of scholarship about Tibet by non-Tibetans was slowly weakening, as a number of Tibetan scholars became familiar with and adopted the methods and perspectives of the contemporary academy, in China and the West, to analyze their own culture and society. A significant result is that in some cases the modern Tibetan author and the scholarly interpreter of Tibetan literature might be the same person. In sum, the several sharp dichotomies that informed writing in and about Tibet just three decades ago have been rapidly blurred or reconfigured in the emerging Tibetan literary world. In its details it is a compelling story, illustrating a leap from pre- to postmodernity in a society that had no occasion to catch its breath in the space that we call the "modern." Nevertheless, outside the circle of Tibet specialists, it is a story that remains largely unknown.

This book, conceived and brought to fruition thanks to the efforts of Lauran Hartley and Patricia Schiaffini-Vedani and collaborators representing the best current scholarship on Tibetan writing, offers for the first time an outstanding guide to the Tibetan literary landscape. Among the valuable contributions found here are introductions to the leading contemporary Tibetan authors and their main works, with insightful treatments of the social background that informs them, and the problems of aesthetics and literary form that the new Tibetan writing has aroused. The perspectives opened up are generous ones, including full and nuanced reflections on contemporary Tibetan literature in its relationships to traditional poetics, as well as such characteristically modern questions as the place of Tibetan writing in the Tibetan diaspora, and in languages other than Tibetan. Mulitlingualism, magical realism, twenty-first-century Chinese urbanism — a lively engagement in these and other themes that resonate far beyond Tibet recommends this work to all who are interested not just in Tibet but in new literatures in

China and South Asia, and beyond this, to those concerned with the emergence of new literatures throughout the world. It calls us to interrogate the meaning of the literary in realms where the aleatory ruptures of the present compel radical innovation, without altogether uprooting the enduring presence of the past.

Matthew T. Kapstein
Paris, May Day 2007

Note on Transliteration

In recognition of the need to standardize the phonetic rendering of the Tibetan language and in keeping with conventions of recent publications, we have primarily employed the Simplified Phonetic Transcription of Standard Tibetan of the Tibetan and Himalayan Digital Library (THDL), created by David Germano and Nicolas Tournadre. While we have adhered to the prescription of the THDL Simplified Phonetics system to "follow the pronunciation of the Central Tibetan dialect based upon the Tibetan spoken in Lhasa," Amdo pronunciations are provided for the many contemporary authors from Tibetan areas in Qinghai and Gansu provinces of the PRC, where the Amdo dialect is spoken. These pronunciations can be found in parentheses following the standard phonetic spelling in appendix 1, "Glossary of Tibetan Spellings." We have also strayed from the THDL Simplified Phonetics system in instances where Tibetan writers outside Tibet, especially those writing in English, use a particular rendering of their name in the English language. This applies to our Tibetan contributors as well, who are widely published in English. Such names are asterisked in the appendix.

Readers may also refer to appendix 1 for the correct Tibetan spellings rendered according to the Wylie system, introduced by Turrel Wylie as "A Standard System of Tibetan Transcription" in the *Harvard Journal of Asiatic Studies* 22 (1959). The Wylie transliteration system has also been used in the text and notes for the purpose of transcribing Tibetan titles, terms, and publishing information.

Chinese names are rendered in the pinyin system of romanization. In the rare case of references to pre-1949 China, the reader should keep in mind that we have used the pinyin system anachronistically deciding to err in the favor of consistency. We have also chosen to render the names of most Sinophone writers, even if they are of Tibetan ethnicity, in Chinese pinyin, with the Tibetan name in parentheses at first mention. This will enable readers to more easily locate their works. Appendix 2, "Glossary of Chinese Characters," provides the Chinese characters for authors, place names, and technical terms found in the text.

Introduction

LAURAN R. HARTLEY AND
PATRICIA SCHIAFFINI-VEDANI

This book of essays on Tibetan comparative literature and cultural studies aims to provide a much needed critical introduction to both the recent emergence of modern literary forms by Tibetan writers and the cultural discourse accompanying and bolstered by this new literature. At the same time, unprecedented social opportunities and challenges inform the writing, contours, subject matter, and reading of these texts. The study of modern Tibetan literature thus touches on a host of related extra-literary topics: rapid but uneven socioeconomic development, minority discourse, education, diglossia, cultural identity, nationalism, diaspora, religious revival, and political vicissitudes. A comprehensive project such as this also raises other concerns, not least the risk of reifying categories still being negotiated among Tibetan writers. For instance, the very definition of Tibetan literature, that is, the set of criteria for conceiving a national literature, has been hotly contested by Tibetan writers, literary critics, and scholars since the mid-1980s. As editors, we have decided to err on the side of inclusion—not to further any particular vision of a national literature, but to provide the reader with material for more critically considering the issues at stake and the multitude of voices and perspectives encountered throughout the Tibetan literary world. The studies in this book thus cross linguistic boundaries, covering works by Tibetan authors writing in Tibetan, Chinese, and English. We have also sought to include a range of geopolitical origins, examining literary works and discourse in the People's Republic of China (PRC) and in the exile communities of India, Nepal, and the western hemisphere.

The inspirational seeds for this reader were planted in March 2001, when five of the contributors (Pema Bhum, Lauran Hartley, Matthew Kapstein, Lara Maconi, and Patricia Schiaffini) participated in the first panel on modern Tibetan literature ever organized at an annual meeting of the Association for Asian Studies. This panel was significant also in that it marked one of the first times in the United States that scholars from backgrounds as different as Tibetology, Sinology, and comparative studies convened to discuss modern literature produced by Tibetan nationals. The success of this collaboration encouraged the editors to conceive a critical volume in which leading researchers in twentieth-century Tibetan literature could provide a comprehensive introduction to this newly emerging field of study.

Although the book is organized by topic, it also follows roughly from past to present to assist the teacher, student, or general reader seeking background and critical perspectives on Tibetan literary works. Part I examines twentieth-century writings that represent early departures from premodern literary practices or closely engage religious and cultural traditions. These essays discuss early vernacular projects, the unprecedented use of Chinese by Tibetan authors, socialist literary discourse, the new literary forms of the 1980s, and religious representations. Part II addresses more recent developments, in particular the head-on engagement with modernity, development, and urbanization, as well as diglossia, magical realism, ethnic and cultural hybridity, writing in the diaspora, and the situating of Tibetan fiction in world literary studies. An extensive list of translations in western languages, including several poems, short stories, novels (excerpts), and essays discussed in these chapters, can be found in the appendices.

Before we touch upon other issues pertaining to this volume, some demographic preliminaries are in order. The administrative unit called Xizang, or the Tibet Autonomous Region (TAR), established by the Chinese Communist government in 1965, is the political entity usually called Tibet today, but it is home for just half of the 5.4 million Tibetans living in the PRC.[1] The majority reside in nomadic areas or rural villages in the Tibetan autonomous prefectures, counties, and other regions of Qinghai, Sichuan, Gansu, and Yunnan provinces. Tibetans living in Qinghai Province, for example, make up 22 percent of the provincial population and 21 percent of the total Tibetan population in the PRC.[2] These demographics and a generally looser political climate partly explain why more than 80 percent of Tibetan-language literary journals are published outside the TAR[3] and a disproportionate number of Tibetophone writers today were born in Qinghai and Gansu Provinces.[4] Other significant locales of Tibetan residence and literary production include cities housing the main nationality publishing centers: Beijing, Xining, Lanzhou, Chengdu, Lhasa, and to a lesser degree the city of Dechen in Yunnan Province. In recent years independently financed Tibetan books have also been published in Hong Kong, and a few publications from Taiwan quietly circulate among Tibetan lay and religious students. Though several important western Tibetological works can be read in Chinese translation, very little Tibetan writing published in exile ever reaches readers in the PRC.[5]

A chronological approach might suggest that the displacement by modern

Tibetan publishing centers in the People's Republic of China. Map by Creative Design Resources.

literary forms of classical Tibetan literary forms is a fait accompli. On the contrary, classical forms continue to thrive, and are now a powerful signifying alternative to the new hegemony of contemporary literary forms. Indeed, one of the most prevalent debates among Tibetan literary critics and writers concerns "the role of tradition in a modernizing society," a theme echoed in art, education, and other social sectors. The implications of modernity—literary or otherwise—are particularly interesting in Tibet, a society that has been idealized (not least by Tibetans and young Chinese intellectuals) as a Shangri-La: a mystical alternative to militarism and a consumerist world economy, a site "where all that was imagined to be good and true about the premodern had been preserved."[6] The characterization of Tibetan culture as rich in tradition but otherwise "backward" (Ch. luohou; Tib. rjes lus) is further underscored by the discourse surrounding the attribution of nationality (Ch. minzu) status in the PRC and by the use of Tibet as an "other" against which to gauge Chinese socioeconomic progress and to strengthen the very construction of a Han majority.[7] The literary strategies by which contemporary writers negotiate such weighty discourse are addressed throughout this book.

As Tsering Shakya (chapter 3) observes: "Literature has become the main arena for intellectual confrontation among competing ideas in Tibet today." The emergence of a civil society, such as that observed by scholars of China,[8] is yet to be seen in Tibetan areas of the PRC, where political restrictions on public meetings and individual or group initiatives remain the norm. Literary magazines and other forms of cultural production thus provide a proxy public forum. A disturbing testimony to the power of modern Tibetan literature to serve as a discursive site and vector of social change is the censorship still faced by writers (both Tibetophone and Sinophone) despite the greater liberalization since Mao. One of the more recent and virulent cases is the ostracism inflicted upon the Sinophone Tibetan writer Weise (Tib. Özer, b. 1966) for the views expressed in her book *Xizang biji* (Notes on Tibet), a collection of essays on Tibetan cultural and religious issues.[9] Banned in September 2003 after the success of its first edition, the book was accused of "exaggerating and beautifying the positive function of religion in social life."[10] Weise herself was criticized for her "faith and reverence for the Dalai [Lama]" and lost her promotion.[11] Though forced to attend reeducation groups to correct her "deviationist" thinking, she still refused to publicly criticize the Dalai Lama and then lost her job altogether.[12] In another case, five monks in Hainan Prefecture (Qinghai Province) were reportedly sentenced in 2004, each for two to three years in prison, after publishing "politically sensitive poems" in their monastery's newsletter.[13] Yet Tibetan writers find creative ways to negotiate their literary freedoms amid these limits on permissible discourse; these have included writing about the past, using humor and satire, and turning to magical realism (for this last topic see chapter 9).[14] Since 1980 more than ten thousand poems, short stories, essays, and novels have been published in Tibetan and another several thousand in Chinese. In both languages the range of subject matter, themes, points of view, and writing styles reveals a Tibetan literary world and intellectual milieu that has only gained in vibrancy, complexity, and self-reflection with its relative unleashing since Mao.

One striking feature of modern Tibetan literature is its late arrival on the timeline of national literatures, including the near-absence of the novel until some twenty years ago. In fact the very term "*rtsom rig*," which is everywhere used to render the concept "literature" in Tibetan today, was coined only in 1955.[15] Although Tibetan writing dates back to the Tibetan Imperial Period (seventh to ninth centuries) and countless volumes of Buddhist philosophy, history, biography, and other belles-lettres have been produced since then (in manuscript and through printing from carved woodblocks), the constructed sense of a Tibetan national literature emerged arguably in the 1980s.[16] This decade also saw the advent of western vernacular literary forms, such as free verse, the short story, and the novel. These literary lacunae are only partly explained by Tibet's remote geographic location. Recent studies have begun to expose the myth of a Tibet completely shut off from the rest of the world.[17] Lhasa in particular, and the far eastern regions of the Tibetan plateau, were cognizant of and took part in world currents by the late nineteenth century— and even earlier if we consider the experiences of religious entourages (sometimes numbering in the thousands) who made the long journey to Peking from Lhasa, Zhikatsé, and monasteries in the Sino-Tibetan border areas. Nor were foreigners (missionaries or otherwise) unknown to Tibetans in the vast lands of what was indigenously called "Greater Tibet" (Bod chen po), including the central regions of Ü and Tsang, as well as the southeastern region of Kham and the northeastern region of Amdo.[18] Not least, the trade route from Kalimpong to Darjeeling, which linked Lhasa to the hill-stations of the British Raj in northeast India and their superior schools, Tibetan aristocratic bungalows, and Tibetan-language newspaper the Tibetan Mirror (f. 1925), provided further exchange with life beyond the Tibetan plateau.[19] And yet, despite Tibet's political, economic, and religious exchanges with its Asian counterparts, few foreign literary models found their way to Tibet, with the towering exception of works originating in India.

Tibetan Belles-Lettres from the Thirteenth Century to the Twentieth

The significance of vernacular developments in twentieth-century Tibetan literature becomes clear when one considers the magnitude with which Indic-inspired conventions have dominated Tibetan classical literature since the thirteenth and fourteenth centuries. Even for Tibetans writing one hundred years ago, Indic models came not from contemporaries living south of the Himalayas but from early Indic masters in the second to eleventh centuries, or at least works attributed to these religious siddhas and monastic teachers in the Buddhist universities of northern India.[20] A range of classical Tibetan genres have their roots in India, and works typically gained authority from these origins: tantric songs of enlightenment based on Indic dohā; aphorisms and pithy advice for royalty and the general populace based on nītiśāstra; popular stories to relay religious teachings based on the jātaka tales; and biographical accounts based on other canonical texts.

This is not to deny the native Tibetan elements of the reworked versions; many Tibetan writings drew on Indic works merely for inspiration or formal conventions. Moreover, there is also a substantial and varied body of material that is notably not so much influenced by Indic models, if at all. Folksongs (e.g. mgur, glu) and oral literature, including the Gesar epic recited from one end of the plateau to the other and in communities on the far Sino-Tibetan border, have played a major role in Tibetan cultural production throughout the centuries. Even the writings of certain religious teachers and adepts contain strong colloquial elements, in terms of both content and vernacular. Writing by early Kadampa teachers such as Geshé Potoba (1031–1105), the biography of the eleventh-century *yogin* Milarepa written by Tsangnyön Heruka (1452/3–1507/8), the "love songs" of the sixth Dalai Lama (1683–1706), and the autobiography of the second Zhapkar (Shabkar) Rinpoché (1781–1851), to name just a few instances, all revel in the everyday. Zhapkar relays humorous anecdotes about greed among the wealthy or religious, sheep who protest their own slaughter for a visiting lama, and yak dung. Likewise, Tibetan landscapes can be the subject of praise verse with no particularly didactic purpose. Janet Gyatso has discussed how one genre in particular opens the possibility for idiosyncratic, individualistic, and realistic (not to mention imaginal and magical) self-expression: autobiography and diary writing.[21] With countless instances of Tibetan autobiographical and biographical writing, dating back to the fifteenth century, it is not surprising that contemporary lay writing both inside and outside Tibet should have been characterized by an explosion of memoirs and other autobiographical works.[22]

Though home for most classical writers was a monastery, religious life was not the sole subject of their literary labors. And as observed by Cabezón and Jackson (1996), "the written tradition was preceded by a well-developed oral tradition that included not only the usual repertoire of epic poetry, folk songs, and legendary narratives, but also material on such areas as law and politics."[23] Contemporary writers have drawn for literary and filmmaking inspiration on such colloquial sources (Milarepa, Zhapkar, folksongs, etc.), and even stories from Tibet's imperial past. Further study of the non-Indic elements in traditional Tibetan literature would surely aid our appreciation of pre-modern and contemporary Tibetan literature.[24]

To the degree that belles-lettres penned by teachers in the most powerful religious institutions, especially the Gelukpa and Sakya schools, were strongly influenced by Indic *kāvya* theory, an examination of these writing styles and rhetorical conventions is also informative for identifying both ruptures and returns in the work of contemporary writers. In the tongue-in-cheek summary of E. Gene Smith, "Poetics in Tibet begins and ends with the *Kāvyādarśa* of Daṇḍin,"[25] Daṇḍin (late 7th c.),[26] who lived in the region of Tamil but wrote in Sanskrit, was a relatively late contributor to the kāvya tradition, which first established itself as a special literary style among Sanskrit and local Prakrit writers in India from 500 to 100 BCE.[27] The *Kāvyādarśa* taught rhetorical and metaphorical conventions to elicit through writing the range of emotions that an actor might prompt on stage. Daṇḍin acknowledged three classes of kāvya: verse (Tib. *tshigs bcad*, Skt. *padya*), prose (Tib. *lhug*, Skt. *gadya*), and mixed prose and verse (Tib. *tshig bcad lhug spel ma*, Skt. *campū*).[28] Kāvya theory as transmitted in Tibet from the thirteenth century maintained this threefold classification.[29]

The study of classical poetry (Tib. *snyan ngag*) as derived from Daṇḍin's treatise and subsequently reinterpreted by Tibetan and Mongolian scholars came to be regarded in Tibet as one of the five minor sciences (*rig gnas chung ba lnga*), and three of the four remaining minor sciences dealt with topics closely related to *snyan ngag*: metrics (*sdeb sbyor*), synonymy (*mngon brjod*), and dramaturgy (*zlos gar*).[30] By the fourteenth century, as noted by Leonard van der Kuijp, *snyan ngag* was regularly studied in the Tibetan monastic curriculum,[31] and knowledge of metrics and synonymy became requisite for a religious or lay man of letters.

The foundation of Indic kāvya theory is derived "through the practical experience of actors in the ancient Indian theatre"[32] and rests on two interrelated concepts: the *rasa* (Tib. *nyams*) and the *sthāyibhāva* (Tib. *'gyur*). The term "*rasa*" could be glossed several ways but most literally means "taste." In poetics it refers to the aesthetic experience enjoyed by the audience or reader.[33] The eight types of aesthetic experience (*nyams*)—sensitive, comic, compassionate, furious, heroic, apprehensive, horrific, marvelous—correspond to eight basic emotions (*'gyur ba*)—love, humor, grief, anger, energy, fear, disgust, astonishment.[34] The audience or reader "tastes" the emotion (e.g. love) and has an aesthetic experience (e.g. sensitivity). In other words, a display or expression of love on stage or in a poem elicits the experience of sensitivity. To evoke these emotions through writing, the poet relies on ornamental poetic figures (Tib. *rgyan*, Skt. *alaṅkāra*), which are based on either phonological considerations (*sgra rgyan*) or semantic considerations (*don rgyan*).[35] One of the peculiarities of Daṇḍin's theory was his outline of ten qualities (Tib. *yon tan*, Skt. *guṇa*) which were to be precisely balanced in fine writing: mellifluent, clear, even, pleasant, delicate, succinct, elevated, weighty, graceful, and profound.[36] The qualities of well-composed poetry as explained in most Tibetan commentaries reflect Daṇḍin's prescription. The faults to be avoided or corrected include irrelevant words, internal contradictions, repetitiveness, uncertainty or hesitation, weak grammar, and poor logic.[37]

But knowledge of kāvya theory was not enough to ensure beautiful writing, even by classical Tibetan standards. The ideals of literary learning laid down by Sakya Paṇḍita Künga Gyentsen (1182–1251) in his curriculum *The Entrance Gate for the Wise*[38] insisted on the study of Daṇḍin's treatise, but also mastery of metrics and synonymy.[39] This tripartite curriculum, as characterized by Matthew Kapstein (2003), "came to define, for later generations, a paradigm of classical learning."[40] The most common form of synonymy in Tibetan poetry is the use of kennings (compound expressions with metaphorical meanings), such as substituting "sky-elephant" (*nam mkha'i glang po*) for the word "cloud," or "quill of the clouds" (*sprin gyi myu gu*) for the word "river." For the educated contemporary Tibetan reader, the synonyms and other rhetorical devices employed in classical Tibetan poetry would remain opaque without tutored study. The written Tibetan language thus often strayed far from the colloquial, and this situation maintained itself well into the twentieth century.

The "New Tibetan Literature"

Only with the founding of Tibetan-language literary magazines in 1980 and 1981 did a new corps of secularly educated young Tibetans find inspiration to begin experimenting with literary forms. Even then, young writers typically turned to folktales, folksongs, or classical verse for literary models—works revived after the Cultural Revolution (1966–76). The first Tibetan free-verse poem, "Waterfall of Youth" (1983), for example, draws heavily on kāvya conventions derived from Sanskrit, especially for its metaphors (see chapter 4). A second pool of inspiration was the new writings of Chinese authors, and scattered verses and short stories by Tibetans writing in Chinese. The latter were published in the Chinese-language magazine *Xizang wenyi* (Literature and arts from Tibet), founded in Lhasa in 1977 and soon renamed *Xizang wenxue* (Literature from Tibet). Indeed, from 1950 to 1980 the bulk of new literary works by Tibetan authors was written in Chinese, as discussed by Yangdon Dhondup in chapter 2. These writings consisted primarily of poems, but also short stories and a few short novels.

Though Daṇḍin himself wrote a great deal of prose, original works of prose fiction were rare in the history of Tibetan belles-lettres; those that did exist were mostly modeled after Indic works.[41] One of the earliest examples of modern Tibetan fiction, a novella entitled *Yeshé Lhamo and Blacksmith Topgyel* (1959), broke with that convention but largely drew its plot from a Tibetan folk story.[42] The first full-length modern Tibetan novel, *Kelzang Metok* (1980), was initially published in Chinese and only two years later in Tibetan.[43] Written by a former member of the People's Liberation Army, it pays tribute to the social transformations enabled by the Chinese "liberation" of Tibet as seen in the life of its young protagonist, after whom the book is titled. The novel *Crown Turquoise* (1985), despite its formulaic scenes of suffering under Tibetan feudal lords in the "Old Society," earned wide readership for its depiction of romantic love and the trials of an aristocratic family in pre-communist Tibet. More recently, the acclaimed novel *The Secret Tale of the Tesur House* (written by a Tibetan aristocrat educated in India and published serially from 1994 to 1996) has also depicted the Old Society, but with fewer ideological messages.[44] Today Tibetophone novels still total fewer than two dozen, but cover a wider range of periods and themes. Ranging from historical realism to magical realism, Tibetan novels in Chinese also tend to find inspiration in Tibet's past. Some of the best examples are the award-winning novels *Wu xingbie de shen* (A god without gender, 1994), by Yangzhen (Tib. Yangdrön, b. 1963), and *Taiyang Buluo* (The clan of the sun, 1998), by Meizhuo (Tib. Medrön, b. 1966).[45] Far from criticizing the old Tibet to promote communism, as happened in the early Sinophone Tibetan novels of the 1950s, the acclaimed female authors of these works humanize and demystify pre-communist Tibet's past to reinforce the importance of Tibetan culture, ways of life, and traditions. A totally different use of Tibet's history is that of the magical realistic novels *Saodong de Xiangbala* (Turbulent Shambala) and *Chen'ai luoding* (Red poppies), by Tashi Dawa and Alai (see chapters 9 and 10).[46] They recreate a chaotic "past" where the alive turn out to be dead and the idiots turn out to be sane, as a means to reflect on the surreal and dislocated elements of Tibet's present.

Tibetan short stories began to proliferate by the mid-1980s, following the lead of Döndrup Gyel (1953–85), a maverick writer from Amdo who took his own life at the age of thirty-two.[47] Translations (via Chinese) of stories by western writers, such as Chekhov, de Maupassant, O. Henry, and Faulkner, as well as Gabriel García Márquez and Borges, were further inspiration during these early years. But Tibetan critics soon argued that "authentic" Tibetan literature must smell of *tsampa* (roasted barley flour), an opinion echoed by the Chinese editors of *Literature from Tibet*, who sought Tibetan literary works "full of the scent of yak butter tea."[48] Such prescriptions continued well into the 1990s and in Tibetan literary practice resulted in a heightened role for the nomad and a clear preference for traditional settings. Stories were typically set in the grasslands or a remote village, rarely the town or city. Yet the majority of Tibetophone writers were living as either students or teachers at minority colleges in cities throughout the PRC: Central Nationalities Institute (Beijing), Northwest Nationalities Institute (Lanzhou), Qinghai Nationalities Institute (Xining), Southwest Nationalities Institute (Chengdu), and Tibet University (Lhasa). They were writing, albeit from minority enclaves, in urban areas.

Campus of Qinghai Nationalities University (formerly Institute) in the provincial capital, Xining. While the vast majority of Tibetan writers in the 1980s were students at this and other "minority institutes" in Beijing, Lanzhou, Lhasa, and Chengdu, writers' origins have been more diverse since the late 1990s. Photo by Riika Virtanen.

Some 80 percent of the Tibetan population in the PRC continues to live a nomadic or rural life. Photo by Lauran Hartley.

This literary fixation on the grassland in the face of rapid development marks a prevailing emotional and literary response, what might be termed "anticipatory nostalgia," among Tibetan intellectuals. David Der-wei Wang (1992) identifies this trend in the context of modern Chinese literature: "In contrast to the conventional theme of nostalgia, which presupposes the loss of the homeland or the beloved, anticipatory nostalgia works only so long as its endearing object still lingers on, contained in the hypothetical *if*."[49] So far, nomadic and semi-nomadic lifestyles have been maintained along-side urban growth. In contemporary Tibetan literature the juxtaposition of land and cityscapes (see chapter 11) draws on the power of place or spatial dimensions to convey temporal concerns: "The passage of time may be more concretely known or experienced through the physical changes in places . . . A geographically remote place awakens the memory of remote times."[50] For this reason urban space and development figure more prominently only in recent Tibetophone literature, and even then often to point to the past.

In the same way that pastoral scenes contribute to a repertoire of tradi-tional motifs, descriptions of Tibetan customs and habits also speak to a dis-tinct Tibetan culture and identity. This tendency is more pronounced among Sinophone Tibetan writers who are apt to *describe* cultural customs for a Chi-nese reader. (Tibetophone writers know that their audience is by and large restricted to Tibetan readers.) Writers have expressed to us that one reason to write about the past is that the present is too sensitive.[51] Another motiva-tion may be to reclaim a perceived golden age when Tibetans were masters of their own destiny, as evident in the growth of Tibetan "historical fiction" since 1995.[52] But with some three thousand short stories in Tibetan alone[53] and dozens of anthologies and collections of short stories by Tibetan writers now available in both Tibetan and Chinese, it is no longer possible to make general statements about their literary content. One conclusion that can be drawn, however, is that the state of Tibetan fiction, at least in terms of the short story, has reached an unprecedented level of quality and variation.

It is poetry, however, that dominated the Tibetan literary output of the early 1980s and 1990s. One reason for this abundance is that language teach-ers in Tibetan schools often encourage students, from as early as middle school, to practice writing poetry as part of their studies in Tibetan litera-ture. The phenomenon has been gently lampooned by the poet Ju Kelzang (see chapter 5): with a wide range of quality, the number of poems submitted annually to any leading Tibetan literary magazine can total in the thousands. Since the publication in 1983 of the first modern Tibetan free-verse poem, "Waterfall of Youth" by Döndrup Gyel, free verse has grown in popularity and now surpasses the production of metric verse, at least in quantity. In the past decade, as younger monks have entered the modern literary foray, many have beautifully employed kāvya forms to express contemporary concerns.

The poetic renaissance in Tibet since the Cultural Revolution raises the question of how writers relate themselves to Tibetan kāvya today and reveals the degree to which modern literary discourse represents an internal struggle among Tibetan intellectuals to negotiate the criteria informing literary craft and other forms of cultural production.[54] Many Tibetan scholars have used kāvya theory or combined it with modern literary theory (usually Marxist) to evaluate pre-kāvya writing, such as ancient mgur found at Dunhuang, as well as modern literature.[55] Other critics have rejected the kāvya model altogether, arguing that it represents an Indic tradition which for several centuries led Tibetan literature far from its roots. Still others argue for a wholly new literary path. In this way, as Kapstein observes, "the formation over many centuries of a culturally valued indianité in Tibetan literature . . . has been at once reaffirmed and contested in contemporary Tibet."[56] As Tibetan writers seek to carve out a unique literary space, they must distinguish themselves vis-à-vis two fronts—the so-called Indianization of their ancestral writing and the Sinocentric or western models prevailing in the Chinese literary world. Yet the realm of comparison is daunting. After juxtaposing their oeuvre of modern literary works in the first instance to Chinese literature and their own classical tradition, and then again to the whole of world literature, some contemporary Tibetan writers express a sense of marginality bordering on despair.

Writing from the Margins

Despite centuries of Tibetan literary production and highly publicized efforts by the Chinese Communist Party (CCP) since the 1950s to promote universal education in Tibet, illiteracy rates in Tibetan areas remain shockingly high. As of 2005 about 45 percent of the population aged fifteen and over in the Tibet Autonomous Region was illiterate, compared with a national average of 11 percent.[57] Tibetan illiteracy among the young may be even higher than reported statistics. According to findings by Kolås and Thowsen (2005), Chinese government documents "give widely disparate figures" for any single statistic and "officials tend to exaggerate enrollment rates . . . and the number of bilingual schools."[58] In one prefecture of Qinghai Province, for example, as many as 70 percent of young and middle-aged Tibetans were illiterate.[59] In Gannan Tibetan Autonomous Prefecture only 34 percent of schools for Tibetans actually teach in Tibetan; the primary language of instruction is Chinese.[60] All indicators point to a relatively small population of potential readers for Tibetan literary works and an even smaller pool of potential writers. Indeed our fieldwork suggests that the primary consumers of Tibetan literature are lay students, monks, and teachers, many of whom have tried their own hand at writing.

The ranks of women writing in Tibetan are even more limited, both in Tibet and in the diaspora. A survey of Tibetophone literary journals based in the PRC reveals that only one out of twenty contributions is by a woman, and the vast majority of these are poems—for reasons yet to be explored in current scholarship. Two of the most prominent female poets, Chakmo Tso (b. 1968) and Zungchuk Kyi (b. 1971), escaped to India several years ago, but continue to write in exile. The number of Tibetan women publishing in Chinese is proportionately greater, and includes Weise (b. 1966), Meizhuo (b. 1966), and Yangzhen (b. 1963), all of whom were highly acclaimed by the 1990s, and emerging young female authors like Ge Yang (b. 1972).

Given the growing importance of a Chinese-medium education to secure employment,[61] and cuts in government subsidies for education and publishing in an increasingly privatized economy, one might have expected the level of Tibetophone cultural production to fall after the renaissance experienced in the 1980s and early 1990s. There are promising signs, however, that the hard-won successes of Tibetan intellectuals in preserving and continuing to develop their culture over the past two decades have taken firm hold. Some one hundred Tibetan-language journals are now being published in the PRC. The majority of these focus on literature and are privately funded. One of the most startling developments has been the reemergence of monasteries as active centers of literary production: the turn of the millennium saw the founding of several monastic journals in Amdo, in part to outline their vision of Tibetan society in the twenty-first century. Whether for lack of funding or because of political pressure, literary journals issued by monasteries in Lhasa or elsewhere in the TAR were just starting to appear as this book went to press. Likewise, privately funded school magazines and local or county-level journals also remain scarce in central Tibet, despite their widespread presence in Tibetan areas outside the TAR. While the print runs of the two most widely read literary journals, Bod kyi rtsom rig sgyu rtsal (Tibetan art and literature), published in Lhasa, and Sbrang char (Light rain), published in Xining, total only seven thousand copies,[62] their influence far exceeds their immediate readership. For twenty years they have been virtual beacons of possibility, motivating writers, scholars, and other would-be publishers alike.

Engaging Traditions

Part I of this book, "Engaging Traditions," opens with a look at literary developments in the early twentieth century that laid the groundwork for the dramatic transformation of Tibetan literature in later decades. Lauran Hartley (chapter 1) singles out Gendün Chömpel (1903–51), one of the most important cultural icons of modern Tibet because of his heterodox writings and literary views. By all accounts he was ahead of his time. Not a visionary loner, he was representative of a small group of progressive intellectuals in Lhasa who sought change. Like many Tibetan aristocrats, the Amdo monk Gendün Chömpel was also inspired by his travels south of the Himalayas. Chapter 1 contrasts his writing with the poems of traditionally trained scholars employed by the new Communist government in the 1950s. This chapter challenges the assumption that all publishing during this decade was politically driven; rather, classical literary projects initiated by these scholars were an important thread of transmission for Tibetan writers in the 1980s — but only after two decades of devastating repression.

The imprisonment of senior Tibetan scholars began with the "Democratic Reforms" launched in Amdo and Kham in 1957,[63] and intensified after the occupation of Lhasa and central Tibet in 1959. Tibetan-language publications waned and came to a standstill during the Cultural Revolution (1966–76), with one exception: *The Quotations of Chairman Mao*. As one Tibetan vanguard notes in his autobiography, "People could criticize Tibetan, they could say that Tibetan language mustn't be used, they could even stop Tibetan language. But, they couldn't stop the translation of Mao's *Red Book*."[64] In most areas this was the sole text to sustain Tibetan literacy until the loosening of party policy at the Third Plenary Session of the Eleventh Party Congress in 1978. This meeting, which marked the rise to power of the reform-minded Deng Xiaoping, heralded a cultural revival, albeit in the pursuit of the Four Modernizations. Tibetan intellectuals were generally enthusiastic, but the pool of Tibetan-literate writers was minuscule. A true upswing in Tibetophone publications took several years to get under way.

Sinophone Tibetan writers, by contrast, had remained active during the revolutionary years. Yangdon Dhondup's "Roar of the Snow Lion: Tibetan Poetry in Chinese" (chapter 2) explores the historical circumstances of the 1930s which gave rise to a new corps of young Tibetans educated in Chinese. The works of these poets, who were generally from poor families in eastern Tibet, would later inspire Tibetans writing in Tibetan. Chapter 2 focuses on Yidan Cairang (Tib. Yidam Tsering), who despite having a background similar to that of other Sinophone writers born in the 1930s, surpassed them by the literary quality of his works and his influence in both Sinophone and Tibeto-phone literatures. Even in the midst of revolutionary fervor he exhibited a sensitivity and insight that would lead him to endure as one of the most respected and beloved Tibetan writers until his death in 2004. Yangdon Dhondup also chronicles the rise of individualism in the poems of later Sinophone Tibetan poets, but notes that the portrayal of self is very much embedded in a Tibetan context, with frequent references to nationality (mi rigs).

Tsering Shakya's "The Development of Modern Tibetan Literature in the PRC in the 1980s" (chapter 3) first outlines the political and ideological forces introduced in Tibet during the 1950s, not only for the "immediate and striking impact" that the changes had on Tibetan language, but for the "dislocation of identity and traditional epistemology" triggered by colonialism. He then traces the rise of new literary forms, delineating a range of influences: Tibetan folk tradition and Indic kāvya in the early Communist period, Chinese short story writing in the years immediately following Mao, print journalism, party dictates for a realist literary style, and Chinese "scar literature" (Ch. shanghen wenxue), which recounted the tragic excesses of the Cultural Revolution. While Communist ideology held sway in the few literary experiments of the 1950s and Tibetan poems and fiction in the early 1980s, literary subject matter eventually diversified. Nevertheless, Shakya argues, a realist approach continued to dominate Tibetophone literature, even into the 1990s. His contrast of the contemporary Tibetan novel with what he terms the "romance" genre of traditional Tibetan narrative (heroic accounts of Gesar, the biographical tradition, and the eighteenth-century precursor to the modern Tibetan novel Tale of the Incomparable Youth)[65] offers a valuable analysis of several landmark texts.

While Shakya highlights Döndrup Gyel's role as a champion of progress, Nancy Lin (chapter 4) draws on her work in Sanskrit studies to follow the writer's ongoing engagement with Tibetan literary tradition or classical models. She deftly resolves the seeming inconsistency of Döndrup Gyel's status as a literary "maverick" and his "obsession with the Rama story cycle." Drawing on ample textual evidence, she advances the hypothesis that Döndrup Gyel's reworking of the Ramayana represented "part of an ambitious project to revive Tibetan literature in the wake of the Cultural Revolution." For Döndrup Gyel, the Indic-derived Ramayana was a vehicle through which he could "advance a new indigenous model of poetry." Her argument is further bolstered by citations from various writings by Döndrup Gyel concerning his views on literary theory.

Many of the earliest pioneer poets—in particular Döndrup Gyel, Ju Kelzang, and Jangbu—in turn inspired their friends and the next generation.

This fueled the flourishing of the "New Poetry," which Pema Bhum (chapter 5) describes in "Heartbeat of a New Generation" as above all a "psychological liberation," both from the rigid and largely Buddhist-inspired prescriptions for content in classical poetry and from the hollow ideological platitudes of eulogies to the Party in the early 1980s. While a poem written in classical verse could conceivably be "new" if it addressed contemporary subject matter and used more vernacular language, in practice the sense of New Poetry was generally conflated with free verse. Pema Bhum's article, first written in Tibetan in 1991 and later published in English in *Lungta*, the groundbreaking journal of the Amnye Machen Institute (Dharamsala), is reprinted here in its entirety. The article spurred a heated debate among Tibetans in exile, mainly by readers who took issue with Pema Bhum's argument that Buddhism and Communism and classical forms had all failed the Tibetan nation and intellectuals. The author also registers strong disappointment in the failure of exile scholars to recognize or approve this development. One issue of the independent exile magazine *New Moon* (Zla gsar) was devoted to an interview with Pema Bhum regarding the controversy and accompanying death threats. We have asked Pema Bhum to revisit his article and to reflect on more recent developments among Tibetan poets. His remarks on the original article and on pennames, women, and monastic writers, and Tibetan literary websites compose chapter 6.

Françoise Robin (chapter 7) also explores the representation of religion, but in Tibetan-medium fiction. She identifies three general attitudes: radical criticism, selective rationalism, and neutral to positive reappraisal. Throughout the course of her historical survey she observes how these same views surfaced in other debates regarding the role of traditions in a modernizing society, for example in art and philosophy. Based on her reading of a vast number of short stories and novellas, she concludes that an anticlerical trend characterized Tibetan-medium fiction in the 1980s, a tendency that must be placed in the context of the campaign of the Four Modernizations.[66] Above all, writers were engaged in denouncing superstition, corruption, and blind faith. Greater nuance is expressed by the late 1990s, when the views of what Robin calls the "selective rationalists" tend to dominate. These writers differentiate between superstition and what they view as commendable religious practices, such as compassion, karma, and genuine meditation. Robin notes how this rationalist approach shares certain "overlap" with official views on appropriate religious practices. However, she argues, broader rationalist trends among Tibetan intellectuals are not merely parroting party policy. Rather, faced with "the systematic denigration" of religion and Tibetan culture, authors and other intellectuals evince a "growing [intellectual] autonomy." More recently, stories have begun to offer a neutral or even positive treatment of religion and religious figures. Some authors treat the very category of "backwardness" with irony. Robin concludes that religion and its representation in Tibetan literature are vehicles through which "the nationality's self-representation and agency is negotiated."[67]

Engaging Modernities

The chapters in Part II address literary developments that engage modernity on its own terms, more so than they engage tradition through the lens of modernity. Tibetan experiences of modernity through the medium of literature are now negotiated and inscripted in two languages in the PRC. Lara Maconi's essay (chapter 8) explores the historical and sociopolitical implications of Tibet's diglossic coexistence of literatures written in Chinese and Tibetan, both by Tibetan writers. By presenting the different discursive positions among Tibetan intellectuals regarding the use of these two languages for literary purposes, Maconi exposes an issue that is at the core of political and ethnic tensions in Chinese-occupied Tibet. She starts by reminding us that the process of political domination begins with language. The Chinese central government has imposed Chinese as the official language in Tibet and has also attempted to "modernize" the Tibetan language to better serve Chinese socialist needs. This process has resulted in the development of two largely separate literary worlds among Tibetan writers, one Tibetophone and the other Sinophone. In the context of this literary diglossia, Maconi writes, "the discussion of questions of language is never a neutral matter for the Tibetan writer." She reinforces this idea by providing an in-depth analysis of the exacerbated debate (which has maintained currency since the 1980s) on whether Sinophone literature should be considered Tibetan literature—a debate that for many Tibetan intellectuals has become an issue of defining Tibetan national identity and ensuring Tibetan cultural survival.

The chapters by Patricia Schiaffini (chapter 9) and Howard Choy (chapter 10) deal more closely with Sinophone Tibetan literature by exploring the literary and personal realms of two of its more famous writers, Zhaxi Dawa (Tashi Dawa) and Alai. Schiaffini reconsiders Zhaxi Dawa's use of magical realism, which previous scholarship attributed to the influence of Gabriel García Márquez in light of his ethnically and culturally hybrid identity. As Schiaffini explains, Zhaxi Dawa, like many other magical realist writers around the world, rediscovers his culture after being educated in a foreign land. It is this Han-educated sensibility that allows him to see and describe the magic he sees in Tibet. But more than a way to perceive Tibet, magical realism has become for Zhaxi Dawa a safe language in which to express the dislocated and absurd reality of Tibet's colonial present. Amid the heated debates over his Tibetanness, Zhaxi Dawa has also found in magical realism a way to transcend his contested hybridity and join the international postcolonial literary scene.

Choy's analysis of Alai's novel *Chen'ai luoding* (translated into English as *Red Poppies*) takes us to Aba (Tib. Ngaba), a region that Choy defines as being at "the interstices of the geological and cultural planes between the so-called Xizang and China's hinterland." But as Choy elucidates, that culturally hybrid region where Chinese and Tibetans have historically cohabited also metaphorically describes Sinophone Tibetan writers: marginal to the centers, syncretic, and always forced to define their identity. Through the figure of the equally hybrid protagonist—half-Chinese and half-Tibetan, considered an imbecile and yet wiser than anyone else around—Choy speculates on the author's intention to destabilize pure Tibetanness and to demand that we address him by his multiple positions.

The primarily realist Tibetophone stories examined by Riika Virtanen (chapter 11) engage modernity not through magical realism or fantasy but by portraying the day-to-day conflicts that arise when science and progress confront local faith practices and mores. Her chapter analyzes stories by Döndrup Gyel, Tenpa Yargyé, Anyön Trashi Döndrup, and Pema Tseten, which are concerned with economic development, modernization, and urbanization vis-à-vis Tibetan traditional culture and ways of life. Virtanen unveils a deliberate juxtaposition of modern and traditional elements as a reflection of the contradictions inherent in present-day Tibetan society. Two antagonistic spaces become signifiers for tradition and modernity: the Sinicized town, which evokes feelings of alienation, displacement, and nostalgia; and the grasslands, which become the repository of Tibetan culture and beliefs. Development is sometimes welcomed as renewal, and sometimes feared as the end of traditional lifestyles. But as Virtanen points out, the authors' belief in education as the means for progress and Tibetan language literacy as the key to cultural preservation prevails over the clashes, contradictions, and negotiations between the old and the new portrayed in their works.

Some younger Tibetophone writers, however, inspired by translations of western poetry and the magical realist and surreal writing of Sinophone writers such as Zhaxi Dawa, have rallied for the value and "prerogative" of writing obscure poetry.[68] They constitute a small modernist or even postmodernist movement among Tibetan writers, and represent a later phase of modern Tibetan literary developments as outlined by Sangye Gyatso in chapter 12. Sangye Gyatso, a well-known poet who publishes under the name

Gangzhün, participated in the debate, arguing largely against the value of obscure (*go rgyu med pa*) or meaningless (*brjod bya med pa*) poetry.[69] Here he dons his scholarly cap to offer a timeline of modern Tibetan literature, including the emergence of modernist cliques. His chapter focuses on the development of literary groups or cohorts in the northeastern region of Amdo. To the best of our knowledge, this phenomenon does not have a literary equivalent in Lhasa, despite an active "salon" life among Sinophone intellectuals in the mid-1980s and the recent formation of artist collectives.

Tibetan writers in the diaspora also face issues of identity, diglossia, and displacement. The very existence of Tibetan language in exiled communities is threatened by the economic leverage to be gained by learning English or the challenges of applying a Tibetan-language education. One Tibetan writer has recently opined: "We have seen the beginnings of a generation that cannot use Tibetan to save its life."[70] However, the establishment of several Tibetophone magazines in India, Nepal, and the United States since 1990 may indicate an improvement in this situation. The founders of most of these literary magazines are writers who left the PRC fairly recently. For example, several major Tibetophone periodicals published in Dharamsala, including the independent paper *Dmangs gtso* (Democracy, f. 1990), its successor *Bod kyi dus 'bab* (Tibet times, f. 1996), and the literary journal *Ljang gzhon* (Young shoots, f. 1990), were all launched by recent arrivals, the majority from Amdo.

The pool of writers in the diaspora is understandably smaller. After the escape in 1959 of the fourteenth Dalai Lama, some 100,000 Tibetans—a very small proportion of the population—also left for life in exile, primarily in Nepal and India. As Hortsang Jigme (chapter 13) describes it, most thought that the exile would be temporary, until control of their homeland was regained. In malaria-infested environs and makeshift living structures, the general populace had little chance to think about creating a national literature. Aristocrats, many of whom had second or family homes in Kalimpong or Darjeeling to which they could flee, might have had more leisure time, but the task of rebuilding institutions and infrastructure—monasteries, schools, hospitals, government offices, etc.—consumed the energies of many of those concerned. When it came to culture, much of the discussion in exile centered on preservation and less on development. As Hortsang Jigme demonstrates, the late emergence of modern literary forms in Tibetan was "not a spontaneous development or evolution." Rather, it was largely inspired by the writing projects launched when a second generation of Tibetans started leaving Tibet in the late 1980s and sought to establish in India cultural forms that they had enjoyed in the PRC (newspapers, literary magazines, etc.) but with a freedom of expression previously unknown.

Indigenous literary developments in exile have been seen primarily in English, ever since the founding of the first English literary journal, *Young Tibet* (later renamed *Lotus Fields*), in Delhi in 1977. While nationalist and political themes still characterize the bulk of Anglophone exile writing, a few select Tibetan writers are perfecting the craft. One such author is a former guerrilla fighter and director of the Tibetan Institute of Performing Arts, Jamyang Norbu. Although he was an early contributor to *Lotus Fields*, he has become more widely known since the publication of his novel *The Mandala of Sherlock Holmes* (1999), which in 2000 won the prestigious Crossword Prize for English Literature. Steven Venturino (chapter 14) takes this novel, which "investigates the murder of people and culture, and the theft of history and identity," as a starting point to examine some of the limitations of theories of postmodernity and postcoloniality in understanding modern Tibetan literature. As he reminds us, Tibetan literature struggles to define itself outside the imposed category of "minorities (Chinese) literature" or the adoption of diaspora Tibetan writing into other national literatures such as Indian, American, French, or German. It is this transnationality of Tibetan literature that supplements notions of "international postmodernism" by calling attention to the cross-border, rather than intrastate, nature of literary exchange. Postmodernism and postcolonialism can only be effective tools for the study of Tibetan literature, Venturino concludes, if we revisit their implicit assumptions of national identity, pay attention to nonwestern forms of colonialism, and read Tibetan literature in the context of Tibetan history and politics.

· · · · ·

The flourishing of literary activity in the PRC, such as we have described, was almost wholly funded from Chinese government coffers in the 1980s and early 1990s. And yet by no means were the writers who published in official journals mere mouthpieces for the CCP, as might have been claimed during the years under Chairman Mao. By 1995, however, smaller journals saw signs that official funding might be withdrawn. Tibetan publications soon faced the same predicament as their Chinese counterpart publications across the PRC: increasing privatization, decreased official funding, and pressure to turn a profit. Coupled with heavy economic incentives for Tibetans to choose a Chinese-medium education, a rational-choice model of group behavior would predict the withering of Tibetan literary production. And yet, despite economic and political pressures, Tibet is experiencing a virtual cultural renaissance.

The creative energy that launched the "Tibetan New Literature" in the 1980s and 1990s can now be seen in other areas of Tibetan culture: religious revival, scholarship, production of music DVDs and concerts, computer programming, internet publishing, blogs and web-based discussion groups, Chinese-Tibetan translation, the dubbing of films in both Lhasa and Amdo dialects, video documentary, and most recently art film. A significant development in Tibetan literary life since the late 1990s is that Tibetan writers have started to apply their talents to this wider range of cultural endeavors.[71] Given low literacy rates in Tibet, some of these forms (e.g. song lyrics or music videos) will reach a far wider audience than poems published in literary journals, for example. And yet for the first time ever, music videos are now allowed to have Tibetan-language subtitles.[72] Not least, foreign funding has also encouraged projects to increase Tibetan literacy rates.

Are these simply the signs of technological advance and the widening of the literary "public forum" to other media? The concentration of these projects outside the TAR suggests that greater political leniency is a contributing factor. But scientific and political advances do not explain the emphasis on production *in Tibetan*. We would argue that in a society whose identity is largely tied to maintaining a distinct religion, culture, and language, the acts of writing, reading, singing, performing, and translating in Tibetan become acts of cultural survival, a public reaffirmation of cultural identity and pride. In the 1980s a Tibetan education assured graduates of a job in a school, nationality institute, or publishing office. As overall education levels improve, however, and seats at these institutions become more competitive, more and more families are choosing to educate their children at Chinese-medium schools. But job competition is stiff in "the real world" of Sinophone society and glass ceilings abound, as they do elsewhere in the world for minority populations. To this degree, social advance and notoriety are doubly hard to achieve. While the 6.4 million Tibetans living in the PRC may not have a common dialect, they do largely have a common written language, religion, and culture. Music has proved to be a strong uniting factor, sometimes with extramusical results. In 2004, for example, in the middle of a grasslands concert held in Gannan Prefecture, representatives from two counties that had been feuding for centuries signed an agreement for cooperation. The lyrics and proceedings were all subtitled in Tibetan.

The field of literature has also been a ground for transcending political and linguistic barriers. In 2005 an anthology of Tibetan women's poetry was published in the PRC with funding from the United States. The volume contains works by Tibetan women poets living in various Tibetan regions of the PRC, as well as the United States and India.[73] In the same spirit, it is our wish that this book—fruit of the close collaboration between Tibet and China specialists who not too long ago still dwelled in separate intellectual and academic worlds — may also provide fertile ground for a continuing discussion of these issues. Our final goal is to stir readers to seek out Tibetan writing, whether in translation or in their Tibetan, Chinese, and English originals. To facilitate further reading in Tibetan literature, we have included in the appendices a heretofore unavailable bibliography of modern Tibetan literary works in translation.

Since this book's inception in 2001, public interest in contemporary Tibetan literature has only grown, and courses in Tibetan literature have newly been offered at major universities. In many ways we feel that this is a book whose time has finally come. We are grateful above all to the patience of the contributors and our families, who supported this endeavor and urged us to the finish line. We also thank Miriam Angress and Fred Kameny, our editors at Duke University Press, as well as Matthew Kapstein for his engaging foreword, which insightfully sketches the emergence of an exciting new field of study.

Notes

1. *Zhongguo renkou tongji nianjian* 2005. The official Tibetan population in the TAR is 2.52 million (in 2004). *Xizang tongji nianjian* 2005, 33.
2. *Qinghai sheng tongji nianjian* 2005, 80.
3. If we were to add the number of school-produced journals, such as those published by students at Qinghai Nationalities Institute (Xining) and Northwest Nationalities Institute (Lanzhou), the percentage would be even higher.
4. That Amdo writers predominate in the Tibetan literary world of the PRC is further indicated by the fact that nearly 40 percent of contributions to the Lhasa-based journal *Bod kyi rtsom rig sgyu rtsal* (Tibetan art and literature) originate from Amdo, but contributions from the TAR rarely appear in the Xining-based journal, *Sbrang char* (Light rain).
5. The most notable exception are the works of Namkhai Norbu, a scholar and philanthropist born in the Degé principality of Kham in 1938 who now resides in Naples. He is the founder of the Zhangzhung Insititute, and his works on the Bön religion, which are also available in the PRC, have contributed to a search for "authentic" Tibetan roots in pre-Buddhist society and literature.
6. Lopez, *Prisoners of Shangri-La*, 10.
7. Gladney, in his *Dislocating China*, deals at length with the construction of the Tibetans and other national minorities in China as "others" in order to homogenize the Han majority. Gladney offers a background on the historical, strategic, and political reasons behind the state's recognition of certain national minorities (6–27) and deals directly with Han representations of national minorities as "ethnic others" (51–96). In Gladney's opinion these visual renderings that emphasize a backward and wild nature for the national minorities are encouraged by the Chinese state

with the aim of defining the Han as the most "modern" and developed nationality in China, and minimizing the strong local differences among the so-called Han majority in order to unify the Chinese nation.

8. For more on the emergence of a civil society in China see *Modern China*, April 1993, and Timothy Brook and B. Michael Frolic, eds., *Civil Society in China* (Armonk, N.Y.: M. E. Sharpe, 1997).

9. Weise, *Xizang biji*. Chapter 9 in this book also addresses how authorities in Tibet exert their control on what writers write.

10. Wang Lixiong, "Xizang miandui de liangzhong diguo zhuyi: toushi Weise shijian."

11. Ibid.

12. Although banned from publishing books and articles, Weise wrote a series of articles on her internet blog (http://blog.daqi.com/weise/) until it was officially disabled in June 2006.

13. "Five Tibetan Monks Jailed in Western China," Radio Free Asia, reported on 13 February 2004.

14. For an anthropological study on the use of humor in Tibet see Makley, "The Power of the Drunk," 39–79. For an example of a short story in Tibetan which exemplifies the use of humor and parody to carry out a sociopolitical critique of modern Tibet see Tsering Dondrup, "A Show to Please the Masses," 61–77.

15. See Hartley, "Ascendancy of the Term *rtsom rig* in Tibetan Literary Discourse," 1–16.

16. The conceptual model for constructing a national literature in Tibet derives primarily from the literary evolutionism taught in the context of Chinese literature since the 1920s. See Zhang, "The Institutionalization of Modern Literary History in China," 347–77, and "Building a National Literature in Modern China," 47–74.

17. See Dodin and Räther, eds., *Imagining Tibet*.

18. Several excellent articles on the topic "Christian Missionaries and Tibet" can be found in *Lungta* 11 (winter 1998), published by the Amnye Machen Institute in Dharamsala.

19. For information on the *Yul phyogs so so'i gsar 'gyur me long/Tibet Mirror*, founded by the Christian convert the Rev. G. Tharchin in Kalimpong, see Tashi Tsering, "The Life of Rev. G. Tharchin." A description of the lively intellectual milieu on the Kalimpong-Lhasa trade route can be found in "A Conversation between Jamyang Norbu and Elliot Sperling."

20. As demonstrated by Kurtis Schaeffer (2005), the alleged transmission of oral teachings later transcribed as literary works (in particular, the songs of tantric yogins) likely involved a collective effort both in the initial composition and in the versions written and rewritten during subsequent centuries, whether by intermediaries in Nepal or translators and commentators in Tibet. See Schaeffer, *Dreaming the Great Brahmin*.

21. Gyatso, *Apparitions of the Self*; and "Autobiography in Tibetan Religious Literature."

22. Nicole Willock has explored how Tseten Zhapdrung writing his memoirs in the

1950s turned to the autobiography of the fifth Dalai Lama for rhetorical framing. See Willock, "A Mellifluous Voice."

23. Cabezón and Jackson, Introduction, *Tibetan Literature*, 14.

24. The editors would like to thank Janet Gyatso for edifying remarks that caused us to reconsider the indigenous elements in early literature and thus expand this section.

25. Smith, *Among Tibetan Texts*, 205.

26. For biographical information on Daṇḍin and selections from his writings see Warder, *Indian Kāvya Literature*, vol. 4, 165–211.

27. Warder, *Indian Kāvya Literature*, vol. 1, 2.

28. Ibid., 183.

29. Tshe tan zhabs drung, *Snyan ngag me long gi spyi don*, 4.

30. The term *mngon brjod*, translated here as "synonymy," has also been translated as "lexicography"; see e.g. Cabezón and Jackson, eds. *Tibetan Literature*, 18, and vander Kuijp, "Tibetan Belles-Lettres," 393. Another gloss for "metrics" (Tib. *sdeb sbyor*) is prosody. The fifth minor science is astrology (*skar rtsis*), with little relevance for our purposes.

31. Van der Kuijp, review of *Snyan-ngag me-long-gi spyi-don sdeb-legs rig-pa'i 'char-sgo*, 212–13.

32. Warder, *Kāvya Literature*, vol. 1, xiii.

33. Ibid., vol. 1, 22.

34. Ibid., vol. 1, 23. Tibetan terms drawn from Tshe tan zhabs drung, *Snyan ngag spyi don*, 17.

35. Van der Kuijp, "Tibetan Belles-Lettres," 397. Cf. Tshe tan zhabs drung, *Snyan ngag spyi don*, 12.

36. Warder, *Kāvya Literature*, vol. 1, 94–95. Tibetan terms drawn from Tse tan zhabs drung, 33–36.

37. Rdo rje rgyal po, *Snyan ngag gi rnam bshad gsal sgron*, 472–75.

38. Tib. *Mkhas pa'i 'jug pa'i sgo*. For a study of section 3 of this text see Jackson, *The Entrance Gate for the Wise (Section III)*.

39. Van der Kuijp, review of *Dag-yig ngag-sgron-gyi rtsa-ba dang de'i 'grel-pa*, 216.

40. Kapstein, "The Indian Literary Identity in Tibet," 776.

41. Two popular examples are Chöwang Drakpa's *Sprin gyi pho nya* (Cloud messenger), based on the *Meghadūta* by Kālidāsa, which has been available in Tibetan since the thirteenth century, and Dokhar Tsering Wanggyel's *Gzhon nu zla med*, written in the early eighteenth century. For an English translation of the latter see Mdo mkhar ba Tshe ring dbang rgyal, *The Tale of the Incomparable Prince*, trans. Beth Newman (New York: Harper Collins, 1996).

42. Rdo rje rgyal po, *Ye shes lha mo dang mgar ba Stobs rgyal* (Beijing: Mi rigs dpe skrun khang, 1980). The story can also be found in the scholar's collected works: *Rdo rje rgyal po'i gsung rtsom phyogs bsgrigs*, 823–89.

43. *Skal bzang me tog* (Ch. *Gesang hua*). The first (Chinese) version was published by the People's Literary Publishing House (Beijing: Renmin wenxue chubanshe) in 1980, the second (Tibetan) by the Nationalities Publishing House (Beijing: Mi rigs dpe

skrun khang) in 1982. See 'Jam dpal rgya mtsho, Afterword to *Skal bzang me tog*, n.p.

44. The English version of this novel follows the original but was slightly revised by the author, who rendered the "translation" himself. See Tailing, *The Secret Tale of Tesur House*.

45. Yangzhen, *Wu xingbie de shen*, and Meizhuo, *Taiyang Buluo*.

46. Zhaxi Dawa, *Saodong de Xiangbala*, and Alai, *Chen'ai luoding*, trans. in English as *Red Poppies* by Howard Goldblatt and Sylvia Li-chun Lin.

47. Chapter 4 examines Döndrup Gyel's classical interests, and chapters 3 and 11 discuss his poems, essays, and short stories. References to his work likewise abound in other chapters, for he was arguably the most influential Tibetan writer of the late twentieth century. For writers today, however, Döndrup Gyel serves more as a heroic icon than as a direct literary model.

48. Chin. *Chong man suyou cha wei er*.

49. Wang, *Fictional Realism in Twentieth Century China*, 280.

50. Lutwack, *The Role of Place in Literature*, 54–55.

51. Schiaffini-Vedani, "Tashi Dawa," 59–61.

52. Robin, "Stories and History."

53. Ibid., 24.

54. For extended discussions on this topic see Kapstein, "The Indian Literary Identity in Tibet," 786–94; and Hartley, "Contextually Speaking."

55. Kapstein, "The Indian Literary Identity in Tibet," observes how the maverick writer Döndrup Gyel took "recourse throughout his work [a thesis on the early *mgur* tradition] to theoretical categories drawn directly from the *kāvya* tradition" (793). See also Kapstein, "Dhondup Gyal," 45–48.

56. Kapstein, "The Indian Literary Identity in Tibet," 751.

57. *Zhongguo renkou tongji nianjian 2006*, 129. There is only a minor difference in this age group between illiteracy rates in the TAR for the urban population (44 percent) and the rural population (32 percent). Ibid., 122–23. There is a greater discrepancy between the illiteracy rate for Tibetan women in the TAR (56 percent) and that for men (33 percent).

58. Kolås and Thowsen, *On the Margins of Tibet*, 17, 26.

59. Ibid., 106.

60. Yang Chunjing, "Qiandan Zang yuwen jiaoxue zai fashan minzu jiaoyuzhong de zhongyaoxing" (A tentative study on the importance of teaching in the Tibetan language for developing national education), *Xizang yanjiu*, no. 2 (1996), cited in Kolås and Thowsen, *On the Margins of Tibet*, 119.

61. Two of the initial studies in western languages to identify this problem are Dicki Tsomo Chhoyang, "Tibetan-Medium Higher Education in Qinghai," and Susan Costello, "The Economics of Cultural Production in Contemporary Amdo."

62. Robin, "Stories and History," 23.

63. For details on the extent of the "Democratic reforms" see Smith, *Tibetan Nation*, 470–80.

64. Jiangbian Jiacuo ('Jam dpal rgya mtsho), *Ganxie shenghuo*, 399.

65. See n. 41, above.
66. "Four Modernizations" (Ch. *sige xiandai hua*), a campaign launched by Deng Xiao-ping in 1978, was aimed at modernizing the PRC in the areas of agriculture, indus-try, the military, and science and technology.
67. An increasingly favorable treatment of religion and faith during the 1990s has also been apparent in the works of Sinophone Tibetan writers.
68. For example, Bya gzhung Dbyangs bha, "Snyan ngag 'tshol ba" (Searching for poetry), *Gangs ljongs rig gnas* (Tibet culture) 1994, no. 3, 82–85; and Skyabs chen bde grol, "Gnam 'og 'di na snyan ngag la kha lo bsgyur thub mang" (Many in this world can control their poetry), *Gangs rgyan me tog* (Snow flower) 1999, no. 2, 54–55.
69. See Gangs zhun, "Go dka' ba snyan ngag gi yon tan yin nam," 124–28.
70. This article appeared in *Bod kyi dus bab* (Tibet Times), 15 September 2005, 3.
71. The Sinophone writer Zhaxi Dawa was one of the first who turned to writing song lyrics and scripts for documentaries and films. Since then he has also produced several documentaries about Tibet. In recent years Tibetophone writers such as Jangbu, Pema Tseten, and Gangzhün have also ventured into the film industry, with considerable success.
72. Feature-length and made-for-television films must still be dubbed and subtitled in Chinese, even if the actors are speaking Tibetan.
73. Dpal mo, ed., *Bzho lung*.

PART ONE

Engaging Traditions

Heterodox Views and the New Orthodox Poems: Tibetan Writers in the Early and Mid-Twentieth Century

LAURAN R. HARTLEY

Any discussion of the so-called modern—whether it be in art, literature, music, or architecture—risks constructing a temporal or aesthetic divide on the basis of political or socioeconomic watersheds, thereby categorizing all preceding forms and phenomena under the heading "tradition." Indeed, critical discourse on modern Tibetan literature often starts with the advent of Communist rule in Tibet (marked by the signing of the Seventeen-Point Agreement in 1951 or the flight of the Dalai Lama in 1959), or more typically with the Third Plenary Session of the Eleventh Party Congress in 1978, which heralded greater leniency in the post-Mao period. It is my purpose here not to challenge these periodizations per se, but to highlight examples of Tibetan writing in the early twentieth century that in certain ways broke with the classical literary norms prescribed by Indic kāvya theory, as discussed in the Introduction. The literary imagination of Tibetan writers in the pre-Communist era dispels the assumption that it was the so-called "liberation of Tibet" which paved the way for intellectual innovation. In particular, we will look at poems by three pre-Communist writers: Gendün Chömpel (1903–51), Giteng Rinpoché (1880/81–1944), and Shelkarlingpa (1876–1913).[1] Their writings are significant as literary expressions of changing times and as models for young poets writing fifty years later under a new political regime.

Western studies also tend to characterize the early Communist era (1949–78) as entailing the cooptation of Tibetan intellectuals, such that "the knowledge and skills of the traditional literary elite could be exploited for the revolutionary cause." In the second half of this chapter we will examine Tibetan verse from the early Communist period which would seem to support this generalization—patriotic poems by scholars whom I have elsewhere described as Tibet's "monastic vanguard."[2] Nevertheless, ambitious initiatives by these same scholars to publish classical texts and draft textbooks for teaching kāvya theory point to ideals that transcend party dictates. With the arrest of leading Tibetan figures in the late 1950s and the campaigns of the Cultural Revolution, these projects came to an end. But when these elderly teachers were finally exonerated in the post-Mao period, their tutelage and the (re)publication of their earlier drafts laid the ground for what would be called the "New Tibetan Literature" (Bod kyi rtsom rig gsar rtsom). This chapter thus seeks to enrich our understanding of Tibetan cultural production in the mid-twentieth century and the role of Tibetan scholars in bridging the pre-Communist era with that following the Cultural Revolution.

Gendün Chömpel (1903–1951)

The popularity of the Amdo-born scholar and monk Gendün Chömpel has grown to almost cultlike proportions. Though imprisoned by the former Tibetan government, in all probability for his radical views, he has posthumously become a hero for many in Tibet and exile alike. Posters now feature his image next to that of Döndrup Gyel (see chapter 4), who is held as the "father of modern Tibetan literature." In 2005 memorials marking the centennial of Gendün Chömpel's birth were held in Beijing and New York City. His life is the subject of Heather Stoddard's Le Mendicant de l'Amdo (1985) and his philosophy the subject of Don Lopez's The Madman's Middle Way (2006).[3] A three-volume collection of his writings published in Lhasa in 1990 was reprinted in Dharamsala the following year, and the second (1994) and third (2000) printings sold out quickly on the streets of Lhasa. The bulk of his poetry can be found in the third volume, along with his famous Guide to India and The White Annals, an imperial history based on Old Tibetan texts found in the caves of Dunhuang.

Contemporary Western scholars tend to emphasize the "modern" cast in the writing of this "progressive and open-minded scholar"[4] and the foreign exposure that he gained through his travels. Toni Huber (2000), for example, has suggested that certain compositional elements as well as features of "actual physical production" in Gendün Chömpel's Guide to India (1939)[5] make the work "one of the very first examples of modern native Tibetan literature. Some of the features which define it as 'modern' are its synthetic and critical approach to providing an up-to-date Buddhist historical geography of Indian sites; its functional guide for visiting them using modern means of transportation; and its inclusion of some of the first examples of modern Tibetan cartography, which Gendun Chöphel himself drew."[6] As Huber (1997) illustrates, the "new modern, rational set of universal crite-

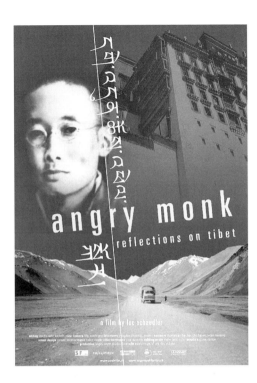

Poster for the feature-length documentary film *Angry Monk: Reflections on Tibet* (2005), which portrays the life of Gendün Chömpel. Photo courtesy of Luc Schaedler of Angry Monk Productions (Zurich).

ria for making authentic identifications of Indian Buddhist sites" promoted by Gendün Chömpel were "borrowed almost entirely . . . from the writings of colonial archaeologists and orientalists,"[7] that is, from the writings of the Maha Bodhi Society, a Theravāda Buddhist missionary organization in India that undertook academic research, the restoration of temples and monasteries, and the publication of journals and books, including the *Guide to India*.[8] Irmgard Mengele (1999) has referred to Gendün Chömpel as "the first 'modern' scholar of Tibet" for similar reasons: "He was the first who not only completed a traditional Tibetan education, but who also was courageous enough to leave the monastic society, travel abroad, learn several new languages and deepen his knowledge by collaborating with scholars of different nationalities."[9]

From a literary perspective, however, the seeds of this progressive monk's "modern" or vernacular writing style may have been planted before the age of nineteen, when he entered Labrang Monastery.[10] Evaluations of Gendün Chömpel's literary skill by Tibetan critics tend to emphasize the indigenous quality of his poetry and local sources of inspiration. For instance, the now-exiled Tibetan literary scholar Pema Bhum (1999) has argued that a lucid writing style, void of kāvya's heavy ornamentation and synonyms, was cause for his popularity in the 1980s.[11] Another scholar suggests that this vernacular quality in Gendün Chömpel's work might be due to the "unusual instruction" he received at the age of fifteen while at Ditsa Trashi Chöding, a monastery in Amdo.[12] Having already studied basic kāvya and demonstrated brilliance in rendering even the most challenging poetic forms in Daṇḍin's third chapter of the *Kāvyādarśa*, Gendün Chömpel was encouraged by his rather visionary teacher Khenchen Gendün Gyatso[13] to continue writing. According to his biographer Rakra Rinpoché, Gendün Chömpel acknowledged the influence of this early instruction on his literary thought: "My teacher Khenchen had a method for teaching poetry that differed from others. During summer vacations or when we would take walks, he would say, 'Gendün Chömpel, look! Those elephants in the sky are tired from carrying water. They can only move slowly on the road of the gods.' He wouldn't say the real names, such as 'water,' 'tree,' 'flower,' or 'mountain.' Rather, he referred to the action of each object, such as 'goes slowly,' 'drinks with its legs,' 'grows from the water,' and 'holds earth.' At first, it just made me laugh and feel a bit uncomfortable. But, thinking about it later, I realized Khenchen's method is an absolute necessity for teaching poetry (*snyan ngag*)."[14]

Khenchen Gendün Gyatso was also unique in not exacting too many illustrations from his students. Rather, he encouraged them to write only when they truly felt moved by some scenery, for example. Gendün Chömpel concluded from these experiences that the best *snyan ngag* was that which "put into writing just what one would say with no extra words."[15]

Eventually Gendün Chömpel applied this close observation and fresh outlook to religious and social ironies, a potent tool when combined with his acerbic humor. In 1927, for example, Gendün Chömpel wrote the poem reproduced below, often referred to as "Bla brang la bskur ba'i ka rtsom" [Acrostic sent to Labrang].[16] This poem is written in an abecedarian acrostic form, the successive lines beginning with successive letters of the alphabet (ka, kha, ga, nga, etc.). Though not found in the *Kāvyādarśa*, this form of wordplay was popular among Tibetan literati for centuries. Yet Gendün Chömpel's writing style is void of the ornate synonyms that characterized most poetry during his time. Moreover, a strong local flavor and sense of humor are evoked by the use of colloquial terms unique to the Amdo dialect, such as *akhu* (monk), *na ning do tshig* (last year, this year), and *ba lang* (cow).

> Ka ye! After I went elsewhere,
> a few monks who will say anything
> claimed, "The Pehar Oracle wouldn't let
> that one stay because of his great arrogance."

If there is a fastidious dharma-protector,
then why does he let stay all those good-for-nothings
who roam about, selling tea,
chang [liquor], livestock, sheep, etc.?

They hoist up their robes [to the height of] palmyra leaves.
They carry mean knives and wooden batons.
Now, *they* are the ones you should expel.
They have grown increasingly numerous in the last few years.

Some say, "He was expelled to another place, because
he hasn't the [pure] faith of Pasang."
Then why aren't the lowest of sentient beings expelled—
such as the cows, female yaks, birds, little birds, and bugs?

There's no reason for the four-fanged oracle-king
to banish in his ignorance
those who would endure heat, cold, drowsiness and fatigue,
to study the teachings of the Buddha.

Though to us it seems there is a big difference between
degenerate monks in good hats, clothing, shoes, etc.
and degenerate monks who eat poor food,
in the eyes of the [dharma] kings above, there is no difference.

Rather than banish hither this arrogant one who knows
the Rwa dialectics and the Bse dialectics,
how much better it would be to banish those arrogant ones
who sell meat, *chang*, and smokes!

Ha! Ha! Isn't it true? Just think about it!
Closely question the geshés.
The one who has spoken here is the Name-Abbot,
the Lion of Logic, Samgha dharma [Gendün Chömpel]!

Gendün Chömpel wrote this poem to address rumors about his alleged "expulsion" from Labrang Trashikyil Monastery, where he had scandalized the assembly by debating *against* the standard curriculum of the monastery's chief hierarch. Shortly after, he left Labrang "encircled by a halo of notoriety."[17] It is said that he wrote this poem en route to Lhasa.[18] Since Gendün Chömpel remained in contact with Jamyang Zhepa, the main hierarch of Labrang Monastery, and several fellow students for the remainder of his life,[19] he likely intended this poem as a hard-hitting but playful joust at the assembly he had left behind, not as a scathing critique. In any case, its content and writing style illustrate the vernacular tendencies of Gendün Chömpel even before his travels abroad.

Gendün Chömpel's travels in India began in 1934, when he was thirty-two years old, at the invitation of his friend, benefactor, and research colleague Rahul Sankrityayan (1893–1963),[20] with whom he also studied Sanskrit. After two years of pilgrimage he arrived in the northeastern hill station of Kalimpong. This bustling trade town was home to several aristocratic Tibetan families and supported an intellectual exchange less fettered than in Lhasa, where conservative religious elements still held fast. With the publishing opportunity offered by the Tibetan newspaper *Yul phyogs so so'i gsar 'gyur me long / Tibet Mirror*, founded ten years previously by the progressive Christian convert Tharchin Babu (1890–1976),[21] Gendün Chömpel became a regular contributor and even briefly worked for the newspaper. Here too his poems evince a conscious departure from the embellished language of classical kāvya, as seen in his poem posthumously entitled "A Vernacular Acrostic" (1936).[22]

Heather Stoddard (1985) describes how Gendün Chömpel avidly studied both Sanskrit and English during his travels in India and applied these skills to ambitious translation projects. These endeavors offered potential avenues for literary influence, from which we can discern three trends.[23] First was his admiration for Kālidāsa's *Śakuntalā*, which he translated[24] and later promoted as a model for students in Lhasa after his return in 1945.[25] One student recalled Gendün Chömpel's advising him and a fellow student: "The author of the *Śakuntalā*, the non-buddhist Kālidāsa, was more expert than Daṇḍin. . . . Therefore, [I] greatly hope you two [students] will accomplish a little with this poetry in the future. Literary works should not be tied up too much with synonyms. The meaning should be succinct as well as clear and easy to understand. It is said that 'The best composition is understood from the first reading.'"[26] Other literary works which he translated from Sanskrit while in India include the *Rāmāyaṇa* and the *Dhammapada* in their entirety, as well as excerpts from the Veda and the Bhagavad Gītā. He was also familiar with the *Kāmā śāstra*, upon which he relied in writing his own expanded *'Dod pa'i bstan bcos* [Treatise on desire].[27]

A second literary influence to which Gendün Chömpel gained access while in India was English literature and English translations of foreign writers such as Pushkin.[28] He even wrote a few poems and essays in English which were published by the Maha Bodhi Society from 1939 to 1941.[29] Yet his Tibetan writings reveal no evidence of direct borrowing. On the contrary, Gendün Chömpel was self-deprecatory about his ability to appreciate

English literature. Arguing that one must understand the spoken language to appreciate the flavor of a nationality's poem, he admitted that he himself did not have a taste for English poetry: "I tried to experience the flavor of poetry written in English, but the understanding such as they experience it never came. Moreover, even when someone else explained it, I never truly got their way of thinking. I thought maybe it would make a difference if I were to try writing in English. But, when I finished writing, the result was strange. Thus, it seems to me that if you have not been accustomed [to using] your own language since childhood, [writing in that language] will be impossible. Thus, [the issue is] whether or not one is familiar with one's own spoken language."[30] By the time he returned to Lhasa, Gendün Chömpel had firm opinions about the need to vernacularize the literary language. He recommended to his students: "If one has also been instructed in the three chapters of the *Me long*, some lines of verse will undoubtedly come, regardless of how little experience or skill one has. However, one will not [necessarily] be able to produce the affective state (*nyams 'gyur*) or flavor such as is required for *snyan ngag*. Specifically speaking, in order to write rich literature (*rtsom*) or poetry (*snyan ngag*), if one isn't deeply familiar with the spoken language of ones own region, it will be difficult to combine meaning and sound in a sonorous and profound way."[31] His prescription was not the "socialist realism" dictated by Mao in 1942, and he did not reject the whole of kāvya theory. Rather, this progressive scholar's concept of the vernacular was rooted in his "selected tradition" from Tibetan literary predecessors. In particular, Gendün Chömpel favored the relatively late commentary by Ju Mipam Gyatso (1846–1912),[32] which he felt was "the clearest, most concise and most complete" understanding of the *Kāvyādarśa*.[33] Upon his deathbed in 1951, Gendün Chömpel requested that his student read two poems: one by Tsongkhapa[34] and the other by Ju Mipam.[35]

A final influence is seen in the poet's return to indigenous forms: the pre-kāvya writings of seventh- and eighth-century Tibetan poem-songs (*mgur*) found in Dunhuang and the *mgur* of later writers, including Milarepa (1040–1123), Shar Kelden Gyatso (1607–1677), and Zhapkar (1781–1851), the latter two from Gendün Chömpel's native Repgong. While Gendün Chömpel would have read the later writers, only his trip to India made the Old Tibetan texts from Dunhuang available to him.[36] We do not have access to Gendün Chömpel's complete works, but the formal influence of mgur seems most prominent toward the end of his career, in the heartbreaking verses that he wrote while imprisoned in Lhasa (1946–49).[37] In one poem he even imitates arcane spelling conventions found in the Dunhuang manuscripts, such as using *myi* for *mi* (e.g. in *myi shes pa*).[38] Alongside his efforts to render the arcane language of the Old Tibetan annals into present-day vernacular, these poems point to Gendün Chömpel's passion for discovering and engaging Tibet's earliest traditions.

Gendün Chömpel was but one brilliant example of progressive thinkers working towards the "improvement" of Tibetan society from the 1930s to the 1950s. Among his acquaintances were a few traditional but socially engaged scholars, such as Akhu Sungrap Gyatso (1896–1982), Geshé Sherap Gyatso (1884–1968), the Mongolian lexicographer Geshé Chodrak (1898–1972), and the aristocrat and publisher Horkhang Sönam Penbar (1898–1972). In her study of Tibetan intellectual currents during these decades, Stoddard (1985) also mentions the nephew of Tharchin Babu, Rikdzin Wangpo, who in 1948 was the first Tibetan researcher invited to the School of Oriental and African Studies in London.[39] Changlochen (1889–197?), another contemporary of Gendün Chömpel and fellow member of the "West Tibet Improvement Party,"[40] was renowned as an aristocrat-poet; and the two students and faithful biographers of Gendün Chömpel, Lachung Apo (1902–75) and Rakra Rinpoché (b. 1925), became skilled men of letters in their own right. Another member of Gendün Chömpel's immediate group of friends was the innovative painter Amdo Jampa (d. 2002), who introduced realism to the art of Tibetan painting.[41]

And yet, however vernacular the language, Gendün Chömpel's poems (always written in metric verse) do not represent a literary rupture, except perhaps in their content. It is a sad fact that Gendün Chömpel's untimely death in 1951 occurred just on the eve of the launching of new Tibetan newspapers and modern-format publishing projects. His literary output did not enjoy the access to print media and wide distribution accorded to scholars writing only a few years later. The reception or influence of Gendün Chömpel thus became widespread only thirty years after his death, when his works were finally published for broader readership.[42] His popularity among writers today can be partly understood as a case of delayed salience, such as Kronfeld (1996) has observed in literary discourse on what she terms "the margins of modernism."[43]

Giteng Rinpoché

Giteng Rinpoché, a contemporary of Gendün Chömpel and a fellow Amdowan, also knew greater fame posthumously. Articles about Giteng Rinpoché (1881–1944) were especially numerous in the early 1990s,[44] when young scholars endeavored to draw his poem "Pho nya gzhon nu Don grub" (Young Döndrup the courier) into the realm of a newly conceived sense of literature. "Young Döndrup" is a poetic "letter" written by Giteng Rinpoché from his residence in Tsekog (Huangnan Prefecture, Qinghai Province) to his student Marnang Dorjechang (1898–1946) at Karing Monastery in Xunhua.[45] Marnang Dorjechang was also the reincarnation of Giteng Rinpoché's teacher, which explains why the elderly lama would expend so much effort in writing to his student and would praise him so highly. This poem is of the Tibetan literary genre called *chab shog*, or epistle writing, typically sent from teachers to students and vice versa.

In Giteng Rinpoché's poem the narrator has conjured an imaginary messenger to deliver this special letter, and the bulk of the poem describes the lands through which the messenger must travel to reach the cherished recipient. The poet's instructions thus serve as a conceit to offer the third-party reader a guided tour through regions intimately familiar to the writer. Along the virtual journey, the narrator extols the merits of particular communities or geographic wonders while elsewhere warning against hazards. The message to be relayed is secondary to the aim of introducing the reader to the terrain.[46] The opening of "Young Döndrup":

> Ten thousand[47] *miles* north of here,[48]
> is the embodiment of Gyelkün Yeshé Tiklé,[49]
> who is [as dear to me as] the eyes on my face and my heart
> inside. His name alone is nectar to my ears.
>
> Could there be a messenger who would swiftly accomplish the
> entirety of the needed task, carrying a letter without delay,
> who if I were to invest upon his head responsibility for this
> poetic letter would have all the great virtues [of a messenger]?
>
> Just then, because the necessary karmic conditions were
> unstoppable, a young white she-cloud smiled and there was
> the son of a *lha* upon whom I could have gazed forever.
> He strolled slowly, like a baby elephant.
>
> "Kye! Kye! You, boy who accomplishes great things.
> Come here! Come here! With this flower of prayer,[50]
> which will ensure for you the auspiciousness of the exoteric
> and esoteric arts, I appoint you fine messenger. . . ."[51]

This poem evokes Indic models most directly in its origins. Giteng Rinpoché modeled his poem after a classical Tibetan work,[52] which in turn was modeled after the Indian *Meghadūta*. The Indian classic is about a treasurer (*phyag mdzod*) who is exiled by a king for his lassitude. Separated from his lover, the treasurer sends messages of longing via the clouds. Giteng Rinpoché also employs Indic metaphors, when describing such local sights as the bustle of city life or the physical beauty of young men and women in town:

> The shine of their moon[-like] faces fully surpassing
> [those of] divine youth, the people fine clothed with a
> spectrum of fine ornaments dangling from their belts
> enjoy themselves immensely.

> Slim-waisted women who move like ducks
> strolling slowly, weighed down from the burden
> of many necklaces on their beautiful young breasts
> are in all ways as beautiful as goddesses.[53]

The reader familiar with kāvya conventions and the use of synonyms in Tibetan poetry will recognize the ubiquitous references to the moon-like face and duck's waddle (a compliment in this context!). Less characteristically, Giteng Rinpoché refers in his poem to the contemporary political climate, including the horrors of the Muslim warlord Ma Bufang's rule in Repgong (Ch. Tongren):

> Having cut off the heads of the hosts of enemies
> who affront them — like ears of wheat —
> the sound of demons smacking their lips in an
> ocean of blood and fat is the music of the night.[54]

To the best of our knowledge, Giteng Rinpoché wrote this poem in 1938.[55] The contemporary references and the literal narration of a land and its people(s) or "imagined communities" cause us to take special notice of this poem. Furthermore, Giteng Rinpoché refers to the two poems on which his own poem is based: "Isn't my poetry a mixture of that by Makhöl and Chöwang Drakpa? Doesn't my *rasa* burn with the youth of the *āryas*?"[56] Such self-referencing also gives this poem a more modern cast.

Students evaluating this piece in the early 1990s praised it for its vernacular qualities, arguing that "Young Döndrup" evinces the qualities of realist literature: use of vernacular language, concern with the natural environment (drawing on Gorky), and detailed character description.[57] Giteng Rinpoché's poem was upheld as a model for contemporary writers of "both short stories and poetry."[58] One poet to take this to heart was Ju Kelzang (b. 1960), who studied with Döndrup Gyel at the Central Nationalities Institute in Beijing and is highly skilled in both classical conventions and modern verse forms.[59] The intended recipient of Ju Kelzang's letter is not a religious student but his parents residing in Golok (Ch. Guoluo), their nomadic home in Qinghai Province. Ju Kelzang conjures up two "magical birds" to serve as messengers in his poem "Poetic Words to Encourage the Illusory Courier." Though the poet was writing from Beijing, he first sends the birds to Lhasa and its magnificent sights and then details from there the journey to Golok. Stanzas in which he describes hazards that will prompt "a dance on the stage of the coward's chest" and the "moon-like faces of beautiful women, who are clothed in rainbows and move like the Sandalwood tree" are clearly inspired by similar passages in "Young Döndrup." Ju Kelzang acknowledges this influence, and in an interview explained how his poem started out as a classroom writing exercise that he later published.[60]

Shelkarlingpa

Early-twentieth-century writers from central Tibet, like their Amdo counterparts, also addressed contemporary subject matter. One work merits special attention: "Lhasa dran glu" (published with the English title "A Song of Lhasa Memories"), a poem composed by H. E. Shelkarlingpa (1876–1913) while he was exiled in Darjeeling with the thirteenth Dalai Lama after Qing troops seized Lhasa in February 1910. Shelkarlingpa was appointed deputy minister in 1912 and soon made cabinet minister, but he died in the following year.[61] Literary writing was a pastime for Shelkarlingpa, as it had been for other Lhasa aristocrats since the seventeenth century.[62] Unlike classical works which typically referred to India, "A Song of Lhasa Memories" is a romantic verse of longing for the author's homeland, specifically the "beautiful and auspicious" site of its capital:

> I miss Lhasa, beautiful, auspicious place:
> On the bare round the eight-petalled lotus,
> The flanks of the hefty hills replete with the eight auspicious signs,
> The heavens round like the shape of the wheel.[63]

He praises its lively market and the "calm dispositions" of its inhabitants, contrasting the milieu to the hubbub of Darjeeling:

> I miss Lhasa: Going around the Middle Circuit again and again,
> Bargaining while looking in the shops;
> Here and there the uncountable wealth of elegant goods
> that vies with Vaiśravaṇa's treasury.

I miss Lhasa: Its careful and dependable ways,
Not awhirl with activity like here;
Its casual folks' calm dispositions,
Mulling over their meals and doing honest work.[64]

What is remarkable about "A Song of Lhasa Memories" is how the contemporary is made tangible in the poet's expression of longing for Lhasa. For centuries, verse had been primarily reserved for religious topics and praise.[65] Though he draws his style and select metaphors from Indic kāvya, Shelkarlingpa applies classical conventions to contemporary subject matter. In a land where only fifteen years previously a respected religious teacher had advised the local king to "stroll like an elephant,"[66] Shelkarlingpa's verse signals a profound shift in Tibetan literary attention to the present. This tendency gained momentum by the 1930s, as seen in the poem "Young Döndrup" and the vernacular preferences of Gendün Chömpel.

As discussed by Janet Upton (1999), Shelkarlingpa's poem is now reproduced in contemporary Tibetan textbooks, having become a model for young writers. Much as Giteng Rinpoché's "Young Döndrup" was reworked by college-age writers to sketch out the ethno-geographic contours for fellow Amdo readers in the 1930s, Shelkarlingpa's poem when read by junior high students now "invokes longings for a Tibet that most students have seen only in their mind's eye: the Tibet of traditional Lhasa."[67]

Tibetan Writing in the Early Communist Era (1949–1976)

In contrast to the vibrant intellectualism of the self-study and projects of Gendün Chömpel and his fellow political progressives, publishers, and artists, the state of literary works published in Tibetan during the first few decades of Communist rule could be bluntly characterized as uninspired. Tibetan literary production from 1949 to 1965 consisted primarily of poetry and secondarily of the collection and editing of folk literature. Only one Tibetan attended the First Minority Literature Conference in Beijing in 1956, and he was not a literary writer.[68] Danzhu Angben (Tib. Dondrup Wangbum; 2001) identifies two "regrettable lacunae" (Ch. *quehan*) during this period: the near-absence of Tibetan novels, plays, and essays; and of literature written in Tibetan.[69] As detailed in chapter 2, most literary works published at this time were by a new cohort of literary pioneers: the first generation of Tibetan poets to write in Chinese. The few pieces written in Tibetan were poems praising the Communist Party, its leaders, and its policy, as was true of the writers' more numerous Chinese-language counterparts.

Geshé Sherap Gyatso giving a public address in Xining, circa 1950. Photo originally published in *Jiefang Qinghai huace* (Images of the Liberation of Qinghai; Xining: Qinghai renmin chubanshe, 1989).

Geshé Sherap Gyatso (1884–1968)—a senior scholar from Amdo who shared a contentious teacher-student relationship with Gendün Chömpel while the two were in Lhasa—was one of the earliest scholars to write such political praise poetry, marking a transition from religious eulogies. Several poems repeat key phrases or refrains, thereby evoking the earlier writing style of aphoristic writing and offering prayers (*gsol 'debs*).[70] This can be seen in one of his best-known poems, "Bslab bya rang byung lha'i rnga bo" (Drum of spontaneous advice):

> With compassion, unable to bear the sight of the country's people
> facing tens of thousands of sufferings, it has taken up the weapons
> of fearless heroes and first defeated the enemy—
> The Communist Party.
>
> Though they have no religion and don't accept it,
> they don't stop others [and grant] religious freedom.
> Politically, though, the way of the party must be followed.
> This is a fundamental tenet of the Communist Party.

All citizens must believe
in the constitution reviewed hundreds of times
by Comrade Mao Zedong and many scholars, in the
Three [Red] Banners[71] and the leadership of the Party.
This is a fundamental tenet of the Communist Party.[72]

The need to distinguish and treat accordingly the two
contradictions: the enemy who must be totally opposed,
and internal contradictions within the organization,
This is a fundamental tenet of the Communist Party.

Making no mistake in clearly turning
a despising red eye towards imperialism
and a white and joyful smile towards socialism—
This is a fundamental tenet of the Communist Party.

America—a paper tiger, a bubble-formation,
feigns a strong and mighty appearance, with not a
sesame seed of truth in it, crumbling under examination
This is a fundamental tenet of the Communist Party.

The need to know that [America] lures with wealth
a few small *preta*-like countries to its side,
while offering a witch's smile to others—
This is a fundamental tenet of the Communist Party.

The need for one's heart to pound [in fear] at
China, these days a technological world power,
flying over the head of imperialist America—
This is a current tenet of the Communist Party.[73]

Sherap Gyatso was also more likely to draw on religious terminology than later writers were. In one poem he even compares the thought of Chairman Mao to the philosophy of the Buddha:

I, Jampel Gyepé Lodrö,[74] have seen
in this holy person named Mao Zedong
a great many of the praiseworthy marvels
found in the untarnished thought of the Buddha.[75]

Another example of religious-inspired verse written praising Mao Zedong is a eulogy by the fourteenth Dalai Lama,[76] who likely presented it during his visit to Beijing in July 1954:[77]

Om Sarasvatī!
O, Triratna, who showers in abundance upon the
Glorious world all virtuous excellences,
Protect us always with your auspicious sacred
countenance which is everlasting and unparalleled.

[You] the people's leader, whose countless good deeds
equal in glory those of Mangkur Gyelpo[78]
and of Brahma the creator of the world,
resemble the sun which illuminates the earth.

May the almighty Chairman Mao,
whose knowledge extends to the horizon
like ocean waves,
live in this world forever.

People regard you as a mother who protects us
and enthusiastically inscribe your image.
May he live forever to show us the good path of peace
through friendship free of bias and wrath (Skt. krodha).[79]

The poem continues for several more stanzas, praising the actions of Chairman Mao and his work in freeing people from their suffering, especially that incurred by "our enemy—cruel imperialism." References to "peace and justice" and the "good path of peace" might signal the Dalai Lama's desire for amicable relations, which tragically only worsened.[80] This poem also suggests that the views of Geshé Sherap Gyatso and other religious hierarchs mentioned here were not extreme deviations from accepted discourse at this time.

Poetry could also be used for persuasion. In the poem "Drum of Spontaneous Advice," Geshé Sherap Gyatso sought to explain Communist policy, to assure Tibetans that the Communist Party would allow religious freedom, and finally to underscore the might of the Communist Party. In two other instances Sherap Gyatso served as a broker through his poetry: on one occasion writing to the monks of Sera, Ganden, and Drepung monasteries, persuading them not to resist the Communist advances; and secondly, during the Great Leap Forward, offering a reinterpretation of Buddhist tradition to convince people that it was acceptable to kill birds and bugs, as required by Communist policy at the time.[81]

Religious references soon waned, however, as seen in the poems of Tsatrül Ngakwang Lozang (1879–1957),[82] despite his standing as a reincarnate lama trained at Sera Monastery and holder of a *geshé* degree (the highest level of education attainable in the Tibetan monastic system). Early in his career he was a private secretary to the thirteenth Dalai Lama, whom he accompanied to various sites in China, including Beijing for an audience with the Qing emperor.[83] In 1911, at the order of the Dalai Lama, he went to Japan and taught at a monastery there.[84] He later worked for many years editing the Tibetan Buddhist canon with Sherap Gyatso. When the People's Liberation Army entered Lhasa in 1951, Ngakwang Lozang became vice-director of the local Cadre School[85] and established the Tibetan Military Regional Office Literary Research Association.

Tsatrül Ngakwang Lozang's poems are viewed by some Tibetans today as examples of "new poetry"[86] for its contemporary content. "G.yu yi ske rags gser kyi zam pa" (Turquoise belt, golden bridge, 1955), for example, was written in honor of the completion of the two highways joining Qinghai and Sichuan Provinces with the Tibet Autonomous Region.[87] The poem begins:

> Mighty rivers in the [valley] depths cut off
> any direct route between [here] and
> the motherland, Khams, and Qinghai.
> The mountains are high and the steep slopes vast.
>
> Though you might like to cross them, as if flying,
> they are dangerous, each steeper than the last,
> and the sharp mountain peaks would cause you
> to tremble, even if you had hawk wings.
>   . . . .[88]

The author's expressions of wonder at the fruits of scientific progress in the poem "Lcags kyi phug ron dngul skya mdog" (Silver hue of the iron dove, 1956) also center on a contemporary image—in this case the landing of an airplane:

> The weather fine, the sun bright,
> a pleasant sound is heard from the northeast horizon.
> When visible overhead,
> We see it is the arrival of a beautiful plane.
>
> It is dove-hued and winged.
> With beautiful cabins and brightly painted stars,[89]
> It hovers and circles over this city.
> I think a gentle eye looks on from afar.[90]

This photo of Tibetans offering barley-beer for the first Chinese plane to land in Lhasa in 1956 was featured shortly after the event in *Mi dmangs brnyan par* (People's Pictorial), a magazine published in Beijing. Image courtesy of Latse Contemporary Tibetan Cultural Library.

Both poems are in metered verse, but void of ornate metaphors. Ngakwang Lozang further evokes a certain "colloquial" quality in his poetry by avoiding the "elliptical" (*'khyog brjod*) forms of kāvya ornamentation; his diction is straightforward.

Chapgak Tamdrin (1999) argues that Ngakwang Lozang's poetry had "no small influence on the development of [Tibetan] literature" and was important in fostering a new literary style that emphasized intelligibility and conveyed emotion.[91] One reason for this influence was that Ngakwang Lozang's poems were published in the *Tibet Daily*, on whose editorial staff he served in the final years of his life. His poems thus set a tone for the political praise poetry that dominated the following two decades of Tibetan literary production. His themes included the need for unity, protecting the motherland, resisting imperialism, and building a socialist China, as evoked in the poem "Gung khran tang gi 'khrungs skar dus chen la bsngags pa brjod pa" (In praise of the commemoration of the founding of the Communist Party, 1956):

> In the vast and happy gardens,
> Under the cool shade of the hoisted white canopy of sky
> The fine clothing of the monks and lay people flap.
>
> Men and women alike wear customary adornments,
> Everyone sings with brotherly love happy songs and melodious refrains.
> The pure and nourishing tea and food are delicious.
> Their hearts are moved by the Communist Party's way.
>
> The Communist Party and its policy are good.
> Under the guidance of the great Chairman Mao, the
> Autonomous Preparatory Committee was established.
> The right path to the good and happy life has been found.
>
> We are completely freed from private ownership.
> In the boat of high-level policy
> We have firmly shifted course towards a good new path.
> May the great society also reach the summit.[92]

Other political praise poems by Tsatrül Ngakwang Lozang include "The Great Unity of the Patriotic Youth," "In Praise of Premier Zhou Enlai," "Song of Praise Offered for Chairman Mao, Leader of the Peoples of All Nationalities," and "In Commemoration of the Founding of the PLA."[93] Not only were his poems propagated through the mass media in the 1950s, they were also among the first works published in the opening issues of Tibetan literary journals founded in the early 1980s.[94] Editors seeking to fill their pages with at least some original Tibetan literary works[95] turned to the writings of early "brokers" of tradition such as Tsatrül Ngakwang Lozang. But this teacher's influence was felt most strongly in the 1980s through the use of his textbook on classical grammar, published in 1959 and again in 1981.[96]

It was through such "applied" activities that these early scholars left their greatest legacy. Sungrap Gyatso (1896–1982), for example, did not write much poetry. He was active in film-dubbing projects, as well as in establishing the Qinghai Tibetan Newspaper and Tibetan programming on Qinghai Radio, both in 1951. He was also a member of the Northwest Culture and Education Committee and vice-director of the Provincial Translation Committee.[97] The poem for which he is best known was written in praise of the city of Changchun, capital of Jilin Province in the northeast part of China, which he visited on three separate occasions from 1953 to 1956 to work on filmmaking projects at its famous studios:

> Flowers of praise are flung for
> the world of the great Changchun,
> in the northeast of what's famed as
> the mighty motherland.
>
> With no deep canyons, here in what
> resembles an immense region or the sky,
> at the center of this vast earth,
> the houses shimmer like constellations.
>
> It is a clear sign of the full achievement
> of the great era in which the population
> of more than 800,000 enjoy
> the glory of the new life of happiness.[98]

While references in this poem to a happy socialist life certainly add a contemporary flavor, the poem reflects classical poetry in its form and praise of place. Moreover, Sungrap Gyatso relies on ornate expressions to represent a particular object; for example, in the brief excerpt above the kenning "holder of wealth" (nor 'dzin) is used for earth.

His poem "Mtsho sngon po la bstod pa" [Praise for Blue Lake], which praises Qinghai Lake, is reminiscent of the *mgur* of Zhapkar and Shar Kelden Gyatso:

> Currents of water like melted blue sky pool into
> a lapis sea, from which spread in all directions
> the great waves of Amdo's Blue Lake, known as
> "The Queen of Ten Thousand Households."[99]
>
> As for the extent of this great lake's surface
> One hears the people of the grasslands say
> that even a good horse needs about eighteen days
> to travel its long circumference.
>
> . . . .
>
> In the clear sky night,
> the form of the moon on the lake and
> the shining of many constellations lead
> one to wonder if this is not the sky itself.[100]

In the final line the poet employs a classic rhetorical device called the "metaphor of doubt" (*the tshom gi dpe*) in which the true subject (the reflection) so closely resembles the object of comparison (the sky) that doubt is raised in the readers' mind as to whether they are viewing the subject or the metaphor.[101] This poem was among the first poems published in *Sbrang char*, the literary magazine founded in Xining in 1981. It also appears in a popular textbook on kāvya by Tseten Zhapdrung, and was thus read for several years by students of Tibetan literature at the six nationality institutes[102] serving as a model for young poets in the 1980s.[103]

The Monastic Vanguard

In 1954 Sungrap Gyatso and several other monastically trained scholars (some of whom were delegates to the first National Peoples Congress) were invited to Beijing to translate political materials, including the Constitution of the PRC and selected works of Chairman Mao. More than four thousand terms were discussed and standardized, prompting Sungrap Gyatso to draft a Chinese-Tibetan dictionary.[104] These efforts mark the first major step in the standardization of terms for Chinese-Tibetan translations during the Communist era. The second step came in 1958 at the Second National Work Forum on Minority Languages; among the resolutions drafted here was one to make Chinese the source language when translating and borrowing new terms and to transcribe foreign words—in particular, the names of people and places—indirectly on the basis of their phonetic rendering in the Chinese pinyin system, a policy maintained to this day.[105] In 1959 the project to translate the complete works of Mao was launched. Jampel Gyatso, describes how this endeavor, which lasted ten years (1959–69) and employed more than one hundred people, elided dialectical differences in favor of a commonly understood vernacular language through an extensive editing process incorporating the work of readers from Lhasa, Amdo, and Khams, and thus set a standard for decades to come.[106]

The bulk of this work fell under the auspices of the Tibetan section of the Nationalities Publishing House (f. 1953) in Beijing, which published hundreds of Tibetan works between 1953 and 1965. For the first two years of operation its publications were strictly political: speeches, legal documents, and bilingual posters. Though the ultimate aim of these and many subsequent projects may have been to "civilize" the Tibetan population or to further "political indoctrination," as emphasized in current scholarship, several Tibetan monk-scholar-translators also initiated projects to make classical Tibetan texts, grammars, poetry, and folktales available to a wider reader-

Tibetan translation team in the mid-1950s. Reprinted from Mi rigs brnyan par (Nationalities Pictorial) (Beijing, 1956).

ship. The quantity of publications by Tibetan authors from Beijing alone is not overly impressive, but if we also consider the publishing houses in Xining, Lhasa, Chengdu, and Lanzhou, then the number of apolitical Tibetan works (classical or otherwise) issued in the 1950s and 1960s is quite extensive.[107] These include grammars, dictionaries, classical Tibetan texts, and studies of traditional poetry, among them *Tale of the Incomparable Prince* (1957), *Story of the Cuckoo* (1958), *The Aphorisms of Sakya Paṇḍita* (1958), *The Story of King Drimé Kunden* (1958), and the *History of the Fifth Dalai Lama* (1957). Other Tibetan texts were drafted but not actually published in the 1950s; these manuscripts were often written for classroom use by scholars on the translation teams who were asked to teach at nationality institutes during this early period. Dungkar Rinpoché, for example, drafted his famous textbook *Opening the Door to the Study of Ornamentation for Writing Poetry* in 1962 while teaching at the Central Nationalities Institute in Beijing.[108] Tseten Zhapdrung's *The Abridged Kāvyādarśa* was published in 1957, and republished in 1981 with 24,000 copies printed in the first year.[109]

More than a few great scholars were optimistic at that time about Communist policy and its implications for increasing Tibetan literacy. In the eastern areas of Amdo and Kham, however, countless middle-aged men including indigenous local leaders were being imprisoned in "Democratic reforms" launched east of the Yangtze River from 1956 to 1958.[110] The campaigns spread, and by the start of the Cultural Revolution in 1966 virtually all publishing in Tibetan had stopped, except for translations of works by Chairman Mao. Many of the scholars mentioned here were arrested and spent more than a decade in prison or in hard labor until their release around 1978. When those who survived the Cultural Revolution were asked again to teach in Tibetan programs reestablished at nationality institutes, their instruction and (re)published works made an important contribution to the renaissance of Tibetan literature after the paralyzing effects of the Cultural Revolution.[111]

While the ideological poems of Tibet's monastic vanguard lacked the brilliance of writings by Gendün Chömpel and others in preceding decades, the issuing of their verse in print media and textbooks (many verses here were apolitical) legitimated the application of kāvya forms to contemporary subject matter. Above all, their efforts while serving on translation committees, on newspaper editorial boards, and in film-dubbing offices furthered the vernacularization of the written Tibetan language and expanded its lexicon. While our discussion does not disprove the significance of the 1980s as a renaissance in Tibetan publishing, it does temper the idea that the initial years of the Communist era were a wasteland for Tibetan literature. The projects of the 1950s maintained a critical thread of continuity from the pre-Communist era, laying the foundation for later literary negotiation. Though I have mentioned only a few well-known figures here, such as Sherap Gyatso, Tsatrül Ngakwang Lozang, Dungkar Rinpoché, and Tseten Zhapdrung, there were also unnamed others in various locales who persisted in teaching Tibetan—sometimes bravely resisting party directives—for whom we have no biographies. Because of their efforts, in the 1980s at least a handful of Tibetans in their twenties had language skills sufficient enough to write verse inspired by kāvyā and to begin experimenting with literary forms, despite the setbacks of the Cultural Revolution and preceding campaigns.

Notes

This chapter is dedicated to the memory of Professor Jamyang Drapka (d. 2008), whose intellect and generosity were testimony to Tibet's great teaching tradition.

1. For the dates of Shelkarlingpa I am citing a biographical account by Shelkarlingpa's grandson, Tshe dbang rnam rgyal, "Bod kyi nye dus kyi grags can snyan ngag pa

Shel gling Mi 'gyur lhun grub kyi snyan ngag rtsom las skor cung zad gleng ba," 61–72. Cf. Petech, who places his birth "circa 1864" in *Aristocracy and Government in Tibet*, 159.

2. See Hartley, "Contextually Speaking," 147.

3. Extensive lists of biographical material on Gendün Chömpel are provided in Huber, *The Guide to India*, 133–52; and Mengele, *dGe-'dun-chos-'phel*, 14–16, 115–27. Two recent biographies should be added to their lists of secondary materials: Rdo rje rgyal, *'Dzam gling rig pa'i dpa' bo rdo brag Dge 'dun chos 'phel gyi byung ba brjod pa bden gtam rna ba'i bcud len*; and Du Yongbin, *20 shiji Xizang qiseng*.

4. Mengele, *dGe-'dun-chos-'phel*, 2.

5. The full title of this work is *A Guidebook for Travel to the Holy Places of India* (Rgya dkar gi gnas chen khag la 'grod pa'i lam yig). Huber details the revisions and publishing of this text from its original conception in 1934/35 and publication in 1939 to its final revised version (1945/46) and publication in 1950; see Huber, *The Guide to India*, 13. The *Guide* is also included in the three volumes of collected works published in 1990 by the TAR Tibetan Antiquarian Books Publishing House (Bod ljongs Bod yig dpe rnying dpe skrun khang), which were then revised and edited by T. G. Dhong-thog for Dzongsar Institute in Bir, India, in 1991.

6. Huber, *The Guide to India*, 19.

7. Toni Huber, "Colonial Archaeology, International Missionary Buddhism and the First Example of Modern Tibetan Literature," 307.

8. Ibid., 302.

9. Mengele, *dGe-'dun-chos-'phel*, 1.

10. Shawo Tsering states that Gendün Chömpel left for Labrang in 1922. See Sha bo tshe ring, "Mkhas dbang Dge 'dun chos 'phel," 61. According to another biographer, he left for Labrang in 1923 at the age of nineteen; see Rdo rje rgyal, *Dge 'dun chos 'phel*, 13. Cf. Stoddard, *Le Mendiant de l'Amdo*, 39, who states that the monk left Ditsa for Labrang circa 1920, when he would have been about sixteen.

11. Pema Bhum, "The Heart-Beat of a New Generation," 6. I have substituted "wording" and "synonyms" for the given glosses "principles" and "expressions." Original text in Padma 'bum, *Mi rabs gsar pa'i snying khams kyi 'phar lding*, 16–17. The full translation is reproduced here in chapter 5.

12. Sha bo tshe ring, "Mkhas dbang Dge 'dun chos 'phel dang khong gi snyan rtsom bshad pa lhag bsam 'o ma'i rdzing bu," 61.

13. This is the name given for the teacher in Bkras mthong, *Dge 'dun chos 'phel gyi lo rgyus*, 17. Cf. Sha bo tshe ring, "Mkhas dbang Dge 'dun chos 'phel dang khong gi snyan rtsom bshad pa lhag bsam 'o ma'i rdzing bu," 61, who states that the teacher's name was Mkhan chen Blo bzang lung rtogs chos kyi rgya mtsho.

14. Bkras mthong, *Dge 'dun chos 'phel gyi lo rgyus*, 17.

15. Ibid., 18.

16. This poem has been published in Dge 'dun chos 'phel, *Collected Works*, 389–90. The given title of the poem, "Bla brang la skur ba'i ka rtsom," was most likely applied by the editor Horkhang Sönam Penbar. Rdo rje rgyal, *'Dzam gling rig pa'i dpa' bo rdo brag Dge 'dun chos 'phel gyi byung ba brjod pa bden gtam rna ba'i bcud len*, 22, mentions

an alternative and more probable title: "Gnas chung zhu 'phrin" (Letter to the Oracle).

17. Stoddard, *Le Mendiant de l'Amdo*, 145.

18. Rdo rje rgyal, *Dge 'dun chos 'phel*, 23.

19. Ibid.

20. For a biographical summary see Stoddard, *Le Mendiant de l'Amdo*, 157–60.

21. See Tashi Tsering, "The Life of Rev. G. Tharchin," 9.

22. A French translation of the poem is available in Stoddard, *Le Mendiant de l'Amdo*, 176–77.

23. Another potential influence which I do not discuss here is suggested by Leonard van der Kuijp: "Dge-'dun-chos-'phel appears to have been considerably influenced by S. K. De's theories"; see his "Review of *Snyan-ngag me-long-gi spyi-don sdeb-legs rig-pa'i 'char-sgo*, by Tshe-tan Zhabs-drung 'Jigs-med rigs-pa'i blo-gros," 213.

24. Tib. "Bya len ma mngon par shes pa'i zlos gar," *Dge 'dun chos 'phel gyi gsung rtsom: A Collection of Miscellaneous Writings by Ven. Gedun Chophel*, vol. 2 (1991), ed. T. G. Dhong-thog, 233–58; and Dge 'dun chos 'phel, *Collected Works* 2, 423–48.

25. Rdo rje rgyal, *Dge 'dun chos 'phel*, 101; and Sha bo tshe ring, *Mkhas dbang Dge 'dun chos 'phel*, 69. Cf. Mengele, *dGe-'dun-chos-'phel*, 8, and Huber, *The Guide to India*, 4, who state that he returned to Lhasa in 1946. I have recorded 1945 here, because Mengele herself cites Horkang Sönam Penbar as stating that he and Gendün Chömpel "met for the first time in 1945." Mengele, *dGe-'dun-chos-'phel*, 15. The issue should be resolved, but it is not critical for our purposes.

26. A critical edition of this biography by Sherap Gyatso (also known as Go 'jo A pho Bla chung, 1905–75) has been translated and researched by Mengele, *dGe-'dun-chos-'phel*, 36.

27. Stoddard, *Le Mendiant de l'Amdo*, 184. Publishing details for these works are provided in Mengele, *dGe-'dun-chos-'phel*. At the same time, we should recall that another work by Kālidāsa, the *Meghadūta* (Tib. *Sprin gyi pho nya*), had been available in Tibetan since the thirteenth century. See Kapstein, "The Indian Literary Identity in Tibet," 22.

28. This observation is made in a literary history by the Central Nationalities Institute, which determined that the "old fisherman" in one of Gendün Chömpel's poems is inspired by Pushkin's children's tale "The Tale of the Old Fisherman and the Goldfish." See Sha bo tshe ring, *Mkhas dbang Dge 'dun chos 'phel*, 81.

29. Three of his poems first published in the *Mahabodhi* (Calcutta) in 1941 have been reprinted by the Amnye Machen Institute (Dharamsala). See "English Poems of Gendun Choephel: Manasarowar, Milarepa's Reply, Rebkong," *Lungta* 9 (1995), 12–13.

30. Bkras mthong, *Dge 'dun chos 'phel gyi lo rgyus*, 19–20.

31. Ibid., 19.

32. The commentary referred to here is entitled "Snyan dngags me long gi 'grel pa dbyangs can dgyes pa'i rol mtsho," entry no. 3333 in Lokesh Chandra, *Materials for a History of Tibetan Literature*, vol. 1.

33. Bkras mthong, *Dge 'dun chos 'phel gyi lo rgyus*, 166.

34. See "Praise of Buddha Śākyamuni for his Teaching of Relativity," trans. R. Thurman, in *Life and Teaching of Tsongkhapa*, 99–107 (Dharamsala: LTWA, 1982), as cited in Mengele, *dGe-'dun-chos-'phel*, 73, 127.

35. "Jam dpal rdzogs chen gyi gzhi lam bras bu," as cited in Mengele, *dGe-'dun-chos-'phel*, 73.

36. Stoddard, *Le Mendiant de l'Amdo*, 183.

37. See poems from the section "Snyan ngag thor bu" (Miscellaneous poems) in Dge 'dun chos 'phel, *Collected Works*.

38. See "Mi rtag pa dran pa'i gsung mgur." Though this poem is entitled as a "*mgur*," the use of the honorific "*gsung*" implies that Horkhang himself probably named the poem. The title is a bit misleading in that the form of the poem (eleven syllables) is *snyan ngag*, and not *mgur*, for which each line typically contains six syllables.

39. Ibid., 219.

40. Tib. *Nub Bod legs bcos skyid sdug*; Chin. *Xizang geming dang*. Note that the latter translates as the "Tibet Revolutionary Party." For more information on this important political initiative, which was closely associated with the Chinese Nationalist Party (Guomindang) and founded in 1946, see Stoddard, *Le Mendiant de l'Amdo*, Goldstein, *A History of Modern Tibet*, and McGranahan, "Empire, Archive, Diary," who draws from the diary of the founder Pomda Rapga (c. 1900–1976). According to McGranahan, Pomda Rapga also wrote on the need for vernacular literature in the introduction to a grammar book in the late 1940s.

41. For more information about this painter (also known as Jampa Tseten) and the significance of his work see Harris, *In the Image of Tibet*.

42. About one hundred handwritten copies of Gendün Chömpel's imperial history based on ancient Dunhuang texts, the *Deb ther dkar po* (White annals), were surreptitiously circulated throughout Tibetan areas during the Cultural Revolution. After the fall of the Gang of Four, cyclostyle copies were privately produced and distributed. Pema Bhum, interview with author, Jersey City, November 2002.

43. Kronfeld, *On the Margins of Modernism*, 32–33. To be more precise, it was not simply a lack of resonance that slowed his reception but also the scattering during the Cultural Revolution of his works, which were retrieved by Horkhang Sönam Penbar only in the 1980s.

44. Reviews of Giteng Rinpoché's writings include Blon phrug Gnam lha rgyal, "Yongs 'dzin Blo bzang dpal ldan gyi snyan rtsom las 'Pho nya gzhon nu don grub' kyi sgyu rtsal gyi khyad chos rags tsam gleng ba," *Bod ljongs zhib 'jug* 1991, no. 1, 43–57; Lha mkhar tshe ring, "Rtogs brjod gser gyi me tog gi khyad chos mdo tsam gleng ba," *Gtsos mi rigs dge thon ched gnyer slob grwa'i rig gzhung dus deb* 1 (1991), 81–88; Stobs ldan, "Rje Blo bzang dpal ldan gyi snyan ngag gi rig rtsal la che long tsam dpyad pa," *Bod ljongs zhib 'jug* 1992, no. 2, 26–37; and Zon thar rgyal, "'Sprin gyi pho nya' dang 'Pho nya gzhon nu Don grub' gnyis la dpyad bsdur gyi gtam rob tsam gleng ba," *Bod kyi rtsom rig sgyu rtsal*, 1992, no. 5, 35–43. For a biographical article see 'Jigs med bsam grub, "'Jam dbyangs bla ma yongs 'dzin paṇḍita blo bzang dpal ldan gyi rnam thar mdor bsdus," *Bod ljongs zhib 'jug* 1990, no. 1, 136–45.

45. I have derived the dates for Giteng Rinpoché from Blo bzang chos grags and Bsod

nams rtse mo, eds., *Gangs ljongs mkhas dbang rim byon gyi rtsom yig gser gyi sbram bu*, vol. 3, 2029–31.

46. "Young Döndrup" was written as a poetic flourish and at times humorous accompaniment to Giteng Rinpoché's actual letter to Marnang Dorjechang, which was a separate text.

47. The two monasteries are not really this far apart. Like much *snyan ngag*, this exhibits the use of hyperbole ('*ud chen po*).

48. This refers to Dorjedzong Monastery, in Huangnan Prefecture.

49. A human emanation of Manjuśri, bodhisattva of wisdom. Marnang Dorjechang (also known as Jikmé Damchö Gyatso) was Giteng's student, as well as the reincarnation of Giteng's teacher, Jikmé Samten (1814–97).

50. Tib. *bden tshig*. Words which are spoken by a lama for someone's safety, success, etc., and have a powerful prophetic effect.

51. The translation of this poem is based on the version that appears in Blo bzang chos grags and Bsod nams rtse mo, *Gangs ljongs mkhas dbang*, vol. 3, 2031–47.

52. This refers to the poem "'Phrin yig ngang mo rnam rtsen" (Letter: Frolic of the swan) by the seventeenth-century Tibetan scholar Mipam Gelek Namgyel. The author is grateful to Pema Bhum for this information. A published version of the poem is not readily available outside the PRC.

53. Blo bzang chos grags and Bsod nams rtse mo, eds., *Gangs ljongs mkhas dbang*, 2039.

54. Ibid., 2036.

55. The reasoning for this was explained to me by Professor Jamyang Drakpa (a student of Tseten Zhapdrung, himself a student of Giteng Lozang Penden) who tutored me on the entirety of this poem in the spring of 2000 during my stay at the Qinghai Nationalities Institute in Xining. According to his biography, Giteng Rinpoché went to Dorjé County (Tshe khog) twice in his lifetime: once when he was forty-four years old and later when he was fifty-seven. It is more likely that he wrote the poem at this later date (in 1938), at which time he was engaged in Vajrabhairava meditation ('jigs byed kyi bsnyen pa).

56. Blo bzang chos grags and Bsod nams rtse mo, eds., *Gangs ljongs mkhas dbang*, 2039.

57. For example see Blon phrug Gnam lha rgyal, "Yongs 'dzin Blo bzang dpal ldan," 46–50.

58. Ibid., 54.

59. 'Ju Skal bzang, "Sgyu ma'i pho nya skul ba'i snyan tshig gzhon nu'i rol rtsed," 35–40.

60. Interview with Lauran Hartley, Xining, February 2001. Giteng Rinpoché's poem was also a model for Sangs rgyas, "Gces su 'os pa'i pha yul."

61. Petech, *Aristocracy and Government in Tibet*, 159. Also see n. 1, above.

62. The cabinet minister Dokhar Tsering Wanggyel (1697–1763), for example, wrote not only his own memoirs and the biography of the great Tibetan leader Miwang Polhané (1689–1747) but also the famous kāvya-inspired *Tale of the Incomparable Prince*, written in prose with mingled verse. In contrast to the works of the twenti-

eth century discussed here, Dokhar's piece for all intents and purposes reads as if it took place in India.

63. This translation is by Janet Upton; see her article "Cascades of Change," 20.

64. Ibid.

65. One exception may be seen in the songs of certain Amdo teachers; Zhapkar, for example, wrote folk-inspired verse of his experiences traveling in nomad areas. Yet even these must be seen as following in the line of Indic, dōha-inspired, religious "songs of realization." Another exception, the "love songs" of the Sixth Dalai Lama, are famous in large part for their uncharacteristically frank and sometimes ribald nature.

66. I am referring here to Ju Mipam's treatise on how a king should rule, the *Rgyal po'i lugs kyi bstan bcos* (1895).

67. Upton, "Cascades of Change," 19.

68. Jiangbian Jiacuo, *Ganxie shenghuo*, 490.

69. Danzhu Angben, *Zangzu wenhua fazhan shi*, 1120. One exception was *Kelzang Metok*, a novel about the arrival of the PLA into Tibet which Jiangbian Jiacuo (Tib. Jampel Gyatso) began writing in Chinese in 1960 (see chapter 3).

70. This point is made in Chab 'gag Rta mgrin, "Krung go gsar pa dbu brnyes pa'i dus 'go'i Bod kyi rtsom pa po grags can 'ga' dang khong tsho'i brtsams chos brjod pa," 23.

71. Chin. *san mian hongqi*, referring to "the general line of building socialism, the Great Leap Forward, and the people's communes." This term was also used as an alternative for The Great Leap Forward (1958–61). White, *Policies of Chaos*, 148.

72. This one stanza has five lines instead of the usual four, for reasons unknown to me.

73. The poem as reproduced here is based on the version in Chab 'gag Rta mgrin, "Krung go gsar pa," 16.

74. This is another epithet for Sherap Gyatso.

75. Shes rab rgya mtsho, *Rje btsun Shes rab rgya mtsho 'jam dpal dgyes pa'i blo gros kyi gsung rtsom*, vol. 2, 598.

76. The Tibetan and Chinese versions of this poem, along with an English translation (evidently derived from the Chinese), is published in Archives of the Tibet Autonomous Region, comp., *A Collection of Historical Archives of Tibet* (Beijing: Cultural Relics Publishing House, 1995), 107–1,2,3,4,5,6,7. My translation (based on the Tibetan original) is quite similar to the official English translation. I am grateful to Professor Elliot Sperling for alerting me to the existence of this poem.

77. The Dalai Lama stayed in Beijing until March 1955. Smith, *Tibetan Nation*, 412.

78. "King of Universal Respect" in the published translation. This title refers to the first king of the world, who was elected by the common consent of the people, according to Indic tradition. Das, *Indian Pandits in the Land of Snow*, 952.

79. I am thankful to Professor Leonard van der Kuijp for suggesting the translation of the Tibetan term *kru rda*.

80. Since the selection here emphasizes the Dalai Lama's praise of Chairman Mao, I am obliged to note that the Dalai Lama clearly asserts his sovereignty by signing

the letter as "the Fourteenth Dalai Lama Ngakwang Lozang Tenzin Gyatso, the unparalleled see who rules the three realms."

81. I am thankful to Pema Bhum (Latse Contemporary Tibetan Cultural Library) for this information.

82. The year and place of birth here are drawn from Rig gnas lo rgyus dpyad gzhi'i rgyu cha rtsom sgrig pu'u, ed., "Tsha sprul Ngag dbang blo bzang gi sku tshe smad cha'i mdzad rnam mdor bsdus," 33–42. Another biographical sketch can be found in Ko zhul Grags pa 'byung gnas and Rgyal ba Blo bzang mkhas grub, *Gangs can mkhas grub rim byon ming mdzod*, 1373–74.

83. Rig gnas lo rgyus, "Tsha sprul Ngag dbang blo bzang," 34.

84. Ko zhul and Rgyal ba, *Gangs can mkhas grub rim byon ming mdzod*, 1373.

85. Rig gnas lo rgyus, "Tsha sprul Ngag dbang blo bzang," 34–35.

86. Ko zhul and Rgyal ba, *Gangs can mkhas grub rim byon ming mdzod*, 1374.

87. The Xikang-Tibet highway was completed in 1955, the Qinghai-Tibet Highway only a few months later. See Dreyer, *China's Forty Million*, 132.

88. Tib. *G.yu yi ske rags gser kyi zam pa*. Rig gnas lo rgyus, "Tsha sprul Ngag dbang blo bzang," 40; and Ko zhul and Rgyal ba, *Gangs can mkhas grub rim byon ming mdzod*, 1374. Cf. Chab 'gag Rta mgrin (1999), who gives an alternate title: "Gser zam g.yu yi lam bu." The poem as reproduced here is based on what I believe to be an excerpt, as cited in Rig gnas lo rgyus.

89. This refers to the stars on the flag painted on the side of the plane.

90. Tib. "Lcags kyi phug ron dngul skya mdog." The poem as reproduced here is based on the version in *Bod kyi rtsom rig sgyu rtsal*, 1984, no. 1, 13–14.

91. Chab 'gag Rta mgrin, "Krung go gsar pa," 29.

92. Tib. "Gung khran tang gi 'khrungs skar dus chen la bsngags pa brjod pa." The poem as reproduced here is based on the version in *Bod kyi rtsom rig sgyu rtsal*, 1984, no. 1, 12–13.

93. Tib. "Tsung li Kra'u En len [sic] la bstod pa," "Rigs so so'i mi dmangs kyi gtso 'dzin Ma'o kru'u zhir bstod glu 'bul," "Dmags 'dzugs dus chen la phul ba." Cited in Ko zhul and Rgyal ba, *Gangs can mkhas grub rim byon ming mdzod*, 1374; and Chab 'gag Rta mgrin, "Krung go gsar pa," 25.

94. For example, two poems by Tsatrül Ngakwang Lozang originally published in 1956 in *Tibet Daily* are published in *Bod kyi rtsom rig sgyu rtsal*, 1984, no. 1, 12–14. One of these is "Silver Hue of the Iron Dove," discussed above.

95. Many of the earliest published literary works in the Tibetan magazine *Tibetan Art and Literature* were actually translations from Chinese and other languages.

96. Tsha sprul Ngag dbang blo bzang, *Sum cu pa'i snying po legs bshad*. His other textbooks include *Sum cu pa'i rtsa 'grel gyi dper brjod* (Illustrations of *sum cu pa* and commentary), and *Syan ngag me long gi le'u dang po dang le'u gnyis pa'i 'grel ba dang dper brjod* (Illustrations related to the first and second chapters of the *Kāvyādarśa*).

97. Chab 'gag Rta mgrin, "Krung go gsar pa," 38.

98. Gsung rab rgya mtsho, "Grong khyer Khran khrun gyi gnas tshul zhu ba'i 'phrin yig." The version here is cited in Chab 'gag Rta mgrin, "Krung go gsar pa," 38–39.

99. For a discussion of this term see the exquisite translation *The Life of Shabkar*, trans. Matthieu Ricard, 152 n. 23.

100. Cited in Chab 'gag Rta mgrin, "Krung go gsar pa," 41–42. A strong regionalist tendency can be seen in the songs of Zhapkar, a yogin from Amdo Repgong who also wrote songs of praise for Lake Qinghai as a pilgrimage site. Later versions seem to shift the emphasis from praise of a religious pilgrimage site to praise of the lake as a symbol or metonym of Amdo.

101. This type of metaphor (*the tshom gi dpe*) is one of thirty-two metaphorical ornaments (*dpe'i rgyan*), as discussed in the second chapter of the *Kāvyādarśa*. My definition here is drawn from Tshe tan Zhabs drung, *Snyan ngag spyi don*, 56.

102. Chab 'gag Rta mgrin, "Krung go gsar pa," 44.

103. See for example Gcod pa don grub, "Mtsho sngon por bstod pa'i glu dbyangs" (Song in praise of Lake Qinghai) in *Brtse dung gi mig chu* (Tears of love) (Chengdu: Si khron mi rigs dpe skrun khang, 1993), 54–62; and Bkra shis phun tshogs, "Mtsho khri phyogs rgyal mor phul ba'i glu dbyangs" (Song offered to Lake Qinghai), *Sbrang char*, 1 (1986), 71–74, repr. in *Sprin gyi sgra dbyangs* (Song of the clouds), Bod kyi deng rabs rtsom rig dpe tshogs (Tibetan modern literature series) (Xining: Mtsho sngon mi rigs dpe skrun khang, 1991), 270–79; and Chab gag rta mgrin, "Khri gshog rgyal mo'i glu dbyangs" (Song of the queen of ten thousand households), *Bod kyi rtsom rig sgyu rtsal*, 1982, no. 5, 23–24, repr. in *Sprin gyi sgra dbyangs*, 264–69.

104. Ye shes rdo rje et al., eds., *Gangs can mkhas dbang rim byon gyi rnam thar mdor bsdus*, 454–55.

105. Jiangbian Jiacuo, *Ganxie shenghuo*, 381.

106. Ibid.

107. Details can be found in Hartley, "Tibetan Publishing in the Early Post-Mao Period," 233–55.

108. Dung dkar Blo bzang 'phrin las, *Snyan ngag la 'jug tshul tshig rgyan rig pa'i sgo 'byed*.

109. Tshe tan zhabs drung, *Snyan ngag spyi don*.

110. Jiangbian Jiacuo, *Ganxie shenghuo*, 490.

111. Perry Link has observed a similar "revival" aspect in Chinese cultural production of the early 1980s; see Link, *The Uses of Literature*, 13.

2

Roar of the Snow Lion:

Tibetan Poetry in Chinese

YANGDON DHONDUP

> The past,
> Ah, how beautiful the past was,
> how beautiful, how beautiful,
> A beauty which cannot be expressed,
> A beauty which cannot be imagined,
> My past,
> Our past, . . .
> How beautiful, how beautiful, how beautiful.[1]
> —Weise (1999)

The past as a time of glory, nostalgic yearning as disapproval and criticism of the present—this imagined Tibet of the past as perfection is an image repeatedly found in the works of Tibetan poets born in the 1960s. These lines by Weise (Tib. Özer), born in 1966, chronicle the sense of loss and the possibility of return to the land from which she has been separated.[2] Weise belongs to this generation of younger poets, many of whom experience themselves as bereft of their past; their way of imagining their land is conditioned by guilt and troubled identity. While a return to the historic culture of Tibet is felt as a source of their identity, they also feel anxiety about reordering themselves by invoking it. This anxiety is in turn fractured because the poets express themselves in Chinese. The ambiguity of allegiance to the land is coupled with the unconscious sense of betrayal generated by this fracturing. The result is a dislocated relationship of the self toward Tibet, the land of their dreams.

This idealistic image of Tibet differs from the vision held by the previous generation of Tibetan poets who had also written their verses in Chinese. Tibet as a romantic construct of the imagination is not visible in their poems.

For them, as I will elaborate later, the past was something to abhor and was associated with the trauma of their experience. In that sense the imagining of Tibet by the younger generation represents a radical change of perception. Nevertheless, since this image of Tibet is born of the anxiety of not belonging, prompted by an inability to express oneself in Tibetan, it echoes the feelings of the older generation. As Tibetans who express themselves in Chinese, younger writers are unconsciously haunted by the predicament of belonging and not belonging. In both generations, deficiency of language has left writers with a shaken confidence evident in their work.

I wish to explore the differing voices and images of the native land and self fashioned by Tibetan poets writing in Chinese. To begin, I discuss the emergence of the first generation of Tibetan poets to write in Chinese. I have used the term "pioneers" to distinguish this group, since their writings were precursors to literary works by Tibetans after 1980 who also wrote in Chinese. In this group I have included five major poets: Wan Zuoliang (Tib. Tamdrin Gönpo), born in Labrang (Gansu Province) in 1934; Yidan Cairang (Tib. Yidam Tsering), born in Tsongkha (Qinghai Province) in 1933; Raojie Basang (Tib. Rapgyé Pasang), born in Dechen (Yunnan Province) in 1935; Geseng Duojie (Tib. Kelzang Dorjé), born in Trika (Qinghai Province) in 1936; and Gongbu Zhaxi (Tib. Gönpo Trashi), also born in Labrang in 1938.[3] I have paid greater attention to poems by Yidan Cairang, since he was an especially influential figure on the literary scene.[4] His publication record exceeded by far the output of his contemporaries. But among all of the Tibetan poets it seems that Tamdrin Gönpo was the first Tibetan to ever publish a poem in Chinese, in 1955.[5]

I then look at poetry from the mid-1980s onward, when a younger generation of poets came to the forefront and took over the newly established practice of writing poetry in Chinese. The poetry of this generation differs in content and form from that of its predecessors. Most importantly, the poets emerged during a time of tremendous political and cultural change. After the death of Mao Zedong in 1976 and the arrest of the Gang of Four, Deng Xiaoping assumed political leadership. His program of reforms had an immense impact among literary circles throughout China. Writers and artists were rehabilitated, and in a speech delivered at the Fourth Congress of Writers and Artists in 1979, Deng Xiaoping "promised an end to interference with artistic creation."[6] This cultural autonomy also extended to minority writers, and for the first time Tibetan writers and poets did not have to demonstrate political allegiance to China in their work.

My aim is to focus first on the educational background of these poets. The history of Chinese-medium education in the border areas of Tibet illustrates the diverse use of language. I will trace how the Republican government (Guomindang) supported education among Tibetans as part of its project to gain control in the shaping of character and moral thinking. The importance of education in consolidating power was clearly visible in the Republican government's policy toward Tibetans in the border regions. I shall then look at how Tibetan poets under the newly established communist system produced certain kinds of work. How are we to understand this literature and how do these Tibetan poets relate to it? As for the younger generation of poets, how do they communicate their social and political environment, and how do they reconcile their medium with their ethnicity?

The Pioneers

The 1930s were turbulent years in the histories of both China and Tibet. The Japanese had occupied Manchuria, the Red Army had begun the Long March in Jiangxi, and the Communist Party had moved to Yan'an. The Tibetan political situation also deteriorated after the death of the thirteenth Dalai Lama in 1933. The interregnum that followed weakened Tibet's political status, and the Chinese Republican government sought to assert power in all Tibetan areas. Huang Musong's mission to Lhasa in 1934 was an important initial contact between the new regime in China and Tibet, leading to a Chinese presence in Lhasa after a near-absence of some twenty years.[7] In the border areas of eastern Tibet, the Tibetan government had long ago lost its jurisdiction, and local chieftains (dpon) were ruling over vast territories.

Amid this political chaos Yidan Cairang was born in 1933, in the little village of Chongtse (Ch. Congzhi) in Tsongkha, nowadays better known as Ping'an County in the province of Qinghai. The area is well known as the birthplace of Tsongkhapa, founder of the Gelukpa school of Tibetan Buddhism, and for the famous monastery of that school, Kumbum. The territory was incorporated as an administrative area in Qinghai Province by the Republican government in 1928. The province was at that time ruled by the Muslim warlord Ma Qi, later succeeded by his sons Ma Buqing and Ma Bufang. Born into a family of farmers, Yidan Cairang had no real prospect of receiving a Tibetan education. The only avenues of education for Tibetans were joining a monastery and studying with a private teacher invited into the home. Since Yidan Cairang's family was relatively poor, his father decided to send him to a Chinese school. The writer recalls that about ten Tibetan youngsters were sent from his village to that Chinese school.[8] Thus the first education he received was in the Chinese language.

The Sinophone Tibetan writer Yidan Cairang (Tib. Yidam Tsering) in cadre clothing, late 1970s. Photo courtesy of Latse Contemporary Tibetan Cultural Library.

It is interesting to note that Puntsok Tashi Takla (1922–2000), who later became the brother-in-law of the present Dalai Lama, was born some years earlier than Yidan Cairang in the same village of Chongtse. In his unpublished memoir he recalls his childhood education:

> When I was five years old, I started studying the Chinese language with Lhamo Dhondup. (Lay children in Tsongkha did not study Tibetan.) Our teacher was a 50-year-old Chinese man, who lived with us. He had come to our area to escape the famine in the neighbouring Chinese area. He taught us in the morning and evening, while herding our sheep during the day.
>
> The elderly Chinese man was well-versed in Chinese literature. Apart from the language, he taught us Chinese history and enchanted us with Chinese stories containing lessons on filial relationship. Since there were no schools in our village, it was very difficult to get textbooks. Our teacher followed the old Chinese pedagogy, in which memorization was very important. Every morning he put us through a test to see if we had memorized the words taught on the previous day. We memorized late into the night by oil lamp.

In 1933–1934, a small Chinese school was opened in the eastern part of C[h]ongtse, where there was a fairly large concentration of Chinese population. The school had more than one hundred students, of whom ten or more were from our village. Altogether, the school had approximately fifteen Tibetan students. Soon the Chinese authorities were announcing that they had opened schools in all the Tibetan nomadic and agricultural areas. As a matter of fact, there were schools only in those areas where the Chinese population predominated.[9]

Another contemporary, Tsongkha Lhamo Tsering, also received his first education in Chinese.[10] Tsongkha Lhamo Tsering, like most Tibetans from the Tsongkha area, had long forgotten his mother tongue and spoke exclusively in the Xining dialect. It was only later that he learned to write and speak Tibetan. After graduating from the Xining Teacher's Training School (Xining jianyi shifan xuexiao) he was sent to the Institute for Frontier Minorities (Bianjiang minzu xueyuan) in Nanjing.[11] Thus the first formal education that Yidan Cairang, Puntsok Tashi Takla, and Tsongka Lhamo Tsering received was in the Chinese language. Tibetans in the Sino-Tibetan border areas were educated in Chinese long before Tibetans in central Tibet were. This exposure to modern education led to the emergence of a group of Tibetans in the eastern regions who were fluent in Chinese. Many were employed as translators, first by the Republican government and later by the Communist Party.

In 1948 Yidan Cairang was sent to Xining to the Kunlun Middle School (Kunlun zhongxue). This school, which had been established by Ma Bufang, recruited mainly Chinese Muslim and Hui students, but some sixty Tibetan students from the surrounding area were also registered at that time.[12] Even though the fees, lodging, and board were paid by the school, life at Kunlun Middle School was extremely harsh. The Tibetan students not only studied but were also trained in combat. They were not allowed to speak in Tibetan among themselves.[13] Ma Bufang's aim in recruiting Tibetan students was to later use them as mediators or translators for his military advance into Tibetan areas. His authority was expanding within Qinghai and into present-day Gansu, placing the Tibetans inhabiting these areas under increasing pressure. Ma Bufang therefore sought to consolidate his power by recruiting Tibetans to serve under him. One method was to make use of education. A number of schools were thus established while Ma Bufang controlled the area.

The Republican government later followed this same strategy: between 1935 and 1937 about ten primary schools were established in the area surrounding Xining, capital of Qinghai Province.[14] This was followed by the founding of a Mongolian and Tibetan State Central School (Meng Zang zhongxin guojia xuexiao) in each county, as well as the Mongolian-Tibetan Middle School (Meng Zang zhongxue), the Mongolian-Tibetan Teacher Training School (Meng Zang shifan xuexiao), and the Government Teacher Training School of Xining (Guoli Xining shifan xuexiao), all in Xining.[15] Most of these schools offered a normal curriculum of mathematics, geography, science, general knowledge, history, Chinese, and also Tibetan language. In Kham, southeastern Tibet, the Republicans had also established a number of schools, such as the Batang Government School (Guoli Batang xuexiao) and the Barkham Government School (Guoli Ma'erkang xuexiao).

In 1934 the Republican government sent Huang Musong to Lhasa to negotiate with the Tibetan government about establishing an office for the Commission for Mongolian-Tibetan Affairs (Meng Zang weiyuanhui) and a school in Lhasa.[16] Though a school already existed in Lhasa, it was reserved for the children of Hui families.[17] The Republican school started enrolling students in 1938 and was in the Tromzikhang, on the north side of the Barkhor. The staff comprised Chinese, Hui, and Tibetan teachers.[18] Baba Püntsok Wanggyel, a progressive pro-Communist Tibetan from Batang (Kham), also taught for a short period in that school.[19]

Though Tibet had a highly sophisticated system of education, it was confined almost entirely to the monasteries. Some wealthier families provided education for their children by inviting teachers to give private tuition, and in the 1940s many of the aristocratic and trading families sent their children to British schools in India. The only two schools established by the Tibetan government were the Potala School (Rtse slob grwa) and the Accounting Office (Rtsis khang).[20] Both schools were, however, reserved mainly for children from the aristocracy or for children of government employees. The curriculum consisted of a rigid system of memorizing texts, calligraphy, law, and accounting.[21] There were a number of attempts to establish other schools, such as the Gyantsé School and the Lhasa English School, but unfortunately these projects were undermined by conservative factions within the clergy.[22]

The Republican school continued until late 1949, when the Chinese mission was expelled from Lhasa. Among those deported from Lhasa was Baba Püntsok Wanggyel, who later became a leading communist official. One of the best-known students in the school was Gyalo Döndrup, elder brother of the present Dalai Lama. Besides him and several other children from the Tibetan aristocracy, there were also a few students from the Nepali and Muslim communities of Lhasa.[23] It must be noted that this school was established mainly for the benefit of the local Chinese population, which consisted largely of merchants and the staff of the Chinese mission.

The Republican's emphasis on education, especially for the non-Han population, can be traced back to the Republican leader Sun Yatsen's "Three People's Principles" (*San min zhuyi*), a summary of his political philosophy. The serious political blows from both internal and external attacks that China had suffered in the beginning of the twentieth century had led many Chinese intellectuals to seek a remedy that would rejuvenate and strengthen their nation, and it was as part of this drive that Sun Yatsen had formulated the three principles of nationalism, democracy, and people's livelihood,[24] based on his conviction that the Chinese people were subjugated not only by the Manchu rulers but also by foreign powers. National consciousness and solidarity were two of the conditions which Sun Yatsen saw as lacking in the Chinese people, and the use of institutions to inculcate feelings of national sentiment and integration was regarded as one way of restoring this national spirit.[25] The Republicans thus emphasized education to arouse nationalism. However, in Tibet it seems that they were equally concerned with the loyalty of the non-Han population: for the Republicans members of the new generation of educated "minorities" were to be mediators for Sun Yatsen's new China. One of the songs taught by teachers at the school in Lhasa, for example, was *Wo ai Zhonghua* (I love China). The students were also instructed to learn the "Three Loves" (*san ai*) — love for China, love for the people, and love for the school.[26] The political insertions within the school curriculum were efforts to mold the Tibetans into individuals loyal to China, representing the dissemination not only of knowledge but of an ideology situating Tibet within China.

As we can see, in the first half of the twentieth century Chinese was being slowly introduced as the language of education and modernization in many Tibetan areas. The location and time were very important for shaping the future education of the poets: it was not an accident that these poets should have emerged from those border areas which had the closest contact with Chinese culture. Moreover, the region of Amdo was cohabited by Muslims, Han, Mongols, Salars, and Tibetans, for whom Chinese was the language of inter-ethnic communication; the Tibet-China borderlands of Amdo and Kham are the points of Tibetan culture and political influence farthest from Lhasa. Even more than location, timing is crucial in understanding the emergence of Tibetans writing in Chinese: the early poets grew up in a period when China was emerging from the collapse of dynastic rule. Concepts of nationhood were introduced and new social relationships between the citizen and the state were being established.

Young Tibetans learned not only a new language but also aspects of the new nation's ideological message. While in colonized territories the first writers to express themselves in the language of the colonial power have often been from the middle class, most of the Tibetans in the eastern Tibetan schools were from relatively poor family backgrounds.[27] This emphasis on the selection of "mediators" served Mao's proletarian ideal by giving the masses the opportunity to be the masters of their own destiny. This class background made them especially receptive to the Communist Party's message of reform and equality. It was as part of the beneficiary class of the communist revolution that the first generation of Tibetan poets would express a deep gratitude toward the party and write in a style that would often conform to China's national trend. This cultural transference reflects the chronology of their writing careers, which encompassed the development of China and witnessed the onset of Tibetan modernity.

Writing for the Motherland

After the Communists moved to Yan'an in 1936, Mao summoned artists and writers for a meeting on literature and art. The talk, which was later publicized as the "Talks at the Yan'an Forum on Literature and Art," set the guidelines for literature and art until the late 1970s. In his talk Mao made clear to the writers that literature must serve the masses and that the writer's task is to produce art that is easily accessible. Yidan Cairang, for example, began his writing career by translating folk stories into Chinese—tales which he had heard from his mother or which were commonly known among Tibetans. Writers, Mao further declared, should learn from the proletariat (then defined as workers, peasants, and soldiers), so that they could produce works with a revolutionary spirit. Restrictions on writers were implicit in his pronouncement that literature is inseparable from politics; literature in the Mao era thus became a political tool.

In the 1950s, when the Communists marched into Tibet, literature and art were important elements in propaganda and in spreading the party's message. Stories and poems depicted how backward Tibetan society was and how the masses had suffered under the "old society." At first these writings were mainly produced by the PLA's "cultural officers."[28] The policies on literature and art were not only intended for Chinese writers and artists but also extended to other nationalities. Tibetans were therefore asked to show their joy at being liberated and their love for Mao. A good example of an early Tibetan poem (written in Chinese) is "Chairman Mao Is Our Beacon":

One thousand lamps, ten thousand lamps,
Chairman Mao is the beacon of all revolutionary people!

One thousand red flags, ten thousand red flags,
The thought of Chairman Mao is the greatest!

One thousand books, ten thousand books,
Chairman Mao's books are the most revolutionary!

Even forests change into brushes, oceans to ink,
They can never express the liberated serfs' love for
Chairman Mao![29]

Like the poets in China, Tibetan poets in the early 1950s and 1960s were producing works that showed their loyalty to the party and Mao. In addition, the voice of the "liberated serf" was important to the party, since it communicated to the public that the "liberation" of Tibet was welcomed by "oppressed" Tibetans and had therefore been necessary.

Yidan Cairang also wrote eulogizing poems in his early career. His poem "Dang a, wode ama" (The party, my mother) praises the Communist Party:

Today, I sing to my heart's content,
The voice which comes from the depths of my heart.

The Party, ah, my beloved Mother!
The mother lives in the heart of the son.

The Party, ah, my beloved *Ama*!
The son grows up in the mother's bosom.

The Party, ah, the mother who lights up the world!
The whole nation is reborn in your bosom.

Ah! In that dark old society
Who could say that we had this status then?

Our nation which has suffered
Is like a "clumsy wild ox" in the mouth of a wild animal.

· · · · · · · · · · · · · · · · · · ·

When the glory of the Party shines on the snow mountain
Ha! Ha! The "wild ox" jumps with exultation in the ranks of the people.

· ·

We are the masters of our time,
We dictate the motion of time's vehicle.

How good! People's time, people's world,
How good to be under the leadership of the Party and the radiance of
    socialism.[30]

This poem in many ways typifies the Communist vision of the relationship between the party and the Tibetan people. The party is represented as a mother who extends her maternal protection to the infant, while the child finds love and protection in the bosom of the mother. This relationship is reinforced by the contrasting use of the past and present, a technique used in proletarian poems and stories to convey the misery of life in the past and the brightness of the present and future. The serf therefore becomes the master in the present. The message of the poem is clear: progress and material wealth could only be achieved because of the leadership of the party.

Unshakable belief in the party can be also seen in Gongbu Zhaxi's "Gaobie mama" (Farewell to mother), in which the poet conveys his love for the motherland while on a visit to Canada with a Tibetan dance group:[31]

The pitiful tears
Drop finally over Canada.
Motherland, you are like a warm current surging in my heart
The red flag, fluttering like a red flame

. . . .

The Great Wall, that loftiness of spirit
Warms my blood.

. . . .

China, the most beautiful flower
Opens up above the Pacific

. . . .

Motherland, ah, Mama!
I am indeed the most beautiful flower among the fifty-six.[32]

This image of the nation as a mother recurs in most poems of this early patriotic type. China is repeatedly glorified in multifarious ways, revealing a deep nationalistic feeling toward China, but little poetic skill. Many of the poems in the early years after the Communist victory were written in a simple and straightforward style. Poetic technique was not put in the foreground, since content was the primary concern. Simplicity of style and form was promoted by the Communist Party so that the political message could be easily understood by the masses.

After the Lhasa uprising in 1959 and the consequent flight of thousands of refugees across the Himalayas, Kelzang Dorjé wrote "Zhebian shi nide jiaxiang" (This is your native place), a poem dedicated to the Tibetans who went into exile in India.[33] In the middle of the last stanza he urges his compatriots to return to their native land:

Come back! This is the place where your loving mother grew up
Compatriot, *Khampas* of Tibet,
There is no need to writhe and hesitate in the mud.
Come back! This is your strong and prosperous motherland.
Compatriot, *Amdowas* of Tibet,
There is no need to shed any more tears by the banks of the Ganges,
Come back!

The early poems by these poets were eulogies to the party and to Mao. The themes were mainly political and expressed in a simple style; the message was direct. It must be noted that these poets were writing during a time when literary creativity and sensitivity were divorced from the artist's personal experience. The poems were published in official party-controlled magazines and journals. Thus the content of the poems reflected the official view rather than an expression of individual sentiment and feeling. The party used early Tibetan writers writing in Chinese as agents to convey political messages to the masses. We can say therefore that historical and political conditions gave rise to this form of poetry and that the works are consequently the product of historical rather than individual circumstance.

The Roar of the Snow Lion: Cultural Nationalism in the Works of Yidan Cairang

Among the earlier generation of poets, only Yidan Cairang was to find a new readership. He became popular among Tibetan readers because his works were readily comprehensible, with frequent references to Tibetan folksongs and stories and a strong folk flavor. This Tibetan flavor can also be seen in the poems of contemporaries, such as Tamdrin Gönpo's "Chun yuan" (Spring wish).[34] Yidan Cairang's use of symbolic motifs, such as the constant reference to "snow" — Tibet is often referred to in Tibetan as the "land of snows" (*gangs ljongs*) and the mythical animal associated with Tibet is the snow lion (*gangs seng*)[35] — and to "nationality," are reminders to the Tibetan readership that his poems show a consciousness firmly centered on Tibet. His long poem "Muqin xinshou de ge" (The song mother taught me) is a good introduction to the story of his life:[36]

The world I was born in,
Was a "pure soil" protected by *Dharma*.
But at the door of the honest and kind-hearted,
One could often hear the howls of the demon.

What the narrator refers to as the "pure soil protected by Dharma" is Tibet before the Chinese arrival, when Buddhism was prevalent, and the door stands for the boundary between Tibet and China. The narrator then becomes an adult and leaves his native place:

> When mother saw me off,
> The morning star was sprinkling sparkling morning dews,
> But the dark and dense fog,
> Suffocates the gorge leading to the river.
>
> When I went on my road and said farewell to my mother,
> I thought the *Sechen* flower covered the way to the mountain road.
> However, like a starving wolf, the bitter winter's snowstorm
> Swallowed me into a bottomless icy hole.
>
> In drowsiness it's as if my mother's voice is telling me
> The story of "Ayé Tsomo and her Mottled Calf."
> ". . . the mottled calf was eaten by the evil spirit for lunch;
> In the evening it will eat all its organs."
>
> "The destitute *Ayé* fortunately,
> Met the magpie, the frog, cow dung and a stone roller,
> Who exterminated the ruthless nine-headed spirit—
> Indeed, she was relying on their wisdom and help."
>
> Now I understand the value of life.
> How can one weep in silence and bear the humiliation?
> These larvae wriggling in the scorching heat
> Will not let your flesh and blood wait for the winter.
>
> Ah, the value of life should be
> Like the fruits ripened in autumn that nourish the soul,
> The good seeds of mankind,
> Sowed into the fertile land of aspiration.

When leaving his home, the narrator soon discovers that the road he is taking is not as beautiful as he imagined. As the tone of the poem becomes more serious, the voice of the narrator acquires growing maturity during his journey. Through his recollection of a popular folk story, he finally comes to understand the meaning of life.

The inclusion of traditional modes of expression, songs, and folk stories is common in Yidan Cairang's poetry. By evoking them he not only shows that he is rooted in Tibetan culture but at the same time tries to make his readership understand that one can find wisdom and redemption in one's own culture. It is exactly this way of thinking—his reference to his own culture as a source of regaining balance and strength—that makes him popular among Tibetan readers.

In the following lines Yidan Cairang refers not only to his situation as a Tibetan but also to developments in China:

> Our path is far away from being straight,
> Sometimes we have to walk repeatedly over the crooked road.
> Among the tens of thousands of rivers heading towards the great sea
> There is not one which is not twisted and narrow.
>
> Our path is also not smooth,
> Sometimes the feet ache from the hard and narrow road.
> If the road ahead were as boundless as the sky,
> Then mother need not have sweated blood to mold me.
>
> It's true, on our road
> We have suffered injustice and woes,
> But the craftsman's hammer in his left hand,
> Accidentally hits the right hand.
>
> I am no longer innocent.
> I cannot believe that in front of me there is no cold stream to numb my
>   feet,
> Yet the iced snow on the heaven's lake has already melted,
> And a flock of wild geese sing from the top of their lungs.

In this poem, written in 1981, the poet alludes in the last two stanzas to an important development at the time. The chaotic years of the Cultural Revolution, ten years that came to an end only in 1976, are described in the first two stanzas. With the death of Mao in 1976, the Chinese leadership slowly began to loosen its grip on the people and removed from power Mao's inner circle, the Gang of Four. The hammer is thus the instrument by which the great craftsman Mao molded his policy (as did, the poem implies, his political successors like Deng Xiaoping), while the Gang of Four is his right hand. Even with the disabling of the craftsman's right hand, the narrator still feels reluctant to believe that life will improve. This hesitancy on the part of the narrator is understandable because of the innumerable political campaigns that China has endured even since the death of Mao: the durability of reform remains uncertain, lasting only until the next political campaign sweeps the country. Interestingly, the last two lines are identical to Döndrup Gyel's lyrics in the famous song "Mtsho sngon po" (The blue lake), verses which praise Lake Kokonor in Amdo and were set to music by the composer Wayemache Chopathar.[37]

Yidan Cairang's poems in the 1970s revolve around universal themes such as love and loneliness, drawing on images from nature. The poet communicates in purely aesthetic dimensions; he sings the song of a snow mountain, a river, or a lonely yak herder on the vast grassland. The tone and rhythms of these poems are gentle, hinting at an almost romanticized depiction of the landscape of Tibet. Inevitably some of the poet's works also included the requisite espousal of politically correct views and upheld the Communist Party in a positive light. However, one poem written even before the Cultural Revolution is remarkable for its expression of a more personal sentiment:

> A black stone soaked in the river cannot be washed white.
> A white stone placed under the sun cannot be darkened.
> Even if they were buried in a pile of ash,
> The rain can still distinguish them!
>
> What is true cannot be falsified.
> What is false cannot be true.
> This indeed is not difficult to understand![38]

These seven lines were part of a group of thirty poems written in 1963. The poet explains in a footnote that the whole poem was burned during the Cultural Revolution and that he was able to retrieve only a fraction of it from memory. The remarkable frankness in this poem reflects the situation of writers and intellectuals during the early 1960s, when campaigns such as the "Hundred Flowers Movement" (1956–57) and the consequent anti-rightist campaign had left people with a sense of disillusionment. Writers and poets active on the literary scene felt the encroaching control and abuse of literature by the party.

The poems written by Yidan Cairang from the 1980s onward reveal a shift in content and style. With the emergence of more liberal times throughout China, writers and poets were able to regain, in limited forms, their literary freedom. As part of the shift in the national trend in poetry, Yidan Cairang's poems became more subjective. He seems not only to have come to see himself as a poet writing for his own self-fulfilment but as a poet with a social conscience. His concern for his own people is visible in many of his works. With wider literacy in Tibet and a growing number of Tibetans capable of reading Chinese, he was at last able to write for a Tibetan audience. The poem "Lu" (Path) is strongly nationalistic and well known among the younger generation of Tibetans:

On the road I relish the speed of a horse's hoof.
In the desert I admire the heavy load a camel carries.
On the snow mountain that frightens the eagle,
I see the yak with its tongue stuck out jumping like a fierce tiger from
    the ravine!

Beneath the feet of those who struggle, there will always be a path!

Please do not think too highly of the one who dives into the water—
The necklaces of my ancestors are the corals deep in that sea![39]

Most of the Tibetans whom I asked about this poem interpreted it as a response to the Chinese. Some also voiced a feeling of pride after reading it. They acknowledged the validity of the poet's dissatisfaction and felt his anger and frustration. The yak, here representing the Tibetan people, is depicted as an animal full of vitality, which even though trapped succeeds in emerging from a deep and narrow place. The poet thus conveys faith in his own people and in those who continue to struggle.

The last two lines deliver the poet's message: it is of no use for others to boast about the profundity of their achievement, since the narrator's ancestors have long since decorated themselves with treasures found in their own culture. The depiction of Tibet as endowed with an ancient and rich culture invokes in many Tibetans a feeling that they need not be ashamed of being themselves. Frantz Fanon summed up this state of mind when he wrote: "Perhaps unconsciously, the native intellectuals, since they could not stand wonderstruck before the history of today's barbarity, decided to back further and to delve deeper down; and, let us make no mistake, it was with the greatest delight that they discovered that there was nothing to be ashamed of in the past, but rather dignity, glory, and solemnity."[40]

The past is also reclaimed as a source of pride in "Dabian" (A reply), in which Yidan Cairang equates Tibetan culture with other great cultures of the world.[41] He then urges Tibetans to renounce the imported culture and return to their cultural origins:

I praise the Amazon which sings the greatness of the native Americans.
I gasp in admiration when the Nile accumulates the splendour of the
    "Thousand and One Nights."
But I do not therefore blame at all my mother,
Because the Yellow River and the Yangtse River gave *Gesar* to a world of
    twinkling stars![42]
The cultural history of each nationality is not bestowed by heaven!

My responsibility is not to dress up my mother with things from faraway
   places,
But to transform my mother's milk into wisdom that inspires epics!

The poem is written in an ecstatic and dignified style, using exclamatory sentences and words such as "nationality" and "ancestors" to invoke dramatic
imageries. Here again the final couplet communicates the message of the
poet—as if Yidan Cairang is making an appeal to reject the modernity that
the Chinese have brought to Tibet and instead to draw strength from one's
own native culture. In another poem the same argument is evident in the last
two lines: "The cake beautifully painted cannot fill the growling stomach /
The coarse *tsampa* will strengthen your red copper-coloured body!"[43] Tsampa,
made of roasted barley, is the staple diet of the Tibetan people. The poet thus
points to a specific and unique ingredient of "Tibetanness." This repeated
insistence on using native elements to strengthen and rejuvenate oneself includes a cry against the Other's encroachment.

   Yidan Cairang's poems are replete with a conscious exploration of his own
cultural ideals. By drinking from one's own cultural reservoir, he argues, one
not only asserts one's identity but also maintains the integrity and conscience
of a people. This moral ideal challenges modernity, a development in which
the poet sees a compromising of his principles. By using terms such as "our
nationality" or "our ancestors" Yidan Cairang is trying to restore Tibetans'
pride in their own culture and tradition, while also urging others to be aware
of that culture and tradition. This nationalistic sentiment can be found in
the literatures of many other peoples who endured a history of colonialism.[44]
Yidan Cairang, whether he appreciated it or not, made a much stronger connection with Tibetan readers when he wrote in that nationalistic tone.

   It is interesting that while the first generation felt a close bond to their
own cultural group, they also retained faith in China, as if their cultural identity lay with the Tibetans and their political allegiance with China. This idea
of belonging to a geopolitical China arises from their upbringing. Theirs was
the generation that saw with its own eyes how China transformed itself into a
modern nation. They experienced the fall of the Republican government and
the rise of the Communist Party. By means of this political integration, they
felt that they were not only part of the history of China but also the makers of
a new Tibet.[45] The Communist Party entrusted them with an education and
the promise of a better and more just world. Having experienced at a young
age the harsh life of the poor, the new generation of educated Tibetans welcomed the eradication of class differences and the possibility of mass education provided by the arrival of the Communists. Education also provided

them with an otherwise unattainable status in their own community. Not only were they the first Tibetans to write in Chinese, they also represented a new type of modern Tibetan literati. The underlying sentiment evoked by their experience was a deep feeling of gratitude and belief in the party's policy of bringing reform and material progress to minority groups.

For some, however, enthusiasm for the party slowly waned after they realized that Tibetans were being treated unequally. For example, although mass education was made available, the Tibetans realized only too late that members of the younger generation were forgetting their mother tongue. Even in some remote areas, only Chinese was being taught in the schools.[46] Thus while Tibetans felt gratitude toward the party, a growing disillusionment was also visible. A realization of the disparity in power and the prevalent Chinese attitude toward Tibetans as second-class citizens triggered in some older Tibetans a reaction of distrust and a collapse of their ideals.

The enthusiasm of many youths in the early 1960s, when Yidan Cairang wrote "We Are the Masters of Our Time," can no longer be seen in his later work.[47] There was a growing realization that Tibetans would always be marginalized. This disenchantment results inevitably from being witness and part of a historical transition; many intellectuals could sense that "it is the privilege and the curse of midnight's children to be both masters and victims of their times."[48] This remark, from Salman Rushdie's *Midnight's Children*, epitomizes the situation of the now older Tibetans. They were born at a time when the old world collapsed and a new order emerged. Their lives encapsulated both mastery and victimization.

At the same time, this recognition opened a different path for some Tibetan poets and intellectuals. For Yidan Cairang, it seems that his frustration led him to write against what he saw as Chinese perceptions. His words suggest a tension, which is embedded in the social situation, between addressing his despair and finding a possible remedy. His courage in openly acknowledging pride in his culture parallels a response among African writers, as summarized by Fanon: "The Negro, never so much a Negro as since he has been dominated by the whites, when he decides to prove that he has a culture and to behave like a cultured person, comes to realise that history points out a well-defined path to him: he must demonstrate that a Negro culture exists."[49] Like the African writers in their early struggle against colonialism, Yidan Cairang is challenging the preconceived belief that Tibetans are barbarians and therefore have no culture. Though educated and raised by the party, he nevertheless managed to reclaim his own culture and values. In this sense Yidan Cairang stood out from all his contemporaries: his style of literary protest, in which the poet reflects on his situation, is unique among the first generation of poets.

Romantic Individualism: The Poetry of the Younger Generation

The younger generation of Tibetan poets was mostly born after the Cultural Revolution (1966–76) and therefore did not experience any of the political campaigns faced by the elder generation. While the elder generation first wrote revolutionary poetry for the party and only later proceeded to write works that did not relate to politics, most of the younger Tibetan poets began writing in the mid-1980s and were relatively free to write for themselves. Unlike the elder generation, younger poets had little political and historical burden to carry.

Most younger Sinophone poets also have limited experience of Tibetan life in the countryside, as they attended schools in metropolitan areas. Some are children from mixed marriages, whose fathers or grandfathers were *lao Xizangren*—Han Chinese who came to Tibet as PLA soldiers or cadres in the early 1950s and settled in Tibet after their retirement—and whose mothers were Tibetan. Others poets from Amdo belonged to the "Seven Villages of Repkong" (*Rong bo sde bdun*), an association of villages in Repgong (Ch. Tongren) with a bilingual Tibetan-Chinese school. Whether one was sent to the Tibetan or Chinese class was entirely dependent on the choice of the parents.

The language barrier meant that when many of these students returned after graduation they found difficulties in adjusting and being accepted by the community. Since they wrote in Chinese, they were inevitably shunned by the Tibetan literary community. The situation has improved considerably during recent years, but some Tibetan critics remain reluctant to accept the former students as "Tibetan" poets. Moreover, growing up among the Chinese seems to have had a particular impact on their identity. In many ways they had to assert themselves as Tibetans among Chinese while at the same time having to reclaim their Tibetanness in their own community.

The term "neither Chinese nor Tibetan" (*Rgya ma Bod*), which originally described Tibetans from the border areas, is sometimes used now to describe these hybrid Tibetans. In Amdo, Tibetan villages with a large number of Chinese residents slowly began to adopt Chinese customs and language—in some villages, for example, Tibetans still practiced Tibetan Buddhism but adopted Chinese customs, such as ancestor worship or burial rituals.[50] The local Chinese dialect was mixed with Tibetan words. Using the term "neither Chinese nor Tibetan" to refer to this group of Tibetan writers shows the equivocality of their position and the emergence of a new cultural subgroup.

One characteristic that differentiates their work from that of the older generation is the much more personal view of their surroundings in the poems of the younger generation, as the loosening of political restraints led to a rise in individualism. A good example of a highly subjective work is the long poem "Qunshan, huozhe guanyu wo ziji de songci" (Mountain range or the song about myself) by Alai, which speaks of the self-conscious search for the self:

I am myself,
I am also not myself either.
I am my own brother, my own lover,
My own child, my entire blood relation.
My fellow countrymen with their roots in the mountain,
My fellow villagers from the village.
When I am myself, I use the name my father has given to me.
When I am myself, my name is Alai,
This is the name fate has bestowed on me.[51]

The poem tells of the lonely journey through the varying landscapes of Tibet. Alai's language is ornate and eloquent.[52] By using his real name in the text, the poet implies that the "I" is the poet himself. (For further discussion of Alai's use of first-person narration see chapter 10.) Although the "I" is indeed a device for emphasizing a self-conscious form of narration, I believe that most of the younger Tibetan poets are defining themselves within a shared community of people, culture, and history, that they are defining themselves as Tibetans. This imagined coherence is represented by their reference to Tibet as their place of origin.

A similar exploration of the self can be seen in the works of other Tibetan poets such as Dodrak (Ch. Duozhi Ge). In his individualistic poem "Wo" (I), the theme of self is counterpoised with the theme of life and death.[53] The poem is a protest against death and ending. Though one discerns a certain naïveté in Dodrak's poems, he nevertheless succeeds in expressing fresh and charming images in simple, outspoken language.[54] In "Dansheng" (Being born), Jikmé Püntsok (Ch. Liemei Pingcuo) describes the hour of his birth in the vast grassland.[55]

Weise recollects the meeting of her past lover in "Ji nian yihou" (After many years).[56] The poem is about two lovers who have taken different paths. It tells the story of separation, of growing up in different worlds, and of the pain and happiness in being reunited. The poet's sense of belonging is redeemed by unification with her lover. Weise was unable to speak Tibetan, since the language spoken at home and outside was Chinese; this changed only when she returned to her birthplace in Lhasa and gradually learned her ancestral language.[57] The process of rediscovering her identity, linked to her return to the traditional center of Tibet, is visible and has inevitably shaped

The banned writer Weise
(Tib. Özer) with Patricia
Schiaffini in Lhasa, 1999.
Photo by Patricia Schiaffini.

her later works. She became a devout Buddhist and many of her poems revolve around religious themes:[58]

> At the monasteries of Labrang and Kumbum[59]
> She recalled a sentence by a poet:
> "The last thing I saw
> Were eyes filled with tears."
> Her eyes full of tears
> Did not pass through the borderline,
> Nor are they among the dead
> In the kingdom of dream.
> Yet, seeing the golden mirage,
> The golden Tara smiles from the corner of her mouth.
> The golden father, Tsering Dorjé,
> is wrapped in a monk's gown.

The narrator describes the sadness of seeing the once famous and flourishing monasteries. The monastic institutions were most strongly affected by
the Chinese arrival. During the Cultural Revolution some were used as pig-
sties, while others were converted into military barracks.[60] Kumbum, once
renowned for its magnificent butter sculptures and its jade-green roof tiles,
has nowadays become a busy tourist site. To earn a living the monks even
offer stalls where Chinese tourists can pose for photographs in Tibetan cos-
tumes. It is therefore not surprising for a devotee like Weise to feel disturbed

by seeing the monastery turned into a site of commerce for hawkers and noisy tourists.

In another poem, Weise tells the story of a monk:[61]

In what kind of mirage
Did I and he meet?
At that time, the sunset glowed like fire,
Like the burning gown.
I see his face—
Ah, a childlike face.
Restrained in this way
He grew up in silent tears.

It is the tale of suffering, a story which appears to be the enunciation of a troubled conscience and the search for a religious ideal. Through the description of the monk's tears, and the hint of repressed pain, the text suddenly becomes a site where social realities are questioned and right and wrong are exposed. This subversive quality in the text is echoed by Suobao (Tib. Söbo), who describes a Tibet bereft of its history: "When the traveller crosses the land of snows, / no footprints are left behind."[62]

Imagining Tibet

The discontinuity and ruptures in the identity of the younger generation have left many to embark upon a journey of self-discovery to find their spiritual and cultural origin. A return to the past and origins is undertaken by some writers through a re-association with actual space. They start their journey by repossessing the land from which they were literally separated. Geographical references therefore become crucial in redefining identity; as Edward Said writes, "the land is recoverable at first only through imagination."[63] The works of the Tibetan poets are therefore replete with images of monasteries, rivers, grasslands, and snow mountains—images that metaphorically stand for Tibet.

The land is described in imagery that is both individualistic and romantic. Banguo (Tib. Banko), a great-grandson of the renowned Amdo chieftain Gyapön Guru Dorjé[64] who now works as an editor at the Qinghai Nationalities Publishing House, describes the grassland as capable of working miraculous effects:[65]

When I walked through the Tawu grassland,
I felt, starting from my legs, my entire body shake like water.

This mysterious shake started spreading over the whole vast land,
And I was captured by the ripples.
At dusk, my eyes filled with tears,
I was standing and gazing ahead at the old wooden barrel.
Ripples were forming at its base.

While Duojie Qunzeng (Tib. Dorjé Chözang) reclaims the river Yarlung Tsangpo:[66]

Yarlung Tsangpo
You are the convulsion of lightning,
You are the rush of despair.

Caiwang Naoru (Tib. Tsewang Norbu) describes his journey to Lhasa and the long-awaited sight of the Potala. Likewise, Zhaxi Cairang (Tib. Trashi Tsering) sings a song about his hometown in southern Gansu Province.[67]

After redefining the landscape, the poets proceed to restore local heroes. Meizhuo (Tib. Medrön), for example, recalls one of Tibet's most famous kings, Songtsen Gampo:[68]

The iron hoof has burned on the fertile wild land
But you, you have chosen the high plateau
Like snow, like a hungry animal, like the intoxicating lake,
to wander around
you are destined for the grassland.

The highland is also destined by the totem
The numerous falling eagles
The snow lion hidden in the forest.

On the map, the wings and hoofs you have amassed
shrink into a deep red color that no one can repeat
The color of the sun, the color of blood,
a color that the next generation will never understand and tolerate.

Even among those who are not to endure, you have endured it.

A long time ago, I was crossing the border of your territory
spreading ancient love,
looking for your beautiful blue sky.

At last I understood,
your lineage is our natural dwelling which we cannot change
Before becoming proud I was haunted by feelings of inferiority.

Tears are hindering my sight
I cannot see the charm and gentleness that is written
a thousand times inside me
I cannot see the magpie that consoles a lonely traveller.

Year after year, you were alone at the edge of the highlands
Charmingly naive you disrobe yourself
amazing a race with your transcendence above the worldly.

You have taken a consort from far away,
and received also your own people's venerated Buddha
You defended the isolated life
You also brought faith through simple prayer.

The country which has risen from the sea,
without gaining strength has become old and feeble.
Is the fire burning in your heart?

Occasionally there are those who awake from your ancestral line
Like you they wake and like you they fall,
at those times you cannot talk, you cannot express the agony
But I am in agony
I repeat my confession many times
I am in agony.

The poet's choice of subject is significant in that the historical figure Songsten Gampo evokes and epitomizes the founding of the Tibetan Empire. His battle with neighboring countries and his thirst for territory to enlarge his empire and power are described in lines 1–12. Words such as "hungry animal," "map," "deep red color," "blood," and "sun" vividly describe the conquests of the emperor. The middle section of the poem (lines 14–19) partly tells of the author's journey of her inward searching. This journey is the travel in time and space of someone who seeks her roots and finally realizes that she is unable to shake away her own past. In the discovery of her cultural heritage she transcends her feelings of inferiority. This passage illustrates her psychological transformation from a member of a marginal group who is vulnerable to cultural and social biases to someone whose confidence is reinforced with the discovery of a rich cultural legacy. The last few lines (31–39) echo the author's regret about the condition of Tibet. Words like "old" and "feeble" are used to describe the state into which Tibet has fallen. The poem ends with a gloomy observation that even those who have the same ability as the king are defeated in the end.

Historical allusions are also prominent in other poems by Meizhuo. In "Tseyang Gyatso: My King,"[69] she addresses her "king," the sixth Dalai Lama Tsangyang Gyatso (1683–1706), who was kept hidden in Tawang for many years to prevent knowledge about the death of the fifth Dalai Lama from spreading. This errant religious hierarch, an inspiration for sentiments that could not be destroyed by Labzang Khan, is still revered by many Tibetans. The poet laments his untimely death at the age of twenty-four. In another poem, she evokes with admiration the eleventh-century poet and yogi Milarepa.

Inevitably the journey of discovery has signified a construction of Tibet that figures only in the imagination. Through this imaginative return a sense of belonging is shaped by what Benedict Anderson calls "an imagined community."[70] It is in this "Tibet" that Tibetan poets writing in Chinese feel a sense of belonging. Their shared personal and cultural experience connects them also with their past, a past which is figuratively invoked in a romanticized imagery. A poem by Lhamo Döndrup (Ch. Lamu Dongzhi) begins by describing how the "heroes" saw the snow mountain. Even though the narrator does not seem to dispute what the heroes tell him, he nevertheless approaches the snow mountain quite objectively. There is almost an uncaring sense when he makes this journey. But what he knows for sure is that one day he will reach the mountain and become part of history. Thus one detects a yearning for the past while simultaneously sensing a vision of altering the present.

> In this world
> The snow mountain is a beautiful place,
> A story which has not been changed for many thousands of years.
> The solidified snow mountain has an eternal form—
>
> Those heroes who walked towards it always say this to us.
>
> But when I walked towards the snow mountain,
> I did not think at all.
> In fact, to think or not, it is all the same.
> Let the wind and snow fill the air.
> While tirelessly walking, I am also filled.
> The far-away snow peak,
> Looks at me with tacit understanding.
>
> Sooner or later I will also cross the snow mountain,
> And turn myself into one. Later,
> Let the people behind me step on me.[71]

Though some might dispute that writers who express themselves in Chinese are "real" Tibetans and bearers of Tibet's cultural heritage, these poets—by positioning themselves as Tibetans and at the same time being confronted as a minority within the larger Chinese group—share the experience of being the Other. Their otherness allows them to perceive continuity in their past history. But historical continuity is also framed with a sense of discontinuity, since their personal identities have not proceeded along a straight line of formation. The poems of Sinophone Tibetan poets are thus situated at a juncture where a sense of disruption meets the perception of continuity.

Another feature which has become important in the poetic expression of the younger generation is their language. With a growing number of Tibetans able to attend universities and writers' training classes, their proficiency in Chinese has become more sophisticated. They seem to have gained more confidence in writing in Chinese than their predecessors. Because the first generation was partially "instrumentalized" by the party to convey a certain ideological vision, the form of their poetry assumed a minor role. Yidan Cairang and Tamdrin Gönpo are exceptions: in their works the inclusion of folk songs, characters from the *Gesar* epic, and metaphors drawn from *Snyan ngag me long* (Mirror of poetry)—a translation of the classical Indian text *Kāvyādarśa*—reveal their effort to be rooted in their own culture. The use of indigenous cultural elements and modes of expression in their works accounts for how popular and well received they are among Tibetan readers. Apart from these two poets, most of the elder generation of poets were trapped by a system which required writing on behalf of an ideology. When their poems became less political, they wrote in a simple language about the grassland, the snow mountains, nomadic life, or love. By emphasizing simplicity, they followed Mao's command to write poetry with mass appeal.

The younger generation's emphasis on eloquence in language reflects the increasing importance of style in contemporary poetry. But this linguistic mastery has had a negative impact on the Tibetan readership: the writings of the younger generation are viewed by some as a mere aesthetic expression of Tibet and not, as they would have preferred, as the voice of a marginalized group. One often hears remarks from Tibetan readers that the poems do not reveal any "Tibetanness." It is indeed the case that the poems written by the younger generation could be mistaken for those of any Han Chinese poet, such as Yang Lian's poem "Potala" or Cai Chunfang's "Momentary Convergence," both of which treat the subject of Tibet.[72]

The accusation by Tibetan readers that the poems of the younger generation and those of Chinese poets are almost identical may be partially true, but I would argue that it reflects an expectation among many Tibetan readers that literature should serve a nationalistic purpose. These readers often look for an overt message: they would like to see a writer or poet writing on behalf of the Tibetans and against the Chinese. But no matter what the readership thinks, Tibetan poets writing in Chinese are invariably in a difficult position, experiencing themselves as Tibetans while not always accepted as such by their own community.

Notes

This chapter is dedicated to the memory of Yidam Tsering (1993–2004).

1. Weise, "Ling yige huashen" (Another embodiment).
2. Weise (Tib. Özer) was born in 1966 in Lhasa, Tibet, and graduated in 1988 from the Chinese department of the Xinan minzu xueyuan (Southwest Nationalities Institute) in Chengdu. Among her major publications are *Xizang zai shang* (To Tibet), a collection of poems, and *Xizang Biji* (Notes on Tibet). As discussed in chapter 1, *Notes on Tibet* was banned around September 2003 by the Chinese authorities for its alleged stance in favor of the Dalai Lama. For more on Weise and *Notes on Tibet* see "TAR Authorities Ban Book by Tibetan Author," www.tibet.ca/en/wtnarchive/2004/3/16_2.html; "Extracts from 'Notes on Tibet,'" www.tibet.net/tibbul/2004/0506/features1.html; "CTA Upset with Chinese Authorities' Action on Tibetan writer," WTN: World Tibet Network News, 30 October 2004; "China Persecuting Tibetan Writer for Pro–Dalai Lama Opinion, Says Human Rights in China," www.savetibet.org/news/news, Tibet News, 27 October 2004; and "Dharamsala Says China's Persecution of Tibetan Writer Is Ethnic Discrimination," www.savetibet.org/news/news, Tibet News, 28 October 2004.
3. T. N. Takla, in his article "Notes on Some Early Tibetan Communists," *Tibetan Review*, June–July 1969, 7–9, mentions Ngakwang Kelzang as being a Chinese scholar and poet. I was unable to find more information on him and have therefore left him out of this analysis.
4. For another excellent study of Yidan Cairang see Lara Maconi, "Lion of the Snowy Mountains."
5. Caiwang Naoru and Wangqiu Caidan, eds., *Zangzu dangdai shiren shixuan*, 19.
6. McDougall and Louie, *The Literature of China in the Twentieth Century*, 334.
7. Goldstein, *A History of Modern Tibet*, 365.
8. Interview, Lanzhou, August 2001.
9. P. T. Takla, unpublished autobiography, translated by Tendar.
10. In 1945 in Nanjing, Tsongkha Lhamo Tsering met Gyalo Döndrup, elder brother of the fourteenth Dalai Lama. From then on he worked with Gyalo Döndrup and became one of the key persons in organizing the clandestine independence movement in Tibet. After the flight of the Dalai Lama to India, Tsongkha Lhamo Tsering was in charge of a guerrilla base for the Tibetan independence movement in Mustang. He later worked for the exile government and became the minister of security. He died in 2000. For more information see Tsongkha Lhamo Tsering, *Btsan rgol*

rgyal skyob: The Early Political Activities of Gyalo Thondup, Older Brother of H.H. the Dalai Lama, and the Beginnings of My Political Involvement (1945–1959), 2 vols. (Dharamsala: Amnye Machen Institute, 1992).

11. Interview with Tenzing Sonam (son of Tsongkha Lhamo Tsering), London, December 2001.

12. Interview, Lanzhou, August 2001.

13. Ibid.

14. Zhu Jielin, Zangzu jinxiandai jiaoyu shilue, 149.

15. Ibid., 148–53.

16. Chang Xiwu, "Guomindang zai Lasa ban xue jianjie," 85–92.

17. Ibid., 85. The school was set up in the early twentieth century and was located in the mosque in the Muslim area of Lhasa.

18. Ibid., 86–87. The Chinese teachers were staff from the Guomindang office, the Hui teacher was the Imam Ma Tingfu, and there were three Tibetan teachers: Gönkar Ngawang, Aba Yingta, and Abu Roro.

19. For more details on Baba Püntsok Wanggyel see Tsering Shakya, The Dragon in the Land of Snows; and Goldstein, Sherap, and Siebenschuh, A Tibetan Revolutionary.

20. Bass, Education in Tibet, 1–3.

21. Ibid., 1.

22. For more detail on the Lhasa English School see Gaxue Qujie Nima and Lalu Ciwang Duojie, "Lasa yingyu xuexiao pochan ji," 27–34.

23. Chang Xiwu, "Guomindang zai Lasa ban xue jianjie," 87.

24. Gray, Rebellions and Revolutions, 233.

25. W. M. Theodore De Bary, Wing-Tsit Chan, and Chester Tan, eds., Sources of Chinese Tradition (New York: Columbia University Press, 1960), vol. 2, 98–117.

26. Chang Xiwu, "Guomindang zai lasa ban xue jianjie," 90.

27. For a discussion of the rise of African Literature see Emmanuel Ngara, Ideology and Form in African Poetry (London: James Currey, 1990).

28. See for example the poems by Xia Chuan, "Jiefang Xizang jinxing qu" (The march for the liberation of Tibet) and "Fanshen nongnu duikou qu" (Emancipate the serfs, a dialogue song), in Xueyu fangge (Songs set free in the Land of the Snows), ed. Xia Chuan (Lasa: Xizang renmin chubanshe, 2002), 1, 22.

29. Lin, Modern Chinese Poetry, 250. Unfortunately the poet's name is not mentioned.

30. Geng Yufang, Zangzu dangdai wenxue, 44–46.

31. Gongbu Zhaxi, Gongbu Zhaxi shiji, 66.

32. The number fifty-six refers to the number of nationalities officially recognized as living in China.

33. Geseng Duojie, "Zhebian shi ni de jiaxiang" (This is your native place), Zangzu dangdai shiren shixuan, ed. Caiwang Naoru and Wangqiu Caidan, 45–47.

34. Ibid., 19.

35. Snow lions also symbolize protectors of the Dharma and are depicted holding a jewel on the Tibetan national flag.

36. Yidan Cairang, "Muqin xinshou de ge" (The song mother taught me), Xueyu de tai-yang, 210–21.

37. Döndrup Gyel (1953–85), one of the best-known Tibetan writers, is credited with having laid the foundations for a new Tibetan literature. For more on the life of Döndrup Gyel see Pema Bhum, "The Life of Dhondup Gyel," 17–29.

38. Yidan Cairang, "Zhende jiabuliao" (What is true cannot be falsified), *Xueyu de taiyang*, 56.

39. Yidan Cairang, "Lu" (The path), *Xueyuji*, 8.

40. Franz Fanon, *The Wretched of the Earth* (New York: Grove, 1968), 210.

41. Yidan Cairang, "Dabian" (A reply), *Xueyuji*, 5.

42. The Yellow River (Rma chu) and Yangtse River ('Bri chu) originate in Tibet. Gesar is the hero of a Tibetan epic.

43. Yidan Cairang, "Xinnian de lunduo" (The steering wheel of faith), *Xueyuji*, 19.

44. Consider the case of Africa and the emergence of the concept of Negritude.

45. This attitude is visible also in Jampel Gyatso's autobiography. See Jiangbian Jiacuo, *Ganxie shenghuo*.

46. Pema Bhum also refers to an encounter such as that experienced by Yidan Cairang while in a nomad area. See Pema Bhum, *Dran tho smin drug ske 'khyog / Six Stars with a Crooked Neck*, 139–45.

47. Geng Yufang, *Zangzu dangdai wenxue*, 44–46.

48. Salman Rushdie, *Midnight's Children* (London: Vintage, 1995), 463.

49. Fanon, *The Wretched of the Earth*, 212

50. A very good example of this can be seen in the documentary film *Stranger in My Native Land* (White Crane Films, 1998) by Tenzing Sonam and Ritu Sarin. When Tenzing goes to see his father's village in Tsongkha, his uncle performs the ritual of burning money in front of his ancestor's grave.

51. Alai, "Qunshan, huozhe Guanyu wo ziji de songci" (Mountain range, or the song about myself), *Zangzu dangdai shiren shixuan*, ed. Caiwang Naoru and Wangqiu Caidan, 79–88.

52. Even though Alai has published an anthology of his poems, he is nowadays better known for his novel *Chen'ai luoding* (The dust settles), which in 2000 received the Mao Dun prize, China's top literary award. For an English translation of his novel see Alai, *Red Poppies*, trans. Goldblatt and Lin.

53. Duozhi Ge, *Xin ganjue / Tshor snang gsar ba*, 14.

54. His published volume on poetry is in Tibetan and Chinese. It seems that he is much more comfortable in the Tibetan language.

55. Geng Yufang, *Zangzu dangdai wenxue*, 87–88.

56. Weise, "Jinian yihou" (After many years), *Xizang zai shang*, 40.

57. Interview, Lhasa, September 2001.

58. Weise, "Qianding de nianzhu' (Predestined rosary), *Xizang zai shang*, 72.

59. Two Gelukpa monasteries in Gansu and Qinghai province.

60. For a more detailed account of the years during the Cultural Revolution see Tsering Shakya, *The Dragon in the Land of Snows*, 314–47.

61. Weise, "Huanying" (Unreal images), *Xizang zai shang*, 3.

62. Suobao, "Xueyu qingxu" (Snowland mood), *Zangzu dangdai shiren shixuan*, ed. Caiwang Naoru and Wangqiu Caidan, 128–29.

63. Said, *Culture and Imperialism*, 271.

64. Guru Dorjé was originally from Bayan (Hualong, Qinghai) and was the chieftain of a hundred families (*rgya dpon*). He set up schools in his area and encouraged Tibetans to study both languages. Some of the better students were sent later to Xining to study at Ma Bufang's Kunlun Middle School. This is the reason why many early Tibetan cadres came from that area. Thus Taktsang is known among Tibetans to be an area from which many Tibetan cadres originated. Meizhuo, the novelist based in Xining, is from Taktsang. Her father is the well-known Tibetan cadre Penjor Tsering.

65. Banguo, "Mutong" (Wooden barrel), *Zangzu dangdai shiren shixuan*, ed. Caiwang Naoru and Wangqiu Caidan, 224.

66. Duojie Qunzeng, "Yalu zangbu" (Yarlung River), *Zangzu dangdai shiren shixuan*, ed. Caiwang Naoru and Wangqiu Caidan, 144.

67. Caiwang Naoru, "Duo nian hou hui you yige zhanzai taiyang cheng zhongxin" (After many years there is someone standing in the middle of the Sun City), *Zangzu dangdai shiren shixuan*, ed. Caiwang Naoru and Wangqiu Caidan, 153; and Zhaxi Cairang, "Heiye luguo Gannan" (Passing across Gannan at night), *Zangzu dangdai shiren shixuan*, ed. Caiwang Naoru and Wangqiu Caidan, 301.

68. Meizhuo, "Songtsen Gampo: Statue of the King of Tubo," trans. Yangdon Dhondup, *Song of the Snow Lion*, ed. Batt and Tsering Shakya, 146–47. For the original poem see Meizhuo, *sanwen shixuan*, 78–79.

69. Meizhuo, "Tseyang Gyatso: My King," trans. Yangdon Dhondup, *Song of the Snow Lion*, ed. Batt and Tsering Shakya, 147. For the original poem see Meizhuo, *sanwen shixuan*, 81–82.

70. Benedict Anderson, *Imagined Communities* (London: Verso, 1983).

71. Lamu Dongzhi, "Zoujin xueshan" (Walking toward the snow mountain), *Zangzu dangdai shiren shixuan*, ed. Caiwang Naoru and Wangqiu Caidan, 113.

72. Barmé and Minford, eds., *Seeds of Fire*, 433–38.

3

The Development of Modern
Tibetan Literature in the People's
Republic of China in the 1980s

TSERING SHAKYA

Only after the establishment of Communist Chinese rule in Tibetan-speaking areas of the People's Republic of China (PRC) did a new Tibetan literature emerge. In addition to establishing political and administrative control of Tibet, the Chinese government brought about Tibet's first encounter with the modern world—specifically, an engagement with a technologically advanced society imbued with a modern and materialistic ideology. The missionary zeal of the new Communist regime was focused on incorporating Tibet into the great "motherland," and in doing so to "civilize" this underdeveloped, backward region. In this regard there are many similarities between western colonial rule and the Chinese colonization of Tibet. In both cases colonialism caused a dislocation of identity and traditional epistemology in the indigenous social system and culture. Like other colonial rulers, China not only asserted territorial claims but also set out to control the minds of the natives.

The notion of underdevelopment (rjes lus) is crucial to understanding the nature of Chinese rule in Tibet. The term implies that Tibet lagged in technology and, more important, that it was culturally stagnant and backward. Therefore "liberation of the serfs" was intended to encompass both economic emancipation and cultural empowerment of the people. In this process language and literature became the focus of colonial exchange. And it was in this context that a new literature emerged in Tibet.

Chinese rule had an immediate and striking impact on the Tibetan language at every level, because initially it was the principal medium used by the Communists to convey their message. At this stage Tibetan intellectuals were recruited as "important patriotic personages"—a class that would mediate between the past and the present. Because many members of the early literary élite were from monasteries and the religious community, the Chinese assumed that they would be trusted by the masses. The Communists also used them and their literary skills to articulate the new course for Tibetan society, and so literary discourse in the early stages was narrowly focused on the question of a new lexicon and terminology (tha snyad). A new Tibetan lexicon was needed to translate the Communist propaganda and Marxist ideology that had driven the Communist revolution in China. It is worth noting that unlike western colonialists, who generally did not intend to overthrow the traditional ideology of their subjugated territories, the Communists came to Tibet with the explicit intention of replacing the existing socio-ideological system.

Modification and reform of the Tibetan language were therefore considered necessary to mold the thoughts and actions of the people. In the early 1950s the Communists acted with the belief that the social transformation would be gradual, and that it would proceed with the consent of the people. Change was to be introduced slowly by both overt and covert means: overtly by appropriating existing institutions and ideology to win over the people, and covertly by undermining the ruling order. The knowledge and skills of the traditional literary élite could be exploited for the revolutionary cause; ironically, the class position given to these writers also made them targets for attack. Indeed, literary production by members of the Tibetan élite was soon used against them, to undermine their privileged position in society.

Thus initially the Communists' concern with the Tibetan language was primarily related to the practicality of governing a country that had been and wished to remain—whatever China's historical and legal justification for claiming Tibet to be a part of China—fundamentally separate. At this time literary activities involved publishing translations of Communist propaganda, and so the literary élite debated how to translate into Tibetan such concepts in the Communist lexicon as *people, democracy, class, liberation,* and *exploitation.* They also discussed whether new terms should be coined based on a written textual basis, or rather derived from colloquial, spoken usages. Clearly, printing technologies and presses were not brought into Tibet by the Chinese to promote literary creativity; rather, they were there for the party and its propaganda needs.

During the Cultural Revolution (1966–76) the Chinese emphatically denied the existence of a separate Tibetan identity, and under the Communist slogan "destroy the Four Olds" all aspects of Tibetan life and custom were attacked.[1] The party imposed total uniformity on culture and lifestyle throughout China. In Tibet almost all publishing in the Tibetan language ceased, except for party propaganda and translations of articles from Chinese news-

"Nongmin ai du Ma-Lie shu" (Herdsmen love to read Marxist-Leninist Books). The banner in this poster from the Cultural Revolution reads: "Diligently read and study in order to understand Marxism." Reprinted by permission of Stefan Landsberger and the International Institute of Social History.

papers. Consequently the sole marker of distinction that remained for the Tibetan people was the spoken language.

Only after the death of Mao and the subsequent emergence of new leadership under Deng Xiaoping did unprecedented change come to China. The party's policy toward intellectuals underwent a transformation, as did its policies toward so-called minorities. The goal of overt assimilation was abandoned in favor of policies of cultural autonomy. These changes had far-reaching consequences for Tibetans.

Tibetans generally agree that when the authorities allowed Tibet some degree of autonomy in expressing its cultural identity—shortly after the Third
Plenum of the Eleventh Central Committee in 1978—modern Tibetan literature began. Tibetan Buddhism, suppressed for over twenty years, was also
revived.[2] The following year, a group of young Tibetans in Lhasa got together
and sought permission from the government to publish Bod kyi rstom rig sgyu
rtsal (Tibetan art and literature); their request was readily granted. The impe-
tus for publishing the magazine was a Chinese edition of Xizang wenxue (Literature from Tibet) that had been in existence for several years. The Chinese
writers and intellectuals residing in Tibet were quick to grasp the opportunity afforded by Deng Xiaoping's change in policy. The greater willingness
of Chinese workers in Tibet to embrace the change reflected not only their
being attuned with the times but also differences in the position and security
of Tibetans and Chinese in Tibet. Almost invariably Tibetans are less likely to
initiate change, demonstrating a cautiousness, a tendency to test the political
waters before taking any initiative.

The existence of a Chinese edition made it easier for the Tibetans to argue
for the right of Tibetans to claim their own space. When Tibetans in Amdo
founded the magazine Sbrang char (Light rain) they made a similar argument.
Gyurmé, the founder and first editor, in an interview mentions that he was
spurred into seeking permission from the authorities because of the large
number of magazines appearing in Chinese at the time.[3] The publication of
the two Tibetan magazines was a watershed, inspiring a new style of narrative
writing in Tibetan during the 1980s. Producing a Tibetan literary magazine
was not an easy undertaking, as it represented above all an attempt to revive
the Tibetan language. All those involved in the endeavor saw their labor primarily as a means to resuscitate the use of written Tibetan, and the use of the
Tibetan language could only be justified by making the project palatable to
the authorities. The reason cited in the petition to the party was the need to
convey the party's new message of reform and modernization. For the party,
the motivation was to confirm that the reforms were genuine and to win
over the support of the people and establish legitimacy. Perry Link argues
that Deng Xiaoping and the new regime made a "political calculation" in
relaxing the party's control over literary production.[4] Under the new regime,
Perry Link rightly argues that the party would "benefit from expressions of
popular support; pent-up popular resentment at the Cultural Revolution was
a resource waiting to be tapped; literature and art were an avenue for chan-
nelling the resentment towards support for the new regime."[5] In this way

Early issue of *Tibetan Art and Literature*, a literary magazine published in Lhasa that was the first in the Tibetan language.

the new regime's need for popular support and the desire of the people for greater freedom created a mutually supportive space, as realpolitik and the opportunity for greater freedom of expression converged.

The inaugural issue of *Tibetan Art and Literature* published by the Tibet Autonomous Region (TAR) Writers' Association in 1980 comprised three short stories: "Dbyangs can" (Yangchen), "Pha yul gyi sa" (Soil of the native land), and "Sdi dbang gis gson pa'i mi" (Honored person), as well as a translated excerpt from the novel *Skal bzang me tog* (Kelzang Metok). All four works had been written several years earlier and already published in Chinese magazines; all were about Tibet and had been written in Chinese by Tibetans. Their primary aim was to persuade Chinese readers of the moral justification for the "liberation" of Tibet by portraying the People's Liberation Army as having freed Tibetans from a "dark period" of feudal exploitation. That the stories were written by Tibetans—the muted voice of Tibetan serfs speaking against oppressive feudal lords—gave them an air of authenticity. All were published widely and used in schools.

The translation of these stories from Chinese into Tibetan suggests that there were no Tibetans writing in their own language at this time. Indeed, when a Swedish journalist arrived in Lhasa about 1975 with the intention of meeting contemporary Tibetan writers, the Cultural Department of the TAR Government was unable to produce a single one.[6] According to Tendzin Namgyel, a former editor of *Tibetan Art and Literature*, this episode had a great impact on Tibetans working in the Cultural Department and inspired them to encourage Tibetans to begin writing stories.[7] Later, critics realized that no Tibetans had been producing fiction primarily because they were unsure what was permissible under party policy. A more cynical observation is that the four stories in the first issue of *Tibetan Art and Literature* were deliberately selected to establish precisely the guidelines on style and content favored by the party; this seemed especially true since all four dealt with the crimes of the Tibetan "feudal" society and the miserable lives of the working class.[8]

Whatever the motive for publication, the first issue of *Tibetan Art and Literature* initiated a burning debate. What is Tibetan literature? What should be the defining factor: the language, the ethnic origin of the author, or the subject matter? (The latter two, the journal seemed to suggest.)

The quarterly *Light Rain* was founded the following year in Amdo, in the far northeastern corner of the Tibetan-speaking world. The title suggests the nurturing of young seedlings and evokes images of fertility, luxuriance, and the regenerative power of rainwater. Aptly titled, *Light Rain* was to become the premier literary journal in Tibet. More than any other publication, it shaped and established the foundation of modern Tibetan literature. The editors of *Light Rain* deliberately challenged the views of *Tibetan Art and Literature* by publishing only stories written in Tibetan. Unlike the editors of *Tibetan Art and Literature*, the editors believed that Tibetan literature should be defined not by the subject matter or the ethnicity of the author, but by the language alone. The readers concurred. One reader insisted that if the journal published stories translated from Chinese, it would lose its unique nature and become neither "a goat nor a sheep" (*ra ma lug tu 'gyur*).[9]

A number of magazines soon emerged, including *Zla zer* (Moonshine), *Bod ljongs mang tshogs sgyu rtsal* (Tibetan popular arts), *Nyi gzhon* (Young sun), *Lho kha'i rtsom rig sgyu rtsal* (Lhokha literature and arts), *Lha sa'i skyid chu* (Kyichu River of Lhasa), and *Gangs dkar ri bo* (Snow mountain). In the words of one Tibetan poet, the magazines "blossomed like spring flowers." These journals were never truly independent, but continued to fall under the control of larger associations. Current examples include *Tibetan Art and Literature*, published by the TAR Writers' Association; *Light Rain*, published under the auspices of the Qinghai Writers' Association; and such magazines as *Snow Mountain*, published by the trade unions. In addition to these journals, many unofficial publications and magazines—from colleges and even monasteries—began to circulate in local areas. In Amdo there was a mushrooming of unofficial publications, such as *Mtsho sngon po'i glu dbyangs* (Song of Lake Qinghai), *Smyug gsar* (New pens), *'Ba' sgra* (Sound of a sheep), and *Shar dung ri / The Eastern Snow Mountain*. Published in cyclostyle,[10] the journals were poorly printed and were distributed only in local areas.

In this early period the subject of a typical story was the evils of the old society. For example, "Bu mo spun gsum gyi rnam thar" (A story of three sisters), written by Kelzang Namdröl and published in *Tibetan Art and Literature*, tells of the sufferings of three sisters—Patok, Bötrik, and Tsamchö—at the hands of a soldier, the son of an aristocrat, and a lama (these representing the three feudal lords of old Tibet). By describing the evil behavior of these three men, the story attempts to show the backwardness and oppressiveness of the old society.

Between 1980 and 1984 such stories condemning the evils of the old society and praising the benefits of the peaceful Chinese liberation were regularly published in *Tibetan Art and Literature*. They were intended to convince the younger generation of Tibetans, those born after 1950, that Communist policies in Tibet were justified. This was particularly important after 1980, because by then most people were complaining not about the evils of feudal Tibet but about the suffering that they and their parents had endured during the Cultural Revolution. Such stories also characterized the earliest contributions to literary columns in newspapers.

Print Journalism and a Realist Trend

Despite the high level of illiteracy in Tibet, the Chinese authorities recognized the importance of print media and worked toward establishing Tibetan-language newspapers. By the mid-1950s there were four Tibetan-language newspapers in circulation in Tibetan areas; by the early 1980s the number had more than doubled, and there were more than a dozen Tibetan quarterly journals. I have elsewhere explored the link between print journalism and Tibetan literature in greater detail.[11] It should suffice here to simply note that in the history of European literatures, the emergence of newspapers in the seventeenth century privileged prose writing, and as theorized by Lennard Davis, periodicals replaced episodic accounts of the distant past with descriptions of contemporary events.[12] Journalism purports to convey accounts of events and people. This aim becomes central to realism, the literary approach previously dictated and still favored by the party. Whether directly inspired by print journalism, Chinese reportage writing, or rhetorical practices during the Cultural Revolution, the earliest short stories published by Tibetans are composed as eyewitness reports of a lived experience. Tibetans were encouraged to write stories as an expression of outrage against the old society. In *Kelzang Metok* (published in Chinese in 1980 and Tibetan in 1982), Jampel Gyatso uses a similar strategy of blurring fact and fiction, with footnotes of actual events. The Chinese authorities encouraged stories of suffering during the old society as the authentic voice of the people.

In accounts of literary practice in Tibet, one term repeatedly used is "reflecting the true condition of Tibetan people" (*Bod mi dmangs kyi 'tsho ba mtshon pa'i brtsam chos*). The new narrative forms of short stories and novels are viewed for their power to reflect a verifiable condition in society. The actual veracity of the story or experience is not important; what matters is the enunciation and assertion that the story is real and a dramatization of an authentic experience. A later, more complex short story by Tenpa Yargyé, "Mgo ras kyi btums pa'i bu mo" (Girl swathed in a headscarf), begins with the narrator's statement: "This is a true story of yesterday's actual event on the grassy plain of Nachen"; later the authenticity of the story is emphasized by the narrator with this statement: "The people in these pages are drawn from my travel diary."[13] Another strategy used by writers is situating their narrative as *nyin tho*, literally "a daily account," a diary or journal kept by the narrator. Among the best examples are Yangtsokyi's "Rtswa thang gi nyin tho" (Diary of the grassland)[14] and Drongbu Dorjé Rinchen's "Lam gram gyi nyin tho" (Roadside journal).[15] In Tsering Döndrup's "Zla ba" (Dawa), the narrative begins with the wedding night of Dawa and Gyatso, who is reading his wife's diary.[16] The entire story is framed as though it were the diary of Dawa. Each entry and section of the story is marked with a date, beginning with the first entry, "1st June 1985." In these texts the readers are invited to share the intimacy of observation and to believe that what is written is actual lived experience. Yet here fact and fiction are blurred and the text serves to reveal the mind of the diarist. The precise recording of time, date, and location also create the effect that the story is a news report. Yangtsokyi's "Diary of the Grassland," which uses a similar effect, opens: "Written in Serzangtang, on the xth day of x, 198x."[17]

In the 1950s newspapers were the only form of mass-circulated reading material for the people. It is not an accident that they were the only forum for the publication of short stories. In the late 1970s three Tibetan language newspapers launched a feature column called "Smyug gsar" (New pens), which carried regular short stories submitted by readers. Initially these contributions were mainly translations from Chinese and stories written by Ti-

Yangtsokyi, author of "Diary of the Grassland," at her home in Gonghe (Qinghai Province). Her story was well received when first published in 1988. The author now works for a legal affairs office. Photo by Lauran Hartley.

betans in Chinese. The stories invariably told of suffering in the old society and the wise leadership of the party. The stories were didactic and related to a particular campaign conducted by the party. What is interesting is that these stories were popular as moral fables: they were used in teaching and school textbooks were filled with them. The traditional folktales of "incorrect" and "suspicious political leanings" were replaced with socialist parables. This amalgamation of news and fictional writing is not simply the accommodation of differing forms in the same medium. It implies that both types of report are authentic and that they mirror historical and lived experience. The short stories present a proposition to the readers: that the old days were bad and characterized by errors in political thinking, but the solution lies in the reports and speeches of the leaders printed on the same page. While in liberal society newspapers and pamphleteering began as a voice of opposition, in Tibet under Chinese rule the opposition was directed not against the colonizing power but at tradition and the Tibetan self.

Another link between journalism and modern fiction in Tibet is that many of the writers began life as journalists. Trashi Penden, author of the novel *Phal pa'i khyim tshang gi skyid sdug* (The joys and sorrows of an ordinary family) and many popular short stories, is a journalist for the *Tibet Daily* and submitted reports from his home village in Rinpung in central Tibet.[18] He acquired his interest in novels from writing news reports and reading short stories in the paper. Other writers also assert that their initial interest came from reading the column "New Pens." After all, this was the only material available to Tibetan readers.

The Tibetan Novel

One work in classical Tibetan is close to the novel in form: the *Gzhon nu zla med kyi gtam rgyud* (Tale of the incomparable youth), written by the eighteenth-century cabinet minister Dokhar Tsering Wanggyel (1689–1763).[19] The subject matter, style, and mode of narrative owe much to Indic-inspired literary principles that had dominated Tibetan literary composition since the thirteenth century. Tsering Wanggyel's "Tale" occupies a unique position in Tibetan literature and marks a shift in the Tibetan narrative tradition. However, as I have argued in greater detail elsewhere,[20] the style of narrative in *Tale of the Incomparable Youth* is closer to what Northrop Frye terms romance literature than to the novel per se. Frye writes, "The essential difference between novel and romance lies in the conception of characterization. The romancer does not attempt to create 'real people' so much as 'stylised figures' which expand into psychological archetypes."[21] As theorized by Frye, romance is concerned with heroes while the novel is concerned with men. Thus the traditional Tibetan narrative was generally a romance in that its subject matter, characterization, and style typically dealt with myth and reflected upon the past. The central subject was the idealization of heroes. The Gesar epic is all about heroism, and even the subjects of most biographies are portrayed heroically. In this respect the *Tale of the Incomparable Youth* is no exception; the life of the prince Zhönnu Damé (lit. "incomparable youth") is narrated in a heroic style, albeit in a manner resembling the life of the Buddha. Indeed, the plot draws heavily from the avadāna and Ramayana traditions, and Tsering Wanggyel locates the story, in terms of both space and time, in the Indic world. Finally, *The Tale of the Incomparable Youth* is written in a mixture of verse and prose characteristic of the kāvya style. The wording is florid and ornate, with an exaggerated tone. Thus Tsering Wanggyel adheres to another trait of traditional epics, for which Ian Watt notes, "conformity to traditional practice [is] the major test of truth" and "the merits of the author's treatment were judged largely according to a view of literary decorum derived from the accepted models in the genre."[22] The *Tale of the Incomparable Youth* departs little from traditional Tibetan (via Indic) form and structure.

The first known Tibetan novella of the twentieth century, *Ye shes lha mo dang mgar ba Stobs rgyal* (Yeshé Lhamo and Blacksmith Topgyel), was also inspired by Tibetan tradition, but it drew on the folk story not the epic, and the literary work's new style certainly identifies it as a modern novella.[23] The work was written by Dorjé Gyelpo, a former monk who had obtained the highest ecclesiastical degree from Trashilhunpo monastery and was highly respected as a grammarian. In 1952 he was recruited to teach in the newly established Tibetan cadre school in Lhasa and two years later was transferred to Beijing to work as a Tibetan editor at the newly established Nationalities Publishing House. As described in chapter 1, the main task of the publishing house was to produce Tibetan translations of Communist Party literature and to translate the works of Mao. Dorjé Gyelpo was among those recruited to edit party literature newly translated into Tibetan.

Yeshé Lhamo and Blacksmith Topgyel was first published in 1959 as new reading material for students at the Central Nationalities Institute in Beijing. Not so coincidentally, the story's subject matter was of the type favored by the party. After 1950 the Communists found that much of the native literature was incongruous to the party's ideology and aims. They began to look for a new literature that could mediate between the native tradition and the new mode of cultural representation favored by the party. The party located the sources of this new literature in folk stories, as they were seen as the embodiment of mass culture and as storehouses of the wisdom of the common people. The Communist Party's cultural cadres began to compile editions of folk stories and publish them. Likewise, Dorjé Gyelpo acknowledges that "the seed for this story was the compilation of folk stories made by Gyentsen Penjor in 1959 at the Nationalities Institute and [this] author has written [this story] in the colloquial speech of the Ütsang region."[24]

Dorjé Gyelpo's novella provides evidence for how folk traditions inspired the earliest writing of modern literature. Before 1950 most native writers were not exposed to any exogenous sources of influence. No modern western or Chinese literature had been translated into Tibetan, and it is most unlikely that any of the writers could read in foreign languages. Therefore when the party encouraged writers to produce literature that was suitable for the party's requirements, writers returned to folk stories and rendered them into modern form. When we look at Dorjé Gyelpo's Yeshé Lhamo and Blacksmith Topgyel we find that the narrative is a folk story couched in new party ideology. Its simplistic plot is narrated in the third person, with a "story-telling" flavor—that is, the narrator tells readers what to read in the story. The characterizations are also simplistic, with obvious good and bad characters. The narrator sets the time of the story during the disintegration of the unified Tibetan Empire after the death of the last Tibetan emperor Langdarma circa 842. The plot concerns the love story between a blacksmith, Topgyel, and Yeshé Lhamo, the daughter of a wealthy manorial lord whose vast holdings and power are described at the outset of the story. From the start the landlord is described as "oppressive" (*gdug rtsub can*), and Topgyel's family ceaseless service as corvée laborers for the landlord leave them with no free time. Topgyel lives with his mother in Lhasa and is summoned to work at the country estate of the landlord. Yeshé Lhamo, the daughter of the landlord, falls in love with Topgyel and becomes pregnant with his child. In Tibetan society blacksmiths are considered an impure caste (*rigs ngan*), and the rules governing social groups are extremely strict. It is forbidden to share cooking and eating utensils with impure castes, and sexual relations with impure castes are regarded as taboo. When the landlord learns of the relationship between his daughter and Topgyel he feels disgraced and believes that his family's honor had been ruined. He summons Topgyel to die under torture, and when Yeshé Lhamo learns of her lover's death she commits suicide.[25]

Neither the plot nor the subject matter presents much complexity. What is interesting is that it imitates the new genre favored by the party and yet the author resorts to a folk method for narrating the story. The flavor is that of a blend of folk story and literary fiction. The language is close to everyday spoken language in terms of both syntax and vocabulary. However, the author finds it to difficult to break totally from traditional literary idiom and usage. In traditional narratives, the protagonist's speech is rendered in verse to heighten emotion. Here the author uses a similar device, but the verses are akin to folk songs underpinned with highly exaggerated emotive language. The depiction of characters lacks the intricacies of a novel. This is partly because there is a strict requirement as to the types of character that can be constructed in fiction, and here we can see that the narrative adheres to the party's guideline. The text is evidence of the beginnings of the construction of new political figures and definitions of Tibetan society. The characters very much conform to the Chinese Communist division of society into three antagonistic classes, the serf owners, the representatives of the serf owners, and the peasant. The landlord is a dark absent figure whose authority is mediated by the "representative of the feudal lord" while the masses are oppressed. In contrast, the protagonist is not only a member of an oppressed class but also a semi-orphan, mirroring a repeatedly used archetype of the new socialist man.

In the concluding paragraph, the author makes explicit the purpose of the text in a polemical verse directing the reader to view the text as a condemnation of the "evil conceited tradition of the ruling class" (*nga che nga btsan dpon po'i lugs ngan*). He goes on:

Any [reader] who can recognize the sense in this story,
Will welcome the auspicious sign of the revolution,
Today under the clear guidance of the Communist Party,
the foundation for prosperity is being planted.[26]

The text is important in the history of the new style of writing that was being promoted by the Communists. Not only is it addressed to the masses, but the didactic message is nothing less than a call for revolution. It became a foundational guideline to future writers about the subject and style favored by the party. Tibetan writers tended to look for a model (*dpe*) for their writings, and Dorjé Gyelpo's text became an important prototype for the subsequent construction of literary images of Tibet. The year of publication is of great importance: 1959 marked a watershed in Chinese colonial rule in Tibet. The nationwide revolt that took place in that year showed the vulnerability of the Chinese in the region and the tenuousness of their hold on the hearts and minds of the people. It is beyond my scope to detail the cause of the revolt. Suffice it to say that the revolt marked an important transition in the method of colonial rule. It was not only the revolt that shifted strategies of Chinese rule but also the move toward hardened leftist policy in China, which was to have a serious effect on Tibet. The "anti-rebellion campaign" began with systematic aggression against Tibetans and their culture, as the authorities abandoned any notion of Tibet as separate from the rest of China. This assault on Tibet reached its most violent form during the Cultural Revolution, which swept throughout China. It is little wonder that the next Tibetan novel was not written until after this tragic decade.

In 1982 the first full-length Tibetan novel was published: *Skal bzang me tog* (Kelzang Metok),[27] by Jampel Gyatso (Ch. Jiangbian Jiacuo), an academic working at the Academy of Social Sciences in Beijing. From a poor family in Batang (Kham), Jampel Gyatso had joined the invading People's Liberation Army at a young age and been trained as a translator. *Kelzang Metok* (the novel is titled after the protagonist, whose name literally means "flower or the auspicious era") is written in the style of socialist realism and has stereotypical characterizations. Set at the time of the Chinese invasion, the novel celebrates the "unwavering service performed by the People's Liberation Army for the Tibetan people" in liberating the masses.[28] In the epilogue, the author states that he wrote the book to depict the sacrifices made by the People's Liberation Army.

The book received much praise and won a prize for the best novel by a minority national in China. Among the Tibetan populace, however, the book was recognized as party propaganda, and the author was criticized for deni-

Jiangbian Jiacuo (Tib. Jampel Gyatso) at Nationalities Writers Conference in Beijing in 1982. Reprinted from *Nationalities Pictorial* (Beijing, 1982).

grating Tibetan society while internalizing the colonizer's image of Tibet as "a hell on earth" before the Chinese invasion. Despite the novel's propagandistic style and content, it nevertheless made innovations in the use of simple and readable language.

In 1985 the second Tibetan novel, *Gtsug g.yu* (The crown turquoise), appeared as part of the celebration of the twentieth anniversary of the founding of the TAR, and it was serialized in *Tibetan Art and Literature*.[29] The author was Penjor Langdün, a great-nephew of the thirteenth Dalai Lama. As a young boy Penjor had studied in Darjeeling, and in the 1950s had traveled to China to further his education. The subject of the novel is the internal rivalries among the aristocracy of the old Tibetan society. The story was intended to portray "the exterior beauty and the internal rottenness of the aristocracy and power holding classes,"[30] and readers were asked to empathize with the suffering of the working class. True to the party line, aristocrats and landlords are once again represented as serving only their own class interests. The protagonist, Penden, is described as a slave with deep hatred for his oppressors. Through Penden's actions, we are shown that the overthrow of the ruling class is natural because the hatred of the working class cannot be suppressed.

Despite its very narrow and superficial theme, *The Crown Turquoise* was an instant bestseller. It is now out of print, and on a recent visit to Lhasa it was impossible to find anyone who would part with a copy. Though propagandistic, the book was widely read and liked by Tibetans for its use of language and its portrayal of old ways of life. Readers tended to dismiss the obvious propaganda in the novel as simply a prerequisite for publication, and therefore focused on the language and how the narrative moved them. The plot has been described as a "turquoise rosary," meaning that it grips the reader.[31]

While the novel follows traditional Tibetan grammatical and stylistic rules, *The Crown Turquoise* also manages to give to everyday conversation a literary flavor. The mixture of colloquial speech and literary form made the novel accessible to the masses; thus it was able to meet one of the new literary criteria. *The Crown Turquoise* and *Kelzang Metok* were thus landmarks in the development of modern Tibetan literature.

Tibetan "Scar Literature"

After 1985 a new theme emerged in Tibetan short stories. This too was not an accident but the result of party policy to "expose the crimes of the Gang of Four and praise the Four Modernizations." The policy allowed Tibetans for the first time to write and speak about the painful period after the "peaceful liberation" of Tibet. A number of stories appeared depicting life during the Cultural Revolution and the suffering endured by the people. Gopo Lin, a critic from Kham writing in *Light Rain* in 1989, called these "the stories of the wounded mind of Tibet" (*Bod kyi sems rma'i sgrung gtam*).[32] The popular term "literature of the wounded" had appeared in China in 1979. A typical story of this kind is Trashi Penden's "Bgres song Tshe ring la go 'dzol byung ba" (Old man Tsering's misunderstanding).[33] The main character, Tsering, is persecuted during the Cultural Revolution for following the "capitalist road"; but afterward his skill as an entrepreneur is appreciated and encouraged.

Most of these stories about the Cultural Revolution were not original and did not critically analyze or explore the deeper experience of that nightmarish period. However, two stories published in the early 1980s in *Tibetan Art and Literature* were exceptional. While they lacked immediate identification as "scar literature," later commentators quickly saw in them representations of the Cultural Revolution. These two stories, "Char shul gyi nags tshal" (Forest after the rainstorm) by Namdröl[34] and "Me tog ldum rwa'i nang gi klan ka" (A dispute in the garden) by Penjor Langdün,[35] are written in an allegorical style and borrow much from folktales and traditional genres, such as "The Dispute between Tea and Beer."[36]

"Forest after the Rainstorm" is written in the style of a folktale (*sgrung*). The narrative is in prose, but the speech of the main characters is in verse. In the story, a group of animals have to rebuild their forest dwellings after a storm, which evidently represents the Cultural Revolution. Remarkably, the characterizations of the animals are reminiscent of George Orwell's *Animal Farm*.

Penjor Langdün's "A Dispute in the Garden" is regarded as one of the finest works of prose written in Tibetan. The language and style of the story are significantly more sophisticated than those of comparable works, and the author makes little attempt to comply with the demand that the language be accessible to the masses. Using old-fashioned language, the narrative has flowers in a garden disputing who is the most beautiful; to claim the coveted title, each behaves selfishly and ruthlessly.

These two short stories resist the standard treatment of the Cultural Revolution in fiction. Rather than merely justify the policies of the new leadership under Deng Xiaoping, the authors look deeply into their own experiences, questioning the nature of humanity and human relationships. The Cultural Revolution, like all traumatic events, brought to the surface the best and worst human emotions, including greed. By depicting allegorically how characters behave in an evil manner to achieve their own goals, the authors ask if human nature is inherently selfish or rather altruistic.

In essence, this opening of literature to other kinds of expression was an invention of the Chinese authorities, designed to serve a political need. The authorities saw a dual role for literature: extolling (*bstod bsngags byas*) the virtues of the revolution and exposing (*ther 'don*) the criminality of feudalism, perpetuated by enemies of the state. The literary revolution that they designed was meant to sever the link with Tibet's past and inaugurate a new period of socialism under the tutelage of the Chinese Communist Party. To this end the reforms were meant to leave no room for ambiguity or freedom of expression.

Ultimately the authorities hoped that literature would establish a secular humanistic tradition to replace religion as the main discourse of public and private morality. And this educational function of literature—to mold people's thoughts and train citizens how to behave—was made a significant part of the burden that a writer under communism was required to shoulder. The emerging generation of Tibetan writers was expected to be the vanguard of socialist modernization, and its work—through exemplary plots and appeals to rationalism—was expected to urge the people, by peaceful means, to open their mental horizons (*blo sgo phye*) and embrace China's socialist modernism (*gsar rje*).

Of course this is the official version of literature's function, and it is disputable whether all writers and artists agreed with it in the 1980s any more than they do today. It was clear, however—as it is now—that without conformity to party policy there was no possibility for publication.

Döndrup Gyel and Literary Innovation

In the period after 1980 the Tibetan intellectual community—traditional scholars educated in the monasteries and a young generation of intellectuals trained in universities in China—emerged from the Cultural Revolution severely traumatized. They had witnessed attacks on every aspect of Tibetan culture and identity. Now, when the party allowed even a small opportunity for expression, the intellectual community plunged into a debate on how best to make use of the degree of openness that the new policies allowed. Traditionalists in the community argued that the weight of intellectual labor should be directed toward restoring what had been lost and destroyed; this group embarked on a mission to salvage and reproduce damaged manuscripts. Consequently, the 1980s saw a renaissance in Tibetan publications, and a large number of rare manuscripts and texts entered the public domain. At the same time, a group of young intellectuals believed that the main task facing Tibet was what they called "innovation." They believed that Tibet had suffered under the hands of the Communists not only because of the military and political might of the Chinese but also because there was an inherent weakness in Tibetan culture: its inability to confront and integrate the forces of change.

Among the writers of the Tibetan intellectual community to emerge from this debate was a young man named Döndrup Gyel (1953–85), now considered the founder of modern Tibetan literature. Born in a small village in Gurong Puwa in the Nangra district of Amdo in 1953, a few years after the Communists came to power. Döndrup Gyel was from the first generation born after the Communist revolution—those who were supposedly its main beneficiaries. However, like so many of his generation, he saw his education come to an abrupt end during the Cultural Revolution.[37]

In 1979 Döndrup Gyel enrolled at Beijing Central Nationalities Institute and began to study under the prominent Tibetan scholar Dungkar Lozang Trinlé, who remembers him as a brilliant student with a perfect memory: "He would sit in the class without opening a notebook, but a few days later he would recall everything he had heard."[38] In 1983 Döndrup Gyel published a poem called "Lang tsho'i rbab chu" (Waterfall of youth), which caused a sensation among Tibetans.[39] The poem was like nothing they had ever read. Not only did it evidence literary innovation, but it contained a bold and nationalistic political statement. The poem fervently appealed to Tibetans to embrace modernism as a means of regenerating their culture and national pride, and besought the youth to shake off the past and march proudly toward their future.

This boldness in style and politics was characteristic of Döndrup Gyel's writings. For the first time the possibility emerged that through the medium of poetry and fiction, a genuine discourse on Tibetan modernity could occur. At stake were the future direction of Tibet and Tibetan identity in the latter half of the twentieth century.

Döndrup Gyel's work was a turning point because while criticism was unacceptable to the Chinese authorities, he showed that it was nevertheless possible to speak implicitly about the "wound inflicted on the mind of the Tibetans" (Bod kyi sems kyi rma), referring to the period under the leadership of the Gang of Four. Furthermore, he was able to raise the issue of Tibet's status as a subaltern, which was intrinsic to a debate about modernization. At this time the founders of literary journals saw their task as nothing less than the regeneration of Tibetan culture and identity, and one of the phrases that dominated Tibetan literature between 1980 and 1987 was mi rigs kyi la rgya (which means "honor," "pride," or "allegiance to nationality"). Literature that raised this subject was possible because indigenous discourse on Tibet's alterity paralleled state-sponsored discourse on modernization—that is, the Four Modernizations. The authorities saw the emerging debate in Tibetan literature as conforming to the party's will—thus lessening the party's fear of a possible challenge to official definitions—but overlooked the larger issues being addressed in the writing.

The debate inevitably produced a confrontation between traditionalists and modernists. While the modernists saw tradition ("old habits") as impediments to change, others pointed out that tradition was the most significant marker of Tibetan separateness from the colonizer. Because of party restraints, traditionalists could not make their counterarguments publicly. However, the actual process and practice of revitalization demonstrated that a large portion of the populace favored the use of tradition as a way to restore Tibet's selfhood and define it as separate from China.

Despite obstacles, the infant literature was audacious, and it is fitting that Tibetan critics should compare the period to the May Fourth literary movement in China, which brought debates about modernity into the forefront of intellectual discourse in the 1920s and 1930s. While a characteristic of this early period of Tibetan literature was writers' condemnation of the "old society," the best work can be distinguished from the turgid style favored by the party and from the stereotyped proletarian heroes and demonic feudal lords prevalent in propaganda. While condemning the past, Döndrup Gyel and other new writers made no attempt to provide a political justification for the present. Nor did they make a clear distinction between a "bad past" and a "good future." Significantly, they portrayed a more complex relationship between past and present; and the imperfections of the old Tibetan society were described along with its accomplishments.

In a number of short stories, poems, and articles, Döndrup Gyel championed modernism. However, his advocacy did not include an official characterization of Tibet as underdeveloped. In his poem "Waterfall of Youth," for example, he demonstrates his feeling that the only role for Tibet to play is that of "the bride of science and technology." In this verse from the poem, he makes it clear that the past cannot be a guide to the future:

> The thousand brilliant accomplishments of the past
> cannot serve today's purpose,
> yesterday's salty water cannot quench today's thirsts,
> the withered body of history is lifeless
> without the soul of today,
> the pulse of progress will not beat,
> the blood of progress will not flow,
> and a forward step cannot be taken.[40]

Tibet's past is compared to "salty water" and a "withered body" that lacks the ability to regenerate itself. In a poem published five years later, "'Di na yang drag tu mchong lding byed bzhin pa'i snying gson po zhig 'dug" (Here also a living heart is beating strongly), he associates the old Tibet with conservatism (rnying zhen), isolationism (bag 'khums), and reactionary thinking. He asks: Why is it so difficult to plant new ideas, new habits, and new doctrines in the Land of Snows?

In short stories and articles as well as poetry, Döndrup Gyel explored the urgent need for Tibet to modernize. His ideas crystallized in a brilliant polemical essay, "Rkang lam phra mo" (A narrow footpath), published in Light Rain in 1984.[41] The essay begins with a group of old men in a village who are gazing toward a narrow footpath that leads away from the village. The footpath is full of historical significance, and the villagers are greatly attached to it. Legend has it that the mythical King Gesar once traversed the path and that the Bodhisattva Monkey, primogenitor of the Tibetan race, also traveled on it. Other villagers assert that the path was created by Lhalung Pelgyi Dorjé, the monk who assassinated the allegedly anti-Buddhist king Langdarma. The narrator of "A Narrow Footpath" is a young boy. He walks on the same path to school every day, wondering why the old people of the village do not use the new road below the village. For him the ancient path evokes wonder at the courage, innovation, and bravery of his ancestors, but it also poses a question: If our ancestors could carve this path, why has the current generation failed to make any improvements and allowed it to fall into such a dilapidated state?

For Döndrup Gyel the narrow path is a metaphor for Tibet's parochialism, conservatism, and confinement. The old people who venerate the past do not want to change. Rather than see history as containing the potential for innovation, the traditionalists insist that their way of life is immutable, and they fear progress. Döndrup Gyel concludes that the narrow path cannot teach contemporary Tibet much about the spirits of science and technology, that traditional cultural monuments cannot provide the Tibetan people with "nourishment and energy for the invention of a new culture." We can understand that it is Döndrup Gyel's own voice calling for change when the boy narrator declares that he will travel to school on the new road.

"A Narrow Footpath" was published under a pseudonym and was seen by many as an attack on traditional culture, which offended conservative sections of the Tibetan community. Döndrup Gyel reportedly received death threats after its publication. However, he remained undaunted and continued to explore the theme of tradition versus modernity. In "Sad kyis bcom pa'i me tog" (Frost-bitten flower),[42] Döndrup Gyel tackles the issue of arranged marriage, describing the old custom as a "tradition without compassion" (snying rje med pa'i goms srol).[43] This short story is divided into seven parts, which collectively relay a story of suffering and unhappiness brought about by arranged marriage. The structure of the story is reminiscent of Akira Kurosawa's film *Rashomon*, as each of the characters tells his or her own version of events. The protagonist, Tsering, starts the first section of the story by declaring that he is telling the sad story in order "to urge our parents and older generation to open their narrow minds." The central tragedy of the story is that despite knowing of Tsering's and Lhakyi's love for each other, the parents force their children to marry other people. Their decision in the end causes great suffering for everyone.

Here Döndrup Gyel states that the custom of arranged marriages negates individual choice and that happiness cannot be achieved by means of blind faith in old customs. The subject matter of the story again reveals the author's concern with the conflict between tradition and change. Lhakyi's father is depicted as a man governed not by feudal superstition but by narrow thinking. Having already promised his daughter to the son of a man who had saved his life, Lhakyi's father is bound by his oath. Yet Döndrup Gyel gives equal weight to the father's story. In fact he is portrayed sympathetically, and readers are urged to accept his reasoning as an alternative truth. In neither "The Narrow

Footpath" nor "Frost-Bitten Flower" does Döndrup Gyel blindly condemn the entirety of "old society." Rather, he encourages readers to question all power and authority, and this gives Tibetan literature a purpose different from that assigned to it by the party.

Related to the question of modernization, another difficult subject for Tibetan writers, was and still is religion. At a practical level the party's policy is to view religion as obstructing economic modernization and its persistence and popularity in society as contradicting socialism. It is through their religion, however, that Tibetans have always found their identity. Consequently, the early party practice of overtly denigrating Tibetan Buddhism was seen by the people as undermining Tibetan selfhood, and it gradually became clear to the party that its direct attacks and coercive methods had completely failed. Therefore in the new period the party decided to challenge the influence of religion indirectly—through literature. Writing that contested the authority of religion and portrayed religious figures negatively was encouraged. (This is why many Tibetan readers continue to see all modern literature as nothing but a tool of the Chinese Communist Party.)

Döndrup Gyel dealt with this question in a controversial story titled "*Sprul sku*" (The reincarnate lama), published in *Light Rain*.[44] Set in a remote village in 1980, the first time after the Cultural Revolution that people were allowed to practice their faith freely, the story begins with the arrival of a stranger who proclaims himself an incarnate lama. The form and content of the story appear similar to those favored by the authorities. The protagonist, an old man named Akhu Nyima, embodies religious faith and is described as "honest and straight as an arrow." His faith is so strong that he distrusts his own knowledge. He sees evidence that the incarnate lama may not be who he claims to be—the lama contradicts himself and shows an imperfect knowledge of Buddhism—but Akhu Nyima accepts the lama's explanations for these lapses and regards his own doubts as evidence of a lack of faith. At the time of its publication, the story was seen by commentators as a good example of modern writing containing antireligious social and moral propaganda. The story appeared to warn people that religion could be used to deceive them. Whether readers interpreted the story as attacking religion or merely reflecting a trend in society, it became the subject of much debate. But Tibetans have always been well aware that there are people who wear the mask of religion to dupe the faithful. Therefore a closer reading of the text—in light of the recent history of Tibet and China—might suggest that the figure of the incarnate lama represents the blind trust that people had placed in Mao and the Communist Party.

Tibetan Literary Content and Change

Though writers in Tibet and China lack freedom to explore the full range of individual sentiments and subjects explicitly, nevertheless their works do not merely follow the diktats of the party, even when written in Chinese and published under the eyes of the censors. Despite the constraints imposed by state and party, Tibetan writers are able to bring burning issues into the foreground, and as we have seen, this stimulates politically charged debate. Although the line favored by the state and the party is compulsory and all authors must seem to conform to be published, when we examine the writings themselves their conformity is not quite so clear-cut. At the same time, literature emanating from Tibet is still maturing, and many works are indeed repetitive or didactic, and follow the party's guidelines on art and literature. Since 1994 control over work produced by Tibetan writers has become increasingly strict, and the creative energy encouraged in the early 1980s has been suppressed in official publications.

Literary production and the cultural landscape in Tibet have undergone a dramatic shift since the initial renaissance of the early 1980s, which was partly in response to the repression of the Cultural Revolution. Today the situation has markedly changed, in terms not only of politics but of larger social factors. Educational reforms and the increasing dominance of Chinese as a language of instruction and profession have had a mixed effect on the use of the Tibetan language in Tibetan intellectual discourse. While a burgeoning of Tibetan publications speaks to persistence and even resistance in projects that support use of the Tibetan language, there are strong pressures to gain a Chinese-language education to become employable, and the publishing industry in China and Tibet has faced cuts in government subsidies. Though Tibetan language publications continue to receive more state subsidies than mainstream Chinese-language publishing in China, Tibetan publishing houses have become more discriminating in their selection process, as resources are severely limited. Today many authors have to meet the cost of publishing their own works. The financial burden is considerable, because the costs cannot be recovered from the sale of books. This is one of the reasons why fewer than fifteen full-length Tibetan-language novels have ever been published. Short stories and poetry still remain the main genres of modern Tibetan literature, with journals offering cheaper forums of publication. Indeed, writers are paid a small honorarium for contributions to the most popular official journals, such as *Tibetan Art and Literature* and *Light Rain*.

Another development that has had an impact on literary activities is the growth of new media for creative channels; the advent of television in Tibet has opened a new avenue for writers. It is also financially more lucrative for writers to produce scripts for television sketches and plays, and now feature films and documentaries. The medium demands changes in subject matter and style, and both have undergone a shift since the last decade of the twentieth century. Where Tibetan literature of the 1980s was frequently used to convey a message (either the official party line or a subtly nationalistic one), now there is an attempt to write texts that dispense with overt social messages and simply narrate a "good story." An example is a novel by Teling Wangdor, *Bkras zur tshang gi gsang ba'i gtam rgyud | The Secret Tale of the Tesur House* (1997).[45] There are no identifiable heroes or stereotypical characters, and the narrator does not pronounce judgment nor direct readers to a certain conclusion. This shift may portend the future direction of the subject matter and style of Tibetan literature.

By all accounts literature has become the main arena for intellectual confrontation among competing ideas in Tibet today. The development of modern Tibetan literature cannot be separated from the politics of identity. Tibetan literature emerged as an assertion of Tibetan space in a period of increasing intrusion by the metropolitan colonial inscription. For Tibetan writers and intellectuals, the Tibetan language alone has the power to preserve and reinvent Tibet.

Notes

This chapter appeared in somewhat different form as "The Waterfall and Fragrant Flowers."

1. For an account of the restrictions placed on Tibetan language and the sometimes humorous misunderstandings that ensued see Pema Bhum, *Dran tho smin drug ske 'khyog | Six Stars with a Crooked Neck*.
2. For background on the political changes that took place in Tibet in the early 1980s see Tsering Shakya, *The Dragon in the Land of Snows*.
3. 'Gyur med, interview with the author, Xining, August 2000.
4. Link, "The Limits of Cultural Reform in Deng Xiaoping's China," 120.
5. Ibid., 120–21.
6. Skal bzang ye shes, "Bod rigs kyi rtsom rig lo rgyus thog gi dus rabs gsar pa" (A new era in Tibetan literary history), *Bod ljongs zhib 'jug*, 1983, no. 3, 64.
7. Bstan 'dzin rgan pa, "Bod kyi rtsom rig gsar pa'i skyed tshal" (The garden of new Tibetan literature), *Bod kyi rtsom rig sgyu rtsal*, 1997, no. 2, 2.
8. Rig dpal, "Dus skabs gsar pa'i Bod yig brtsams sgrung gi 'phel phyogs" (Directions in Tibetan stories in the new era), *Bod kyi rtsom rig sgyu rtsal*, 1992, no. 1, 28–30.
9. *Sbrang char*, 1984, no. 3, 90.

10. Apart from manually recorded copybooks, cyclostyle printing (Tib. *rnum par*, lit. "oil printing") was the most common form of private duplication in the 1980s. The process consists of writing with a stylus on was wax paper and then screen printing onto paper.

11. Tsering Shakya, "The Emergence of Modern Tibetan Literature—*gsar rtsom*."

12. Davis, *Factual Fictions*, 71–78

13. Bstan pa yar rgyas, "Mgo ras kyi btums pa'i bu mo" (Girl swathed in a headscarf), *Byang thang gi mdzes ljongs* (Lhasa: Bod ljongs mi dmangs dpe skrun khang, 1995), 89. See appendix 3 for an English translation of this work.

14. *Mtsho sngon mang tshogs sgyu rtsal*, 1988, no. 3, 1–9. See appendix 3 for an English translation of this work.

15. 'Brong bu Rdo rje rin chen, *Sbrang char*, 1992, no. 3, 17–24. See appendix 3 for an English translation of this work.

16. Tshe ring don grub, *Tshe ring don grub kyi sgrung thung bdams bsgrigs*, 43–62.

17. *Mtsho sngon mang tshogs sgyu rtsal*, 1988, no. 3, 1.

18. For a brief biographical introduction to Trashi Penden see the back cover of *Sbrang char*, 1994, no. 4.

19. Mdo mkhar Tshe ring dbang rgyal, *Gzhon nu zla med kyi gtam rgyud* (Lhasa: Bod ljongs mi dmangs dpe skrun khang, 1987). For an English translation see Tshe ring dbang rgyal, *The Tale of the Incomparable Prince*, trans. B. Newman.

20. Tsering Shakya, "The Emergence of Modern Tibetan Literature."

21. Frye, *Anatomy of Criticism*, 304.

22. Watt, *The Rise of the Novel*, 13.

23. Rdo rje rgyal po, *Rdo rje rgyal po'i gsung rtsom phyogs bsgrigs*.

24. Ibid., 823.

25. The text of the story I used is reprinted in Rdo rje rgyal po, *Rdo rje rgyal po'i gsung rtsom phyogs bsgrigs*, 817–89.

26. Ibid., 889.

27. 'Jam dpal rgya mtsho, *Skal bzang me tog*.

28. Ibid., 545.

29. Dpal 'byor, *Gtsug g.yu*.

30. Rig dpal, "Dus skabs gsar pa'i Bod yig brtsams sgrung gi 'phel phyogs," 30.

31. Ibid., 31.

32. Go po lin, "Dus skabs gsar pa'i Bod kyi sgrung gtam gyi brjod bya'i bstan don skor rags tsam gleng ba," 145–68.

33. Bkra shis dpal ldan, "Bgres song Tshe ring la go 'dzol byung ba," 3–12.

34. Rnam 'grol, "Char shul gyi nags tshal."

35. Ibid., 1–8.

36. Tib. *Ja chang lha mo'i bstan bcos*. For an English translation see Bon grong pa, *The Dispute between Tea and Chang*, trans. A. Fedotov and Sangye Tandar Naga (Dharamsala: Library of Tibetan Works and Archives), 1993.

37. Pema Bhum, "The Life of Dhondup Gyal," 17–29.

38. Discussion with author, London, 15 August 1996.

39. *Sbrang char*, 1983, no. 2, 56–61.

40. Ibid., 58.

41. *Sbrang char*, 1984, no. 3, 1–6.

42. Don grub rgyal, *Collected Works*, vol. 2, 218–88.

43. Ibid., 218.

44. *Sbrang char*, 1981, no. 3, 3–34.

45. Bkras gling Dbang rdor, *Bkras zur tshang gi gsang ba'i gtam rgyud*. An English translation by the author has also been published in the PRC under the title *The Secret Tale of the Tesur House*.

4

Döndrup Gyel and the Remaking
of the Tibetan Ramayana

NANCY G. LIN

> Our scholars have a weakness which is to rely as much as possible
> on India for our cultural and historical origins. In general, there is
> a close relationship between Tibet and India in all sorts of aspects.
> But to think that all we have came from India would mean that
> Tibet has nothing of its own history, own culture, own characteris-
> tics, own thinking, own customs, etc. More than thirty years have
> passed since [Communist] liberation, but we still haven't been
> able to resist this view. We youth should be ashamed of this and
> our nationality should be ashamed as well . . . in my view, if Daṇḍin
> could write a *Kāvyādarśa* [Mirror of poetics], why can't we write a
> Tibetan *Mirror of Poetics?*
> —Döndrup Gyel, letter to Sanggyé published in *Sbrang char* (Light
> rain), 1984[1]

Memorialized as the father of modern Tibetan literature, Döndrup Gyel
(1953–85) is best remembered for composing the first free-verse poem in
Tibet and for rousing national consciousness among succeeding generations
of Tibetan youth. He was the undisputed literary sensation among Tibetans
during his brief career, and his work was canonized on both sides of the Chinese border.[2] His impassioned appeal to release Tibetan literature from its
alleged cultural colonizer, India, is characteristic of the stirring rhetoric that
contributed to his heroic status. Given the tireless zeal with which Tibetan
writers and students celebrated him in the 1980s and 1990s, one might believe that Döndrup Gyel single-handedly created the basis for a new Tibetan
literature. Appraising his oeuvre, Trashi Penden asserts that the iconic free-
verse poem "Lang tsho'i rbab chu" (Waterfall of youth) "completely over-
came the fetters of old ways of writing and delivered the system of liter-

Döndrup Gyel.

ary composition entirely to a new land."[3] Pema Bhum captures this popular image of Döndrup Gyel as a trailblazing culture hero: "in the minds of young writers and intellectuals in Tibet today Dhondup Gyal is not only the founder of a new literary path but he has become something of a model for courage against oppression and a fighter for national honor."[4]

English-language scholarship has tended to support this portrait of Döndrup Gyel as a thinker whose nationalist vision depended on resolute innovation. Tsering Shakya cites a verse from "Waterfall of Youth" in which Döndrup Gyel "makes it clear that the past cannot be a guide to the future . . . Tibet's past is compared to 'salty water' and a 'withered body' that lacks the ability to regenerate itself."[5] In her anthology of translated stories, Riika Virtanen introduces Döndrup Gyel's story "Sad kyis bcom pa'i me tog" (Frost-bitten flower) as "a powerful cry for individual freedom of choice and a critique of the old customs."[6] Mark Stevenson and Lama Choedak T. Yuthok published a translation of "Rkang lam phra mo" (A narrow footpath), an essay that gained prominence through its protagonist's choice of modernization and progress at the expense of tradition and cultural heritage.[7] Following a particular Tibetan reception of Döndrup Gyel's work, these selective translations and assessments reiterate the consistent theme that modernization requires a radical break with the past.

Countering this trend, Matthew T. Kapstein has suggested that Döndrup Gyel "struggled to find a new voice not by rejecting Tibet's literary past, but by immersing himself within it and revaluing it."[8] Kapstein's reassessment hints at why Döndrup Gyel worked intensively on the Ramayana, the epic tradition that has been hailed as "something like the living sum of Indian culture"[9] and placed foremost in the canon of Sanskrit literature in its form attributed to Vālmīki. Scholars have recognized the existence of the Ramayana as a distinct tradition in Tibet since at least the ninth century, commonly known as the Story of Rāmaṇa. Nonetheless, Tibetan tellings continue to be regarded as a sign of Indianité[10] by Tibetan and western scholars alike owing to the Indian origin of their form and content. This might make Döndrup Gyel's obsession with the Ramayana—which extended to no less than five literary projects—even more puzzling in light of his claim that Tibetans had relied too heavily on Indian culture and needed to develop a distinctive literary culture of their own. How indeed were Tibetans to extricate their national literature from Indian cultural influence, and if one was seeking to do so, why turn to the Ramayana?

I propose that Döndrup Gyel's work on the Story of Rāmaṇa was part of an ambitious project to revive Tibetan literature in the wake of the Cultural Revolution. Döndrup Gyel positioned the Story of Rāmaṇa as a suitable narrative to affirm the legitimacy and continuity of the classical Tibetan literary tradition. He considered the Indian origins of both the Story of Rāmaṇa and classical Tibetan poetics less important than their historic role and their potential for transformation. At the same time he reworked the Story of Rāmaṇa to advance a new model for poetry, one that sought to replace the élitist, Indianized reputation of classical poetics (Tib. *snyan ngag*) with the nascent principles of an indigenous poetic theory. This process entailed greater selectivity with regard to classical poetic conventions, retaining basic elements while stressing ease of understanding, a direct style, and the influence of song-poetry. In light of Döndrup Gyel's approaches to the Story of Rāmaṇa, I conclude by reconsidering some of his more prominent publications.

The Legacy of Rāmaṇa in Tibet

The Story of Rāmaṇa in Tibet is but one of many narrative traditions drawing from a loose collection of Indic legends, a central representation of these being the Sanskrit Rāmaṇa attributed to Vālmīki (in circulation by the first century CE). This collection of legends spread throughout much of Asia, with distinctive literary and performance traditions appearing in multiple languages, societies, and religious contexts. Since the diversity and influence of the Rama story cycle has been well documented elsewhere,[11] there is no need to discuss its numerous variations, but here I recount salient points for ensuing plot discussions.

The prince Rāma, son of King Daśaratha, marries the princess Sītā and is later exiled to the forest with Sītā and his brother Lakṣmaṇa. The demon-king Rāvaṇa abducts Sītā and takes her to the island of Laṅkā. Rāma enlists the alliance of a monkey tribe, and a monkey with extraordinary powers named Hanumān finds Sītā. Rāma defeats Rāvaṇa in a major battle, is reunited with Sītā, and returns to rule his kingdom. In some versions Sītā is later banished because of doubts about her chastity during her period of abduction; she raises two children who eventually succeed Rāma to the throne. From an early stage the characters were sometimes accorded religious significance, with the dominant paradigm identifying Rāma as an incarnation (Skt. *avatāra*) of the supreme deity Viṣṇu. Rāma has also been identified as a previous life of the Buddha, e.g. in the *Daśarathajātaka* of the Pāli canon.

In Tibetan the earliest evidence of the Rama story cycle consists of the fragments of two recensions extracted from the Dunhuang cave complex in the desert of northwestern China, likely written down during the Tibetan occupation of the region from 787 to 848.[12] Literary examples of the Rama story resurface from the thirteenth century, when a reference to Bödrok (Skt. Rāvaṇa) in *Legs par bshad pa rin po che'i gter* (Treasury of elegant sayings), the collection of aphoristic verses by Sakya Paṇḍita Künga Gyentsen (1182–1251), generated numerous retellings of the story by commentators. Best known among these is the commentary by Sakya Paṇḍita's disciple Martön Chökyi Gyelpo (ca. 1198–ca.1259).[13] Upon Sakya Paṇḍita's statement that Bödrok was known to have been killed because he was attached to desirable things, Martön relates the story in a lively and straightforward prose style. Ulrike Roesler has shown that while Martön's plot is closer to the Dunhuang version than the Vālmīki Rāmāyaṇa, certain details suggest that Martön relied on a widespread oral tradition with parallels in Indian, Khotanese, and Southeast Asian versions.[14]

Martön's account is strikingly free of didactic overtones considering that it belongs to the genre of aphorism (Tib. *legs bshad*, Skt. *subhāṣita*). As Roesler observes, Martön is more interested in reporting Indian mythology than in making the story conform to Buddhist views.[15] Martön apparently relishes the reporting, vividly recounting the mischievous escapades of Hanumantha (Skt. Hanumān) in Laṅgkā (Skt. Laṅkā) as he upends fruit trees, tricks demons, and burns down the island with his tail. Indeed, Hanumanta emerges as the hero of the story, while Rāmaṇa plays little part in the action. While some of Rama's more troubling actions found in both the Vālmīki Rāmāyaṇa and the Dunhuang recensions—such as killing the monkey chief or banishing the blameless Sita—are lacking, he is not accorded any special status as the Buddha, Viṣṇu, or even a particularly distinguished king. The sheer fun of good storytelling is in greater evidence than moral rigor or a move toward Buddhist adaptation.

The Story of Rāmaṇa was also made to serve the aesthetic concerns of poetics. A key figure in the literary arts of his era, Sakya Paṇḍita also introduced to Tibetan scholars in the 1220s the Mirror of Poetics (Tib. Snyan ngag me long) of Daṇḍin, a seventh-century treatise on Sanskrit poetic theory (Skt. kāvya, Tib. snyan ngag) with extensive references to the Vālmīki Rāmāyaṇa.[16] The Mirror of Poetics was adopted as the standard treatise for snyan ngag—one of the five minor disciplines of monastic education[17]—and guided Tibetan literary composition not only in poetry but in such areas as philosophy, biography, and letter writing. Commentaries on the Mirror of Poetics, such as that of Ju Mipam Gyatso (1846–1912), incorporated poetic examples drawing from the Rāma story cycle.[18]

By far what became the best-known work treating the Rama story cycle in Tibet is Dri za'i bu mo'i rgyud mang gi sgra dbyangs [Song of the gandharva maiden's lute], composed in 1438–39 by Zhangzhung Chöwang Drakpa (1404–69). A Gelukpa disciple of Tsongkhapa (1357–1419) and Khedrup Jé (1385–1438), Chöwang Drakpa used a plot with considerable similarity to that of Martön, suggesting a commonly recognized version of the Rāmaṇa narrative in Tibet. Yet in matters of style he parts ways, writing in metered verse and emphasizing the display of ornamental figures of speech (Skt. alaṅkāra, Tib. tshig rgyan), as prescribed by the Mirror of Poetics, in a highly elaborate and deliberately obscure manner.[19] In his classification of five schools of poetic composition, the research scholar Tashi Tsering ranks Chöwang Drakpa's style as the most difficult, assessing it as "a much sought after style of composition—among the Tibetan intellectuals . . . as it was beyond the grasp of the common people and gave an elitist touch."[20] With Chöwang Drakpa's tour de force, the Story of Rāmaṇa became a formidable literary challenge, both to read and to emulate. The fame of Song of the Gandharva Maiden's Lute continued well into the twentieth century, aided by the commentary of Alak Zhelshül Ngakwang Tenpé Gyatso (d. 1920s) of Labrang Trashikhyil Monastery.

Throughout its career in Tibet, the Story of Rāmaṇa was never fully domesticated. Although it may have enjoyed some popularity in oral storytelling, it has been overshadowed in this role by other narratives such as the Gesar epic, popular Buddhist biographies, dramas, and local folktales. As a non-Buddhist story that was retold rather than properly translated from an authoritative source—the Vālmīki Rāmāyaṇa—it never gained inclusion in the

Buddhist canons that formed during the fourteenth to eighteenth centuries. Such a place was reserved for loftier narrative works such as the *Jātakamālā* [Garland of birth stories, Tib. Skyes rabs so bzhi pa] of Āryaśūra and the *Bodhisattvāvadānakalpalatā* [Wishing vine of bodhisattva stories, Tib. Byang chub sems dpa'i rtogs brjod dpag bsam 'khri shing] of Kṣemendra, which related past lives of the Buddha and were translated directly from finely wrought Sanskrit. While these Buddhist narratives were actively taught in monastic curricula, by comparison the Rama story cycle remained an exotic object to most Tibetans. The scholarly giant Jonang Tāranātha Kunga Nyingpo (1575–1634) cited two Sanskrit scholars from Bengal as his source for learning the *Rāmāyaṇa* along with the other major Indian epic *Mahābhārata*,[21] while Chöwang Drakpa's elaborate reworking of the Story of Rāmaṇa—despite being written in the Tibetan language—earned him the reputation in Tibet of being the foremost Sanskrit scholar of his day. Small wonder that the accomplished monk-intellectual Gendün Chömpel (1903–51) preferred authentic Sanskrit sources for the *Rāmāyaṇa* when he commenced a new translation into Tibetan in 1936.[22]

Döndrup Gyel and the Story of Rāmaṇa

Before tracing Döndrup Gyel's involvement with the Story of Rāmaṇa, a few biographical details of his life may bear recounting. Born in 1953 in Gurong, Amdo, he completed middle school in Repgong in 1969, during the traumatic ruptures of the Cultural Revolution. After a three-year stint at the Qinghai Broadcasting Station in Xining, he was sent to study at the Beijing Central Nationalities Institute (CNI) in a political climate that was actively hostile to intellectualism. Although classical Tibetan literature was prohibited as "poisonous weeds," Döndrup Gyel secretly kept several books, including the commentary of Mipam Gelek Namgyel (1618–85) on the *Mirror of Poetics*—possibly his first exposure to the Story of Rāmaṇa. He returned to the Xining radio station in 1976 and began publishing his writings when cultural restrictions relaxed at the official close of the Cultural Revolution.

From 1979 to 1981 he returned to the CNI and trained with the illustrious scholar Dungkar Lozang Trinlé (1927–97). Upon obtaining his master's degree he remained there to teach Tibetan language classes. It was at this time that he actively taught Story of Rāmaṇa materials for his advanced class of Amdo middle school teachers, including *Song of the Gandharva Maiden's Lute* and his own poetic rendition, *Rā ma ṇa'i rtogs brjod go bder sbyar ba mgur dbyangs blo gsar rna ba'i dpyid glu* (Spring song for youthful ears: a melodious and accessible composition on the story of Rāmaṇa). In 1984 he was transferred to the Nationalities Teacher Training School in Chapcha, where he complained of isolation and grew increasingly depressed. In November 1985 he took his own life.[23]

Educated in Tibetan and Chinese, Döndrup Gyel worked on five distinct projects related to the Story of Rāmaṇa: the aforementioned *Spring Song for Youthful Ears*, an incomplete commentary on Chöwang Drakpa's *Song of the Gandharva Maiden's Lute*, an incomplete translation of Romesh C. Dutt's English verse rendition (1899) of the Ramayana, via the Chinese translation of Sun Yong,[24] a reworking of the Dunhuang Story of Rāmaṇa manuscripts, and an essay concerning the Ramayana tradition in India, Tibet, and worldwide, which serves to introduce Döndrup Gyel's *Spring Song for Youthful Ears* and his unfinished translation from Chinese. Published posthumously in his collected works, the five projects were likely written during the years 1979–85 while he was a graduate student and teacher.[25]

Döndrup Gyel's extensive work on the Ramayana occurred during the official "warming" of literary activity encouraged by the Chinese Communist Party after the "freeze" of the Cultural Revolution. Along with the publication of literature in Chinese and minority languages, the policy shift sanctioned the translation of foreign literature under the slogan "Make the past serve the present and foreign things serve China" (Ch. *guwei jinyong, yangwei zhongyong*).[26] Sun Yong's translation of Dutt's *Ramayana* was published in 1978 by the People's Literature Publishing House in Beijing, the same year that the complete works of Shakespeare, Cervantes's *Don Quixote*, Balzac's *Le Père Goriot*, Tolstoy's *Anna Karenina*, and Goethe's *Faust*—to name but a few— were published in Chinese translation.[27] A complete translation of Vālmīki's Rāmāyaṇa into Chinese soon followed, with the first volume published in 1980.[28] In the meantime a handful of classical works in Tibetan were being reprinted, such as *Gzhon nu zla med kyi gtam rgyud* (The tale of the incomparable prince) by Dokhar Tsering Wanggyel (1697–1763) in 1979, commentaries on the *Mirror of Poetics* in 1980 and 1981, and *Mi la ras pa'i gsung mgur* (The one hundred thousand songs of Milarepa).[29]

The climate seemed favorable for the monastic scholar Mugé Samten (1913–93) to publish Chöwang Drakpa's *Song of the Gandharva Maiden's Lute*, together with Ngakwang Tenpé Gyatso's commentary, through the Sichuan Nationalities Publishing House in February 1981. Its early release and unusually high print run of 8,500 copies testified to its anticipated role in reviving Tibetan literature in the wake of the Cultural Revolution. In the preface Mugé Samten noted its status as a world-famous narrative that had been translated into English and Chinese, as well as its presence in Tibetan literature as evidenced by the Dunhuang manuscripts and numerous Tibetan compositions based on the Rama narrative.[30] The publication of *Song of the Gandharva Maiden's Lute* stimulated discussion about the national identity of the Ramayana and the validity of the Tibetan Rāmaṇa tradition. In an article published twice in 1982, Lodrö Gyatso marks its identity as specifically Indian, stating that "in India, the Story of Rāmaṇa is known and has been heard by every household and by every man and woman, elder and child . . . a great many people place their faith in Rāma, and reckon him to be a god."[31] He further claims that if Sanskrit- and Hindi-language versions had been translated into Tibetan, "this would have effected an unsurpassed benefit to our own culture."[32] Picking up on the heightened interest in foreign literature during the past few years, Lodrö Gyatso justifies his discussion of the Ramayana by invoking its value and status as a foreign object that can serve cultural progress in China. In addition, he implies that Sanskrit-language versions such as the Vālmīki Rāmāyaṇa are superior to Tibetan ones.

Döndrup Gyel, by contrast, employs the more inclusive rhetoric of world literature: "The Story of Rāmaṇa not only attained great value and status in the history of the development of Indian literary arts, it also attained great value and status in the history of the development of world literary arts . . . it spread around the world so that most national literature is influenced by it. For that reason, the Story of Rāmaṇa is a famous work of the literary arts of each people of the world. It is a precious intellectual treasure of each nationality of the world."[33] To reinforce the point that the Ramayana has transcended its Indian origins, Döndrup Gyel goes on to list the numerous languages into which it has been translated. Moreover, in his essay he calls into question Vālmīki's authorship, asserting that the work was originally created by the collective "wisdom and labor of the common people" and that learned people other than Vālmīki, who remain anonymous, contributed to its later elegant style.[34] Döndrup Gyel deliberately chooses not to follow the preeminent Indian authority for the Rama story cycle, the Vālmīki Rāmāyaṇa. For him the Ramayana does not belong exclusively to India, nor to Vālmīki; it belongs to the world, with a Ramayana to enrich every nation.

Perhaps wittingly, Döndrup Gyel's choices reflected ongoing debates about the Ramayana tradition in international scholarship in the twentieth century. Paula Richman has called an early approach the "Valmiki and Others" model, in which Sanskrit philologists privileged the Vālmīki Rāmāyaṇa as the original and authoritative source from which all other versions were derived, and by which they were to be measured for their deviations. A second approach, the "Many Ramayanas" model, acknowledges the diversity of the Ramayana tradition and treats each telling as valid in its own right.[35] Publications sympathetic to this model make conscious efforts to foreground non-Sanskrit and non-Hindu tellings, identifying them by their respective languages: hence the Hindi Ramayan, the Thai Ramakien, the Tamil Iramavataram, and so on. Döndrup Gyel's inclusive view of the Ramayana tradition as multi-authored and multinational is consistent with the "Many Ramayanas" response to the "Valmiki and Others" model.

Continuing in this vein, Döndrup Gyel cites the antiquity of the Tibetan versions and the subsequent development of the literary tradition in Tibet: "Now, if one asks whether there was a version of the Story of Rāmaṇa in our snowy homeland of Tibet, there was . . . in the trove [of manuscripts] found from Dunhuang, four fragments of the Story of Rāmaṇa emerged . . . After that, there were a great many writings by former Tibetan scholars which were versions of the Story of Rāmaṇa, either in verse or prose . . . [these] renditions, commentaries, and poetic exemplars like the stars of the sky are too innumerable to count."[36] The use of a rhetorical question at the beginning of the passage indicates that Döndrup Gyel is weighing in on a debate, in favor of the antiquity of the Rāmaṇa tradition in Tibet based on the Dunhuang evidence. His acknowledgment of the highly developed Tibetan literary tradition constitutes an implicit parallel to the celebrated Indian literary tradition. Tibetans would not need to rely on Sanskrit or other Indian sources for access to the Ramayana: their own sources were venerably ancient, sustained by impressive iteration, and in short amounted to a distinctive and legitimate literary tradition.

By recognizing that not all Ramas are created equal, Döndrup Gyel anticipated the third and most recent "Questioning Ramayanas" model delineated by Richman. This model is attentive to the ways that particular tellings of the Rama story negotiate "power, status, and access to information and/or knowledge" in hierarchical social contexts. For Richman, the Rama story is "inherently political" because it sets forth normative ideals for kingship, social behavior according to rank and status, and utopian society.[37] This formulation presupposes the universal familiarity and depth of sociopolitical influence with which the Ramayana tradition has permeated Indic societies. As we have seen, the Story of Rāmaṇa was largely restricted to an educated élite trained in poetics, with little influence in the social or religious fabric of Tibet at large.

It is this very outcome of literary reception in Tibet that brings Richman's formulation to bear on Döndrup Gyel's Rāmaṇa writings. Pema Bhum recalls that during Döndrup Gyel's period of writing activity in the aftermath of the Cultural Revolution, "everyone was competing to write in the style of Snyan ngag me long [Mirror of Poetics]," and that Chöwang Drakpa's Song of the

Gandharva Maiden's Lute was considered one of the highest expressions of this poetic style.[38] Given the official persecution of Tibetan-language education and materials that had just taken place, however, it was rare for the youth of Döndrup Gyel's generation to have received sound training in the complexities of restricted meter, metaphor, simile, and other conventions of *snyan ngag* (poetics). Döndrup Gyel's initial choice to even undertake writing and teaching the Story of Rāmaṇa based on *snyan ngag* principles constituted an affirmation that the heights of Tibetan literature could be recovered in the wake of calamitous cultural disruption.

The choice to focus on the Story of Rāmaṇa over other possibilities is telling of the political pressures of the day. In his master's thesis on the indigenous genre of song-poetry (*mgur glu*), Döndrup Gyel criticizes Tibetan composers for their religious tendencies, including the yogi-saint Milarepa (1052–1135), Jonang Tāranātha, and the madman-saint Drukpa Künlek (1455–1529): "Since they were people who put faith in Buddhism, the song-poems they composed were full of Buddhist views. From time to time they wrote on authentic social life, class struggle, conflict between religious sects and so on. However, overall most of their work is in contradiction with realism. Moreover, the romanticism in their work is clothed with the thick odor of deluded religious faith."[39] This indictment of famous works of song-poetry stresses their incompatibility with the socialist values to be promoted in literature—secularism, realism, and the devaluation of anything not sufficiently populist.[40] The contrast with Döndrup Gyel's endorsement of the Story of Rāmaṇa as a globally inclusive literary phenomenon forged by anonymous hands is stark, if not utterly convincing. Surely the irony of placing Chöwang Drakpa's élite composition within the Ramayana tradition of the common people was apparent. Nevertheless, as several trends converged in the late 1970s and early 1980s—the vogue for translating world literature into Chinese, the continued antireligious sentiment of the Communist Party, and the search for the roots of Tibetan literature—the Tibetan Story of Rāmaṇa emerged as one of the most appealing options for public consumption and endorsement. Whatever his personal views on religion and elitism, Döndrup Gyel found in the Rāmaṇa tradition an acceptable inspiration for the revival of Tibetan literature.

Yet Döndrup Gyel was not satisfied with merely preserving Tibetan renditions of the Story of Rāmaṇa that had, after all, been subjected to the Indian *Mirror of Poetics*. Lauran Hartley has observed that Döndrup Gyel was the earliest proponent of an indigenous Tibetan poetic theory.[41] This was based not on his innovative free verse, which had created a literary sensation, but on a reconsideration of *snyan ngag*. In his published letter to Sanggyé, a colleague who had recently published a controversial master's thesis on *snyan ngag*, Döndrup Gyel responded:

> In the fifth chapter of your work, *Magic Key*, [you give] a critical examination of the strengths and weaknesses of the *Mirror* that hadn't come to mind for Tibet's scholars ever since *Mirror of Poetics* theory spread in Tibet. Even if it did occur to them, it was a new view that they didn't dare to state. Although there is a little bit of selectivity (*blang dor*) done by Sa[kya] Paṇ[ḍita] in *Entryway into Scholarship*, you state, "Although [he] translated here and there and also explained through commentary . . . the difficult poetic figures based on phonetics, etc. can't be applied to Tibetan language, like [applying] a design for silk brocade onto a homespun woolen cloth." SaPaṇ's work of selectivity (*blang dor*) wasn't complete. Although there are a lot of things to understand and think about in your writing, the essence of your thinking is that Tibet needs a treatise on the science of poetic figures that accords with its own characteristics.[42]

His audacity to join in a critique of Sakya Paṇḍita, who was instrumental in developing *snyan ngag* in Tibet, is modulated by his esteem for Sakya Paṇḍita's early efforts. On one hand he affirms that Tibetans still need to develop their own distinctive poetic theory, relying on Sanskrit poetic theory only when appropriate; on the other, he defends Sakya Paṇḍita and the *Mirror of Poetics* by including verse, prose, and mixed prose and verse in his definition of *snyan ngag*—against Sanggyé's limitation of *snyan ngag* to verse only.[43]

Döndrup Gyel's use of the term "selectivity" (*blang dor*)—literally, "accepting and rejecting"—anticipated its currency as a phrase in the late 1990s. The term is now used by those self-identifying as "selectivists" who choose to "keep what is good from tradition as a base and adopt what is useful from 'modern world culture' . . . [but] to reject what is 'bad' or 'useless' of tradition."[44] This is expressed as a moderate stance between those who are considered either too traditional or too modern. Here Döndrup Gyel uses the term in a more restricted literary sense, accepting from Sanskrit poetic theory what is appropriate for Tibetan language, while rejecting anything that is not. By asserting that Sakya Paṇḍita had begun the work of selectivity, but had not gone far enough, Döndrup Gyel suggests that a more rigorous process of selection as a discursive tool is key to realizing a Tibetan theory of poetry. Presumably this theory would be the basis of the Tibetan *Mirror of Poetics*, for which he had so poignantly expressed his yearning in his letter to Sanggyé.

What then would guide this process of selection? A recurring theme is that poetry should be easy to understand (*go bde*). Three of Döndrup Gyel's Story of Rāmaṇa projects incorporate this phrase into their titles: his long narrative poem *Spring Song for Youthful Ears*, the verse translation of Dutt from Chinese, and the Dunhuang reworking which consists of mixed prose and verse. He reinforces the notion in his essay introducing the former two works: "Now, to foster the understanding of our new generation, I who bear the name 'teacher'—disregarding my own poor level and abilities—have based a narrative on the Chinese translation of the *Story of Rāmaṇa* in an easy-to-understand (*go bde*) manner, and another [rendition] on the narrative of Zhangzhung Chöwang Drakpa, *Song of the Gandharva Maiden's Lute*, in easy-to-understand (*go bde*) verse, called *Spring Song for Youthful Ears*, and also written in this way."[45] The principle of writing easily understood poetry departs from Zhangzhung Chöwang Drakpa's deliberately obscure style, which included the use of riddles (*gab tshig*) to puzzle an élite circle of literary connoisseurs. Placed in the urgent circumstances of cultural survival, and likely influenced by the vernacularization of Chinese literature,[46] Döndrup Gyel was committed to making poetry enjoyably accessible rather than dauntingly difficult for an emerging generation of Tibetan intellectuals.

Given that Döndrup Gyel based *Spring Song for Youthful Ears* on Chöwang Drakpa's *Song of the Gandharva Maiden's Lute*, comparison of the two texts presents an opportunity to observe his ideas at work. Döndrup Gyel followed the *Song of the Gandharva Maiden's Lute* so closely that his lines can be made to correspond with those of Chöwang Drakpa. At times Döndrup Gyel has borrowed the content almost verbatim, as in this descriptive verse:

[On the] sorrowless tree (*rkang 'thung*)
the beaming (*'dzum dkar*) flowers laughed (*dgod byed pa*),
shameless [as] the chime
of a courtesan's (*tshogs can ma yi*) anklet.[47]
　　　　　　　—Chöwang Drakpa

Atop the tree (*ljon shing*) called "Sorrowless"
the beaming faces of the flowers laughed.
The radiance of sun and moon could not match
their charms flaunted like the chime
of a prostitute's (*smad 'tshong ma'i*) anklets meeting.[48]
　　　　　　　—Döndrup Gyel

Döndrup Gyel's modification of the verse closely matches Ngakwang Tenpé Gyatso's commentary on the *Song of the Gandharva Maiden's Lute*. Ngakwang

Tenpé Gyatso glosses *rkang 'thung*, translated from the Sanskrit kenning *pādapa* ("foot-drinking"), with *ljon shing* (tree). He further clarifies the reference by marking "Sorrowless" (Tib. *mya ngan med*, Skt. *aśoka*) as the name of the tree. Döndrup Gyel follows suit in these cases, as well as in Ngakwang Tenpé Gyatso's substitution of a more colloquial term for "courtesan" and the inclusion of the word "meeting" (*reg pa*) to reinforce the idea that her anklets clink together. Döndrup Gyel's third line is lifted from Ngakwang Tenpé Gyatso's comment that "the blossoming (*dgod par byed pa*) of the bright smiles ('*dzum dkar*) of the flowers cannot be matched even by the shining of the sun and moon."[49] The comment draws attention to the sensual richness of Chöwang Drakpa's second line, which plays on the figurative meanings of "laughing/blossoming" and "beaming (smile)/beaming (light)" to highlight the visual as well as the aural qualities of the verse. With the incorporation of Ngakwang Tenpé Gyatso's glosses and some well-placed prepositions, Döndrup Gyel facilitates and enriches the reader's understanding of the verse.

Lest we judge this a case of plagiarism according to western professional standards, it is worthwhile to consider these lines in the context of Tibetan literary history. As José Cabezón has pointed out, the classical Tibetan notion of authorship was often collaborative rather than individual, and the common practice of borrowing without attribution could be explained by three considerations: the pedagogical emphasis on verbatim memorization, the commentarial nature of many texts, and the traditional reverence for the work of previous masters.[50] Döndrup Gyel's teacher, Dungkar Lozang Trinlé, had trained in the Buddhist monastic system to which Cabezón refers and conveyed its values in his teaching. He considered the *Song of the Gandharva Maiden's Lute* one of the major works of classical poetry and wrote annotations to Ngakwang Tenpé Gyatso's commentary, which he praised as "exceedingly clear."[51] Döndrup Gyel learned the *Song of the Gandharva Maiden's Lute* well, quoting passages from memory while teaching at the Central Nationalities Institute in Beijing. In view of his literary heritage, *Spring Song for Youthful Ears* may be considered a sort of commentary that explains the *Song of the Gandharva Maiden's Lute* and responds to the commentary of Ngakwang Tenpé Gyatso.[52] Döndrup Gyel's profound admiration for Chöwang Drakpa and Ngakwang Tenpé Gyatso comes to light through his sustained engagement with them, laboriously rewriting the *Song of the Gandharva Maiden's Lute* line for line and teaching these materials to his students.

Armed with intimate knowledge of Tibetan classical literature, Döndrup Gyel takes previous Tibetan poets to task for being "unable to produce many new and novel poetic compositions that are easy to understand (*go bde*), facilitating comprehension . . . the treatises and model-books of kāvya (*snyan ngag*) were bound up with many unknown or poorly known synonyms and archaisms, and adorned with incomprehensible poetic ornaments."[53] Döndrup Gyel does not oppose the use of imagery, figurative language, and poetic figures, as evinced by the verse above. Yet as already noted, he replaces "foot-drinking [tree]" (*rkang 'thung*) with the colloquial "tree" (Tib. *ljon shing*) — that is, a tree obtains water through its roots, or feet. Although a reader would require neither Sanskrit-language training nor an Indian cultural background to guess at the suggested meaning of "foot-drinking," confusion on this point would detract from the alluring mood of the passage. A second example is Döndrup Gyel's replacement of "body-born" (Tib. *lus skyes*, Skt. *aṅgaja*) with the plural "fur" (Tib. *spu'i tshogs*).[54]

As for difficult poetic figures and expressions that would be considered archaic by Tibetans of his day, Döndrup Gyel makes short work of them in the first lines of his narrative:

> The one following the goose Jambudvīpa,
> Is Cāmara (*rnga yab*), the leader of gander[s].
> Desiring the rising red one,
> The one who followed it is Adi's youngster.[55]
>   — Chöwang Drakpa

> Once, in a very early time,
> to the west of the southern subcontinent of Jambudvīpa
> there was an island where demons and demonesses dwelled.
> Its name was Yak's Tail Island (*rnga yab gling*).[56]
>   — Döndrup Gyel

Chöwang Drakpa's verse refers to Jambudvīpa, the world as it was known to Indic civilization, and uses the alternative name Cāmara (yak-tail fly whisk, Tib. *rnga yab*) for the island of Laṅkā. "Adi's youngster" is a reference to the sun, which in Indian mythology is considered the son of Aditi. As Ngakwang Tenpé Gyatso's commentary explains, the gander and goose are metaphors for Cāmara and Jambudvīpa. This is followed by corresponding similes: as a gander might chase after a goose, so the island appears to chase after the continent; likewise, the sun follows the rising red hue visible at daybreak.[57] In short, to understand this verse one would need familiarity with Tibetan translations of Sanskrit mythological references, have sufficient acquaintance with the Story of Rāmaṇa to recognize its setting, and successfully interpret the complex literary devices being employed.

Here Döndrup Gyel has transformed an extremely opaque verse into an equally straightforward one. He retains the name Jambudvīpa (Tib. *'dzam gling* or 'dzam bu gling), which continues to be used in literary Tibetan to refer to the world at large. However, again following the commentary, he explicitly marks the Tibetan rnga yab as the name of an island—and not a fly-whisk made from a yak-tail, as it literally means. He further sets the scene for action by identifying it as the dwelling of demons. Döndrup Gyel abandons the metaphor of the gander and goose altogether, as well as the simile of sun and sunlight that supports it. They have been replaced by a simple (if geographically questionable) description of the location of the island in relation to Jambudvīpa, i.e. the South Asian subcontinent. In short, Döndrup Gyel has recast or jettisoned all the references that would render the verse unintelligible to those unfamiliar with the Indian cosmological universe, and has replaced interlocking poetic figures with straightforward diction and description.

Elsewhere in the text, Döndrup Gyel has similarly removed or streamlined various references to Indian deities. For Śiva, the god who grants the boon of virtual immortality to the demon king Bödrok, Chöwang Drakpa uses numerous epithets translated from Sanskrit, including Deché (Skt. Śaṅkara), Drakpo (Skt. Ugra), Lhachen (Skt. Mahādeva), Dechung (Skt. Śambhu), and Ganggé-chuter (Skt. Gaṅgādhara). Döndrup Gyel replaces these with the common epithet Wangchuk (Skt. Īśvara) and occasionally uses the variant Wangchuk Chenpo (Skt. Maheśvara). Chöwang Drakpa refers to the goddess Sarasvatī by both her well-known Tibetan name, Yangchen, and an epithet, Ngangwé Bumo (Skt. Haṃsinī) referring to her association with swans; Döndrup Gyel excludes this latter reference. All the above epithets enhance the status of the *Song of the Gandharva Maiden's Lute* as a text cognizant of the finer points of Indian mythology: even the title of the work itself alludes to Sarasvatī, who is associated with calling the celestial beings gandharvas and bears a lute. Döndrup Gyel, on the other hand, finds it unnecessary to employ Sanskrit references which are unrecognizable to most contemporary Tibetan readers, and which could be omitted without affecting the plot.

Chöwang Drakpa's text also includes descriptive references from Indian botany and geography, many of which Döndrup Gyel removes altogether. Among those deleted are the fruit of the kiṃśuka tree (Tib. keng shu'i 'bras), the fruit of the tindu tree (Tib. tun ta'i 'bras bu), and a common epithet of the Ganges River, Jāhnavī (Tib. dza hu'i bu mo).[58] That is, two strategies common to nationalizing narratives, territory and its attendant mythology, have been largely excised of their Indian markers in Döndrup Gyel's rewriting of Chöwang Drakpa. As Döndrup Gyel stated that Sakya Paṇḍita had not been selective enough (blang dor), he might also have said that Chöwang Drakpa had not gone far enough in his dor, rejecting, for Döndrup Gyel's project of reconstructing Tibetan literature. It is worth emphasizing that Döndrup Gyel's project was not to xenophobically purge the text completely of its Indian-*ness*. Rather, the terms that he tends to preserve may have been adopted from India but continue to enjoy broad literary usage in Tibetan, such as the example of the world as Jambudvīpa (Tib. *'dzam gling*). The overall effect is a text more familiar to his audience of Tibetan students training in the secular state educational system.

Döndrup Gyel's tendency to vernacularize the *Song of the Gandharva Maiden's Lute* is evident in the following pair of passages, in which Wangchuk's wife is sent to give the power of immortality to the demon king Bödrok (Tib. *'Bod grogs*), the "Bellower":

> Struck by a ray of sunlight—the lord's injunction—
> the lotus garden—Uma—
> offered honey—the supreme boon—
> [to] the extremely prideful "Bellower" (Tib. *sgra dbyangs can*).
> A swaggering many-limbed elephant,
> the six-legged [bee] drunk with honey
> pierced the flower [with] spears.
> Ten-Necks [said], "O gander's daughter [Sarasvatī],
> [I] desire the pure white in
> the lotus garden of Brahmā.
> Who would enter the darkness of deceit?"[59]
>
> > —Chöwang Drakpa

> As for that, the mighty god Wangchuk said,
> "Uma, quickly go
> to Ten-Necks, king of demons,
> grant him the power of immortality,"
> thus he ordered his wife.
> The goddess Uma undertook
> her master's command and said to Ten-Necks,
> "You shall receive the power from me."
> Then the powerful ten-necked demon,
> haughty like a conceited rogue elephant,
> arrogance extending long as a trunk,
> replied to the goddess Uma's pleasant speech,
> "As for me, I wish to attain the power of immortality
> only from the mighty god himself.
> Woman, there's no chance I'll fall
> into the trap of your deceitful words."[60]
>
> > —Döndrup Gyel

Here the dialogue written by Döndrup Gyel—again indebted to the commentary of Ngakwang Tenpé Gyatso—replaces a string of metaphors and is remarkably close to the rhythm of colloquial Tibetan, while simultaneously maintaining the seven-syllable meter common to *snyan ngag* and some of the formal usage of literary Tibetan. Although Döndrup Gyel was unwilling to completely forgo the characteristic features of *snyan ngag*, he was willing to modify them significantly to accommodate a contemporary Tibetan audience.

In his letter to Sanggyé, Döndrup Gyel proposes a new classification of literary style, direct style (*kha gsal ba'i lugs*) and concealed, or indirect, style (*kha dam pa'i lugs*). Although he does not elaborate on what he means here, his friend Nya Lodrö Gyentsen takes up this distinction in his preface to Döndrup Gyel's collected works. After profusely praising the *Song of the Gandharva Maiden's Lute* as "the pinnacle among poetic works like the tip of a victory-banner on the slopes of snowy-mountained [Tibet]," Nya Lodrö Gyentsen judges it "indirect," citing its use of synonymy and ornaments, its roughness of phrasing, and the lack of clarity in subject matter. Döndrup Gyel's *Spring Song for Youthful Ears*, on the other hand, is "suitable for enjoyment by many—as such it is a sure direction for the composition of contemporary literature."[61] The features of *Spring Song for Youthful Ears*—which emphasize clarity over subtlety, ease of understanding over ambiguity and suggestion—indicate that Döndrup Gyel preferred a direct style for his own writing.

Contemporary Tibetan intellectuals who dislike classical *snyan ngag* style are critical not only of its heavy use of Indian references and poetic figures but of its metrical rhythms, which feel artificial compared to colloquial diction.[62] Prescribed meters consist of lines of equal length forming four-line stanzas; seven- and nine-syllable lines are the most common, but longer meters are also used. The metrics observed in song-poetry (*mgur glu*) are more relaxed: stanzas can vary in their number of lines, lines within stanzas can be of equal or unequal length, and the number of syllables in a line can be even or odd. In *Spring Song for Youthful Ears* the stanzas consist of three, four, or five lines, which are of equal length. Döndrup Gyel makes greatest use of seven-syllable and nine-syllable lines, although lines of up to fifteen syllables appear. Lines with an even number of syllables are relatively rare but a few stanzas of six- and eight-syllable lines may be found, e.g. in chapters 3 and 21. Döndrup Gyel's work on the prosody of song-poetry suggests that he considers this flexibility an advantage. He asserts that when translating Indic poetry into Tibetan, "if unequal-syllable forms are used, the aesthetic experience (*nyams*) of the original composition can be maintained."[63] The *Spring Song for Youthful*

Ears has the features of an experimental work and is not executed with perfect consistency. Nevertheless, Döndrup Gyel's incorporation of formal aspects of song-poetry is significant as an alternative model to free verse that is more open in form than classical *snyan ngag* but retains traditionally recognized poetic structures.

In the chapter of his master's thesis addressing the content (*srog*, literally "life") of song-poetry, Döndrup Gyel argues: "If we wish to transform that backward genre, [we] definitely need good recognition of the content (*srog*) of literary arts (*rtsom rig sgyu rtsal*). Works of literature—the life of society— are authentic productions of reflections in the minds of authors. And works of Tibetan literature—the life of Tibetan society—are authentic productions of reflections in the minds of Tibetan authors. *Snyan ngag* and song-poetry are classifications of Tibetan literature that constitute two distinct literary expressions. So if literature (*rtsom rig*) is created anew based on these types of distinct literary expressions, [it] should certainly scrutinize and analyze authentic social life."[64] We may infer that personal experiences and thoughts should inform the content of one's writing. While *Spring Song for Youthful Ears* largely preserves the content of *Song of the Gandharva Maiden's Lute* and Nga-kwang Tenpé Gyatso's commentary, Döndrup Gyel approaches these materials with a critical mind and creates a new work based on his own criteria. More provocative for our discussion is the suggestion that a new literature (*rtsom rig*) might be created by combining the modes of expression used in *snyan ngag* and song-poetry. One may recall that Döndrup Gyel uses the terms for song-poetry (*mgur* and *glu*) in the full title of *Spring Song for Youthful Ears*. Yet the essential place of *snyan ngag* in Döndrup Gyel's literary life is apparent, given that most of his poetry uses prescribed *snyan ngag* meters and poetic figures, and that his participation in literary debates of his time is couched in terms of *snyan ngag*. Moreover, the term *rtsom rig* is not further developed here or used consistently in his thesis: it often appears synonymous for "literary arts" (*rtsom rig sgyu rtsal*), a broad term that can also encompass folktales, drama, film, and so on. In the absence of sustained theorizing on Döndrup Gyel's part, we return to his literary creations.

Reviving Tibetan Poetry for the Times

Brought into dialogue with his more famous works, Döndrup Gyel's *Spring Song for Youthful Ears* and his musings on poetic theory can lend fuller insights into his motivations and agendas. Revisiting "Waterfall of Youth," we can appreciate his explicit commitment to Tibet's literary heritage, particularly the elements of classical *snyan ngag* poetry:

Do you hear me—Waterfall?
Do you hear these questions of the young people of Tibet, the Land of
Snows?
What to do if the great horse of poetry (snyan ngag) is suffering
from thirst?
What to do if the elephant of prosody (sdeb sbyor) is tormented by
heat?
What to do if the lion of synonymy (mngon brjod) is afflicted with
pride?[65]

Despite Döndrup Gyel's use of the free-verse medium, he is unwilling to
abandon the category of snyan ngag merely because it has reached a sorry
state in contemporary times. In his letter to Sanggyé, he gives the definition
of snyan ngag wide berth, including prose writing along with metered verse
and asserting that "whatever the form of snyan ngag, it needs good content
(srog)."[66] Although "Waterfall of Youth" is now celebrated as the first instance
of free verse (tshig rkang rang mos) in Tibet, this would not have precluded Döndrup Gyel from including it in his conception of snyan ngag.[67]

That Tibetan traditions should be simultaneously preserved and modified
is expressed more strongly later in the poem:

And how can yesterday with its salt-water
quench the thirst of today?
If the corpse of history, which is hard to locate,
Is bereft of the life-force (srog) appropriate for the times,
The pulse of development will never beat,
And the heart and blood of the avant-garde will never flow,
Not to mention the march of progress.[68]

The corpse, which might be taken to include literary traditions such as snyan
ngag and song-poetry, is "hard to locate," suggesting the recovery period following the suppression of Tibetan language and traditions during the Cultural Revolution. But like the bodies of the horse, elephant, and lion, this
corpse can be reinvigorated with life-giving substances of blood and water
in this vulnerable historical moment, rather than discarded for something
new.

Döndrup Gyel invokes the role of srog in distinguishing good poetry from
bad in his caustic poem "Impressions after Reading Praise," written in seven-
syllable snyan ngag meter:

It is really pitiable, this business about saying
that a lama is more than a lama, or

that a blind person has one thousand eyes,
that a crippled person can run quickly.

. . . .

As if trying to breathe life (*srog*) into a corpse,
these poems are coherent (*rjod byed*) but have no consciousness.
Words empty of content (*srog med rtsom*) are like literary corpses
One can't decide if they are real (*don dang ldan*) or not.[69]

In Döndrup Gyel's view a poem cannot qualify as good poetry on account of a few (garbled) metaphors. His own creative and critical selectivity in rewriting the Story of Rāmaṇa serves as his example of the meaningful use of literary devices to "breathe life" into an old work. As we have seen in the Spring Song for Youthful Ears, these devices are not to be indulged in for their own sake, but only if they are coherent (*rjod byed*) and meaningful (*don dang ldan*), and hence easy to understand (*go bde*).

Döndrup Gyel's reappraisal of Tibetan tradition can be further understood through another of his famous works, "A Narrow Footpath." Stevenson and Choedak have translated the final line as follows: "A beautiful and dazzling array of a thousand beams of light shone before my eyes and revealed a path to me, and I was compelled to walk toward the direction of the highway"[70] (*nga'i gom pa'ang rang dbang med par gzhung lam gyi phyogs su spo dgos byung*).[71] The English translation "compelled to walk" is ambiguous enough to lend itself to differing interpretations. Translating more forcefully if not elegantly, Stevenson and Choedak describe the narrator as "involuntarily (*rang dbang med par*) coerced to move (*spo dgos byung*)" toward the road symbolizing progress, not from an impulse of his own will but by some outside force. This would differ significantly from the popular understanding that the protagonist deliberately rejects the old path in favor of modernization, progress, and whatever else the new road might symbolize. However, my reading is consistent with an earlier passage, in which Döndrup Gyel articulates the possibility of retaining the old path: "That they were unable to leave behind them anything other than this threadlike path has nothing to do with the stupidity of the people of ancient times. On the contrary, it is we who should be ashamed when we have not been able to widen and level the surface of this footpath for tens of thousands of years. The threadlike path we have inherited from them is no ordinary footpath. Throughout Tibetan history it has carried the fame of the Tibetan race beyond the mountain peaks."[72] Had the original footpath been improved upon, there would have been no need for the new highway. This tone of regret pervades the story, as the protagonist witnesses missed

Döndrup Gyel, before his
untimely death in 1985.
Reprinted from *Dpal Don grub
rgyal gyi gsung 'bum*, vol. 2
(Beijing: Mi rigs dpe skrun
khang, 1997).

opportunities to repair and broaden the old path, which might be interpreted
as Tibet's cultural heritage.

The symbolism of the old footpath lends itself well to Döndrup Gyel's
selective approach to perpetuating Tibet's poetic heritage. As we have seen,
Döndrup Gyel positioned the Story of Rāmaṇa as an ancient and legitimately
Tibetan narrative tradition, dating back to the Dunhuang period. He studied
and taught the *Song of the Gandharva Maiden's Lute* as the primary exemplar
of this tradition, while simultaneously recognizing its limited appeal and
applicability for Tibetans interested in reading and writing literature. The
strategy was then to rewrite it as the *Spring Song for Youthful Ears*, in such a way
as to broaden its popular appeal and smooth out the rough areas—complex
metaphors, obscure synonyms, ambiguous diction, and little-known Indian
references—for a contemporary Tibetan audience. An analogy may also be
drawn between the two roads and the debates about defining *snyan ngag* versus the new term *rtsom rig* ("literature") in the late 1990s.[73] These debates
came after Döndrup Gyel's time, but his own work testifies to his support
for continuing and revising *snyan ngag* to accord it contemporary relevance,
rather than founding the entirely new literary path ascribed to him.

As the richness and variation of the Ramayana tradition resists reduction
to a metonym for India, so Döndrup Gyel in all his literary range resists reduction to an emblematic figure onto whom Tibetan national desires can be

projected. A more balanced understanding of Döndrup Gyel can be reached by considering his lesser-known works along with his famous ones. Döndrup Gyel's sustained encounter with the Tibetan Rāmaṇa tradition marks his claim to an illustrious literary lineage which, through the rewriting of the Story of Rāmaṇa, was to attain the heights of literary excellence and a surge in popularity. His personal contributions to this lineage were to draw out its Tibetan-*ness* and, complementarily, to recruit it in the project of developing contemporary Tibetan literature. Döndrup Gyel may be understood as a bridge between classically trained monastic scholars such as his teacher Dungkar Lozang Trinlé and the new generation of Tibetan writers active after the Cultural Revolution. Although mainstream Tibetan literary discourse has since shifted its focus to defining the term *rtsom rig* in ways that generally privilege western literary theory,[74] Döndrup Gyel's efforts on the Story of Rāmaṇa offer a glimpse into an alternative discourse committed to developing a Tibetan-based form of literary theory.

Notes

Many teachers helped me in the course of this project. I especially thank Geshe Lozang Jamspal and Tenzin Norbu for their patient guidance through the initial phase of translation, and Lauran Hartley for her sustained advice and mentorship.

1. Don grub rgyal, "*Bod kyi tshig rgyan rig pa'i sgo 'byed 'phrul gyi lde mig bklags pa'i myong tshor*" (Impressions after reading *Magic key opening the door to the study of Tibetan poetic figures*), *Sbrang char*, 1984, no. 2, 89, translation by Lauran R. Hartley in "Contextually Speaking," 224–25.
2. Don grub rgyal, *Don grub rgyal gyi lang tsho'i rbab chu dang ljags rtsom bdams sgrig*; Don grub rgyal, *Dpal don grub rgyal gyi gsung 'bum*.
3. Bkra shis dpal ldan, "Don grub rgyal gyi brtsams 'bras dang des Bod rigs kyi rtsom rig gsar par thebs pa'i shugs rkyen skor," 70.
4. Pema Bhum, "The Life of Dhondup Gyal," 28.
5. Tsering Shakya, "The Waterfall and Fragrant Flowers," 37.
6. Riika J. Virtanen, introduction to *A Blighted Flower and Other Stories*, 21.
7. Döndrup Gyel [Rang grol], "A Threadlike Path."
8. Kapstein, "Dhondup Gyal." For an earlier article on Döndrup Gyel which offers a useful overview of his wide range of literary interests see Stoddard, "Don grub rgyal (1953–1985)."
9. R. C. Prasad, quoted in Philip Lutgendorf, *The Life of a Text: Performing the Rāmacaritmānas of Tulsidas* (Berkeley: University of California Press, 1991), 1.
10. I borrow this term from Matthew T. Kapstein, "The Indian Literary Identity in Tibet," 747–802.
11. See for example Richman, ed., *Many Rāmāyaṇas*, and Richman, ed., *Questioning Ramayanas*. For more information on the Rama story cycle in Southeast, Central,

and East Asia see Raghavan, ed., *The Ramayana Tradition in Asia*; Raghavan, *The Ramayana in Greater India*; Bailey, "The Rāma Story in Khotanese," 460–68; Bailey, "Rāma"; and Bailey, "Rāma II."

12. See de Jong, "The Story of Rama in Tibet," and Kapstein, "The Indian Literary Identity in Tibet," 758–62.

13. Sa skya paṇḍita Kun dga' rgyal mtshan and Dmar ston chos rgyal, *Legs par bshad pa rin po che'i gter dang de'i 'grel pa* (Treasury of elegant sayings and its commentary) (Lhasa: Bod ljongs mi dmangs dpe skrun khang, 1982; repr. Gangtok: Sherab Gyaltsen, 1983), 190–96. The verse is numbered 322 in this edition. Davenport has translated Dmar ston's narrative in full, although it is apparently framed by the commentary (1972) of Sakya Khenpo Sanggyé Tenzin. Davenport, trans., *Ordinary Wisdom*, 206–9.

14. Roesler, "The Great Indian Epics in the Version of Dmar ston chos kyi rgyal po," 442–48.

15. Ibid., 448. On Dmar ston's literary work see also Roesler, "Not a Mere Imitation."

16. Portions of the text were first made available in Tibetan through Sakya Paṇḍita's *Mkhas pa 'jugs pa'i sgo* (Entryway into scholarship). For a study of the relevant chapter of this work see Gold, "Intellectual Gatekeeper," 182–218, 261–316. Credit is also due to Shongtön Lotsāwa Dorje Gyentsen and Lakṣmīkara, who translated the text in full under the patronage of Sakya Paṇḍita's nephew, Pakpa Lodrö Gyentsen (1235–80), between 1267 and 1270; van der Kuijp, "Tibetan Belles-Lettres," 395.

17. See for example Ngag dbang blo bzang rgya mtsho, *Dalai Lama V, Gsan-yig of the Fifth Dalai Lama / Gsan yig Gang+ga'i chu rgyun* (Delhi: Nechung and Lhakhar, 1970), vol. 1, 28–29.

18. E. Gene Smith, "Mi pham and the Philosophical Controversies of the Nineteenth Century," *Among Tibetan Texts*, 231.

19. For brief discussions of Zhangzhung Chöwang Drakpa's style see van der Kuijp, "Tibetan Belles-Lettres," 398–99, and Kapstein, "The Indian Literary Identity in Tibet," 782–86.

20. Tashi Tsering, "Tibetan Poetry down the Ages," 48.

21. van der Kuijp, "Tibetan Belles-Lettres," 399, 405 n. 3.

22. Stoddard, *Le Mendiant de l'Amdo*, 174; Dge 'dun chos 'phel and Rak ra Bkras mthong, trans., *Gsar bsgyur Rā ma yā ṇa'i rtogs brjod* (A new translation of the Ramayana) (Beijing: Mi rigs dpe skrun khang, 2005). Although Gendün Chömpel's translation only became available to me as this book was going to press, a brief review confirms that its structure and content follow the seven books (kāṇḍa) of the Vālmīki Rāmāyaṇa more closely than previous Tibetan versions did.

23. This summary is based primarily on Pema Bhum's article "The Life of Dhondup Gyal," along with Stoddard, "Don grub rgyal (1953–1985)," and Virtanen, *A Blighted Flower and Other Stories*, 16–17.

24. Sun Yong, trans., *Lamayanna Mahapalada* (The Ramayana and the Mahabharata) (Beijing: Renmin wenxue chubanshe, 1978). I have not yet been able to consult this book, but the bibliographic information indicates that it is translated from Dutt. Also, Döndrup Gyel's Tibetan translation closely follows Dutt's version.

Dutt, *Ramayana, Epic of Rama, Prince of India*, reproduced in Romesh C. Dutt, *The Ramayana and the Mahabharata* (London: J. M. Dent and Sons, 1953).

25. Don grub rgyal, *Collected Works*, vol. 1, 12–89, vol. 5, 306–48, vol. 4, 179–204, vol. 6, 51–88, and vol. 1, 1–12. I am indebted to Matthew T. Kapstein for calling attention to these in "Dhondup Gyal: The Making of a Modern Hero." Don grub rgyal's incomplete commentary was also published in the literary journal *Zla zer* in 1990. Don grub rgyal, "Rgyal po rā ma ṇa'i rtogs brjod kyi 'grel ba blo gsar ngang mo'i rol mtsho zhes bya ba bzhugs so (Pleasure-lake of swans: a novice commentary on the story of King Rāmaṇa)," *Zla zer*, 1990, no. 1, 68–81, 61.

26. Eber, "Western Literature in Chinese Translation," 52–53.

27. Gálik, "Foreign Literature in the People's Republic of China between 1970–1979," 68–69.

28. Ji Xianlin, *Luomoyanna* (Ramayana) (Beijing: Renmin wenxue chubanshe, 1980–84), repr. in Ji Xianlin, *Ji Xianlin wenji* (Collected works of Ji Xianlin) (Nanchang: Jiangxi jiaoyu chubanshe, 1995–98), vols. 17–24.

29. Stoddard, "Tibetan Publications and National Identity," 143, and Hartley, "Contextually Speaking," 171–72.

30. Dmu dge bsam gtan rgya mtsho, Preface to Ngag dbang bstan pa'i rgya mtsho, *Rā ma ṇa'i rtogs brjod / Zhang zhung ba Chos dbang grags pas brtsoms / Ngag dbang bstan pa'i rgya mtshos 'grel bshad byas* (The story of Rāmaṇa by Zhangzhung Chöwang Drakpa with commentary by Ngakwang Tenpé Gyatso), 2nd printing (Chengdu: Si khron mi rigs dpe skrun khang, 1983), 4.

31. Blo gros rgya mtsho, "Rgyal po rā ma ṇa'i rtogs brjod bsil ldan kha ba can gyi ljongs su ji ltar dar ba'i tshul rags tsam brjod pa gangs ri kun tu dga' ba'i gtam zhes bya ba bzhugs so" (An account to please the snowy mountains, roughly relating how the story of King Rāmaṇa spread in the cool Himalayas), *Bod ljongs zhib 'jug*, 1982, np. 3, 106–7. A nearly identical copy of this article appeared under the same author and title in *Bod kyi rtsom rig sgyu rtsal*, 1982, no. 2, 37–52.

32. Ibid., 119.

33. Don grub rgyal, *Collected Works*, vol. 1, 8–9.

34. Ibid., 1–4. One might be inclined to dismiss this as obligatory lip service to socialist ideals, except that he repeats both points several times; furthermore, many Ramayana scholars agree with this argument and consider the Vālmīki Rāmāyaṇa the result of an oral tradition, with narrative layers added over the course of several centuries.

35. Richman, *Questioning Ramayanas*, 3–5.

36. Don grub rgyal, *Collected Works*, vol. 1, 11–12.

37. Richman, *Questioning Ramayanas*, 5–6.

38. Pema Bhum, interview with author, New York, 21 February 2003.

39. Don grub rgyal, *Collected Works*, vol. 3, 519. The thesis was first published as Don grub rgyal, *Mgur glu'i lo rgyus dang khyad chos* (History and features of song-poetry) (Beijing: Mi rigs dpe skrun khang, 1985).

40. In the same passage he states that a few of the better works may be salvaged, including the song-poetry of Dunhuang, the song-poetry of the Sixth Dalai Lama

Tsangyang Gyatso (1683–1706), and folksongs. Milarepa was another of his great interests, and although denounced here he is frequently discussed in Döndrup Gyel's thesis. See also Don grub rgyal, *Collected Works*, vol. 3, 27–53, vol. 5, 215–305.

41. Hartley, "Contextually Speaking," 224.

42. Don grub rgyal, "Impressions after reading *Magic Key*," 88. Translated with Lauran Hartley and Pema Bhum.

43. Ibid., 83–89, 118. Jonathan Gold argues that Sakya Paṇḍita "Buddhicized" *rasa* theory, a major element of Sanskrit poetics, to appeal to his Tibetan readership. However, Sakya Paṇḍita does not characterize this process as an indigenous one, and more investigation is needed to determine the reception of his work. Gold, "Intellectual Gatekeeper," 190.

44. Hartley, "Inventing 'Modernity' in Amdo," 10. The phrase *'dor len* is a common synonym, using the verbs in present tense and reversing the order. Ibid., 8.

45. Don grub rgyal, *Collected Works*, vol. 1, 12.

46. See Stevenson, "Paths and Progress," 57–60.

47. Ngag dbang bstan pa'i rgya mtsho, *Rā ma ṇa'i rtogs brjod*, 39–40. Cited passages from the *Song of the Gandharva Maiden's Lute* have been translated with Geshe Lozang Jamspal; any remaining errors are my own.

48. Don grub rgyal, *Collected Works*, vol. 1, 18. Cited passages from Döndrup Gyel's *Spring Song for Youthful Ears* have been translated with Tenzin Norbu; any remaining errors are my own.

49. Quoted in Ngag dbang bstan pa'i rgya mtsho, *Rā ma ṇa'i rtogs brjod*, 40.

50. Cabezón, "Authorship and Literary Production in Classical Buddhist Tibet," 251–52.

51. Dung dkar blo bzang 'phrin las, *Snyan ngag la 'jug tshul tshig rgyan rig pa'i sgo 'byed*, 567.

52. Gnya' Blo gros rgyal mtshan uses the term *'grel pa* (commentary) to describe *Spring Song for Youthful Ears*. Gnya' Blo gros rgyal mtshan, Preface to Don grub rgyal, *Collected Works*, vol. 1, 7. Another example of a literary reworking that has been classified as a commentary (*'grel*) is the *Dpag bsam 'khri shing* (Wishing vine) of Padma Chos 'phel, which gives prose accounts of the stories in Kṣemendra's original. Mkha' 'gro tshe ring, ed., *Rtogs brjod dpag bsam 'khri shing gi rtsa 'grel* (Wishing vine of bodhisattva stories: Root text and commentary) (Xining: Mtsho sngon mi rigs dpe skrun khang, 1997).

53. Kapstein, "The Indian Literary Identity in Tibet," 792–93.

54. Zhang zhung ba Chos dbang grags pa quoted in Ngag dbang bstan pa'i rgya mtsho, *Rā ma ṇa'i rtogs brjod*, 36; Don grub rgyal, *Collected Works*, vol. 1, 17.

55. van der Kuijp, "Tibetan Belles-Lettres," 398. For the Tibetan see Ngag dbang bstan pa'i rgya mtsho, *Story of Rāmaṇa*, 17.

56. Don grub rgyal, *Collected Works*, vol. 1, 13.

57. van der Kuijp, "Tibetan Belles-Lettres," 398–99.

58. Zhang zhung ba Chos dbang grags pa quoted in Ngag dbang bstan pa'i rgya mtsho, *Rā ma ṇa'i rtogs brjod*, 19, 31, 24.

59. Zhang zhung ba Chos dbang grags pa quoted in Ngag dbang bstan pa'i rgya mtsho, *Rā ma ṇa'i rtogs brjod*, 27–28.

60. Don grub rgyal, *Collected Works*, vol. 1, 15.

61. This and the preceding quotation are from Gnya' Blo gros rgyal mtshan, Preface to Don grub rgyal, *Collected Works*, vol. 1, 6–7.

62. Pema Bhum, "The Heart-beat of a New Generation: A Discussion of the New Poetry," 2–16.

63. Don grub rgyal, *Collected Works*, vol. 3, 512.

64. Ibid., 515.

65. Don grub rgyal, "Lang tsho'i rbab chu"; Hartley, "Contextually Speaking," 188.

66. Don grub rgyal, "Impressions after Reading *Magic Key*," 87.

67. For remarks on the formal aspects of "Waterfall of Youth" see Robin, "Tibetan Free Verse Poetry," 453.

68. Don grub rgyal, "Waterfall of Youth," 56–61; Hartley, "Contextually Speaking," 189.

69. Don grub rgyal, "Bstod pa bklags pa'i 'char snang."

70. Döndrup Gyel, "A Threadlike Path," 65.

71. Don grub rgyal, *Collected Works*, vol. 6, 7.

72. Döndrup Gyel, "A Threadlike Path," 63.

73. See Hartley, "Contextually Speaking," chapter 7.

74. Ibid.

"Heartbeat of a New Generation":

A Discussion of the New Poetry

PEMA BHUM

TRANSLATED BY RONALD SCHWARTZ

This essay was first delivered in 1991 at a conference on Tibetan language and literature, organized by Chögyel Namkhai Norbu in Archidosso, Italy. Because of its influence and the controversy that it engendered in Tibetan exile society, the article was later published in book form; see Pad ma 'bum, Mi rabs gsar pa'i snying khams kyi 'phar lding (Dharamsala: Amnye Machen Institute, 1999). The English translation was also published by the same institute; see Lungta 12 (summer 1999), 2–16. We have reprinted it here, slightly revised, with the consent of the translator. Certain details have of course changed (e.g. the total number of Tibetan journals), and the past decade has seen further literary developments among Tibetans living in the PRC and abroad. For this reason we have asked Pema Bhum, now director of the Latse Contemporary Tibetan Cultural Library in New York City, to revisit his article in chapter 6.

1

In relation to what comes earlier, we generally say that what comes later is new. It is like that with the Tibetan "new" and "old" poetry. Compared to the songs (*mgur*) of the Dunhuang manuscripts, the poetic compositions (*snyan rtsom*) of the "discoverers of hidden treasures" (*gter ston pa*) were new; and compared to these, the "mystic songs" (*gsung mgur*) of the yogis were new; and when compared to the mystic songs, the poems in the style of the Kāvyādarśa (*Snyan ngag me long*) were also new. In this essay, I am not speaking of this sense of "old" and "new," a topic familiar to all scholars. Rather, I will focus on the New Poetry, which many scholars (both old and young) dwelling in exile have neither familiarity nor desire to examine. The few who do show a slight interest have difficulty recognizing the flavor of traditional Tibetan poetry, which is embedded in this style of composition.

Less than ten years have passed since this new style of writing began to spread. According to the documents we have, the first poem was composed by the brilliant writer Döndrup Gyel (1953–85) and appeared in the second issue of *Sbrang char* (Light rain) in 1983. Even now we still lack a common name for referring to this style. Some call it the "new poetry" (*snyan rtsom gsar pa*), some "free verse" (*rang mos snyan ngag*), and some "contemporary poetry" (*deng rabs snyan ngag*). Yet the vigor with which this writing has spread is remarkable. The phenomenon was observed by the poet Ju Kelzang in 1991: "The educated write contemporary poetry. The uneducated also write contemporary poetry. University students write contemporary poetry. Elementary school students also write contemporary poetry."[1] What he says here is very true. There are nearly thirty newly established journals within the three traditional provinces of Tibet. In 1984 and 1985 alone more than forty pieces of New Poetry appeared in *Light Rain*. Likewise, if we were to include all the pieces published thus far in other literary journals, official and unofficial, we can estimate that the total number would be huge. Now, those who favor the new writing style can only roar with victory and those who dislike it let out a long sigh of disappointment.

The writers of the new style have been patient, but regrettably, scholars both inside and outside Tibet have not given them the attention they deserve. It is difficult to say whether there are even ten scholarly articles on New Poetry inside Tibet.[2] The Library of Tibetan Works and Archives in Dharamsala has received no more than three scholarly articles about the New Poetry from Tibet, and the majority of scholars in the exile community have adopted the principle of completely ignoring the phenomenon.

In his introduction to the Tibetan translation of the *Gītañjali* by Rabindranath Tagore (1861–1941), Samdong Rinpoché shows his irritation with the lack of development in Tibetan poetry: "Because of the gradual spread over ten centuries of the principles of 'ornamental words,' many new literary forms were unable to find a place in the Tibetan language. We are still hiding behind the veil of Daṇḍin's theory, and for the last thousand years have continued in the steps of *kāvya* ornamentation (*tshig don rgyan*).[3] Rinpoché expressed these sentiments on 18 June 1983. That year, in the second issue of *Light Rain*, the first piece of New Poetry appeared in Tibet: "Lang tsho'i rbab chu" (Waterfall of youth). However, Rinpoché did not notice this event. Nine years have passed since then, and some hundreds of poems have appeared, yet regrettably he remains silent on this subject.

2

Poetry (*snyan ngag*) is a literary genre, and everything in literature depends on the labor of the mind. When we ask where this "mind" comes from, our sophists, with their dry intellectual formulae, proudly give explanations. However, they are mistaken. The dry terminology teaches nothing except a general system of mental phenomena applicable to the minds of all human beings in all epochs. The mind in literary composition requires a psychology through which it is impossible to substitute one particular place, time, or person for another. Feelings of joy and sadness from ancient times cannot take the place of contemporary feelings. A variety of modern sensations fills the modern mind, and in these lie its inner meaning and character.

We must therefore conclude that the psychology revealed in the New Poetry is determined by the modern condition. The question naturally arises: What are the characteristics of this psychology revealed by the New Poetry, or put another way, what psychological causes and conditions give rise to New Poetry? This question broadens and deepens the problem we need to resolve. There is no way to adequately address this question in a short space, but after even a bit of research, we are able here to assert a few preliminary ideas.

All Tibetans, both inside and outside Tibet, share a common sorrow— their homeland is occupied by another. In addition to this, Tibetans inside bear the sorrow that comes from being forced to hide the anger they feel toward the plunderers of their homeland and the murderers of their fathers; they can never show their real face and must bow respectfully to those in power. There is also a special suffering for writers and poets. Suppressing the fire of hatred in their hearts and pretending to smile, they must use their pen, which is like their soul, to sing songs of praise to the bloody hand that murdered their fathers. Tibetans in exile, though they are unable to take revenge, have the desperate satisfaction of expressing their anger by cursing and exposing the crimes of their enemies. However, poets inside Tibet are denied this satisfaction. I think that this suffering that fills the mind is being experienced by Tibetan scholars for the first time in Tibetan history. Material prosperity can only partially erase it, but to overcome the suffering, a basis for belief and hope is required.

Scholars inside Tibet are presented with two formerly prevalent doctrines. The first is Marxism-Leninism. However good or bad it is in reality, it was brought to Tibet by armed military force. When a doctrine comes associated with military might, people inevitably fear it. Actually, in order to spread this doctrine, an ocean of blood has been spilled and a mountain of corpses raised. In order to ensure its consolidation in Tibet, the communist Chinese have applied the theory of "without destruction nothing can be established." Our contemporary writers remember in minute detail all the damage done to classical Tibetan culture, the torture of scholars, and so on. In short, this doctrine is associated in the minds of all Tibetans with destruction, torture, poverty, and famine. A doctrine which provokes fear cannot possibly help to remove the suffering of the mind.

The other doctrine is Buddhism. This has been associated with the history of Tibet for over a thousand years. It is difficult to estimate fully how much human life and material prosperity the Tibetan people have expended on its development. Though this doctrine has brought some unrest and warfare to us, it has also provided not a little happiness and hope. Regrettably, the crucial question of the life or death of the Tibetan people will also determine the life or death of Buddhism. Let alone save the Tibetan people, Buddhism cannot even save itself. On the other hand, everyone clearly understands that the Tibetan people have sacrificed much in order to sustain religion. Now made desperate by their condition, when they query Buddhism, the answer they receive is "Your experiences are the fruit of your actions." Poets inside Tibet know what kind of difficulties their ancestors went through in order to bring Buddhism to Tibet, and how they honored and served religion from generation to generation. Wearing sheepskins, their ancestors made offerings of fine silk; drinking plain tea, they made offerings of butter and milk. Dwelling in yak-hair tents, they constructed countless temples. Now Buddhism is unable to offer another answer. They are disappointed and think for the first time: "Well, what use is Buddhism? In this world there is no hope for refuge except in oneself."

The minds of the poets are cold and empty. Though they have experienced defeat, they have also achieved victory. As for the defeat: being without a foundation and refuge in one's mind is like being a young calf abandoned on an empty field. As for the victory: being without any limitations on thought is like being a bird set free from a cage. Speaking of the disappointment poets feel now toward both Marxism and Buddhism:

Sophists, your profound systems have opened the
Door of my mind.
Thank you. Prophesiers of the future,
With your grandiose predictions,
And your fierce arrogant minds,
You have provided me with stimulation.
Thank you. Powerful gods of my destiny,
What a good joke you've played on me. Thank you.[4]

For this generation of poets the separation from the above-mentioned "sophists," "prophesiers," and so on will not be brief. They will certainly never return. They will foretell their own future; their own destiny will be their guide.

3

Whenever a reader encounters a piece of literature (*rtsom rig*) or religious commentary (*bstan bcos*), a title comes associated with it. What are these titles that the reader encounters? Ancient Tibetans paid attention to them, and when Atīśa (982–1054) came to Tibet he too inquired about the way the titles of religious commentaries were chosen. The Tibetans gave several answers. Both the questions and the answers at that time were directed toward the theory of religious commentary. Therefore they cannot be compared with the attributes of imagery and feeling as in poetic composition. There is also no special custom of giving a title to the rare type of small poem that does not satisfy the definition of a "chapter" (*sa rga chen po*) according to the theory of the *Kāvyādarśa*. Nor is there a custom of giving a title to the "songs" (*mgur*) of the yogis that were not influenced by the *Kāvyādarśa*. For example, in the Collected songs of Jé Milarepa (1040–1123) and of Drukpa Künlek (1455–1529), though we expect a general title for the collection, it is rare that a title is given to a particular song.

Tibetan literary titles were transformed due to the influence of the *Kāvyādarśa*. In such titles I would suggest there are two components: a "base" (*khyad gzhi*) and "attributes" (*khyad chos*). For example, in the case of the fifth Dalai Lama's *Annals: Song of the Queen of Spring* (*Deb ther dpyid kyi rgyal mo'i glu dbyangs*), "Annals" (*deb ther*) is the base, "Song of the Queen of Spring" (*dpyid kyi rgyal mo'i glud dbyangs*) the attributes. In all titles of this kind, the attributes are regarded as more important than the base. For example, although the *Golden Rosary of Elegant Sayings* (*legs bshad gser 'phreng*) is only the attribute-component of a title, this religious commentary is known by this title. The base-component shows the type of contents of the literary work; the attributes-component indicates, for the most part, how the contents of the work, and its mode of expression, will benefit the reader. This kind of title brings to mind advertisements on the benefits of commodities in modern newspapers and journals. Without taking the reader into consideration, the authors of these literary works have already decided the benefit their works will have. This is the reverse of the procedure in contemporary culture. With contemporary literature the reader is the one who appraises the comparative value. Readers appraise the value through the feelings produced while reading and by the specific features they show in comparison to other literary works. However, these appraisals are never transmitted in the titles of the work. Before the reader encounters the work, he has appraised the value of the author's literary work. Moreover, the appraisal of the value of a literary work from the title is characteristic of the influence of the *Kāvyādarśa* in Tibet up until now.

In general, the giving of titles is changing in all contemporary fields of literature. In New Poetry a complete transformation has taken place. New titles have appeared along with the new way of composing poetry. Writers do not consider their poems to be like the *Song of the Queen of Spring*; nor do they think about following the experts on "ear ornamentation" (*rna rgyan*), etc. The title does not come from these sources, but from three others: (1) the feelings, sensations, and thoughts expressed in their literary works, and how these appear to their minds; (2) how they are able to attach or impart these feelings, sensations, and thoughts to specific external objects; and (3) how these feelings, sensations, and thoughts can be clearly and powerfully expressed by some phrase in the composition or its title. Whichever of these three applies, the feelings, sensations, and thoughts expressed within the work are the basis for the choice of a title. At this point we may define the principal difference between titles in the New Poetry and in traditional literary works. Traditional writers give titles by anticipating the feelings that will come to the reader. In the New Poetry, writers choose them in accordance with their own mental processes. In the former, titles are given while thinking about how to get the attention of the reader; in the latter, titles are given while thinking about the way thoughts appear in the writer's own mind. The titles of traditional literature need long expressions, while in the New Poetry a few short words or just a single one is allowed. Here is the principal distinction. Formerly, the attributes of the title became more important than the base, and it was possible to have several attributes for one base. Further, one attribute could not be expressed without using a lot of words—i.e., by one word alone or a few words. Now the base of the title has come to be regarded as more important than the attributes—so much so that the status of title is not even given to the attributes. Because there is nothing but this base, the title has no use for a lot of words.

4

After many hundreds of years, we have become accustomed to metrical composition with an equal number of feet and equal meter. Now in the face of new writings styles, suddenly the habits of many hundreds of years are completely contradicted. We see the length of line and meter expand freely without discipline; we feel we do not know how to read these poems and we do not know how to appreciate their flavor. In fact, such metrical styles are not unknown in Tibetan literature. In the Dunhuang "treasure songs" (*gter mgur*) and in the early songs (*mgur*) of the yogis we also see unequal numbers of lines, unequal numbers of syllables, and unequal meter. However, there are important differences between the metrical composition of earlier times and their contemporary forms. Most ancient poems did not consist just of words, but had melodies (*dbyangs rta*) associated with them. Now, when we say "*glu*," "*mgur*," and "*gzhas*," in fact these are distant cousins of ancient metrical compositions. In these there is not a great deal of freedom in the choice of words that fit the associated melody. The words must accord with the rhythm, the pauses, the modulation of breath, etc., of the "*glu*" or "*mgur*." Therefore it is possible to derive the meter and length of verses from the meter and length of the melody. Not only that, but it is likely that *glu* and *mgur* were also performed as dance (*bro*), so at that time metrics had no choice but to harmonize melody, dance, and words. There is no counterpart in contemporary poetry, which derives primarily from modulations of the mind. We all have similar experiences. In the rhythmic changes and modulation of the mind there are variations in duration and force. We are not able to manipulate these in the same manner as we manipulate a composition. If we want to adjust the flow of the mind to accord with the rhythm of composition, then we must greatly limit and modify it. The traditional writer ignores much of the reality of his mind when he composes a poem; in order for us to read and appreciate this literature we must likewise artificially restrict our mental experience.

Writers of contemporary poetry believe that mental sensations are more important than the combinations of words in the creation of poetry. Composition is a tool for clarifying or expressing the living mind; therefore, composition must follow the mind. Since the modulation and force of feelings are independent, it is not possible for them to be determined by the requirements of meter, as in our traditional poetry. Thus, if we make poetry whose composition respects from the outset the rhythms of the sensations in the mind, then we will have inexhaustible flavors. Conversely, if we let the feelings of the mind strictly guide us through the individual composition, it will be impossible for that poem to express artificial conceits and inflated heroics.

Contemporary poets believe that the words of a poem will follow the succession of feelings as they fully unfold and develop. Through their rhythmic power they are able to express these feelings entirely with just a few words. By the force of the earlier sentences the meaning of the later ones comes naturally. Thus, if the earlier lines are long, then the later lines may be shorter, and if the earlier lines are short, the later may be longer, etc. In Döndrup Gyel's "Waterfall of Youth," the writer illustrates this by drawing the attention of the reader to a waterfall on a steep rock face:

Look.
A pure white billowing stream of bubbles
Drops of light, patterns on a peacock feather
A parrot's wings
A painting on silk
A rainbow.[5]

Here do we think that because the second and third lines of this short poem are longer and the last three lines shorter, it lacks the flavor of poetry? If we were traditional poets, it is possible that we would adorn the last three lines with unnecessary word ornamentation to make them compatible with the two earlier lines. Is this necessary? If a short line is able to express completely what is said in a longer line, then it has fulfilled its responsibility. From the point of view of words, the sign of unadulterated poetry is when there is not one word too many, not one word too few. From what has been said here, if we add to just the right number of words this ability will be lost.

In his biography of Gendün Chömpel (1903–51), Rakra Rinpoché quotes Gendün Chömpel's opinion that although one might understand a foreign written language, if one does not understand the spoken language, one is unable to appreciate the flavor of that poetry.[6] This implies that even if one does not use the spoken language in poetry, it should not be held in contempt. The prime reason why many readers find the poetry composed by Gendün Chömpel pleasing is that it is somehow in harmony with the spoken language. When in the course of our lives we speak of the warmth of the sun in the day and the clear light of the moon at night, we are giving expression to the living form of both the sun and the moon as we have perceived them. But in school we learn to use "jewel of the sky" (nam kha'i nor bu) for the sun and "lord of the stars" (rgyu skar bdag po) for the moon, and practice substituting one name for the other. In the first case, a human subject encounters an object and acquires experience through sensations in the mind and body; then the sensations come to be associated with the name. In the second case, there is no way we can experience sensations of the mind and body by just learning a name in isolation. Therefore, in poetic compositions that value images and feelings, the use of words and names that can draw the experiences of the body and mind into the imagination is very important. However, under the influence of the *Kāvyādarśa* it was difficult to incorporate Tibet's own spoken language. Now the New Poetry has changed that. Although wording (*tshig 'gros*) and expressions (*mngon brjod*) of the *Kāvyādarśa* continue to be used, the spoken language is much more in evidence.

The natural speech of a people is not learned in books. Natural speech is directly learned from nature and from human society. The ways that a people perceives nature and society have been absorbed into its speech and writing; through these we recognize the many mental experiences of pleasure, suffering, hatred, depression, etc. that occur in nature and human society. Thus external images and the inner living mind permeate natural speech. This is the foundation of the literary composition of a people. To the extent that it is close to a people's natural speech and conveys the life and experience of the people, it will be easily understood; likewise, to the extent that literary composition is removed from a people's actual speech and is weak in the life and experience of the people, then it will be difficult to understand. Although eight hundred years have passed since the *Kāvyādarśa* was translated into Tibetan, our poetic expression has been unable to move beyond the circle of a few experts and monasteries. Although not even ten years have passed since the spread of the New Poetry, now both scholars and non-scholars, as well as university and even school-age students, enjoy writing the New Poetry. The reason for this lies in what has been explained above.

5

Section 2 above describes how the thinking of young contemporary poets inside Tibet has freed itself from political and religious ideology. The characteristics of this new way of thinking are revealed through the stages of composition or exposition—and especially in the choice of subject matter for poetry.

Before Tibet was transformed by the Chinese communists, most traditional poets just followed Buddhism. When they looked at the world and at their own lives, they were not able to look through their natural human eye. Not only did they see the outer world as if through saffron-colored glass [i.e. the color of monasticism], but they also viewed their own minds in the same way. Because the eye was always saffron-colored, every subject of composition was saffron. Tibetan poets looked at nature, human society, and their own mind through a psychology laden with Buddhist theory and doctrine, and this provided the foundation for their choice of subject matter. Their poetry contained little apart from praise for the Three Jewels [Buddha,

Dharma, and Sangha] and explanations for the accumulation of merit and Buddhist philosophy. Because their psychology was bound by Buddhism, their poetic composition was also bound by its theories. Poetry itself was not able to achieve an independent status.

The pioneering efforts of contemporary poets have been to liberate themselves from religious poetry. They see the whole domain of poetry as their mission, and have their own ways of viewing the world, society, and human life. When the world of poetry is looked at through the eye of religion, all one can see are dry definitions buried in the analytical mind, not the multitude of living images from experiences of direct perception. Thus the Tibetan poet Ju Kelzang writes:

> For advice, there is no one above one's parents.
> To show reality, there is no one better than a lama.
> To share a secret, only a friend will do.
> But look somewhere else for a poet.[7]

In this way the New Poetry movement is a revolution striving for freedom in the domain of consciousness.

As soon as they are liberated from the constraints of religious and political ideology, poets experience feelings that exceed the bounds of the old world, which they must abandon for a new one. This is expressed in their poetry:

> Oh, friend!
> Friend who delights in poetry,
> Do you know where poetry is?
> Do not search for poetry in books.
> It is in life's immensity.
> Do not imagine that learned explanations in books
> Are really poetry.[8]

We must understand four dimensions of the "life" spoken of here: (1) the dimension of the mind of a particular person, (2) the dimension of the relationship between people, (3) the dimension of the relationship between a person and society, and (4) the dimension of the relationship between a person and nature. The power of the poetic eye must reach out to each of these dimensions; the soul or "life-force" (*srog dbang*) and physical vitality of poetry must be sought in them. By so doing, contemporary poets have enlarged the psychological range of both the mind and the external world. When these poets investigate human psychology, the mind is devoid of the thinnest layer of religious or political doctrine. They have penetrated the innermost layer of the human mind. Thus in their poetry the variety of joys and sorrows of the unembellished mind, symbolized by love between man and woman, are presented to the reader in tangible form. Here the mind of the traditional poet never ventures: "Exposing one's insides / To the wide world. / How sad!"[9] This lament clearly illustrates the differences between the psychology of the old and new poets. Such openness has no place among traditional poets. Through their efforts in shaping consciousness within the areas of religion, history, and poetry over the last thousand years, they and their ancestors succeeded in covering the real nature of the mind of the Tibetan people in saffron. Now, these efforts have been interrupted for just a short time and the new literature arrives, tearing away the covering. When the inner mental layers are mined and displayed for others, the laments [of the traditional poets] arise spontaneously.

Contemporary poetry is not merely a political platform for praising the Communist Party and its policies, the party's birthday, the nation's birthday, etc. Nor is it a religious tool for expressing repulsion at samsara (cyclic existence) or the wish to be reborn in the heavenly realms. For the New Poets, who are liberated from politics and religion, the range of expression of the mind has been enlarged and, similarly, the range of the world of external objects has been very much enlarged. Traditional poets are necessarily limited, both because their consciousness is shaped by religion, and thus they have the same views of nature, society, and life, and because their method of composition finds its common origin in the *Kāvyādarśa*. Except for the embellishment, there is not much difference in the views or procedure of traditional poets in composing a poem on any particular subject.

It is not like this with the New Poets. Whey they express something in poetry, their outlook is not based on religion or politics; it is possible for one subject to symbolize various meanings and to express each meaning in different ways, depending on the feelings of the poets. For example, Döndrup Gyel's "Waterfall of Youth" and Rinchen Trashi's "Rbab chu" (Waterfall) are two compositions with the common subject of a waterfall.[10] However, the actual meanings of these two poems, and what is symbolized by the waterfall, are different. In the former, the nature of the waterfall expresses Tibetan youth; the latter poem shows how the poet, while appreciating the evanescence of a cascade of water falling into a gorge, realizes that if he wants to find the way forward in life, he must come to terms with the fear of death.

Because one subject is able to provide different meanings drawn from life, other poets viewing the same subject at different times and places are able to derive still other forms. This is also one reason why contemporary poets take on a broad range of subjects. For example, if a "snow mountain" were the subject of a poem, traditional poets would do little but gaze upward from its base. Contemporary poets, however, are able to capture a rich image of this snow mountain, by considering it at different times and from different places. For example, in the poem "Sa sgang sngas su byas pa'i skar ma 'od chen" (Starlight shining on the pillow of the earth) Dondrup Wangbum imagines flying; when he looks down from the sky, the mountain takes on a new form:

> Oh, oh! This flower of a mountain,
> So big, so beautiful.
> Sweet fragrance rising.
> Soft white petals, loose and free.
> Your stem, pure clear water flowing.
> Verdant fields of grass, your leaves.
> Deep firm earth protects your roots.
> The sky-blue ocean moistens your heart.[11]

Another reason for the wider range of subjects in the New Poetry is that the aim is not to eulogize but to represent experience. In the poems of traditional poets, the objects of praise and how they are praised are all the same, except for a little variety in embellishment. It is irrelevant if the poet's sensibilities have truly been shaped by experience; instead, poets compose poetic words of praise on the basis of what is found in books or known by convention. Though you will never meet the beneficent and familiar Tibetan yak in the poems of traditional poets, they will compose many words of praise for the unfamiliar Indian elephant. By contrast, contemporary poets are guided not by what is conventionally known but by their own experience and imagination. Therefore, we meet not only yaks but yak dung in their poetry. Since they rely on a multitude of directly lived experiences, instead of what is conventionally taught, the range of their poetry necessarily widens.

6

It is not possible to discuss poetry separately from the poem itself. As we have not yet examined a full poetic composition, we shall do so now, line by line; our analysis will consider the poem's structure as a sample of New Poetry, and other characteristics rarely found in traditional poetry.

The title of the poem we shall examine is "Dar srin dang dar zab" (The silkworm and the silk).[12] The poet composed this poem after observing a dancer preparing for a performance. Initially, the poet focuses on the silk costume rather than the dancer. This is how the costume appears to him:

> Drops of melting sun,
> The moon a ball of ice,
> A slice of rainbow cuts across
> A gown woven of dusk clouds.[13]

The poet speaks of the great beauty of the sun, which furnishes humanity with a variety of images, illusions, memories, and hopes. This beauty is revealed through four of its aspects (sun, moon, rainbow, and dusk) in the brilliant luster of the costume. The silk costume is then rendered even more beautiful by combining the beauty of the words "melted" (zhu ba), "frozen" ('khyags pa), "sliced across" (phred du gtubs pa), and "woven" (thags su bkrun pa). Next the poet tells us who is wearing that costume: "Oh, slowly dress your body / Beautiful girl who sweetens my heart."[14] Now the beautiful costume and the beautiful girl "who sweetens my heart" align harmoniously. When these two great beauties are joined, beauty is added to beauty, and the effect is ravishing. Now the poet writes:

> Stirring desire even in a recluse, young sapling body
> Making even the peacock jealous, garment of rainbow cloud
> Melody of youth, spangled colors,
> Oh, yes! A rain of nectar in the eye,
> In the heart, a cloud-vessel of honey.[15]

The dancer's body weakens even the resolve of a recluse. The costume outshines even the beauty of a peacock. Collecting these two beauties together is so powerful that human society is infused with the "melody of youth" and the "spangled colors." The whole world is moistened by the "rain of nectar" through joining these two beauties. All hearts are wrapped in the "cloud-vessel of honey." In thought and action no one can resist being drawn into each subtle movement of such a beautiful form. Thus, the poet too "Finds pleasure in your joyous dance. / I will make music along with you. / Even then—."[16]

Remembering past suffering when one is happy and past happiness when times are bad, however, is a perpetual condition of the human mind. At this point the poet writes: "Circling ripples in a pool of memories. / Once more, faded images of things past. / Undulating, clearly moving."[17] What moves?

> A silkworm eats a leaf from the generous tree,
> Wriggling body, panting breath,

The instant its life-movement stops, the last instant . . .
A cocoon of new silk thread
Is vomited in a stream from its mouth.[18]

The dancer and the spectators are lost in beauty, drunk with beauty. The suffering of human life has vanished completely from their minds. However, in the poet's vision, as the beautiful form of the dancer fades the image of the silkworm vomiting silk thread appears, with its "wriggling body" and "panting breath." This is the truth, of course. Clothes beautify a person and a saddle embellishes a horse; accordingly, the silken cloth enhances the dancer's beauty. But the silk cloth is made from the thread that is vomited as the silkworm ends its life. All the ornaments that have become things of beauty for human beings are the result of the suffering of other beings. The suffering of one is the origin of the happiness of another; the happiness of one is the origin of the suffering of another. Here the poet, beholding the reality of so-called human happiness, becomes weary and sighs. He cries at the sight of the silkworm at the end of its life, with its wriggling body and panting breath, vomiting a silk thread.

Witnessing this scene, the dancer and spectators ask the poet, "What is wrong?" and the poet suddenly wakes from his recollection of things past. So as not to spoil their pleasure, he wipes away the tears and with a feigned smile answers:

Oh, it's nothing.
If I am too sad, I laugh.
If I am overjoyed, tears flow.
Enjoy your lovely dance with all your heart,
I will sing a melody along with you.[19]

Listen to the poem. Such truth in these lies; falsehoods are necessary at such moments. When we actually perceive the reality of human happiness it vanishes. To be happy we must depend on lies and hypocrisy. The imagination of the poet enables us to perceive the vital image of the happiness that is behind suffering and the suffering that is behind happiness. It is the nature of poets to experience uncommon joys and sufferings; thus, in the past some poets were also considered crazy. A real poet does not just share with us beautiful figures of speech; he provides new ways to perceive human experience.

We are able to identify three stages in the development of the poem that we have analyzed above. In the first stage the poet starts with the costume of silk; then he moves on to how the costume adds beauty to the dancer. From there the poet moves on to the enjoyment of beauty that the dancer provides to the world. From one beauty to another the poet has moved toward human happiness and the radiance of human life. In the second stage, which begins after his remark "Even so—," the leaping imagination of the poet moves from happiness to unhappiness and from brilliance to the realms of darkness. Seeking the origin of the silk, the poet sees in his imagination a miserable silkworm, with its wriggling body and panting breath, vomiting a silk thread as it expends its life. Now tears instead of ink flow from the poet's pen. From the two vital images of the miserable silkworm and the beauty of the silk, he sees the reality of human happiness. The meaning of the poem deepens, and here we are able to see a new strength. Relying on neither politics nor religion, the poet seeks the truths of human life through the leaps and turns of poetic imagination. These truths which he seeks are not hidden within dry definitions, but are revealed to humanity through vital images from direct experience and through the cries of happiness and the lamentations of sorrow which suffuse them.

In the third stage of the development of the composition, the poet expresses a new meaning. So far the poet has unambiguously and movingly conveyed two images: the dancer wearing the beautiful silk and the miserable worm. The experience of much human happiness, when we must smile even as we cry and laugh while we choke, exemplifies the contradictions of human life. While everyone enjoys the beauty of the dancer, the poet is seized by the image of the life expended vomiting silk thread. His eyes are filled with tears, his throat choked up with sorrow. The poet finds himself in both of these two opposing mental worlds.

The inner meanings of these three stages deepen and sadden from the earliest lines to the end. As sadness increases, one feels closer to what is true in life. These three stages depend on each other. As the poet moves from the earlier lines to the later ones, the meaning expands and the images become clearer; at the same time, the earlier lines take on more power. For example, once the image of the miserable silkworm appears, the earlier lines on the beauty of the silk costume are imbued with the life of the silkworm.

Now that we have read the later lines and experienced their flavor, reading the poem again enables us to appreciate more fully the beauty of the words with which he praises the dancer's silk costume. On the first reading, we did not appreciate how many lives had been spent. On the second reading, however, we see how many silkworms have died, with panting breath and wriggling bodies, vomiting silk thread to produce that silk costume. We thus feel the presence of the countless lives that have expired in making this costume.

The subject of the poem is enlarged in this way. The deep meaning of this poem is achieved through two leaps (mchong stabs) of the poet's imagination from the initial starting of the silk itself. After establishing a firm foundation for the poem, the poet's imagination leaves the silk and moves temporarily to the silkworm vomiting the silk thread. Looking at this for an instant, he jumps again to the dancer. Because this long leap of the imagination occurs so suddenly, many readers are unable to follow and feel that this type of poem is difficult to read.

As illustrated in this composition, not only is the content of the poem determined by its initial starting point and the two leaps, but so too are the movement (rtsom 'gros) and structure (rtsom sgrom). The structure of New Poetry is determined by leaps of the imagination like those seen here, not by figures of speech (rjod byed tshig). Figures of speech are only tools to amplify the images and forms apprehended by the imagination. Likewise, the structure of the poem is produced by the stages of the poet's experience and the way his imagination unfolds. For instance, in the poet Jangbu's "Zhog glu" (Morning song),[20] the structure of the composition is produced in accordance with the development of the poet's feelings of happiness and suffering. It is the same with his poem "Smon 'dun" (Wish).[21]

Having arrived at this point, we are now able to see the principal structural difference between traditional and contemporary poetry. When traditional poets think about structure, they think about figures of speech and a structure [prescribed by] theory. This is clearly illustrated in the Tibetan tradition of abecedarian poems (ka rtsom), in which each line begins with a successive letter of the alphabet, and by other difficult poetic forms embellished through prescribed conventions for the incorporation of vowels and consonants (bya dka' ba'i sgra rgyan).[22] For this type of poem, a poet primarily considers how to arrange the letters and sound ornaments; he thinks less about the progression of the specific meanings that he wishes to express. The poet determines the organization of the letters and the sound ornaments before he decides the specific meanings that he wishes to convey. If he does settle on the meaning first, then he must zigzag back and forth [between content and form] to express himself. Likewise, when the poet praises a lama or the Buddha, he follows the order of "body," "speech," "mind," "blessing," etc. in accordance with specific religious doctrine. There is no other progression available to the poet. If we want to explain this type of poetry, we are forced to set aside the poetry itself and discuss religious doctrine.

We may identify yet another difference. For the most part, when traditional poets express overt feelings of happiness and suffering, they do not express the progressive intensification and transformation of these feelings; therefore we likewise do not see a firm relationship between these feelings.

For example, with many traditional poems no damage is done if we delete a few stanzas, or add a few stanzas. Even if we were to invert the order of the stanzas, we would not sense that the order is wrong. By contrast, the New Poetry overtly expresses feeling; but more importantly, it expresses subtle feelings, the transformation and intensification of feelings. Because the mental experiences, feelings, and images continuously mix with one another, adding or subtracting a word, or changing the word order, must accord with the intensification and transformation of feelings.

7

Enjoying something through direct experience is not the same as enjoying it through poetry. When we enjoy an object that we perceive directly, the object itself cannot affect our mind except to make us think: "That!" However, when we enjoy something through poetry, the object comes alive. Teeth bared and brow furled in anger, throat choking and tears flowing from sorrow, eyes popping out and mouths dropping with surprise—not only are such feelings experienced as if in our own bodies, but our minds cannot resist undergoing these experiences of anger, sorrow, and surprise. Here what is expressed by letters on a page and formed from matter receives the power of life. Like a magician who uses material phenomena to create an illusion, a poet instills words with the power of life, and the effect arouses a variety of feelings within the reader. Tibetan scholars were amazed by this. Unable to find an explanation, they were ultimately forced to conclude that "for the poet, everything is beautiful" (snyan ngag mkhan la ci yang rgyan).

This proposition has been the conventional wisdom of Tibetan scholars for nearly a thousand years, but we have yet to unravel its secret. For the most part, our scholars take this proposition for granted and offer no explanation. But the saying poses three difficulties. First, we need to understand what it is that we call "poetry." What basic conditions must be filled to call a work poetry? Second, we should understand what kind of person is this "poet." Do we call a "poet" anyone who practices the principles of the Kāvyādarśa and makes such statements as "the earthworm below the castle wall is a dragon" (mkhar rting gi sa 'bu nag ring la 'brug) or "the butterfly on top of the wall is a garuda" (mkhar kha'i phye ma leb la khyung)? What internal and external conditions must be fulfilled to be considered a "poet"? Third, we must interrogate the traditional assumption that "for the poet, everything is beautiful"—how is it that something is beautiful? Does beauty inherently reside in the object even before the poet looks at it? If so, why can only the poet see this beauty and not we? Or is it that the external object is void, and the poet himself imbues it with beauty? If so, why do we experience similar feelings when presented with these objects?

Only by clarifying the first and second issues [the meaning of "poetry" and "poet"] can we begin to solve the third [the nature of aesthetic experience]. We cannot resolve all these difficult points in one short essay. But to illustrate the difference between how the principle "everything is beautiful" operates in traditional poetry and how it operates in the New Poetry, we must deal briefly with the question of aesthetics.

First, we must understand that the word *rgyan* [lit. "ornament"] in "everything is beautiful" (*ci yang rgyan*) means "pleasing to the mind" (*yid du 'ong ba*). "Beautiful" here is not the same as "beautiful" in the case of a human subject encountering an object with the five sensory pleasures. The "beauty" of objects that can be seen, touched, felt, heard, or tasted comes through the five sense organs. Phenomenal beauty, such as pleasing flavors, sounds, beautiful sights, softness, etc., reside in the object itself and are characteristics that all beings can experience in common. As for the principal characteristics of beauty in poetic composition, aside from letters strung together in lines, there are sweet tastes, beautiful sights, or sounds to experience directly. However, a variety of pleasures are produced in the mind as if experienced through the direct perception of the reader.

This is not the main cause, however, of the "beautiful" in poetry. It is more important that the human mind be immersed in the subject of the poem. For example, the sixth Dalai Lama Tsangyang Gyatso (1683–1706) wrote:

The season of flowers is over
Bee, don't be sad
My lover's life is spent
I should not be sad[23]

If we just look at a flower and a bee, it is difficult to say whether they are beautiful. However, there is no one who fails to recognize the beauty of joining these in this song. Through the flower and the bee we are able to appreciate the torment of the lover mourning the death of his beloved. Here is where their beauty lies.

Beauty in poetry does not simply copy the objects of the five sensory pleasures. It moves from the real base (*brten gzhi ngo ma*) of the human mind and its constituents to reside on a new base, the subject matter of the poem. The specific material reality of a poem's subject does not have its own innate power of life; expressing himself, the poet brings this power to the subject, creating new images with new life. The ability to see new images that combine previously unexperienced thoughts and feelings is the reason for the beauty of poetry.

This kind of beauty cannot be destroyed by place, time, or condition. The beauty of an object of direct perception is established in dependence on place, time, and condition; the beauty of poetry is established by breaking free from these constraints. The life force of the flower is defeated by the seasons; however, when human life enters into that flower through the poem, the seasons can no longer affect it. The human mind is swayed by the desire for food, clothes, and fame; however, when it moves through the poem into the flower, it is no longer affected by these. Beauty in poetry occurs to the extent that both the base [brten gzhi, the subject of the poem] and the phenomena attributed to the base [brten chos, the human feelings conveyed through the base] are completely merged with each other. The "beauty" of poetry is not experienced through logical terminology; it is experienced through directly perceived images. Because all the secrets of the human mind appear within the images and in each letter of each line that comprises the poem, the images and words that are produced by the poet's pen are like a pure crystal globe in which we are able to see the inside from the outside and the outside from the inside.

When sensations remain in the human mind, some are muddy and unclear, some are mixed with others and unable to stand alone, some are unstable and come and go easily, some are never revealed because they are just mental experiences that most people cannot express, and some are basically good but corrupted by attachment. These faults are overcome when sensations in the mind are conveyed through the poem such that clear, well-defined, pure feelings are displayed. However, because peoples, generations, poets, and places differ, the feelings conveyed and the images and expressions suffused with these feelings will also differ.

Even for two poets born at the same time, in the same place, and of the same nationality, both the feelings that they choose to convey and the subject matter through which they express these feelings may differ. In the compositions of a single poet as well, the feelings and subject matter may differ. Broadly speaking, however, poetry and poets in a given place and time share certain fundamental characteristics. If so, then what features are typical of New Poetry? What feelings are conveyed in this poetry, and what subjects are used as a base to express them? We discussed the new conception of the base in section 5, when examining the subject (brjod gzhi) or topic (rtsom gzhi) of a poem. As for the variety of feelings conveyed in the New Poetry, we do not see this in traditional poetry; this may be because of an inability to perceive such feelings or simply because the views of traditional and modern poets are wholly antithetical. Nevertheless, we may speak about three characteristics which point to a new direction in Tibetan poetry.

It is not possible to decide what is New Poetry simply on the basis of whether it is "free verse" (tshig rkang rang mos). First, we must consider whether the new psychology has combined with the new soul or "life force" of poetry. A new "life force" does not automatically result in a new writing style. However, its presence is sometimes signaled in a poem when the old outer covering is ripped away by the strength of this new force.

When we read contemporary Tibetan poetry, the first thing we sense is the heartbeat of the Tibetan people. In the images and expressions we are able to see the living courage of those who return to the battlefield to risk their lives, with bandaged wounds in body and mind. In Döndrup Gyel's poem "Waterfall of Youth," the image of the waterfall is suffused with the courage of the Tibetan people. The "body" is the waterfall and the "life force" is the heart of Tibet. This life force is conveyed through the image of the waterfall. The poet gazes in amazement, exclaiming: "Oh, oh! / The youth of the waterfall. / The waterfall of youth."[24] As he says this, the poet takes the inner love of his heart and mentally transfers it onto the waterfall. The waterfall is no longer governed by laws of nature; its power comes from the courage of the Tibetan people. Their courage rises above the desire for food, clothes, and fame; it takes on the character of the waterfall, flowing continuously, leaping with pride and together forming a new stream.

Inspired by "Waterfall of Youth," young poets born inside Tibet have composed a large number of poems suffused with the new courage of their people. Because of this, some readers are now unable to feel the beauty of a poem unless they can hear the courageous heartbeat of the Tibetan people in the images and expressions of the poet. This national courage has opened the door for new forms of composition and contributed to the widespread popularity of the New Poetry.

The love between man and woman is another feeling expressed by contemporary poets. Because most traditional poets were imprisoned by religious views, love between man and woman was regarded as an affliction; therefore most traditional poetry does not praise love between man and woman. Though not considered a worthy subject for a poem, this kind of love was sometimes used to symbolize or illustrate the world's faults, or as a metaphor for the relationship between lama and disciple or for one's faith in religion. Traditional poets hold narrow and ultimately repressive views about the real love between man and woman. Because contemporary poets are not bound by any views, they treasure human nature as it really is. They see that love between man and woman is a major component of life. The supreme example of the ability of the human mind to abandon everything and lose itself is the complete submersion of a man and a woman in pure, passionate love. When pure love enters the mind, there is no room for desiring food, clothes, or fame. The impressions of the person also transform the external world in accordance with his desire; he is able to hear the wings of a bee sadly proclaiming the end of the flower's season, and his lover's words in the sound of falling water.

Because love between man and woman is the supreme love in the minds of contemporary poets, love itself, or any part of it, is no cause for shame and there is no need to repress it. Seeing contemporary youths loving openly, old people who are bound by traditional views "Shake their heads from side to side. / The world has turned upside down."[25] Contemporary youth answers:

Oh,
No need to be surprised.
No need to feel shame.
What is happening
Is a joyous step
In harmony with the march of history.
Angry eyes and damning curses,
Do not obstruct and interfere.
What is happening
Is a blow struck by the fist of freedom
On the head of conservatism and cowardice.[26]

For contemporary poets engaged in this confrontation between new and old views, the love between man and woman is not just an illustration used to praise something else; in many poems the object of praise is love itself. The poets elevate and convey pure and passionate love through the images and expressions of their poems.

The use of different means to convey the noblest human virtues — loving others over oneself, the courage to accept hardship, humility without pride, diligence without weariness, etc. — also distinguishes contemporary and traditional poets. In traditional poetry, when the Three Jewels, for instance, are made the subject of praise, the attributes of conventional objects (e.g. wish-granting tree, lion, sky) are singled out and used as metaphors. How is this different from contemporary poetry? Traditional poets apply the attributes of an object to the subject of the poem; the subject is thus made to take on a new form. Contemporary poets select various elements of human experience and use these to imbue an external object with new "life force." Traditional poets reconstruct formerly existing images of the subject itself with attributes from the object. Contemporary poets combine features that belong to the object with feelings that arise in the mind, thereby creating a new image that belongs to neither subject nor object alone. The difference between these two approaches is clearly demonstrated by comparing a poem such as "Ljon pa'i phugs bsam" (Ideals of a tree) by the contemporary poet Tigta (also known as Ju Kelzang) with invocations (mchod brjod) in religious commentaries (bstan bcos) composed by traditional poets.[27]

By comparing the works of traditional and contemporary poets we are able to identify another difference—that is, in the very objects used to convey feelings. When traditional poets use an object to exemplify the noblest human virtues, they consider only its conventional attributes; they do not consider whether it has practical value in their own lives. Although Tibetan poetry contains many references to the lotus flower, "wish-granting tree," "cow that provides all the milk one desires," lion, elephant, and so on, none of these have any value for Tibetan society. Human virtues were conveyed through these images simply by following what appeared in books. By contrast, contemporary poets select objects that have practical value in their lives and natural environment; they can thus express human virtues through these objects without relying on literary convention. This approach is well demonstrated in the poem "Nga rang sbar chog" (May I burn), written by Jangbu (aka Dorjé Tsering).[28] Here the poet takes as the subject of his poem cattle dung, which has the attribute of giving light and warmth inside the tents of Tibetan nomads as it consumes itself and turns to ash. In a straightforward manner, Jangbu thus illustrates the human sentiment of loving others rather than oneself.

Notes

1. 'Ju Skal bzang, "Deng rabs snyan ngag ngo sprod rags bsdus," 15.
2. The reader should recall that this piece was written in 1991, and "New Poetry" has been the subject of dozens of articles in the preceding decade. —Ed.
3. Zam gdong Rinpoche, "Introduction," Glu thal sbyar ma (Gītañjali), by Rabindranath Tagore, trans. Dngos grub (Delhi: Tibet House, 1984), 8.
4. Ljang bu (Rdo rje tshe ring), "Dmar po khrag gi glu" (Song of red blood), Sbrang char, 1987, no. 3, 72.
5. Rang grol (Döndrup Gyel), "Lang tsho'i rbab chu," 56.
6. Bkras mthong Thub bstan chos dar, Dge 'dun chos 'phel gyi lo rgyus, 19.
7. 'Ju Skal bzang, "Deng rabs snyan ngag ngo sprod rags bsdus," 15.
8. Nor sde, "Snyan ngag de gang na 'dug shes sam" (Do you know where poetry is?), Sbrang char, 1986, no. 4, 72.

9. 'Jigs med theg mchog, "Cong sgra'i 'grel ba rang ngo gsal pa'i me long" (A mirror clearly showing one's face: Commentary on "The Sound of the Gong"), *Sbrang char*, 1987, no. 1, 94.

10. Rin chen bkra shis, "Rbab chu" (Waterfall), *Sbrang char*, 1987, no. 1, 94.

11. Don grub dbang 'bum, "Sa sgang sngas su byas pa'i skar ma 'od chen" (Starlight shining on the pillow of the earth), *Bod kyi rtsom rig sgyu rtsal*, 1986, no. 2, 12.

12. Tig ta ('Ju Skal bzang), "Dar srin dang dar zab" (The silkworm and the silk), *Sbrang char*, 1987, no. 3, 78–79.

13. Tib. *nyin byed dkyil 'khor zhu ba'i this pa/ zla shel 'od dkar 'khyags pa'i gong bu/ 'ja' tshon phred du gtubs pa'i khugs pa/ mtshams sprin thags su bskrun pa'i sham bu/.*

14. Tib. *sku la dal bur gsol rogs gnang dang kye/ snying la ro mngar ster ba'i nu rgyas ma/.*

15. Tib. *drang srong chags pa slong byed gzugs kyi 'khri shing/ mdongs mtha' zhe sdang skyed byed gos kyi 'ja' sprin/ lang tsho yi rol dbyangs/ tshon ris kyi 'gyur khugs/ a ho/ mig la bdud rtsi'i gru char/ snying la sbrang rtsi'i sprin phung/.*

16. Tib. *kho mo dga' ba'i zhabs bror rol song/ ngas kyang yi rang dbyangs snyan los 'then / de lta na'ang—.*

17. Tib. *dran snang lteng ka 'khyil ba'i rlabs phran gyi ngogs su / 'das don gyi gzugs brnyan mog po de slar yang / lham lham du g.yos byung / wal wal du g.yos byung /.*

18. Tib. *lhag bsam shing lo zos pa'i dar srin zhig / lus nyugs nyugs / dbugs lhem lhem / tshe srog rgyu ba 'gags pa'i skad cig / skad cig tha ma . . . / da dung dar skud gsar ba'i chun 'phyang zhig / zhal nas nar mar skyug bzhin 'dug /.*

19. Tib. *'o / ci yang ma red / skyo ches na gad mo 'tshor / dga' drags na mig chu 'thor / khyed rang snying nas dga' ba'i gar la rol dang / kho bos yi rang dbyangs kyis ram bu 'degs 'ong /.*

20. Ljang bu, "Zhog glu" (Morning song), *Sbrang char*, 1983, no. 2, 56.

21. Ljang bu (Rdo rje tshe ring), "Smon 'dun" (Wish), *Sbrang char*, 1986, no. 4, 66–67.

22. These include palindromes, lines with vowels left out that can be read in more than one way, and other kinds of word-puzzles.—Trans.

23. Tib. *me tog nam zla yal bar/ g.yu sbrang sems pa ma skyo/ byams pa'i las 'phro zad par/ nga ni skyo rgyu mi 'dug.*

24. Rang grol, "Lang tsho'i rbab chu," 56–61.

25. Ljang bu, "Chu rtsed kyi glu" (Song of water-play), *Sbrang char*, 1985, no. 1, 36.

26. Ibid., 38.

27. Tig ta ('Ju Skal bzang), "Ljon pa'i phugs bsam" (Ideals of a tree), *Sbrang char*, 1987, no. 3, 79.

28. Ljang bu, "Nga rang sbar chog" (Let me burn), *Sbrang char*, 1985, no. 1, 41–42.

6

"Heartbeat of a New Generation" Revisited

PEMA BHUM

TRANSLATED BY LAURAN HARTLEY

In "Heartbeat of a New Generation," I noted that there was not yet any uniform term for the poetic writing style of that time. I recalled three names for this phenomenon: the "new poetry" (*snyan rtsom gsar pa*), "free verse" (*rang mos snyan ngag*), and "modern poetry" (*deng rabs snyan ngag*). During the fifteen-odd years that have since passed, the number of terms has only increased, now also including "liberated verse" (*grol ba'i snyan ngag*), "unfettered verse" (*ma bcings pa'i snyan ngag*), and "unmetered verse" (*rkang bas ma bcad pa'i snyan ngag*); no standard could be realized. Except for the term "modern poetry," all these names emphasize the greater freedom allowed in terms of the length of lines. Though sound reasons lie behind the coining of all, when many Tibetans speak they naturally opt for *rang mos snyan sngag*. How this term came about and why it feels natural merits investigation.

The term *rang mos snyan ngag* is a direct calque of the Chinese *zi you shi* (free verse); that is, *rang mos* was used to translate *zi you* (freedom) and *snyan ngag* was used to translate *shi* (poetry, poem). But, the term *rang mos* is not a native Tibetan word. It does not appear in Geshé Chödrak's *Brda dag ming tshig gsal ba* (Orthographical dictionary), compiled in 1949 and published in 1957; nor in the *Dag yig gsar bsgrigs* (New orthography), compiled during the Cultural Revolution, more than ten years after the term was first propagated (as discussed below). It was only in 1985, with the publication of the *Bod Rgya tshig mdzod chen mo* (Great Tibetan-Chinese dictionary), which defined *rang mos* as "at one's own will," that the word was first inscribed in the accepted Tibetan lexicon.

Generally speaking, when one glosses the Chinese term *zi you* (freedom), the first Tibetan word that comes to mind is *rang dbang*. However, in the first volume of the *Tha snyad gsar sgrigs* (Dictionary of new terms, 1954)—the first Chinese-Tibetan dictionary with terms expressing Chinese communist ideology—the term *rang mos* appears together with *rang dbang* as the translation for *zi you*. Further, the second volume of the Tibetan edition of *Selected Works by Chairman Mao* (1960) includes a speech entitled "Rang mos ring lugs la ngo rgol byed dgos"; this is a translation of the original Chinese title "Fandui ziyou zhuyi" (Oppose liberalism).[1] Perhaps *rang mos* was used to translate *zi you* to distinguish the "liberalism" opposed by Mao Zedong from the sense of "freedom" in Tibetans' minds when they heard, for example, Sakya Paṇḍita's "If one is free (*rang dbang*) all is happiness. If one is controlled by another (*gzhan dbang*) all is suffering."[2]

Mao Zedong's "Oppose Liberalism" had to be studied many times over by everyone—whether literate or not—during the various political campaigns launched throughout China and Tibetan areas. I encountered it in the 1970s and remember one incident especially related to this speech, which illustrates how widely known it was among Tibetans.

The year was 1974 or 1975. I was teaching at Malho (Ch. Henan) Mongolian Autonomous County Nationality Middle School in Qinghai Province. The Cultural Revolution had begun, and for a time there was a policy of inviting representatives of the People's Liberation Army, workers, or nomads to supervise the school's affairs, especially in terms of ideology. In that year two nomads were invited to our school. One was more than seventy years old. Though completely illiterate, he had a strong understanding of Mao Zedong's speeches. During one of the many political movements at that time, all the teachers and students at our school were required to study "Oppose Liberalism." I was assigned the task of reading the article aloud to students, and then the "representative nomad" would offer commentary. Though I had earlier read excerpts in the "little red book," *Quotations of Chairman Mao*, I was not familiar with the entire speech.

After I finished reading the article to the assembled students, the elderly nomad proceeded to explain the text. He broke the general meaning down into four topics: the source of liberalism among the revolutionary ranks, the manifestations of liberalism among the revolutionary ranks, the negative effects of liberalism among the revolutionary ranks, and ways to clear the negative effects of liberalism among the revolutionary ranks. I was amazed that this unschooled person could relay such a clear, systematic, and thorough commentary. Though there were many political study sessions and readings of Mao's works during the Cultural Revolution, this particular article was never studied so intently that an illiterate person could offer such an explana-

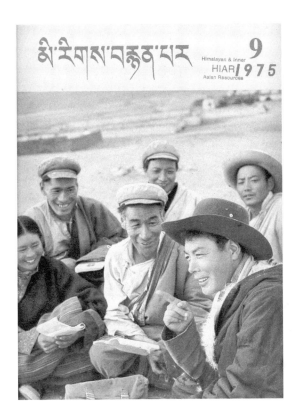

མི་རིགས་བརྒྱན་པར 9
HIAR / 1975

The cover of this issue of *Nationalities Pictorial* (Beijing, 1975), depicts a political study session with Tibetan nomads, such as those carried out during the Cultural Revolution (1966–76). Photo courtesy of Latse Contemporary Tibetan Cultural Library.

tion. I think now that there must have been an active campaign to study this particular speech *before* the Cultural Revolution; for I did not read the article before 1974 but had heard the title many times. I would guess that this older, illiterate man was able to offer such a commentary because the speech had been read again and again for uneducated audiences and explained at each reading. If so, then educated Tibetans would have been all the more familiar with the term *rang mos*, because it would have been their responsibility to read the speech to the uneducated people in their areas.

I would suggest that the frequent references to *rang mos* during the campaign to oppose "liberalism" account for why the term *rang mos snyan ngag* has gained greater currency than any other term for free verse among Tibetans in the PRC. In September 1992 I attended the Second International Conference on Tibetan Language in Archidosso, Italy. After I presented my article "Heartbeat of a New Generation," the great Tibetan scholar Dungkar Lozang Trinlé—who survived the Cultural Revolution and was invited again to teach at nationality institutes in the 1980s (see chapter 1)—expressed his opinion that it was appropriate to refer to the new poetry as *rang mos snyan ngag*. By contrast, the term *rang mos* is rarely used in oral speech or writing by Tibetan intellectuals who grew up in the diaspora, especially India, and who of course never experienced the Cultural Revolution.

Poems by Tibetan Monastics and Women

The pool of poets writing free verse has diversified since I wrote "Heartbeat of a New Generation." The most dramatic change has been an increase in women writers and an unprecedented number of monks publishing verse, in both classical forms and free verse. We would be hard-pressed to find a writer who was not a monk or at least a lay religious practitioner. Only a few writers, such as Dokhar Tsering Wanggyel (1697–1763) and Dorjé Gyelpo (b. 1913), could be considered truly lay writers. As contemporary literary styles took firmer hold in the late 1970s and 1980s, the number of lay writers increased considerably, but monastic writers had dwindled almost to the point of non-existence. Certain senior monastic scholars, such as Tseten Zhapdrung (1910–85), Mugé Samten (1923/4–93), and Jikmé Tekchok, wrote poems during this period, but their works were all in metered verse—and monastic circles never evinced the great surge of would-be writers that occurred among lay students at secular middle schools and colleges. This disparity characterized the Tibetan literary world in the PRC—and even in exile—for many years.

Another recent and significant transformation in modern Tibetan poetry has been the entry of younger monks among the ranks of new poets. Lay classical writers used to follow religious models in lamenting the meaninglessness of samsara. Now monks inspired by the free expression of contemporary poets write of the trials of monastic life. Lhachap Jinpa, for example, writing from Labrang Monastery in 1999 (he is now living in exile), voiced such concerns in his poem "Dpyid dus kyi snga dro zhig la ngas 'di ltar lab" (I say this on one spring morning). After expressing his preference for writing about women in his poetry, he notes: "Though elders often scold me / saying 'You wear the robes of a monk on the outside, / but inside your mind is a wolf'/ I don't want to change my true personality."[3] Chen Rangsé, a well-known monk-poet (his pen name literally means "Self-Awakened from Chentsa"), expressed similar sentiments when a collection of his poetry was refused publication by Qinghai Nationalities Publishing House because the poems about women were "excessively graphic" (Tib. *dmar rjen yin rgyu thal drags*). In a public letter of objection he argued that such topics were "human nature" and expressed "what is most beautiful about poetry." He vowed to persevere and "absolutely offer this type of poetry" to his readers.[4]

These monks and now hundreds of others are searching for new meaning through the medium of free verse—engaging content rarely expressed

The monk-writer Gyadröl (left) and Sinophone writer Dorjé (right) review a Tibetan women's literary newspaper, *Gangs can skyes ma'i tshags par*, while on break at a Tibetan writer's conference in Qinghai in 2005. Photo by Françoise Robin.

in classical poetry. Whereas religious poetry in the past often comprised verses of praise for teachers or lamas, such poems account for only a small fraction of poems written by contemporary monks. Now monks often focus on social issues, such as the environment, the need for education, etc.—the same concerns addressed by secular students. While several monastic writers have published prose essays, most have turned to poetry. This trend has been spurred by the growth of literary magazines issued by local monasteries, especially in Amdo. Many monks also use this new medium to express pride in the virtues of monastic life, but in unconventional ways. One monastic poet, for example, expressed his love for the stone plaza on which the monks debate: "Standing on this stone, you will break the system of hells and open the door to paradise." Monks also echo their lay counterparts in idealizing the role of the poet in society as a conveyor of raw emotional insight or as a "lone wolf"—a social critic writing from a place of religious and worldly detachment. Older monks have tended to be less receptive to these developments. I have been told of discreet negotiations between senior and younger monks in exile which resulted in compromises at one magazine in order to continue publishing.

When monks first started publishing in literary magazines in the mid- to late 1990s, frequently under pen names, they primarily wrote in metered verse. Though a larger number now write in free verse, many still opt to embody contemporary content in traditional forms. In any case, monks now form a major component of Tibetan literary writers and the development deserves greater research by literary scholars.

Female poets were also sorely underrepresented in Tibetan literary circles when I was writing "Heartbeat of a New Generation." There were only a few, and they wrote almost exclusively in metered verse; women experimenting with free verse were extremely rare. I could not identify a single example in the publications available to me in Dharamsala. One sign of positive change in this area was signaled in 2006 when Pelmo, a female professor at Northwest Nationalities University (formerly Institute) in Lanzhou, published the anthology Bzho lung.[5] The title refers to the practical but also ornamental metal double hook worn by nomad women on their belts to carry milk buckets. The anthology (mentioned in the Introduction) includes poems by twenty-three Tibetan women ranging in age from twenty to sixty, and is unique for being the first collaborative project with exile writers. The editor consulted writers in the diaspora and included poems by four women outside the PRC. Funding was provided by a nonprofit organization founded by Lobsang Rabgey, a female Tibetan scholar in the United States. Half of the poems are in free verse.

Tibetan female poets are still relatively few in comparison to the vast number of male poets, but in just fifteen years the number has greatly increased. We also find a much higher proportion of women working at all levels of the publishing industry. To cite just two examples: the main editor at Gansu Nationalities Publishing House is Tamdrin Tso, and Pelhamo, whose poems are published in Bzho lung, is a senior editor for Tibetan Art and Literature. There are also many Tibetan women translators. Some journals have sought ways to encourage more contributions by women. Sbrang char (Light rain), for instance, started a special section featuring works by Tibetan women writers in 1996. According to the editors, many more poems of high quality were submitted after the column first appeared, and the practice has been repeated every two years or so.[6] As summarized by Pelmo, editor of Bzho lung, poems by Tibetan women frequently discuss four topics: 1. the nationality's past, present, and future; 2. women's fate [in terms of social status and domestic responsibilities]; 3. the environment; and 4. the emotional world of women, especially loss and suffering in love affairs.[7] I have also noticed several poems reflecting on maternal feelings and experiences.

The poets we refer to here are only those more widely published in the leading Tibetan literary journals. However, if we were to consider local or privately funded journals, we would find many more women writers who are not as well known or frequently published. Recent developments suggest that a corps of Tibetan women writers has formed, and it is likely their numbers will only increase.

The poet and editor Pelhamo at the editorial offices for *Tibetan Art and Literature* in Lhasa. Photo by Lauran Hartley.

Pen Names

The practice of using pen names developed as soon as the new Tibetan writing emerged. I could have explored this practice in *Heartbeat of a New Generation*, and its continued proliferation prompts me to examine it more closely here. The use of pen names was adopted by Chinese writers and for the most part copied by writers in Tibet. But the Chinese term *biming* did not appear in any Chinese-Tibetan dictionary until 1991, when the Tibetan term *gsang ming* (lit. "secret name") was used for the term *biming*. A direct calque, which in Tibetan would be *smyug ming*, was never coined. I do not know if the term *smyug ming* was used in articles when the dictionary was published, but it was certainly current in oral Tibetan.

Tibet has long known of the practice of an author signing a work with a name other than his or her own. Dungkar Lozang Trinlé identified five methods by which classical Tibetan writers signed their works: (1) the author's given name, or the name by which the author was commonly known; (2) the name granted upon reaching a certain level in the study of Sanskrit grammar; (3) a name that accords with the religious vernacular of one's school; (4) a name that praises one's teacher or students; and (5) a secret name, such as one granted after an esoteric tantric initiation.[8] In the 1980s and 1990s Tibetan college students had the opportunity to adopt the second method, the use of grammar-names. During these two decades a large number of scholars—both government-sponsored and private—worked to revive the ten traditional sciences, especially Sanskrit grammar and poetry, and many students received grammar-names. For example, there were fifteen students in my class when I studied at Northwest Nationalities Institute in Lanzhou from 1985 to 1988. Though our main focus was the Old Tibetan language, we also studied Sanskrit grammar, and all of us were given grammar-names by our teacher. Although most of us continue to write to this day—especially research articles—only Repgong Dorjekhar, who has published several times under the name Dorjé Drayang Gyatso, continued to use a grammar-name.

Another type of traditional pen name, one not identified by Dungkar Rinpoché, is more prevalent today: the prefixing of birth names or monastic names with geographical references. There are many such instances among classical writers and lamas, such as the names of the early scholars Sakya Künga Gyentsen and Tsongkha Lozang Drakpa, whose names identify Sakya and Tsongkha as their the home regions. A major reason for applying a geographic name to one's given name is that certain Tibetan given names are extremely common. Again, when I was studying at Northwest Nationalities Institute, there were two writers named Dorjé Tsering, so one prefixed his given name with the toponym Chapgak (an area in Hainan prefecture in Qinghai Province): he still writes under (and is popularly known by) the name Chapgak Dorjé Tsering. Likewise, there were two writers named Könchok Tseten, and so one published under the name Nyagong Könchok Tseten. Countless examples of this can be found among both classical and contemporary authors.

These days, however, the affixing of geographic names has changed in two ways that mimic the use of western surnames as typically transcribed in Chinese. The standard for denoting such names in Chinese (and subsequently in Tibetan) has been to write the first name, followed by a large dot, and then the surname. Thus the English name Jack London would be written Jack • London. Tibetan writers have recently adopted this convention and write their names as Zho-ong • Kelzang Gyatso, for example, where Zho-ong is the writer's birthplace. While this method was adopted in Chinese to signal a foreign name, the large dot is used in Tibetan to distinguish between the place name of a writer and his or her given name. The second change has been the shortening of the place name to one syllable. Chentsa Rangsé thus becomes Chen Rangsé.

Dungkar Rinpoché also mentions the use of names that signal the sectarian affiliation of classical writers. While this practice may seem irrelevant in the context of lay writers today, we can also identify ways that writers use pen names to signal an ideological stance or affiliation. I will mention only a few.

First, some writers add the word "liberated" (grol) or the word "crazy" (smyon) to their names. If someone familiar with Tibetan modern literature heard the name "Rangdröl" (Rang grol), the writer Döndrup Gyel would immediately come to mind. Dondrup Gyel first used this name in 1981 for a poem entitled "Rtsom gyi mtsho mor rlabs kyi me tog dgod" (On the lake of writing blooms waves of flowers), which was published in the second issue of *Light Rain* that year. From then on Döndrup Gyel wrote many works under the name Rangdröl, including the poem "Waterfall of Youth," which laid the path for the new writing in the form of free verse (see chapter 4).

As used by the fifth Dalai Lama (1617–82), when he wrote under the name Gang shar rang grol, or by Zhapkar, who wrote under the name "Tshogs drug rang grol," the word "rangdrol" has deep tantric meaning, yet "dröl" (Tib. grol) in Tibetan is usually understood to mean the liberation from bondage of both body and mind. Döndrup Gyel chose the name for himself with this understanding. Though Communist Party policy was looser in the early 1980s than during the Cultural Revolution, freedom that would satisfy the more daring writers, such as Döndrup Gyel, was still well out of reach. Many courageous Tibetans such as Döndrup Gyel could not accept the forces of conservatism in Tibetan society. For example, when Döndrup Gyel's short story "Sprul sku" (Reincarnate lama) was published in *Light Rain*, many Tibetans felt that it satirized and ridiculed lamas and so they criticized Döndrup Gyel. He was sent threatening letters and it was said that his life was at risk. It may be that Döndrup Gyel chose his name to say that if others would not give him freedom, he would liberate himself. It seems that Döndrup Gyel was not the only one seeking freedom. Others followed Döndrup Gyel's lead and chose names containing the particle dröl: "Freed from Ignorance" (Rmongs grol), "Awakened and Liberated" (Sangs grol), "Liberated from the Net" (Rgya grol), and so forth.

Other names also signal the views of writers. One name, drawn from classical precedent, is the affix "Crazy" (Tib. smyon), which has also been used by yogin practitioners, most commonly in the Kagyü school of Tibetan Buddhism. While the term is multivalent and has roots in profound Buddhist philosophy, it might nevertheless be understood at one level as a means of distancing onself from present or mundane reality. The same can be said for the use of this term among contemporary writers, whether they seek to break from conventional norms or political and social realities. To cite just a few: "Crazy Pen" (Smyug smyon), "Crazy Lu [a tribal name]" (Klu smyon), and "Crazy person from the Land of Snows [Tibet]" (Gangs smyon).

One last trend is to adopt pen names that convey pride in being a "real" Tibetan or in having a strong attachment to Tibetans and Tibet. Though earlier writers called Tibet the "Land of Snows" (Gangs can gyi ljong) and one ornamental term for Tibetans was "The People of the Snowland" (Gangs can pa), only now has the affix "Snow" (Tib. *gangs*) been used in pen names: "Snow-Son" (Gangs sras), "Snow-Child" (Gangs phrug), "Love Snow [or Land of Snows]" (Gangs dga'), etc. Less direct, but equally evocative, pen names that have appeared in recent years refer to the Tibetan imperial period. The pen name "Song-Bö" (Srong-bhod), for example, draws its first syllable from Songtsen Gampo, the first dharmaraj or imperial king of Tibet responsible for militarily uniting the Tibetan plateau in the seventh century, and the second syllable from the old pronunciation of the term for Tibet (Bod), which Gendün Chömpel spelled "bhod" in his *White Annals*.[9] I intend to explore the significance of these names in greater detail in a future study.

Venues for Tibetan Poetry

If fifteen years ago, when I wrote "Heartbeat of the New Generation" (1991), someone had wanted to read all or most of the contemporary poetry published in Tibetan, the notion would have been feasible, not overly ambitious. Official literary magazines and newspapers at that time numbered fewer than ten, and only twelve years had passed since the founding of Tibet's first literary magazine, *Tibetan Art and Literature* (Bod kyi rtsom rig sgyu rtsal). Most of the other literary periodicals had publishing histories of less than ten years. Granted, a handful of college students were privately publishing cyclostyle journals,[10] but these were thin issues, few in number, and usually short-lived. One rarely saw privately issued collections of poetry. Though there were a few anthologies, most of the poems they contained were simply selected from what had already been printed in journals.

If today someone proposed to read all of the Tibetan poetry published thus far, the suggestion would be audacious. Several literary observers have made the comment, whether accurate or not, that there are now more writers than readers of poetry in Tibet. One primary outlet for poetic writing is journals. While the number of official literary magazines has not much increased, they have now been published for more than two decades, and poems still dominate these magazines. The journal *Gangs rgyan me tog* (Snow flower), for example, claims to publish literary works of all varieties, but for many years has focused almost exclusively on poetry. With the spread of computers in Tibetan areas since the late 1990s, however, the opportunities and capacity for individuals and smaller groups to publish their own journals and books have increased tremendously. It is true that unofficial magazines are not published as frequently as official titles; and several such endeavors were abandoned after only one or two issues. However, in terms of variety the private publications have gone much further than official journals. According to a comprehensive list of the journals received by our library, just from 2003 to 2006 some sixty-five unofficial journals were newly founded. This includes Tibetan titles only and journals published in the PRC, not in exile. If we add those journals published before 2003, the number of unofficial Tibet-related journals published in the PRC totals nearly one hundred. Another few dozen private journals have been published in exile.

Fifteen years ago there were also several unofficial cyclostyle magazines, as mentioned above. For the most part the founders were private groups of students in Tibetan language and literature departments at various nationality institutes. This is no longer so. The private groups who launch such publishing projects today are just as likely to be from monasteries, middle schools, and intensive training programs—although primarily in Amdo, and to a lesser degree in Kham. In 2007 the first couple of private journals were issued in central Tibet. An increasing number of literary journals are also starting to be issued from monasteries in south India by monks who escaped from Tibet in recent years.

The publication of unofficial poetry collections and anthologies has also greatly expanded. It was not easy to publish a book of poetry fifteen years ago. First, one needed to have enough poems for a book; and of course the editor at the publishing house would have the right to decide which poems were worthy of inclusion. There was no way to publish a book without going through an official publishing house. This situation was greatly changed by the proliferation of computers. If a writer now wants to publish a small book of poetry—and is willing to do so without an International Standard Book Number (ISBN)—then it is just a matter of having enough poems to publish and enough money to cover the publishing costs. Again, let us consider the experience of Latse Library: in 2006 we received from the Xining area alone forty-five books on a variety of subjects which were not published by an official publishing house. Of these, fifteen were privately funded collections of poetry by a single author.

Before the founding of *Tibetan Art and Literature* and *Light Rain* in 1980 and 1981 the primary venues for poetry in Tibetan were the literary columns in *Bod ljongs snyin re'i tshags par* (Tibet daily), published in Lhasa, and *Mtsho sngon Bod yig gsar 'gyur* (Qinghai Tibetan news), published in Xining. But the flourishing of new literary magazines does not seem to have hurt literary features in newspapers. *Qinghai Tibetan News* launched a special literary supplement in 1999 as one means to increase its readership and profitability, and the Northwest Nationalities Institute has published sixty issues of *Snyan ngag tshags par* (Poetry newspaper) since the paper's inception in 1989.

Perhaps the newest of all venues is the internet. In keeping with the importance of this media outlet for literary, artistic, and news production worldwide, poetry by Tibetan writers in both Tibetan and Chinese has begun to establish its presence on the web. The web site "Mchod me: Bod kyi rtsom rig gi dra ba" (Offering lamp: A Tibetan literary website) is but one of several web sites and blog forums, not to mention individual blogs, where Tibetan literature representing a range of literary styles continues to appear. On these sites we find poems not published elsewhere. Many of these works are more radical than the poetry published in print. And the blogs, of course, can be quite spontaneous and humorous. This new medium has allowed much greater exchange between writers and readers — in both Tibetan and Chinese. Writers ask for responses and they get them. When a review is too harsh, other readers will chastise the critic. Among the most active sites is tibetcm .com, which features primarily poems but also literary news, articles, and music.

In short, such a variety of publishing venues for poetry has never been available in Tibet. The result is a more engaged readership, but also less editorial control in terms of both content and quality; there has been a virtual flood of poetry both in and outside Tibet. For better or worse, the day has passed when a single scholar could hope to read the majority of published poems and analyze them as a cohesive whole. In the "Heartbeat of a New Generation," I wrote: "Now, those who favor the new writing style can only roar with victory and those who dislike it let out a long sigh of disappointment." This assessment caused quite a controversy, at least in exile. Some people understood my remark to mean that classical poetry had somehow lost and would soon disappear. Their objections led me to clarify my thoughts on this topic. There were many critics (especially in the older generation) then who claimed that contemporary poems written in free verse were not Tibetan — they were "neither goat nor sheep." My acknowledgment of "victory" was to say that despite their protests the new poetry had secured a foothold in the Tibetan literary world. If the statement held true then, it is even more apt now. If we look at the number of poets writing free verse, the countless free-verse poems now published, and the ever-increasing number of venues devoted to free verse, it is no longer a matter of liking or disliking the genre. Tibetan free-verse poetry can no longer be dismissed.

Notes

1. The Tibetan translation literally reads: "[We] need to oppose liberalism." The convention of adding "*byed dgos*" to verbs was adopted during the Cultural Revolution to render the many imperatives espoused during political campaigns. We do not find this usage in previous writing.
2. Tib. *Rang dbang thams cad bde ba ste/ gzhan dbang thams cad sdug bsngal lo*. This popular saying is drawn from the aphorisms of Sakya Paṇḍita. For an English translation see Davenport, trans., *Ordinary Wisdom*.
3. Lha chab sbyin pa, "Dpyid dus kyi snga dro zhig la ngas 'di ltar lab" (I say this on one spring morning), *'Od lnga'i gur khang* (The rainbow tent) 1 (1999), 94–95.
4. Gcan Rang sad, *Lang tsho'i zhabs rjes*, 253.
5. Dpal mo, ed., *Bzho lung*.
6. *Sbrang char*, 1996, no. 4, 89.
7. Dpal mo, Introduction, *Bzho lung*, 2.
8. Dung dkar Blo bzang 'phrin las, "Bod kyi dkar chag rig pa," 72–98. One could argue that the five names identified by Dungkar Rinpoché differ from contemporary pen names because they are not created by the author.
9. Dge 'dun chos 'phel, "Deb ther dkar po," *Collected Works*, vol. 3, 212. For an English translation of this text see Gedun Choephel, *White Annals*, trans. Samten Norboo (Dharamsala: Library of Tibetan Works and Archives, 1978).
10. In cyclostyle reproduction a sharp stylus is used to scratch into wax paper, which becomes the stencil for screen printing.

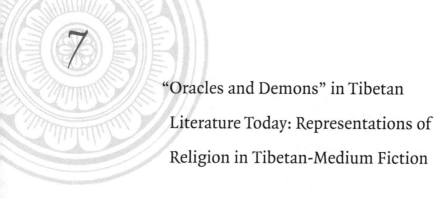

"Oracles and Demons" in Tibetan Literature Today: Representations of Religion in Tibetan-Medium Fiction

FRANÇOISE ROBIN

In 1946 the Tibetan National Assembly in Lhasa sent a nine-point communiqué to Chiang Kaishek, which stated: "There are many great nations on this earth who have achieved unprecedented wealth and might, but there is only one nation which is dedicated to the well-being of humanity in the world, and that is the religious land of Tibet which cherishes a joint spiritual and temporal system."[1]

A few years later, in 1950–51, forces of the Chinese People's Liberation Army invaded eastern Tibet, and by 1959 the Dalai Lama was in exile. The American missionary Robert Ekvall made an enquiry in 1960 among Tibetans refugees from all walks of life ("from lamas to nomads"),[2] which led him to underscore five criteria that defined for the Tibetans he interviewed a "Tibetan cultural self-consciousness" and expressed their "strong cultural awareness."[3] Paramount among these criteria was sameness of religion (chos lugs gcig).[4] Forty years later a university professor from Amdo, when interviewed by Lauran Hartley, named religion as a key component of Tibetan civilization: "Culture, religion and language are the glue that holds us together as a nationality. Without these, our nationality will disappear."[5]

Ever since researchers in the West began to survey contemporary Tibetan fiction, they have noted a tendency that characterizes most colonial environments: Tibetan writers have had to compromise between their creative impulses and the social and political frame into which their writing must fit.[6] The literary output of such a renowned writer as Döndrup Gyel (1953–85) illustrates this duality. One of his earliest writings, "Pad mtsho" (Petso), published in 1981,[7] underscores the lack of access to education for girls; "Sad kyis bcom pa'i me tog" (Frost-bitten flower, 1982–83), which the Tibetan studies specialist Tsering Tar has rated the best medium-length short story in Tibetan,[8] is a moving and dramatic appeal for free choice of one's life partner, especially from the girl's perspective. "'Brong stag thang" (Plain of the wild yak and tiger, 1981) narrates the thwarted love between two youngsters hailing from neighboring but antagonistic clans.[9] It exposes a Tibetan herders' custom that the Chinese Communist Party (CCP) has repeatedly addressed and tried to redress: the bloody feuds between clans, perpetuated from generation to generation in merciless vendettas. "Sgrung pa" (The bard, 1981)[10] narrates the moving life story of a Gesar Epic singer persecuted during the Cultural Revolution, and is one of the very first instances of Tibetan-medium "scar literature" (Ch. *shanghen wenxue*)—a term describing literary works settling accounts with the Cultural Revolution, which were encouraged by the Chinese state in the late 1970s as a means of achieving collective and individual catharsis through literature. The impact of these works on the readers' minds remains to be assessed, but it is interesting to note that Hartley found in the course of her valuable survey on tradition and modernity in Amdo that two of the four themes, namely traditional restrictions on women's rights and lack of widespread education, were rejected by a majority of persons as "bad" or "useless" aspects of Tibetan tradition.[11] A majority of interviewees also disapproved of "what they labeled as superstitious beliefs."[12] This leads us to our main concern: in what way is religious belief,[13] which is by tradition so closely associated with Tibetan culture as exemplified above, treated and represented in Tibetan-medium fiction written under the auspices of a Communist Chinese state that grants little agency to its Tibetan writers?[14] By examining a selection of short stories and novels published since the early 1980s—mainly in Amdo (roughly covering a major portion of today's Qinghai and a part of Gansu and Sichuan) and to a lesser degree in the Tibet Autonomous Region (TAR)[15]—we will see that fictional writings display three attitudes toward religion: radical criticism, selective rationalism, and neutral to positive reappraisal. We will then assess how these attitudes fit into today's polymorphous and rapidly changing Tibetan society, and the purposes they serve.

Radical Criticism

Generally speaking, Tibetan-medium short stories focus mostly on herders, peasants, teachers, or students, rather than on religious characters exclusively. This may be because when realistic fiction is at an early stage, as in Tibet,[16] authors tend to write mainly of people and situations with which they are familiar. I do not mean to say that clerics are not engaged in literature. They are indeed, but they tend to dedicate themselves mainly to poetry. One reason for this rather clear-cut literary orientation may be that clerics are offered better chances to master classical Tibetan language (mainly traditional Buddhist poetry originating from India and absorbed by Tibetans since the thirteenth century),[17] whereas laymen have often followed classes on modern literature in the course of their lay training. Another reason is that the bulk of canonical Tibetan literature includes no treatise on the subject of prose fictional writing. Therefore, if a cleric were to engage in the composition of prose fiction, he might be accused of rang bzo (lit. "one's own fabrication"), which the Great Tibetan-Chinese Dictionary defines as "an activity devoid of foundation, and subjective,"[18] the sort of activity that the orthodox Tibetan religious world traditionally frowns upon since it is "opposed to authenticity in recognized traditions . . . devoid of acknowledged authority and without a lineage going back to an original master."[19] Although clerics did write fictional works in pre-1950 Tibet, they would explain their endeavor in an introduction, usually by saying either that their works had been written at the request of their masters, for the benefit of all beings, or that they had felt compelled to resort to storytelling for the benefit of people of "little understanding"[20] like them; indeed most "fiction" written then was edifying stories in which Buddhist principles were expounded in a popular way.[21] The consequence is that the religious world and the religious characters, when represented, are often seen today through the eyes of laymen (or laywomen) writers—a kind of "secondhand" representation.[22]

If we attempt to establish a rough chronological divide, we can say that a derogatory stance toward Buddhism and the Tibetan clergy in general is usually found in writings published in the 1980s, or by a certain group of writers. Tsering Döndrup,[23] for instance, is famous and rather controversial in Tibet for his anticlericalism.[24] One of his main and recurrent characters is called Alak Drongtsang, which can be translated as "Wild-Yak Rinpoché."[25] When the former editor in chief of the magazine Sbrang char (Light rain), Sanggyé, criticized him for choosing this name, Tsering Döndrup argued somewhat mischievously that it was the only way to avoid confusion in the readers' minds between his fictitious "Wild-Yak Rinpoché" and some lama who really existed.[26] One of his first and most famous short stories, "Gzhon nu'i rang sgra dbyar gyi rnga gsang" (Sound of a young man: The secret drumming of summer),[27] has as its protagonist a young man from Amdo named Tsering. A fan of Lu Xun and Gorky and a member of the Young Communists League, he is forced by his parents to join them on a trip to Lhasa when a lama prophesies that his father will recover if he goes on pilgrimage to the Jokhang Temple.[28] After protracted discussions,[29] Tsering yields to their pressure and drops school, as well as his political responsibilities. Once in Lhasa he compares unfavorably the dim and flickering lights of the Jokhang with the bright electric lamps in his school, and describes his prostrating mother as a leaning tree. The pilgrimage over, the family returns home, but Tsering's father, far from recovering, dies at the hospital. The young man has to spend as hospital fees the money he had planned to use for his own education, and is left with no option but to become a herder, a social condition he had hoped to escape by gaining a modern education.[30] His smashed hopes and ensuing troubles are all blamed on religion.

In 1988 the same author published another short story, "Rtse chus khrel dgod byed bzhin" (Ridiculed by the Tsechu River),[31] in which a reincarnate lama, Alak Chömpel, takes a seventeen-year-old girl as his mistress. He answers to gossip by claiming that far from indulging in the sensual pleasures of a common relationship, he and his partner are engaged in tantric practices. When she becomes pregnant, he escapes this thorny situation by recognizing the child-to-be as a reincarnate lama or rinpoché.[32] In another story published the same year, "Lha ba 'dre ston" (The oracle shows a demon),[33] Tsering Döndrup describes how a community oracle attributes a girl's sickness to a malevolent spirit (nad bdag, lit. "master of disease"). After telling the believers with scrupulous precision what "propitiatory offerings" (lha srol 'bul rten) are required (meat, butter, a sleeveless coat, six silver coins), the oracle then calls for the "master of disease." The nad bdag replies in a ghostly voice. With the hope of nabbing the demon, a villager rushes toward the place from which the demoniac voice is coming, only to discover that the "nad bdag" is none other than another villager hired by the oracle for one yuan. In the end the narrator, a young man who has been listening to this story recalled by old Penden, bursts into laughter along with the others. But his hilarity is not due to the sham itself: it is directed at "men who, like old Penden, are not liberated from the invisible formless net."[34] Old Penden is so deeply entrenched in the net of "superstition" that his faith in oracles is not even shaken by this incident.

The short story "A shel Bde chen mtsho mo" (Elder sister Dechen Tsomo),[35] also published in 1988 but by a woman writer named Tredrön, shows a young woman from Amdo moving to Lhasa and being abused by a lama who takes advantage of her youth and inexperience. Lhakpa Püntsok, a critic and writer who has held high political positions since the 1980s (he now belongs to the governing body of the China Tibetology Center in Beijing), dedicated more than twenty laudatory pages to this short story.[36]

Another short work famous for criticizing not so much corrupt lamas as blind devotees is "Ca ne" (The bowl), by Repgong Dorjekhar.[37] It makes fun of old Drukgyel's attachment to a bowl given to him by a lama before "Liberation." To the old man the container is so infused with the lama's blessings (*sbyin rlabs*) that any tea poured into it has a distinctive taste. This short story was selected for several Tibetan anthologies and even appears in a university-level textbook on Tibetan literature published as late as 1998. In the same vein, the famous short story "Sprul sku" (Reincarnate lama, 1981) by Dön-drup Gyel[38] denounces the blindness of Tibetan believers: a community falls prey to a fake *tülku* whose dishonest activities are made possible by the villagers' devotion and lack of discernment in religious matters.

This simplistic anticlerical trend is common in fiction published in the 1980s, a time when, according to Tsering Shakya, "writings that contested the authority of religion and portrayed religious figures negatively were encouraged."[39] One should not forget that for most Tibetan writers of the early 1980s, social(ist) realism was a new literary genre imposed from above and executed under the guidance of cultural institutions: "They put a pen in our hands and said: 'Now you write! And you criticize your traditions!,'" a prominent Tibetan writer once confided.[40] It should also be recalled that the Cultural Revolution had just come to an end. During that ten-year period (1966–76), radical criticism of tradition and religion was a regular and compulsory activity; it can be surmised that new writers still deemed it safer in 1980 to keep in line with this criticism, in case the liberalization policy sweeping across China at the time was unexpectedly reversed.

Still, we cannot say that all radical authors write under pressure. Hartley's study on modernity in Amdo identifies an informal group which she describes as "radical modernists," intellectuals opposed to roughly all aspects of Tibetan Buddhism (both popular and classical) in the name of the survival of Tibetan civilization, for whom "the monastic community is a special target."[41] Their views are encapsulated in the writings of a critic called Zhok-dung who admonished Tibetans in 1999 to get rid of "old propensities" (*bag chags rnying ba*) that "have repeatedly cast darkness which blocks the youth who have ideas."[42] Zhokdung defined these propensities as "the ancient religion of worldly deities which trusts in the guidance of *lha, klu, gnyan, btsan,* etc. of this world; the belief in deities, *mo*-divination and astrology; the use of curses, hexes and spells; the teachings of no-self and *karma,* etc. — such views by which the gods (*lha*) and demons (*'dre*) claim ownership of us."[43]

Selective Rationalism

The second group of writers, whose approach I would call selective rationalist, evoke themes that approximate the approach of what Hartley describes as "moderate/selective modernists." Defined as "seeking to keep what is good in tradition as a base and adopt what is useful from 'modern culture,'"[44] this position was largely defended by Amdo intellectuals at the end of the 1990s.[45] Hartley explains further that "selective modernists" are "more ready to reject . . . what they label . . . as superstition"[46] in religion—contrary to the "radical modernists" who reject both "popular superstitions" (belief in invisible creatures, such as lha, 'dre, klu, and gnyan) and "universal" Buddhist beliefs (e.g. karma, selflessness). For this reason I have chosen to label these writers "selective rationalists": their works differentiate between what is deemed a "respectable" or "authentic" religious practice (e.g. compassion, belief in the law of cause and effects, power of meditation) and what should be condemned (e.g. belief in nāga[47] and faith in popular practitioners of Buddhism, such as oracles and divinators).[48]

A few short stories will illustrate this point. In " 'Dris yun ring na re khengs mang" (A long acquaintance leads to many hopes, 1999), by Anyön Trashi Döndrup,[49] the narrator is a young graduate student who acts as an attendant for Akhu Samten, an old, respected, and knowledgeable teacher, himself an ex-monk.[50] After a flattering description of the old man, the narrator begins to question his disinterest toward material goods, as Akhu Samten seems heavily disturbed when someone steals one hundred yuan from him. The story ends with the old teacher finally explaining the reason for his sorrow: he feels sad for the thief. The reader is meant to infer that according to the karma theory, this theft will undoubtedly lead its perpetrator to suffering in a next life. The old teacher's magnanimity provides an unexpected ending: first, the twist in the story itself, and second, the positive treatment of a religious figure. We could surmise that the same story written in the early 1980s would have underscored the gap between charity as a key Buddhist quality and the meanness of the old teacher, thus discrediting the whole institution.

Tsering Yangkyi[51] is a female author[52] from Zhikatsé (Ch. Rikaze, TAR). Her "So nam shor ba'i ljang bu" (Neglected sprout, 1998) narrates the story of Wangdor and his only son Namgyel. Wangdor is sent to work in inner China for six months.[53] Upon his return he learns that his wife is pregnant by another man. She leaves Wangdor, who gradually takes to gambling, a not uncommon occurrence in Tibetan society today. After the sudden demise of his grandfather, who was the pillar of the family, young Namgyel slowly drifts away from his father, skips school, starts begging in tea stalls, and roams the streets of Lhasa. His father beats him severely on several occasions when the teacher informs him of his son's disastrous results at school. In the end Wangdor realizes that his son needs care and attention. He takes him to the Jowo Rinpoché, the most sacred statue in all of Tibet, for both of them to pray and swear that they will resume a normal life, without gambling or begging. Note the shift between Tsering Döndrup's "Sound of a Young Man"

The writers Tsering Yangkyi and Trashi Penden with their family at home in Lhasa in 1997. Trashi Penden is also editor of the Tibetan version of the newspaper *Tibet Daily*. Photo by Lauran Hartley.

and Tsering Yangkyi's "Neglected Sprout": in "Sound of a Young Man" the Jowo statue in Lhasa symbolizes the bone of contention between the hero and his parents, and attachment to old ways and backward ideas; in "Neglected Sprout" (written some fifteen years later), the same statue represents the locus of reconciliation between father and son, and the promise of an improved life in the future.

Other writings that I would classify as selective rationalist mix and contrast "classical Buddhism" and "popular Buddhism": see for instance "Gangs dabs kyi gtam rgyud" (Story at the foot of the snow mountain),[54] written by Rangdra.[55] This short story tells of the plight of Lewang Drölma, a woman who mistakenly picks up, for domestic use, a few dry twigs fallen from the village holy *nāga*-tree (*klu sdong*). At the very same time, an incredibly violent storm devastates the village and a thunderstorm strikes and burns the holy tree. The local tantric practitioner (*ngags pa*) declares that one of the very twigs picked up by Lewang Drölma hosted a *nāga*. He predicts that *nāga* spirits will seek revenge and inoculate Lewang Drölma with a "*nāga* disease" (*klu nad*), elsewhere in the text explicitly referred to as leprosy (*mdze nad*). The villagers collectively decide to expel her from the village. The violent scene is made even more poignant as Lewang Drölma hears, from a distance, her young son call "Mother!" after she has gone. So far the plot recalls the anticlerical stance of radical critics seen previously. But the angle shifts when the author describes the heroine waiting in loneliness for her husband and her son. She prostrates untiringly to the great local mountain-god Machen Pomra; she makes mudras (ritual and symbolic hand gestures) and circumambulates holy places. When after many years her husband and her son finally find her, they discover a skeleton (rus sgrom). But the skeleton is not scattered all over the earth: it is sitting on a heap of stones, in the lotus position with hands in a mudra gesture and face turned toward the village, an attitude reminiscent of Buddhist meditation posture. Also, when excited villagers drive Lewang Drölma away from the community, the author describes the scene as follows: "Generally speaking, men and women from Lewang Village would respect the law of cause and effect and were very compassionate, but that day, it was as if they had been really possessed by demons. Stones, sticks, handfuls of earth, etc., fell on Lewang Drölma's body like rain pouring down."[56] Obviously the author wishes to oppose and contrast popular religious practices (symbolized here by the belief in nāga and the violence and misery that it generates) and a kind of "purer" Buddhism (illustrated by Lewang Drölma's practice of Buddhism once expelled from the community). This example is by no means unique: even Tsering Döndrup, an author who is usually hard on religious matters and characters, occasionally shows a certain leniency toward a non-popular Buddhism. His first and recent full-length novel Mes po (Ancestors), published in 2001,[57] recounts, without any sarcasm on the author's part, the story of Lumokyi, a young woman respected for her sanctity and dedication to Buddhism, who at a young age moves to a cave where she practices Buddhism.

What these rationalists criticize is a certain type of popular Buddhism, and more globally "superstition." In part, their attitude reflects the official Chinese attitude toward religion, a position expounded in the White Paper issued on 22 June 2000 regarding "The Development of Tibetan Culture" in the TAR. It stated that "the state respects and safeguards the rights of Tibetans and other ethnic groups in Tibet to live their lives and conduct social activities in accordance with their traditional customs, and their freedom to engage in normal religious activities and major religious and folk festival celebrations . . . The central people's government and the government of the Tibet Autonomous Region have all along paid special attention to respect for and protection of the freedom of religious belief and normal religious activities of the Tibetan people."[58] An article published in 1995 in the Chinese edition of Xizang ribao (Tibet daily) stated that "normal religious activity" was clearly opposed to "common concepts of ghosts and gods, . . . feudal, superstitious activities,"[59] which were elsewhere explained as "oracles and divination."[60] We have just seen that oracles and astrologers were a favorite target of a certain group of writers. This attitude is particularly obvious in writings by someone like Rangdra. For instance, his "'Dre rkang rto" (The limping devil, 1996)[61] narrates how a demon called "Limping Devil" is believed to haunt a remote village in Amdo. At the end of the short story, the three prominent persons of the village—the soothsayer (mo pa), the astrologist (rtsis pa), and the oracle (lha ba)—confirm each other's diagnosis: the "Limping Devil" is to blame for the village misfortunes. But the reader, through rather humorous authorial narration, soon understands that contrary to what the three characters collectively think—or pretend they think—it is not so much the mysterious and malevolent "Limping Devil" who jeopardizes the harmony in the community as greediness, jealousy, and above all, belief in that very spirit. In "'Pho 'gyur" (Changes), by the same author (first published in 1998),[62] a group of tantric lay practitioners (ngags pa) gather to summon Chammo, the local deity, who is to speak to them through the mouth of the village oracle. After some time, during which the oracle fails to go into trance, they resort to persuasive and even coercive means: "They warned him: 'If today you are not possessed, we will stop paying the oracle lot (that is, the measure of cereal grains that each family must give yearly to the oracle) for one whole year!' At first, the oracle was somehow dumbfounded, but after a while, a 'Khag, khag' sound came from the bottom of his throat, and his head shook like a damaru. When they saw his body jerk and shake and jump into the air, they understood that the oracle was indeed possessed by the deity."[63]

What links can be established between the CCP's charge against superstitious beliefs, and the radicals and selective rationalists' all-out attack on them? There seem to be three main reasons why the CCP condemns "superstitious beliefs" so firmly. In the first place, these beliefs are seen as economically counterproductive. In an article published in the official and national Chinese daily Guangming ribao (Guangming daily), "feudal superstitious" activities are condemned because they are "unmercifully swallowing up pitiful resources and funds."[64] But economic extravagance is not the only reason why oracles and astrologists should be opposed: faith in such "superstitious" aspects of Buddhism contradicts science. An editorial of the official Tibet Daily dated 26 November 1996 accuses religious circles and religious party members of "oppos[ing] any kind of scientific development," and reproaches them with "not send[ing] their children to school but to the monasteries, because they don't want them to receive scientific teachings."[65] Last—but certainly not least—"superstitious beliefs" are the target of the government all over China because of their association with social and political unrest. Illegal sects, according to the same article in the Guangming Daily, "endanger the spiritual building" of the communist country and threaten "social stability." One immediately thinks of the Falun Gong cult, but there are many other examples. In the case of Tibetan Buddhism, the association between "superstitious beliefs" and "splittism" by the "Dalai clique" is openly asserted and often repeated. As for popular religion, Ronald Schwartz argues, "the political content is expressed through religious themes, and religious longing becomes a substitute for effective political power."[66] He adds that "increasingly, in the period since the declaration of martial law [1989], expressions of this kind of popular religion have reappeared, with reports of spirits-possessions and 'manifestations' of deities."[67]

Criticisms of popular religions, and more precisely oracles and seers, as formulated by some radical critics and selective rationalist writers overlap with official CCP guidelines when it comes to economy and science. An example of a condemnation of "superstitious beliefs" on economic grounds can be found in a short story called "Shog thang" ([Religious] paper scroll) published in the 1980s, which describes how an old man decides to spend his family's savings to acquire an expensive *tangka* (religious painted scroll) instead of spending money for the benefit of his family and his cattle, as his son suggests.[68] The lack of (and sometimes obstruction to) scientific thinking is denounced in "The Sound of a Young Man," in which a lama's erroneous prophecy is contrasted with the doctor's accurate diagnosis of the father's ailment and treatment, and in "Limping Devil." The political side of the attack on "superstitious" beliefs, however, is not encountered in short stories, for the simple reason that politics are never mentioned directly in Tibetan works.

Thus up to a certain point it can be surmised that Tibetan radicalists and rationalists, like most writers living in colonized societies, "have adopted reactive perspectives which lock them into a reductive position whereby they can return the colonial gaze only by mimicking its ideological imperatives and intellectual procedures";[69] or, to put it differently, "the colonized speak in accents borrowed from their masters."[70] A majority of today's writers are intellectuals who have attained a certain level of education in the Tibetan language, while reading and being raised under the guidance of Marxist theory; many have experienced life in a Chinese megalopolis. In a way they have seen Tibetan culture reflected through a Chinese, Marxist, socialist, materialist credo. Without totally rejecting religion, selective rationalists are sensitive to materialism and science as extolled in China. They have internalized a certain idea of modernity as presented through colonial cultural values and its "naturalized oppositions between us and them, science and barbarity, modern and traditional."[71] As representatives of the "educated middle-class . . .

drawn into the colonial cultural world,"[72] they are receptive to the colonial cultural discourse which calls for a reform of Tibetan Buddhism and preaches in favor of a "rational" approach, and would certainly not disagree with the official Chinese White Paper on "The Development of Tibetan Culture" (2000), which condemned all superstitious practices in Tibet as a hindrance to "modern civilization," "healthy life," and "development of Tibetan culture in the new era."[73]

But colonialism and the encounter with Communist Chinese anticlericalism do not suffice to explain the rejection of a certain type of religious beliefs among Tibetan intellectuals: this condemnation of "superstition" by some literary circles must be seen here against the background of "the inexorable and universal forces of science, progress, rationality and modernity"[74] usually associated with the modern world and technology to which Tibet is slowly gaining access. It implies, in the area of Buddhism, the promotion of a "scientific," "rational," "tamed" Buddhism, based on knowledge and reason—a "civilized" Buddhism versus a "popular," irrational, or "wild" Buddhism epitomized by trance and divination. Certain sectors of Tibetan society are experiencing now what was experienced over a century ago by Hindus as they faced a modernity embodied by the British colonial force. At the time "opposition to idolatry was a major idea around which religious reform in the nineteenth century was organized and propagated."[75] More examples could be drawn from a vast number of other colonized societies.

Reappraisal of Religion from the Mid-1990s Onward

When the twentieth-century reformer, intellectual, and iconoclast Gendün Chömpel (1903–51) first encountered Theravāda Buddhism in Sri Lanka in the late 1930s, he was "deeply impressed by [the] simplicity" of this type of Buddhism and "considered Buddhism as it was practiced in Tibet at that time as degenerated."[76] Gendün Chömpel was not then faced with any kind of Chinese communism or colonialism (although Sri Lanka was under British rule), but he came face to face with a "sober" kind of Buddhism which offered him a new perspective on his own tradition. Still, Gendün Chömpel later changed his mind again: "he had second thoughts about this point of view, realized that each tradition had its own value, and claimed that any reform of current Tibetan Buddhism would in itself mean a debasement of tradition."[77] Following a similar evolution of thought as that experienced by Gendün Chömpel, several writers have recently published short stories that seem to depart from the search for "rationality" and accusations that Tibetan Buddhism is lacking in it; rather, the scale is tilting back toward a renewed appreciation of popular religious traditions. Two short stories will be discussed here to illustrate how widely shared religious beliefs (in these stories, reincarnation and healing through rituals) are portrayed more favorably in light of this reappraisal.

Trabha's short story "Re smon" (Wish, 1995)[78] is divided into four scenes. The first shows villagers talking about an old woman who has just died. They recall how before her death Grandmother Drölma showed signs of senility, once asking her grandson Tsering to wait for her and marry her. The second scene shows her some time before her death, asking Tsering to listen to a story (*gna' gtam*). He refuses, as she has already narrated it twice. Tsering tells his parents that Grandmother Drölma called him Böddé on that day. The third scene introduces a new character, Böde, talking with a young woman named Drölma. She tries to talk him out of taking part in a fight but he insists: he is renowned as a young and brave community leader, so how could he not fight? Moreover, the local lama, Alak Khadingtsang, has given him an indestructible protective coat of mail (*srung ba rdo rje mgo khrab*). The fourth and final scene shows Grandmother Drölma and Alak Khadingtsang. Fifty-three years have passed since Böde's death. She has already consulted seventeen lamas about his rebirth, and all agree that he was reborn in a condition lower even than that of an animal—which old Drölma cannot accept. In contrast, Alak Khadingtsang tells her that Böde was reborn as a human being: as her grandson Tsering. Grandmother Drölma prostrates to the lama's feet: she confesses that until then she had lost faith in him, as she believed that the armor given by him (by which she means the lama's previous incarnation) had failed to protect Böde. The short story ends with Grandmother Drölma begging the lama to grant her a rebirth in a girl's body, in a family distant enough from Tsering's so that they might marry later. This last scene is the key to the puzzling preceding scenes. Not only is this a moving and original short story—consisting only of dialogue—but it is noteworthy in that it ridicules neither Tibetan Buddhism nor popular Tibetan beliefs in trülku, which as we have seen are regular targets for some writers. Here again it can be surmised that a more anticlerical author would have opted for a sarcastic attitude, tone, or angle, taking advantage of this story to make fun of traditional beliefs and the overly "credulous" or "superstitious" grandmother.

In the short story "Grong khyer gyi 'tsho ba" (Life in town, 2003), by Pema Tseten,[79] young Rikden Gyatso is bedridden. His educated parents try their best to find a monk or lay ngakpa to recite the prayers prescribed by Alak Gönpotsang, a Buddhist hierarch who occupies high political and religious positions in the Chinese city where the story takes place. The couple ends up "hiring" a lay tantric practitioner whom they find at the bus station. They invite him to their home, where he performs the required healing ceremony—

but Chinese neighbors turn up at eleven o'clock and again at midnight to complain harshly about the prayers and drum beatings coming from their Tibetan neighbors' flat (one neighbor asks if they are performing drama, *zlos gar*). Finally, to make sure that little Rikden Gyatso will recover, the main character's father-in-law asks the tantric practitioner how to perform a *tse-tar*[80] in a big town. The religious officiant advises the family go to a public park, buy fifty fish, and throw them into the river. They do as requested, prompting a number of comments on the part of Chinese passersby. Soon the child recovers.

How can we account for and interpret this "neutral"—and even positive—treatment of religion or religious figures? The terms "folklorization" or "indigenism" have been used by some western literary critics to describe fiction writing from Haiti, in which Haitian motifs figure prominently, and to describe the practice of lending prominence to testimony and socioethnic information, to the detriment of aesthetics and fiction. I believe we should be cautious when comparing Tibetan contemporary fiction to other "third world" literature. While many influential "third world" authors address a non-autochthonous public, expressing themselves through a language borrowed from the colonizer (English, French, Spanish, Chinese, etc.), Tibetan authors who write in Tibetan know that they are addressing only their fellowmen, and a small number at that, as hardly any Chinese or westerner can (or bothers to) read Tibetan-medium literary production, and few modern Tibetan literary works are actually translated. Moreover, their reading public hails from such backgrounds as those described in the narratives; second-generation urbanites are very few. Thus there is no need to introduce a supposedly "typical" traditional Tibetan way of life to sympathetic but ignorant readers—as happens in works meant for a "foreign" public.

Hartley once used the term "ethnicization"[81] to characterize the inclusion of religious motifs in Tibetan contemporary literature. She defined the term as "the use of religious symbols as cultural markers."[82] It is a fact that in most short stories, one comes across a community elder sitting in a sunny corner and turning his or her prayer wheel, mumbling endless *Om ma ni padme hum* and counting mantras on a rosary. But I think that the inclusion of religious scenes can be seen not as "cultural markers" but as an expression of a certain kind of *cultural nationalism*, defined by Partha Chatterjee as a cultural construct that enables the colonized to posit their difference and autonomy, well before and outside the realm of political nationalism. Commenting upon Bengali "cultural nationalism" in late nineteenth century, Chatterjee wrote that cultural nationalism's "most powerful, creative and historically significant project [is] to fashion a 'modern' national culture that is nevertheless not

Western. If the nation is an imagined community, then this is where it is brought into being. In this, its true and essential domain, the nation is already sovereign, even when the state is in the hands of the colonial power. The dynamics of this historical project is completely missed in conventional histories in which the story of nationalism begins with the contest for political power."[83] I believe, *mutatis mutandis* (change "Western" into "Chinese" in the above quotation), that this can equally apply to the group of writers, or more accurately writings, that I have characterized above as "neutral" and "positive"—and to a certain extent, to radicalists and rationalists as well. This is even truer in a colonized Tibet, where direct political opposition is unthinkable—in contrast to nineteenth-century Bengal, which knew of political groups opposed to or at least able to discuss British rule. Of course, "cultural nationalism" and the fashioning of a modern national culture through literature do not necessarily require a neutral or positive assessment of folk culture. Again Chatterjee offers a pertinent example: he describes how in the nineteenth century, Bengali intellectuals (the "middle class") gradually grew dissatisfied with the sharp criticism of Bengali culture presented by the colonizing power, and how this criticism prompted a backlash: "For the colonized middle-class, caught in its 'middleness,' the discourse of 'Reason' was not unequivocally liberating. The invariable implication it carried of the historical necessity of colonial rule and its condemnation of indigenous culture as the storehouse of unreason . . . made the discourse of Reason oppressive."[84]

I tend to think that the reappraisal of religious characters and activities—both popular and learned—can be explained by a similar wariness and weariness at the systematic denigration of what belongs to the heart of Tibetan Buddhism, and what differentiates it from other types of Buddhism. This discussion should be seen in the wider context of the debate on backwardness (*rjes lus*), a key notion with which Tibetans have often equated their own culture in the last fifty years and which often surfaces in modern fiction. Not incidentally, this very concept seems to be undergoing the same process of reevaluation in the opposite direction, as will be exemplified by a comparison of three short stories published in 1983, 2000, and 2002. The first is Tsering Döndrup's "Sound of a Young Man." Tsering, the protagonist, makes a stopover in Xining, the capital city of Qinghai Province, while on his way to Lhasa. Among his fellow travelers is an old man, Gönpo, who after eating his *tsampa*[85] wipes his bowl with the upper part of his overcoat. A Chinese passerby comments on the scene: "After eating *tsampa* they wipe their bowl with the upper part of their coat, and after shitting they wipe their ass with the lower part of their coat!"[86] Tsering, who understands Chinese (he went to school), is tempted to smash the passerby in the face, but he refrains, remembering the eighth point of the tenth section of his schools' disciplinary code ("Do not fight").[87] He also concedes that the Chinese man's remark is true, and laments to himself: "Ah, Tibetan people! Tibetan people! Ah, grassland! Grassland! When will you rank among advanced people?"[88] The Chinese perception of Tibetans as backward, what has been referred to as the "stigmatized identity"[89] of the colonized people, is clearly accepted and internalized in this narrative. But in a short story published seventeen years later, we can see the shift from acceptance of one's so-called backwardness or inferiority to irony toward this category of judgment: in "Sha yu mo she'u" (Fawn) the protagonist has a one-night affair with a Chinese woman.[90] Later, the woman confides to a Chinese friend: "These Tibetans are indeed backward, but when it comes to seducing girls, they are quite advanced!"[91] The idea of progress, when applied to such a private domain as flirtation and lovemaking, reveals itself as an irrelevant and groundless category.[92] The third short story, published two years later, goes even further: it shows a young Chinese traveler-cum-artist on a visit to Tsetang (TAR) wistfully commenting to his Amdo Tibetan fellow travelers: "How much I would like to be Tibetan like you!"[93] He had explained earlier in the narrative: "You Tibetans are really an artistic people. I like you, Tibetans!"[94]

This general reappraisal can be interpreted as a sign of the growing autonomy of Tibetan writers, as I have argued elsewhere:[95] writers are learning how to use for their own design a tool placed into their hands by the colonizing force, and they are beginning to model a perception of themselves increasingly independent of the official Chinese Marxist view of Tibetan culture. Authors use fiction as a locus for discussing, negotiating, and contesting present and future visions of Tibet. This occurs in the framework of confrontation or negotiation with the colonizing power and negotiation with colonized compatriots. In that perspective, religion should not be seen solely as a subject debated among writers, but rather as a "site" or forum where the nationality's self-representation and agency are negotiated.[96] This use of fiction as a site for negotiation can be explained by three special conditions which circumscribe Tibetan-medium fiction writers today: first, they belong to a Chinese environment, where little space for expression is offered to the civil society and the public sphere; second, theirs is a colonized context where the confines of discussion are decided by the ruling Other; third, they must take into account "the framed tensions between the pulls of tradition and the inexorable push of modernity"[97] that are shaking Tibetan society today.

For these reasons, Tibetan-medium fiction today merits our attention; it is a forum where points of view, however divergent, are all directed toward the same concern: pondering, negotiating, shaping, and elaborating not only what "Tibet" and "Tibetan civilization" mean, but how to fit in their Chinese and world environment, and with what degree of actual or virtual agency.

Notes

I purposely borrow here the title of a celebrated Tibetological work, *Oracles and Demons of Tibet*, by R. de Nebesky-Wojkowitz.

1. Quoted in Goldstein, *A History of Modern Tibet*, 542.
2. Ekvall, "The Tibetan Self-Image," 634.
3. Ibid., 629.
4. Whether it means that *bönpos* are excluded from the range of Tibetanness, or that Bön belongs to the same overall religious frame, is not clear. After religion came the same food habits (*kha lugs gcig*) and then language (*skad lugs gcig*). The feeling of belonging to the same ethnic group (*mi rigs gcig*) ranked only fourth, followed by the same environment (*sa cha gcig*). Ekvall, "The Tibetan Self-Image," 629–30.
5. Hartley, "'Inventing Modernity' in Amdo," 15.
6. As suggested in the title of Tsering Shakya's article "Literature or Propaganda? The Development of Literature since 1950."
7. Don grub rgyal, "Pad mtsho," 289–301.
8. Tsering Thar praises the work with these words: "It stands like a tiara on the top of the head, like the master of constellations." "Bod kyi deng rabs brtsams sgrung las 'phros pa'i gtam chu yi zegs ma," 87. For an English translation of this short story see Don grub rgyal, "A Blighted Flower," *A Blighted Flower and Other Stories*, comp. and trans. Riika Virtanen, 31–74. For a French translation see Thöndrupgyäl, *La Fleur vaincue par le gel*, trans. Françoise Robin (Paris: Bleu de Chine, 2006). For the original Tibetan text see Don grub rgyal, "Sad kyis bcom pa'i me tog."
9. Don grub rgyal, "'Brong stag thang."
10. Don grub rgyal, "Sgrung ba."
11. Hartley, "'Inventing Modernity,'" 10.
12. Ibid.
13. It should be noted that by "religion" I mean mostly Tibetan Buddhism, since *bön* appears only exceptionally. The only instance to my knowledge is Padma tshe brtan, "Grong khyer gyi 'tsho ba" (City life), *Sbrang char*, 2003, no. 1, 5–42, in which a Tibetan intellectual couple, Yungdrung and Dekyi, end up divorcing when Dekyi's parents discover after many years that their son-in-law is from a *bönpo* background.
14. It has been a recurring complaint among Tibetan writers writing in Tibetan that under political conditions prevailing in the last decade of the twentieth century and the first decade of the twenty-first, their range of freedom is more limited than that of their ethnic Chinese counterparts and ethnic Tibetan writers who write in Chinese. In other words, some Tibetan writers feel that they cannot express as many opinions or explore as many topics as their Chinese colleagues.

15. One of the reasons for this imbalance may be that the literary scene in the TAR has been less active than that of Amdo in the last decade, for several reasons (mainly educational policy and the tense political atmosphere) that I cannot delve into in the scope of this article.

16. The first Tibetan realistic short story was published in 1981 and the first ever full-length novel in 1985. Thus it can be said that as paradoxical it may seem for a people who have been extremely prolific literarily in the last thirteen hundred years — Tibetan script was devised under royal patronage in the seventh century — Tibetan writers may be the last in the world to enter the realm of literary fiction.

17. Three of the five minor sciences (*rig gnas chung ba lnga*) that clerics are supposed to master concern poetics: *snyan ngag* (ornate poetic composition inherited from Sanskrit *kāvya*), *mngon brjod* (lexicography), and *sdeb sbyor* (prosody). Another of these five minor sciences, dance and drama (*zlos gar*), also entails, at least theoretically, the mastery of language; Isabelle Henrion-Dourcy has noted that drama is described by Tibetan scholars as "not being ignorant of languages" (*skad rigs la mi rmongs*) or as "the art of verbal expression" (*smra ba'i sgyu rtsal yongs su rdzogs la dpal dang yon tan ldan pa*). Isabelle Henrion-Dourcy, "Ache lhamo: Jeux et enjeux d'une tradition théâtrale tibétaine," vol. 1, 138.

18. Tib. *khungs med rang 'dod kyi bya ba*. Zhang Yisun et al., *Bod rgya tshig mdzod chen mo*, 2657. A Tibetan proverb illustrates the stance toward creation: *bya ba thams cad lad mo yin / lad mo'i nang nas su mkhas yin* (All activities are imitations; let's see who is best at it!).

19. Stoddard, "Le maître spirituel, l'artiste et le saint-fou," 267.

20. Tib. *thos chung*, as found in the introductory part of the Tibetan drama *Chos rgyal Nor bzang gi rnam thar* (The life of the religious King Norsang), for instance.

21. This includes the Gesar epic, of which written versions were often composed by clerics and which included religious statements and references.

22. The representation of religious characters in modern fiction awaits study.

23. Tsering Döndrup has been introduced to the western public in Yangdon Dhondup, "Writers at the Cross-roads," 225–40.

24. I shall demonstrate below that his criticism is not as systematic as one might think at first glance.

25. A *drong* (*'brong*) is a wild yak. *Alak* and *tsang* are appellations used in the Amdo Tibetan dialect to show respect for a lama; they are equivalent to the term *rinpoché*, literally "precious," used for the same purpose in central Tibet and the diaspora.

26. Tshe ring don grub, interview by author, Sog po (Qinghai), August 2002. The intellectual and writer Dorjé Tsering (also known as Jangbu) confirmed during a casual conversation that because the genre of realist fiction was young and almost unheard of in Tibet until the early 1980s, some readers in the early years actually sought out in real life the fictional characters and places described in stories (interview by author, Paris, May 2004).

27. Tsering Döndrup, "Gzhon nu'i rang sgra dbyar gyi rnga gsang" (Sound of a young man: The secret drumming of summer), *Tshe ring don grub kyi sgrung thung bdams bsgrigs* (Selected short stories by Tsering Döndrup) (Xining: Mtsho sngon mi rigs

dpe skrun khang, 1996), 1–19. This story was originally published in Tibetan in 1983. A Chinese translation was published in the following year in *Minzu wenxue* (Nationalities literature). Between 1984 and 1985 it was awarded at least three literary prizes in three provinces or regions: the *Bod kyi rtsom rig sgyu rtsal* (Tibet literature and art) prize for works published in the magazine of the same name in 1982 and 1983; an award granted to commemorate the anniversary of the foundation of Qinghai Province in 1984; and a prize in Chengdu (Sichuan Province) awarded in 1985 to a number of Tibetan-medium literary works published between 1976 and 1983 in the four provinces (Qinghai, Gansu, Sichuan, Yunnan) and the TAR. The acclaim of this short story shows how anticlerical works were officially supported at the time.

28. The Jokhang is the the most sacred Buddhist temple in all of Tibet.

29. Not incidentally, Tsering resorts to political and scientific arguments to counter his parents, driven by religious faith: first, he claims that only the CCP and the masses have raised him, not the gods nor the lamas; and second, he reminds his parents that the doctor has asked the father to get some rest. This dispute synthetically sums up the thread of tradition versus modernity that runs through the story.

30. Tsering Shakya, whom I wish to thank for his insightful comments on this article, wrote to me that "many stories about families wasting money on religious offerings . . . in the 1980s were deliberately selected as a means to counter the growing strength of religion in Tibet" (e-mail to author, 26 November 2004).

31. Tshe ring don grub, "Rtse chus khrel dgod byed bzhin."

32. See note 25, above.

33. Tshe ring don grub, "Lha ba 'dre ston."

34. *A mes Dpal ldan dang 'dra ba'i gzugs med kyi dra ba las ma grol ba'i mi rnams.* Tshe ring don grub, "An Oracle Showing the Devil," 22.

35. Bkras sgron, "A shel Bde chen mtsho mo."

36. Lhag pa phun tshogs, "Bud med rtsom pa po zhig gi snying dbus kyi 'bod sgra."

37. Reb gong Rdo rje mkhar, "Ca ne."

38. Don grub rgyal, "Sprul sku." In an article taking this novella as a starting point, Matthew Kapstein has shown that the expression of doubt or criticism of the *trülku* (reincarnation) establishment within Tibet was not unknown before 1950. See Kapstein, "The Tulku's Miserable Lot."

39. Tsering Shakya, "The Waterfall and Fragrant Flowers," 39.

40. Name of interviewee, date, and place of meeting withheld.

41. Hartley, "'Inventing Modernity' in Amdo," 13.

42. Ibid., 10.

43. Zhogs dung, "Rmongs skran 'joms pa'i gtar kha: bag chags rnying rul la rgol ba'i gtam" (Blood-letting that will overcome the tumor of ignorance), *Mtsho sngon Bod yig gsar 'gyur* (Qinghai Tibetan news), 2 May 1999, 3–4; quoted in Hartley, "'Inventing Modernity' in Amdo," 19–20. Note that in Xinjiang, another "problematic" autonomous region of China, the most radical intellectual fringe of the population is generally hostile to Islam, which is condemned as an instrument of social regression: "the majority of intellectuals are anti-Islamic and believe that science

and western education are the means by which to bring progress to the Uyghurs. Several Uyghurs believe that the resurgence of Islam among the Uyghurs peasants would place them in a position analogous to that of the American Indians. 'What are we to do?' one Uyghur political official asked, 'retreat into our culture so that Hans can come watch us like animals in a zoo? No! We must compete with the Chinese on their terms.'" See Rudelson, *Oasis Identities*, 144.

44. Hartley, "'Inventing Modernity' in Amdo," 10.

45. Although Hartley's study focused mainly on the Amdo region, her analysis is relevant because the majority of today's fiction writers are from there.

46. Hartley, "'Inventing Modernity' in Amdo," 10.

47. Nāgas are beings said to live underground and in rivers. Tibetans take great pains not to disturb them, for fear of punishment (in the form of skin diseases, etc.).

48. Tertön (treasure discoverers) do not seem to have been targeted by Tibetan authors, to the best of my knowledge. Interestingly, the thirteenth chapter of the famous and traditional Amdo folktale cycle *Mi ro rtse sgrung* (Corpse stories), entitled "Mo ston phag mo" (The soothsayer with a pig head), ends with this reflection: "The saying that goes: 'oracles, soothsayers and magicians are the three fibbers [Tib. *rdzun rkyal*, "bags of lies"] in this world' is true indeed!" (*Lha ba / mo pa / sgyu ma gsum / 'jig rten khams na rdzun rkyal gsum zer ba ci mi bden*). See *Mi ro rtse sgrung*, 118. For a French translation with original Tibetan text see *Les Contes facétieux du cadavre*, trans. Françoise Robin in collab. with Klu rgyal tshe ring (Paris: Langues et Monde—L'Asiathèque, 2005). I have heard this saying in Amdo from a number of informants, so it can be surmised that it is a popular saying and that religious practitioners have somehow aroused suspicion among Tibetans, even in general circles. At the same time, it could also be that the saying gained popularity since the publication of this immensely popular edition. Note that the saying does not appear in the closely resembling episode belonging to the famous *Ro sgrung* anthology, *Mo ston pa dbu gtsug phag mgo can gyis rgyal rgyud chad la khad pa'i srog bslus nas srin po bza' mi btul ba* (The soothsayer with a pig face on its head saves a dynasty on the brink of extinction and tames a couple of demons), *Ro sgrung* (Lhasa: Bod ljongs mi dmangs dpe skrun khang, 2000), 154–67, nor in the version published in India in 1968 (Lama K. S. Tulku, ed., *The Tibetan an* [sic] *Professor Tales* (n.p., 1968), 41–57). This discrepancy could have arisen because *Mi ro rtse sgrung* was published in the 1960s, when religion was already under severe attack in Tibetan areas and China in general. This statement against popular religion might have been added by the editor, so as to make publication of this traditional folktale easier. On that subject see Robin, "Les Jeux de la sapience et de la censure."

49. A smyon Bkra shis don grub, "'Dris yun ring na re khengs mang." Anyön Trashi Döndrup (the first part of his name means "the crazy man from Amdo") was born in Khri kha (Ch. Guide) in Qinghai Province in 1967. He entered the Tibetan section of the Northwest Nationalities Institute (Tib. Nub byang mi rigs slob grwa chen mo, Ch. Xibei Minzu Xueyuan) in Lanzhou, Gansu Province, in 1986 and graduated in 1990. Since then he has been working for the literary magazine *Light Rain* while regularly publishing short stories.

50. This is not explicitly stated in the short story, but the reader understands that he was made to disrobe (possibly in 1958 or during the Cultural Revolution), since he is still a bachelor and wears red garments.

51. Tsering Yangkyi teaches Tibetan language and literature in a high school in Lhasa. She has published a number of articles focusing on education in specialized journals in the TAR and Qinghai, and a number of short stories. She is married to Trashi Penden (b. 1962), a celebrated author from Zhikatsé (Ch. Rigaze) who has long worked for *Bod ljongs nyin re'i tshags par* (Tibet daily) in Lhasa. Trashi Penden published the longest Tibetan novel, *Phal pa'i khyim tshang gi skyid sdug* (Joys and sorrows of an ordinary family), in 1991.

52. That two female authors are introduced in this article is misleading: there is a paucity of Tibetan-medium female fiction writers today.

53. Tshe ring g.yang skyid, "So nam shor ba'i ljang bu." This short story received an important literary award, the Light Rain Prize, in 2001.

54. Rang sgra, "Gangs 'dabs kyi gtam rgyud."

55. He was born in 1964, in Kawasumdo (Tib. Ka ba sum mdo, Ch. Tongde) in today's Qinghai Province; his real name is Tsegyel (Tshe rgyal). Engaged in writing literature (short stories, poetry, prose, essays) since 1985, he has been working for the literary and cultural magazine *Mang tshogs sgyu rtsal* (Art of the masses) since 1991. In 1999 he published a historical biographical novel, *Thon mi Sambhota* (on which see Robin, "Stories and History").

56. *Spyir Las dbang sde ba'i skyes pho mo rnams las rgyu 'bras brtsis zhing / byams snying rje che ba sha stag yin na'ang / nyin der kho tsho ngo ma 'dres bzung ba dang mtshungs par Las dbang sgrol ma'i lus steng la rdo dang dbyug pa / spo tho sogs char ba 'bab 'bab byas.* Rang sgra, "Gangs 'dabs kyi gtam rgyud," 64.

57. Tshe ring don grub, *Mes po.*

58. www.tibetinfo.net/news-updates/nu260700.htm (emphasis added). Although this white paper deals mainly with the TAR, we can extend its position to all Tibetan-populated areas.

59. Excerpt from an article entitled "A Few Policy Demarcation Lines That Need to Be Strictly Grasped to Correctly Deal with the Religious Issue," published in *Xizang ribao* (Tibet daily), Chinese edition, 27 February 1995, as reported by "Summary of World Broadcast" (BBC), 15 March 1995.

60. www.tibetinfo.net/news-updates/nu220199.htm.

61. Rang sgra, "'Dre rkang to."

62. Rang sgra, "'Pho 'gyur."

63. *De ring lha 'bab rgyu ma byung tshe / lha pa'i lo phyi nang gsum gyi lha skal (lha pa'i yon du lo rer khyim tshang re nas 'bru rigs bre gang re 'bul dgos pa de la zer) chod" ces mngon bsgrags byas tshe / dang po lha pa had se btang na yang / cung zad nas lha pa'i mgrin pa las khag khag gi sgra zhig grags / Mgo bo da ru ltar g.yugs / Lus po sig sig tu 'dar bzhin gnam lding sa lding byed pa la bltas na / da lta lha pa dngos su lhas bzung yod pa rtogs thub.* Rang sgra, "'Pho 'gyur," 376–77. Note the use of parentheses by the author to explain to the readers what is meant by the term *lha skal* ("oracle's lot").

64. Quoted in www.tibet.ca/en/wtnarchive/1995/1/7_1.html.

65. Quoted in www.tibet.ca/en/wtnarchive/1996/12/5_5.html (emphasis added). In a speech delivered in 1998, Ragdi (then deputy secretary of the TAR party committee) illustrated this position by quoting the following anecdote: "In one village in Linzhou [Tib. Lhundup] county in 1997, a peasant asked a lama to perform a divination before the wheat harvest. The lama said that the harvest could not start, which had an adverse effect on the farming season by leaving the wheat subject to a disastrous hailstorm. Such religious interference, causing production losses that *affect the dissemination of new technology*, is quite common throughout Tibet. Emancipating the masses from such superstition, to firmly stop and root out such sorcery, is a principle that we Party members and officials need to pursue" (emphasis added). Speech printed in the *Tibet Daily*, 24 November 1998; see www.tibetinfo .net/news-updates/nu220199.htm.

66. Schwartz, *Circle of Protest*, 226.

67. Ibid., 226. In 1993 a fifty-eight-year-old Tibetan female oracle was arrested for uttering overt anti-Chinese slogans when in a trance, and sentenced to eight years of reform through labor (www.tibet.ca/en/wtnarchive/1994/5/31_2.html). In 1996, summing up the CCP's opinion, the TAR party secretary Chen Kuiyuan (1992–2000) "warned that superstitious beliefs had made a recent comeback in the region because the Dalai Lama had used religion to drug the people." Quotation from *Tibet Daily*, 12 November 1996, according to Reuters news dispatch, "China Vows to Fight Hostile Foreign Forces in Tibet," Beijing, 21 November 1996.

68. The author of this short story is called Lhundrup. It seems it was published in 1985 in the literary magazine *Bod kyi rtsom rig sgyu rtsal*. As I have not been able to obtain a copy, I am relying on Adrian Moon's summary in "Modern Tibetan Fiction," part 2, 8.

69. Ania Loomba, *Colonialism/Postcolonialism* (London: Routledge, 2002), 256.

70. Ibid., 231.

71. Dirks, *Colonialism and Culture*, 8.

72. K. N. Panikkar, "Creating a New Cultural Taste: Reading a Nineteenth-Century Malayalam Novel," *Tradition, Dissent and Ideology: Essays in Honour of Romila Thapar*, ed. R. Champakalakshmi and S. Gopal (Delhi: Oxford University Press, 1996), 95.

73. See www.tibetinfo.net/news-updates/nu260700.htm.

74. Dirks, *Colonialism and Culture*, 7.

75. Panikkar, "Creating a New Cultural Taste," 104.

76. Stoddard, *Le Mendiant de l'Amdo*, 181–82.

77. Ibid., 182.

78. Bkra bha, "Re smon." Trabha was born in 1963 into a peasant's family near Chapcha (Ch.: Gonghe) in Qinghai and entered school at the late age of thirteen. There he met Anyön Trashi Döndrup (see note 49, above). After graduation in 1986 he worked as a journalist for the Qinghai People's Radio until 1998, when he joined the Qinghai Nationality Institute for a three-year training course. He graduated in 2001 and has been working at the Central Nationality Institute (Beijing) since then. He has been writing and translating texts since 1986 and has published more than

one hundred pieces of literature, as well as a middle-length novel, *Srin po G.yu rngog dang Nyi ma Lha sa* (The turquoise-maned demon and Sunshine Lhasa).

79. Pema Tseten was born in 1968 in Trika (Tib. Khri ka, Ch. Guide) and graduated from the Northwest Nationalities Institute. He has been writing in both Tibetan and Chinese since 1991. Having graduated from the Beijing School of Cinema in 2004, he is the director of *Rtswa thang* (Grassland), the first-ever feature film entirely directed and acted by Tibetans in China. In 2007 his film *Silent Stones* was shown in New York City. For a discussion of the film see Robin, "Silent Stones as Minority Discourse."

80. The Tibetan term *tshe thar* (lit. "liberation of life") refers to a popular ritual that consists of buying an animal, especially one destined to be killed (e.g. cattle, fish), to rescue it. Merit gained by this rescue can be dedicated for the sake of a sick person, for instance.

81. Hartley, "Themes of Tradition and Change in Modern Tibetan Literature," 40.

82. Ibid.

83. Chatterjee, *The Nation and Its Fragments*, 6.

84. Ibid., 55.

85. Roasted barley flour, the Tibetan staple food.

86. *Thu ba thog ma des rtsam pa zos rjes dkar yol 'byid byed dang | thu ba 'og ma des skyag pa btang rjes bshang lam 'byid byed red.* Tshe ring don grub, "Gzhon nu'i rang sgra dbyar gyi rnga gsang," 11–12.

87. The western reader does not know whether the comical effect of quoting this school regulation is deliberate.

88. Tib. *Kho'i sems la Bod rigs ang | Bod rigs | Rtswa thang ang | Rtswa thang | Khyed ga dus sngon thon mi rigs kyi gras su tshud dam snyam.* Tshe ring don grub, "Gzhon nu'i rang sgra dbyar gyi rnga gsang," 12.

89. Harrell, *Cultural Encounters on China's Ethnic Frontiers*, 6.

90. Bkra bha, "Sha yu mo she'u." While the title of this short story literally means "fawn," it refers to the lyrics of a popular song in Amdo. Whenever the protagonist is asked a question that resembles lyrics in the song (such as "Where are you going?"), the questioner adds as a nonsensical joke: "*sha yu mo she'u.*" We can imagine that these last syllables are sung.

91. Tib. *Bod pa 'di tsho mi rigs rjes lus shig yin rung | mo 'gugs kyi thabs sna tshogs thad nas ha cang sngon thon red.* Bkra bha, "Sha yu mo she'u," 31.

92. The link between minority nationalities' backwardness and eroticism has been exemplified and analyzed in the Chinese context in Gladney, "Representing Nationality in China," 92–123. More generally, the articulation between primitive culture and loose sexual behavior is a colonial cliché that needs no further comment here.

93. Tib. *Nga'ang khyod tsho ltar Bod mi zhig yin na ci ma rung.* Pad ma tshe brtan, "Rtse thang la 'gro."

94. Tib. *Khyod tsho Bod ni ngo ma sgyu rtsal la mkhas pa'i mi rigs shig red | Nga khyod tsho Bod la dga'.* Pad ma tshe brtan, "Let's go to Tsetang," 10. I have found a number of striking similarities between Pema Tseten's sympathetic view of "traditional" Tibetan

culture and the overall tone of 'Jigs med 'phel rgyas, "Nu bo sprul skur ngos bzung rjes" (After my younger brother was recognized as a reincarnate lama), Sbrang char, 1996, no. 4, 3–49, which was translated from the original Chinese. In this novella trülku-hood is never criticized, mainland and Hong Kong Chinese characters worship unquestioningly the new incarnate lama, and one Chinese character is even made to tell the Tibetan protagonist: "What's wrong with becoming Tibetan? I like Tibetans" (Tib. Bod mir gyur na mi legs pa ci zhig yod / Nga rang Bod mir dga' ba yin). See 'Jigs med 'phel rgyas, "Nu bo sprul skur ngos bzung rjes," 29. It may be no coincidence that both authors live in Beijing, write in Chinese (Pema Tseten writes in both Tibetan and Chinese, but Jikmé Pelgyé seems to write only in Chinese), and usually address a Chinese-educated and sympathetic readership, be it Han Chinese or Tibetan.

These sympathetic writings by authors expressing themselves in Chinese largely contrast with works written by Tibetans in Tibetan which are more critical toward religious figures, such as in Khedrup (Mkhas grub), "Btsun ma Bstan 'dzin chos sgrol" (The venerable nun Tendzin Chödröl), Bod kyi rtsom rig sgyu rtsal, 1997, no. 3, 95–105. I wish to thank Pema Bhum of the Latse Contemporary Tibetan Cultural Library in New York for having kindly provided me with a copy of this work. The author, himself a trülku, was born in the Lhokha (Ch. Shannan) area of the TAR in 1957 and has published a number of poetic works which have been awarded numerous literary prizes. In "The Venerable Nun," Khedrup shows how a girl, who drops out of school after it is discovered that she had an affair with a classmate, enters the local nunnery. Soon disillusioned with the lack of discipline, frivolity, and self-interestedness of her fellow nuns, she forsakes the nunnery altogether to return to her former lover and bears a child. Khedrup's story points to flaws in religious life and behavior, without noting that some monasteries and nunneries have become empty shells because of political constraints, especially in the TAR. The critical tone might also be due to the greater scrutiny to which fiction works published in the TAR are subject compared to other Tibetan-populated regions.

95. See Robin, "Stories and History."

96. See for instance what happened in India when fiction writers grasped the subject of the plight of Indian woman and the custom of sati. "What was at stake was not women but tradition," Lata Mani writes in her article "Contentious Traditions," 115.

97. Dirks, Colonialism and Culture, 10.

PART TWO

Negotiating Modernities

8

One Nation, Two Discourses:

Tibetan New Era Literature and

the Language Debate

LARA MACONI

> *Yo quiero mar y montaña hablando mi propia lengua*
> *Y a nadie pedir permiso pa' construir la patria nueva*
> —Cueca de la Confederación Unida de los Trabajadores, Chile

Tibetans writing literature under Chinese rule since the 1950s have faced a new phenomenon: the widespread composition of belles-lettres in Chinese by Tibetan-national Sinophone writers.[1] The development has spurred Tibetan intellectuals in various milieux, especially since the 1980s, to question the very nature and categorization of this brand of literature. Markedly disparate views have made it difficult to agree on a definition of "Tibetan literature."

In this chapter I draw on interviews with Tibetan writers and publishers in the People's Republic of China (PRC), as well as critical articles and literary works, to explore the historical contours of Tibet's diglossia and its significance for Tibetan writers. First, I outline the social and cultural context of what I call the "language debate" in contemporary Tibetan-national literature. Second, I identify the main linguistic issues of debate in Tibetan literary circles and the discursive positions of different generational cohorts—at official and unofficial levels—with respect to their literary views and their language of literary expression (Tibetan or Chinese). Third, I argue that the literary language debate in Tibet, far from being the speculative activity of formalist or essentialist intellectuals, expresses concrete concerns with tangible implications for every aspect of Tibetan literary life—in the practices of creating, publishing, and reading literature. Today Tibet is a diglossic society where the "other" language (Chinese) reigns as the official means of communication, and the negotiation of linguistic idiom is never a neutral matter.

A nation is a soul or spiritual principle. These are but two aspects of the same thing. One is in the past, the other in the present. One is the common possession of a rich legacy of memories; the other is the present consent, the desire to live together, the wish to continue to assert the undivided heritage that has been handed down. A nation is therefore a huge solidarity, constituted by the feeling of sacrifices that have been made, and which will continue to be made. It supposes a past, but it nevertheless comes down to the present in a tangible fact: the consent, the clearly expressed desire to continue living together.[2]

In "Tibetan Publications and National Identity," Heather Stoddard first adopted this definition of a nation by Ernest Renan to observe, "Tibet stands at the present time as a nation . . . It is a divided nation."[3] Nevertheless, many Tibetans share the perception of a common heritage, a sense of group belonging, and a repertoire of symbols of this belonging. Together with kinship patterns, religious and social affiliations, and cultural values and practices, the Tibetan language stands among those symbolic elements whose practical utility has been seriously undermined by the recent Tibetan-Chinese confrontation. In the early 1950s Chinese was adopted as the official language in all Tibetan areas of the PRC, but the Chinese government took a gradualist approach with regard to educational development in Tibet and support of bilingual Sino-Tibetan education. This softer policy was halted with the implementation of democratic reform (Ch. *minzhu gaige*) in 1959 after the Lhasa uprising and the flight of the Dalai Lama to India. Mao's "red" and "egalitarian" educational strategy was then implemented in Tibet; Tibetan culture and language were considered unpatriotic and élitist, and Tibetan was relegated to a secondary language in both policy and practice.[4] Besides the introduction of Mao's revolutionary policies, a host of diverse and complex factors account for this linguistic shift in Tibet. In the 1950s many illiterate Tibetan youngsters recruited into the People's Liberation Army (PLA) were fed, dressed, and "educated" in Chinese (free of charge). And for many years of the Cultural Revolution (1966–76), Tibetan was officially forbidden. Under liberalization policies since the early 1980s, Tibetans educated in Chinese have had a better chance of gaining a higher education and a more rewarding professional career. Learning Chinese generally increases one's wealth and status, one's access to Chinese publications and media, and the possibilities for communicating with greater China, as well as other countries. Tibetan access to the modern world, in terms of economic, social, intellectual, and educational development, has been organized in such a way that the filter of the Chinese apparatus is perceived as unavoidable by Tibetans living in the PRC. The privileging of the Chinese language for securing an education, a job, and information, as well as for accomplishing the simplest of social or administrative tasks, has been used as a not-so-subtle means of persuasion to meld two potentially distinct concepts: a modernized Tibet and a Sinicized Tibet.

In *The Post-Colonial Studies Reader*, Ashcroft, Griffiths, and Tiffin argue, "Language is a fundamental site of tension for discourses on political and cultural domination because the domination process itself begins in language."[5] For the Chinese central government, the promotion and development of socialism and a socialist consciousness in Tibet have above all been a question of language; that is, a question of both communicating through a shared language and controlling the use of language(s). The issue of how to modernize the "old-fashioned" Tibetan language and adapt it to the "new" and "progressive" socialist context was soon raised in the 1950s as a critical requisite for furthering propaganda objectives. A new lexicon was introduced to accommodate socialist ideology and promote a new and modern Tibet in Tibetan and Maoist terms.[6] A new grammar and literary style that more closely reflected colloquial Tibetan, as well as a simplified orthographic system, were created.[7] Translating a great quantity of propaganda documents and pamphlets into Tibetan and teaching Tibetan to the first Chinese officials sent on mission to Tibet are but some of the practices that China adopted in the early 1950s to enable politically oriented "communication" with Tibetans. Nevertheless, history has shown that this early policy of preserving and developing the national language in Tibet was the starting point for the large-scale implementation of an assimilationist policy in the economic, social, and cultural life of all the national minorities in the PRC. Given that the primary goal of education in the greater PRC is "to guarantee the unity and territorial integrity of China,"[8] the Chinese establishment considers education in Chinese to be paramount. As Arienne Dwyer points out, standard Chinese rests at "the pinnacle of a metalinguistic hierarchy which mirrors the vertical basis of power in China today, [and] state language policies establish official minority language under the arching umbrella of the Chinese state."[9] In this context, the control of language becomes a prerequisite for the central power, and linguistic and literary issues become sensitive political questions. In policy and practice the coexistence of the Chinese and the Tibetan languages in present-day Tibet does not presuppose an equal footing. Tibetan has an inferior sociopolitical and cultural status. Consequently, diglossia rather than bilingualism is a better term for current Tibetan linguistic practice in the PRC. The cultural shock to Tibetan society caused by the weakened status of

Tibetan is even more evident when one considers that for almost a millennium (since around the thirteenth century) Tibet was the spiritual center for several peoples of Central Asia, and the Tibetan language was a prerequisite for the scholastic education of those peoples. As A. I. Vostrikov notes: "In the course of the last three centuries, the Tibetan literary language had acquired almost the same significance among the Mongols, Oirats, Tanguts and other peoples, as Latin in medieval Europe . . . [It] was so widely spread that various Tangut, Mongol and other non-Tibetan scholars wrote even the histories of their own countries in full or in part in Tibetan."[10]

Diglossia in the Tibetan New Era Literary Arena

In both content and language, Tibetan literature has mirrored the social, cultural, and linguistic tensions experienced by Tibetan society since its recent confrontation with China and the modern world. Tibetan literary content, since the 1950s—and even more widely since the 1980s—has been nurtured by previously unheard-of philosophical and artistic movements, ranging from socialist realism and revolutionary romanticism, to free-verse poetry, stream of consciousness, and black humor, to self-centered humanism, modernism, and post-modernism. Linguistically the national Tibetan literary arena has reproduced the diglossic panorama that society has experienced in various spheres of life and culture. Though literary composition in Tibetan has never been abandoned, new generations of Tibetans have been educated in Chinese and have begun to write in it. Thus since the 1950s a Tibetophone and a Sinophone literature by Tibetans have developed in parallel. This linguistic disjunction lies at the root of a long-standing debate between the Tibetophone and Sinophone Tibetan literary worlds. From the early 1980s a public discourse on the relationship between a national language and a national literature was colored with tones of national affirmation that went beyond purely literary considerations.

The Tibetophone and Sinophone literary worlds share official organisms (central and local associations of writers, cultural bureaus, literary magazines, publishing houses for national minorities), but are separated in terms of logistics, economic support, literary practice, expectations, effective possibilities of evolution, and range of influence. The result is two parallel and linguistically distinct spheres of Tibetan literary activity, which are organized in distinct ways, receive different types of governmental economic and political support, develop different literary themes, styles, and forms, evolve according to different rhythms, and are addressed to different readerships. As suggested above, Tibetan literary life in the PRC is the expression of a diglossic reality in which Chinese is openly encouraged as the language of literacy. Tibetan writers, critics, and publishers who work in the Tibetan-language sections of cultural and educational work units (publishing houses, magazines, schools, translation bureaus) are required to be educated in Chinese even if their professional specialization concerns Tibetan projects. In no case is literacy in Tibetan considered sufficient. Chinese is necessary in official meetings, to communicate with Chinese officials, and to accomplish the many bureaucratic tasks that educated people and artists are required to undertake. Publications in Tibetan, as well as other "minority" languages, always provide bilingual (Tibetan and Chinese) bibliographic references, while Sinophone publications on Tibetology provide only Chinese references. Whereas Tibetophone literary magazines provide an additional table of contents in Chinese,[11] no Tibet-related Sinophone magazine, including *Xizang wenxue* (Literature from Tibet, f. 1977) provide a table of contents in Tibetan.

Together with their regional origins, the language that writers use in composition has been of paramount importance in the process of literary affiliation—that is, the formation of intellectual circles sharing literary affinities and experiences. Throughout central Tibet, Kham, and Amdo, Tibetan writers belong to one of two linguistically demarcated groups with distinct activities and interests. Literary communication and exchange between the two have been rare (especially since the 1990s), and common literary initiatives encouraging literary intranational exchange are generally considered neither useful nor interesting.[12] Well-known authors who write (or wrote) in Tibetan include Döndrup Gyel (1953–85), Penjor (b. 1941), Trashi Penden (b. 1962), Ju Kelzang (b. 1960), Jangbu (b. 1963), Orgyen Dorjé (b. 1961), Lhagyel Tsering (b. 1962), Tenpa Yargyé (b. 1971), Ramtsebo (b. 1970), and many others. Well-known authors who write (or wrote) in Chinese include Yidan Cairang (1933–2004), Zhaxi Dawa (b. 1959), Sebo (b. 1956), Alai (b. 1959), Weise (b. 1966), Yangzhen (b. 1963), Danzhu Angben (b. 1955), and Meizhuo (b. 1966).[13]

Literary observers in the PRC have noticed among the youngest generations of Tibetan writers a trend toward writing in Tibetan more than in Chinese. The use of Chinese in full-time literary practice appears to be primarily limited to Tibetan writers educated during the Cultural Revolution. A glance at literary publications reveals that recently the number of Tibetan Sinophone writers in the PRC has not grown significantly. This is quite evident if one compares the number of submissions to literary magazines: the editorial board of the Tibetan-language literary magazine *Sbrang char* (Light rain) estimates that since 1981 it has received approximately five thousand works by some one thousand Tibetophone authors (a good portion of whom are very young amateur writers), whereas the editors of Tibetan Sinophone magazines frequently complain of the serious lack of literary works submitted for publication.[14] Recently there has been a growing trend among the youngest generation of Tibetan writers to launch Tibetan-Chinese bilingual literary projects, and a small number of writers consistently engage in bilingual creative activity. Jiangbian Jiacuo (Tib. Jampel Gyatso, b. 1939), Tsedor (b. 1949), and Pema Tseten (b. 1968), for example, write in both Tibetan and Chinese. Teling Wangdor (b. 1934) is perhaps the only bilingual writer in the PRC who writes in both Tibetan and English. Such bilingual literary activity is still relatively rare, however, and most literary works by Tibetan nationals are written in Tibetan.

Intranational literary activities or initiatives between the Tibetophone and Sinophone spheres of Tibetan-national writers in the PRC appears to be sporadic. In Lhasa the distance between the two Tibetan language-demarcated literary worlds is more striking than in Amdo. This is partly because the few Tibetan Sinophone writers who still reside in Lhasa (e.g. Zhaxi Dawa, Da Danzeng) were raised and educated in inland China. They cannot speak Tibetan. Moreover, since the early 1990s some have lost enthusiasm for literary composition (Zhaxi Dawa) or have left Tibet (Sebo, Weise, Yangzhen). Even when their artistic energy was at its peak in the early 1980s, no Tibetophone writers took part in the activities of Lhasa Sinophone literary circles. The brilliant artistic salon (Ch. *shalong*) inspired by Ma Yuan in the early 1980s drew Chinese and to a lesser extent Tibetan Sinophone artists with diverse orientations (mainly painters and writers). An oil painting by Yu Xiaodong entitled *Ganbei Xizang* (A toast to Tibet) portrays in vivid detail the members of the Lhasa salon in the early 1980s. Not a single Tibetophone writer is presented in this visual dedication to Lhasa intellectuals.

In Amdo, on the contrary, the literary environment is more dynamic, with greater solidarity and collaboration between the Tibetophone and Sinophone literary circles of Tibetan-nationality writers. Examples of this collaboration include the publication of bilingual volumes such as *Hainan wenxue zuopin jingxuan* (The essence of Hainan literary works), a collection of works in Tibetan and Chinese written mainly, but not solely, by Tibetan authors,[15] or the bilingual collection of poems by Gönpo Trashi (b. 1938),[16] translated from Chinese into Tibetan by Repgong Dorjekhar (b. 1958), an official translator from Amdo and a prolific Tibetophone writer now living in Beijing.

The financial and intellectual solidarity manifested by one language group toward the literary initiatives of the "other" language group is also indicative of Tibetan intranational activities. This brand of solidarity is exemplified by the publication of the Yidan Cairang's *Xueyun ji* (Snow rhymes collection,

Ganbei Xizang (A Toast for Tibet, 1996), painting by Yu Xiaodong. From left Ma Lihua (writer), Wang Haiyan (numismatist), Li Zhibao (artist), Luo Hao (photographer), Li Xinjian (artist), Se Bo (writer), Feng Shaohua (calligrapher), Pi Pi (writer), Che Gang (photographer), Han Shuli (artist), He Zhong (writer), Gong Qiaoming (writer, deceased), Tian Wen (writer, deceased), Hong Liwei (military officer), Ma Yuan (writer), Yu Xiaodong (artist), Mou Sen (film director), Tashi Dawa (writer), Jin Zhiguo (writer), Liu Wei (writer), Li Yanping (artist), Pei Zhuangxin (artist), Cao Yong (artist). Reprinted with permission by the artist.

1996);[17] this collection of poems in Chinese, which was released as an edition for restricted readership (Ch. *neibu*), was logistically and financially supported by the Tibetophone literary magazine *Zla zer* (Moonshine), based in Hezuo, Gansu Province. The critical participation of one language group in the literary activities of the "other" language group (by writing introductions to the "other" language group's publications, for instance) is also an important expression of Tibetan intranational literary practices. Yidan Cairang, for example, wrote the introduction to *Skya rengs lha mo'i 'bod brda'* (Call of the Goddess of Dawn),[18] a collection of poems in Tibetan by Lhagyel Tsering. These few examples illustrate that a certain degree of reciprocal literary interest animates the two Tibetan linguistically demarcated literary worlds in Amdo. In Kham, Tibetan-language writers do not constitute a significant group in terms of size or influence. Contemporary literature in Kham is better represented by the so-called "Khampa" Sinophone literature, as heard through the voices of well-known authors like Alai, Jiangbian Jiacuo, Liemei Pingcuo, and Zhangge Nima.[19]

TIBETAN EDITORIAL WORLDS

The official (that is, state-implemented, state-supported, and state-controlled) editorial world in all the main Tibetan areas in the PRC (and in China as a whole) is structured according to the two-language pattern. In Lhasa, for example, the Sinophone literary magazine *Literature from Tibet* and the Tibetophone literary magazine *Bod kyi rtsom rig sgyu rtsal* (Tibetan art and literature, f. 1980) function as two editorial poles for the same organization: the Association of Writers of the Tibet Autonomous Region (TAR). Equally, in the Labrang district of Amdo, the Sinophone magazine *Gesang hua* (Flower of the good era) and the Tibetophone magazine *Moon Shine* are the two literary magazines published by the Cultural Bureau (Ch. *wenhua ju*) in Hezuo, seat of the Gannan Tibetan Autonomous Prefecture in Gansu Province. The Chinese editorial pole is meant to guarantee the existence and "correct" functioning of the magazine.

Until recently Tibetophone magazines without a Sinophone counterpart were rare;[20] those that did exist were usually nongovernmental and based in small Tibetan areas. With an increasing number of privately funded magazines, their numbers have increased since the late 1990s in areas where the readership is mostly literate in Tibetan, and it is easier for local people to organize cultural projects with locally based agreements and support. This is the case, for instance, with *Chos bzang dga' tshal* (The paradise of good dharma), a magazine featuring both traditional and modern Tibetan literature and edited by Taktsa Monastery in Dzögé, Sichuan Province. In exceptional cases

Tibetophone operations stand alone in larger towns and are supported by the government. For example, in the Kokonor area of Amdo, where Tibetan language magazines are widely spread among the Tibetan population, no Tibetan-national Sinophone literary magazine significantly competes with the Tibetophone magazine *Light Rain* (f. 1981). The Tibetophone magazine *Mtsho sngon mang tshogs sgyu rtsal* (Art and literature of the Qinghai masses), which is also based in Xining but published by the Qinghai Cultural Bureau (Ch. Qinghai wenhua ju), lost its complementary pole when the Chinese magazine of the same name (*Qinghai qunzhong wenyi*) was shut down for publishing "pornographic" material in 1989. Similarly, *Shannan wenyi* (Lhokha art and literature)—the Sinophone magazine of the local Association of Writers in the Lhokha region of the TAR—was short-lived after the release of its first few issues in the 1980s; it was shut down for lack of readership. Its Tibetophone counterpart, *Lho kha'i rtsom rig sgyu rtsal*, however, continues to be regularly edited by Orgyen Dorjé, one of the most widely appreciated contemporary poets in all of Tibet. In Kham no Tibetan language magazine significantly competes with *Gongga shan* (Gangkar mountain), a Chinese-language magazine edited in Kangding. Its Tibetophone counterpart, *Gangs dkar ri bo*, is published irregularly and for domestic use (*neibu*).

Following this same structure but multilingually, the publishing houses of all national minorities within the PRC include a Sinophone editorial section together with others for diverse minority languages. A brief look at their editorial activity shows that this coexistence is not really balanced, and publications in Chinese are usually more numerous. The China Tibetology Research Center in Beijing publishes in Tibetan, Chinese, and English. Its *Catalogue of Chinese Publications in Tibetan Studies (1949–1991)*[21] lists 1,497 Tibetological publications edited by two hundred publishing houses in the PRC: 813 in Chinese, 663 in Tibetan, and 21 in English. The center's catalogue for the years 1992–95 lists 716 Tibetological publications: 411 in Chinese, 297 in Tibetan, and 8 in English;[22] the same catalogue for the years 1996–2000 lists 956 publications: 520 in Chinese, 429 in Tibetan, and 7 in English.[23]

TRANSLATION

Intranational translation (the practice of translating literary works by Tibetan writers from Tibetan into Chinese and from Chinese into Tibetan) provides another measure of literary exchange between the two literary worlds. Translations from Chinese into Tibetan are far more numerous than those from Tibetan into Chinese.[24] Certain editorial policies of *Light Rain* regarding translations are quite telling in terms of how the relationship between language, literature, and nationality is negotiated in the prevailing cultural and political context. For Tibetan translation of works by Tibetan-national Sinophone writers, the Sinophone nature of the original work is not mentioned, nor is the identity of the translator. It is thus impossible for a nonacquainted reader to determine if a literary work by a Tibetan writer published in *Light Rain* is a translation from Chinese or an original Tibetophone work. The magazine employs this practice only for Tibetan-national writers, while detailed references (the nationality of the writer and identity of the translator) are provided when the author of a translated work is of non-Tibetan nationality. In summary, the practice of intranational Tibetan translation in the PRC is not developed well enough to assure thorough communication between the Tibetophone and Sinophone spheres, which together constitute the Tibetan-national literary world of the PRC.

Tibetophone writers in the PRC, thanks to their "necessary" bilingualism, can and do read in Chinese. Chinese literature thus offers models of modern and avant-garde writing for Tibetan authors seeking new literary horizons, but Sinophone readers have little access to works in Tibetan, aside from translated religious texts. Translations into Chinese are very few, and Tibetan Sinophone literature receives much more official support, as illustrated in the recent acclaim of Alai's novel *Chen'ai luoding* (The dust settles),[25] which is discussed in detail by Howard Choy in chapter 10. Even when Chinese translations of Tibetophone literature are available, they are mainly read by a Sinophone readership of Tibetan nationality, which is more directly concerned with intranational Tibetan literary questions. The vast majority of Sinophone readers in the PRC are unaware of the very existence of a modern Tibetophone literature. There is no evidence that modern Tibetan-language literary works (either in the original or in translation) have had any consistent influence on the Chinese or Tibetan Sinophone literary world. By contrast, some Tibetan Sinophone writers, such as Zhaxi Dawa and more recently Alai and Weise, have managed to acquire a prominent and influential place in the all-China literary world.

A few Tibetan-national bilingual writers in the PRC consistently translate their own works. As the majority of these writers usually write in Tibetan, and less frequently in Chinese, the orientation of their self-made translations is more often from Tibetan into Chinese. Pema Tseten (Ch. Wanma Caidan, b. 1968) from Hainan Prefecture in Qinghai Province, is one example. His short stories in Tibetan and Chinese have been published in diverse magazines without mention of whether they are original compositions or self-made translations. These magazines do not indicate whether the Chinese versions of Pema Tseten's works are in fact direct translations. Only by comparing publication dates does one notice that the Tibetan version is earlier. Pema Tseten has translated at least ten of his own short stories.

The well-known poet Jangbu has also translated some of his own works into Chinese, such as the short story "Wu" (Lacuna) and the poems "Kha bar nyan pa" (Listening to the snow; Ch. Ting xue de fangshi), and "Rkang gling 'bsud mkhan" (The flutist; Ch. Gudishou). When publishing his Chinese translations Jangbu purposely obscures the identity of the author and translator. Playing with the Chinese transliteration of his Tibetan given name (Dorjé Tsering, Ch. Duoji Cailang) and his two pen names (Jangbu, Ch. Jiangpu, or "sprout"; and Seru, Ch. Siru, or "rhinoceros"), Jangbu variously names the author and translator of his texts according to his personal inspiration. In so doing he emphasizes the translated nature of his Chinese texts without revealing the link between the writer and the translator.

Other Tibetan bilingual writers write variably in Tibetan and Chinese, such as Tsedor, an assistant editor at the Tibetophone literary magazine *Tibetan Art and Literature* who is also a writer, translator, and critic. For Tsedor the choice of language at the moment of composition is no arbitrary practice. His policy regarding linguistic choice consists in first considering the readership(s) to whom he addresses his work, the language of their literacy, and their specific sensibility and understanding of the subject; consequently, he never translates himself. In Tsedor's words, "translating is creating."[26] Even when treating the same subject, but in two languages, the writer has to enter a spirit of creation. In the Tibetan version of his essay "Lhasa's Barkor" (Tib. Lha sa'i bar skor), the author seeks to retrace the atmosphere of the Barkor in more intimate terms, as if speaking to people familiar with the place, its history or histories, its cultural value, and its current role in everyday life. The aim is to establish a sympathetic dialogue with the reader. The Chinese version (Ch. Lasa de bajiao jie) is conceived to address people less familiar, or quite unfamiliar, with the place. The narrative is more descriptive of local customs and terms, the tone more explanatory.

Writing in two languages as a means of explaining to the "other" one's cultural distinctiveness was first employed by a few Tibetan writers in the early 1980s. Jiangbian Jiacuo (author of the first novel by a Tibetan in Communist China), for example, initially published a Chinese version of *Gesang Meiduo* (Kelzang Metok) in 1980, and then edited a Tibetan version of the same novel (Tib. *Skal bzang me tog*) in 1981. The only example of Tibetan-English literary bilingualism in the PRC is the recent publication of a novel by Téling Wangdor, a Lhasa nobleman educated in a Jesuit school in India from 1946 to 1953. After the publication in Tibetan of his novel *Bkras zur tshang gi gsang ba'i gtam rgyud* (1997), he undertook his own English translation of the novel *The Secret Tale of Tesur House* (1998).[27] Employing the same strategy as his colleague and friend Tsedor, Téling Wangdor revised certain parts that might puzzle an English reader less familiar with Tibetan history and customs. Translingual and transliterary practices like these point to the difficult position of the Tibetan contemporary intellectual who tries to find his place in a society where diglossia and cultural marginalization are a reality.

LITERARY CRITICISM

Young Tibetan writers (both Tibetophone and Sinophone) often denounce a lack of perceptive criticism concerning their literary production, and a lack of insight into the true Tibetan nature of their work. The few critics literate in Tibetan whom I met bemoan the absence of a tradition of literary criticism in Tibetan, and the difficulty in obtaining an adequate specialized education in the field (that is, an education capable of providing new formulations, categories, and terminology for the modern aspirations of Tibetan contemporary literature). Criticism relating to Tibetan literature in the PRC shows three main trends: when Tibetan writers in the PRC write critical articles on literature, these are mostly about works written by Tibetan-national authors; articles on Tibetan-language literature are mostly written by Tibetan-national critics; and Tibetan critics educated in the Tibetan language prefer to write about Tibetan-national Tibetophone literature rather than Sinophone literature. One of the few exceptions to these recurrent practices is a collection of critical articles entitled *Gezhe wuhui* (The singer does not regret)[28] by the Amdowan bilingual critic Dekyitso (Ch. Dejicuo). This book, though written in Chinese, concerns mainly Tibetophone writers. Of the fifteen articles in her volume, twelve are concerned with Tibetophone writers, two with Tibetan Sinophone writers, and one with a bilingual writer.[29] Conversely, Zhaxi Dongzhu's critical essay on Tibetan contemporary fiction, "Dangdai zangzu xiaoshuo sikao" (Reflections on contemporary Tibetan fiction),[30] awarded the China National Minorities Literary Prize for "débutant works and writers, critics section" in 1990, approaches the subject of Tibetan contemporary prose by taking into account only Sinophone writers. This kind of approach, which ignores works written in Tibetan, is quite widespread in the PRC. Zhaxi Dongzhu's position mirrors both the government's understanding of the Tibetan contemporary literary world and the perception that China's inland critics often have of a "minority" literature. Zhaxi Dongzhu's essay has been highly criticized by the Tibetan young intelligentsia.

The attention paid by inland Chinese literary critics to Tibetan literature is extremely limited. and the few Chinese Tibetologists educated in Tibetan are more interested in traditional, ancient, classical, and folk aspects of Tibetan culture than in modern literature. One exception is Geng Yufang,[31] author of various essays and books on modern Tibetan literature. His book *Zangzu dangdai wenxue* (Tibetan contemporary literature),[32] is possibly the first study in Chinese of both Tibetophone and Sinophone Tibetan writers, albeit with a Marxist conception of Tibetan history. Ma Lihua's book *Xueyu wenhua yu Xizang wenxue* (Snow Land culture and Tibetan literature)[33] is another rare example in that the author explicitly admits her linguistic incompetence in Tibetan and defines at the outset the limits of her investigation. One should also note that the Chinese critics who were educated in Tibetan in the early 1950s are mainly persons who have some long-term experience of Tibet. They are the so-called *lao Xizang*, or veterans of Tibet. For example, Gao Ping, Li Jiajun, and Geng Yufang (all involved in literary activities) arrived in Tibet in the 1950s and 1960s, and lived on the Tibetan plateau for more than twenty years. Their interest in Tibetan literature is nurtured by a manifold nostalgia of Tibet with sentimentalist, exotic, and heroic tones. Their essays express both a pride of living in contact with a native culture still rich in genuine qualities and human sensibilities (a kind of myth of the noble savage) and a sense of being charged with a "civilizing" mission in Tibet in the name of socialist ideals, justice, and modernity. Their approach is often permeated with the expectation that Tibetan literature is the "characteristic" (Ch. *you tese de*) representation of a frontier or marginal people.

In light of the diglossia defining Tibetan literary life in the PRC and the lack of translingual activity, the discussion of language is never a neutral matter for the Tibetan writer. The writer develops a linguistic hyperconsciousness, and writing itself becomes primarily an "act of language."

THE DEBATE ON LANGUAGE AND LITERATURE IN
TIBET AFTER THE CULTURAL REVOLUTION

With greater freedom of expression in the new political and cultural environment of the 1980s, Tibetan intellectuals began to ask critical questions regarding literary development: Is Sinophone literature by Tibetan-national writers a part of Tibetan literature? What is the link between a national language and a national literature? What is the value and function of a national language? Is language a mere channel of communication, or is it the core of a national culture? Does its main function lie in its capacity to communicate with the greatest number of people, or does it contain those "symbolic values" which, in Renan's words, are the very constituents of a nation? What are the role and status of a language spoken by a small number of people when confronted with the force of a widely spoken language? How can a clear difference be made between a "minority" language (a political fact) and a "minor" language (a value judgment)? What is the role of the writer who finds himself at the crossroads of manifold antagonist forces (languages and cultures, political allegiances and artistic aspirations)? Fueled by complex feelings of injustice and frustration amid a crescendo of statements about national and cultural identity, this discussion was indirectly nurtured by thirty years of Maoist campaigns, which denaturalized Tibetan society and denigrated Tibetan culture and language.

The debate on Tibetan language and literature after the Cultural Revolution took place against a shifting cultural backdrop. At its start in the 1980s the language debate was much more animated than in the 1990s. After the First Tibet Work Forum, held in Beijing in April 1980, and Hu Yaobang's visit to Tibet (and thanks to the strong support of the tenth Panchen Lama), policies were introduced to encourage the use of Tibetan, to ensure the right of nationalities to use their own language, and to support the notion of cultural distinctiveness. The time was considered politically ripe to give intellectuals the chance to show their national solidarity, above and beyond linguistic and cultural considerations, without fear of chauvinism and nationalism. In the early years of the New Era writers were encouraged to express themselves freely, reflecting a broader religious and cultural leniency. In 1985, for example, the celebration of the Great Prayer Festival (Mönlam Chenmo) was allowed again after being banned for twenty years.[34] These important signs of change fostered optimism among Tibetan intellectuals.

Tibetans launched diverse initiatives to culturally affirm Tibetan intranational unity. The sixth issue of the Sinophone magazine *Literature from Tibet* in 1986, entitled "Zangzu xiaoshuo zhuanhao" (Special edition: Novels by Tibetans), represented one such initiative.[35] The declared aim of the publication was "to collect works from different Tibetan areas in the PRC and encourage the constitution of an intellectual solidarity among Tibetans from different areas."[36] Titles of Tibetan publications during the early 1980s frequently used the word *zangzu* (Tibetan nationality) rather than *Xizang* (Tibet), which would emphasize the geographic origin of the writers (and could also include Han writers living in Tibet). The use of the word *zangzu* indicated the priority attached in those years to "national characteristics" (Ch. *minzu tese*) in literary activity.

The policy of encouraging Tibetan aspirations for cultural preservation and development (which had emerged in the 1980s as compensation for the devastations of the Cultural Revolution) eventually came to an end. By the early 1990s, as noted later by the Tibet Information Network (UK), "TAR

Party deputy secretary Tenzin described the Tibetan language policy as 'not working' and 'at a stalemate.' In the political sphere, after the Third Forum on Work in Tibet in 1994 . . . closer connections with the interior and the centre were to take priority over the notion of cultural distinctiveness."[37] With the resurgence of nationalist unrest all over the PRC, patriotism, cultural assimilation, and amalgamation became the dogmas of the 1990s. A series of Patriotic Education Campaigns were carried out in the TAR in 1990, 1994, and 1997 to "reconstruct a sense of national esteem" (the "nation" in question being the PRC).[38] Consequently the intellectual isolation of the young Tibetan literati in the PRC deepened, as did their skepticism about their chances of contributing culturally to the reconstruction of a Tibetan nationhood. The language debate in Tibet since the 1990s has lost its liveliness, not because it is less timely but because language has been perceived, more than ever, as a sensitive issue contributing to national tension.[39]

The contours of the language debate in various Tibetan regions of the PRC have been markedly different. The political atmosphere in the eastern areas of Amdo and Kham has been more relaxed than in the TAR, making the culturally oriented affirmation of national belonging through literary activities easier in eastern Tibet, even in the 1990s. Likewise, the linguistic and literary debate regarding Tibetan Sinophone literature can be discussed more openly. In Amdo nationally oriented literary activities include the publication of books such as *Zhongguo dangdai zangzu zuojia youxiu zuopin xuan* (A selection of the best works by Tibetan contemporary writers from China),[40] *Bod kyi deng rabs rtsom rig dpe tshogs* (Tibetan contemporary literature series),[41] and *Zangzu dangdai shiren shixuan* (Selected poems by Tibetan contemporary poets).[42] During my discussions with them, editors involved in these projects confirmed their intention to group together the main voices of the Tibetan literary world within the PRC, thereby forming a coherent ensemble of Tibetan-national literary works. Strong artistic quality and the Tibetan nationality status of the writer were prerequisites for selection.

In the TAR, by contrast, official discourse on literature since the 1950s has encouraged the constitution of a cultural "Tibetan-ness" separate from nationality status. This is especially true for the Sinophone sphere of Tibetan literature, where the notion of a *Xizang* literature (that is, a literature of Tibet, or more literally of the TAR) has been introduced to replace the notion of a *zangzu* literature (that is, a literature by Tibetans). By this "rectification" of categories, the attention has shifted from the nationality of the writer to the geopolitical notion of the TAR, including the multiethnic nature of its contemporary literature. Publications such as the newspaper *Xizang ribao* (Tibet Daily, f. 1956), and the Sinophone literary magazine *Literature from Tibet*, as well as works like *Xizang xin xiaoshuo* (New fiction from Tibet)[43] and *Lingting Xizang* (Listening to Tibet),[44] exemplify this. A rise in the number of non-Tibetan writers in the Sinophone publications of the TAR has highlighted the gap between a *Xizang* literature and a *zangzu* literature in Central Tibet; this was especially so in the 1990s.[45]

THE TIBETAN LANGUAGE DEBATE AND LITERARY THEORY IN THE NEW ERA

The question of how to define Tibetan-national Sinophone literature is but one aspect (possibly the most widely argued) of a larger debate on language and literature which has unfolded in greater China since the early 1980s. It has concerned both the renewal of Tibetan literature as a whole (Tibetophone and Sinophone) in terms of content and style, as well as the renaissance of all the literature produced in the PRC. From different perspectives and with distinct terms for each nationality, the question of language has become a central issue in the cultural reconstruction of New Era literature in greater China.

In inland China the *yuyan re* (language fever) phenomenon—that is, the emergence of language as a new and central problematic for literary criticism—became the main feature of the debate on aesthetic modernism in 1982. The publication in September 1981 of Gao Xingjian's *Xiandai xiaoshuo jiqiao chutan* (A preliminary enquiry into the techniques of modern fiction) was the landmark event that consolidated the formal and linguistic orientation of modernism in the PRC.[46] Language came to be studied as a system of culturally significant signs, and the old formula of socialist realism—"content determines form"—was reversed; formal issues acquired subtler and deeper meaning. In early 1989 Li Tuo's *Mao wenti* (Mao style theory) provided a new framework for examining Maoism as a social phenomenon structured semiotically through linguistic codes.[47] In China of the 1980s the language fever debate, together with the debate on humanism during the same period, brought to the fore the contradiction between realism and modernism, which has constituted the real debate of all literature in the PRC since the Cultural Revolution.

By reexamining the cultural value of a language and questioning its mere instrumental function, the formal, modernist approach to literature offered Tibetans a suitable context in which to discuss specific Tibetan language and literary issues concerning both the Sinophone and the Tibetophone spheres of Tibetan literature. For Tibetans, inscribing Tibetan language and literary questions in a debate that concerned greater Tibet helped to assure a stable intellectual ground for questions hardly tolerated by the official discourse.

In the dual confrontation between the formal and cultural notion of a language, Tibetans have emphasized the importance of the "cultural" meaning of a language, a meaning that in Tibetan terms has acquired obvious "national" colors. As a consequence, the core question of the debate in the intranational Tibetan arena has been the very Tibetan nature of Sinophone literature by Tibetan writers. This has been perceived as the most problematic issue in the Tibetan literary world since the 1950s.

While it is true that the language debate in Tibet has focused on Tibetan-national Sinophone literature, Tibetan-language literature has also been deeply concerned with linguistic questions since the early 1980s. Here the debate has mainly questioned the traditional relationship among language, national representations, and modernity. Tibetan calls for language standardization, modernism (as an alternative to socialist realism), and modernization of content and language (as an evolution from classical Tibetan literature) have been clearly expressed in Tibetan language publications since the 1980s. Support by the Tibetan intelligentsia for these recommendations has not, however, been unanimous.

PERSPECTIVES AMONG TIBETOPHONE WRITERS

The question of how to modernize the Tibetan language and adapt it to the new artistic aspirations and necessities of Tibetan New Era literature is a key concern in the Tibetophone sphere of the Tibetan literary realm. Together with the necessity of creating a modern standard literary Tibetan, two other reforms are viewed as paramount. On the one hand, young writers voice the need for new literary styles and forms to better express modern feelings; on the other hand, literary critics feel the need to develop a critical lexicon to express new ideas and modern literary categories.[48] To "borrow and learn" from other literatures has been perceived by Tibetans as an important strategy for cultivating a new literature and critical space. Thus in the early 1980s advocates for translating western and other foreign literature into Tibetan launched a debate on translation as a prerequisite for creation. To date, however, the practice of translation has been quantitatively feeble, and undertaken on the basis of previously made Chinese translations.[49]

Tsedor has been one of the most energetic advocates of translation in the context of Tibetan New Era literature. His articles are illuminating on two main points: his awareness that modernizing Tibetan language is a prerequisite for modernizing Tibetan literature; his understanding of how to renew Tibetan literature and language without betraying its Tibetan nature, its national essence. In "Zangwen chuangzuo ji fanyi" (Composing and translating into Tibetan), Tsedor argues that to accelerate "the slow evolution of Tibetan literature and the construction of a national literature in Tibetan language" it is necessary to improve and spread Tibetan education, elaborate a modern literary Tibetan language, translate Chinese and foreign literary masterpieces (classical and modern) into Tibetan, and elaborate a set of modern literary theories rich in national specificity.[50] In a later article, published in 1994, Tsedor recalls the example of Pushkin, who thanks to his translations "opened the path of the great modern literary tradition in Russian language."[51] Making much the same argument, Dorjé Rinchen (1994) quotes Wen Fu, Lu Xun, and other Chinese intellectuals who at the beginning of the twentieth century elaborated a modern national Chinese literature in the vernacular (Ch. *baihua*) based on massive translation activity and the imitation of foreign literary models.[52]

More conservative advocates for preserving a traditional classicism in literature have denounced this brand of literary and linguistic innovation. Fearing the development of a *no man's literature* in a *no man's language*, they have denounced the Sinicized and westernized features of Tibetan New Era literature and predicted the decline of the rich Tibetan poetic tradition. Sangdak Dorjé, professor of Tibetan classical poetics at Tibet University, is one of the most vocal opponents of modernizing the Tibetan traditional poetic lexicon and style. In his book *Mig yid rna ba'i dga' ston legs bshad gter gyi 'bum bzang* (Feast for the eyes, mind and ears: The excellent treasure vase of elegant writing), a critical reexamination of Dandin's *Kāvyādarśa* (The mirror of poetics), he criticizes the formal innovations of free-verse poetry by young Tibetans. He explains that writing irregular verses (which he calls "halting verses" because of the different length of each poetic line; Tib. *rkang pa ring thung shor ba'i skyon*) has always been considered a serious poetic imperfection.[53] After denouncing a few rare examples of this imperfection in the classical tradition (614–15), he vigorously attacks present-day free-verse poetry, and denounces its Chinese-imported flavor. He cites the following poem, "Mother," as an example of non-Tibetan poetic sensibility (the author is not identified):

Ah!
Ocean
My Mother
You
All in All[54]

Sangdak Dorjé comments: "If one does not know Chinese he does not get the feeling [of the poem]. The poem becomes unintelligible if one is not well educated in Chinese. How can one say that this is Tibetan literature? Tibetan literature possesses specific features, [comes from] the very heart of Tibetan people, its expression is the Tibetan language."[55]

In Sangdak Dorjé's view, young Tibetan poets should learn how to express new content in a classical style and language, so as to express a modern Tibetan sensibility and preserve a true Tibetan literary essence.[56] He suggests the following as a classical reformulation of "Mother":

Mother
Far-off Mother
My country
I miss you
The sweet calls of the cuckoo and
The plaintive sound of my recalling you
mingle together.[57]

Many of Sangdak Dorjé's other poetic exercises in classicism are meant to show the pertinence and beauty of combining tradition (in poetic language and style) with modernity (in content). He cites one untitled quatrain in which the poet uses the metaphor of water in a pitcher; the poet denounces the stupidity and ignorance of petty officials whose heads (the pitchers) are full of inculcated principles and ideas (water), which are poured mechanically from one "pitcher" to the other.[58]

Sangdak Dorjé's resistance to modernism is not an isolated case. Generally speaking, however, literary classicism and literary modernism are promoted simultaneously. Many Tibetan literati do enjoy and practice different styles of literature, both traditional and modern. Thus Lhundrup Namgyel (b. 1945), former editor of the Tibetophone Lhasa literary magazine *Tibetan Art and Literature* and a writer of neoclassical poetry,[59] is one of Jangbu's greatest fans, and welcomes literary innovation and modernity. Recently at Labrang monastery in Gansu province, some traditionally educated monks formed two groups of poets: *Srol rgyun srol nag* (the stubborn traditionalists) led by Sangkok and Penden, and the modernist *Rang mos rkang lo ma* (the limping free-wheelers),[60] led by Lhachap Jinpa, who writes free-verse love poems and novels. I was told that representatives from the two sides regularly had traditional quasi-monastic debates over modern literary subjects. Other examples of a desired and happy cohabitation of tradition and modernity in literature can be cited. Writers like Döndrup Gyel and Ju Kelzang, widely known for the modernity of their literary production, have shown an uncommon mastery of classical composition as well. Acrostics, verse alternating prose, and other classical literary devices are frequently used by the youngest generations of Tibetan Tibetophone writers. A comparison of Döndrup Gyel's free-verse poem "Lang tsho'i rbab chu" (Waterfall of youth) and his more classical "Rgyal srid sna bdun la 'sbyar ba'i 'bel gtam" (Sermon on the seven royal emblems)[61] demonstrates that young Tibetan writers can experiment and obtain remarkable results in both classical and modern styles. Lhagyel Tsering's collection of poems *Call of the Goddess of Dawn* is an example of what I call a "conciliatory" style:[62]

> Guided by the eye of Venus which shows me the path
> I come, my feet kicking, scattering the light of dewdrops on grass
>   blades.
> Like a trumpet waking those still fast asleep at cock crow
> I come, knocking at the door which seems to be locked from inside.[63]

In his verses, the poet searches for a happy medium between the danger of stagnant poetic mannerism and the oddity of obscure poetic experimentalism.

PERSPECTIVES AMONG TIBETAN SINOPHONE WRITERS

Whereas the Tibetophone side of the language and literary debate has called for linguistic innovations in literary form, style, and lexicon without implying a radical change in the nature of the Tibetan language, the Sinophone side has called into question the very emergence of an "other" language literature written by Tibetans. As noted above, these faces reflect one and the same concern: how to preserve Tibetan cultural identity when confronted with a difficult politico-cultural cohabitation, and with the changes which have accompanied the modern world.[64]

When discussing Tibetan-national Sinophone literature, writers often express their positions with unease. Generally speaking, Tibetophone writers reject the idea that Sinophone literature by Tibetans should be considered Tibetan literature per se. The terms immediately shift from literary concerns to politico-cultural issues of Sinicization and cultural suppression.[65] Tibetan-national Sinophone writers, conversely, tend to regard their literature in Chinese as "Tibetan literature," but their discourse is not univocal. Some are reluctant to affirm the Tibetan-ness of their Sinophone literature on the mere basis of their Tibetan nationality. While they acknowledge an incongruity between their nationality (that is, what Tibetans "are" and "feel") and the expression of their intimate and creative self (that is, their Sinophone literature), they also explain that at the crossroads between illiteracy in Tibetan and the hope of getting a larger readership in Chinese, they have little choice. A Tibetan-national Sinophone writer likened the situation to that of a child who would learn how to run fast and free even in a place unfit for running (for example, among the trees in a deep forest), if only he could satisfy his unquenchable desire to run. Any means for literary practice is good insofar as it serves the ultimate wish of the writer to fully express his or her artistic self.

Many young Tibetan-national Sinophone writers feel that literary issues should be taken up in literary and artistic frameworks. Some writers refuse to take a position in what they call a "sterile outdated question" which "has nothing to do with literature and art."[66] These writers defend the right of the author to seek intellectual freedom and artistic quality through whatever means he or she possesses, including language. In their opinion, nationality-related questions are not literary questions.

The influence of nonliterary concerns when evaluating literature was far more evident in my conversations with Tibetophone intellectuals than with Tibetan Sinophone intellectuals. The reputation that a writer has (among both literati and general readers) and his or her views on intracultural and national issues are often considered more important than the artistic quality of the writer's literature. Not only the language of composition but the writer's personality, outlook, social engagement, and mode of expression appear to be important in evaluating the Tibetan-ness of a literary work. This is so for the Amdo poet Yidan Cairang (Tib. Yidam Tsering), whose poetry in Chinese is appreciated by the majority of the Tibetophone intelligentsia in Tibet because of his openly affirmed national engagement. Yidan Cairang is considered a Tibetan writer, and his poetry in Chinese is considered an expression of Tibetan literature.[67] This is not the case for the internationally well known writer Zhaxi Dawa. As Wandekhar explains in his article "On the Need for a Connection between the Tibetan Nationality's Own Characteristics and Its Modern Literature," even if the literary quality of Zhaxi Dawa's Sinophone fiction is generally appreciated in Tibetophone literary circles, the Tibetan-ness of his literature is not acknowledged.[68] (Zhaxi Dawa is further discussed by Patricia Schiaffini in chapter 9.)

Among the earliest critical voices to question the Tibetan-ness of Sinophone literature was that of Sanggyé, who in his essay "When Writing New Tibetan Literature It Must Be in Tibetan" affirms in apocalyptic tones that language is the defining factor in determining the national nature of any given literature.[69] He rejects any possibility of including Tibetan-national Sinophone literature in greater Tibetan literature. Sanggyé's view was fundamentally shared by Yidan Cairang (though he himself is a Sinophone poet), as illustrated in his article "On the Development of Tibetan Contemporary Mother-Language Poetry: Reading the Collection of Poems *The Call of Dawn*

Goddess."[70] Yidan Cairang's discourse is more conciliatory, however, and expresses deeper insight into the specifics of contemporary Tibetan history. Yidan Cairang first considers Tibetan literary diglossia in an international perspective. He shows that literary diglossia has emerged in minority literatures all over the world, including the Anglophone literature of the Tibetan diaspora. Yidan Cairang, in the name of national solidarity, argues for the importance of recognizing the Tibetan-ness of all Tibetan-national writers—Tibetophone, Sinophone, Anglophone, and other. In his view literary realities affected by diglossia, such as those of Tibet, should be understood as the expression of transitory periods in the history of nations. Tibetan-national Sinophone literature should thus be included in the literary history of the Tibetan nation. At the same time, Yidan Cairang explains, historical events should not hinder peoples from being aware of societal and cultural forces and engaging in cultural preservation. Because literature and texts are in the first order a matter of language, all Tibetan intellectuals who are illiterate in Tibetan should learn their mother language. Reforms should be made in the educational system so that Tibetans may close this linguistic gap. In Yidan Cairang's terms, only through a pertinent educational policy can literary diglossia remain as a parenthesis in the history of the Tibetan people's literature. He predicts an imminent increase in Tibetophone literary production in Tibet, the natural result of a literary evolution in which literature reappropriates its natural functions, that is to be the "expression of the heart and soul of his people."[71]

A profound personal, literary, and national engagement explains Yidan Cairang's reluctance to unconditionally deny the Tibetan-ness of all Tibetan-national Sinophone literature. Though he wrote in Chinese, he spoke fluent Tibetan. He knew very well the difficulty of expressing in "another" language one's personal makeup.[72] In his attempt to redefine a literature that is sometimes able, though written in Chinese, to show the Tibetan-ness of its origins, Yidan Cairang put forth the expression I have adopted here: "Tibetan-national Sinophone literature" (Ch. yong Hanwen xie de Zangzu wenxue).[73]

In his foreword to the anthology New Fiction from Tibet (1989), the Chinese critic Zhang Jun discusses in more critical tones the question of how to consider Sinophone literature written in Tibet.[74] He approaches literature in regional terms, paying special attention to various novels written in Chinese in the TAR by both Chinese and Tibetan authors. One of Zhang Jun's most interesting insights concerns the monolingual (Chinese) but multiethnic nature of the anthology itself. Zhang Jun regards the linguistic homogeneity of the volume (which results from the use of a common Chinese language by all the writers) not as a successful expression of multicultural exchange in Tibet but as "the tangible manifestation of the deep crisis in recent Tibetan litera-ture"—a literature, he continues, that "is inevitably born handicapped in its very nature."[75] The "handicap," Zhang Jun argues, consists of the intrinsic linguistic fracture, and the lack of communication between Tibetophone and Sinophone Tibetan writers. Zhang Jun's pessimistic assessment of Tibetan language and literature is an exception among Chinese critics.[76]

· · · · ·

Of the secondary literature that I have studied, Sōnam's article "Rtsom rig gi mi rigs khyad chos dang Bod rigs rtsom rig skor gleng ba" (On national characteristics in literature and Tibetan literature)[77] is one of the most inter-esting and comprehensive articles on the language debate in the Tibetan lit-erary world. In many respects Sōnam represents a summing up of the essays already discussed: he refuses to apply the epithet of "Tibetan literature" to Sinophone literature written by Tibetans; he expresses the need to consider it with "other" categories, and yet he accepts this brand of literature as a form of cultural production by Tibetans living in a specific context and period. In quoting Gorky, Sōnam defines literature as the "art of language. Without linguistic abilities, no literature can be produced. Without a national lan-guage, no national literature can be produced."[78] In his terms the language of literature is not only the national language of a writer and the mirror of the feelings of a nation; it should also be artistically beautiful. Sōnam openly criticizes the use of a hybrid language (Tibetan-Chinese code switching) in literature. He argues that the linguistic solutions adopted by some Tibetan Sinophone writers in an attempt to "translate" their intimate Tibetan self into the Chinese language (translation, transliteration, compound solutions, loan words, etc.) are examples of "anti-literature" because they are unintel-ligible to both the Tibetophone and the Sinophone reader. He illustrates his views with an excerpt from a short novel by a Tibetan Sinophone writer: "*Aba he ama daizhe ajia dao agu de kangba he tuba.*"[79] This sentence, which is quite awkward in Chinese, is a linguistic combination of Chinese syntactic and grammatical key words (*he* = and; *daizhe* = to lead sb. swh.; *dao* = to go; *de* = of; *he* = to drink) with phonetic transposition from Tibetan into Chinese of the words *aba* (father), *ama* (mother), *ajia* (sister), *akhu* (uncle), *kangba* (house), and *tuba* (noodle soup). Only by understanding each word in the language of reference (be it Chinese or Tibetan) can one comprehend this compound sentence: "The father and the mother took the sister to uncle's to have some soup."[80]

Younger generations of Tibetan writers in both the Tibetophone and Sino-phone spheres of Tibetan literature have shown a less essentialist opinion of

Tibetan-national Sinophone literature in the PRC. Jangbu, for instance, has written an article entitled "Sin rga phur sger langs thob rjes kyi lo ngo bco lnga'i ring gi (1965–1980) Dbyin yig rtsom rig" (On anglophone literature in Singapore since it achieved independence, 1965–1980), which examines linguistic hybridity in Singapore literature and implicitly compares it to that of Tibet. This approach succeeds in changing the terms of the language debate in Tibet from its specific and local context to a more global reflection on "other" cultures all over the world.[81] His discussion of why identity issues similar to those faced by Tibetans exist elsewhere in the world is emblematic of the interest that young Tibetan intellectuals have for the so-called dominated cultures and their literatures (e.g. Indian, Jewish, African, black American) in the international arena. This article mirrors the wish—which is growing among young Tibetan intellectuals—to understand the Tibetan situation from a more global and detached point of view.

The disparate views on language held by Tibetan intellectuals have thus far hindered any satisfying definition of "Tibetan literature." In the Tibetophone literary sphere the profound linguistic and literary innovations marking New Era literature (Tib. *gsar rtsom*) have not led to any questioning of whether New Era literature belongs to Tibetan tradition in a meaningful way. However, with regard to Tibetan-national literature in Chinese, the great number of expressions used to even name this literary phenomenon points to the difficulty in negotiating any single definition. The classificatory labels have included *Zangzu wenxue* (literature by Tibetans), *Zangqu wenxue* (literature from Tibetan areas), *Xizang wenxue* (literature from the TAR), *Xizang difang wenxue* (literature from the area of the TAR), *Xueyu wenxue* (literature from the Land of Snow), *Zangyuwen/Hanyuwen wenxue* (Tibetophone/Sinophone literature), *yong Zangyu/Hanyu xie de Zangzu wenxue* (literature written by Tibetans in Tibetan and Chinese), *shaoshu minzu wenxue* (national minorities literature), *Xibu wenxue* (literature from the west [of China]); *Xiyu wenxue* (literature from western [China]), *Xibei wenxue* (literature from the northwest [of China]), *Xinan wenxue* (literature from the southwest [of China]). All suggest that the question of how to consider, and where to locate, Tibetan-national literature in Chinese is not merely a question of the "rectification of names." Finding relevant terms to describe a literary phenomenon that challenges traditional and accepted critical categories and definitions remains a complicated issue in both the Tibetan and Chinese literary arenas.

Tibetan-national Sinophone literature has been perceived as a cacophonous manifestation in the present-day Tibetan diglossic context. One wonders whether new critical frameworks—frameworks which leave room for plurality, hybridity, and "otherness"—might not offer greater insight into the harmonious combinations of a literature capable of transforming its marginality into creative energy.

Notes

1. I further explore this subject in my Ph.D. dissertation, "Frontières de l'imaginaire: La Problématique de l'identité culturelle dans la littérature tibétaine d'expression chinoise en PRC," which focuses on cultural identity in Tibetan Sinophone literature. My purpose is not to support an "ethnic-centered" discourse on contemporary Tibetan literature but to consider how Tibetan-national writers, critics, and editors negotiate their role as literary actors in the present-day PRC. I use the expressions "Tibetan-national Sinophone writer" (or literary spheres, or literature, etc.) to distinguish between the nationality of the writer (Tibetan) and the language (Chinese) in which he or she writes. The terms "Sinophone," "Tibetophone," and "Anglophone" denote the language of composition, not the writer's spoken language.
2. Ernest Renan, "What Is a Nation?," *quoted* in Stoddard, "Tibetan Publications and National Identity," 122.
3. Stoddard, "Tibetan Publications and National Identity," 122.
4. For more information on PRC language policy in Tibet see Bass, *Education in Tibet*; Kolås and Thowsen, *On the Margins of Tibet*, 93–131.
5. Ashcroft, Williams, and Tiffin, eds., *The Post-colonial Studies Reader*, 283.
6. Tsering Shakya argues that the Tibetan translation of the word "counter-revolutionary" (Tib. *gsar brje'i ngo log pa*) illustrates how language can be used as a means of covert persuasion. *Gsar brje*, literally "changing toward the new," is now a well-established term for "revolution." "Counter-revolutionary," that is, an "enemy of the state committed with the goal of overthrowing . . . the socialist system" (Chinese Criminal Code, 1980, Article 90) was translated into Tibetan as *gsar brje'i ngo log pa*, literally "turning against the new changes" (that is "modernity"). The political and moral implication embedded in this expression is that turning against *gsar brje* means not only turning against "revolution" (that is, being counterrevolutionary) but also refusing the "new," that is, "modernity." The equation subtly suggested is that socialist revolution *is* modernity. See Tsering Shakya, "Politicisation and the Tibetan Language," 161.
7. For a detailed analysis see Tsering Shakya, "Politicisation and the Tibetan Language."
8. Yang Wanli, "Xizang kecheng jiaocai yanjiu de teshuxing jiqi duice" (The countermeasure and particularity of research on teaching materials), *Xizang yanjiu* 58, no. 1 (1996), quoted in Bass, *Education in Tibet*, 100.
9. Dwyer, "The Texture of Tongues," 68.
10. Vostrikov, *Tibetan Historical Literature*, 9–10.
11. A few magazines, such as *Bod kyi rtsom rig sgyu rtsal* (Tibetan art and literature), provide a third table of contents in English.

12. I draw this conclusion from interviews and other fieldwork conducted in the cities of Lhasa, Xining, Lanzhou, Chengdu, and Beijing from 1995 to 1997 and in 1999.

13. For translations of works by writers mentioned in this chapter see appendix 3.

14. These findings are derived from field research conducted during 1995–97 and 1999.

15. Rdo sbis rdo rje, ed., *Mtsho lho'i rtsom rig brtsams chos gces bsdus.*

16. Gongbu Zhaxi, *Gongbu Zhaxi shiji.*

17. Yidan Cairang, *Xueyun ji.*

18. Lha rgyal tshe ring, *Skya rengs lha mo'i 'bod brda.'*

19. Jianbian Jiacuo and Zhangge Nima also write in Tibetan.

20. For reasons beyond the scope of this chapter, the production of independent Tibetophone journals has dramatically increased in Qinghai and Gansu provinces since the late 1990s.

21. Ma Huiping, ed., *Catalogue of Chinese Publications in Tibetan Studies (1949–1991).*

22. Ma Huiping, ed., *Catalogue of Chinese Publications in Tibetan Studies (1992–1995).*

23. Ma Huiping, ed., *Catalogue of Chinese Publications in Tibetan Studies (1996–2000).*

24. Based on the abundant but incomplete material and information that I collected during fieldwork (as of late 2000), I estimate that between 1980 and 2000 at least fifty-two contemporary Tibetan-language works by twenty-two writers were translated into Chinese (self-made translations included), whereas 192 contemporary Chinese-language works representing thirty-four writers of Tibetan nationality were translated into Tibetan (self-made translations included). Excluding self-translating writers (discussed later in this chapter), the Tibetophone authors most frequently translated into Chinese are Döndrup Gyel (seven works), Püntsok Trashi (four), and Penjor (four). The Tibetan-national Sinophone writers most often translated into Tibetan are Yidan Cairang (fifty-two works), Danzhu Angben (twelve), Gazang Caidan (ten), Gesang Duoji (seven), Yixi Zeren (five), Zhaxi Dawa (five), and Gongbu Zhaxi (whose collection of sixty-one poems was translated in its entirety by Repgong Dorjékhar). These data are only suggestive. For an analysis of Tibetan translation practices in the context of New Era literature see Maconi, "Une longue marche translinguistique: Présence française dans la nouvelle littérature tibétaine: Modes de médiation et d'intégration, réception, intertextualité," 205–36.

25. Alai, *Chen'ai luoding* (The dust settles). For an English translation of this novel see *Red Poppies.*

26. For a detailed explanation of Tsedor's theory and practice of translation see Ci Duo, "Zangwen chuangzuo ji fanyi" and "Yuelun zangzu wenxue he wenxue fanyi"; Tshe rdor, *Skyed ma'i bka' drin*; and Maconi, "Une longue marche translinguistique."

27. Tailing, *The Secret Tale of Tesur House.* In 1998 this novel was published by the same publishing house in Chinese under the title *Zhai sufu miwen.*

28. Dejicuo, *Gezhe wuhui.*

29. The twelve Tibetophone writers are Döndrup Gyel, Tsering Dondrup, Dorjé Rinchen, Ju Kelzang, Khedrup, Repgong Dorjekhar, Lhagyel Tsering, Dorjé Tsering, Dekyi Drolma, Nordé, and Orgyen Dorjé. The two Sinophone writers are Alai (Tib.

A legs) and Liemei Pingcuo (Tib. Jikmé Püntsok). The bilingual writer is Zhangge Nima (Tib. Lcangs skya Nyi ma).

30. Zhaxi Dongzhu, "Dangdai zangzu xiaoshuo sikao."

31. In the early 1950s Geng Yufang was sent on a cultural mission to Tibet, where he learned Tibetan. He is now a retired professor of Tibetan literature at the Beijing Central University for Nationalities.

32. Geng Yufang, *Zangzu dangdai wenxue.*

33. Ma Lihua, *Xueyu wenhua yu Xizang wenxue.*

34. This festival was first instituted by Tsongkhapa, founder of the Gelukpa school, during the fifteenth century and held in the Jokhang Temple in Lhasa. Though held under Communist rule during 1985–88, it was then banned again for political reasons.

35. So far I have not been able to find no. 6 (1986) of *Literature from Tibet*. In many big university libraries of the PRC there is a lacuna of documentation for the year 1986, possibly because the time was marked by a peak of intellectual openness and by student protests that the Chinese government eventually suppressed.

36. Li Shuangyan, "Yang Zhen yu ta de gaotian houtu," 316.

37. Tibet Information Network, "Language and Tibetan Identity."

38. This is the third of the four goals of patriotic education as defined in the handbook "Guidelines for Patriotic Education," quoted in Bass, *Education in Tibet,* 55.

39. During the fall of 1999 I asked a group of ten writers in Xining to debate the question of the Tibetan-ness of literature written in Chinese by Tibetan writers. At first they categorically refused; then an animated debate ensued.

40. Xue Li, ed., *Zhongguo dangdai zangzu zuojia youxiu zuopin xuan.*

41. 'Gyur med, ed., *Bod kyi deng rabs rtsom rig dpe tshogs.*

42. Caiwang Naoru and Wangxiu Caidan, eds., *Zangzu dangdai shiren shixuan.*

43. Feng Liang, ed., *Xizang xin xiaoshuo.* This volume contains novels by eighteen writers based in Central Tibet: eleven are Han Chinese, six are Tibetans, and one is Yi.

44. Huang Pingtang and Yang Zhen, eds., *Lingting Xizang.*

45. This geopolitical grouping of literary works is not exclusively applied to the TAR. Every province in the PRC publishes a collection of *zuopin jingxuan* (selection of the best pieces of literature); see for example Qinghai sheng zuojia xiehui, ed., *Qinghai wenxue zuopin jingxuan* (Xining: Qinghai renmin chubanshe, 1999). What is striking about Sinophone literature in central Tibet is the obviously decreasing participation of Tibetan-national writers in literary activity.

46. Jing Wang, *High Culture Fever,* 145.

47. See Li Tuo, "Mao Style and Its Political Institutionalization," unpublished proposal for research, Duke University, spring 1993; quoted in Wang, *High Culture Fever,* 145, 314.

48. Many Tibetan-language publications have feature sections or articles that establish a modern literary lexicon and new critical categories by translating, transliterating, or transposing new terms for previously unheard-of literary genres, trends, and movements from Chinese into Tibetan. Sometimes traditional expressions are recuperated and adapted to the needs of modern literature. The regular feature

"Tibetan-Chinese Glossary of Literary Terms" (Rtsom rig ming tshig Bod Rgya shan sbyar) in *Light Rain*, for example, introduces the reader to new literary terms such as *rang lab* (monologue), *ma 'ong ring lugs* (futurism), and *ta ta ring lugs* (dadaism). Some literary terms patently derive from Chinese expressions: *gnas zhu'i rtsom rig* (Ch. *baogao wenxue*, reportage), *lo rgyus kyi snyan rtsom* (Ch. *shishi*, epic), *dmangs khrod rtsom rig* (Ch. *minjian wenxue*, folk literature), *dpyad rtsom* (Ch. *pinglun*, literary criticism). Others come directly from the Tibetan literary tradition: *ka bshad* (acrostics), *snyan ngag* (poetry), *sgrung* (tales), *legs bshad* (aphorisms).

49. For an analysis of the debate regarding translation and modernity, including the practice of translating foreign literature into Tibetan, see Maconi, "Une longue marche translinguistique."

50. Ci Duo, "Zangwen chuangzuo ji fanyi," 29–30.

51. Ibid.

52. Gcan tsha'i Rdo rje rin chen, "Rtsom rig gi lad 'bri sgyu rtsal gyi skor rags tsam gleng ba."

53. Gsang bdag rdo rje, "Mig yid rna ba'i dga' ston legs bshad gter gyi 'bum bzang," 617.

54. Ibid., 619.

55. Ibid., 619–20.

56. I recall Sangdak Dorjé's astonishment during one of our conversations in Lhasa in 1999 as he read some of Jangbu's poems, such as "H₂O" (p. 8), "Zhe mer mer" (Nausea; 86), "Nga rang sbar chog" (Let me burn; 11); see Ljang bu, *Ljang bu'i rtsom btus.*

57. Tib. A ma lags / thag ring du bzhugs pa'i a ma / bdag gi mes rgyal / ngas khyed dran byung / khu byug gi gsung snyan dang/ khyed rang dran pa'i smre ngag / mnyam du 'dres song. Gsang bdag rdo rje, "Mig yid rna ba'i dga' ston legs bshad gter gyi bum bzang," 615.

58. Ibid., 569.

59. See for instance his collection of poems *Ka bshad bung ba dga' tshal.*

60. *Rkang lo ma* in Amdo dialect means "to limp." Note the puns: *rang mos* in *rang mos snyan ngag* (lit. "poetry according to one's own free-will," that is, free-verse poetry); *rkang*, "foot," as a prosodic unit; *rang mos rkang lo ma* (the limping free-wheelers).

61. For a summary in French see Robin, *Don grub rgyal.*

62. Lha rgyal tshe ring, *Skya rengs lha mo'i 'bod brda'*

63. Tib. Lam lam tho rangs skar chen bgrod lam 'tshol ba'i 'dren byed du bsten te / Bdag gis rtswa 'go'i zil ba 'od kyi rdog pas gtor zhing gtor zhing 'ongs / Bya pho'i mgrin sgra gnyid du 'thoms rnams slong ba'i dung brda' ru byas te / 'Dag gis nang lcags brgyab pa'i dra ma sor mos rdung zhing rdung zhing 'ongs. Lha rgyal tshe ring, *Skya rengs lha mo'i 'bod brda,'* 2.

64. Possibly because the debate over language and literature in Tibet concerns the sensitive subject of Tibetan identity, oral information has been particularly precious in attempting to put it in its just perspective and avoid reducing it to a polemic among intellectuals. During fieldwork I only managed to collect a little literature on the subject, especially in Chinese.

65. The difficulty expressed by a part of the Tibetan intelligentsia in accepting Sino-phone literature as part of Tibetan literature is not new. One may think of the polemics raised by the "Sino-Tibetan" theory in the field of linguistics. This theory has been questioned in the West and yet fully adopted as part of the PRC's official linguistics policy. Because the theory includes Tibetan in the same family as Chinese, Thai, and Burmese, it raises sensitive questions of national assimilation. For more information on the Sino-Tibetan theory see R. A. Miller, Review of *Introduction to Sino-Tibetan. Parts 1 and 2* (Wiesbaden, 1966–67, by R. Shafer), *Monumenta Serica* 27 (1968), 398–435, quoted in Beckwith, *The Tibetan Empire in Central Asia*, 3–5.

66. Anonymous, Chengdu, 1996 and 2002.

67. See n. 17, above.

68. Ban de mkhar, "Bod kyi mi rigs rang mtshan pa'i khyad chos dang deng rabs rtsom rig gnyis kyi rten 'brel gyi dgos pa syi bshad," 63–64. I thank Lauran Hartley for sending me this article.

69. Sangs rgyas, "Bod rigs kyi rtsom rig gsar rtsom byed na nges du Bod kyi skad dang yi ger brten dgos"; see also *Bod ljongs zhib 'jug*, 1987, no. 1, 119–26, 144. I did not have access to the Tibetan article but was able to get an unpublished, abridged Chinese translation made by a Chinese critic working on Tibetan contemporary literature: Sang Jie, "Zangzu wenxue chuangzuo bixu yong Zangyuwen."

70. Yidan Cairang, "Cong shiji *Liming tiannü de zhaohuan* kan zangzu dangdai muyu shige de fazhan."

71. Ibid.

72. For a detailed analysis of how this Sinophone writer managed to express his Tibetan self in an "other" language, see Maconi, "Lion of the Snowy Mountains."

73. Yidan Cairang, "Cong shiji *Liming tiannü de zhaohuan* kan zangzu dangdai muyu shige de fazhan."

74. Zhang Jun, "Rumo de shijie."

75. Ibid.

76. In his article Zhang Jun points to other Chinese misconceptions of "Tibetan literature": the frequent confusion between "Tibet" and the "TAR," and consequently between "Tibetan literature" and "literature from the TAR"; the notion of Tibetan literature as China's "far-western literature" (Ch. *Xibu wenxue*); the outsiders' view of Tibet among Lhasa-based writers, many of whom are from inland China.

77. Bsod nams, "Rtsom rig gi mi rigs khyad chos dang Bod rigs rtsom rig skor gleng ba."

78. Ibid., 206.

79. Ibid., 204.

80. Since the Chinese *tuba* literally means a "handful of earth" instead of "[Tibetan-style] soup," the meaning of the sentence could be twofold: the father and the mother took the sister to uncle's to have some soup (alternatively: a handful of earth!).

81. Bse ru (Ljang bu), "Sin rga phur sger langs thob rjes kyi lo ngo bco lnga'i ring gi (1965–1980) Dbyin yig rtsom rig."

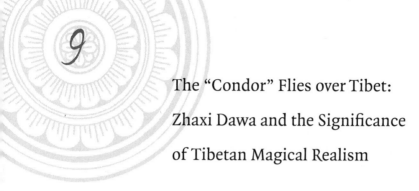

The "Condor" Flies over Tibet:

Zhaxi Dawa and the Significance

of Tibetan Magical Realism

PATRICIA SCHIAFFINI-VEDANI

The end of the Cultural Revolution triggered a major effort to translate for-eign literary works into Chinese, making possible the arrival of a few key works of Latin American magical realism to the Tibetan Autonomous Region (TAR). In the early 1980s several Lhasa-based authors, led by the Sino-Tibetan writer Zhaxi Dawa (Tashi Dawa, b. 1959), produced short stories in Chinese dealing with traditional Tibetan culture and way of life. Their mixture of real and dreamlike episodes attracted the attention of literary critics, who viewed the development as signaling the emergence of a Tibetan magical realism. In a culturally effervescent period when Chinese intellectuals were still ana-lyzing the roots of the Maoist catastrophe, the refreshing mixture of magic, authenticity, and primitivism within these stories fascinated China's young cultural élite. Zhaxi Dawa soon became the most famous Tibetan writer in China, and his style a synonym for modern Tibetan literature. But his popu-larity has also been contested. Many doubted the Tibetan-ness of Zhaxii's works, which were written in Chinese; others defined his magical realism as foreign to Tibet and a mere imitation of western literature; and still others simply took issue with his hybrid Sino-Tibetan identity.

This chapter examines Zhaxi Dawa's magical realism in relation to his cultural and ethnic hybrid identity, and the sociopolitical circumstances of modern Tibet. It will also analyze some of the ambiguities and contradictions that his hybrid Sino-Tibetan identity has created in his works.

Magical Realism: The Subversion of Realist Literature

Magical realism emerged in Latin America in the 1940s as a response to the crisis of literary realism. A young generation of Latin American writers, heavily influenced by European aesthetic trends, realized that new literary means of expression were needed to reflect the richness of Latin American cultures. After long periods of fascination with European arts and letters and years of living abroad, many of these writers returned to their native Latin America and began the process of rediscovering their own cultures. Like tourists in their own lands, they felt delighted by the colors, images, and diversity of the indigenous traditions, and astonished by the coexistence of native traditions and the culture imposed by the colonial powers. Unlike surrealism, which resorted to the invention of artificial worlds, they chose to focus on the most marvelous elements of real life and to elaborate on native beliefs, thus creating a new literary genre that came to be called magical realism.[1]

Magical realism arrived to the Tibetan plateau in the early 1980s, at a time when writers were still coming to terms with the atrocities of the Chinese Cultural Revolution. As their Latin American counterparts had done before, writers in China were desperately searching for literary alternatives to realism. Socialist realism had dominated the literary spectrum of China since 1949, and a succession of political campaigns had suffocated most attempts at artistic innovation and social engagement on the part of writers. The first works of magical realism translated into Chinese—Juan Rulfo's *Pedro Páramo* and García Márquez's *One Hundred Years of Solitude*—exerted a powerful attraction for young intellectuals. The appeal of these novels was that they offered a socially and politically concerned literature that also, unlike socialist realism, emphasized aesthetics, the importance of local cultures, and the preeminence of the subjective experience.

The higher degree of freedom initiated by Deng Xiaoping's reforms in the early 1980s allowed for the translation and dissemination of literary works from afar and the diffusion of aesthetic and philosophical trends. This invigorating political and cultural climate, together with the strong need to vent after decades of governmental repression and abuses, led Chinese writers to explore new literary avenues. Maybe the most influential result of this quest was the "search for roots" (Ch. *xungen*) movement. By focusing on forgotten traditions, and returning to the "authenticity" of the primitive and of nature, the *xungen* writers tried to recreate (or create altogether) a time when social conventions, politics, and urban life had not yet repressed man's emotions and desires.

In spite of their huge interest in Latin American magical realism, Chinese writers soon moved on to other literary pursuits. The *xungen* movement, although very successful in invigorating modern Chinese literature during the early 1980s, was short-lived. Beyond it, very few people have ever made a case for the existence of a Chinese magical realism.[2] It seems as if magical realism had passed through China only to take root in Tibet: during the 1980s and 1990s the Tibetan writer Zhaxi Dawa was more or less considered the sole representative of magical realism in China. More recently this role seems to have fallen to another Tibetan writer, Alai (Tib. A legs; see chapter 10), whose very successful novel *Chen'ai luo ding* (The dust settles), recently translated into English as *Red Poppies*, has also been linked to magical realism.

Becoming Tibetan

Zhaxi Dawa was born in 1959 in Batang, a Tibetan area in what is now Sichuan Province, to a father of Tibetan ancestry and a Han mother. He was given a Chinese name, Zhang Niansheng, and regarded as Han until he was an adult. Since he spent most of his childhood in Chongqing (Sichuan) and attended Chinese schools, he never got a chance to learn Tibetan. It was not until he moved as a teenager with his family to the TAR that Zhaxi Dawa became acquainted with Tibetan culture. Deprived of the opportunity to attend college by the Cultural Revolution, he enrolled in the Exhibition Center of the Tibetan Autonomous Region to study painting. He worked as a stage designer for Tibetan theater and later as an editor. In 1978 he was awarded a one-year scholarship to study at the prestigious Chinese Opera Institute in Beijing. There he familiarized himself with contemporary Chinese literary trends, especially the "literature of the wounded" (also known as "scar literature," Ch. *shanghen wenxue*), detailing the atrocities of the Cultural Revolution; he also read recent translations of Russian, French, and German literature. Back in Lhasa in 1979, he began publishing short stories in Chinese.

The late 1970s were a period of exuberant optimism and hope for Tibet. After a decade of fierce Chinese political control and cultural assimilation, the Chinese government had officially acknowledged the rights of China's ethnic minorities to preserve their languages and cultures. In 1977, after official directives, the Chinese-language journal *Xizang wenyi* (Literature and arts from Tibet) was created with a mandate to promote artistic and literary development in the Tibetan plateau. However, the key to the revitalization of Tibetan arts and letters seems to have been Hu Yaobang's visit to Tibet in 1980, during which Hu publicly blamed the Chinese Communist Party (CCP) for the poor conditions in modern Tibet. Most Tibetan and Han writers whom I interviewed in the TAR during the fall of 1999 referred to Hu Yaobang's speech as "honest" and "deeply moving," and emphasized how at the time they felt that Hu's visit paved the way for a new era of openness and prosperity in Tibet.[3]

Although Han cadres in Tibet had been instructed during the Cultural Revolution to do away with Tibetan culture in order to promote Communism and fight "superstition," now they were officially entrusted with promoting Tibetan culture at all costs. As people all over China were bursting into the spontaneous writing of literature as a way to share their tragic experiences of the Maoist era, Han cadres in Tibet anticipated a similar literary boom by Tibetans. However, initially very few Tibetans answered the Chinese literary call.

The shortage of Tibetan writers had historical and political causes. Under the old Tibetan regime literacy was not widespread, and after 1959 most of those who were literate fled to India to escape Communist rule. With the Chinese takeover, efforts were made to spread education in Tibet at first, but during the Cultural Revolution schools were closed and Tibetan culture suffered severe damage under the campaign to eradicate the "Four Olds."[4] Another hindrance to the development of a literary culture was that the Tibetan literary tradition, extremely rich in religious texts, was almost bare in secular texts.

In 1979, frustrated by the initial lack of literary response from the Tibetan people, Zhou Yanyang, an editor with *Literature and Arts from Tibet*, received the draft of a story by a twenty-year-old writer called Zhang Niansheng. The former literary critic Zhou Shaoxi, son of Zhou Yanyang, recalls how his father advised the young writer to claim a Tibetan identity: "My father read the draft of the first short story by Zhaxi Dawa, who in those days went by the surname Zhang. He thought it was a good story so he wanted to meet him. Zhaxi Dawa was very young. When my father realized that Zhaxi Dawa's father was a Tibetan, he told him he should use a Tibetan name. . . . From that time on he began signing his works as Zhaxi Dawa."[5] Zhaxi Dawa was not the only ethnically hybrid writer officially encouraged to relinquish his Han identity. So were two writers who at the time resided in Lhasa: Xu Mingliang (Ch. Sebo, Tib. Gsal po, b. 1956),[6] son of a Tibetan mother and a Han father, was also urged to write under a Tibetan pen name, while the half-Yi half-Han female writer Feng Liang (aka Jihu Shini, b. 1963) was urged to write under a Yi name.[7] While the actions of these early editors at *Literature and Arts from Tibet* can be attributed to their concern about the initial lack of Tibetan writers and their overzealous eagerness to promote minority cultures, later editorial practices in China have proven to be not so well intentioned. The generalized practice of "Tibetanizing" book titles or requiring Sinophone Tibetan writers to write almost exclusively about Tibet proves that Chinese publishing houses take advantage of the alluring fascination that Tibet exerts on Chinese readers.[8]

Although the first step in becoming "Tibetan" was acquiring a Tibetan name, Zhaxi Dawa's earlier stories reveal that leaving his Han cultural back-

江那边

扎西达娃

感拉近了。

象绸缎一样光滑的流水，一望无边，庄严低沉，无尽无休地流向不为人知的远方。

江这边，一个贫瘠的村庄，七八十户人家。用石头垒成的房子零乱地座落在山坡上，墙壁贴着牛粪饼，几只鸡在房顶上啼鸣，从雪山流下的一股小溪穿过庄子。村口，一棵古老高大的菩提树，大约是几百年第一个来这里定居的流浪人种下的。每过一些日子，人们就从江那面的供销社买回一些极需极简单的日用品：糖、茶叶、白布、针线。

早晨。河边，一弯细长的沙滩。一个男青年和一个小姑娘正把一只牛皮船推下河。他们相差十多岁。

"带我去，单增哥。"姑娘漫不经心地说。她不知过过多少次，到现在已成为习惯了。

"你还小。"他也习惯地回答，因为她要天天放羊。

"江那面的庄子大吗？"

"大。"

江面很宽，象湖泊，象海洋，象平原。对岸远山下的村庄隐现在视野中，缥缈，模糊。然而，河滩上那几星绿色的斑点——那是几棵孤独的柳树，把江这边和那边的距离

12

Illustration for Zhaxi Dawa's short story "Jiang nabian" (The other side of the river), by the artist Luo Lunzhang. *Xizang wenyi* 5 (1982), 12.

ground and assumptions was not easy. Critics have bestowed no attention on Zhaxi Dawa's early works (1979–84), which still retain some of the conventions of socialist literature. However stale these stories may seem from a literary point of view, they are an invaluable resource for tracing the evolution of his representation of Tibet, which parallels his own evolution in the quest for a Tibetan identity.

In these stories a still culturally Han Zhaxi Dawa, who is just becoming acquainted with Tibet, tends to describe Tibetan people as being rightfully "modernized" by the CCP. Most of Zhaxi Dawa's Tibetan characters in this period are young women, a common trend in Han representations of ethnic minorities at the time.[9] The images of infantilized minority people vis-à-vis older Sinicized females or older Han male figures—a juxtaposition which Louisa Schein has insightfully associated with the dependence and submission of minorities to the Han state—abound in Zhaxi Dawa's early writings.[10] The most characteristic example is "Daoyan yu Sezhen" (The director and Sezhen), the story of a Han theater director in his fifties who struggles to educate a childish Tibetan actress.[11]

Although "Chenmo" (Silence, 1979) was Zhaxi Dawa's first short story in terms of chronology, this work has been mostly overlooked or forgotten by Han critics. What may seem at first a careless omission may shed some light on the process of Zhaxi Dawa's Tibetanization. The protagonist of "Silence" is a Chinese girl named Hai Ping, who takes refuge in Tibet after losing her best friend during the brutal repression of a peaceful demonstration in Beijing.[12] This story is a typical example of the "literature of the wounded" (Ch. *shanghen wenxue*) in China, characterized by predictable plots aimed at denouncing the abuses perpetrated during the Cultural Revolution. The story has only one Tibetan character, an unnamed girl who befriends the Han protagonist. While the novice writer is able to describe both how violence takes place in Tian'anmen Square and the impact of this violence on the psyche of the Han girl, he cannot produce a convincing description of the Tibetan girl or the Tibetan background. "Silence" is clearly the product of a young Han mind, alienated from Tibetan culture, history, and current problems, that recreates the general denunciation of the Maoist oppression prevalent in China at the end of the 1970s.

Maybe it is not coincidental that Zhaxi Dawa himself,[13] as well as most Han critics, editors, and writers whom I interviewed in the course of my research, have forgotten that such a "Chinese" story was Zhaxi Dawa's literary début.[14] Instead, all of them mention "Chao fo" (Buddhist pilgrimage), published in 1980, as his first short story.[15] "Buddhist pilgrimage" represents Zhaxi Dawa's first attempt to portray what he thought were the quandaries and aspirations of modern Tibetans. The story centers on a traditional and vulnerable Tibetan teenager who has just arrived in Lhasa from the countryside, and her mentor, a Han-looking modern, educated, and independent Tibetan woman. "Buddhist pilgrimage," a story fully developed in Tibet that features only Tibetan characters, marks the author's personal transition to a Tibetan identity. Overlooking the Chinese story "Silence" meant forgetting Zhang Niansheng and embracing Zhaxi Dawa. But what was the real importance of embracing Zhaxi Dawa's new Tibetan identity? For the Han editors in Lhasa, who deeply regretted the systematic destruction of Tibetan culture during the Cultural Revolution, finding a promising Tibetan author like Zhaxi Dawa meant redemption from the past and hope for the future. For Zhaxi Dawa himself, becoming Tibetan opened a myriad of literary possibilities imaginable to only a very few aspiring Han writers at the time.

The still superficial understanding of Tibet and its culture, and the exoticized way in which Zhaxi Dawa represented the Tibetan people in his early stories, clearly unveils an outsider sensibility. However, the situation began to change in the first half of the 1980s. At that time Zhaxi Dawa's fellow Chinese writers engaged in cultural introspection (Ch. *wenhua fansi*) to expose and correct what they thought were the inherent maladies of the Chinese tradition—for which they blamed the abuses of the Maoist era. Zhaxi Dawa, who had steadily partaken in mainstream Chinese intellectual discourse, progressively broke away from these trends to engage in an introspection that would culminate in his embracing his new Tibetan identity. Immersed now in Tibetan culture and in the complexities and contradictions of modern Tibet, Zhaxi Dawa realized that many of the social and political improvements promised by the Chinese in 1980 would not materialize. Zhaxi Dawa was already in his mid-twenties, departing from the naïveté of his teenage encounter with Tibet and with literature.

The Origins of Zhaxi Dawa's Magical Realism

The idealized and generally positive mood of Zhaxi Dawa's early works begins to fade around 1985. His stories become more abstract as realism gives way to the legendary and the supernatural—occasionally even to the surreal. While Zhaxi Dawa's early stories portrayed Tibetan reality in Han terms, he now makes a conscious effort to understand how Tibetans perceive their surrounding world. A genuine curiosity for Tibetan traditional culture and an amazement with it lead him to search for literary inspiration in Tibetan beliefs, which for the first time he tries to present without judgments or opinions. His works now place equal weight on the supernatural and the natural, and they attempt to disrupt conventional understandings of time, space, and structure. Although dichotomies still abound, they are of a completely different nature: Zhaxi Dawa leaves behind his reductive plot lines—good versus evil, correct versus incorrect—to engage in a deeper analysis of the antagonisms between the indigenous and the colonized.

This rather radical change has been generally attributed to the literary influence of Latin American magical realism or efforts to imitate Gabriel García Márquez.[16] However, Zhaxi Dawa rejects being a conscious follower of magical realism: "I do not object when critics call my works magical realistic, that is their choice. But actually, we never said we were followers of magical realism. That all originated when some editors of [the journal] *Literature from Tibet*, as a commercial stunt, published a monographic issue devoted to magical realism in Tibet, which included stories by Sebo, Jin Zhiguo, myself and others."[17] Zhaxi Dawa admits that during the 1980s North American and Latin American novels in China encouraged young writers to reflect on cultural, spiritual, supernatural, and psychological issues. He acknowledges that he probably read more foreign literature in translation than most of his peers, and he points to Faulkner as one of the strongest influences.[18] But more than anything else, Zhaxi Dawa states, it is Tibetan reality that has inspired him: "Tibetan culture and traditions are able to provide a writer with all reality and magic s/he wants; we do not need to look for them abroad; we just need to look outside the window."[19] A similar view has been expressed by the innovative and highly acclaimed Tibetophone writer Dorjé Tsering (also known as Jangbu) who in an interview in 1999 affirmed that "those [supernatural] beliefs and phenomena that critics would label as magic, in Tibet are part of daily life."[20] The presence of legendary elements and religious beliefs in daily life is, in Zhaxi Dawa's opinion, one of the many characteristics shared by Latin American societies and modern Tibet. He also sees similarities in terms of their historical processes and the richness of their religions, traditions, and cultures. That is why he affirms that "the appearance of a magical-realistic literature in Tibet would be a very logical phenomenon."[21]

The survival of magical realism in Zhaxi Dawa's stories for almost two decades indicates that the adoption of this form of expression was much more than a literary fad. While Zhaxi Dawa seems to find an explanation for it in the similarities of the historical processes of Latin America and Tibet, while his critics allege an imitation of Gabriel García Márquez, this essay explains Zhaxi Dawa's magical realism as a natural response to his cultural hybridity. The explosive mixture of local oral literatures and imported literary techniques, the syncretism of native beliefs with borrowed or imposed ideologies, and traumatizing colonial experiences, are not the only similarities between Tibet and Latin America. They also have in common the phenomenon of intellectually and ethically hybrid writers, who although educated under the culture of the colonial powers are still linked to their native lands. As these writers look to their native worlds with the cultural sensibilities of outsiders, their hybrid cultural baggage allows them to see "magic" in what for insiders is just reality. Zhaxi Dawa explains how Tibetan reality overwhelms the senses of the newcomer: "As soon as a writer enters deeply into modern Tibet, s/he will come to forget that what it is in front of her/his eyes is reality. S/he will think that it seems more a product of a hallucinating imagination."[22] Zhaxi Dawa's first reaction to this unknown and uncomprehensible reality was, as exemplified by his early stories, to try making sense of it with a Chinese-educated frame of mind. However, by the mid-1980s Zhaxi Dawa's works begin to reflect a deep change in perspective: the writer now attempts to situate himself inside Tibetan parameters to explore the beliefs and phenomena that previously seemed surreal to him. His extensive travels around Tibet and reflections on the situations and phenomena that he encounters lead him to the realization that in spite of the Chinese promises of progress, Tibetans are not yet the masters of their destinies. As in centuries before, they are still subject to the despotic whims of nature and the prevailing authority.[23] Thus Zhaxi Dawa distances himself from his previous idealism, and begins to challenge the concepts of reality, progress, and linear history.

Temporal Ambiguity

Zhaxi Dawa's magical realistic world is defined by temporal ambiguity, as he often confronts characters that appear to come from different times. In "Xizang, ji zai pisheng jieshang de hun" (Tibet: The soul tied to the knots of a leather rope) some characters seem to live in an old, legendary Tibet, a land of Gesar, pure ideals, and religious fervor, while others live in a modern time of tractors, calculators, and radios broadcasting the inauguration ceremony of the Olympic games.[24] Although the characters interact at certain points of the story, they are unable to understand each other; they have thoroughly different aims, beliefs, and priorities in life. It is almost as if characters from Tibet's past had been taken hostage in a confusing future.

Subject to mysterious forces, Zhaxi Dawa's characters seem to jump from one temporal dimension to the next, from one reincarnation to another. In "Shiji zhi yao" (The invitation of the century) the protagonist leaves his home, in what seems to be modern Lhasa, and heads to the countryside to attend the wedding of his best friend. Upon his arrival he realizes that his trip has not only been one in space, but also one in time: he has entered his friend's former life. He finds that his friend is not a shy history professor in a modern city anymore, but a compassionate landlord from older times who has been sentenced to prison for his opposition to the oppressive rule of a prince. Although our protagonist has been dragged into this time dimension without possibility of escape, his friend seems able to manipulate time on his own behalf: refusing to live in the unfair world of oppressors and oppressed, his friend has started a physiological regression in time by which he gets younger, until he becomes a fetus and enters the womb of a woman, the reincarnation of his future mother. His final goal is to be reborn fifty years later in what he hopes will be a better world. The "liberation" of his friend has tragic consequences for our protagonist: he remains trapped in the past and is forced to serve the imprisonment to which his friend was previously sentenced.[25]

Altering the linear timeline of realism, Zhaxi Dawa's works often present the idea of a circular history. History seems to repeat itself in the lives of characters that are predestined to live like their parents. Both "Meiyou xingguang de ye" (A night without stars) and "Fengma zhiyao" (The glory of the wind horse) are about sons forced to kill the assassins of their fathers, knowing in their turn that the victims' sons will soon come to avenge them. A dialogue from "A Night without Stars" illustrates this point:[26]

> [Agebu.] . . . So you came to avenge your father.
> [Vagabond.] I have finally found you, after ten years. Look at me, I have nothing on me, just the knife my father left me to revenge.
> [Agebu.] And . . . , what happens if tonight you die under my knife?
> [Vagabond.] Oh! When my son grows up he will come looking for you, and if you are already dead, he will look for your son. We are both Kamba men, you know well our traditions.
> [Agebu.] One generation after another, an enemy that cannot be defeated.[27]

In front of the crowd gathered to view the duel, Agebu decides not to fight and kowtows in front of his rival, in an attempt to break the never-ending circle of revenge. The vagabond accepts Agebu's kowtow as a symbolic defeat. Both men express their desire to become friends and leave behind their parent's rivalry. But when the vagabond steps into the woods, somebody— presumably Agebu's wife trying to redeem the shame of a husband who has refused to fight—stabs him to death. The two men's attempt not to repeat their parents' history has failed: the vagabond's family, assuming that Agebu is the killer, will eventually send a son to avenge his father. With a last breath of life the vagabond asks Agebu to keep his hat: "If my son finds you some day, give him [this hat]; he would then know that you and I finally became friends."[28] The vagabond dies without knowing whether this last attempt will finally break the revenge circle between the two families. Vengeance is one of Zhaxi Dawa's resources to present a cyclic time, a history that repeats itself only to perpetuate the mistakes of the past.[29]

Is Zhaxi Dawa, by disrupting conventional timelines, just trying to escape the fixed boundaries of realism, or is he also opposing the concepts of linear history and Marxist evolution, so often used by the Chinese authorities to justify their "liberating" and "progressive" presence in Tibet? One thing is certain: Zhaxi Dawa's magical realistic stories portray a different conception of time, one not linked to the conventional idea of progress prevalent in Chinese society. They present Tibetans as not interested in using revolutions or wars to bring about material change; as a nationality not invested in using violence to impose their beliefs on others; as individuals concerned with daily life, the performance of family and religious duties, and the continuity of inherited traditions and values. Contrary to the ways in which Chinese socialist literature (and Zhaxi Dawa's early works) represented Tibet, his magical realistic novels try not to make judgments on Tibetan society or impose alternatives to the Tibetan ways of life. However, these same representations that seem to encourage tolerance and respect for Tibetan culture sometimes cast a shadow of pessimism and passivity, as characters appear trapped in a circular dominium that forces them to repeat their progenitor's lives.[30]

Ideological Ambiguity

The few scholars in the West who have studied Zhaxi Dawa seem to disagree on the interpretation of his works. Barmé and Minford, for instance, affirm that the author uses Tibetan culture to serve Chinese Communist purposes: "Zhaxi Dawa is a Tibetan imbued with the ideology and literary trendiness of the Chinese, [and who] uses Tibet's religious culture in the service of Marxist-Leninist Modernism."[31] Lü Tonglin, on the contrary, points to Zhaxi Dawa's desire to negate Chinese Communism by representing Buddhism: "Buddhism in Zhaxi Dawa's fiction gains its identity by negating the cultural and ideological domination of Communism . . . The negation of Communist ideology in Zhaxi Dawa's world of fiction becomes the *raison d'être* for the positive existence of Buddhism."[32] I contend that Zhaxi Dawa represents

Buddhism and Communism not to endorse one over the other, but to reflect on what he perceives to be the clash of two diametrically opposed belief systems in modern Tibet. Educated among Han people, Zhaxi Dawa is part of that ideologically orphaned generation whose members during the Cultural Revolution were either Red Guards or street hooligans. During the Cultural Revolution they were taught to despise religion; after it, they came to despise politics. With such an iconoclastic background it is not surprising that during the 1980s, when Zhaxi Dawa was writing his magical realistic stories, his position toward ideology should have become one of true skepticism.

The speculation about Zhaxi Dawa's ideological grounds arises from the deliberate ambiguity of his magical realist writings. He represents elements of both Buddhism and Communism, but contrary to his earlier preference for modern Chinese values and attitudes, in his later stories he tries not to take sides. This is an authorial reticence typical of magical realist writers who oppose the judgmental side of realism, but also fits perfectly with Zhaxi Dawa's desire (and survival need) to avoid addressing directly ideological and religious issues. When I once asked about his beliefs, Zhaxi Dawa smiled and avoided a direct answer by talking about that in which he did not believe: "I am not a member of the Communist party [and] I am not interested in politics . . . I am not a Buddhist believer. I am more interested in the role of religion in Tibetan culture than in religion *per se*."[33] In terms of ideological preferences, not much can be inferred from his characters either: most of them are devoted and honest Buddhists, but as devoted and honest as the fewer Communist cadres he portrays. This is exemplified by the two main characters in "A Night without Stars." The vagabond is supposed to embody Tibetan traditional values and religious beliefs, while the Communist cadre Agebu represents the new Tibet. Both are portrayed in equally good terms. They are honest, capable of noble acts, and willing to make sacrifices: the Communist cadre risks his honor when he kowtows to the vagabond to avoid the spread of violence; a dying vagabond refuses to incriminate his killer so as not to sadden Agebu. In spite of their different ideas the two are finally able to understand each other—although, as we have seen, this understanding comes only after the vagabond relinquishes his tradition-based desire for vengeance. We may say that Agebu and his "modern" ideals triumph over the most "backward" elements of Tibetan tradition. Nevertheless, the vagabond's death, presumably at the hands of Agebu's wife, who wants to fulfill the tradition of revenge, suggests that "progress" for Tibet will not be easily attained. This would be the most obvious message of the story. However, Zhaxi Dawa's deliberate lack of clarity always leaves an opening for different interpretations, and as we will see, this ambiguity has worked to his benefit.[34]

One effect of Zhaxi Dawa's ideological skepticism is that most of his magical realist stories present instances when Communism and Buddhism clash without finding grounds for an understanding. "Tibet: The Soul Tied to the Knots of a Leather Rope" exemplifies this when an old Tibetan man tells of how some people sought a mysterious paradise called "Communism": "In 1964 they began organizing People's Communes here. Everybody was talking about going towards Communism, [but] at that time nobody could explain clearly what it was. In any case, it was definitely a paradise. But where was it? Nobody knew. When asked, those coming from central Tibet said it was not there; those coming from Ngari said it wasn't there. Those from Kham said they have never seen it either. In that case, there was only one place where nobody had gone before, Mount Kailash. Some villagers sold all they had, took with them a bag of tsampa, and left saying they were going to [look for] Communism. They never came back."[35] On a symbolic level, this episode refers to the suffering and death of those who looked for the ideal of Communism; on a more practical level, it also shows how unfathomable the concept of Communism must have been for common people in Tibet. Another story portrays Tibetan herdsmen hanging up in their tents, together with other religious symbols, the pictures of Mao Zedong given away by the People's Liberation Army (PLA): since Mao was so venerated by the Communist soldiers—the herdsmen reasoned—he ought to be an enlightened being. These same herdsmen, after listening to the propaganda about the PLA, began referring to it as "the army of Buddha." If it was as good as the propaganda said, obviously it could not be called anything else.[36] In their encounter with such an incomprehensible set of beliefs, the logical reaction was to use their own religious and social standards to interpret it.

But in Zhaxi Dawa's magical realist stories Tibetans are not the only ones unable to understand foreign ideas; more often than not the Communist Chinese also fail to understand the Tibetan way of thinking. In "Xizang, yinmi suiyue" (Tibet: The mysterious years) a young Chinese UFO researcher arrives at the desolate mountain where an old Tibetan man lives. Speaking in Chinese, he tries to explain the aim of his scientific visit to Tibet: "I am a member of the Chinese Association for the Study of UFO. I have my credentials here, they are authentic. . . . You see, this place is very similar to [Peru's] Nazca plain. It is possible that my organization can prove that this spot, in ancient times, was in fact a landing place for life forms from [all over] the universe."[37] The old man does not understand Chinese. He defensively addresses the young stranger who is picking up rocks in a land Tibetans consider sacred: "What are you doing? If you were an exhausted traveler passing by, I would treat you as my guest. But your eyes are constantly looking at the ground, looking for something. This is not right. I will not allow you to blaspheme this land using your demoniac magic."[38] The scene ends in a climax of mutual frustration: the young Chinese scientist leaves the mountain crying, powerless to explain the importance of his research to that "old herdsman, who does not understand Chinese, does not understand law, let alone understands what UFO means."[39] There is no possibility of understanding between the two of them, not even at the last moment, when the old Tibetan man gives up his hostile attitude and tries to call the researcher back: he talks in Tibetan, a language the Chinese man does not understand. Even if the Chinese scientist had known Tibetan, in Zhaxi Dawa's magical realist universe he most likely would have failed to comprehend the importance of religion for Tibetan people. With examples like this the writer is clearly showing the surreal situations created by the impossibility of understanding between two radically different dogmas.

Zhaxi Dawa's ideological skepticism shows also in his attitude toward the validity of Communism and Buddhism for the progress of Tibet. His "Tibet: Soul Tied to the Knots of a Leather Rope" provides the best example. The story begins when the first-person narrator, a rather presumptuous socialist writer, realizes that the characters of one of his unfinished short stories have somehow acquired life. In his story a religious man and his girlfriend are wandering around Tibet in search of a legendary Buddhist paradise. The writer, lacking imagination, had stopped the story just when the characters were about to cross to the other side of a sacred mountain behind which the paradise was supposed to be. Now, certain that he will find his characters in that same spot, the narrator decides to begin a real journey to the mysterious mountain so that he can join his characters. When he is finally able to find them, the male character is dying from a fatal injury caused, ironically, by a tractor—an unmistakable symbol of socialist progress. The narrator, being a socialist writer, regrets having created characters so imbued with religion and "superstition." He asks himself why he has not been able to create "new people" instead: strong, positive, and productive characters who can serve the needs of this "glorious" socialist era. At the end he realizes that there is still hope for him as writer: after the death of his male protagonist the writer takes the female character back with him, promising to create a "new woman" in her. The story ends with the confused woman following the narrator on the journey back to the socialist world, as submissively and aimlessly as she had followed her boyfriend in his quest for a Buddhist paradise. For Zhaxi Dawa the fate of this female character symbolizes the fate of Tibet: first led to believe in the promise of Buddhist salvation, then forced to follow the path toward a socialist paradise.

Magical Realism in the Sociopolitical Context of Tibet

The revival of Tibetan culture and the relative freedom of expression during the early 1980s were followed by a tightening of Chinese control at the end of the decade. This was Beijing's response to pro-independence uprisings in the Tibetan territories and to political statements made abroad by the exiled government of the Dalai Lama. The alternating periods of repression and relative relaxation, as well as the implementation of contradictory party policies, left Tibetan writers little room for free expression.

Although China lacks an official censorship organ producing periodical guidelines about what is and is not allowed to be written, as in other totalitarian regimes, party representatives often express publicly what is expected from intellectuals.[40] Party leaders from the Tibetan Autonomous Region, for instance, have often criticized the tendency of writers to overemphasize Buddhism in their works.[41] Their criticism signals an official fear of religion, rooted in both the obvious ideological distrust of religion by the CCP and the close relationship between Buddhism and the Tibetan independence movement. Writers are encouraged to portray modern Tibet, especially the improvements introduced by Communism. This is the predicament that writers face in modern Tibet: they are advised not to talk about the past, but neither can they speak their minds about Tibet's present. (See the Introduction for the recent example of the banning of a book by the female Tibetan writer Weise (Tib. Özer), accused of overemphasizing the importance of Buddhism and the figure of the Dalai Lama in Tibetan society.)[42]

Besides political concerns, writers in Tibet also have to contend with powerful ethnic pressures. Literary misrepresentations of Tibet are contested by Tibetan intellectuals who wish to defend Tibetan culture publicly, and by the Chinese authorities who want to avoid social unrest in Tibetan-populated areas. The most representative example in this regard was the scandal concerning a short story by the Han writer Ma Jian in 1987. The short story "Liangchu ni de shetai huo kongkong dandan" (Stick out the fur of your tongue or it is all a void), which misrepresented Buddhist concepts and traditions, led to angry responses by Tibetan intellectuals and the Chinese authorities, and eventually to the author's self-exile in Hong Kong.[43] In addition, Tibetan writers who portray a darker side of Tibetan tradition will definitely upset members of their own communities. This was the case with certain stories, poems, and essays by Döndrup Gyel, who was not only accused of attacking Tibetan culture and religion but also received death threats from radical members in the Tibetan community.[44]

The works of Zhaxi Dawa, however, have not yet received such polemical critiques. An intricate magical realist style allows him to address sensitive sociopolitical issues with a certain degree of freedom. His works, usually more appealing to experimental and avant-garde writers, young editors, and heterodox university students, are difficult for old-fashioned readers to understand. In the course of my research I interviewed older intellectuals and party members employed in cultural work units in central Tibet, Chengdu, and Beijing. Many of them confessed that they had not read one of Zhaxi Dawa's works in its entirety; those who had made the attempt usually said either that they had not understood his stories (Ch. *kan bu dong*) or that after reading some pages they were not able to keep reading any longer (Ch. *kan bu xia qu*). These readers, usually more fond of realistic literature, complained that in his fiction it was hard to pinpoint what was reality and what was fantasy, when the events took place, and what was the moral of the story, if any.[45]

The mixture of real and dreamlike episodes, the use of complex images and metaphors, and an obvious ambiguity in time, space, and themes allow Zhaxi Dawa to breach political, religious, and even sexual taboos. "The Glory of the Wind Horse" presents the dark panorama of the "progress" brought to Tibet by the Communist regime: a carnival of witches, baby monsters, cruel police, Khampa thieves, and people living in rubbish dumps.[46] *Saodong de Xiangbala* (Turbulent Shambala), his first full-length novel, contains explicit sex scenes in the form of dreams and hallucinations that surpass those of the Han novelist Jia Pingwa's controversial novel *Fei du* (The abandoned capital), published only a couple of months earlier in Beijing, and banned for its sexual content.[47] Zhaxi Dawa's story "Weigan dingshang de zhuiluo zhe" (Those fallen from the mast) refers to the even more sensitive issue of homosexuality inside monasteries.[48] But although the topics were potentially controversial, these works encountered no criticism, neither from the Chinese government nor from Tibetan intellectuals and religious authorities.[49]

In an intellectual environment that prohibits both praise of Tibet's past and criticism of Tibet's present, Zhaxi Dawa's use of magical realism, by design or not, has allowed him a considerable degree of creative freedom. By creating atemporal worlds where tradition mingles with modernity and magic melts with reality, Zhaxi Dawa has been able to write about highly sensitive issues which very few of his peers dare to explore. By conveying for the reader the impression of entering an imaginary territory, the author cleverly avoids being held politically or ethnically responsible for what happens there.

· · · · ·

Zhaxi Dawa's magical realism is a product of his hybrid identity and the sociopolitical and ethnic climate of modern Tibet. More often than not, Zhaxi Dawa's use of magical realism has been understood only as a stylistic choice based on imitation of Latin American literature. But like many other magical realist manifestations in world literature, Zhaxi Dawa's literary style is above all, rooted in Tibet's colonial present. It is based on his "insider's will" to portray Tibet outside the realistic and descriptive framework traditionally used by the colonizers. Like many other magical realist writers in Latin America and Africa, Zhaxi Dawa can perceive the "magic" side of Tibet precisely because of the literary and artistic training that he received from the colonial metropolis. Thus many Tibetophone writers—perceived to be more "authentic": they have not succumbed to Chinese influences—tend to deny the existence of magical elements in traditional Tibetan culture and ways of life. As Dondrup Wangbum (Ch. Danzhu Angben) explains: "Actually, the 'mystery' of Tibet is the 'mystery' of Tibetan culture, and this mystery stems from ignorance. Once it is understood, it is no longer mysterious. A Tibetan never thinks of himself or his life as a mystery."[50] As an intellectual who has been equally exposed to two different cultures, Zhaxi Dawa cannot fully participate in either. Brenda Cooper's description of West African magical realist writers summarizes well the sometimes contradictory situation of intellectuals caught between the worlds of the colonizers and the colonized: "Insiders and outsiders, traitors and champions of resistance, these writers are cultural hybrids, who grapple with the demands created by national atrocity and with the attractions inherent in contributing to national pride; these writers inscribe in the narrative guts of their fictions their moral and political uncertainties."[51] Zhaxi Dawa's hybridity renders him ethnically "impure" in the eyes of many, both inside and outside Tibet and China. He is not accepted as a Han among Hans, nor as a Tibetan among Tibetans. When we consider how the writer deals with this predicament, the character Sangie, from Zhaxi Dawa's "The Invitation of the Century," again comes to mind. Unhappy with the role that life has forced him to play amid sociopolitical unrest, Sangie begins a physiological regression of time until he becomes a fetus and enters the womb of his mother, intending to be reborn fifty years later in a better world.[52] For Zhaxi Dawa, magical realism has been a protective womb in which he has been able to hide, a womb that has nurtured his creativity and allowed him to escape the harsh reality of modern Tibet. If not to be reborn in another time, at least magical realism has allowed him the rare opportunity of transcending the boundaries of Tibet and China. His magical realist stories have been translated into several languages, and in the 1980s and early 1990s Zhaxi Dawa received more international attention than any of his counterparts in Tibet, and many Chinese writers in the hinterland.

Zhaxi Dawa's contributions to the modern literature produced in Tibet, as well as that produced in China, have been many. After the Cultural Revolution his magical realist stories played an important role in the successful subversion of socialist realism, and in the defense of a writer's right to creativity and expression. From a strictly literary point of view, he has influenced a whole generation of Tibetan and Chinese writers. Moreover, his works have attracted Chinese readers' attention to Tibetan culture, and to the works of other Tibetan writers. As the Chinese literary critic Zhang Jun put it: "'Tibet: The Soul Tied to the Knots of a Leather Rope' opened a door to Tibet for many people [in China]. It presented us, for the first time, with some of the concerns of the Tibetan people. For example, I used to think that Tibet was a backward place, but after reading these stories I understood that this was not the case. I learned that Tibetan society had traditionally emphasized the development of spirituality over the pursuing of material concerns. The works of Zhaxi Dawa taught me the importance of spiritual development and spiritual satisfaction for the Tibetan people. I believe this is one of Zhaxi Dawa's most important contributions."[53] However, very few Tibetans see Zhaxi Dawa's contributions in such a favorable light. His magical realist renderings of Tibetan ways of life sound unnecessarily exotic and sometimes even misinformed for many educated Tibetans. And yet it is not the content of his writings, but above all his Sino-Tibetan hybrid identity and his writing in the Chinese language, that place Zhaxi Dawa at the center of this ongoing literary but identity-centered debate.

Notes

1. For more on the portrayal of the marvelous elements of indigenous reality, see the Cuban writer Alejo Carpentier's "manifesto" of 1949 for a new Latin American literature: Alejo Carpentier, Preface to El reino de este mundo (The kingdom of this world).

2. Although for many scholars xungen and magical realism are different movements, a few critics seem to think of them in similar terms: for example, Zhang Xudong (Chinese Modernism in the Era of Reforms, 137) includes Zhaxi Dawa in the xungen move-

ment, while the Chinese anthology *Mohuan xianshi zhuyi xiaoshuo* (Magical realist novels), edited by Wu Liang, also incorporates short stories by Han Shaogong and Mo Yan, Chinese writers traditionally considered to be the initiators of the *xungen* movement.

3. Hu Yaobang's Lhasa speech on 29 May 1980 led to a climate of unprecedented openness in the TAR. Here is an excerpt of the message that he conveyed to the Tibetan people: "Tibetans still live in poverty. In some areas living standards have even gone down. We comrades in the Central Committee . . . feel that our party has let the Tibetan people down. We feel very bad! The sole purpose of our Communist Party is to work for the happiness of people, to do good things for them. We have worked nearly thirty years, but the life of the Tibetan people has not been notably improved. Are we not to blame?" Quoted in Wang Yao, "Hu Yaobang's Visit to Tibet," 287–88.

4. The campaign to smash the "Four Olds," which began about 1967, called for the eradication of traditional ideas, culture, morals, and customs.

5. Zhou Shaoxi, interview by author, Lhasa, 27 October 1999.

6. For more on Sebo see Schiaffini-Vedani, "Changing Identities."

7. The Yi are concentrated mostly in parts of Sichuan, Yunnan, Guizhou, and Guangxi. Some Yi groups live in the proximity of Tibetan communities in Sichuan province.

8. It is not coincidental that the two short stories that made Zhaxi Dawa famous in China, "Xizang, ji zai pisheng jieshang de hun" (Tibet: The soul tied to the knots of a leather rope) and "Xizang, yinmi suiyue" (Tibet: The mysterious years)—and after which his two most popular anthologies are named—are precisely the only stories that have "Tibet" in their titles. Years later, when Zhaxi Dawa was already an experienced writer and wrote his first novel, he made a point of referring to Tibet in the title *Saodong de Xiangbala* (Turbulent Shambala) (Beijing: Zuojia chubanshe, 1993). Editorial insistence on Tibetan references in titles also affected Feng Liang when a prestigious Chinese publishing house asked her to change the title of her novel *Zanghonghua xiang* (The scent of saffron) to *Xizang wuyu* (A Tale from Tibet) (Beijing: Zuojia chubanshe, 1998).

9. For Chinese ethnic minorities represented by the figures of "sensuous women" see Gladney, "Representing Nationality in China." For minorities represented as innocent girls see Schein, "Gender and Internal Orientalism in China."

10. Schein, "Gender and Internal Orientalism in China," 90. Interestingly, the illustrations that accompanied Zhaxi Dawa's works in this period, made mostly by Han artists working for the journal *Xizang wenyi* (Literature and arts of Tibet), support Zhaxi Dawa's personification of Tibet in the images of young and submissive female characters. For example, figure 1, the most important illustration in Zhaxi Dawa's story "Jiang nabian" (The other side of the river, 1982), was drawn by the artist Luo Lunzhang and shows an innocent and smiling Tibetan girl in a kneeling position that unequivocally denotes fragility and submission.

11. Zhaxi Dawa, "Daoyan yu Sezhen."

12. Zhaxi Dawa, "Chenmo."

13. Zhaxi Dawa, interview by author, Lhasa, 21 October 1999.

14. The Chinese critic Zhang Jun, and the prominent editors and writers Ma Lihua and Jin Zhiguo (all interviewed in Chendgu and Lhasa during the months of October and November 1999) are among the ones who recalled "Chao fo" as Zhaxi Dawa's first short story.

15. Zhaxi Dawa, "Chao fo."

16. In this regard Barmé and Minford (*Seeds of Fire*, 450) affirm: "[Zhaxi Dawa] became known for a number of short stories that attempt to imitate the magical realist style of Latin American literature which was introduced to China during the early 1980s." Similarly, many scholars link Zhaxi Dawa to the Colombian writer García Márquez. In this regard, Barmé and Minford claim, "Zhaxi Dawa sees himself as the Chinese Gabriel Garcia Marquez" (452). Lü Tonglin compares a passage from "Tibet: The Soul Tied to the Knots of a Leather Rope" to García Márquez's *Cien Años de Soledad* (One hundred years of solitude) in *Misogyny, Cultural Nihilism and Oppositional Politics*, 111. Alice Grünfelder, a pioneer in the study of Zhaxi Dawa, argues that "novels like *Xizang, xi zai pishun shang de hun* 'Tibet, Soul Tied to a Leather Cord,' *Xizang, yinmi suiyue* 'Tibet, Mysterious Years' and *Guzhai* 'Old Manor' gained the attention of the whole nation and can be seen as works in the tradition of Marquez' '100 Years of Solitude.'" Grünfelder, "Zhaxi Dawa and Modern Tibetan Literature," 340.

17. The journal volume to which Zhaxi Dawa is referring here is *Xizang wenxue* (Literature from Tibet), 1985, no. 6. Zhaxi Dawa, interview by author, Beijing, 3 February 1994.

18. Previous scholarship has noted some similarities between Faulkner's works and those of magical realist writers; see for example Ude, "Forging an American Style," 56–57:

> We can see . . . common elements of Magical Realism most clearly in [Faulkner's] *Go Down, Moses*. First Faulkner firmly rejects the confines of traditional realism; in its place we find a multidimensional metaphysical as well as physical reality . . . Second, the mythical or legendary as well as the historic past becomes an actual presence in contemporary life . . . In the process, Faulkner seeks to fabricate poetic recreations, a third characteristic of Magical Realism, rather than mere imitations of reality. Fourth, he seeks to distort time, space, and identity as those elements are understood in conventional realism. . . . Faulkner mixes mystical or magical elements with the everyday details of commonplace reality in an attempt to generate in the reader a firm belief in the validity and genuineness—the reality—of his fiction. These are also the traits we recognize in both South and North American Magical Realism.

19. Zhaxi Dawa, interview by author, Beijing, 3 February 1994.

20. Dorjé Tsering (Jangbu), interview by author, Lhasa, 10 October 1999. In a recent paper Franz Xavier Erhard also quotes Dorjé Tsering on the issue of magical realism in Tibet: "Since Tibetans believe in gods (*lha*), demons ('*dre*) and magic (*sngags, mthu*) [Dorjé Tsering] insists that his stories are more realistic (*dngos yod*) than

magical realistic (*sgyu 'phrul dngos yod*)." See Erhard, "Magical Realism and Tibetan Literature," 143.

21. Zhaxi Dawa, "Xizang xiaoshuo = 'mohuan xianshi zhuyi?'"
22. Ibid.
23. Interview by author, Beijing, 3 February 1994.
24. "Xizang, ji zai pisheng jieshang de hun," 174–98. In 1986 this short story won the "All-China Excellence Award for Short Stories" (Quanguo youxiu duanpian xiao-shuo jiang) conferred by the Eighth Conference of the Chinese Writers Association (Zhongguo zuojia xiehui di ba jie), one of the most prestigious literary awards in China. This together with its innovative style, which mixed seemingly real events with almost surreal episodes, brought Zhaxi Dawa to literary prominence and led him to be labeled a follower of magical realism.
25. Zhaxi Dawa, "Shiji zhi yao," 119–33.
26. Zhaxi Dawa, "Meiyou xingguang de ye," 68–78. There is an English translation, although rather incomplete, in *China's Tibet*, 1995, no. 3, 32–35. See also Zhaxi Dawa, "Fengma zhi yao," 93–118. For an English translation see Stewart, Tsering Shakya, and Batt, eds. *Song of the Snow Lion*, 96–113.
27. Zhaxi Dawa, "Meiyou xingguang de ye," 72.
28. Ibid, 77.
29. The idea of history repeating itself in Zhaxi Dawa's works has also been noted in Lü, *Misogyny, Cultural Nihilism and Oppositional Politics*, 117: "Zhaxi Dawa seems to tell us that everything in his story is bound to be repeated—hopelessly."
30. "Meiyou xingguang de ye" addresses the topic of revenge and its devastating impact on generations of the same families. The story "Tibet: The Mysterious Years" presents a similar case, that of a daughter whose life has been ruined by the burden of having to continue her mother's religious duties after she died. Zhaxi Dawa, *Xizang, yinmi suiyue* (Wuhan: Changjiang wenyi chubanshe, 1993), 1–46.
31. Barmé and Minford, *Seeds of Fire*, 416.
32. Lü, *Misogyny, Cultural Nihilism and Oppositional Politics*, 104.
33. Zhaxi Dawa, interview by author, Beijing, 3 February 1994.
34. Steven Venturino proposes another interpretation: "Agebu and Lhajig's family conflict, personal confrontation, and subsequent reconciliation represent the independent choices of Tibetans to negotiate the past and develop new ties with each other, perhaps as a way of uniting against an enemy stronger than those arising from Tibetan tradition. The character of [Agebu's wife] Kamzhub then comes to be seen as a figure of Chinese provocation, fanning the fires of the old traditions in order to once again pit Tibetans against themselves." See Venturino, "Reading Negotiations in the Tibetan Diaspora," 116.
35. Zhaxi Dawa, "Xizang, ji zai pisheng jieshang de hun," 190. Zhaxi Dawa bases this anecdote about a "Communist paradise" on old slogans used in Tibet by the CCP. As Åshild Kolås explains: "Reforms which were launched in Tibet, whether in agriculture, family planning or road building, were formerly portrayed as 'a step in the path towards the Socialist Paradise' (*spyi tshogs ring lugs zhing khams*)." This socialist paradise, a new society without classes, was also presented as a prosperous and

developed society: "The Chinese People's Government is our Great Mother. Yuan-notes are falling like rain." See Kolås, "Chinese Media Discourses on Tibet," 70.

36. Zhaxi Dawa, "Xizang, yinmi suiyue," 33.

37. Ibid, 38–39.

38. Ibid, 39.

39. Ibid. Note how the Han character places Chinese language, law, and science together as the paradigms of Chinese culture and progress, something he believes is out of the Tibetan man's reach.

40. For more on literary control in the PRC see Link, *The Uses of Literature*, 56–97.

41. An example of this is the famous speech that the TAR party secretary Chen Kuiyuan gave in Lhasa in July 1997, celebrating the return of Hong Kong to the PRC. His speech, addressed directly to the intellectual community of Tibet, was an official reminder of their duties toward the state and the party. He took up what he considered the four major problems of the writers and artists of Tibet: divorce from reality and from the problems of the working class; emphasis on artistic form and pleasing the public while neglecting political thought; a wrong interpretation of the Tibetan tradition and of what constitutes ethnic characteristics; and the inclination of "a small number of people" to echo the opinions of the Dalai Lama. For the whole speech see *Xizang ribao*, 16 July 1997. This part of the speeeh was understood by Tibetan writers and artists to be a critique of those whose works emphasize traditional Tibetan ways of life and Buddhist practices.

42. Those Tibetan writers who in spite of all difficulties have persevered in their pursuit of literary endeavors have often developed "survival skills" to write without risking their careers; this chapter deals with one of them, the use of magical realist abstraction and metaphors. Nevertheless, humor also appears to be a powerful means for carrying out an incisive social critique without raising official suspicion. The success of the Tibetan writer Püntsok Trashi exemplifies this. He uses the Chinese genre of brief sketches (*xiaoping*) and comic cross-talks (*xiangsheng*), but usually writes the texts in the Tibetan language so that they are accessible to common people when performed in public places and on television. The contents are usually humorous but also poignantly critical of social vices such as gambling and alcoholism. The humorous language serves two important purposes: it allows the author to portray the social evils that Tibet suffers under Communist rule without receiving official criticism; and it allows his works—as well as his social criticism—to reach a much wider Tibetan audience, people of all ages, literate and illiterate. His works have even been translated into Chinese in an anthology called *Pingcuo Zhaxi xiaoping xiangshen xuan* (Selected sketches and cross-talks by Püntsok Trashi). For more on this author see Schiaffini, "Realism, Humor and Social Commitment," 67–69. For more on the uses of *xiangsheng* in China as a sociopolitical weapon see Link, "The Genie and the Lamp," 83–111; and Link, *Evening Chats in Beijing*, 88–89.

43. Ma Jian. "Liangchu ni de shetai huo kongkong dandan" (Stick out the fur on your tongue or it is all a void). For a comment on the incident and a translation of the most controversial pages of Ma Jian's story see Barmé and Minford, *Seeds of*

Fire, 439–47. A complete translation of the story can be found in Batt, trans., *Tales of Tibet*, 235–54. For the official reaction to Ma Jian's story see the article by the Tibetan Branch of the Association of Chinese Writers and Artists, Zhongguo zuojia xiehui Xizang fenhui, "Yipian chouhua, wuru zangzu renmin de liezuo."

44. See Pema Bhum. "The Life of Dhondup Gyal," 17–29. For an example of the controversial writing of Döndrup Gyel see "Rkang lam phra mo," trans. Stevenson and Lama Choedak T. Yuthok.

45. Series of interviews with intellectuals, editors, and writers in the TAR, Chengdu and Beijing, fall 1999.

46. "Fengma zhi yao," 93–118. For an English translation see Stewart, Tsering Shakya, and Batt, *Song of the Snow Lion*, 96–113.

47. The works mentioned are Zhaxi Dawa, *Saodong de Xiangbala*, and Jia Pingwa, *Fei Du*.

48. Zhaxi Dawa, "Weigan dingshang de zhuiluo zhe."

49. Not coincidentally, the work by Zhaxi Dawa that aroused more official suspicion was one of his earliest and more *realistic* short stories, "Basang he ta de dimei men." The story, which portrays the life of a young girl in charge of her younger siblings, caught the attention of the authorities when it was filmed as a TV series. Wishing to depict as closely as possible the life of a Tibetan city in the early 1980s, the TV series was filmed entirely in Lhasa, with an all-Tibetan amateur cast and under the close supervision of Zhaxi Dawa, who also acted in the series. Although the topic fit the officially encouraged representation of modern Tibet, the series encountered critics soon after being aired. The authorities were not content about a TV program that reflected so closely the real living conditions in Lhasa. Zhaxi Dawa, interview by author, Beijing, 3 February 1994.

50. Dondrup Wangbum, Preface to *A Soul in Bondage*, 11.

51. Cooper, *Magical Realism in West African Fiction*, 217.

52. Zhaxi Dawa, "Shiji zhi yao."

53. Zhang Jun, interview by author, Chengdu, 3 November 1999.

In Quest(ion) of an "I": Identity

and Idiocy in Alai's *Red Poppies*

HOWARD Y. F. CHOY

In Tibetology the inquiry of minority identity is inevitable, an inquiry in both the collective and individual senses of the word "identity": the quality of a person recognizable as the "same"—from Late Latin *identitâs*—as other members of a group and at the same time the "sameness" of an individual always being him- or herself rather than someone else. Thus identity refers paradoxically to both collective characteristics and distinct individuality. Disoriented in the identity crisis between Chineseness and Tibetanness, the self of such a Chinese Tibetan as the writer Alai (Tib. A legs) is so confused that he can only present fictionally and fictitiously his identity in idiocy. "Idiocy" is a derivative of Greek *ídios*, meaning "personal, private." With the etymological reference of Greek *idiôtês* "private individual" extended to a layman with no specialized knowledge (hence the Middle English derogatory sense of "idiot" as an "ignorant person"), idiocy is commonly defined today as a psychological state of being unable to learn language or defend against dangers. It takes a political turn, however, when it comes to the colonial condition: being incapable in the heritage of one's native dialect or in acquisition of the "national" language, and being incompetent to guard against foreign invasion. Alai is a poet of idiocy in search of identity.

A native of Four Chieftains (Ch. Situ), officially known as Markham County today, Alai 1997 finished his maiden novel *Chen'ai luoding* (The dust settles), which has been translated into English as *Red Poppies*. Whereas his novella "Jiunian de xueji" (Bloodstains of the past, 1987) narrates a fallen headman family, *Red Poppies* relates the end of the age of chieftains by focusing on the last Maichi Chieftain and his dramatic rivalry with the other three chieftains on the Tadu River, namely Wangpo, Lha Shopa, and Rongong.[1] Ten years in quest of a lost, or more precisely imagined, identity of a "Tibetan" have led the author further into the backwoods of local history. *Red Poppies*, a creative celebration of the chieftains' last carnival in the Republican period (1912–49), tells the story of the sudden flourish and collapse of the Maichi Chieftain from the point of view of his younger son, who is believed to be retarded. As the fool's fictive autobiography develops, however, we find the first-person protagonist-narrator a round character growing from a mere moron to a wise fool, who magically manages to save his people from starvation, expand his family's turf, and remodel a border fortress into an open market, bringing peace to the marginal region. The first capitalist hero—in fact, the wealthiest person—in the history of chieftains, he redefines the word "fool" as a synonym of good fortune. His triumphant return from the frontier turns out to be a Rabelaisian fool's festival: "a pair of strong men lifted me onto their shoulders, and suddenly I was riding above hundreds of bobbing heads amid deafening cheers. I towered over the crowd, drifting on an ocean of human heads and tossed by raging waves of human voices."[2] But being a fool, he fails to seize his day by taking power. After the liberation of Tibet in 1951, he is murdered by his father's feudist.

The theme of the historical novel may be explored by means of a pair of core questions frequently enunciated from the middle of the work through the end: "Where am I?" and "Who am I?" (192/204–5). They are raised in the morning—the moment of transitioning from drowsiness to soberness, from subconsciousness to consciousness, from dream to reality—when "I" wakes up and feels lost. Since "Where am I?" is posed before "Who am I?," my identity is predetermined by my position. Often when these core questions are cast, the protagonist is put in a different place as the plot opens out: the first time is when he is sent by his father to the northern border of Maichi territory to compete with his brother in the south for heirship; the second time is when he is kidnapped and taken to the female chieftain Rongong's camp during the food bargaining on the border; then, he awakes again at home after missing the golden opportunity to direct the people's craze to usurp the Maichi chieftainship; lastly, however, after he has returned to the border, these two everlasting questions no longer bother him, as he finally knows where and who he is before being assassinated. As an ethnically and culturally hybrid writer, Alai seems to suggest that one can only find one's position and identity in repeated exiles, that a second exile is actually a comfortable homecoming, and that to define and shape one's Tibetanness against the background of Han society, it will be necessary to be elsewhere, away from home, so as to be considered a true Tibetan.

The powerful and wealthy Maichi chieftain gains his legitimacy not from the religious center of Lhasa to the west, but from his political ties to China in the east. This is reflected in the beginning: when Maichi files a complaint against his neighbor, Chieftain Wangpo, he goes to the military government of the Republic of China with an official seal conferred by the former Qing dynasty (1644–1911) emperor and a map. It is not the official title inscribed on the seal, but the geographic location defined on the map that determines the political inclination of the marginal subordinate—a subordi-Nation to both the political authorities of Beijing and the religious orthodoxy in Lhasa, whose scholastic Gelukpa School stands in contrast to Bön and other traditions that predominate in Jiarong. Though Wangpo also has a seal from Beijing, he always goes on pilgrimages to Lhasa as a result of his geographic ignorance in believing that his chiefdom is bigger than China. In any case, "even though they [the chieftains] considered themselves kings, they still had to kneel before those in power in Beijing and Lhasa" (97/102). Despite the proverb "the Han emperor rules beneath the morning sun, the Dalai Lama governs beneath the afternoon sun," the black-turbaned Tibetans' proximity to the immense Chinese territory has influenced the Maichi for their geopolitical position: "We were located slightly to the east under the noonday sun, a very significant location. It determined that we would have more contact with the Han emperor to the east than with our religious leader, the Dalai Lama. Geographical factors had decided our political alliance" (18/20–21).

Geographical factors indeed contribute to the black-turbaned Tibetans' ambivalent positioning and ambiguous identity. The Aba (Tib. Rnga ba) Tibetan and Qiang Autonomous Prefecture, one of the two Tibetan autonomous prefectures in Sichuan province reestablished during the 1980s on the basis of the previous Sichuan Tibetan Autonomous Region and Aba Tibetan Autonomous Prefecture, is a polyethnic gray area between the eastern edge of the Tibetan Plateau and the hinterland of China, a heterogeneous locus of the unified nation. It is in this "in-between space" in the midst of mountain folds, as Alai admits in his travel notes, that his stories unfold.[3] The special region, known as Jiarong (Tib. Rgyal rong), "was considered an uncivilized, barbarous wilderness, be it in the view of the westward expanding Tang dynasty [618–907], or from the perspective of the eastward extending Tibetans."[4] Following the Qiang (fourth century BCE) and the Tibetans (eighth century CE), the Han began to settle in this land on a large scale during the tenth century, as the Hui then did in the fourteenth. Different religious forces, including various sects of Tibetan Buddhism, Bön, Daoism, Islam, and Christianity, contend with each other to evangelize the polyethnic inhabitants. At the juncture of the provinces of Sichuan, Gansu, and Qinghai, Aba derives its name from the Chinese (mis-)transliteration of Awa, which in turn is short for Aliwa, meaning "migrants from Ali," an area in the westernmost Tibetan region.[5] Thus, in view of its diasporic history, the place and its nomenclature are already inscribed with an alien and heterodox Tibetan identity.

Geologically the Aba area, lying amid the Eurasian plate, the Indo-Australian plate, and the Pacific plate between the Yangtze platform and the Tibetan fold, is frequently under the influence of two fault zones.[6] A total of twelve tremors over 5.0 on the Richter scale were recorded there in the 1930s and 1940s, with the first epicenter right in Markham, which is identified by geologists as one of the five major seismic areas in the region.[7] What do the complex tectonics of earth's history tell us about the problematics of ethnic identity? If the two fracture zones can be interpreted as the Sino-Tibetan tensional forces that have been tugging the Aba Tibetans, then there is no doubt that Alai deftly employs the violent shakings of the earth's crust caused by tectonic collisions as a metaphor of political subduction.

When asked about the implications of the two earthquakes in the epic, the Chinese critic Bai Ye sees the second seism, starting with the maniacal movements of the adulterers and adulteresses, as a condemnation of morbid lust.[8] Rather than incline to moral judgments, I perceive the tremors as presages of the political upheaval. The scene immediately before the first quake, when Chieftain Maichi attempts to find a spot in the field to make love to his third wife, can be seen as a colonial allegory of territorial violability: "Let me remind you that this impatient man was the master of boundless lands, yet he could not find a place to lie with his beloved woman. The empty spaces were all taken up by animals of unknown origin" (64/68). One wonders what on earth these "animals of unknown origin" are in the colonial history on the fringe of the Tibetan Plateau. They abruptly appear when the mysterious, fragrant, flaming flowers from China form a spectacular carpet across the Maichi manors. These foreign species suddenly occupy the Tibetan territory. Although its gigantic stone structure survives the temblors, the chieftain's seemingly unshakable estate is razed to the ground by the PLA's artillery fire in the end. As the dust settles, these eastern Tibetans are no longer under the rule of their kings but are identified as the subjects of an alien authority.

In effect, as the story develops, Alai demonstrates a subtle shift of influence on the Tibetan periphery from West to East by first exhibiting an array of Indian imports (balms, incense, snuff, tiger-skin capes, gem-studded daggers, fruits, flowers, drugs) and then gradually enumerating Chinese products (poppy seeds, firearms, wax, candy, tea, china, silk, sedan chairs). Among these exotics, especially noteworthy are the last Indian item and the first Chinese item found in the fiction, namely the pink pills that cure syphilis and the red poppies that bring as much wealth as dearth. From the place which the Tibetans refer to as Gyakar (Tib. *Rgya dkar* or *Rgya gar*), the Land of White Robes, i.e., India, comes the medicine as remedial as Buddhism; from Gyanak (Tib. *Rgya nag*), the Land of Black Robes—China—comes the narcotic as addictive as power. The opium poppies transplanted by the Chinese emissary stupefy the chieftains, making them believe that they have control over their lands. Thus the poppy plant, its giant blossoms rapidly reddening the gray area between the white and black lands, is not only a hallucinogen and an aphrodisiac[9] but also a biological metaphor and color code for a new form of Chinese colonization. Introduced into the Four Chieftains area around 1938,[10] poppy planting was finally banned with the abolition of chieftaincy and the advent of communism, for the Red Chinese now prescribe their red utopia as a more effective opiate than red poppies.

Furthermore, the territorial aggrandizement of the colored Chinese is also metaphorically associated with the sexually transmitted disease that follows the spread of poppies: "Before falling asleep, I kept thinking about syphilis and about 'them.' I'd take a stroll on the street as soon as I got up the next morning to see if I could spot the colored Han" (369/393). Instead the narrator runs into a family feudist, whose brother enlists as a Red Tibetan to avenge their father's death from injustice upon the Maichi. At the end, "I" is killed not by "them," the Red Han Chinese, but by one of "us," his Red Tibetan compatriots—that is, not by the colonizer other but by the colonized self. So though I am *here*, here has now become a domain of *there*, as *we* have become a part of *them*, and I, a stranger within myself. This leads our attention to the loaded question of colonial identity.

"Who Am I?" The Idiocy of Identity

To answer the question "Who am I?" is to identify "I," to define "I"; and to define the self is to describe *it* not as a subject but as an object, that is, to objectify it or differentiate it as the other. This does not seem to be a problem in the beginning, when in the first quarter of the novel "I" is a member of an ethnic group which is casually distinguished from the Chinese by the foreign missionary Charles: "If, *like the Chinese*, you are worried about the intentions of Westerners, then wouldn't Wangpo Yeshi's religion be a good one for you? Isn't his derived from the teachings of your religious leader, the Dalai Lama?" (94/99; my emphasis). By comparing the Tibetans with the Chinese, the westerner actually makes a statement contradictory to the imperialistic claim that the Tibetans and their territories are within the boundaries of, and therefore belong to, China. Yet it soon becomes an issue when the Maichi family is accused by other chieftains of being "traitors to the Tibetan people," even though the accusers themselves have also been granted their fiefdoms by the Chinese emperors (104/113). The concept of "traitors" (Ch. *pantu*), which can just as easily, if not more effectively, be used by the Chinese government to condemn the Tibetan separatists, reveals the acute anxiety arising not only from the conflicts of interests between the two peoples but from the struggle for power within an ethnic group. Interestingly, it challenges the idea and role of a fixed identity, suggesting a split identity under the double pressure of expectations from both sides, for traitors are traders of dual identity.

The postcolonial theorist Homi Bhabha has felicitously argued that the singular identity is unsettled by hybridity, which he defines spatially as the margin where continuous contacts and conflicts of cultural differences would release an identity from its stable construction based on oppositional categories such as race and class, giving rise to an "in-between identity."[11] Conceived when his father was drunk, the idiot I-narrator is the child of a chieftain and his second wife, a Han prostitute who becomes a Tibetan aristocrat through interracial marriage. Hybridity is found in his mixed blood as well as in his noble and low origins. Trapped between Tibetanness and Chineseness, nobility and lowliness, his ethnic and class status—two of the key components that constitute an identity—are problematic, though the class concern is not emphasized as much as the ethnic question in the story. Identity hybrids are also found in his parade, including two maidservants, an adulterine slave, an executioner-photographer, a priest-turned-historian, and a disloyal wife of noble birth. Together these complex characters represent a highly hybrid humanity that casts in carnivalesque light the complexities of collective identity formation.

The literary critic Yue Gang further interprets the nitwit-narrator as an alter ego of the author himself by reading into Alai's multiple hybrid biography: "Above all, the 'hybrid' would be the easiest way to characterize an obvious point: the protagonist and I-narrator of the novel is the son of a Tibetan father and a Chinese mother. In fact, Alai himself is 'hybrid' twice over, of Tibetan and Hui parents, raised in a Tibetan village but formally schooled as a teacher of Chinese and married to a Han teacher of English. His cultural hybridity engenders something different from, if not entirely beyond, the concept of ethnic identity developed in our academic discourse. His is a position of an epistemological order that blends a deep-seated folk wisdom with a distanced position of prophecy and culminates in an aesthetic of historical melancholia."[12] Such "an aesthetic of historical melancholia," as I understand it in the fool's epic, originates from the narrator-writer's nostalgia for the Tibetan empire's early colonization.

Pained enough in his identity questions/quest as he suffers from amnesia in the detritus of history, the protagonist-narrator only barely remembers the glorious past of the independent Tibetan kingdom during the seventh and eighth centuries, when his nomad ancestors settled in northwest Sichuan.[13] The disintegration of the Tibetan empire left in the vast Jiarong region as many as eighteen chieftains registered under the Ming and Qing sovereignties. Ethnologists tend to adopt among diverse theories the explanation that Jiarong is an abbreviation of the Tibetan place-name Jiamu chawarong, which means "the agricultural area (*chawarong*) under the mountains of local gods (*jiamu*)," whereas the epicist prefers to interpret *jia* as a Tibetan reference to the Han people, who lived nearby the agricultural valley (*rong*).[14] While the ethnologists' view is rather religious, that of the epicists points directly to the Other, whom the nomadic settlers encountered. The Jiarong Tibetans were first localized by the Sichuan natives and then Sinified to become farmers during many centuries of colonization. As the colonizers yesterday, they were counter-colonized then and are recolonized today. Colonization is therefore never unidirectional, nor does it occur only once.

Such processes of colonization are epitomized in the epic by the lama-turned-historian Wangpo Yeshi, whose *tongue* is cut twice as punishment for his frank criticisms of Chieftain Maichi. Historically, the Jiarong Tibetans also became mute twice. First, being counter-colonized, they suffer from aphasia of their distinct dialect: "Later, when the Tibetan kingdom fell, nearly all the aristocrats who had come here had forgotten that Tibet was our homeland. And we gradually forgot our mother tongue. We spoke the language of the conquered natives. Of course, there were still signs of our own language, but they were barely perceptible" (96/101). Then, being recolonized, they adopted but did not acquire Chinese as their metropolitan language: to show the support of the Manchu and Republican rulers, an imperial plaque with a Qing emperor's Chinese inscription, "INSTRUCT AND ASSIMILATE BARBARIANS" (Ch. *daohua qun fan*), and a poem claiming the chieftains' territories by the Nationalist government's special emissary are proudly displayed in the guestroom of Chieftain Maichi, who ironically "knew nothing about poems, let alone one written in a tongue he didn't understand" (38/42). The Maichi idiot is not interested in learning Chinese either, when his Han mother offers to teach him. For the Tibetan chieftain, what matters are not the meanings of the Chinese characters but the authority and superiority that the *foreign* language as a master code represents. For the Tibetan writer, it is precisely the foreign national language that facilitates his narration of the native colonial history, when the native language is forever forgotten.

With the "national" language foreignized from the native perspective, the unified notion of "nation" is problematized in the meta-narrative: "Please note that Father used the word *nation*. That doesn't mean that he really believed he ruled an independent nation. It's all a matter of language. The word *thusi*, or *chieftain*, is a foreign import. In our language, the closest equivalent to *chieftain* is *gyalpo*, the term for 'king' in ancient times. Chieftain Maichi had used the word *nation* instead of other terms, such as *territory*" (37/41).[15] The official language is thereby estranged as consisting of senseless, if not entirely empty, signs. Questions about a total national identity and ideology for a strong, unified country are beyond the concern and knowledge of the local kings: "even the smartest person in this land would appear to be a moron as far as such issues were concerned, because not a single chieftain had ever really wanted to know what nation and nationality were" (351/374). In idiotism the dominant discourse of nation and nationality is regarded as grand nonsense, because the moron could not have the slightest idea of these modern notions.

Nor does "liberation" appear in its legitimate sense in the fiction. While the official chronicle *Aba zhou zhi* (Gazetteer of Aba Prefecture) highlights the PLA's distributions of relief grain during the liberation,[16] Alai satirically suggests that this has been done by the chieftain's idiot son before the advent of the communists. Moreover, the Maichi moron has announced his insane plan to set his slaves free on the eve of liberation: "The Liberation Army, which was fighting for the rights of the poor, had not yet arrived, and the slaves were acting as if they'd already been liberated. . . . the steward said, 'If this is how things are going to be, the Communists won't have anything to do when they get here'" (389/416).[17] So when the Communists come to "liberate" the area, they are in a rather embarrassing situation: "That upset the soldiers, for wherever they went, they had been greeted by loud cheers. They were the army of the poor, who made up the majority of the world's population. The poor people cheered because they had finally gotten an army of their own. But not here, where the slaves opened wide their foolish mouths to cry for their masters" (402/428). It is such "foolishness," or in a more literal sense of the Chinese original, *yu bu ke ji*, "stupidity in the extreme," that disavows the mammoth myth of the colonial liberation. Stupidity in the extreme is not merely a gesture of political sublation but a vision of alternative history that seeks to rewrite the region in the imagination with a possible past.

In fact, such dumb idiocy can be comprehended in the Daoist idiom of "great wisdom appearing slow-witted" (Ch. *da zhi ruo yu*). It is not a simple synthesis of sagacity and stupidity but the oxymoron of "a wise fool" in an upside-down world, where "an idiot was thinking for everyone else" (244/261). Portrayed as prophetic and passionate, the imbecile hero of Si-chuan Tibet is intended to embody a primitive wisdom that is dead and gone. The Tibetan slow-witted wisdom is found in the practice of tolerance: first, the mentally challenged Maichi discovers the magic that he feels no pain if someone hits him with hatred; later, when his family's implacable enemies make an attempt on his life, he thinks not of killing them in revenge; lastly, when he is murdered, he calls the avenger his friend. In the reality of Aba, it is such a spirit of lenience that yields a syncretism, which allows differing religions or sects to coexist in one temple.[18] This position of idiocy resists religious fundamentalism and destabilizes pure Tibetanness. To those who criticize or ridicule him for not being a real Tibetan, Alai laughs like an idiot.

Hence idiocy is a way of denying that one is identical or identifiable with any single group, be it the Chinese or the Tibetans, for the dunce is doomed to be simultaneously neither Tibetan nor Chinese. The French critic François Pitavy has observed in his study of the Faulknerian idiot: "The idiot . . . is the one without the Other, confined to the order of the imaginary, without the ability to rise to the order of the symbolic, since the 'I' is immutably related to an ideal self."[19] Indeed, by virtue of its inabilities and ignorance, idiocy opens a space for a mixed—instead of a fixed—identity and allows conflicting characteristics to fill in the identity vacuum. Yet it persistently resists the master narrative as, to borrow Bhabha's words again, "colonial nonsense."[20] The idiocy of identity is not an answer to "Who am I?" but a strategy to interrogate the institutional nationality imposed by the great Nation (like the bloody purple garment of a wronged slave's spirit that mysteriously wraps the protagonist's body, making his movements involuntary) and to recognize and repudiate at the same time the colonial otherness within oneself for the newly liberated generation, a generation bereft of a proper, ideal identity.

· · · · ·

It is from the interstices of the geological and cultural planes between the so-called Xizang and China's hinterland that a historic hybrid identity emerges. The idiotic identity that Alai attempts to articulate is an undecidable and yet undeniable self-positioning. It is not a cross-cultural identity found in any homologous sense but an in-between nonidentity existing as a heterologous presence. Wild folly prevents such identity from being ideologically identified and defined. And such is an "I"-idiot, who in spite of his occasional clear-headedness never informs us of his name in his narrative game, demanding that our sensibility address him by his multiple positions—because the question "Who am I?" would be unanswerable without also asking: "Where am I?"

Notes

I should like to express my gratitude to Nicole Elizabeth Barnes for taking the time to read my manuscript, and to Patricia Schiaffini-Vedani and Lauran Hartley for their intelligent editorial efforts.

1. For an analysis of Alai's "Bloodstains of the Past" read my "Historiographic Alternatives for China: Tibet in Contemporary Fiction by Tashi Dawa, Alai, and Ge Fei," *American Journal of Chinese Studies* 12, no. 1 (April 2005), 81–83. The four chieftains in history were Zhuokeji, Suomo, Dangba, and Songgang, the first being the most influential on the eve of liberation. See Sichuan sheng Aba Zangzu Qiangzu zizhizhou difangzhi bianzuan weiyuanhui, eds., *Aba zhou zhi* (Gazetteer of the Aba prefecture), vol. 1, 762–63, for an official account of the "peaceful liberation" of Situ in 1951.

2. Alai, *Chen'ai luoding*, 276; Goldblatt and Lin, trans., *Red Poppies*, 294. Hereafter page numbers in the text refer to this Chinese edition and then to the English rendition.

3. Alai, *Dadi de jieti*, 28.

4. Ibid., 29. The Jiarong region includes the Aba area.

5. See Yan Songbo and Que Dan, *Aba diqu zongjiao shiyao*, 3; also Alai, *Dadi de jieti*, 35.

6. Yan and Que, *Aba diqu zongjiao shiyao*, 1; "Aba Zangzu zizhizhou gaikuang" bianxiezu, comps., *Aba Zangzu zizhizhou gaikuang*, 4.

7. Sichuan sheng, *Aba zhou zhi*, vol. 1, 314, 316–17.

8. Bai Ye, "*Bailuyuan, Chen'ai luoding ji qita*—Dangqian xiaoshuo chuangzuo dawenlu," 201.

9. The Singapore historian Zheng Yangwen, in her *The Social Life of Opium in China*, 10–24, discusses how opium was initially consumed at the Chinese court as an aphrodisiac during the middle period of the Ming dynasty (1368–1644).

10. Sichuan sheng, *Aba zhou zhi*, vol. 1, 108.

11. Homi K. Bhabha, Introduction to his *The Location of Culture*, 18.

12. Gang Yue, review of *Red Poppies* (April 2005), at Modern Chinese Literature and Culture Resource Center (http://mclc.osu.edu/rc/pubs/reviews/yue.htm), listed under "Book Reviews." Alai's words of aspirations are quoted in Ran Yunfei and Alai, "Tongxiang keneng zhilu," 9; and in the Translators' Note to *Red Poppies*.

13. Modern western Sichuan is composed of parts of Amdo and Kham, two of the three provinces of historic Tibet. Thus an important effect of Alai's work is suggested by Bhabha's observation: "Remembering is never a quiet act of introspection or retrospection. It is a painful re-membering, a putting together of the dismembered past to make sense of the trauma of the present." "Interrogating Identity: Frantz Fanon and the Postcolonial Prerogative," *The Location of Culture*, 63.

14. Yan and Que, *Aba diqu zongjiao shiyao*, 7–9; Alai, *Dadi de jieti*, 13–14.

15. I have altered the English translation of *guojia* from "country" to "nation" for the sake of consistency with the quote that follows and because of its political implication of a particular people and territory that were formerly independent and are currently colonized.

16. Sichuan sheng, *Aba zhou zhi*, vol. 1, 36.

17. Here I resume using, from the Chinese original in the novel, the term "Liberation Army" (*Jiefangjun*), a short form of the Chinese People's Liberation Army (PLA), adopted in 1945. The English translation "Red Army" (*Hongjun*), short for the Chinese Workers' and Peasants' Red Army (*Zhongguo gongnong hongjun*), is an earlier designation used only in 1927–37.

18. For a study of syncretism and syncretic temples in the Aba Tibetan and Qiang Autonomous Prefecture see Yan and Que, *Aba diqu zongjiao shiyao*, 107–12, 430–35.

19. François L. Pitavy, "Idiocy and Idealism," 102.

20. Bhabha, "Articulating the Archaic: Cultural Difference and Colonial Nonsense," *The Location of Culture*, 123–38.

Development and Urban Space

in Contemporary Tibetan Literature

RIIKA J. VIRTANEN

The development taking place in Tibetan communities throughout the People's Republic of China (PRC) has been rapid, especially in urban areas. When traveling in the Tibet Autonomous Region (TAR) and Amdo (Qinghai Province) during the summer of 2005, I noticed clear and ample signs of infrastructural development: well-maintained roads, a reliable water supply, electricity, beautiful school campuses, modern buildings, hospitals, and lively business centers. Outside of Lhasa, a long traffic tunnel piercing a mountain was being opened to quicken the journey to Gongkar Airport. From the road near Damzhung one could see sections of the new railway supported by strong pillars with trainwagons on top, announcing the imminent opening of the railway connecting Lhasa and Golmud to the north.[1] The railway construction project has spurred widely differing opinions that mostly center on its long-term effects, as the railway connection will make the TAR more accessible to an influx of Chinese visitors, migrants, and others.

Tibetans have experienced dramatic changes during the years since the Chinese communist takeover of Tibet and the establishment of the TAR in 1965. Nevertheless, the modern and the traditional still coexist in Tibetan areas, leading to a certain tension and dialogue.[2] It is thus interesting to ask how these changes in the lives of the Tibetan people are reflected in literature. This chapter examines modern literary works to identify and better understand Tibetan responses to economic development, modernization, and urbanization, as inscribed or represented in short stories and novels.

Socioeconomic change can be identified in virtually every arena of Tibetan life. Education, for example, has been secularized and made more accesible since the Chinese takeover of Tibetan areas. Yet Tibetan illiteracy rates and school attrition remain alarmingly high.[3] Linguistically, the coexistence of Tibetan and Chinese has had a further bearing on education, administration, and the job market (see chapter 8). A third factor is the effect of urbanization. Traditionally many Tibetans have been nomads, and to this day nearly 85–90 percent of the population is still engaged in farming and pastoralism.[4] How is the strong contrast between modern, urbanized lifestyles and the age-old lifestyles of nomadic herders reflected in modern writings?

Tibetan Literature and Social Change

Tibetan modern literature (*Bod kyi deng rabs rtsom rig*) is a relatively new development: the literary works examined in this chapter were all written during the past twenty-five years. Most scholars consider modern writing styles to have begun in Tibetan areas only in the 1980s, after the Cultural Revolution and the advent of a certain leniency of policies in the PRC. Because the field of modern Tibetan literature is vast, I have had to limit the scope of my discussion to the literary works of four Tibetophone writers: Döndrup Gyel (Don grub rgyal), Tenpa Yargyé (Bstan pa yar rgyas), Anyön Trashi Döndrup (A smyon Bkra shis don grub), and Pema Tseten (Pad ma tshe brtan). All are well known among Tibetan readers; Döndrup Gyel in particular has become a legend and is popularly considered the founder of modern Tibetan literature.[5] Trashi Döndrup's stories are set in Amdo while those of Tenpa Yargyé are set mostly in the Northern Plain (Byang thang). Pema Tseten's novella, on which I shall focus when discussing his literary work, describes Tibetans in a very different kind of environment: the big city.

Most of the prose writings discussed in this chapter can be described as realistic, though Pema Tseten employs other styles as well, such as magical realism. Most stories take place in Tibetan societies and most of the characters are Tibetans. I have examined these literary works for any connection with the subject of socioeconomic development, whether it be events described in the stories, depictions of the milieu and thoughts of the characters, or figurative speech, such as metaphors and similes, that convey images of development and progress.[6] While the expressions found in these literary works are indicative of Tibetan views on development, literary works can of course be interpreted in different ways by different readers. The interpretations provided below are those of this author (unless otherwise indicated).

The ways in which art represents reality is the central problem for theories of representation or mimesis.[7] Literature is always a representation of something: it reflects either the outside world or the inner world of thought.[8] How faithfully it does so varies, as some literary works rely more heavily on fantasy and other works correspond more closely to the actual world or human thought and opinions. Though the characters and events in a work of fiction are imagined, these imaginings relate to or have their "roots" and inspiration in reality. Reality is thus modeled to a certain extent in the imaginings and thoughts of human beings.[9] Laurence Lerner has identified in *The Literary Imagination: Essays on Literature and Society* three constitutive factors that collectively shape a literary work: personal factors, factors concerning tradition, and social factors.[10] The writer who creates literature is a member of the society in which he or she lives; this socially embedded quality, in addition to personal and traditional factors, determines his or her literary expression. Moreover, the characters in the literary works themselves are usually people functioning in human societies; and the reading and reception of a literary work also connects it to society.[11] Once a literary work is published, through its reading it begins to influence the attitudes and ideas of the members of actual societies.

The term "development" as used here refers to certain changes in society, in people's environment and lives, which could also be denoted by the word "modernization."[12] I have concentrated on representations of the "new" and modern in these literary works, but have also paid attention to any lack of these representations. The description of a foreign nongovernmental organization (NGO) in one novella provides material for a brief discussion of the artistic representation of international cooperation in development initiatives. When the word "development" is taken to mean "modernization," the contrast between "modern" and "traditional" is highlighted. The word "development" can also be thought of as "improvement"; but to speak about "improvement" implies that the past was somehow inferior or undeveloped. I emphasize that my understanding of the term does not imply that the new is better than the traditional or that Tibetan communities in the past were "undeveloped."

Literary responses to the relations between the traditional and the modern have also been made in Chinese society. Min Lin (1999) has researched how Chinese intellectuals from a wide range of fields have responded in a multitude of ways in negotiating the divide between tradition and modernity.[13] Her study is relevant for the study of Tibetan responses to modernity, since Tibetans now live within the jurisdiction of the PRC and many Tibetan intellectuals receive their education at Chinese universities. Apart from the Tibetan and Chinese context, the clash between modernity and tradition seems to have arisen in places far apart around the globe. Wendy Griswold, for example, has identified in her study of Nigerian novels thematic elements that could be immediately found in several modern Tibetan literary works, such as the "city versus village," "conflict between individuals and families over marriage," "the aspirations of educated young people," "magic," and "confusion."[14] At

More than a decade of economic development has transformed the streets of towns in Central Tibet, such as the former wool trading post of Gyantsé (pop. 15,000) at 13,000 feet above sea level. Photo by Rebecca Best.

the same time, it is interesting to ask whether there are any peculiarities or special Tibetan features in Tibetan responses to modernization and development. When considering the theme of development in Tibetan areas, for example, the reader should keep in mind that writers in the PRC do not enjoy complete freedom of speech and that it is inadvisable for them to directly criticize certain government policies.[15] Yet it is sometimes possible for them to address socially important topics in ways that are open to various interpretations.

Döndrup Gyel and His Writings: Dreaming about a New Way of Thought

The short stories, essays, and poems of Döndrup Gyel seem to speak for renewal and development. Döndrup Gyel was a writer from the Amdo region (Qinghai), born in 1953 in Gurong Puwa. For the short duration of his life, prematurely ended by his suicide in 1985 (see chapter 4), the writer was prolific. His collected works consist of six volumes of short stories, poems, essays, translations, commentaries, and research papers. Since his death he has become a kind of legend. Posters with Döndrup Gyel's image are respectfully displayed in Tibetan shops in Xining and Lhasa, so highly valued that their owners refuse to sell them.

Many passages in Döndrup Gyel's works are related to the desire for renewal and innovation,[16] a theme expressed strongly in the writer's free-verse poems, often with the help of vivid imagery. The development that Döndrup Gyel desires is more generally conceived; he is more concerned with mental attitudes, and the poems do not specify the fields of social life where changes should be implemented.[17] The scenery of development is that of the mental world, from where all newness starts. The poem "'Di na yang drag tu mchong lding byed bzhin pa'i snying gson po zhig 'dug" (Here also is a living heart strongly beating) laments how difficult it is "in the socialist Land of Snow"[18] to introduce "a new way of thinking," "a new view," "a new way of believing," and "a new custom." To describe how the changes are almost impossible to achieve, the poem makes use of images of nonexistent things such as "a lotus in the sky" and "a rainbow on earth."[19] However, the poem also presents a beautiful image for progress (sngon thon). Progress is represented by the metaphorical image of a gentle rain (sbrang char),[20] a positive image that evokes the nourishing of fields and plants in anticipation of an abundant harvest. Though the poem expresses a strong desire for renewal, it also contains passages admiring the tradition and history of the Tibetan imperial period (seventh to ninth centuries).[21] Thus the poem can be interpreted in terms of cultural continuity, achieved not merely through preservation of the past but through cultural renewal and innovation to keep the culture alive. It is notable that the poem lends itself to a nationalistic reading. Yet in the interpretations stressing the affirmation of Tibetan identity, renewal is also seen as essential. While the poem laments the difficulty of introducing the new, it is nevertheless hopeful about the possibility for positive developments; toward the end of the poem the "I" sees in front of him the "nectar of happiness," hears "the livelihood of future," and, most importantly, sees that "the living heart is still beating."

Other free-verse poems of Döndrup Gyel also contain images of development and progress. The poem "Lang tsho'i rbab chu" (Waterfall of youth) uses the images of a beating pulse and the heart's blood to express the vital importance of development and progress.[22] Toward the end of the poem metaphoric images of the road or path are employed, generally hailing the "path of the future," "a new road for moving forward," and "a luminous highway." While all these images express optimism about finding a way to a better future, the poem also admits the possibility of difficulties: "On the road of the future there might be bigger curves than before."[23]

The image of a cloud, which is metaphorically addressed as the "messenger of the century" and the "happiness of the people,"[24] can be seen as a reference to modern change, development, and innovation. In the poem "Sprin dkar gyi 'dab ma" (Petals of white clouds), for example, the cloud "declares the good news of a new prosperous time arriving to the realm of snows" as it predicts the arrival of a new day.[25] The cloud "praises the great changes of the snowy high plateau" and is described as conferring the "glory of the power of creativity."[26] Change and renewal are cast in a strongly positive light. The free-verse poems of Döndrup Gyel can be interpreted by combining two frameworks, one rooted in a desire for renewal and creativity and the other in nationalism. That is, the poems express a desire for a future of both greater freedom and a greater degree of modernization and scientific rationality. At the same time, the poem "Petals of White Clouds" evokes a more individual interpretation connected with creative work, a prayer that the creative inspiration will stay in one's heart: in the last lines of the poem, the speaker prays that the cloud will "always float in the sky of his mind" and "stay as the ornament in his heart."[27]

These poems hardly mention any external or visible signs of development, except for the image of a road. Their imagery, like the images of gentle rain, clouds, and pulse, can be classified under the thematic categories of nature and living organisms. The poems speak about renewal in a natural way, a far cry from any type of western futuristic poetry with references to industrial and technical achievements. And yet the poems are future-oriented in their expression of great hope for progress. Recall that these poems were written in the 1980s, and that there have been many external developments, as well as certain intellectual changes, since then.

While in Döndrup Gyel's poetry modernization is portrayed more in terms of thought and mental attitudes, in his stories we can identify specific realms in which the writer desires change and encourages people to think critically.[28] The Tibetan customs of arranged marriage and blind religious belief, for example, are targets of the writer's criticism. The stories "Sad kyis bcom pa'i me tog" (Frost-bitten flower) and "Sems gcong" (Depression)[29] contain scenes of parents agreeing with the prospective spouses' parents about the marriage of their children. The children learn of decisions only afterward. In "Frost-bitten Flower" the children revolt against their parents' decisions. The advocated "modernization of thought" is characterized as "being freed from the trap of deluded thinking," a fate which the narrator in the first chapter wishes on the elder as a result of listening to the story that he has to relate.[30]

Most of Döndrup Gyel's stories are set in the countryside and populated with nomads or ordinary farmers living in villages. But the short story "'Brug mtsho" (Druktso)[31] provides an opportunity to reflect upon Döndrup Gyel's description of urban space, as the opening scene is set in the urban environment of Xining: "The summer morning in the town of Xining was filled with attractive characteristics in this way. The sky was blue and clear and in the eastern horizon were visible the clouds colored by sunrise. All the surroundings of the town were encircled by various species of trees giving it a green appearance. On the great bridge on the western gate of Xining cars of various sizes were passing to and fro giving out pleasant horn sounds. The women and men riding bicycles drove on the road ringing the bells of their cycles. In the midsts of trees on the roadside people were exercising and flower sellers were freely engaged in their own activities. All this added a new natural spendour to this ancient fortress town of the high plateau and made it into a vivid painting beautiful to behold" (*Collected Works*, 2: 302). In this passage Döndrup Gyel's view of urban space is aesthetic. The town is likened metaphorically to a beautiful painting, the urban center as "ancient" but with "a new natural splendour." The town with its objects and inhabitants is thus imbued with the ability to renew and transform itself. The story describes additional characteristics of Xining: its blocks of flats, wide roads, marketplaces, and even sweets and fruits.[32]

Although the urban space is given many attractive qualities, the "I" of the story has a liking for nomadic areas. The story opens with the narrator beholding the morning scene in Xining. He is on his way to the bus station, from where he will leave to visit a small community in the grasslands. From the start he is "inexpressably happy to go to do interviews in a nomadic area."[33] Furthermore, the "I" of this short story expresses his preferences by explaining that "even though his body has been in Xining, his mind has not for a moment been separated from the nomadic areas."[34] The story describes the narrator's bus journey, his approach and arrival at the destination. It paints the grasslands with beautiful images of fragrant flowers, horses, sheep, yaks, and singing herders in an idealized light.[35] Despite his longing for the grasslands, "I" has remained thus far in Xining because his job demands it. However, in the story he distances himself from the town; in this way the story describes a movement away from town, quite the opposite of what characterizes the modern phenomenon of urbanization. While other themes such as education and romance are also addressed in this story, for our purposes I have considered only the relationship between the town and nomadic areas—and the story expresses a clear preference for the grasslands over urban life.

Though the poems discussed earlier did not contain any concrete proposals and development is discussed at a more abstract level, Döndrup Gyel clearly considered education a basic requirement for development. Education and study are central themes in several of Döndrup Gyel's writings. Not least, the poems "Slob grwa'i zhogs pa" (Morning at school) and the free-verse poem "Rig pa'i dpa' bo rnams la phul ba'i bstod tshig" (Praise offered for the heroes of the intellect)[36] contain several metaphorical and favorable images of education and knowledge. The theme of education is also strongly present in many of the writer's short stories, including "Druktso" and "Frost-bitten Flower," as well as "Brtse dungs kyi rba rlabs" (Waves of love).[37] Typically the theme of education intermingles with romantic themes.

The last lines of the poem "Morning at School" contain a hopeful, almost exhilarated image of the development of education, expressed in the form of a simile:

Oh, the spring morning of the school
illuminated by ten million good signs!
This is the sign of the education of nationalities
waxing like the new moon. (*Collected Works*, vol. 1, 199)

Because high illiteracy rates continue to prevail among Tibetans in the PRC, it is plausible that education figures so prominently in the works of contemporary writers as a means of inspiring the reading public to engage in activities that would raise their level of education.

The crucial importance of native language skills for successful communication and understanding in achieving development is the focus of a lesser-known work by Döndrup Gyel entitled "Bod yig slob pa" (Studying Tibetan).[38] This short work is unique among the writer's works, as it is written in the Amdo dialect, imitating the colloquial idiom even in its spellings. It is structured in the form of a humorous dialogue between two persons whose turns of speech have been simply marked with *ka* and *kha*.[39] The dialogue centers on their dispute about the importance of studying Tibetan. One person argues for the need to study one's own language, while the other sees no benefit in such study. The curious situation of Director Wangchen, as relayed in this dialogue, is amusing. The director reads aloud documents in Chinese for Tibetan nomads who do not fathom the desired meaning.[40] But when he goes to a provincial meeting, he delivers his report about the difficulties faced by the "minority people" in Tibetan for the Chinese cadres. Although the situation seems quite ridiculous and elicits laughter from readers, the message is clear: a person who is able to communicate would achieve much more, and Tibetan nomads and farmers would learn more about development policies, if they could understand the speeches. The second person, *kha*, explains the importance of one's own language for development: "The communist party tells us how the level of science and learning of the people of the PRC should be improved. What we have in Tibet are the Tibetan letters. What we speak is the Tibetan language. How can one study Tibetan subjects without speaking and reading Tibetan? If one doesn't have a certain standard of education, how could one understand science? If we do not have a certain level of scientific understanding and learning, we will not be able to realize the 'four modernizations'"[41] (*Collected Works*, vol. 6, 49). For this reason the person in the dialogue who sees the value of Tibetan language stresses how everyone in society, irrespective of sex, age, or position, should acquire an education in Tibetan and study its literature and writings.

Nomads and Disappearing Ways of Life in Tenpa Yargyé's Prose

Tenpa Yargyé's writings present a much different view on life and development. He was born to a nomad family in the region of Nakchu in the Northern Plain (Byang thang) of the Tibet Autonomous Region in 1962. His first job was as a schoolteacher, and he later worked for several years at the Nakchu Cultural Bureau. In 2003 he moved to Lhasa, where he is engaged as a songwriter and scriptwriter at the Institute of Performing Arts of Tibet.[42] He has written many short stories and one novel, and has researched folk traditions of the Northern Plain.[43] His collection of short stories is entitled *Byang thang gi mdzes ljongs* (The beautiful northern plain), and a new collection will be published soon.

Most writings by Tenpa Yargyé deal with the life of the people of the Changtang or Northern Plain, the high, cold region north of Lhasa where the vast majority of the population is engaged in nomadism. Foremost is the recently published novel *Thag ring gi sbra nag* (A distant nomad tent), also set in the Northern Plain and depicting the life of hunters.[44] The main characters, Wangchen and his son Drandül, have left their home village and are wandering in the hostile and cold high plateau. They get their food by hunting. The culture of the hunters, their customs, beliefs, and songs, is described in naturalistic detail. The novel also contains hunting scenes and descriptions of taking revenge on enemies.

While reading *A Distant Nomad Tent* I could not at first determine when the events were taking place. Only toward the end of the narrative is there a clue: as Wangchen's son Drandül joins the Tibetan troops on their way to oppose the intruders,[45] there is a mention of the British armed mission to Tibet, which was commanded by Colonel Francis Younghusband in 1903–4.[46] Thus the book is set in a period when man was very much part of nature, void of modern technology (except guns). Though direct representations of development are missing, by looking back toward the ancient and traditional the work marks a perspective quite contrary to that presented in the writings of Döndrup Gyel.

When I discussed this novel with the author, he pointed out that the hunters' way of life is vanishing in Tibet, since the hunting of wild animals has been prohibited by law. One aim of his book was to describe this old way of life and thus preserve some knowledge of the culture and traditions of hunters. Recent Tibetan literature has also evinced an interest in folk traditions. The old is seen as valuable and interesting, and some writers like Tenpa Yargyé include detailed, ethnographically colorful descriptions of folk customs and beliefs in their literary works. In the background are worries that distinctively Tibetan culture is being displaced by modernity, often influenced by Chinese and global culture.

The narratives of the short stories of Tenpa Yargyé take place in more recent times. The short story "'Char snang" (A strange occurrence), published in *Tibetan Art and Literature* in 2003, reflects well the contrast between the traditional life of nomadic people and the modern, "developed" urban life. Even though the traditional and the modern coexist, differences between them are so great that communication and understanding can be difficult. "A Strange Occurrence" tells about a nomad's visit to a town. This is his second visit there: during his first visit he had lost to gambling, drinking, and women all the money that his family had earned by gathering a medicinal herb. The story revolves around the simple event of a nomad searching for a restaurant that serves yak-meat noodle soup. Instead of the restaurant he is searching for, the nomad finds a discothèque. The narrator comments: "as if a magician had performed a magic trick on this small town, even a trace of its former visage was not visible."[47] The town has undergone a complete transformation.[48] The nomad's bewilderment becomes evident for the reader when the nomad cannot interpret properly a scene of dancing couples and a band playing on a television screen. For him, the dancers dancing close to each other appear like "Siamese twins practising walking" and the musicians are perceived as "men who are almost naked and resemble women and women who resemble men looking as if possessed by demons."[49] The nomad's attempt to order his favorite meal is rebuffed by the waitress, who explains that the restaurant has only "karaoke." The nomad tries in vain to order "a bowl of karaoke."[50] The nomad refuses the waitress's offer to bring spirits and exits the restaurant.

Out on the street he is "almost 'bitten' by a small car." As the nomad encounters the decadent world of nightclubs, the reader senses his estrangement and alienation, and the misinterpretations that often result when different cultures collide.

The collection *The Beautiful Northern Plain* (1995) contains eight short stories depicting the lives of nomads in their natural environment in the Changtang. The material goods of modern life such as motorcycles, wristwatches, and tape recorders sometimes appear in passing in the stories, even as the nomads of the stories are mostly engaged in traditional tasks such as milking dris,[51] fetching water, taking care of sheep while armed with a sling ('ur rdo), going to a salt-lake for a salt expedition.

One story which makes skillful use of modern objects is "'Gyur khug mang ba'i mdza' glu" (A melodious love song). A commonplace object such as a tube of toothpaste becomes a representation of modernity, or at least something new and strange, against the traditional background of the nomads. The story tells how Lhabu, one of the main characters, has just returned from the army. One morning Pelmo, a young woman, notices something unusual: "That day while Pelmo was going to fetch water passing near the door of the village chief Nyima, Lhabu was wearing a clean white shirt and washing his teeth holding a glass in his left hand. As he moved the small brush back and forth in his mouth, bubbles resembling the color of milk emerged. She stopped there. Having seen something which she had never seen before she stayed looking there for a while greatly astonished" (31). Lhabu presents Pelmo with a tube of toothpaste and the girl starts to dream about him, hiding the tube under her pillow. Her plan is to open the tube on their wedding day. When she later suspects that her wishes won't come true, she opens the tube, only to find to her horror that the contents are not toothpaste but black shoe polish.

Here the "modern," against the background of very traditional ways of life, is a source of astonishment and humor. In a story set in a town it might be difficult to create this startling effect with such a simple object as toothpaste.

In this story most of the modern objects are owned by Lhabu, who has returned after four years outside his native place. At the end of the story his cassette recorder plays the "melodious love song" which is also the title of the story. Thus modernity seems to leak slowly from outside, even as the nomads carry out their traditional activities such as taking care of the sheep and embroidering tent cloths.

Another short story in the same collection, "Rtswa thang gi glag phrug"

A bilingual street sign on the campus of Qinghai Nationalities University in Xining reads "Knowledge is Power" in Chinese, Tibetan, and Mongolian. Photo by Riika Virtanen.

(Young eagle of the grasslands), centers on education. It begins by praising the development in Nakchu, a town in the Northern Plain, described as the "sky and earth changing places." The writer comments, "Who wouldn't scatter words of praise and lift his thumb in appreciation?"[52] For outer signs of progress characterizing an urban environment, this text mentions the modern multistoried buildings, networks of roads, factories, modern machines, and marketplaces. The school where the protagonist, a poor nomad boy named Nakto, is working is "standing magnificently like a snow mountain."[53] A recurring image throughout the story is "the young eagle of the grasslands." This refers to Nakto, a good student and later an exemplary teacher who earns a prize for his work in education. Nakto is a kind of pioneer, said to be the first child from his village to go to school and also the first to enter university.[54] At the end of the story Nakto flies in a "silvercolored iron bird" to Beijing to receive an "outstanding teacher" award. By portraying the modern school building as a snow mountain and an airplane as a bird, the writer employs imagery connected with nature to depict modernity. In describing Nakto's career and studies the writer is clearly encouraging the young generation of nomads to engage in studies and thus sees the primary importance of education for development. The story ends with the exclamation of the narrator, or perhaps rather the the writer: "Oh, the young eagle of the grasslands, I pray that you will rise higher and higher showing the skills of your wings."[55]

Trashi Döndrup's "The Sound of Autumn": Contrasting Tradition and Modernity

Trashi Döndrup's pen name is Anyön (*a smyon*). This means a "mad [person from] Amdo" (*A mdo smyon pa*). According to the writer, the madness in his pen name refers to his way of thinking differently about many matters.[56] Now I shall look at the views on development and Tibetan society in general that emerge through his writings and whether they differ somehow from the writings of the other writers examined in this chapter.

Trashi Döndrup was born in 1967 in Trika (Tib. Khri ka; Chin. Guide), in an area of great natural beauty on the bank of the Machu River (Rma chu), a two-hour bus journey from Xining. Many of his stories are set in this immediate area or in more distant places throughout his home region of Amdo. Trashi Döndrup has been working as an editor for the literary magazine *Sbrang char* (Light rain) since 1990 and is the author of many short stories and poems, several of which appeared in this publication. Here I shall examine several stories in a collection called *Ston gyi rang sgra* (The sound of autumn), paying special attention to how they relate to development and modernization. The collection contains thirteen short stories and two novellas. In several of the works it is possible to perceive a dominant tension between the traditional and the modern, the "old" and the "new," around which the story has been built. For example, in the short stories "Sems nad" (Depression) and "'Pho 'gyur" (Change) the modern and the traditional are contrasted in such fields as agriculture, livelihood, health issues, customs and beliefs, the environment, and education.

Health is central in the short story "Drin chen ma" (Mother), which reflects on how traditional and modern methods of treating illness still coexist in Tibetan society at large and even inside a single family. The mother of the main character, Teacher Khedrup, has a long history of stomach pains. Khedrup and a healer called Akhu Menpa (Uncle Doctor) see the benefits of treatment in a modern hospital, whereas Khedrup's father is a believer in traditional healing methods. The traditional healing methods described in the story entail the recitation of religious scriptures in the presence of the sick person. The father has also invited two long-haired ngakpas (*sngags pa*)[57] to perform rituals in their house. The story describes a dispute between father and son about whether it was wise to take the mother to a hospital for an operation. In the persons of the son and the father, modern and traditional views clash. There is a clear gap between the thought and actions of characters belonging to different generations. At the end of the story both the traditional and modern treatments fail, and the final scene suggests that the mother has died.

As for development in the field of agriculture and general living conditions, the stories contain several episodes in which the young wish to realize some modern trends and manage to do so, despite opposition from the elders. In the short story "Depression," an old woman named Pemakyi has lost her husband in a car accident. Wishing to know the causes behind this sudden death, she consults a *ngakpa* or tantric practitioner who performs a *mo*-prediction. According to the prediction, "it is not good to dig earth and turn stones."[58] Before his death, the husband had cut trees and leveled a mound in the shape of a *stupa* to obtain clay for constructing walls. Believing the prediction, Pemakyi takes it as her cause to refrain from any work that would disturb the earth. Members of the younger generation of her family disagree. Against the wishes of their grandmother, they construct a fruit garden and also an irrigation channel to bring water to a potentially fertile corner of land. They hope that the grandmother will later see the benefits. Yet in the last scene of the story the grandmother is crying.

This story seemingly contrasts old ways of thinking with newer ones, belief in supernatural predictions with the modern use of advances like irrigation. And yet the story takes no stand on which approach is better. It can be also interpreted as an environmentally cautionary tale, one that warns of the undesirable consequences of excessive change. In parts of Amdo the tilling of earth to increase arable land has spurred erosion. The story "Change" also discusses the relation of agricultural work and technological advances.[59] Toward the end of this story, however, another kind of development work is described: the renovation of old Buddhist sites and monasteries, as the main character, Lugu Gyel, decides that the time has come to speak for the renovation project of an old stupa, which was ruined during the Cultural Revolution.

The title story, "The Sound of Autumn," is an epistolary novella of well over one hundred pages, placed last in the collection.[60] Detailing the correspondence between four old schoolmates, the story focuses on development of several kinds, educational, cultural, and economic. Of special interest is that the story also concerns the involvement of a foreign NGO in Amdo.

Most descriptions of the cooperation between local Tibetans and the foreign agency are contained in the letters of a character named Trelgen Lozang. After completing his university education, he has been sent to work in a remote nomadic area. There he has been observing the life of nomads and comes up with the idea of opening factories in the community that will produce carpets, powdered milk, and shoes.[61] After a successful proposal, which is supported by the local leaders, the community manages to get funding of over two hundred thousand yuan and machinery from an American charitable organization (simply called *dbul skyob tshogs pa*, literally "association protecting from poverty").[62] Trelgen is nominated as the factory manager, and the story describes the cooperation between "foreign specialists," factory workers, and other local people.[63] The story gives a very positive image of the cooperation taking place, as it describes how the prosperity of the area increases. The factory buys wool from the nomads, and new restaurants and shops are built. The attitudes toward the carpet factory project of the local people, ranging from leaders to ordinary nomads, are highly positive; the story describes the people as "filled with one hundred thousand joys."[64]

The character Trelgen Lozang has even written an article concerned with development, entitled "On the Benefits of Establishing a Factory in the Nomadic Area."[65] In their letters to him, his friends praise the article and his focus on "the future of Tibetan society" instead of its past.[66] The novella ends with an invitation to Trelgen Lozang's wedding that he sends to his old schoolmates. He will marry a teacher, Yangchen Drölma, and the ceremony will be held in the assembly hall of the carpet factory, organized through the cooperation of the local people and the American organization.[67]

The short stories of Trashi Döndrup also contain scenes related to education, although it remains a secondary theme. In several of the stories it is not at all self-evident to the elder characters that the children should acquire an education at all. The parents often seem to think that the children should engage in work benefiting the home. For example, in the short story "Btson ma zhig gi snying gtam" (The heartfelt talk of a prisoner) the main character Thöpaga has to stop his academic career even before completing the first grade to look after his family's sheep. In a story entitled "G.yul bcag pa'i gtam rgyud" (Tale of winnowing the harvest), the son who looks too much at his school papers gets scolded, and the father suspects that his attending school has negatively affected his work in the field. In another story, "Spyang ki lug rdzi dang kho'i chung ma" (The wolf-shepherd and his wife),[68] the main character, a shepherd named Tselo, recalls how a university student once tried to look after his sheep. The student suffered from high altitude symptoms and once, in a hurry to escape the mountains, left his books in the mountain hut. In all these scenes the elders are seen as not clearly realizing the value of education.

Trashi Döndrup's stories reveal an appreciation of traditional customs and beliefs, as illustrated in the story "The Wolf-Shepherd and His Wife," which contains strong elements of folk-religious belief. Here the shepherd and his wife come to believe that the wolf killed by the shepherd was the guardian dog of Sinpo Dzagen (Srin po rdza rgan), a mountain also believed to be a local god. The shepherd has to invite ngakpas to perform rituals in his house, and he himself must perform offerings at the local god's temple and offer incense at the site where he buried the wolf. Another story, "Gangs ljongs—rnam shes kyi 'jig rten" (Snowland—The world of consciousness), centers on the old custom of making a mark on a person who is about to die and then searching for a child who bears a similar mark on his body. In spite of his appreciation of old customs, there is one custom against which this writer seems to revolt much in the same way as Döndrup Gyel and many other Tibetan writers did. This is the custom of arranged marriages. In the novella "Nga dang Sgrol ma rnam gsum gyi gtam rgyud" (The tale about me and the three Drölmas), the parents' involvement in the marital plans of their children causes a great deal of unhappiness.

The characters of Trashi Döndrup's stories who side with modernity and those who side with traditional life share certain features and characteristics. For example, ngakpas abound in these stories, representing traditional customs and folk beliefs. On the other hand, those persons who have managed to acquire an education and are often living in a town (like the son working as a teacher in the short story "Mother") represent the modern way of thinking. While the author typically contrasts the views of the elder and the younger characters, there are moments when the elders begin to appreciate the deeds of the young, as in "The Tale of Winnowing the Harvest," in which the father finally admits that his son has been right in his wish to hire a machine to help in the agricultural work.

It is indicative of the extent and rapidity of development that it is possible to create these kinds of stories, in which the central tension is between the traditional and the modern, the elder and the younger. Generally speaking, the society described in Trashi Döndrup's stories seems to stand somewhere between modernity and tradition, reflecting the situation prevailing in Tibetan communities. His view of society and development can be seen as lying somewhere between those of Döndrup Gyel (who was strongly forward-looking) and Tenpa Yargyé (who highlights tradition). Trashi Döndrup portrays situations in which "new" and "old" exist in the same community, often with no clear indication of which is to be preferred.

Tibetan Urban Lives: Pema Tseten's Novella "Life in Town"

Pema Tseten is a writer and award-winning film director from Amdo.[69] Several of his short stories have appeared in literary magazines such as *Light Rain*, *Mang tshogs sgyu rtsal* (Folk art and literature), and *Lho kha'i rtsom rig sgyu rtsal* (Lhoka literature and art). He writes in two languages, Tibetan and Chinese, but the stories mentioned here are all in Tibetan.[70] Initially his stories caught my attention because of the experiments in narrative technique employed in some of them. For instance, his short story "Chos sgron dang mo'i bu Blo ldan" (Chödrön and her son Loden) has several intertwining layers, some recounting the "stories" themselves and others the process of producing and hearing about the stories. Thus the story of a mother and her son, who has been sentenced to death for stealing, is told through the "fictional" writing of the "I"-narrator and through the "real" story (with a highly absurd final scene) as told by the people of the village. The story compares the "fictional" and the "real," but of course both tellings are fictional. There is even reference to a third telling of the story, in which the "I"-narrator promises to write a version based on the "real" events.

I shall concentrate on Pema Tseten's novella "Grong khyer gyi 'tsho ba" (Life in town), published in *Light Rain* in 2003, while adding a few words about the short story "Gangs" (Snow).[71] The latter is exceptional for its magical realist style compared to the other prose writings discussed in this chapter; it also contains artistic representations of the effects of capitalist ideology and westernization.[72] "Life in Town" describes Tibetan lives in urban contexts.[73] Its realistic style makes it appear quite conventional, except for a striking scene relaying the dream world of one of the main characters and a rather bizarre passage in which advice is offered on "how to remove arrogance from three kinds of women."[74] "Life in Town" mainly describes the life of a single Tibetan family in a big town. The members of the family are the husband Yungdrung, his wife Dekyi, and their son Rikden. Through the telling of their life unfolds a picture of the challenges often encountered by Tibetans in urban environments. The name of the town where the novella is set is not mentioned; it is identified only as a "big town" where a few Tibetans live.[75] It is also a place associated with education, where one can see all kinds of material objects and phenomena. A friend of Yungdrung explains these as the cause of the "innate pride" of women living in town.[76] The "big town" is thus not only a physical domain that can be contrasted with milieux and places outside urban areas but also a cultural and sociological domain.[77]

This rather long novella broaches a startling number of issues concerning development and social change. Several scenes address educational and linguistic debates, traditional and modern approaches to health and medicine, unemployment among Tibetan graduates, and conflicts between traditional Tibetan beliefs and customs and mainstream Chinese urban culture. If we compare this literary work to the stories of Tenpa Yargyé set in the Northern Plain, we see a striking contrast in the way the relationship between the traditional and the modern is portrayed. In the stories about nomadic communities, the modern is something "new and exceptional"; but in "Life in Town," the traditional customs and practices of Tibetans become "the other," that which differs from the surrounding cultural environment and provokes reaction, whether it be irritation, amazement, or hostility. Even the society where the Tibetan characters of the novella are living is essentially non-Tibetan.

The tendency to regard Tibetan customs and beliefs as falling far outside the norm is well illustrated in a scene where the young couple, Yungdrung and Dekyi, with their son Rikden, perform the traditional tsetar (life liberation) practice in the middle of a public park in town. In this religious practice merit is accumulated by releasing animals who might otherwise be killed. The family engages in this practice, in hopes that Rikden, who has also received treatment in a modern hospital, might be healed. An elderly person, Dekyi's father, has consulted a lama for a mo-prediction; according to the prediction, a tsetar practice and certain recitations must be performed to ensure the child's complete recovery. They also receive instruction from a ngakpa, who has performed the prescribed recitations (causing much resentment among the Chinese neighbors). The ngakpa advises the family on how to perform the tsetar in town: it is more practical to release fish rather than bigger animals in an urban environment. The next day Yungdrung, Dekyi, and Rikden go to the park to do the tsetar practice according to the instructions: "After the number of fish had reached fifty, Yungdrung still bought a few more. They had Rikden throw the fish one by one into the water. The fish that were thrown into the water shook their bodies quickly and vanished from sight. At first, the people standing around the pond looked at this with amazement. Eventually, they began whispering and some people were making negative and sarcastic comments in hushed voices. Though Yungdrung and Dekyi wished to tell the surrounding people about the virtue of saving lives, when they thought about it in detail, the fish were being released into the pond and it was certain that fishermen would again catch them. Unsure if this were an actual saving of life, they said nothing; holding Rikden by his hand, they hastily made their way through the crowd and returned home" (26). In this scene even the relatively young Tibetans who are performing the traditional religious practice are not completely free of doubts about the sensibility of their actions. Moreover, this practice negatively effects Yungdrung's career: he gets reprimanded at his workplace for his involvement in a superstitious practice and has to confess his mistake in writing (27). As in the prose of Trashi Döndrup, this story portrays ngakpas as representatives of the traditional culture. However, in an urban environment they are scarce: the young couple must search for a passing ngakpa in the town's bus station.

The novella also resembles Trashi Döndrup's stories in its focus on the gap between the generations, and how they differ in their actions and ideas. In the story it is Dekyi's father who behaves more traditionally. For example, after his daughter succesfully delivers a child (through a ceasarean section), he seeks out a lama to request a name for the child. In another scene Dekyi's contraceptive pills are destroyed by her mother, who wants her daughter to get pregnant.

Pema Tseten's stories often contain an unexpected turn of events or change in the flow of narration. In this story the surprise is in the content: the reader is not likely to expect that a story about a young, well-educated Tibetan couple living in an urban environment will end with a dramatic conflict between Bön and Buddhist beliefs. Dekyi's family finds out that Yungdrung comes from a Bönpo family, and after negotiating with their daughter, the parents and Dekyi together scold and threaten Yungdrung, expelling him from their house. He is prohibited from even seeing his child. It is a kind of explosion of old religious suspicions and prejudices in the midst of life in a modern city, suggesting that such prejudices are difficult to erase and can affect the lives of even highly educated people. The crisis in the main characters' marriage introduces the theme of what constitutes the Tibetan nature in a modern environment. From Pema Tseten's perspective, their inner worlds of thought have not become so "modern and rationalized"; old beliefs are still deep-rooted. Education and language are also key concerns in the novella. One of several subplots is the choice of language in which Rikden should be educated. In predominantly Chinese-speaking surroundings, the Tibetan skills of the boy do not develop properly—a cause of worry for his parents. Only when Rikden gets the chance to spend time in his father's native place, a Tibetan community in the grasslands, does he learn to express himself in Tibetan. The father's and son's trip to the grasslands can be described as the journey from a domain seen as "other" than Tibetan to a domain that is essentially Tibetan and affirms the identity of the child.

A large gap between the worldviews of Tibetans born in the countryside and those born in urban centers is reflected in the different childhood experiences of father and son. Yungdrung remembers his first visit as a child to a town and how he was afraid of a car. At the same time, like many Tibetan children growing up in an environment where the Chinese language is dominant who are losing their Tibetan language skills, Rikden has some difficulties recognizing species of animals in the countryside. A Sunday class is arranged to teach the Tibetan language to children, who attend it with great enthusiasm. Rikden is lucky in that when he attains schoolgoing age, a Tibetan primary school is established in his town. To prove the need to know one's own native language, the novella employs the logic of communist ideology: it invokes Stalin's four conditions which a nationality must fulfill—one of which is a common language—and mentions linguistic rights allowed by law.

The situation facing Tibetans living in urban environments is a difficult one: to be successful in a dominant Chinese society it is necessary to be fluent in Chinese. Tibetans who want their children to receive a Chinese-medium education are depicted at length in another short story by Pema Tseten, "Gza' nyi ma" (Sunday). The story recounts the events of one Sunday in the life of the first-person narrator, a poet named Gyentsen. Among the people whom Gyentsen meets is his old schoolmate, accompanied by his wife and son. The couple first treat Gyentsen to drinks and a good meal and then request his help in transferring their child from a Tibetan-medium school to a Chinese-medium school. The father reasons that Chinese-language skills ensure a better future for the child. Though a "cold shiver" runs through Gyentsen's body, he cannot refuse to help. Together the father and the poet visit Künzang, the principal of the Chinese-medium school. Künzang is from the same village as Gyentsen. The father gives beer and a white silk offering-scarf (khata) as a gift to the principal, who eventually agrees to accept the child, but only on the condition that he start one grade lower than his level at the Tibetan-medium school. As the three men continue to drink, the principal remarks on how useless it is to know Tibetan. In return, Gyentsen asks, "Is not the language that you were just speaking now Tibetan?" The opinions of his old schoolmate and the principal so irritate Gyentsen that he leaves the school building. Outside he is again beset with "cold shivers."[78] These stories reveal the conflict between wanting to preserve one's native language and culture and wanting one's children to be able to find jobs.

Another short story by Pema Tseten, "Chödrön and her Son Loden," points in the same direction as his other works discussed here. The "I"-narrator has to travel away from a town to his native place to collect material for his writing. He explains that he never feels like "an urban person" and gets his inspiration when thinking about life and events in his native place.[79] The countryside, and its agricultural and nomadic communities, here is a kind of cultural model of Tibetanness vis-à-vis the town, which is described as more Sinicized. This could explain why many Tibetan writers, even if they live in urban centers (a common occurrence), still set most of their stories in nonurban locations.[80]

In "Gangs" (Snow, 1999), Pema Tseten tells the story of a boy and a girl who both have the name "Snow" and resemble each other, like twins. Another unique characteristic that they share is that their bodies are completely transparent—one of the supernatural features of the story. The theme of capitalism enters the story when the grasslands where they work as teachers receive excessive snowfall and the cattle and people suffer under difficult conditions. To alleviate the suffering and to buy food for the people and animals, the "Snows" decide to put on a show, selling tickets to people wishing to see their transparent bodies. Events take a bumpy turn when westerners who show up are allowed to photograph the the transparent body of the boy called "Snow" but not the two "Snows" together, though they are willing to pay a big sum for the privilege of doing so. The westerners come across as highly stubborn and even appeal for the government to achieve their purpose.

Toward the end of the novel the local leader and other government officials decide that the next morning both "Snows" must allow the westerners to take a photo, even if force is necessary. That night all members of the grassland community, including the government officials, have a dream in which the "Snows" are "the offspring of the snowmountain"; it is revealed that "it is time for them to return to their final abode, the snowmountain."[81] As these unique Tibetans vanish into the snowmountains, the author seems to express his concern that traditional Tibetan culture will succumb to the influx of global and western cultural influences and capitalist ideology, which believes in the power of money and measures everything by it.

· · · · ·

What conclusions might we draw from examining the literary works of these four Tibetan writers, with regard to their representation of development and a rapidly changing society? In all the works the authors have juxtaposed, in similar settings and periods, traditional and modern elements present in Tibetan society. Though Döndrup Gyel's writings typically argue for reform and are critical in their approach, the social milieu in which he situates many of his stories lies outside the town, most often in small villages where the local inhabitants (farmers and nomads) pursue traditional livelihoods. The fiction writing of Tenpa Yargyé is typically set in nomadic communities, where life still seems very traditional. In stories temporally located in the near-present, the modern usually makes sudden appearances in a still very traditional society, sometimes in the form of modern objects which elicit wonder from the characters. In the stories of Trashi Döndrup the tension between the modern and the traditional is often central to the plot. Pema Tseten's novella, by contrast, describes the life of Tibetans in a big town. Yet he too contrasts traditional customs and beliefs with life in a modern urban environment, the countryside with urban centers. The tendency of these four writers to juxtapose the modern and the traditional can be considered a reflection of present-day Tibetan society, in which the traditional still plays a role. However, the degree to which the modern and the traditional coexist varies in these literary works, as does the mood or attitude with which the encounters between them are depicted.

In light of the material examined in this chapter, it appears that there is considerable diversity in how Tibetans view development. Even a single short story may contain widely varying views, as when some characters oppose modernization and development while other characters actively engage in them. Similarly, the perspectives of the writers themselves vary: the views presented in their works range from a desire for renewal (without losing one's cultural roots) to worries about the disappearance of old ways of life. Even those works which express a desire for change also acknowledge the value of tradition. At the same time, when old customs and beliefs are described and even upheld in a work, we cannot assume that the author would speak against all forms of development. Rather, these authors seem to point toward a form of development that preserves traditional folk culture and ways of life. On the whole, the picture that emerges is that of an all-encompassing but nuanced combination of modernity and tradition.

References to Tibetan folklore and traditional Tibetan ways of life can also be interpreted as assertions of Tibetan cultural identity, a need that arises in the PRC, where Tibetans are considered "a minority" and their culture "a minority culture." But Tibetans in the PRC lack the freedom to decide the direction of development and modernization, and face political restrictions on how these themes can be presented in literature. One strategy adopted by Tibetophone writers has been to juxtapose urban environments with rural or nomadic environments. In the writings examined here, towns were described as sites of rapid transformation (even to the point of unrecognizability), resulting in feelings of alienation, displacement, and nostalgia for the native region. Furthermore, the difficulty of maintaining Tibetan practices and Tibetan-language skills in urban environments leads to interpreting the domain of a town as non-Tibetan by its nature. The grasslands thereby become a symbol of Tibetanness.

These literary works suggest that the most crucial question related to development in Tibetan areas is how to preserve the valuable and beautiful aspects of traditional life while providing people with modern comforts and advances. All four writers regard education as essential for improvement and development. They emphasize the need to build and maintain schools, but also the urgency of promoting Tibetan-medium education. As for the role of foreign NGOs and other external agents in development, the stories suggest that in addition to socioeconomic awareness, organizations must be conscious of local cultural matters and beliefs, and highly sensitive to them.

All the writers discussed here raise the question: Can the old and the new coexist continually, or is Tibetan society progressing toward a modernity that will gradually rob it of its past, its unique flavor, its folk culture and beliefs? Their collective answer is that it will be immensely challenging to strike a harmonious balance between modern advances and the preservation of valuable elements in Tibetan culture, some aspects of which may soon vanish from the Land of Snows amid the fervor of rapid development.

Notes

This is a considerably expanded version of a paper originally presented at the seminar "Civil Society, NGOs and Development," arranged by the Sasakawa Association on 15 October 2005 at the University of Helsinki. Its abridged version, "Representations of Development in Contemporary Tibetan Literature," is to be published in a volume of the proceedings edited by H. Katsui and R. Wamai. I am grateful for the comments and advice of Professor H. K. Riikonen, Dr. Gray Tuttle, Dr. Lauran Hartley, Lhundup Dorje, Franz Xaver Erhard, Dr. Hisayo Katsui, Dr. Richard Wamai, Minna Hakkarainen, and members of the Civil Society Study Group. I also remain deeply grateful to the Sasakawa Young Leader's Fund for the scholarship which made possible my fieldwork in Qinghai and central Tibet in 2005.

1. The railway opened on 1 July 2006.
2. For a discussion of the current situation of Tibetan communities in Qinghai, Sichuan, Yunnan, and Gansu see Kolås and Thowsen, *On the Margins of Tibet*. For the situation in Amdo (Qinghai) also see the various articles in Huber, ed., *Amdo Tibetans in Transition*.
3. For instance, according to a recent item by TibetInfoNet Update (27 September 2005), based on the 2004 *China Statistical Yearbook*, the illiteracy rate of the adult population in the TAR was as high as 54.9 percent in 2003 ("Illiteracy and Education Levels Worsen in the T.A.R. despite Development Drive"). However, statistics differ and rates vary in other areas. Another source, an official Tibetan-language publication, states a lower rate: 32.5 percent. See *Bod ljongs deng rabs can du 'phel rgyas 'gro bzhin yod* (Tibet is modernizing) (Beijing: Krung hwa mi dmangs spyi mthun rgyal khab kyi rgyal srid spyi khyab khang gi gsar thos gzhung las khang, 2001), 29. Kolås and Thowsen mention low school enrollment among children of school-going age in several areas populated by Tibetans outside the TAR (*On the Margins of Tibet*, 102–3).

4. Kolås and Thowsen write that most sources estimate the total number of farmers and herders to be as high as 85–90 percent of the Tibetan population (*On the Margins of Tibet*, 154).

5. See Tsering Shakya, "The Waterfall and Frangrant Flowers," 36; and Pema Tsering, "A Deceitfully Erected Stone Pillar and The Beginnings of Modern Tibetan Literature," 112.

6. For a discussion of similar themes in the writings of Döndrup Gyel, Lhagyel Tsering, Drongbu Dorjé Rinchen, Yangtsokyi, Tsering Döndrup, and others see Hartley, "Themes of Tradition and Change in Modern Tibetan Literature."

7. A classic study of representation theory is Erich Auerbach's *Mimesis*, first published in 1946. It examines the relations between reality and its representations in literature in a large number of western literary works from different periods, beginning with the *Odyssey*.

8. Eagleton has pointed out how the role of representations has grown in modern societies with the age of computerization and the worldwide web (*After Theory*, 49).

9. See Walton, *Mimesis as Make-Believe*, 21. On page 74 he writes illuminatingly: "Reality can be the subject of fantasy."

10. Lerner, *The Literary Imagination*, 1–23.

11. See Milner, *Literature, Culture and Society*, 185.

12. The Tibetan language has more than one word for development, including *yar rgyas*, *'phel rgyas*, and *mdun skyod*. *Yar* means "upward," *rgyas* "to widen," *'phel* "to increase," and *mdun skyod* literally "to move forward." These words are quite general and can be used in a variety of contexts.

13. Lin and Galikowski, eds., *The Search for Modernity*.

14. Griswold, *Bearing Witness*, 3–4.

15. Consider the discussion of Özer in the Introduction of this book.

16. Some of these works have also been translated into western languages. Tsering Shakya has translated "Waterfall of Youth" into English in Stewart, Tsering Shakya, and Batt, eds., *Song of the Snow Lion*, 9–13. A Finnish translation of this same poem has appeared in *Kirjo* 2 (2002), 10–11. Mark Stevenson and Lama Choedak T. Yuthok have translated the "Narrow Footpath" into English. See Rang grol (Döndrup Gyel), "A Threadlike Path," *Tibet Journal* 22, no. 3 (1997), 61–66. See also Stevenson's essay "Paths and Progress."

17. Abu (A bu), also known as Dobi Chökyong (Rdo sbis Chos skyong), has characterized Döndrup Gyel's views as evincing "special courage" (*thun min gyi snying stobs*). See A bu, "Don grub rgyal bsam blo ba yin min skor gleng ba," 4. Abu has written a book, which should appear soon, about Döndrup Gyel and his writings. Parts of it have already been published in *Mtsho sngon bod yig gsar 'gyur* (Qinghai Tibetan News).

18. *Collected Works*, vol. 1, 90–94. An English translation of this poem is available in Virtanen, comp. and trans., *A Blighted Flower and Other Stories*, 141–44.

19. *Collected Works*, vol. 1, 92.

20. Ibid., 93. The word *sbrang char* is frequently translated as "honey rain." [According

to Alak Tseten Zhapdrung, however, *sbrang* refers to the insect fly (*sbrang ma*). Thus *sbrang char* is a rain light enough for a fly to navigate. (Conversation with Pema Bhum, New York City, 20 January 2008.)—Ed.] *Sbrang char* is also the name of a popular literary magazine in Amdo in which many of Döndrup Gyel's works first appeared.

21. Ibid., 90–92.
22. Ibid., 135.
23. Ibid., 136.
24. Ibid., 232.
25. Ibid., 231.
26. Ibid., 232.
27. Ibid., 235.
28. Two of Döndrup Gyel's stories are in English translation in Virtanen, comp. and trans., *A Blighted Flower and Other Stories*. Dr. Françoise Robin has translated a selection of this writer's stories into French; see *La Fleur vaincue par le gel* by Döndrup Gyel (Paris: Bleu de Chine, 2006).
29. *Collected Works*, vol. 2, 218–88, 1–17.
30. Ibid., 219.
31. Ibid., 302–17.
32. Ibid., 303.
33. Ibid., 302.
34. Ibid.
35. Ibid., 312–13.
36. Ibid., vol. 1, 195–99, 147–56.
37. Ibid., vol. 2, 18–55.
38. Ibid., vol. 4: 43–50.
39. These are the first two letters of the Tibetan alphabet and are here used to mark the speakers in the same way as an English dialogue might use "A" and "B."
40. Kolås and Thowsen, *On the Margins of Tibet*, 142, report a similar "real-life" occurrence in Jyekundo (Skye rgu mdo) during a horse race. A Tibetan officer gave a speech in Chinese to Tibetans, most of whom could not understand it.
41. Tib. *deng rab can bzhi*.
42. Tib. *Bod ljongs glu gar tshogs pa*.
43. In works associated with folklore, like collections of folksongs, this writer has used the pen name Thang sras yar rgyas, the first part of which can be translated as "Son of the Plain."
44. This novel first appeared under the title *Khrag gi zegs ma mkha' la 'phyo ba'i gangs ri dmar po* (A red snow mountain spraying drops of blood towards the sky) and was published serially in the literary magazine *Bod kyi rtsom rig sgyu rtsal* (Tibetan art and literature). In 2005 it was published as a book by the Nationalities Press in Beijing, its title changed to *A Distant Nomad Tent*.
45. Bstan pa yar rgyas, *Thag ring gi sbra nag* (A distant nomad tent) (Beijing: Mi rigs dpe skrun khang, 2005), 425 n. 1, 428.
46. Smith, *Tibetan Nation*, 156–60.

47. Bstan pa yar rgyas, "'Char snang" (A strange occurrence).

48. The theme of metamorphosis can be observed in connection with descriptions of urban environments in different parts of the world. Veivo (*The Written Space*, 178) has used the concept of metamorphosis to describe one aspect of the representations of a French town in his book. For a comparison of Tibetan and European representations of urban environments see Blanchard, *In Search of the City*.

49. Bstan pa yar rgyas, "'Char snang," 44.

50. Ibid.

51. A female yak, *'bri*.

52. Bstan pa yar rgyas, *Byang thang gi mdzes ljongs*, 146–47.

53. Ibid., 147.

54. Ibid., 151.

55. Ibid., 169.

56. For further discussion of Tibetan writers and the use of pen names see chapter 6.

57. Ngakpas are lay tantric practitioners. They usually belong to the Nyingma-school (*rnying ma*) of Tibetan Buddhism and are often invited to perform various rituals in people's houses.

58. A smyon, *Ston gyi rang sgra* (The sound of autumn), 72.

59. This short story originally appeared in *Sbrang char*, 1998, no. 1, 4–14. The same issue of this literary magazine also contains two other short stories bearing the same title, one written by Trabha (Bkra bha) and the other by Rangdra (Rang sgra).

60. A smyon, *Ston gyi rang sgra*, 293–431. This novella first appeared in *Sbrang char*, divided into two parts published in no. 1 (1999), 4–53, and no. 2 (1999), 4–25.

61. A smyon, *Ston gyi rang sgra*, 350–51.

62. Ibid., 402.

63. Ibid., 410–11.

64. Ibid., 402.

65. Ibid., 351.

66. Ibid., 382, 406.

67. Ibid., 431.

68. Ibid., 112–34. This short story was first published in *Sbrang char*, 1993, no. 1, 4–16.

69. For information about his new film *The Silent Mani Stone* see Li Huijuan, "Silent Mani Stone wins a prize at Pusan Film Festival" (web site of China Tibet Information Center, 26 October 2005). This short article spells Pema Tseten's name as pronounced in Chinese: Wanma Caidan. His film is said to be "the first Tibetan dialogue film in China's film history."

70. According to the literary critic and scholar Dula Gyel, many of Pema Tseten's literary works have appeared in Chinese literary magazines such as *Minzu wenxue* and *Xizang wenxue*. See Bdud lha rgyal, "'A khu thod pa la bcar 'drir phyin pa' zhes pa'i sgrung gtam la 'brel ba'i gtam," 135.

71. Pad ma tshe brtan, "Gangs."

72. For further discussion of this short story see A bu, "Sgrung gtam 'Gangs' las 'phros pa'i gtam."

73. At least five other stories bearing the same title have been published in *Sbrang char*

during recent years. One is the novella *Chengshi shenghuo* (City life) by Li kra'o kreng (Ch. Li Zhaozheng), originally published in Chinese; see the Tibetan translation, "Mi dmangs rtsom rig" (lit. Literature of the people), *Sbrang char*, 1999, no. 4, 36–58, and 2000, no. 1, 30–74. See also short stories written by Trabha in *Sbrang char*, 2003, no. 2, 4–16; Anyön Trashi Döndrup in *Sbrang char*, 2004, no. 1, 28–66, 82; Rangdra in *Sbrang char*, 2003, no. 1, 4–34; and Takbum Gyel in *Sbrang char*, 2003, no. 4, 4–17.

74. Pad ma tshe brtan, "Grong khyer gyi 'tshoba" (Life in town), 12–13, 34.

75. Ibid., 5.

76. Ibid., 12.

77. For a theoretical discussion on representations of space see Veivo, *The Written Space*. In particular, "The Matrix City" (170–85) outlines his view of space or setting in a literary work as something more than just a mere description of place. Space can be seen as a cultural model and used for thematic purposes. Veivo writes, "Representing space works toward cultural models, ideals and fixed situations, reaffirming or refusing the tradition the writer is situated in" (172).

78. Pad ma tshe brtan, "Gza' nyi ma" (Sunday), 9–12.

79. Pad ma tshe brtan, "Chos sgron dang mo'i bu Blo ldan" (Chödrön and her son Loden), 6, 7, 10.

80. Also Kolås and Thowsen, *On the Margins of Tibet*, 153, write about the image of "grasslands Tibet" and its function of affirming Tibetan identity.

81. Pad ma tshe brtan, "Gangs," 36.

12

Modern Tibetan Literature
and the Rise of Writer Coteries

SANGYE GYATSO (GANGZHÜN)

TRANSLATED BY LAURAN R. HARTLEY

From 1980, after the Cultural Revolution, Tibetan literature saw the spread of new and unprecedented forms. Short stories, poetry, essays, and plays began to evince rich writing styles and vivid content, such that Tibetan literature started to develop in accord with other literatures in the People's Republic of China (PRC) and overseas. At the same time, Tibetan literature maintained its own characteristics, and the new forms evolved more perfectly into the new Tibetan literary forms we see today.

It is my purpose here to more closely examine the development of modern Tibetan literature and to identify six stages or periods since 1980: a preparatory stage, or the Dungkar Rinpoché Period (1980–84); a founding stage, or the Rangdröl Period (1983–86); a trial stage, or the Jangbu Period (1987–89); a stage of continuity, or the Ju Kelzang Period (1988–93); an expansionary stage, or the "Four Demons of the Old Fort" Period (1993–96); and a mature stage, or the Period of Plurality (1996 to present). I have delineated these stages or periods based on my own analysis of the development of modern Tibetan literature. Each of these six periods, except for the last, is dominated by certain artistic qualities that characterize the works of writers from this time. Four of the periods have been named for representative literary figures, that is, authors who served as models for younger writers. During the final two stages, The Period of the Four Demons (1993–96) and the Period of Plurality (1996 to present), several literary cliques or coteries of Tibetan writers came into being. This phenomenon is unprecedented in Tibetan literary history, and I shall thus devote greater space below to discuss these formations.

The Dungkar Rinpoché Period (1980–1984)

What we call "contemporary Tibetan literature" (*da lta'i Bod kyi rtsom rig*)[1] can be dated from around 1980, when Tibetan writing flourished again after the stultifying excesses of the Cultural Revolution (1966–76). The first stage in the development of modern Tibetan literary forms lasted from 1980 to 1984. This was a transitional period during which the "old" and "new" were forged in the transmission of literary thought and instruction. I have named this period after Dungkar Lozang Trinlé (1927–97), whose use of traditional writing styles to describe and critique contemporary social life characterizes literary production during this time. Dungkar Rinpoché, who obtained his *geshé* degree from Sera Monastery in 1957, served on translation committees in the early communist period. Like many other scholars he was imprisoned during the Cultural Revolution and exonerated only in the late 1970s, when he was asked to teach Tibetan literature and history at the Central Nationalities Institute. In 1985 he moved back to Lhasa, where he was a professor of Tibetan history at Tibet University.[2] What distinguishes Dungkar Rinpoché from his predecessors is that they wrote mostly about religious issues while his writing seeks to reflect society; his poems concern topics such as communism and describe the lives of peasants and herdsmen. He transformed literary themes to reflect the concerns of the Tibetan people, and he wrote in a language more closely resembling that spoken by the common people. His greatest contribution is the book *Snyan ngag la 'jug tshul tshig rgyan rig pa'i sgo 'byed* (Opening the door to the study of ornamentation for writing poetry) (Xining, 1982), which is still widely studied today.

Other important writer-scholars from this period include Tseten Zhapdrüng (1910–85), Mugé Samten (1923/4–93), Dorjé Gyelpo (1913–92), Khyenrap Ösel (b. 1925), Druprik Khyumchok (b. 1930), and Tupten Nyima (b. 1943). I would also include in this list Alak Dorzhi (b. 1935/6), who continues to teach at Northwest Nationalities Institute in Lanzhou (Gansu Province), as well as Lugyel Bum and Jamyang Drakpa, who teach in the Tibetan graduate program at Qinghai Nationalities Institute in Xining (Qinghai Province). Collectively these teachers have dedicated themselves to providing the younger generation with a cultural education and have thus played a critical role in equipping later writers with the requisite skills. Döndrup Gyel (1953–85), for example, studied with Dungkar Rinpoché at the Central Nationalities Institute from 1978 to 1981. When his first collection, *'Bol rtsom zhogs pa'i skya rengs* (The dawn of clear and simple writing), was published by the Nationalities Publishing House in January 1981, Dungkar Rinpoché wrote the foreword. Many of Döndrup Gyel's early poems were quite classical in form, reflecting Dungkar Rinpoché's training.[3] Indeed, Dungkar Rinpoché's textbook on kāvya theory, which includes many of his original verses as illustrative examples, is still used in Tibetan literature classes in the PRC.

The Period of Rangdröl (Döndrup Gyel) (1983–1985)

"Rangdröl" (rang sgrol) which literally means "self-liberation," was the pen name of the well-known writer after whom I have named this period, Döndrup Gyel. Since he is the focus of a separate chapter in this book and the subject of other informative studies,[4] I shall refrain from providing biographical details on his life and untimely death in 1985. He is an emblematic figure, not least because of the innovativeness of his writings. The writers of this experimental period made courageous progress in the realm of short stories, poetry, and essays. In the mid-1980s innovative works with little precedent in classical Tibetan literature slowly began to appear, many inspired by Döndrup Gyel's free-verse poem "Lang tsho'i rbab chu" (Waterfall of youth), his essay "Rkang lam phra mo" (The narrow path), and his short story of a tragic rape and social change, "Sad kyis bcom pa'i me tog" (The frost-bitten flower).

Other writers representative of this period are Nordé, Penjor Langdün, Repgong Dorjekhar, Chapgak Dorjé Tsering, and Chöpa Döndrup. These authors paid more attention to content in their works, because they still lacked the necessary artistic training and experience to develop sophisticated literary forms. They emphasized that literature should reflect society and wrote about their nationality's right to exist, encouraging Tibetan youth to take up constructive causes that would help the Tibetan people.

The importance of these writers' earlier works was to enable Tibetan literature to proceed on a wholly new path. Though their writing careers began in college nearly two decades ago, several of these writers are still actively publishing. Repgong Dorjekhar, who now works for a translation bureau in Beijing, has recently written two novels: Rnam shes kyi dgod sgra (The laugh of consciousness, 1996) and Rkyal ba'i 'jig rten du nyul ba'i gtam rgyud (The tale of wandering in a swimming world, 1998). Members of this older generation of writers are distinguished from later writers not only by their age but in their writing styles, which are more strongly influenced by realist literary theory.

The Jangbu Period (1985–1989)

These five years were important for the advance of Tibetan literature on a path toward wholly new forms. Forgoing praise poetry and artifice (tshul chos), writers in the late 1980s closely analyzed the reality of their time and employed such writing styles as magical realism (Ch. *mohuan xianshi zhuyi*, Tib. *sgyu 'phrul dngos yod ring lugs*) and critical realism (Ch. *piping xianshi zhuyi*, Tib. *dgag gyag dngos yod ring lugs*). Many works of high quality appeared at this time, such as Jangbu's "Sog rus las mched pa'i rnam shes" (Consciousness from Mongolian bones)[5] and "Gangs dkar lha mo'i bslu brid kyi dbang gis" (Under the spell of the White Snow Goddess),[6] and Patsé's "Gna' bo'i cong rnying," (Ancient bells).[7]

I have highlighted Jangbu (Dorjé Tsering) because his work has been the most influential among all these writers. During the late 1980s he was well-known for his obscure poetry, representing a radical break from realist dictates. He drew inspiration from the Chinese "Misty Poets" (Ch. *menglongshi*). Writers of this generation had a very good command of the Chinese language, so they benefited from reading modern Chinese literature and world literature in Chinese translation, including works by Whitman and Pushkin. Some of the writers—such as Jangbu, Rinchen Trashi, and Tsering Döndrup—were greatly influenced by magical realism as well, in part through the magical realist works of the Tibetan Sinophone writer Zhaxi Dawa (see chapter 9). Soon younger Tibetan writers rallied to this style to distinguish themselves from the preceding generation of writers. Generally speaking, they expressed their sense of social responsibility more subtly than the previous generation; they never used slogans in their writings. Although content was important for them, they paid special attention to form (for the first time in modern Tibetan writing). These writers were more experimental, more open to trying new techniques, in closer touch with the outside world. In the 1990s their writings inspired a series of debates about the relative value of obscure poetry, with Jangbu's admirers arguing for the right to pen "meaningless" works.[8] In recent years Jangbu himself has returned to a more reflective and often satirical writing style. Since 2005 he has been teaching Tibetan language and literature at the Institut National des Langues et Civilisations Orientales (INALCO) in Paris. His latest projects include a documentary film entitled *Tantric Yogi*, which in *vérité* style follows the exchanges of local villagers preparing to attend the great gathering of yogis in Huangnan Prefecture (Qinghai Province) in the summer of 2003. In 2006 he cowrote the script for Sherwood Hu's acclaimed film *Ximalaya wangzi / Prince of the Himalayas*.

Other major writers from this period include Patsé, Rinchen Trashi, Lhagyel Tsering, Tsering Döndrup, Namsé, Gönpo Trashi, and Orgyen Dorjé. While these writers did not write obscure poetry, they were largely contemporaries of Jangbu, more innovative in their writing styles. Many of these writers were classmates or knew each other well, and ultimately they came to

The poet and scriptwriter Jangbu (center) on the set of *Ximalaya wangzi* (Prince of the Himalayas), 2005. Photo courtesy of Dorjé Tsering.

influence each other. Tsering Döndrup writes fiction only: a prolific number of short stories and more recently a few novels. Orgyen Dorjé is unique in that he is from the Tibetan Autonomous Region, whereas the other writers mentioned are all from Amdo. He writes both poetry and short stories. His themes are profound and often hard-hitting.

The Ju Kelzang Period (1988–1993)

Ju Kelzang is an extraordinary writer who has been influential ever since the first period (the Dungkar Rinpoché Period), during which his skill in classical Tibetan literary forms drew public attention. At the same time, it is only fitting to include his work in the category of contemporary Tibetan literature. Like the writing of his contemporaries, Ju Kelzang's works during the period from 1988 to 1993 were pure literary art, as seen in his poems "Acrostic Machine," "Thoughts," and "Gendün Chömpel." I thus call this the Ju Kelzang Period. It was a time when love for nationhood, natural law (*chos nyid kyi bden don*), and society were fused and when writers drew on the strength of their intelligence, abilities, and experience. Other representative writers include Trashi Penden, Tenpa Yargyé, Khedrup, Baré, Chepa Tamdrin Tsering, Könlo, and Durbu Namdrak. Several of these writers were from the Tibet Autonomous Region, including Zhikatsé, Nakchu, and Lhoka. This was a more conservative period, during which writers focused mostly on the characteristics of Tibetan nationality and were skeptical of borrowing too many influences from outside. They made an effort to use the Tibetan language without calquing, or literally translating words and ideas from other languages, as the previous generation had sometimes done. They took for their model the figure of Gendün Chömpel, an outstanding intellectual who believed in innovation but never lost his Tibetan characteristics. Although this generational cohort of writers is smaller than the previous one, it became very influential—primarily for its emphasis on returning to the essence of Tibetan culture.

The "Four Demons of the Old Fort" Period (1993–1996)

A fifth or expansionary stage in the development of modern Tibetan literature can be delineated by the advent and contribution of the first major literary group to emerge in the PRC. "The Four Demons of the Old Fort" (gna' mkhar 'dre bzhi) is a collective name coined in 1993 for four friends who all worked and wrote in Xining, the capital of Qinghai Province. The Four Demons were Chen Metak, Drong, Zhidé Nyima, and Dodrak. As literary and intellectual models for young Tibetan writers in the Xining area, they played no small role in helping to pioneer a Tibetan "New Era" literature (Bod kyi dus rabs gsar ba'i rtsom rig) in Amdo. Moreover, they lent their energy to a wide expansion of writers and literary publications.

The term "old fort" refers to the ancient wall or city fort of Xining when it was an imperial outpost during the Qing Dynasty. A small section of this fortified wall remains visible today, beside the highway just south of the city center. The term "demon" was used primarily because the writers tended to oppose norms of thought and behavior and wrote of difficulties in accepting current society. The Four Demons promoted their literary project in Xining. Poems accounted for the bulk of their literary output and were always in free verse. The many song lyrics that they produced, including Drong's "Gsol 'debs" (Offering) and Zhidé Nyima's "Nga'i gangs ljongs yul la ltad mor phebs" (I went to visit my Snowland) became influential works.

The Four Demons of the Old Fort based their writings on the literature of their own nationality, but were also strongly influenced by foreign literary theory, including imagism, romanticism, magical realism, futurism, and surrealism. They thought that focusing merely on issues pertaining to nationality was to impose limits on poetry. For these writers, poetry had to look into humanity's deepest concerns. Thus they tended to portray some of the darkest problems of society. This made them very different from writers of the two previous generations: although writers such as Jangbu and Ju Kelzang differed significantly in their literary philosophies and styles, both had a positive attitude toward the issues that they portrayed. The Four Demons of the Old Fort, on the contrary, purposely wrote about negative aspects of society with the didactic aim of pointing out behavior that people should not emulate. They adopted poetic elements from the likes of Baudelaire, Eliot, Pound, Rilke, and the Chinese *menglongshi* (obscure) poets, in particular Haizi (Zha Haisheng, 1964–89). In this way they forged a new artistic method for expressing subtle changes in the primordial mind, with theoretical influence from western literary thought. Many excellent writings were published during this period, including "Ngang ba ser bo" (Golden goose), "Nga dang nga'i grogs po tsho" (My friends and I), "Sgyu rtsal gyi dad ldan" (Artistic faith), and "Tshor snang gsar ba" (New sensations). The Four Demons movement was no small force in the Tibetan literary scene from 1993 to 1996, and for this reason I have chosen to distinguish it from other coteries of writers described below. The Four Demons and their writings inspired the emergence of other literary groups. And each of the four has continued to produce a remarkable number of comedic scripts, monologues, and lyrics. Chen Metak, for example, who now lives in Golok, remains a prolific poet.

Chen Metak (Sönam Tenpa) is also known by friends as Rje btsa' ro ba, a rather humorous nickname that likens the tone of his skin to rust. He was born in 1969 in Lhasa Village of Nangkhok Township in Chentsa county in Qinghai Province. His pen name literally means the "Fire Spark from Chentsa." He entered primary school at the age of seven and the Chentsa Nationality Middle School in 1981. After graduating from middle school in 1985 he took the entrance exam for Qinghai Nationalities Teachers Training College, from which he graduated in 1989. Since then he has worked as a Tibetan teacher at the Golok Teachers Training School and the Golok Tibetan Middle School. He is a member of the Qinghai Writers Union. It was while staying in Xining from 1993 to 1994 that he became friends with Drong, Zhidé Nyima, and Dodrak, and the four were named the Four Demons of the Old Fort at that time.

Chen Metak began writing poetry around 1986, at the age of fourteen. Several of his poems appeared in *Lang tsho* (Youth), the literary magazine of the Qinghai Teachers Training School, from 1986 to 1989. His poem "Nyi zla ri bo'i snyan tshig" (Verse of Sun–Moon Mountain) was published in *Sbrang char* (Light rain) in 1991.[9] Though this was his first work to appear in a major literary magazine, the poem is exceptionally beautiful, and Chen Metak's reputation began to spread. In the following year his famous poem "Lho bzhud kyi chu 'dzin" (Southern clouds) was published in *Light Rain*.[10] Many readers were amazed by its excellence in terms of thought and artistry, and he became widely recognized for his writing style. From 1993 Chen Metak's style of poetry began to change under the influence of the aesthetics that came to characterize the Four Demons of the Old Fort. Unlike his earlier poetry, some of Chen Metak's work from this period is hard to understand; the content is intentionally obscure. For this reason its reception among other writers varied. Some praised it for being innovative, while others said that it was not even Tibetan literature, as it revealed no Tibetan consciousness. (I myself was among the poem's detractors at the time.) Later one could see many works by young writers who had imitated this poem. From 1995 to 1996 Chen Metak published such poems as "Phag gi ngang tshul" (Pig manners) and "Da dung 'bri" (Still write). His poems were rarely published after 1997, but in 2001 when I met Chen Metak in Golok, he showed me more than thirty new poems. Only then did I recognize his talent, and he has since made a comeback. Chen Metak grounds his work in Tibetan culture and even religious teachings, and his poetry aims to describe the fate of humans in a chaotic society. He writes directly of his realizations, which are deeply grounded in history and real life. His writing style evinces the straightforward wording of Tibetan folk literature, love songs (*la gzhas*), and other folksongs (*glu shags*), as well as the detailed but concise writing of modernism, and has thereby been strengthened. His poetry has a supple nature and conveys a sense of intimacy.

Drong (Druklha Gyel) was born into a nomadic family in Changshekhuk Township on the southern shores of Qinghai Lake. Since graduating from Hainan Nationality Teachers Training School in 1987 he has worked as an announcer and reporter for Qinghai People's Radio Broadcasting Station. He is a member of the Qinghai Writers Union and began writing poetry around 1987. Though he has published only a dozen or so poems, he was popular among readers because of his sense of humor and the simple wording, logic, substantive content, and real-life quality of his writing. In particular his poems "Che chung" (Size) and "Chung ma gnyid zin / Ngas snyan ngag 'bri bzhin yod" (My wife is sleeping, and I am writing poetry) have been very influential and widely imitated. Other popular poems include "Kha ba" (Snow), "Nga dang nga'i grogs po tsho" (My friends and I), and "Dbyangs can ma" (Sarasvatī).

Drong is a straightforward man of few words. For this reason his poetry, like his personality, has few slogans or clichés; his poems are free of ornamentation and rather transparent in meaning. He typically writes only two or three poems a year. Though many people press him to write more, Drong once told me that it was impossible to write a lot of poetry, or in any case that he did not know how. He then added that he often consoled himself by thinking that although he is not a prolific writer, he is rich in feelings and thoughts.

Zhidé Nyima (also known as Sa gzhi) is known by his friends and family as "Lord Wolf" (Rje spyang ro ba) because of his tall, lean stature and toothy grin. He is a member of the Qinghai Writer's Union. Zhidé Nyima began writing around 1985 and has since published hundreds of poems and short stories. His poetry has been especially successful. In his writing he criticizes tradition and the decrepit, and rather forcefully expresses his dislike for power and oppression. His best-known poems include the above-mentioned "Golden Goose," as well as "A ma lags phyir rang khyim du phebs shog" (Mother,come back to your home!), "Gnam 'og 'di na" (Under this sky), "Sde chen po rtse ra nang na" (In the village on the peak), and "Lha tshogs kyi gtam gleng" (Conversation of the gods). An anthology of his poetry entitled *Zhi bde nyi ma'i snyan ngag* (The poetry of Zhidé Nyima) was published in 2001. He has also written beautiful lyrics for several popular songs, and his scripts for short comedy skits are widely popular in Tibet. He has stated that the content of his poetry is defined by his reflections on the human condition and its vicissitudes.

Dodrak (also known as Dorjé Drakpa) was born in Chamdo (TAR) in 1970. After graduating from Qinghai Teachers Training College at the age of twenty-three he was hired by the Qinghai Television Broadcasting Station, where he continues to work today. Dodrak began writing in middle school. He too has published hundreds of poems and short stories. An anthology of his poetry entitled *Tshor snang gsar ba* (New sensations) was published by Gansu Nationalities Publishing House in 1993. It includes works in both Tibetan and Chinese. He is the youngest of this group of writers and so far has not been as influential as his counterparts.

The Period of Plurality (1996 to Present) and Writer Coteries

As described above, the first literary group or clique to emerge in the history of modern Tibetan literature was the Four Demons of the Old Fort, based in Xining. The influence of these four writers was felt particularly strongly from 1993 to 1996. Their radical departure from traditional norms marks a threshold after which Tibetan literature seems to have experienced a certain liberation. Tibetan writing has since diversified and been enriched by a greater variety of influences. Having burgeoned like mushrooms after a rainstorm, published writers are now found in a range of social arenas: schools, monasteries, offices, and factories.

Especially noteworthy is the appearance of other influential groups of writers on the Tibetan literary stage, all in Qinghai Province, including the "Four Crazy Brothers" in Gonghe (Tib. Chapcha), the "Four Owls of Rongwo Monastery" (individually known as the Tiger, Lion, Garuda, and Dragon) in Tongren (Tib. Repgong), the "Immortal Eternal-Youths" in Hainan Prefecture (Tib. Sumdo Mang Ba Cha), and three recent graduates nicknamed the Falcon, the Eagle, and the Wolf. The emergence of different literary groups and a diversification in influence is a defining characteristic of what I term the Period of Plurality and a sign that contemporary Tibetan literature and its authors have matured to some degree. Moreover, the rise of literary groups reflects a shift from stubborn faith or reliance on a single literary figure or exemplar to a period in which new forms are contested by a host of writers and scholars.

THE FOUR CRAZY BROTHERS (SMYON PA SPUN BZHI)

The Four Crazy Brothers, Tsokyé, Menla Kyap, Dowi Dorjé and Sölo, are models and leaders for Tibetan writers in the area of Chapcha (Ch. Gonghe) in Hainan Prefecture (Qinghai Province). Though they have also contributed to the development of the Tibetan New Era literature, overall they have been less influential than the other coteries discussed here. The name was coined in 1993; the term "crazy" (smyon) has special connotations in Tibetan culture and has sometimes been applied to religious adepts who attained a high level of spiritual realization, such as the "crazy yogins" Druknyön Künga Lekpa (1455–1529) and Tsangnyön Heruka (1452–1507). Although the four writers are not related by birth, they are called brothers because of their similar intellectual stances. From a literary point of view, each writer is unique. The four frequently discuss their works with each other and exchange ideas, but we cannot discern a significant degree of mutual influence. All of these poets work or have worked in Chapcha, not far from the shores of Qinghai Lake. The majority of their literary output consists of poems, almost solely in free verse. This coterie is different from others in that two of its writers write in Tibetan (Tsokyé, Menla Kyap) while Dowi Dorjé writes in Chinese, as did Sölo.

Tsokyé (Döndrup Tsering) was born in a nomad area on the shores of Lake Qinghai in 1968. Though he started school only at the age of nine, he continued his education, and after graduating from the Hainan Nationalities Teacher's Training School he enrolled at the Northwest Nationalities Institute

(Lanzhou). Since his graduation in 1990 he has worked as a Tibetan teacher at the Qinghai Nationalities Normal College in Chabcha. He is a member of the China's Minority Writers Union and the Qinghai Writers Union. He is also the editor of the *Journal of the Qinghai Nationalities Normal College*. Tsokyé started writing in 1985 and has since published more than one hundred poems, essays, articles, and translations in Tibetan and Chinese.

Menla Kyap was born in Guinan (Qinghai Province) in 1963. He also publishes under the pseudonyms "Little Flint" ('*Bar rde'u*), "Snow Boy" (*Gangs bu*), and "Generate Happiness" (*Dga' skyed*). His education includes studies at Qinghai Nationalities Teachers Training School and the Shanghai Conservatory of Performing Arts. Currently he resides in Xining and works at the Haixi Nationalities Recording House in a number of capacities: translator, actor, scriptwriter, voiceover announcer, office manager, and editor. He is a member of the China Minority Writers Union and the Qinghai Writers Union, as well as the Qinghai branches of the China Performers Union and the China Translators' Union. Menla Kyap started writing in 1982 and has since published more than 350 short stories, poetry, essays, scripts, song lyrics, and comedy sketches. He is virtually a household name in Amdo for his comedy routines, which are widely distributed on cassette tape. The most popular of these are *Sgyu rtsal ba* (Artist), *'Tshol* (Searching), *Lha sar 'gro* (To Lhasa!), and *Ru sde phra mo* (Small village). He has also produced two cassettes of folktales: *Ri bong 'jon ldan* (The clever rabbit) and *Cang shes rta bshad* (The know-all horse). Menla Kyap's first and only collection of poetry, *Brag ri'i sras mo* (Princess of Draga Mountain), was well received, especially among younger readers.[11] Menla Kyap has said that poetry flows in his blood together with a heap of delusions. For this reason he feels compelled to write.

Dowi Dorjé (Ch. Daowei Duoji) writes only in Chinese. He is also a member of the Qinghai Writers Association. Söbo (Ch. Suobao) also wrote in Chinese and was a member of the Qinghai Writers Union until his death in the mid-1990s. Although these two writers actively participated in literary exchanges with their counterparts and friends, Tsokyé and Menla Kyap, because they wrote in Chinese they have been much less known in Tibetan literary circles and much less influential in the development of modern Tibetan literary trends.

THE FOUR OWL-SIBLINGS OF RONGWO
(RONG BO 'UG PA MING SRING BZHI)

Chen Rangsé, Dong Chushel, Chimé, and Yumkyap are also collectively known as the "Tiger, Lion, Garuda, and Dragon," although none of the four creatures corresponds to a specific author. These four writers are literary models and leaders for Tibetan writers in the area of Repgong (Ch. Tongren). At the same time, they have made contributions to the development of a new Tibetan literature in general. The majority of their works are poetry, both metered and unmetered. This group is unique in that it includes a woman, who publishes under the pen name "Eternal" (Chimé). When they began to be identified as a group the writers would spend days and nights together writing poetry. As people learned of their late-night writing sessions, the four were eventually called the "owl-siblings of Rongbo." Rongbo is the famous Gelukpa monastery, converted in the seventeenth century, which helped to make Repgong an influential cultural center in Amdo. In fact the group's more traditional use of language may be due to a monastic influence: Chen Rangsé and Dong Chushel were originally monks (from Rongbo Monastery) who have now returned to lay life.

Chen Rangsé (Khyungtruk Gyel) was born in 1972 in Achung Village in Chentsa County. His village is the site of the famous nunnery Achung Namdzong and also home to many lay tantric practitioners (sngag pa). At the age of seven he started elementary school and from 1988 he continued his education at Hainan Teachers Training School. Upon graduation in 1990 he took vows and became a monk at Ditsa Monastery with the ordination name of Jampa Gelek. In 1994 he transferred to Rongwo Monastery, where he studied for another seven years. In 2001 he returned to lay life and has since been studying English. He started writing poetry about 1990 and is a member of the Qinghai Writers Union. He writes both metered and free verse and has published some one hundred poems, including "Zla ba lha mor phul ba'i snyan tshig" (Verses offered to the moon) and "Chos 'dzin dbang mo" (Chödzin Wangmo). He has two collections of poetry: Sham bha la'i cong sgra (The bells of Shambhala) and Lang tsho'i zhabs rjes (Footprints of youth).[12] His pen name refers to his birthplace (Chentsa) and the Buddhist concept of anatman, that is, "to extinguish the self" (rang sad; see chapter 6).

Dong Chushel, whose birth and ordination name is Tendzin Drakpa, was born in 1971 in Gyelwo village in Repgong. At the age of twelve he entered Rongwo Monastery, where he studied for some thirteen years. In 1996 he gave up his vows and went to work at a publishing house in Beijing. He currently works as an editor in Chengdu, Sichuan. He began writing poetry (both metered and free verse) in 1990, and although at present he does not live in Qinghai he remains a member of the Qinghai Writers Union. He has published some one hundred poems, including "Lhan 'dzoms" (Gather together) and "Bag chags de'i dbang gis ngas phyi mig bltas" (Because of these karmic imprints, I look back).

Yumkyap Gyel was born in 1968 in Nyenzang Village in Repgong. As a child he had no opportunity for formal study beyond elementary school, but he continued studying on his own at home. When he was seventeen years old he was finally able to attend high school. In 1993, at the age of twenty-three, he decided to earn an undergraduate degree, and he graduated from Qinghai Nationalities Institute in 1996. Yumkyap Gyel started writing both metered and free verse about 1990. He has since published dozens of poems, including "Chu mo'i phar tshur" (The water's ebb and flow) and "A khu Dar rgyas kyi skyo glu" (The sad song of Akhu Dargyé). He has published three collections of poetry, including *Kha ba'i rmi lam* (Snow dream) and *Byang 'brong gi rmig sgra* (Hoofbeats of the northern wild yaks).[13] He is a prolific writer and a member of the Qinghai Writers Union.

Chimé (Pematso) was born in 1967 in Repgong. After graduating from Qinghai Nationalities College in 1987 she worked as a middle school teacher at the Gonghe Nationalities Middle School in Hainan Prefecture. She currently teaches at the Tongren Nationalities Middle School in Repgong. Chimé also began writing in 1990, primarily free-verse poetry. She has since published dozens of poems, the best-known of which include "Srod dus kyi dran gzhigs" (Nighttime reminiscing), "Nga dang nga'i las dbang" (I and my fate), "Mchi ma 'di khyod kyi las dbang yin nam" (Are these tears your fate?), and "Dran shes dmar po zhig gi gsang ba" (Secret of a red memory). She is a member of the Qinghai Writers Union, and in 1994 she won an award in the Second Light Rain Literary Awards. Although she does not write much at present, for a time she was one of the most influential members of this coterie. Her writings mostly address women's concerns and world.

THE IMMORTAL ETERNAL-YOUTHS ('CHI MED RGAS MED TSHO)

The "Immortal Eternal-Youths" are a group of writers from Sumdo Mang-Ba-Cha (Hainan Prefecture) in Qinghai Province: Takbum Gyel, Mengwu, and Yangbha. A radical group of writers who refuse to abide by social norms, they have been literary models and leaders for young writers in their area and have helped to develop a modern Tibetan literature. The name Immortal Eternal-Youths refers to their unflagging commitment to literary courage (*spobs pa*) and practice (*lag len*). They faced a great deal of social and familial pressures to discontinue their literary endeavors. Nevertheless, they courageously insisted in pursuing writing and opposed more conventional and prosaic ways of life. The name seems to have been first applied to them about 1997, and they are considered to have continually improved their writing over the years.

Takbum Gyel was born in 1966 in Mangra Township in Guinan County. He graduated from Hainan Nationalities Teachers Training School in 1986 and two years later went to Lanzhou for further studies at Northwest Nationalities Institute. In 1990 he graduated, and he has taught ever since at a middle school in Sumdo. He is a member of the Qinghai Writers Union and began writing short stories about 1987. Since then he has published dozens more, including "Nyin gcig gi cho 'phrul" (One day's magic) and "Wang dge rgan" (Teacher Wang). Takbum Gyel's first novel, *Rnam shes* (Consciousness), was published serially for several issues in the literary magazine *Light Rain*. It is considered the first Tibetan novel by a writer from Qinghai and was honored in the Second Light Rain Literary Awards in 1997. A revised version of the novel was then published as a whole under the title *Lhing 'jags kyi rtswa thang* (The deep blue grassland) by Qinghai Nationalities Publishing House in 1999. Highly skilled from an artistic point of view, Takbum Gyel describes extremely well the Tibetan ways of life.

Mengwu (Döndrup Tsering) was born in 1969 in Chamdo Township in Guinan County. After graduating from Northwest Nationalities Institute in 1992 he became a teacher at Hainan Tibetan Middle School. In 2001 he entered the graduate program at Qinghai Nationalities Institute. Mengwu began his writing career about 1990 and is a member of the Qinghai Writers Union. He writes poetry in both free and metered verse. Among the hundreds of poems he has published he is best known for "Bor mi chog pa'i khas len" (The unforgettable answer) and "Khang ba sngon po'i gtam rgyud" (Tale of the blue house). He enjoys writing poetry enormously and is extremely enthusiastic about his avocation.

Yangbha was also born in Chamdo in Guinan County in 1968. Since graduating from Hainan Nationalities Teachers Training school in 1988 he has worked as a teacher at the Kardrong Tibetan elementary school in Guinan County. In 2003 he was admitted for further studies at Northwest Nationalities Institute. Yangbha began writing around 1990 and is a member of the Qinghai Writers Union. He writes both essays and free-verse poetry. He is particularly well known for his essays in prose verse. He has published some one hundred essays and poems, including "Sa bon" (Seed) and "Sbra nag / kher rkyang gi gtam rgyud smug po" (Black-haired tent: Dark tale of loneliness).

There are other Tibetan literary groups, for example "Hawk, Eagle, and Wolf" (Khra glag spyang gsum), and the "Seven Brothers of the North Star" (Byang skar spun bdun). And of course there are other important writers from this last period who are not associated with a particular style or group.

. . . . .

The tendency of Tibetophone writers to form natural groupings seems limited to areas outside the TAR, and Qinghai Province in particular. At the same

Four writers in their twenties from the self-designated "Third Generation": from left Gadé Tsering (also known as Lake-Son Gadé), Kyapchen Dedröl, Tsering Trashi (also known as "Harsh Arrow"), "Ré Shinbone-Horn." Photo courtesy of Dorjé Tsering.

time, this is admittedly the area that I know best. Lhasa did have a thriving literary salon scene, in particular during the 1980s. This drew a few writers from Amdo, such as Jangbu, who then settled and continued writing in Lhasa. More recently coteries such as those I have described have formed in artistic circles, with the opening of unofficial art galleries. Although Lhasa has been home for several famous Tibetophone writers (e.g. Jangbu, Trashi Penden, Püntsok Trashi) and Sinophone writers (e.g. Zhaxi Dawa, Weise), it would be hard to say that it has a vibrant literary scene.

Such groupings continue to spontaneously rise in Amdo, and have begun to diversify beyond the literary sphere. The trend now is toward informal groupings of friends and intellectuals united by common projects. The latest group to be nicknamed is the "Four Scholars," friends who have demonstrated a strong commitment to educating other Tibetans in western philosophy as a means of eradicating what they view as "ignorance" and "superstition." In light of their extremist views, the nickname is gently derisive.[14]

Very recently, during the summer of 2005 in the course of the Second "Waterfall of Youth" Poetry Recital at Qinghai Lake (Lake Kokonor), a new group of poets in their twenties emerged. They announced that they had formed another poetry group called the "Third Generation" (Tib. Mi rabs gsum pa). When asked about their characteristics, philosophy, and ideals, these rather radical writers replied that they did not have defined characteristics or common goals—but were united in not seeking to write in particular about Tibetan national characteristics. The history of their formation and their ideological platform published on the internet. According to the web site, members (tshogs mi) of the group met formally for the first time in Xining in July 2005. Some ten writers, including Tri Sempa ("King Brave-Mind"), Rekangling ("Ré Shinbone-Horn"), and Datsenpo ("Harsh Arrow"), were in attendance. The group contends that if Döndrup Gyel represents "the first generation of Tibetan poets" and Ju Kelzang represents the second, they represent the third generation. (They make no mention of Tibetan poets writing for hundreds of years before Döndrup Gyel.) The web site reiterates that the group has no unique or defining philosophy. According to its member Kyapchen Dedröl (who grew up in Luchu in southern Gansu Province), they are "the ones who clamor" (ku cho 'don mkhan); and Tri Sempa writes that the group seeks to "discard/destroy whatever systems or methods that exist in Tibetan poetry."[15] The group met for a second time on 3–6 August 2007 in Rebgong. At this meeting the authors resolved to collectively praise works that express "the lost soul, obsession" and that "turn [reality] on its head, mix time and space, and revolt."[16] Apparently poems such as Datsenpo's frankly written "Khang pa 'd i'i nang nas" (From inside this house) exemplify this group's poetry. Book-length collections by writers who identify as members of the "Third Generation" include Tsong chu'i gram gyi snyan ngag (Poems from the shore of the Tsong River) by Khu byug sngon mo ("Blue Cuckoo"), published by the Gansu Nationalities Publishing House in 2007. Many say that the advent of the Third Generation group marks the latest and one of the most significant developments in modern Tibetan literary history—only time will tell.

Notes

The first part of this article is based on a previously published essay by the author in Lta ba, bsam blo, lag len, ed. Gangs zhun and Rdo lha (Lanzhou: Kan su'u mi rigs dpe skrun khang, 2000), 209–16. The editors thank Pema Bhum for contributing details for the concluding paragraphs.

1. A more commonly used term to render this concept is "deng rabs Bod kyi rtsom rig."
2. Tibet Information Network, "Tibet's Leading Scholar Dies," Tibetan Review, September 1997, 13–16.
3. See chapter 4 for Nancy Lin's discussion of Döndrup Gyel's interest in classical literature.

4. Studies available in English include Pema Bhum, "The Life of Dhondup Gyal," Kapstein, "Dhondup Gyal," Stoddard, "Don grub rgyal," and Virtanen, comp. and trans., *A Blighted Flower and Other Stories*.

5. Ljang bu, "Sog rus las mched pa'i rnam shes," *Sbrang char*, 1986, no. 2, 1–7.

6. Ljang bu, "Gangs dkar lha mo'i bslu brid kyi dbang gis" (Under the spell of the White Snow Goddess), *Bod kyi rtsom rig sgyu rtsal*, 1987, no. 2, 19–25.

7. Dpa' rtse, "Gna' bo'i cong rnying," *Bod kyi rtsom rig sgyu rtsal*, 1987, no. 1, 15–16.

8. See for example Skyabs chem bde 'drol, "Gnam 'og 'di na snyan ngag la kha lo bsgyur thub mang" (Many in this world can command their poetry), *Gangs rgyan me tog*, 1999, no. 2, 54–55.

9. Gcan Me stag, "Nyi zla ri bo'i snyan tshig," *Sbrang char*, 1991, no. 2, 39.

10. Gcan Me stag, "Lho bzhud kyi chu 'dzin," *Sbrang char*, 1992, no. 2, 39–40.

11. Sman bla skyabs, *Brag ri'i sras mo* (Princess of Draga Mountain) (Lanzhou: Kan su'u mi rigs dpe skrun khang), 1995.

12. Gcan Rang sad, *Sham bha la'i cong sgra* (The bells of Shambhala) (Hong Kong: Then mā dpe skrun khang, 2000); and *Lang tsho'i zhabs rjes*.

13. Yum skyabs rgyal, *Kha ba'i rmi lam* (Snow dream) (Lanzhou: Kan su'u mi rigs dpe skrun khang, 1996; and *Byang 'brong gi rmig sgra* (Hoofbeats of the northern wild yaks) (Xining: Mtsho sngon mi rigs dpe skrun khang, 2004).

14. Tib. *Mkhas pa mi bzhi*. This refers to Menla Kyap, Zhokdung (Morning Conch), Lhamo Kyap, and Pakmo Trashi. Zhokdung (or Tragya, born in Chentsa) is an editor at the Qinghai Nationalities Publishing House and the author of several controversial articles and books. Menla Kyap (already discussed in detail) is included here because of his close friendship with the others and support of their views. Lhamo Kyap and Pakmo Trashi both work in the media in Xining. Pakmo Trashi in particular has initiated several interesting translation and film projects.

15. http://www.tibetcm.com/news/2006725205502.htm, April 29, 2007.

16. http://www.tibetcm.com/news/2007811171255.htm.

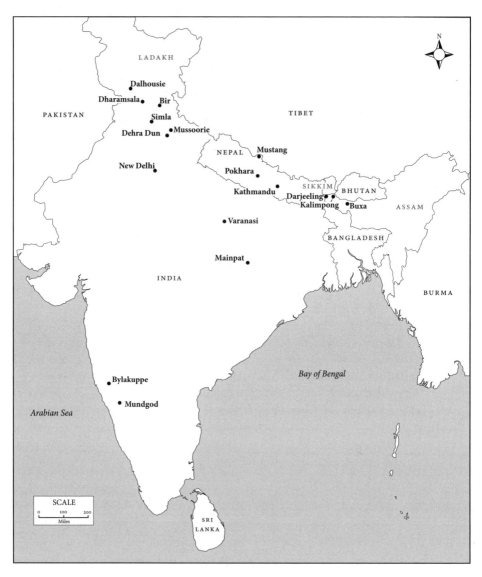

Major Tibetan settlements in South Asia. Map by Creative Design Resources.

13

Tibetan Literature in the Diaspora

HORTSANG JIGME

TRANSLATED BY LAURAN R. HARTLEY

While it is generally held that the writing of Tibetan literature in exile began in 1959, it is important to recall that when Tibetans first sought refuge in India, circumstances required that their great numbers, totaling some eighty thousand, be divided into smaller groups and settled in various localities throughout the vast realm of India. Most of the refugee camps were in the middle of jungle forests otherwise inhabited by wild boars, elephants, and the like. The earliest Tibetan refugees had no proper residences, water, or electricity; rather, they stayed under canvas canopies hoisted amid the trees. These Tibetans, who had just arrived from one of the coldest inhabitable places on earth, suddenly found themselves in a very hot climate. With neither knowledge of the hygiene necessary in such heat nor the resources to take precautions, people daily fell ill or died. Others were killed by snakes, elephants, or malaria-carrying mosquitoes. Despite these conditions, people began to cultivate the land by chopping down trees and digging up roots. Eventually they built temporary homes, and many men and women joined road construction crews in northern India. For more than a decade Tibetans in exile were fully consumed with the challenges of surviving and then leading a life in India.

When the most urgent needs facing exiled Tibetans were constructing a hut for shelter and finding food, it is no wonder that few people were writing, let alone writing literary works. For similar reasons, the situation was not yet conducive to founding new literary styles. Schools were only beginning to open. Aside from a few aristocrats, lamas, and monks, it was rare to find people in the general population who could read and write. Though some members of the religious clergy may have written a few pieces regarding rituals, teachings, or their lineage, there is no evidence from the 1960s or 1970s of the burgeoning literary activity that we see today. While in other spheres of Tibetan exile, religious institutions, practices, and festivals were carried on by teachers and students who first escaped to Bhagsa in Uttar Pradesh and Dalhousie in Himachal Pradesh[1] from their monasteries in Tibet, to the best of my knowledge there is no record of any new literature at that time.

Literary Forms in Exile: The Early Days

Exiled Tibetans worked quickly to publicize the Tibetan cause in international circles. At the same time, they faced the equally daunting task of setting up an infrastructure for Tibetan life in the diaspora: establishing settlements in India and Nepal; building monasteries, schools, hospitals, and even small factories; and managing all of these enterprises. Only after several years did certain monastic scholars who had studied literature in their homeland of Tibet resume their writing of religious texts in literary fashion. The seventh volume (ja) of the Collected Works (gsung 'bum) of a principal teacher of the Dalai Lama, Trijang Rinpoché (1901–82), for instance, contains an inventory in metric verse of tangka paintings.[2] The volume also includes propitiatory verses to various great lamas, aphorisms, songs (mgur), and letters, as well as introductions to the deeds of the Buddha written for India Radio. Trijang Rinpoché wrote a variety of works in kāvya style, including a compendium of dakini teachings, discourses on mandalas, and acrostic verses (kun bzang 'khor lo).

Another monastic scholar, Dzemé Trülku (1927–96), wrote verses praising the Dalai Lama, Trijang Rinpoché, and others teachers, using a poetic figure (gzugs can gyi rgyan) by which the referent (e.g. a face) takes the form of the metaphor (e.g. a lotus); he also wrote maxims, songs of experience, and verses using the semantic-based ornaments described in the second chapter of the Kāvyādarśa (Mirror of poetry). All these writings can be found in his Collected Works, which total six volumes, along with poems written to illustrate metric verse conventions and several "grid-poems."[3] A few other religious teachers and students from the various traditions (Gelukpa, Sakya, Kagyü, Nyingma, and Bön) wrote literary works modeled after the sutras and tantras, letters using classical kāvya conventions, expressions of praise for special gods, propitiations for the speedy reincarnation of various lamas, and other poems in kāvya style. Whereas we see a phenomenal amount of fiction, new poetry, prose poetry, and dramas in Tibetan society today, the literary writings of these religious teachers in exile never veered from classical literary norms.

Although many geshes and other religious teachers in exile society were learned in Buddhism and its related teachings, including the five traditional sciences, very few wrote literary works. This is largely due to the demands of religious practice and debate and the bias in monastic learning, which downplayed the literary sciences. As noted by Georges Dreyfus (*The Sound of Two Hands Clapping*, 2003): "Monastic circles . . . have concentrated on the first two branches [Buddhism and logic and epistemology] to the partial neglect of literary studies, which are considered more appropriate to the aesthetic inclinations of the few highly educated laypeople. Thus, the opposition between philosophy and rhetoric in premodern Tibet led not to an internal debate but to the creation of two distinct educational traditions: a lay focus on belles lettres and a monastic emphasis on religious and philosophical subjects."[4] While this distinction is more pronounced in central Tibet (many religious hierarchs in eastern areas did write poetic works) we may nevertheless observe that generally speaking, the average monk, let alone the average nun, was not taught to write at an advanced level, because the traditional monastic curriculum did not emphasize active writing. Lamas and geshes who wrote religious texts were more numerous. The collected works of Nyingma teachers in particular abound with prophecies, "hidden texts" (*gter yig*), and pure vision texts. This situation was sustained for hundreds of years. Only very recently have a few religious teachers or students written modern literary works.

Starting in the 1970s some religious teachers in exile had the opportunity to travel overseas, including to western Europe, America, and Japan, and began to study western languages and cultures. One who was especially prolific in his output of modern Tibetan writing was Chögyam Trungpa, who published in English many religious works as well as other writings, such as an anthology of his poetry entitled *First Thought, Best Thought*.[5] Trungpa Rinpoché reached many western students at the famous Naropa Institute in Boulder, Colorado. Two of his students, Allen Ginsberg and Anne Waldman, founded the Jack Kerouac School of Disembodied Poetics in 1974, and its writing program remains a vital component of the institute (now a university). Though Chögyam Trungpa's influence was not strongly felt in the wider Tibetan community at the time, he now has a greater following. Based on firsthand observation in my Dharamsala bookstore, I have noticed that Tibetans who are in their twenties and fluent in English are frequent purchasers of his religious essays and literary works.

Other Tibetan teachers, whether religious or lay, were influential through their teaching positions at various universities. For example, the fourteenth Dalai Lama's older brother, Professor Thubten Jigme Norbu (also known as Taktser Rinpoché, b. 1922), first traveled to the United States in 1950. As a professor of Tibetan studies at Indiana University from 1965 to 1987 he was one of the earliest and most influential teachers in the United States, and he produced several studies of Tibetan folk culture and literature, including a translation of the play *Gcun po Don Yod / The Younger Brother Don yod*. However, a biography makes no mention of any original literary works.[6] Another Tibetan scholar who has resided in America for many years is the Sakya teacher Dhongtog Tenpai Gyaltsen in Seattle. He has written many works over the years, including an English-Tibetan dictionary and several philosophical refutations. His most recent project is to compile a Tibetan history. In France, Karmay Samten, an internationally renowned Tibetan scholar, has written countless articles and book-length monographs. Domepa Yönten Gyatso was another prolific scholar who lived in Paris until his death in 2002. Though he never published a collection of poetry, his beautifully written verses, all in metered verse and using classical techniques, can be found as opening verses of praise or invocations (*mchod brjod*), poems of interlude (*bar skabs tshigs bcad*), and closing poems (*mjug rtsom*) in his scholarly writings. Among the many books published by the religious teacher and scholar Namkhai Norbu (b. 1938), who has long lived in Italy, one also finds scattered literary works, most notably a book of poetry in English entitled *The Little Song of "Do as You Please"* (1986).[7]

Rakra Tetong Thupten Chödar (b. 1925), who now resides in Switzerland, has been perhaps the most active scholar of the older generation in terms of his interest in and writing of literary works. Rakra Rinpoché studied *snyan ngag* with Gendün Chömpel, later imprisoned by the Tibetan government in the late 1940s (see chapter 1). His biography of Gendün Chömpel is one of the most widely read works in exile.[8] He has also written a commentary on the eight branches of Tibetan grammar (*Gnas brgyad rtsa 'brel*),[9] completed Gendün Chömpel's colloquial version of the *Rāmāyaṇa* from Dunhuang, and updated Gendün Chömpel's version of the *Deb ther dkar po* (White annals). Throughout his life Rakra Rinpoché has demonstrated a strong interest in *snyan ngag* and has written several works in kāvya style. Many of his own poems can be found in his biography of Gendün Chömpel.

Other older scholars, notably Zamdong Rinpoché (b. 1939), former director of the Central Institute for Higher Tibetan Studies and now head minister of the Tibetan exile government, have remained in India to assist with school administration and exile government affairs. Over the years Zamdong Rinpoché and others have voiced their concern about the rather stagnant state of Tibetan literature in exile. Like the late Yönten Gyatso, Zamdong Rinpoché has written poems that can be found as prefaces, interludes, and conclusions to his longer prose writings.

New Generation Writers in Exile

Generally speaking, not many young Tibetans living in exile have the capacity to write literature in their mother tongue. One reason for this sad fact is that Tibetans in the diaspora total fewer than 140,000, most of whom live in scattered locations throughout the vast expanse of India, which has a population of about one billion. A lack of appropriate textbooks for young children and persistent traditional influences in the education system have further hampered the acquisition of Tibetan literacy by the younger generations in exile. Above all, there is greater incentive to excel in English and little infrastructure to promote literacy in Tibetan. Daily life rarely requires knowledge of written Tibetan; this is certainly so in India, not to mention America, where some ten thousand Tibetans relocated in the 1990s. The threats to Tibetan literacy in exile parallel the situation of young Tibetans in the PRC, who increasingly must be fluent in Chinese to obtain employment. Finally, young Tibetans born in India have little or no firsthand experience with life and environment in their homeland. They can barely imagine the Tibetan environment described in classical and Tibetan folk literature: the grasslands, craggy mountains, and snow peaks. Their foundation and inclination to write poetry in the Tibetan style is weak, and the amount of artistic writing has been nominal for many years.

Pema Tsewang Shastri is one exception.[10] We can attribute his skills to the training he received at the Central Institute of Higher Tibetan Studies in Varanasi, India, coupled with sixteen years of teaching and administrative experience. Regarding his motivation, he has written: "As a published writer my inspiration comes from my stubborn interest and attachment in all things Tibetan, and also from my attraction towards beautiful words and phrases. Inspiration is also drawn from my interest in reading Hindi novels. My late mother, who was able to sing and tell volumes of Gesar stories by heart, had a huge impact upon me and on my use of the language and style of writing."[11] He acknowledges that "hard work and the wise use of leisure time" allowed him to realize his literary aspirations and publish three novels.

Pema Tsewang Shastri's first novel, *Nub kyi grang reg dang shar gyi drod 'jam* (Cold west and warm east), was published in 2000.[12] It portrays Tibetan refugee life, primarily in India and the United States. The protagonist, Trashi, was born in Tibet but raised and educated in India. Like many young Tibetans he serves the exile government after graduation. He works for the Home Department in Dharamsala, where he meets a young woman named Chökyi. After a brief official-turned-romantic trip to Kullu they marry. Their life together and eventual emigration to the United States brings mixed experiences. One literary critic has noted: "The primary virtue of this novel is that its contents cover a broad scope . . . people from all walks of life in Tibetan exile society . . . and yet it is not scattered."[13] Pema Tsewang Shastri then published a second novel, Mi tshe'i bro ba mngar skyur (The sweet and sour taste of life) — the story of Lozang, who was born in Tibet during the Cultural Revolution but soon orphaned by the death of his parents at the hands of the Chinese.[14] With the help of his aunt, Lozang is smuggled into India and attends a Tibetan school in Kalimpong. The story revolves around his school life, friends, a secret trip back to Tibet to see his aunt, and his job at the Education Department of the Central Tibetan Administration in Dharamsala following graduation from Delhi University. After studying a modest amount of Buddhist literature, Lozang ultimately rejects the material and sensual lures surrounding him and becomes a monk, thus fulfilling both the wish of his aunt and his own aspiration. The author's third book (forthcoming) is Nga ni Bod yin (I am Tibet), an autobiographical narration of Tibet.[15] In it Tibet is personified as a mother who tells her life story to seven types of audience, powerfully and eloquently, focusing on her past, present, and future. The theme revolves around the vicissitudes of her long life. The work is a mixture of fact and fiction in content, poetry and prose in structure, and traditional and modern in style. Its language is simple and succinct.

Pema Tsewang Shastri has also written some beautiful poetry, all in metric verse, and undertaken several scholarly articles and translation projects, including a Tibetan translation of Charles Dickens's Great Expectations (Tib. 'Dun pa chen po).[16] Though raised and schooled in India, Pema Tsewang Shastri did not start publishing his literary works until the late 1990s, when a model had been set. He is part of a new wave of writers in exile, many inspired by the introduction of modern Tibetan literature in exile by recently arrived refugees.

New-Arrival Refugee Writers

From 1979, with the easing of policy in China, relations between Dharamsala and Beijing were resumed, and representatives of the Dalai Lama and the government-in-exile conducted a fact-finding tour of China and Tibet. As there had been no means for twenty years of maintaining contact with Tibetans living inside Tibet, Tibetans in the diaspora knew very little of the situation inside the PRC. Only when Tibetan refugees were allowed to return to their homeland for a visit could they learn whether relatives whom they had left behind were still alive. A very small number of Tibetans in Tibet also had the opportunity to visit relatives in India.[17]

The new situation raised many questions for young Tibetan intellectuals born and raised under the Chinese Communist regime: Are we Chinese or Tibetan? If we are Tibetan, what was the real Tibetan historical situation? What is this "Tibetan Government-in-Exile" which is seated in India? Who is its leader—the Dalai Lama? For example, only at the age of twenty, while studying at Labrang Monastery (Gansu Province) in 1986, did I come to know that the fourteenth Dalai Lama was still alive. Around that time, the phrase "national pride" (mi rigs kyi la rgya) began to appear with greater frequency in writings by young Tibetan intellectuals. When drinking or otherwise gathered together, certain young Tibetan writers, such as Döndrup Gyel, would discuss "national pride" and related issues. Until then the Tibetan situation had been such that for an interminable twenty years there was absolutely no room for discussing any such ideas. Thus most Tibetan youth still firmly considered themselves people of China (rgya nag yul mi) and felt no inclination to even raise the issue of national pride.

In the early 1980s an increasing number of young Tibetans began escaping to India. After picking up bits of information about His Holiness the Dalai Lama and the exile communities, they opted for life in India or Nepal, rather than a life of working without freedom as a cadre under the Chinese government. Many held only a general sense of "Tibetan national pride" and no certain ideology, but their political views eventually sharpened in India through discussions that had been prohibited in Communist China. They came with the desire to write, to enjoy a freedom of speech they had never known. When they arrived in India, however, they found not typeset books but only handwritten manuscripts reproduced by the Library of Tibetan Works and Archives and the Cultural Printing Press in Dharamsala, general or religious histories distributed by the Central Institute of Higher Tibetan Studies (Varanasi) and various monasteries, and books for the daily recitation of prayers. There was little to read in Tibetan aside from these texts and a few collections of teachings by His Holiness the Dalai Lama. The new arrivals who were illiterate were not greatly concerned about this situation. Their focus was mostly political, and they were content with being able to criticize or denounce China free from repercussion. However, recent arrivals who had followed the new literary happenings in Tibet found it hard to be deprived of a contemporary literary scene.

Soon after their arrival in Dharamsala, these young intellectuals began to focus more on promoting literature than on securing proper food or clothing.

Dressed in ratty shoes and pants worn at the knees (and sometimes required to stay in cowsheds offered for a small fee as lodging by Indian villagers), these newly arrived intellectuals would hang out on the steps of the Nechung Cafe, on the grounds of the Gangchen Kyishong administrative offices, or at the Tsongkha Restaurant to share notes and gossip about writers in Tibet: Döndrup Gyel, Jangbu, Ju Kelzang, Dondrup Wangbum (Ch. Danzhu Angben), and others. They would discuss the literary magazine *Sbrang char* (Light rain) and lament or criticize the absence of such writers and writings in exile society. They wistfully thought how great it would be if new arrivals could get together and launch similar magazines in exile. But since they had just arrived in Dharamsala and knew no one outside their circle interested in literature or capable of this sort of project, nor how to raise money themselves, they never put their ideas into practice.

It was under these conditions that in June 1990 a group of new arrivals from Amdo, including Pema Bhum, Tsering Döndrup, Tenzin Gönpo, and Kunsang Gyal, launched the first independent newspaper in exile society: *Dmangs gtso* (Democracy). Though the periodical consisted of only a single sheet (i.e. four pages), it was clearly a newspaper and not a literary journal; the earliest issues printed news items alongside poetry and literary works. This changed in December of the same year, when Pema Bhum, Tsepak Rigdzin, Dorjé Tseten, and Palden Gyal founded the magazine *Ljang gzhon* (Young shoots). Although a few other journals existed, only *Young Shoots* was dedicated to literature in Tibetan, with poetry, fiction, essays, and prose poetry. A novelty for the Tibetan diaspora, it exerted an influence that was soon felt in exile society—not only writers but even Tibetan officials and government staff took notice of its fresh approach to literary Tibetan. It is rumored that upon reading the preface to the first issue of *Young Shoots*, entitled "Words of a Young Shoot," Sönam Topgyal (former chief cabinet minister) remarked, "That's odd. There is also Tibetan writing like this?" I would argue that the founding of *Young Shoots* provided the first introduction for exile society to what was being called "contemporary literature" (*deng rabs rtsom rig*) in Tibet. Thus modern Tibetan literature was not a spontaneous development or evolution in exile society. On the contrary, new forms of literary writing were carried from the other side of the Himalayan ranges by young refugees starting in about 1985. Though Tibetan writing in exile has never achieved the intensity or fervor of writing in Tibet during the 1980s, new literary forms now have a firm hold in the exile magazines and other publications. In 2003, when the Literary and Cultural Research Center of the Norbulingka Institute in Dharamsala published *Writings on the Occasion of the Centennial of Gendun Choephel*, *Writings in Memory of Jigme Tekchok*, and *Writings in Memory of Shardong*

Lobsang Shedrup Gyatso, all three volumes displayed the influence of free-verse poetry.

New arrivals (especially from Amdo) have continued to produce a great deal of new literature, albeit of varying quality. They have also been largely responsible for other literary magazines and newspapers recently started in exile.[18] Previously any poetry written in exile was metric verse, and Tibetan fiction was limited to folktales, vetala stories, and the works *Gtam padma'i tshal gyi zlos kar* (Opera in the flower garden) by Dza Peltrül (1808–87) and *Gzhon nu zla med kyi gtam rgyud* (Tale of the incomparable prince) by Dokhar Tsering Wanggyel (1697–1763). New arrival refugees lamented that for thirty years Tibetan writing in exile had neither advanced nor spread beyond these classical works. Eventually these objections compelled Tibetan society and the Tibetan government in particular to pay more heed to the state of Tibetan writing in exile. The cabinet minister Sönam Topgyal repeatedly acknowledged this situation at both official and private meetings.

A sudden boost for the spread of new literature in exile was further provided by an article entitled "Heartbeat of a New Generation: A Discussion of the New Poetry" (this article has been reproduced in chapter 5). Delivered in September 1992 by Pema Bhum (then director of the Amnye Machen Institute) at a conference in Archidosso, Italy, this paper introduced the subject of contemporary literature in Tibet to readers in exile. Shortly after his return the article was circulated in mimeograph form in Dharamsala and elsewhere in India. While most would agree that the article is not inherently controversial, but substantial and well detailed, nevertheless a group of religious extremists and archconservatives were incensed, and demonized both the article and its writer. One spokesperson for detractors of the article remarked in an interview that taking the life of the author was not out of the question.[19] As the debate intensified, people who had never before heard the term "contemporary literature" quickly became familiar with the concept, and people with no interest in modern literature were now compelled to read contemporary writing, if only through excerpts in the controversial essay.

Three years later, in 1995, a new stage in the recognition of modern Tibetan literature in exile was marked when the Amnye Machen Institute hosted the First National Conference of Tibetan Writers. With more than sixty attendees, the conference was held for three days in a local hotel in the hill-station town of Dharamsala. The theme of the meeting was "Literature for Freedom: Role of the Tibetan Writer in the Freedom Struggle," and the topics of the various panels were primarily political, including prison literature, courage in writing, literature versus propaganda, and the social and political limits of contemporary literature. Sessions were also held on Gendün Chömpel, modern Tibetan women writers, and Tibetans writing in English, Chinese, Urdu, and Sanskrit. According to the organizers the event drew a wide range of participants: "Elderly lama scholar/writers from Switzerland and Seattle mingled freely and deliberately not only with younger monk writers, but also with long-haired bohemian poets. Everyone thoroughly enjoyed each other's company. Sober academics and writers from Ladakh and a Nepalese editor of a Tibetan language paper, added to the variety in peoples. . . . Many younger writers expressed great satisfaction in being able to meet, many for the first time, better-known writers living far-away or abroad, and discuss their works with them. Many of the senior writers also expressed their pleasure."[20] Two resolutions of the conference were to join PEN International and to grant the Gendun Choephel (Literary) Award to his Holiness the Dalai Lama.

The release of several Tibetan literary anthologies in exile coincided with the conference; some were surely inspired by it. One year before the gathering I published four small volumes of my own poetry in Tibetan under the collective title Hor gtsang 'Jigs med kyi snyan rtsom phyogs bsgrigs (An anthology of poems by Hortsang Jigme).[21] This was the first collection of poetry in Tibetan by a single lay person either inside or outside Tibet in its history. Previous collections had all been by famous lamas or geshes. The book was well received by readers both in Tibet and throughout the diaspora; people discussed the books, memorized certain verses, and even debated the contents. In this way the volumes strengthened the foundation for poetry writing in exile society. Over the next few years several collections featuring the work of a single poet were published: Beri Jikmé Wanggyel's Zungs khrag (Blood),[22] Lunyön Heruka's Sham bha la'i dud sprin (Letter from Shambhala), and Zang zing gi 'jig rten (Chaotic world),[23] Shawo Gyurmé's Lho ru 'khyams pa'i rnam shes (Southward wandering consciousness),[24] Kelzang Khedrup's Gangs ljongs kyi dge mtshan (Virtues of the Land of Snows),[25] collections by Ngawa Chodrak,[26] Pema Tsering's Gangs seng 'tshol du phyin pa (In search of the snow lion),[27] Chapdrak Lhamokyap's Dbyangs can sprul ba'i glegs bam (Volume [inspired by] the Transformation of Sarasvatī),[28] Draknyön Yamarādzā's Mi yul gyi skyo gdung (Suffering of the human realm),[29] and Lutsang Lozang Yeshé's Tshor ba'i pha bong (Boulder of feeling).[30]

In addition to the virtual absence of Tibetan modern literature in exile until the late 1980s, another lacuna should be noted: the absence of any women writers. This too has changed in recent years. We can now count several young women poets who are actively writing in exile. Collections by women writers include Kelsang Lhamo's Drang srong bsti gnas kyi rmi lam yun ci / Dreaming at the Sage's Abode: Biographical Sketches of Four Living Tibetan Nuns,[31] Chukyé Drölma's Sprin bral zla b'ai 'dzum rlabs (Smile of the cloudless moon),[32] Tsering Kyi's Tshe *ring skyid kyi rtsom btus* (Collection of poetry),[33] and a couple of collections by Zungchuk Kyi.[34] Kelsang Lhamo is a pen name for Chödzin, formerly a nun in Dharamsala who now lives in New York. Chukyé Drölma works as a teacher at the Drölmaling nunnery near Dharamsala. Tsering Kyi was Miss Tibet 2003 and now lives in Europe. Zungchuk Kyi, an excellent writer who was widely published in Tibet before her escape in 2001, now writes in exile. Most other Tibetan women writers in exile also escaped from Tibet in the late 1980s or early 1990s.

English Writers in the Tibetan Diaspora

Though the social conditions and environment in exile have not been conducive to fostering many young authors writing in Tibetan, there has been a much larger pool of Tibetans writing in English and other foreign languages. To the best of my knowledge, the earliest efforts to collectively publish these works began in 1977, when a group of Tibetan students enrolled at Indian universities—Kalzang Tenzin, Samphel, Tenzin Sonam, and Gyalpo Tsering—launched the magazine *Young Tibet*. The first issue of this unprecedented forum for Tibetan literature in English included fourteen poems by only three writers: eight by Gyalpo Tsering, four by K. Dhondup, and two by Tenzin Sonam. No short stories or other literary genres were included. These are not the very first instances of English writing by Tibetans. During his stay in India in the 1930s, Gendün Chömpel tried his hand at English verse with poems such as *Manasrovar*, and *Milarepa's Reply* (see chapter 1). It is quite likely that British-schooled Tibetan aristocrats also experimented in English verse or prose, though I am not aware of any published works.

For the second issue the magazine, published only two years later in 1979, the name was changed to *Lotus Fields* and the editorial board was expanded to include K. Dhondup, Tashi Tsering, and Norbu Chophel. In addition to poems by Gyalpo Tsering, K. Dondup, and Tenzin Sonam, the magazine published translations of fourteen Tibetan folksongs and an article about Tibetan poetry by Tashi Tsering entitled "Tibetan Poetry Down through the Ages," which focused on classical writers. No contemporary writers from Tibet were mentioned or published in the magazine. The third and last issue of *Lotus Fields* was published in 1980. Though the main title of the magazine was still given in English, a Tibetan translation (*Padma thang*) was also provided. This last issue included the works of several new writers, such as a short story by Samphel and folktales compiled by Norbu Chophel. No other English literary magazine has appeared since in Tibetan exile society.

Only in recent years have we seen a resurgence of literary interest by Anglophone Tibetan writers. One of the most prolific and outspoken is Tenzin Tsundue, born in Manali in Himachal Pradesh in 1975. As a child he studied at the Tibetan Children's Village School in Pathlikuhl and later in Dharamsala. In 1997 he began graduate work at the University of Mumbai, where he earned an M.A. in English literature and later an M.A. in philosophy. It was in the large coastal city of Mumbai that he first began attending poetry readings, and in July 1999 his first book of poetry, *Crossing the Border*, was published. He has written of Mumbai: "I share a very strong relationship with the cosmopolitan city. I lived in eight different places in Mumbai in the span of five years. The city people were very kind to Tibet, such sensitive response and support to Tibet. There was no place for me to stay, and yet I wanted to stay on to learn more and also to keep feeding Mumbai with more and more of Tibet."[35]

In 2001, while yet again searching for a place to live, Tenzin Tsundue wrote the poem "Space Bar—A Proposal."[36] In this poem and others, Tenzin Tsundue explores the concepts of home and identity, complicated by the multiple positions he holds as a member of the diaspora. His observations are often tinged with sarcasm and some humor, as in the poem "Tibetanness," in which he writes: "Tibetans: the world's sympathy stock. Serene monks and bubbly traditionalists, one lakh and several thousand odd, nicely mixed, steeped in various assimilating cultural hegemonies."[37] Political themes figure prominently as well: "Kill my Dalai Lama and I will believe no more" and "Thirty nine years in exile. / Yet no nation supports us. / Not a single bloody nation!"[38] Tenzin Tsundue has been general secretary of the Friends of Tibet in India since 1999 and has participated in several acts of civil disobedience in exile. His media stunts and political activism earned him recognition from *Elle* magazine in July 2002 as one of "India's 50 Most Stylish People." In 2001 his essay "My Kind of Exile" won the Outlook-Picador Award for Non-Fiction, garnering first place in an all-India contest out of nine hundred entries. His collection of poems, together with a few essays and short stories, is entitled *Kora* (2002) and is now in its third printing, with a total of six thousand copies.[39] Tenzin Tsundue's writings have been published in dozens of periodicals, including *International* PEN, *Indian* PEN, *Indian Literary Panorama*, *Little Magazine*, *Outlook*, the *Times of India*, the *Indian Express*, the *Hindustan Times*, *Better Photography*, the *Economic Times*, *Tehelka*, *Mid-Day* (Mumbai), *Afternoon* (Mumbai), the *Daily Star* (Bangladesh), *Today* (Singapore), *Tibetan Review*, *Tibetan Bulletin*, *Freedom First*, *Tibetan World*, and *Gandhi Marg*. He represented Tibet in the Second South Asian Literary Conference in New Delhi in January 2005, organized by the premier Indian literary association, Sahitya Academy.[40]

In 2003 Tenzin Tsundue moved to Dharamsala, where he became active in organizing readings and other events with fellow writers. The first such event, "Celebrating Exile," was held in 2002, while Tenzin was commuting between Mumbai and Dharamsala.[41] The idea was to bring together poets, writers, painters, and other people interested in the arts. The event was held at a museum in Dharamsala and drew more than eighty people, many of whom had to listen from the ground floor to the proceedings upstairs. The attendees read primarily in Tibetan and English, and some were fluent in Chinese and Hindi as well. The artist Karma Sichoe exhibited his latest creation, *Sipa Khorlo*, a contemporary painting, six by five feet in size, inspired by the "wheel of life" motif of traditional *tangka* painting. Since then "Celebrating Exile" has been held another five times (most recently in 2006), organized primarily by Friends of Tibet and Students of Tibet groups in India. Writers who have presented at these later gatherings include Anglophone writers such as Namgyal Phuntsok, Bhuchung D. Sonam, and Tsering Wangmo Dhompa, and Tibetophone writers such as Yangkhong Gya, Zungchuk Kyi, Tsering Kyi, and Tsamchö Drölma. One of the readings was organized by tibetwrites.org, a literary web site dedicated to Tibetan literature and co-ordinated by Bhuchung D. Sonam. The works of Bhuchung D. Sonam can be found in his collection *Dandelions of Tibet* (New Delhi, 2002), and he is the editor of the most comprehensive volume of English poetry by Tibetans, *Muses in Exile* (2004).[42] This anthology also includes writings by earlier writers such as Gendün Chömpel and Chögyam Trungpa, as well as poems published earlier in *Lotus Fields*.

One of the most accomplished writers in the anthology *Muses in Exile* is Tsering Wangmo Dhompa, who grew up in the Tibetan communities in India and Nepal and received her M.A. from the University of Massachusetts and her MFA in creative writing from San Francisco State University. Her work has appeared in several American magazines, including the *Atlanta Review*, *Boston Review*, *Mid American Review*, *26*, and *Zyzzyva*. She has also published a small number of chapbooks. In 2002 a collection of her poetry, *Rules of the House*, was published by Apogee Press (based in Berkeley), and in the following year she was a finalist for the Asian American Literary awards. Her work has been praised by a leading American poet as being "full of song" and "interestingly fractured, cross-genred narrative poetry."[43] *Rules of the House* bears intimate witness to the experience of a girl and then young woman growing up in exile. In one work she notes the "sounds we cannot hear but understand in motion."[44] The book is dedicated to her late mother (called "M" in these poems), who "when the thermos shatters, she knows the direction of its spill."[45] While some of her poems are political, her nationalist

The Anglophone writer Tsering Wangmo Dhompa in San Francisco. Photo by Elaine Seiler.

messages are less strident than those of Tenzin Tsundue, for example. In the poem "Member" she further recalls her mother: "Every day could be an end, she'd say, as though stray mutts would take over the government. We were instructed where to go if anything happened to her and F. We were not citizens of the country we lived in, nor did we have refugee papers. M wanted us to belong to a place."[46] Tsering now lives in San Francisco, where she works for a Tibetan aid organization and continues to write.

Other scattered volumes published in the United States have also included works by Tibetan poets writing in English. For example, in addition to translations of Tibetan poems by imprisoned nuns, the works of the Anglophone writers Chögyam Trungpa and Ngodup Paljor (a long-time resident of Alaska) were featured in a recent anthology, *What Book?! Buddha Poems from Beat to Hip Hop* (2005). Both writers are now deceased. Writings published in such volumes are often translations or original English works written by popular dharma teachers. We may count among these the aforementioned book of poetry *The Little Song of "Do As You Please"* (1986) by Namkhai Norbu, whose religious center is based in Arcidosso, Italy.

The most widely acclaimed of Tibetan authors writing in English is Jamyang Norbu. He has written several political essays and books, the most famous of which is the novel *The Mandala of Sherlock Holmes* (1999). In 2000 the novel was awarded the Crossword Prize for Fiction of India, given to five literary works a year in India. The book was released again by Bloomsbury in

England and in America as *Sherlock Holmes: The Missing Years*. Since the contents and significance of this novel are detailed in chapter 14, I will not discuss the book here, except to mention that the author has described it as his "tribute" to three writer of the Victorian era: Arthur Conan Doyle, Rudyard Kipling, and Ryder Haggard.[47]

Another Tibetan writer now living in America is Palden Gyal, an employee of Radio Free Asia who has published several books as an author, editor, or translator. Among his publications are a biographical account in English entitled *Fire under the Snow* and a volume in Tibetan entitled *Mchod* (Offering), published by the Amnye Machen Institute as part of its poetry series in 1997. He was also the editor of an anthology of Tibetan poems released by the independent newspaper *Bod kyi dus bab* (Tibet Times). Entitled *Mchod me* (Offering lamp), the book is a tribute to Thupten Ngodup, a relatively unknown older man who immolated himself in protest against the Chinese occupation of Tibet. Similar books in Tibetan and English—not least *Tomorrow and Other Poems* (New Delhi, 2003), by the former president of the Tibetan Youth Congress, Lhasang Tsering—reflect the political focus of most Tibetan literature in the diaspora. More recently nationalist themes have been augmented by writers (mostly in English) who address the more personal dilemmas of growing up in exile.

Tibetan Publishers in the Diaspora

While only a few Tibetan publishing houses in exile have published a substantial number of literary works, it seems worthwhile to provide an overview. As far as I am aware no history of exile publishing is available in Tibetan or English, and the establishment of these publishing houses marks a greater degree of democracy in intellectual endeavors in exile. For many years, most institutions were funded by the government in exile, or by outside sponsors contributing through official channels. Since about 1990, however, there has been a growth of private cultural institutions which receive little or no government money. The bulk of my data here was drawn from brief interviews with staff at the various organizations and through archival research.

When the Dalai Lama met with Prime Minister Nehru in September 1959 to negotiate the terms by which the Government of India would accept some one hundred thousand Tibetan refugees, it was agreed that there would be separate schools for Tibetan children to maintain their language and culture. The effort began with fifty schools, and eventually the number increased to eighty. These schools were important in cultivating a corps of young Tibetan scholars, writers, and researchers who have since studied at Indian universities or overseas but have fairly good grounding in Tibetan, in addition to English, Hindi, and other languages.

One of the earliest publishing enterprises in exile began under the auspices of the Library of Tibetan Works and Archives (LTWA), founded in Dharamsala in 1970 by the Tibetan government in exile. For more than thirty years the various departments at the LTWA have served both Tibetans and Westerners in religious education, cultural research, and classical and contemporary publishing. The library has published books on Tibetan sayings, songs, and local traditions, as well as episodes of the Gesar epic, oral histories of aristocrats and other documents, English-Tibetan dictionaries, and Tibetan-language textbooks. The LTWA has also reprinted certain works by scholars in Tibet. To this day the LTWA remains an official and vital organization and has made an invaluable contribution to the discussion and research of Tibet and Tibetan culture. The administration had already founded two other important cultural institutions elsewhere in India: the Tibet House in Delhi, with an initial donation of thangka paintings, statues, and other religious objects by the Dalai Lama in 1965; and the Central Institute of Higher Tibetan Studies in Varanasi in 1966. During this same period other centers, such as the Buddhist Institute of Dialectics in Dharamsala, were formed as centers of religious and cultural preservation for Tibetans and Westerners alike.

Other long-established presses of the Central Tibetan Administration include the Snar thang Press, which publishes the widely read magazine *Shes bya* (Object of Knowledge). This magazine is devoted to issues in exile and can now be read online.[48] Finally, one of the most prolific publishers in exile has been the Cultural Printing Press, another official press of the CTA. It has been in existence for many years and published handwritten manuscripts through offset printing. In 1990 it began to typeset its publications.

The first institute to break the official stronghold on cultural institutions was the Amnye Machen Institute (AMI), which was founded on 28 June 1992 by Tashi Tsering, Pema Bhum, Jamyang Norbu, and Lhasang Tsering. In only one decade the institute published a great number of literary, historical, and political works, in addition to various newspapers and periodicals, though some intermittently. In 1993 the institute officially took over the Tibetan independent newspaper *Democracy*, discussed above, until the paper ceased publication in 1996. Under AMI the paper was published bimonthly. *Young Sprouts*, the literary magazine founded in 1990, also fell under AMI auspices beginning in 1994. Twelve full issues of this magazine have been produced. Under the editorship of Tashi Tsering, AMI in 1993 founded G.yu mtsho (Turquoise lake), a women's studies journal, but only three issues have been produced to date. In terms of literature AMI has been especially active in providing Tibetan translations of important works in English and other languages, such as Thomas Paine's *Common Sense*, Gandhi's *Hind Swaraj*, and Aung San Suu Kyi's *Freedom from Fear*.[49] Four volumes have been published in its Tibetan Literature Series, launched in 1993—Kelsang Lhamo's *Dreaming at the Sage's Abode*, Pema Bhum's *Heartbeat of a New Generation* (see chapter 6), selected writings by Döndrup Gyel, and oral literature from Nyarong (Kham)—as well as two volumes in its Poetry Series, launched in 1996. AMI has also released essential works in Tibetology, such as the English-language journal *Lungta*, and its Occupied Tibet Studies Series.[50]

In contrast to the institutions mentioned above, the Amnye Machen Institute has focused not only on preserving but "developing" Tibetan culture. It works toward "informing and raising the cultural and intellectual awareness of the Tibetan people, both in Tibet and in exile."[51] Focusing on "secular subjects with emphasis on the contemporary and neglected aspects of Tibetan culture and history,"[52] their publications ventured where none had yet trodden and were widely welcomed in exile. The institute has been less prolific in recent years, primarily because of lack of funding and staff. Nevertheless, its work has inspired many other ventures.

In June 1997, partly inspired by the work of Amnye Machen, the Tibetan Literary and Cultural Research Center was opened at the Norbulingka Institute, which had long committed itself to cultural preservation and was part of the Central Tibetan Administration. I myself was head of the center and general editor for *Nor lde* (Key to jewels), a monthly cultural newsletter, and *Nor 'od* (Precious light), the institute's literary magazine. The center also published a scholarly journal, *Nor mdzod* (Store of jewels), and an encyclopedia. Its contributions to the field of literature include a literary history and a few anthologies of poetry.

The full range of publications in exile, many marked by a short lifespan, cannot be covered here. I have merely been able to sketch major developments. However, a few conclusions may be drawn. Generally speaking, Tibetan literature in the diaspora is dominated by political themes. While the production of English poems and short stories marked the earliest years of literary experimentation in the late 1970s, we now see a greater burgeoning of Tibetophone writing, largely inspired and undertaken by writers who left Tibet in the last ten to twenty years. Their writings seem to have taken a firm hold, despite challenges to maintaining Tibetan literacy in exile. While Tibetan authors publishing in English are not numerous, a select few have earned high awards from India's and the world's literary establishment.

Notes

1. His Holiness and the Tibetan government (Central Tibetan Administration) officially moved to Dharamsala on 29 April 1960.
2. Khri byang Blo bzang ye shes bstan 'dzin rgya mtsho, *The Collected Works of Khri byang Rdo rje 'chang Blo bzang ye shes bstan 'dzin rgya mtsho* (New Delhi: Mongolian Lama Gurudeva, 1985).
3. Dze smad Blo bzang dpal ldan, *Collected Works of Kyabje Zemey Rinpoche* (Mundgod, India: Zemey Labrang, Gaden Shartse Monastic College, 1997).
4. Dreyfus, *The Sound of Two Hands Clapping*.
5. Chögyam Trungpa, *First Thought, Best Thought*. Though the book was published in English, the author also applied a Tibetan title: *Sems kyi zla ba* (Moon of the mind). Additional poems can be found in the book *Timely Rain*.
6. Mdo smad pa Yon tan rgya mtsho, *Gong sa rgyal mchog bcu bzhi pa chen po'i sku'i gcen po sku 'bum khri zur stag mtsher mchog sprul Thub bstan 'jigs med nor bu'i thun mong mdzad rim bsdus don dpyod ldan yongs la gtam du bya ba sngon me legs bshad nges don sprin gyi pho nya* (Bloomington: Tibetan Cultural Center, 1989).
7. Norbu Namkhai, *The Little Song of "Do As You Please"* (Archidosso, Italy: Shang Shung Editions, 1986).
8. Bkras mthong Thub bstan chos dar, *Dge 'dun chos 'phel gyi lo rgyus*.
9. The root text was written by Chekyidrug (Tib. Lce khyi 'brug) in the mid-eighth century.
10. The material in this section is drawn from written correspondence with Pema Tsewang Shastri, 19 January 2006.
11. Ibid.
12. Pad ma tshe dbang shāstri, *Nub kyi grang ngar dang shar gyi drod 'jam*. The initial print run of five hundred copies sold out quickly, and another five hundred copies also sold out. Apart from collections of religious prayers, this novel has become the best-selling book in exile.
13. Pad ma 'bum (Pema Bhum), Review, *Nub kyi grang ngar dang shar gyi drod 'jam*, (Bod kyi dus bab, 2000), back cover.
14. Pad ma tshe dbang shāstri, *Mi tshe'i bro ba mngar skyur*.
15. Pad ma tshe dbang shāstri, *Nga ni Bod yin*.
16. Charles Dickens, *Great Expectations*, trans. Padma Tshe dbang shāstri as *'Dun pa chen po* (Dharamsala: Tibetan Children's Village School, 1993).
17. This opportunity has expanded in recent years, as allowed by a loosening of PRC policy. In January 2006, for example, thousands of people were granted permission to travel to India for the Kālachakra Initiation led by His Holiness the Dalai Lama.
18. For example, *Dmangs tso, Bod kyi dus bab, Ljang zhon, Rtsam pa, Nor mdzod*, and *Nor 'od* (all published in or near Dharamsala), as well as *Shākya 'od nang* (Mundgod) and *Gangs rgyun* (Varanasi), were founded by recently arrived refugees. One exception is the founding in 2006 of a literary magazine, *'Od* (Light), in Varanasi by a Tibetan born and raised in exile.
19. The first part of the essay was published only in January 1993 in *Zla gsar* (New

moon), an independent journal in Dharamsala, alongside interviews with the writer, government officials, and opponents of the article. Ultimately one would be hard-pressed to find the specific cause of their protest. It is likely, however, that certain conservatives objected to Pema Bhum's assertion, "Let alone save the Tibetan people, Buddhism cannot even save itself." He further argues that poets inside Tibet "are disappointed and think for the first time: 'Well, what use is Buddhism? In this world there is no hope for refuge except in oneself'" (see chapter 5).

20. http://www.amnyemachen.org/.

21. I have recently self-published my fifth volume of poetry, *Gdon 'phrul lta bu'i bzi kha* (Drunk as a demon) (Youtse Publishing House, 2002).

22. Be ri 'Jigs med dbang rgyal, *Dus rabs gsar pa'i rtsom rig pa zhig gi snying khams nas phos pa'i zhungs khrag* [Drops of blood from the heart of a writer in the new era] (Mundgod: Blo gling dpe skrun khang, 1995). This collection of poetry is among the best in Tibetan exile society.

23. Although I was not able to obtain copies of these books in time for publication, it seems to me that the first was published circa 1996 and had a rather large number of fans. Lunyön Heruka's second collection of poetry, *Zang zing gi 'jig rten* (Chaotic world), was self-published around 1997.

24. Sha bo 'gyur med, *Lho ru 'khyams pa'i rnam shes* (Consciousness wandering southwards) (Dharamsala: S. Gyurme, 1995). The writer died shortly after publication.

25. Skal bzang mkhas grub, *Gangs ljongs kyi dge mtshan* (Virtues of the Land of Snows).

26. Ngawa Chodrak (Rnga ba Chos grags) published a series of three books in 1998: *Snyan ngag: g.yag rog zhol chen khros pa'i har sgra* (Poems: Angry snort of the yak), *Sgrung rtsom snying gi zungs khra khol ba'i rba rlabs* (Short stories: Wave of boiling blood from the heart), and a third which I have been unable to obtain.

27. Although the publishing details are not clearly recorded in this book, I recall that it was published around 1998.

28. Chab brag Lha mo skyabs, *Dbyangs can sprul ba'i glegs bam* (Volume [inspired by] the Transformation of Sarasvati). The author has adopted a convention from the Amdo poet-yogi Zhapkar (1781–1851), who would title his volumes after various deities.

29. Brag smyon Ya ma rā dzā, *Mi yul gyi skyo gdung* (The suffering of the human realm) (Kathmandu: Yeshe Yamaradza, 2003).

30. Klu tshang Blo bzang ye shes, *Tshor ba'i pha bong*.

31. Skal bzang lha mo (Chos 'dzin), *Drang srong bsti gnas kyi rmi lam yun ci / Dreaming at the Sage's Abode.*

32. Chu skyes sgrol ma, *Sprin bral zla ba'i 'dzum rlabs.*

33. Tshe ring skyid, *Tshe ring skyid kyi rtsom btus* (Collection of poetry) (n.p. [?Dharamsala], 2002).

34. Zungchuk Kyi (b. 1974) gained her fame as writer while living in Qinghai Province. Her background is uncommon (if not unique) in that she never attended an undergraduate college but has attained renown as an accomplished writer. Widely published in various Tibetan literary journals in the PRC, she had a collection of her poetry published under the collective title *Byu ru'i las dbang* (Fate of the coral).

More recently she has published a second volume of poetry in exile: 'Jags mi srid pa'i rlabs rgyun (The wave that cannot be stilled).

35. Written correspondence to Lauran Hartley (editor), dated 20 November 2005. To publish the book *Crossing the Border*, Tenzin notes that he "begged and borrowed from classmates while studying in Mumbai."

36. Tenzin Tsundue, "Space Bar—A Proposal," *Kora: Stories and Poems*, 19.

37. Tenzin Tsundue, "My Tibetanness," *Kora: Stories and Poems*, 15.

38. Tenzin Tsundue, "Desperate Age," *Kora: Stories and Poems*, 14.

39. Tenzin Tsundue, *Kora: Stories and Poems*.

40. These bibliographic details are drawn from the web site of the Friends of Tibet support group in India. See http://www.friendsoftibet.org/tenzin/.

41. Readers at the event included Tenzin Tsundue, Lhamo Kyap, Lhakyap Jinpa, Dorjee Wangchuk, Tseten Gyal, and Lhasang Tsering.

42. Bhuchung D. Sonam, ed., *Muses in Exile*.

43. Anne Waldman, review, *Rules of the House*, back cover.

44. Tsering Wangmo Dhompa, "She Is," *Rules of the House*, 24.

45. Ibid.

46. Tsering Wangmo Dhompa, "Member," *Rules of the House*, 60.

47. "A Conversation between Jamyang Norbu and Elliot Sperling," 15.

48. See http://www.tibet.net/sheja/.

49. For a discussion of AMI's translation activity see Venturino, "Reading Negotiations in the Tibetan Diaspora."

50. More information on the Amnye Machen Institute can be found at the organization's web site, http://www.amnyemachen.org/.

51. http://www.amnyemachen.org/.

52. Ibid.

14

Placing Tibetan Fiction in a World

of Literary Studies: Jamyang Norbu's

The Mandala of Sherlock Holmes

STEVEN J. VENTURINO

It is said that when Colonel Francis Younghusband led an invasion into Lhasa in 1904, he brought along his beloved copy of Rudyard Kipling's *Kim*. Indeed, the story of an Indian-born Irish boy who becomes involved in the "Great Game" of Central Asian politics, travels across borders at will, and discovers what Kipling understood as the deepest secrets of Tibetan Buddhism served to underwrite the imagination of more than one adventurer and political figure. Since its publication in 1901 the novel has established much of the imaginative territory identified as "India" and "Tibet" for readers around the world.[1] Kipling's Tibet spoke in the voice of the "Teshoo Lama," quietly but persuasively echoing across a mysterious landscape toward the whole of British India and beyond. The novel's ability to create a compelling world-view, into which Tibet would be placed, was enhanced by the politicians, soldiers, writers, scholars, and ordinary readers from many countries who contributed to the contradictory and powerful legacy of the western presence in Asia. Perceval Landon's firsthand account of Younghusband's invasion, *The Opening of Tibet*, a nearly five-hundred-page work filled with reportage, scientific data, and Orientalist scholarship, even concludes with a full-page advertisement for Kipling's novel, urging readers to refer to *Kim* to arrive at "a most concise idea of the relationship between Tibet and India."[2]

In examining the specific importance of *Kim* to diplomacy and geopolitics, Patrick Williams describes what he calls "the Kipling effect," drawing on Edward Said's analysis of the culturally constitutive power of colonial texts. Said argues that "the experiences of readers are in turn determined by what they have read, and this in turn influences writers to take up subjects defined in advance by readers' experiences. . . . Most important, such texts can *create* not only knowledge but also the very reality they appear to describe."[3] Elaborating on these general principles, Williams recalls the influential British

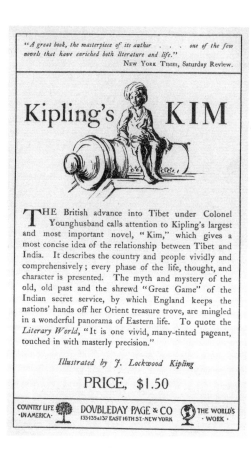

Advertisement for Rudyard Kipling's *Kim* as it appeared in the American edition of Perceval Landon's *The Opening of Tibet* (New York: Doubleday, 1905).

intellectual Leonard Woolf's "inability to distinguish" between Kipling's characters and the models from which they had been drawn.[4] Williams also notes that Lord Birkenhead, the secretary of state for India from 1924 to 1928, who was strongly opposed to Indian self-rule, had never actually visited the country but instead developed his "feel" for the inferiority of Indians by way of "an intensive reading of Kipling's India books with their wonderful descriptive passages."[5] Such examples, Williams asserts, indicate the importance of tracing Kipling's impact on "far-reaching policy decisions" affecting early-twentieth-century imperial politics.[6]

Now, more than a century after Younghusband's invasion, and at a time when political commentators are noting the return of the "Great Game,"[7] it seems equally important to consider again just who is carrying whose books into the battles that continue to erupt along Tibet's politico-cultural borders. Imaginative constructions of Tibet, increasingly the object of academic research, appear daily to affect cultural, political, and scholarly decision making. Chinese dissidents point out that official depictions of Tibet and

Tibetans in the PRC suffer from "one-sided propaganda" in which "chauvinism and nationalism predominate,"[8] while western support groups tend to nurture visions of Tibet in which the country's "complexities and competing histories have been flattened into a stereotype" of a timeless Shangri-La.[9] It should therefore come as no surprise that Tibetan literature should also find itself in significant ways already placed in the antagonistic world of literary studies. Literary critics, including this one, can only situate works of Tibetan literature on maps already informed not only by popular opinion and official policies but by motivated interpretations of global trends in literary theory. The categories that both enable and contain scholarly discussions of emerging Tibetan literature, I suggest, principally include those formed by existing debates on postmodern and postcolonial literature. This chapter therefore offers a critical examination of some of the important forces at work in constructing specific contexts for reading Tibetan literature and the ways in which Tibetan literature both supports and challenges these forces.

While works of Tibetan literature are productively approached by way of existing critical theories of postmodernity and postcoloniality—virtually all of which have been developed without regard for Tibetan literature—the unique aspects of Tibetan works should lead us to reevaluate and revise these approaches in light of their implicit assumptions of national identity and an insufficient attention paid to nonwestern forms of colonialism. Adding urgency to this project are the parallels that obtain between reading Tibetan literature and reading Tibetan history and politics. Placing Tibetan fiction in a global setting and allowing existing literary maps to be redrawn, in other words, may also help to revise flawed assumptions about the global place of Tibet's politics and culture.

In important ways, Tibetan fiction both participates in and challenges what has become a worldwide dialogue of literary studies in which the dominant subfields are "national" literatures defined by the borders of recognized nation-states and their majority languages.[10] On the one hand, Tibetan literature is written in the context of long-standing circumscriptions of "Chinese literature" privileging Han traditions, while on the other hand Tibetan writing in the diaspora is faced with adoption into other national literatures—Indian, American, French, German—or grouped with other "nonwestern" texts whose only distinguishing feature seems to be that they are "nonwestern."

Postmodern and postcolonial approaches to literature are particularly dominant forces, not only for creating the existing interpretive contexts for Tibetan literature but for self-consciously examining the limitations of these contexts as well. Postmodernist writing, for example, has been read as a discursive and political challenge to dominant, totalizing narratives of individual character as well as national identity. Certain strains of postcolonial theory directly confront the hegemonic practices, including discourse, that are essential to maintaining social and political hierarchies. Here I outline the present state of literary affairs as one in which Tibetan fiction can clearly be included in discussions of postmodernism, even as certain premises of "international postmodernism" actually frustrate this inclusion by confining the analytical field of literary works to recognized national boundaries. I contend that Tibetan fiction supplements notions of "international postmodernism" by calling attention to the transnational (cross-border) rather than international (between states) nature of literary exchange.

Postcolonial literature and criticism concerns itself with negotiating a return to place or adapting to a place that is "returned" after colonial occupation. For contemporary Tibetan writers colonialism means either exile—a stateless place—or occupation—an antagonistically shared place. British colonialism has become a part of Tibetan literature written in India, while Chinese colonialism is often at the heart of Tibetan writing in China, manifesting itself in part as "magical realism" or a postmodern clash of modernity and "tradition" defined as premodernity. Each of these fields of colonialism begs the importance of seeing Tibetan history, as well as the Tibetan nation, not as a traditionally coherent historical narrative but as a complex and polyvocal narrative of engagement with the world.

The development of the modern nation, and its privileging of place, find contemporary Tibetan fiction in the important epistemological position of being informed by more than one place at one time. Postcolonial approaches to literature, emphasizing either colonial discourses of the past—whose influence is still very much a matter of the present—or neocolonial strategies conducted through present-day projects of cultural imperialism, globalization, and power politics, tend to direct literary interpretation in these two general directions. Beyond this, however, is a postmodern colonialism suggested by Tibetan literature, in which the temporal dimension of colonialism fuses past and present, while the cultural dimension must negotiate the discursive and social colonizing projects of the East as well as the West.[11]

Currently, scholarly study of Tibetan literature is largely conducted by Tibet specialists pursuing a variety of disciplines, including anthropology, religious studies, sociology, and Asian studies. The International Association for Tibetan Studies over the past decade has devoted increasing attention to contemporary Tibetan literature. Seminar panels and publications sponsored by the IATS, as well as those sponsored by its affiliated organizations and members, have led to significant cross-disciplinary fertilization and an appreciable expansion of the scope of traditional Tibetological concerns.[12] The same cannot be said of literary studies as such, in which Tibetan literature remains acutely underexplored, in part because of the relative dearth of accessible texts, and in part because of the difficult institutional decisions — demanded of western and Chinese critics alike — involving Tibet's status within China. Indeed, when literary and cultural critics are invited to China to participate in conferences devoted to postcoloniality and globalization, discussion of Tibetan literature is carefully policed.[13] Yet I believe that we are at a turning point of sorts, and the appearance of Jamyang Norbu's *The Mandala of Sherlock Holmes* is one sign of a new era in Tibetan literary studies.[14] As I will discuss below, this is a novel that highlights the bridges already existing between disciplines, and these bridges draw critical attention to themselves as well as the destinations they connect. By addressing the issue of Tibetan literature's place in globalized literary studies, I hope to show that while the field of Tibetan studies continues to be influenced by other disciplines (provoking the very kinds of research illustrated by this book), Tibetan studies also influences other disciplines. This is particularly true with regard to theories of postmodernist literature and postcolonial writing, which have yet to meaningfully acknowledge Tibet's history, politics, and literature in a globally informed literary criticism. It is hoped, therefore, that Tibet scholars interested in contemporary literature and criticism will find themselves in a position to contribute to broader cultural debates, while literary critics will discover the importance of including Tibetan literature in their consideration of international comparative criticism.[15]

The Tibetan studies specialists José Ignacio Cabezón and Roger R. Jackson, editors of an important earlier survey of Tibetan literature, acknowledge that "there is an 'imaginative' element to the concept of literature in the West that narrows considerably the range of what may be counted as literary" in Tibetan writing.[16] Works that they want to consider in their review of Tibetan literature do not fit the model of literature as circumscribed by "an essentially foreign concept" of the literary, and therefore "the Euro-American concept of literature may itself have to be modified."[17] While Cabezón and Jackson address a very broad field of texts, primarily in Tibetan and largely historical, my concern is to specifically consider how existing approaches to literary study — whether identified as Euro-American, western, or Chinese — establish the contexts for interpreting new Tibetan fiction, and how this fiction in turn modifies concepts of the literary. That is, "Tibetan literature," as an object of knowledge-making for global academic study, is being constructed in the here and now, often on the basis of contemporary works either composed or circulated in western languages. As critical attention is turned to literature written by and about Tibetans, familiar frameworks for interpretation will influence how Tibetan literature will be "sold" to our colleagues and students. Yet as postmodern and postcolonial approaches to literary analysis suggest, these frameworks are hardly static, and Tibetan literature highlights the restive array of cultural, political, institutional, aesthetic, and ideological interests underwriting the very categories of "Euro-American," "western," and "Chinese."

Of course modifying these interpretive frameworks has its risks. In the United States disagreements over the agents of representation of national culture are called "culture wars," while anxiety over national cultural heterogeneity in China may provoke charges of "foreign meddling in domestic affairs" or outright sedition. But it is the propaganda wars that continue daily to figure most highly in Tibetan debates, with China's official images of a peacefully liberated, happily developing, new Tibet on the one side and western images of a threatened spiritual paradise on the other. Contemporary Tibetan fiction is noteworthy in that it does not simply ignore or deny the narratives implicit in these two perspectives, but instead finds ways of inviting readers to hear these narratives merge in new combinations, expressing complex truths of a global Tibetan society that is both product and producer of the world's texts.

Postmodern (Re)Writing

Two of the defining features of postmodernism, despite widespread debate over definitions as such, are the revisiting of earlier narratives, particularly narratives of history, and the consequent disruption of totalizing structures. "All that has been received, if only yesterday," the philosopher Jean-François Lyotard warns, "must be suspected."[18] The historian Hayden White notes that postmodern theories "dissolve the distinction between realistic and fictional discourses based on the presumption of an ontological difference between their respective referents, real and imaginary."[19] And the literary critic Linda Hutcheon emphasizes that postmodern narratives expose and challenge the "totalizing representations" of existing historical narratives, especially those attempting to conceal the interested aspects of literary and historical representation: "The narrativation of past events is not hidden [in postmodernist texts]; the events no longer seem to speak for themselves, but are shown to be consciously composed into a narrative, whose constructed—not found—order is imposed upon them, often overtly by the narrating figure. The process of making stories out of chronicles, of constructing plots out of sequences, is what postmodern fiction underlines."[20] By highlighting the extent to which all narratives are exercises in managing representation, postmodern writing, according to Hutcheon, may also serve to expose the totalizing forces of political and social narratives. While discussions elaborating this argument proliferate in literary scholarship around the world, significant exceptions arise when criticism of historical narratives is labeled as dangerous, and gaps also appear in the very framing of the "international" scope of postmodernist writing.

In a book published in 1997 the International Comparative Literature Association (ICLA) took on the task of representing the many varieties of "international postmodernism." Essays in it address the founding positions of postmodernism and survey "the reception and processing of postmodernism" in North America, Latin America, western and southern Europe, central and eastern Europe, Africa, and Asia.[21] For each of these regions essays focus on specific countries, with the section devoted to Asia comprising essays examining postmodernism in India, China, and Japan. I will further discuss the essay on Chinese postmodernism below, but at this point it is important to note that virtually no attention is given to literature that cannot be definitively associated with a nation-state, such as Tibetan, Palestinian, or Roma literature. Indeed the very absence of concern for writing of this sort affords us the opportunity to consider how Tibetan literature reflects as well as challenges some of the established approaches to "international postmodernism."

In the ICLA book Matei Calinescu first grounds postmodern rewriting in "the view that the world, and not only the literary work, can be seen as a text."[22] He explains that postmodernist writers "read" histories and events as existing texts to be rearticulated in new texts. Historical parody, in particular, can be read as an exercise in "continuing the past while distancing itself from it," because the (re)writer recognizes his or her inability to completely withdraw from existing texts.[23] Calinescu maintains that while the rewriting of texts, in the broad sense of commentary, parody, and other familiar forms, is nothing new, what distinguishes postmodern rewriting from past forms is "a certain playful, hide-and-seek type of indirection, a tongue-in-cheek seriousness, an often respectful and even honorific irony, and an overall tendency toward oblique and even secret or quasi-secret textual reference."[24] Postmodern writers, that is, (re)create texts that ask us to accept them as "new" even as we recognize familiar references and texts that we are in fact rereading. The Argentinian writer Jorge Luis Borges, for example, mixes real texts with fictional ones in his story "The Garden of Forking Paths," and in "Pierre Menand, Author of Quixote," Borges depicts a fictional writer who recreates, word-for-word, the work of Cervantes.[25]

Interlacing facts and fictions, Jamyang Norbu's *The Mandala of Sherlock*

Holmes not only "recovers" two missing years in the life of Arthur Conan Doyle's detective, but also rewrites aspects of Kipling's *Kim*, Tibetan history, and Jamyang Norbu's own life.[26] The novel is set in the closing years of the nineteenth century: the great detective travels to Tibet, where the British government suspects Chinese meddling in what the British consider their own territory for meddling. Holmes discovers that the specific reason for his trip is to protect the life of the thirteenth Dalai Lama—the previous incarnation of the current Dalai Lama—from Chinese assassination. The novel's initial reception was one of instant recognition by aficionados of the "source texts." As illustrated by a brief sampling of early reviews, readers of the novel are drawn to the fusion of texts—smatterings of dialogue, description, and even footnotes from Doyle and Kipling are transplanted directly into the novel—and prompted to remark on Jamyang Norbu's firm grasp of history and "facts" as he leads them on this new adventure-fantasy:[27]

> Norbu takes to pastiche with grace and elan. . . . Norbu's style is racy yet elegant, measured yet breathless. The author allows these apparent contraries to repose in comfort, lighting up his story with touches of sudden, leavening humour. In a way *Mandala* is like meeting an old friend after many years. He seems altered by time, yet he seems the same as we knew him a long time ago. Things change, things remain the same. . . . If you have time, head for your favourite chair and curl up with *Mandala* and a mug of coffee. If you don't have time, make time for this book. You won't regret it. (*The Telegraph* 19 November 1999)

> A gripping mix of Holmesian drama and Tibetan mythology. (*India Today* 25 October 1999)

> Truth is said to be stranger than fiction. However, when fiction itself assumes the verisimilitude of truth in dexterous hands the result can be even more fascinating as Jamyang Norbu has so capably shown in this gripping account of the exploits of Sherlock Holmes in Tibet. . . . What makes the book fascinating is the depth and extent of research. From a description of gas-lit Bombay of 1891, from the dock-side to horse-drawn carriages, the journey by the Frontier Mail to Ambala and thence to Simla by tonga and finally the long trek initially through the Hindustan Tibet Road past Manasarovar to Lhasa no detail is spared and nothing suffers from inaccuracy. Indeed since Salman Rushdie considered G V Desani's All About Hatter to be the best English fiction written by an Indian, Norbu's Huree could be regarded by Rushdie as a close competitor. (*Business Standard* 21 October 1999)

The author's own formidable knowledge of Tibet and its neighbouring culture, and a successful evocation of India during the zenith of the Raj also plays a major role in making this story eminently readable. (*Economic Times* 7 November 1999)

A ripping tale of deadly intrigue and dastardly crimes that travels from the shores of the Arabian sea at Bombay to the Ice Temple of Shambala on the roof of the world. Norbu argues that *The Mandala of Sherlock Holmes* is pure escapism, yet the book challenges the tendency of Western literature to treat Tibet simply as a fantastic backdrop for the spiritual quests or daring adventures of white people. (*South China Morning Post* 30 October 1999)

Yet within this "ripping tale" and contributing to the complexity of the action in the novel are three primary narrative concerns. The first is the detective tale focusing on discovery and capture of the persons responsible for several murders and the threats on the life of the Dalai Lama. The second narrative involves the events and geopolitics of the turn-of-the- century "Great Game," as Chinese and Western interests clash in Tibet. Finally, the third line is a framing narrative that voices unequivocal protest against the present-day colonization of Tibet by the Chinese government. These protests, which open and close the novel, are offered in the voice of "Jamyang Norbu."

What makes this detective story of interest to those studying postmodern rewriting is of course the way these narrative lines are structured around superimposed texts of history and fiction. The author, Jamyang Norbu by name, explains that he is only the book's editor, while the narrative of the novel's action belongs to Hurree Chunder Mookerjee, a character drawn from the "Babu" of Kipling's *Kim*. Also from Kipling's texts appear the characters of Captain Strickland, Colonel Creighton, and others, who along with Mukherjee were themselves based on historical figures.[28] From Doyle's Sherlock Holmes tales come Holmes, his brother Mycroft, his nemesis Professor Moriarty, and others.

Like the Holmes stories, as well as the Dupin stories of Edgar Allan Poe, Jamyang Norbu's novel confirms that "of all forms of 'light literature,' the detective story is the most inescapably concerned with moral issues."[29] Sherlock Holmes is crafted to address extremely complex and sober questions, which the author signals in the preface by taking on a startlingly bold responsibility: "Tibet may lie crushed beneath the dead weight of Chinese tyranny, but the truth about Tibet cannot be so easily buried; and even such a strange fragment of history as this, may contribute to nailing at least a few lies of the tyrants."[30] It is at this early point in the novel that the reader must decide whether Jamyang Norbu is to be taken seriously: Does he really think that a detective adventure-fantasy mixing facts with fiction will threaten "Chinese tyranny" with "truth about Tibet"? And it is at this early point in the novel, at the narrative level of the author's personal engagement with contemporary history, that the singularity of postmodernist writing leads us to answer in the affirmative. Jamyang Norbu's novel signals a challenging recognition that the persistence of colonial force in historical narratives is based on the texts created in fiction as well as in fact. As a sustained illustration of this, the novel insists that factual and fictional texts alike must serve as the materials on which to base both analysis and response. The novel resembles the present-day Tibetan situation—both are formed by the superimposition of texts, events, and textual events, and both are revealed in the persistence of actual figures, stereotypes, and imaginary landscapes. Jamyang Norbu's novel emphasizes that the narratives—or criminal "plots," to acknowledge the detective genre—emerging from these superimposed layers must be confronted, rather than ignored or deemed superfluous, if a rewritten narrative is to reveal the "missing years"—or hidden truths—of Holmes and Tibet.

There is a long tradition, akin to that attached to Kipling's Kimball O'Hara, of readers responding to the "actual" Sherlock Holmes. Surveying the impact of Doyle's famous detective, Christopher Clausen writes that since his first appearance in 1887, Holmes has become the most "real" character in Victorian literature: "Even among those who have never read any of the stories or seen the film and television adaptations, there must be very few people over the age of ten in the English-speaking world who have never heard of Sherlock Holmes, or of his equally imaginary chronicler, Dr. Watson. As T. S. Eliot pointed out in the *Criterion* in 1929, Holmes is *real* in a way that only the greatest fictional characters ever achieve. Less sophisticated readers think so, too: letters of admiration and requests for help are still addressed to the mythical rooms of a man who, had he ever lived at all, would now [1986] be a hundred and thirty years old. No other Victorian literary character, not even Alice, has maintained so powerful a hold on so many twentieth-century readers' imaginations."[31] While readers of the Holmes stories post letters to Baker Street, Clausen reminds us that the more serious aspects of Holmes's "existence" include the reinforcement of notions of law and order for British society, as well as the idea that criminal acts are signs of "chaos lurking below the surface of civilized life, waiting for the opportunity to reassert itself."[32] Clausen's study focuses on these thematic connections as they relate to British society, rather than on the material and historical consequences of Holmes as a signpost in historical memory, which he disparages by remarking that Holmes "has been the subject of the most tedious pseudoscholarship in the history of letters, most of it premised on the facetious assumption that Holmes was a historical character whose biography needs filling in."[33] Of course Jamyang Norbu's novel is precisely an example of filling in a gap in Holmes's biography—during which, the detective says, he "traveled for two years in Tibet"[34]—but this "pseudoscholarship" serves to expose the power of those "facetious assumptions" that continue to influence Tibet's political and cultural history.

As Clausen argues, Holmes's non-threatening stance toward society as such emphasizes the individualistic nature of crime, since "crime and disorder result from a failure of individual responsibility, not of institutions."[35] *The Mandala*, on the other hand, insists on the complicity of institutions as an essential part of individual as well as social behavior. The "crimes" perpetrated on Tibetan history are among other things matters involving legal, political, and even literary institutions. Jamyang Norbu's "own" history, as narrated in the novel, includes exile from Tibet, a Jesuit upbringing in India, the reading of English books, and the establishment of Tibetan schools in Dharamsala, leading Jamyang Norbu to explain that "mainly due to the peculiar circumstance of my birth, I came into possession of this strange but true account."[36]

Holmes is indeed real, and in ways that readers may not fully recognize. His reality is felt, heard, and seen in the endless maze of texts that compose the British empire generally and Tibet's place in politico-cultural memory specifically. He is real because he operates not only on the cultural imagination but on the political imagination as well. The nineteenth-century British presence in India is a matter of real consequences for today's national political structures, foreign policies, and military strategies, as well as for the texts that will determine future developments.

Ulrich Broich contributes to the ICLA book on international postmodernism with a discussion of intertextuality. Broich notes that intertextuality, like rewriting, is not unique to postmodern literature, but what distinguishes the new forms from the old is the suggestion that the postmodern form "serves new functions, and it is connected with a different concept of literature," including an interest in illustrating "a radically new concept of the text" and therefore of the text's relationship with the world.[37] These new concepts and relationships can prompt a kind of vertigo encountered by fictional characters and by readers who "realize they are suddenly part of a different world."[38] The author's role in *The Mandala* combines the responsibilities of an editor, a fictional character, and a historical figure. Similarly, the Holmes character emerges from and operates on several planes of existence: novels and short stories are cited to confirm specific aspects of his biography, while characters from Kipling's fictional works and historical events around the

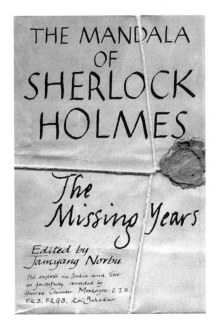

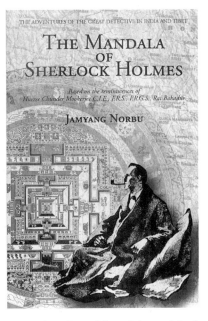

"Wraparound" cover of *The Mandala of Sherlock Holmes: The Missing Years*, by Jamyang Norbu. London: John Murray, 2000.

Cover of the first edition of *The Mandala of Sherlock Holmes*, by Jamyang Norbu. New Delhi: Harper-Collins India, 1999. Design by Christophe Besuchet.

world help to supplement his life story. The novel's vertiginous combination of fact and fiction—and blending of sincerity and farce—suggests the unsettling realization that writers and readers of Tibetan fiction may not always be capable of claiming a distinction in kind between them and the texts they engage.

By the novel's end, the reader actually discovers the "editor," again Jamyang Norbu by name, in the presence of Holmes's reincarnation. Holmes has been revealed to be a Tibetan lama living at the time of the novel's nineteenth-century action, and it is this Holmes who travels with Hurree to Tibet. In the late-twentieth-century setting of the novel's epilogue, the lama has found a new abode in the person of a monk visited by Jamyang Norbu in his attempt to gain further details of Holmes "history" in Tibet. Holmes is placed in both time schemes—as a Tibetan—because he is a bridge for important aspects of Tibetan history and even Tibetan spirituality. The vertigo of intertextuality in this novel therefore leads us to reject totalizing assumptions regarding a single "proper place," or even dimension, for a person, nation, story, or memory. Kipling, Doyle, Jamyang Norbu, British India, and Tibet are each shown to result in and be the results of superimposed texts. As with many other

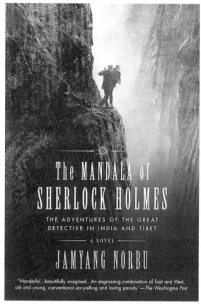

Sidney Paget, "The Death of Sherlock Holmes." Illustration for *Strand Magazine*, December 1893. Reprinted in *The New Annotated Sherlock Holmes*, vol. 1, ed. Leslie S. Klinger, 743. New York: W. W. Norton, 2005.

Paperback cover of *The Mandala of Sherlock Holmes*, by Jamyang Norbu. New York: Bloomsbury, 2003. Illustration is of the painting *Derrida Queries de Man*, by Mark Tansey (1990).

postmodernist texts, we are prompted to acknowledge a significantly "decentered" notion of subjectivity, in which a stable self cannot be identified on the basis of a single given epistemological plane. It is moreover the Chinese component, woven into the matrix of Anglo-Indian references and revisions, that really sets this novel apart in exploring the place that Tibet occupies in a literary world. Holmes's nemesis, Professor Moriarty, is revealed to be in collusion with "Imperial China," and it is only in defeating this particular manifestation of evil that Holmes will emerge victorious and the Dalai Lama will be saved. Moriarty, like Holmes, is revealed to be a spiritually powerful Tibetan monk, rescued from his apparent death by Qing officials who, as he explains, "helped establish me in Europe to avenge themselves against the nations that had humiliated China."[39] In this way the novel reestablishes Moriarty as well as Holmes in an epistemological matrix that demands recognition of the multiple spatial and temporal aspects of both the protagonist and the antagonist of his narrative. Holmes, a decentered, postmodern pastiche of British and Tibetan textual experience, must battle a similar foe, one who cannot be reduced to a single western or Chinese sensibility, but arises from the same postmodern layering of narrative memory and (as discussed below) the transnational dimensions of colonial history.

Scholarly studies have focused on issues of literary postmodernism in Chinese contexts, but none of them thoughtfully take up the challenge of Tibetan literature, even when the opportunity to do so is presented by the arguments made in the studies themselves. The ICLA book devoted to international postmodernism, for example, represents China with an essay by Wang Ning, who argues that while "there is no postmodernist movement" in China, literature of the post-Mao "New Era" does show some signs of postmodernist influence from the West. Wang describes six themes as corroborating this influence, each of which clearly begs the question of Tibet's challenging presence in the People's Republic of China, but none of which is pursued with that challenge in mind.[40] In another collection of essays, Rey Chow also raises important issues regarding postmodernism and Chinese literature, pointing out that any consideration of postmodernity must account for the significance of colonialism in formations of modernity itself. Chow argues that "issues of 'modernity' and 'modernism' in Chinese literature . . . have to be rethought precisely because they are inextricably bound up with imperialism."[41] Her concern, voiced in this influential essay and elsewhere, is that China is following a unique trajectory for modernism and postmodernism because of western imperialism, yet Chow does not explore how Tibet's presence in China and the world destabilizes "Chinese postmodernity" in ways paralleling her convincing argument that China's presence redefines "Western postmodernity."

More ambitious projects of elaborating postmodernist literature in China similarly ignore minority voices within the PRC, yet they suggest theoretical perspectives that should be supplemented with discussions of Tibetan literary works. Arif Dirlik and Xudong Zhang argue that addressing postmodernism in China "also requires an examination of the Chinese situation with reference to the modernity-postmodernity shift globally."[42] A collection of essays edited by these critics considers this shift with regard to specific issues, including the formation of China's "mysterious others" in Fifth-Generation Chinese films, a study that could be productively complicated by interrogating the use of Tibetan "folk life" as a metaphor of Chinese otherness and innocence.[43] Another critic, Xiaobing Tang, valuably foregrounds the oppositional nature of postmodernist literature as he argues that this literature can be used explicitly to confront hegemonic discourses: "To talk about postmodernism, to engage in an intellectual activity that prolongs a productive and diversifying, although occasionally agonizing 'culture crisis,' is necessarily a political choice. No matter how vague or controversial it may be, postmodernism, as a periodizing concept first of all, turns out to be a discursive formation conveniently at the service of a counterhegemonic commitment."[44] This perspective invites us to see Tibet's presence in debates on postmodernism and postmodernity as one that is intimately related to *two* fields of colonial discourse, western as well as Chinese. The task then becomes one of articulating—in criticism as well as fiction—the transformations of Tibetan society that distinguish its unique postmodernist characteristics, which in turn shape any configuration of international postmodernism. Consequently, "international postmodernism" is exposed as an overdetermined field of analysis, limited by its reliance on the boundaries of nation-states, even as its theoretical perspectives suggest that key features of stateless or exile literature call attention to non-national aspects of creating, maintaining, and crossing borders.

The Tibetan writer and critic Pema Bhum describes a new approach to contemporary Tibetan poetry, and I would argue that a central argument of his discussion also points to what is at stake in Tibetan fiction. Pema Bhum suggests that contemporary Tibetan poets are able to direct technical and emotional energies away from earlier conventions involving politics and religion and toward the circumstances surrounding a poet's own experience: "For the New Poets, who are liberated from politics and religion, the range of expression of the mind has been enlarged, and, similarly, the range of the world of external objects has been very much enlarged."[45] Pema Bhum then quickly qualifies the term "politics and religion" by arguing that contemporary poets "are not guided by what is conventionally known, but by their experience and imagination. Therefore, we meet yaks in their poetry. Not only that, but we also find yak dung in their poetry."[46] Tibetan writers therefore produce their texts out of "the experience and imagination" of people who, while freed from overdetermined conventions of traditional religious poetry and models of socialist realism, remain intimately in touch with new, manifold narratives of Chinese colonialism, cultural and religious transformation, and discursive alteration.

This kind of postmodern colonialism is a condition in which the postcolonial legacies of the past crisscross with the colonial projects of the present. For the Tibetan writer in exile, this temporal dimension delineated by past and present colonial projects is also superimposed with a spatial dimension formed on the one side by Anglo-Indian colonialism's influence on politics, literature, and language and on the other side by Sino-Tibetan colonialism's domination of the same. It is to this condition, disclosed and yet concealed by investigations into "Chinese postmodernism" as well as "British India," that I now turn.

(Post)colonial Discourses

Three key perspectives of postcolonial theory are particularly relevant to Tibetan literature in a global marketplace, especially, again, because these theoretical approaches to colonial writing and postcolonial literature have been formed without regard to Tibet's colonization or the work of Tibetan writers who identify themselves as exiles from a colonized nation. These perspectives include the idea that the historical archive should be taken up as a source of texts helping to shape colonial discourse, the argument that mimicry and hybridized discourse are important to the study of texts from colonized societies, and the debate over English as an appropriate language for postcolonial writing.

The notion of "reading the archive" recalls discussions of postmodern rewriting in suggesting that texts of all types help to shape historical memory and contemporary politics. Reading archival material—the notes, journals, official communications, and other documents that are required for colonial administration—as "literature" helps us to see how complex narratives of power, race, and national identity are perpetuated in what are traditionally seen to be "neutral" or "merely factual" texts. Jamyang Norbu's *The Mandala*, as we have seen, turns this formulation on its head, or perhaps simply acknowledges that "facts" can turn out to be transformed literary texts, such as the fictions of Kipling and Doyle, as they become parts of the colonial archive. Gayatri Chakravorty Spivak has argued that the importance of directing "literary reading" to archival material lies in the need to investigate "the object of representations that becomes a reality":

> In that a hegemonic nineteenth-century European historiography had designated the archives as depositories of "facts," and I proposed that they should be "read," my position could be consonant with [Hayden] White's. The records I read showed the soldiers and administrators of the East India Company constructing the object of representations that becomes a reality in India. This is "literature" in the general sense—the archives selectively preserving the changeover of the episteme—as its condition; with "literature" in the narrow sense—all the genres—as its effect. . . . On a somewhat precious register of literary theory, it is possible to say that this was the construction of a fiction whose task was to produce a whole collection of "effects of the real," and that the "misreading" of this "fiction" produced the proper name "India." The colonizer constructs himself as he constructs the colony. The relationship is intimate, an open secret that cannot be part of official knowledge.[47]

Jamyang Norbu's novel illustrates the "whole collection of 'effects of the real'" that is manipulated to construct a place for Tibet's history, politics, and people. The relationship, as Spivak warns, is "intimate, an open secret," a point illustrated by Holmes's identity and the identities of all the British and Chinese characters implicated in the novel's historico-fictional construction. "For the early part of the nineteenth century in India," Spivak adds, "the literary critic must turn to the archives of imperial governance to supplement the consolidation of what will come to be recognized as 'nationalist' literature."[48] Similarly, for the critic of Tibetan literature it becomes crucial to acknowledge the redoubled effect, evident in Jamyang Norbu's novel, of fictional texts that influence the archive of historical facts. The Mandala suggests that for Tibetan history, the "archives of imperial governance" include texts such as Kim and the Holmes stories, in addition to—and in collusion or contestation with—Tibetan archival materials and narratives from the western imagination. A reading of these interlaced texts prevents the "consolidation" of what would be a delusive "Tibetan national literature" based solely on "indigenous" writing. A Tibetan history devoid of the signs of China and the West does not exist, yet when these seemingly "non-Tibetan" aspects of Tibetan history are read as supplements to an essentializing formation of national literature, an irreducibly essential "Tibetan literature" truly emerges.

This sort of national literature therefore emerges as a physical, material force, shaped by the people and material texts that make up Tibetan history, rather than as an abstract vision of "Tibetan identity" unaccountable to manifestations in place and time. When Jamyang Norbu, as the editor of The Mandala, describes the discovery of Hurree's manuscript (the "narrative" itself) he does so by describing the discovery of a physical object, strings attached. What Hurree's great-grandson finds for Jamyang Norbu is in fact a package of texts, a history in a "rusty tin dispatch box" whose story would not be confined by either the box or the now collapsed wall in which it had been lodged: "Extricating it from the debris, he found that it contained a flat package carefully wrapped in wax paper and neatly tied with stout twine. He had opened the package to find a manuscript of about two-hundred pages in his great-grandfather's unmistakably ornate running script, and he had excitedly commenced to read it, not pausing till he had finished the story, sometime in the early hours of the morning. And it was all there."[49] There is a materiality to this text that is emphasized right from the start. Approaching this work as a (post)colonial object that can operate as a text in circulation recalls the argument that the struggle for a "free Tibet" cannot be simply a struggle for the continuing existence of Tibetan culture or even Tibetan Buddhism, since this may to varying degrees be achieved in the global diaspora even if Tibet is never recognized as a sovereign nation-state.[50] By insisting on the materiality of textuality, *The Mandala* argues against overvaluing the ephemeral, even spiritual aspects that have become so closely associated with Tibet, along with the view that material concerns may be abandoned in favor of "what really matters."

Reclaiming Tibet as a political and geographical entity, controlled by Tibetans and recognized as such, finds a parallel in the central plot line of *The Mandala of Sherlock Holmes*, the attempt to possess not only the signified, spiritual *meaning* of a sacred mandala but the signifying, material mandala itself, since attached to the mystical drawing is a set of instructions for acquiring "great power." Both Holmes and Moriarty struggle for this supplemental "key" because of its material rather than its sacred importance. In the novel Tibetan Buddhism may help rescue the Dalai Lama and "save the day," but other, explicitly material forces will be required if Tibet and its contemporary population are to be saved. In fact Jamyang Norbu's Holmes, when first asked to protect the life of the young Dalai Lama, replies, "you require the services of an army, Sir, not a consulting detective."[51] And the great detective himself, the novel informs us, ends up in exile in India, living the contemplative life of a monk. Holmes himself is not to be the final answer to the novel's conflicts; instead the novel's own multilayered materiality, its circulation among readers, and its effects on future narratives serve as responses to the novel's own challenge.

The materiality of a text does not mean that the text is without important fissures and thematic ambiguities. Postcolonial theories suggest instead that these features may be self-consciously emphasized as the irreducible aspects of hybrid identity. Homi Bhabha has written that personal identity, under colonial conditions, is not a matter of a stable, original selfhood but of negotiating the texts contributing to identity as such: "We are no longer confronted with an ontological problem of being but with the discursive strategy of the moment of interrogation, a moment in which the demand for identification becomes, primarily, a response to other questions of signification and desire, culture and politics."[52] "Repeating with a difference" is how Henry Louis Gates Jr. describes the strategy of "signifyin(g)" on a dominant discourse.[53] In addition to its postmodern qualities, Gates emphasizes the importance of signifying for African American slaves as a means of rewriting the so-called neutral discursive structures that in very real ways perpetuate the slaveholder's power. The American slave could not simply respond or reply to a master's question that is itself an instrument of social and political dominance.[54]

The implications for writing undertaken by Tibetans seem clear. Pema

Bhum has written that during the Cultural Revolution in China, Tibetan students would use poetry as a form of subversion against Chinese control of education, language, and even aesthetics. Folksongs that had been banned by the government were rewritten by Tibetans to include adoring references to Mao and the communist revolution, thereby allowing the songs to continue even as the revisions were understood by Tibetans as a form of speaking out against the very subjects being "celebrated."[55]

Notions of hybrid identity and signifying on dominant discourses have also been addressed to a considerable extent in readings of Kipling's Kim. The hybrid, polyvocal Hurree Babu character, correctly identified by Edward Said as a "grimacing stereotype of the ontologically funny native, trying to be like 'us,'" is also, according to Abdul JanMohamed, one of many Anglo-Indian figures who are "masking their real purposes and identities while trying to probe beneath the appearances of Indian political life."[56] In The Mandala the Bengali scholar-spy who had explained in Kim that "I am only Babu showing off my English to you" (231) is now reintroduced as a transnational, transhistorical voice caught in the irreducible overlapping of fact and fiction.[57] In fact, this real-fictional hybrid is placed in the absolute epistemological center of The Mandala of Sherlock Holmes. As if to directly challenge critics as well as admirers of "Babu-speak," Jamyang Norbu as editor remarks in the preface that "the Babu was an experienced and competent writer, with a vigorous and original style that would have suffered under too heavy an editorial hand."[58] It is not in spite of but because of his subversive, signifying discourse that Hurree stands as the epistemological fulcrum of The Mandala, allowing "factual" and "fictional" ways of knowing to revolve around him.

Another significant aspect of hybrid identity and discourse is its relevance to the colonizer as well as the colonized. "Babu-speak," as postcolonial critics have pointed out, manifests in voices of colonizing hybridity as much as colonized hybridity.[59] Kipling himself was said to be anxious over his own reputation as a "babu" born in India and taking on matters above his station, as intimated by Francis Younghusband.[60] Similarly, Jamyang Norbu's representative of the colonial center, Sherlock Holmes, suggests the hybridity of the colonizer and—very specifically—the Indo-Tibetan aspects of British (western) identity. The great British detective and all that he represents are revealed to be subject to the same fundamental discursive paradox as Babu/ Hurree. Holmes is out of his familiar place yet in control, and his speech integrates words and phrases from nearly a dozen languages. Even Holmes's spirituality (as an incarnated lama) is not simply Tibetan because it is convenient, at hand, or shocking—it is Tibetan because of Tibet's role in the spiritual imaginary that shaped geopolitics in Britain and British India at the turn of the century. In other words, with regard to the world of literary studies the very place described as "Anglo-Indian" is in fact a landscape best described by British, Indian, *and Tibetan* interests, particularly as it emerges in *Kim*. Defining South Asian hybridity as merely a dual subject involving Britain and India is insufficient when talk of "British India" turns to spirituality and the future of the empire, as a distinctly Tibetan presence enters the narrative.

Moreover, by revealing Moriarty to be a hybrid colonial figure adopted by Chinese officials, Jamyang Norbu's novel acknowledges the too-often-ignored significance of Chinese colonialism in what is typically framed as simply "British" India and its imperial legacy. Chinese colonialism in fact supplements British colonialism, in the novel as well as in Tibetan history. This development in the novel, fanciful as it is, contributes to a productively complicated picture of modernity, in which Chinese modernity is not only distinguished from western modernity but shown to possess features unique to Tibetan history.⁶¹ Moriarty is revealed as Tibet's transnational historical "nemesis" merging the legacies of western as well as Chinese imperial projects, just as Holmes's "British" sensibility is shown to deconstruct itself into a play of western imaginaries involving rationality and detection on the one hand and spiritualism and Orientalist scholarship on the other.

Distinctions of Chinese modernity also figure into the shape of the literary world by way of the critical perspectives explicitly recommended for reading Tibetan works. For example, the English-language collection of stories by Zhaxi Dawa (Tashi Dawa), *A Soul in Bondage* (originally written in Chinese), is introduced with a critical assessment of how the author depicts young people in Tibet. According to Dondrup Wangbum (Ch. Danzhu Angben), Zhaxi Dawa "articulates their thoughts and the conflicts raised by the tension between the demands of modernization and traditional culture, new and old values. . . . First, he sharply contrasts modern civilization—the outside world—with the reality of life in Tibet, a technique which leaves a deep impression on readers who do not know this part of the world."⁶² The assumption is that "modern civilization" only exists outside Tibetan society and must therefore be brought in by benevolent institutions and programs. Yet this colonial narrative, familiar from official Chinese statements on Tibet, is undercut by the texts of Tibetan modernity—the very "articulations" produced by Tibetan youth, which stand to reflect at least as ambiguous a loyalty to the colonial center as the title of Zhaxi Dawa's book does.

The introduction to Zhaxi Dawa's stories also directly links him with Latin American magical realism, highlighting Zhaxi Dawa's interest in the works of Gabriel García Márquez and Jorge Luis Borges: "Tashi Dawa," writes Dondrup Wangbum, "has put his finger on the pulse of Tibetan society, where religion and science, the new and the old, and the advanced and the backward co-exist."[63] Then, remarking on worldwide popular interest in Tibet's "mysterious" nature, Dondrup Wangbum notes: "Actually, the 'mystery' of Tibet is the 'mystery' of Tibetan culture, and this mystery stems from ignorance. Once it is understood, it is no longer mysterious. A Tibetan never thinks of himself or his life as a mystery; Tashi Dawa's 'magical realism' satisfies people's desire to know Tibet, and the strange descriptions arouse empathy."[64] In other words, the critical guidelines suggest, Tibet's secrets are demystified by removing ignorance—in a way, by "just going there"—a refrain very familiar to westerners who are told that their opinions of Tibet's oppression are based on misunderstandings that can be clarified by simply visiting Tibet. Elsewhere, however, postcolonial approaches to magical realism have emphasized the argument that a dominant language may be unable or unwilling to express the reality of a colonized society, making a nondominant discourse or text seem by definition "unreal" or "magical."[65] Postcolonial critics will explore how writers exploit this distinction between realities to question the totalizing "reality" constructed by a dominant language or discourse. This critical approach, offering opportunities for epistemological investigation and contestation of totalizing discourses, contrasts distinctly with Dondrup Wangbum's overdetermined prescription for the empirical validation of "imaginative" fiction.

Zhaxi Dawa's stories, Jamyang Norbu's novel, Pema Bhum's memoir, and this discussion all raise the question of what is the proper language for Tibetan literature.[66] There is a long-standing debate among postcolonial writers regarding the use of the English language by writers associated with non-English societies, and this debate benefits enormously by including Tibetan voices. The writer and critic Chinua Achebe argues that "African literature" ought not be seen as a single, narrowly defined field but "as a group of associated units—in fact the sum total of all the national and ethnic literatures of Africa," in which "a national literature is one that takes the whole nation for its province and has a realized or potential audience throughout its territory. In other words a literature that is written in the national language. An ethnic literature is one which is available only to one ethnic group within the nation."[67] In this view, the use of English in writing African literature becomes an instance of writing in a language that has been "inherited" by African nations and ethnic groups. And while Achebe acknowledges that English may be "the world language which history has forced down our throats," he recognizes it as an important discursive field on which to negotiate new expression: "the English language will be able to carry the weight of my African experience," he writes, "but it will have to be a new English, still in full communion with its ancestral home but altered to suit its new African surroundings."[68]

Another African writer-critic argues that the goal of "enriching" the English language with non-English conditions is misguided: "We never ask ourselves: how can we enrich our languages? How can we 'prey' on the rich humanist and democratic heritage in the struggles of other peoples in other times and other places to enrich our own?"[69] Ngũgĩ wa Thiong'o directly opposes Achebe's program, yet it is not difficult to understand that in practice, writers from Africa and many other locations around the world find themselves at times siding with one argument and at times the other.

Jamyang Norbu's *The Mandala of Sherlock Holmes* and stories by Zhaxi Dawa illustrate that it is crucial to write in "dominant" or "world languages" to acknowledge the influence of those languages on the very subjects presented in the narratives. At the same time, a self-conscious treatment of the ambiguous place of Tibetan experience within dominant language fields modifies and productively destabilizes those languages. Tibetan texts help to shape the "new English" and the "new Chinese," which in turn become the new discursive fields on which all other writers must contend.[70] Writing in Tibetan, on the other hand, can clearly be a process of "preying" on other traditions and histories to enrich the Tibetan language. Examples of just such a process include Pema Bhum's writing, as well as the series of translated works produced by the Amnye Machen Institute in Dharamsala.[71]

· · · · ·

During Francis Younghusband's invasion of Tibet in 1904, lamas told the Tibetan soldiers that by carrying specially blessed charms into battle, the fighters would be protected from the enemy's bullets. These charms consisted of magic words written on paper, enclosed in small boxes hanging from the soldiers' necks. The Orientalist L. Augustine Waddell, who accompanied Younghusband on the invasion, reported that the charms did not stop any bullets: "Every one of the warriors who opposed us at Guru had these new charms hung round their necks in amulet-boxes. But it all failed pitifully. Neither the Lamas' chorus of curses, nor their charms, had the slightest effect. On the contrary, as if in bitter irony of fate, many at Guru received their death-wounds through their charm-boxes. The Lamas afterwards excused themselves on the plea that they had given only a charm against leaden bullets, whereas ours contained some silver in their composition, and hence the charms proved ineffectual on that occasion; but this defect would be rectified in the charms they would issue in future, which would be found infallible."[72] Decades later, During the First World War, a French soldier was saved from a German sniper's attack by a copy of Kim that the soldier kept in his jacket pocket. In gratitude, the soldier mailed his war medal and the martyred book to Kipling, asking him "to accept both the book and the medal for thus saving his life, and as a token of his devotion to Kim."[73]

Literature always invites multilayered explorations of narratives that simply cannot be read "in one place." It is a matter not only of what texts mean but of *where* they mean and what they do—or fail to do—in these different places. Kipling's Kim and Doyle's Holmes, along with voices drawn from the works of authors as varied as Edgar Rice Burroughs, Harriet Beecher Stowe, Raja Rao, Ralph Ellison, and Lu Xun, have existed as fictions of human experience, but they have also been enlisted as material forces in shaping culture, politics, and the literary world. Sherlock Holmes, for one, "could grow to full stature only in a time when crime could plausibly be seen as the greatest threat to order and its detection the greatest of services, when the police were widely believed to be ineffectual, when science was viewed by its enthusiasts as a new force crusading for progress against ignorance and unreason—above all, when the prospect of a devastating war could seem less menacing than an unsolved robbery or murder."[74] Jamyang Norbu's *The Mandala of Sherlock Holmes* takes these appropriations very seriously. A crime is afoot in twenty-first-century Asia, and Holmes is brought back as a material system of facts, fictions, images, and discourses to investigate the murder of people and culture, and the theft of history and identity. Police are effective only in perpetuating criminal behavior, and talk of war—or even open intervention by other countries—does not threaten existing international politics. Only the unsolved and unpunished crimes remain, though perhaps followed by a new kind of detective and a new kind of justice, both developing out of Tibet's place in the world.

Notes

1. Hopkirk, *Quest for Kim*. See also Bishop, *The Myth of Shangri-La*; and "Not Only Shangri-la," 207–8.
2. Landon, *The Opening of Tibet*, 485.
3. Quoted in Williams, "Kim and Orientalism," 481, original emphasis and ellipses.
4. Ibid.
5. Frederick Smith, Second Earl of Birkenhead. *F. E.: The Life of F. E. Smith, First Earl of Birkenhead* (London: Eyre and Spottiswoode, 1960), quoted in Williams, "Kim and Orientalism," 481.
6. Williams, "Kim and Orientalism," 481.
7. See for example Margolis, *War at the Top of the World*.
8. Cao Changching, "Brainwashing the Chinese," 25.

9. Lopez, *Prisoners of Shangri-La*, 10.

10. See Venturino, "Where Is Tibet in World Literature?," 51–56.

11. Silbey elaborates on "postmodern colonialism" as a preferred term for "globalization": "I regard globalization as a form of postmodern colonialism where the worldwide distribution and consumption of cultural products removed from the contexts of their production and interpretation is organized through legal devices to constitute a form of domination." See Silbey, "'Let Them Eat cake.'" My own use of the term "postmodern colonialism" more specifically considers how colonialism, as a system involving "the implanting of settlements on distant territory" (Said, *Culture and Imperialism*, 9), relates to postmodernism in Tibet.

12. See Venturino, ed. *Contemporary Tibetan Literary Studies*. In addition, an important conference held in Dharamsala, India, in 1995 brought together Tibetan writers and critics. See http://www.amnyemachen.org/.

13. See Venturino, "Inquiring after Theory in China."

14. Jamyang Norbu's novel has also been published under the title *Sherlock Holmes: The Missing Years*. For *The Mandala* Jamyang Norbu was awarded the Crossword Book Award 2000 for best English fiction. Also included on the short list for the award, which has been described as the "Indian Booker Prize," were such writers as Amitav Ghosh, Pankaj Mishra, Shashi Deshpande, and Susan Visvanathan.

15. One example of the growing presence of Tibetan literature in college curricula: *The Longman Anthology of British Literature* now includes an excerpt from *The Mandala of Sherlock Holmes* in the volume devoted to Victorian literature. See David Damrosch and Kevin J. H. Dettmar, general editors, *The Longman Anthology of British Literature*, 3rd edn., vol. 2B, ed. Heather Henderson and William Sharpe (New York: Longman, 2006), 1572–76.

16. Cabezón and Jackson, eds., *Tibetan Literature*, 17.

17. Ibid., 20.

18. Lyotard, "Answering the Question," 44.

19. White, *The Content of the Form*, x.

20. Hutcheon, *The Politics of Postmodernism*, 66.

21. Bertens and Fokkema, eds. *International Postmodernism*, xiv–xvi.

22. Calinescu, "Rewriting," *International Postmodernism*, 245.

23. Ibid.

24. Ibid., 243.

25. Borges, *Labyrinths*.

26. For a more comprehensive reading of Jamyang Norbu's novel and its literary antecedents see my *Novelistic Revisions: Formal Exchanges in Literature and Culture* (in progress).

27. Excerpted from *World Tibet Network News*. 15 December, 1999, <http://www.tibet.ca/wtnarchive/1999/12/15_2.html>.

28. In fact the Babu and Hurree of *The Mandala* are both modeled after Sarat Chandra Das, the Bengali scholar-spy and author of dozens of books and articles. See Hopkirk, *Quest for Kim*; and Chandra Das, *Indian Pandits in the Land of Snow* and *A Journey to Lhasa and Central Tibet*.

29. Clausen, "Sherlock Holmes, Order, and the Late-Victorian Mind," 68.

30. Jamyang Norbu, *The Mandala of Sherlock Holmes*, xv–xvi.

31. Clausen, "Sherlock Holmes, Order, and the Late-Victorian Mind," 66.

32. Ibid., 82.

33. Ibid., 67.

34. Arthur Conan Doyle had described Holmes's apparent death in "The Final Problem," but public demand prompted the author to resurrect the detective in "The Adventure of the Empty House," in which Holmes tells his surprised companion, Dr. Watson, "I traveled for two years in Tibet, therefore, and amused myself by visiting Lhassa, and spending some time with the head lama." See Doyle, *Sherlock Holmes*, 670.

35. Clausen, "Sherlock Holmes, Order, and the Late-Victorian Mind," 75.

36. Jamyang Norbu, *The Mandala of Sherlock Holmes*, ix.

37. Ulrich Broich, "Intertextuality," 249.

38. Ibid., 251, 254.

39. Jamyang Norbu, *The Mandala of Sherlock Holmes*, 197.

40. Wang Ning lists the following themes suggestive of postmodernism in literature: "the loss of the self and the counterculture," "going against established linguistic conventions," "binary oppositions and deconstruction of meaning," "the return to the primitive and nostalgia," "blurring the demarcation between elitist and popular literature," and "parody and ironic description of violence and death." See Wang, "The Reception of Postmodernism in China," 503–7.

41. Chow, "Rereading Mandarin Ducks and Butterflies," 473.

42. Dirlik and Zhang, "Postmodernism and China," 1–2.

43. See Chen Xiaoming, "The Mysterious Other."

44. Tang, "The Function of New Theory," 296.

45. Pema Bhum, "The Life of Dhondup Gyal," 21.

46. Ibid., 24.

47. Spivak, *A Critique of Postcolonial Reason*, 203.

48. Ibid., 205.

49. Jamyang Norbu, *The Mandala of Sherlock Holmes*, xv. Appropriately, the image of a manuscript bound by wax paper and twine serves as the wrap-around cover art for the British edition of *The Mandala*, published in London in 2000 (see figure, page 312). The cover of this edition emphasizes the materiality of the narrative "faithfully recorded by Hurree Chunder Mookerjee," "edited by Jamyang Norbu," and "delivered by hand to John Murray, Sherlock Holmes's loyal publisher and friend." Taking a different approach, the cover of the first edition of the novel, published by Harper Collins India in 1999, highlights the novel's intertextuality by setting Sidney Paget's famous image of Holmes against the background of an intricate Tibetan mandala and a map of the Himalayas (see figure, page 312). The current American paperback edition of the novel, first published by Bloomsbury in 2003, takes this intertextuality to its postmodern limits by parodying Sidney Paget's illustration (1893) of Holmes and Moriarty struggling at the Reichenbach Falls (see figure, page 313). The cover reproduces a painting by Mark Tansey, "Derrida

Queries de Man" (1990), in which the philosopher Jacques Derrida and the literary theorist Paul de Man (central figures associated with deconstruction) nimbly stand on a precipice formed by text (see figure, page 313). They, like the novel, seem to dance in the abyss of the language that circumscribes their situation.

50. See for example Lazar, ed., *Tibet*.
51. Jamyang Norbu, *The Mandala of Sherlock Holmes*, 160.
52. Bhabha, *The Location of Culture*, 49–50.
53. Gates, *The Signifying Monkey*.
54. See also Venturino, "Signifying on China."
55. Pema Bhum, *Dran tho smin drug ske 'khyog / Six Stars with a Crooked Neck*.
56. Said, *Culture and Imperialism*, 153; JanMohamed, "The Economy of Manichean Allegory," 100.
57. Kipling, *Kim*, 231.
58. Jamyang Norbu, *The Mandala of Sherlock Holmes*, xv.
59. See Bhabha, *The Location of Culture*; and Spivak, *A Critique of Postcolonial Reason*.
60. Lycett, *Rudyard Kipling*.
61. From such a perspective, for example, Pema Bhum's memoir of the Cultural Revolution highlights those experiences of Chinese modernity that were unique to Tibetans, particularly with regard to language, books, writing, communication, and the question of modernizing a society (*Six Stars with a Crooked Neck*).
62. Dondrup Wangbum, Preface, *A Soul in Bondage*, 10–11.
63. Ibid., 7, 10.
64. Ibid., 11.
65. D'haen, "Postmodernism," 287.
66. On the issue of languages and Tibetan poetry see the editor's introduction in Bhuchung D. Sonam, ed., *Muses in Exile*.
67. Achebe, "The African Writer and the English Language," 429.
68. Ibid., 433, 434.
69. Ngũgĩ wa Thiong'o, *Colonial Discourse and Post-Colonial Theory*, 435.
70. Consider for example the Chinese short story "Meetings," which revisits the events surrounding Younghusband's invasion of Tibet in ways that prompt an examination of the "triangular" relationship between China, Tibet, and the West. See Ge Fei, "Meetings."
71. See http://www.amnyemachen.org/. For a relevant theoretical approach to minority language use and Bengali literature see Spivak, *In Other Worlds*, 179–96.
72. L. Augustine Waddell, *Lhasa and Its Mysteries*, 174–75.
73. Hopkirk, *Quest for Kim*, 1.
74. Clausen, "Sherlock Holmes, Order, and the Late-Victorian Mind," 89.

Appendix 1:

Glossary of Tibetan Spellings

This list includes primary authors and texts, selected secondary authors, and place names, as well as special terms spelled phonetically in the chapters. Entries are alphabetized letter by letter, ignoring word and syllable breaks. For names usually pronounced in the Amdo dialect, the phonetic rendering for the dialect is provided in parentheses after the Tibetan Himalayan Digital Library (THDL) Simplified Phonetics version. Names followed by an asterisk (*) retain the popular phonetic spelling used in English publications by these scholars. For names typically appearing in Chinese, the pinyin romanization is provided in parentheses after the THDL Simplified Phonetics version.

PHONETIC SPELLING	TIBETAN SPELLING
Achung Namdzong	A 'byung rnam 'dzong
Akhu Samten	A khu Bsam gtan
Alai (Ch. A lai)	A legs
Alak Chömpel	A lags Chos 'phel
Alak Dorzhi	A lags Dor zhi
Alak Drongtsang	A lags 'Brong tshang
Alak Gönpotsang	A lags Mgon po tshang
Alak Khadingtsang	A lags Mkha' lding tshang
Alak Zhelshül Ngakwang Tenpé Gyatso	A lags Zhal shul Ngag dbang bstan pa'i rgya mtsho
Amdo	A mdo
Amdo Jampa	A mdo Byams pa
Amnye Machen*	A myes Rma chen
Anyön Trashi Döndrup	A smyon Bkra shis don grub
Baba Püntsok Wanggyel	Ba ba Phun tshogs dbang rgyal
Baré	Ba res
Batang	Ba thang
Beri Jikmé Wanggyel	Be ri 'Jigs med dbang rgyal

Bödé	Bod lde
Bödrok	'Bod grogs
Bön	Bon
Bönpo	Bon po
Chakmo Tso	Lcags mo 'tsho
Chamdo (Shamdo)	Bya mdo
Chammo	Lcam mo
Changlochen	Lcang lo can
Changshekhug	Chang shes khug
Changtang	Byang thang
Chapcha	Chab cha
Chapdrak Lhamokyap	Chab brag Lha mo skyabs
Chapgak Dorjé Tsering	Chab gag Rdo rje tshe ring
Chapgak Tamdrin	Chab 'gag Rta mgrin
Chazhung Yangbha	Bya gzhung Dbyangs bha
Chen Metak	Gcan Me stag
Chen Özer	Gcan 'Od zer
Chen Rangsé	Gcan Rang sad
Chentsa	Gcan tsha
Chepa Tamdrin Tsering	Chas pa Rta mgrin tshe ring
Chimé	Chi med
Chödzin	Chos 'dzin
Chögyam Trungpa*	Chos rgyal khrung pa
Chongtse (Ch. Congzhi)	Cong rtse
Chöpa Döndrup	Gcod pa Don grub
Chöwang Drakpa	Chos dbang grags pa
Chukyé Drölma	Chu skyes sgrol ma
Damzhung	'Dam gzhung
Datsenpo	Mda' btsan po
Dawa	Zla ba
Deché	Bde byed
Dechen (Ch. Deqin)	Bde chen
Dechung	Bde 'byung
Degé	Sde dge
Dekyi	Bde skyid

Dekyi Drölma (Dejé Drolma)	Bde skyid grol ma
Dekyitso (Ch. Dejicuo)	Bde skyid 'tsho
Dhongtog Tenpai Gyaltsen*	Gdong thog Bstan pa'i rgyal mtshan
Ditsa	Ldi tsha or Dhi tsha
Dodrak (Ch. Duozhi ge)	Rdo grags
Dokhar Tsering Wanggyel	Mdo mkhar Tshe ring Dbang rgyal
Domepa Yönten Gyatso	Mdo smad pa Yon tan rgya mtsho
Döndrup Gyel (Döndrup Jya)	Don grub rgyal
Döndrup Tsering	Don grub tshe ring
Dondrup Wangbum* (Ch. Danzhu Angben)	Don grub dbang 'bum
Dong Chushel	Ldong chu shel
Dongtruk	Ldong phrug
Dorjé Chözang (Ch. Duojie Qunzeng)	Rdo rje chos bzang
Dorjé Drakpa	Rdo rje grags pa
Dorjé Drayang Gyatso	Rdo rje Sgra dbyangs rgya mtsho
Dorjé Gyelpo	Rdo rje rgyal po
Dorjé Rinchen	Rdo rje rin chen
Dorjé Tsering	Rdo rje tshe ring
Dorje Tseten*	Rdo rje tshe brtan
Dowi Dorjé (Ch. Daowei Duoji)	Rdo sbis Rdo rje
Draknyön Yamarādzā	Brag smyon Ya ma rA dzA
Drakpo	Drag po
Drandül	Dgra 'dul
Drölma	Sgrol ma
Drong	'Brong
Drongbu Dorjé Rinchen	'Brong bu Rdo rje rin chen
Drukgyel	'Brug rgyal
Druklha Gyel	'Brug lha rgyal
Druknyön Künga Lekpa	'Brug smyon Kun dga' legs pa
Drukpa Künlek	'Brug pa Kun legs
Druktso	'Brug mtsho
Druprik Khyumchok	Grub rigs khyu mchog
Dungkar Lozang Trinlé	Dung dkar blo bzang 'phrin las
Durbü Namdrak	Dur bud rnam rags
Dza Peltrül	Rdza Dpal sprul
Dzemé Trülku	Dze smad sprul sku
Dzögé	Mdzod dge

PHONETIC SPELLING	TIBETAN SPELLING
Gangzhun	Gangs zhun
Gelukpa	Dge lugs pa
Gendün Chömpel	Dge 'dun chos 'phel
Gesar	Ge sar
geshé	dge bshes
Geshé Chödrak	Dge bshes Chos grags
Geshé Potoba	Dge bshes Po to ba
Geshé Sherap Gyatso	Dge bshes Shes rab rgya mtsho
Gönpo	Mgon po
Gönpo Trashi (Ch. Gongbu Zhaxi)	Mgon po bkra shis
Gurong Puwa	Dgu rong phu ba
Gyadröl	Rgya grol
Gyalo Döndrup	Rgyal lo don grub
Gyalpo Tsering*	Rgyal po tshe ring
Gyanak	Rgya nag
Gyantsé	Rgyal rtse
Gyapön Guru Dorjé (Ch. Guolie Duojie)	Rgya dpon Gu ru rdo rje
Gyatso	Rgya mtsho
Gyelkün Yeshe Tiklé	Rgyal kun Ye shes Thig le
Gyelrong (Ch. Jiarong)	Rgyal rong
Gyelwo	Rgyal bo
Gyentsen Penjor	Rgyal mtshan dpal 'byor
Gyurmé	'Gyur med
Hanumanta	Ha nu man tha
Horkhang Sönam Penbar	Hor khang Bsod nams dpal 'bar
Hortsang Jigme*	Hor gtsang 'Jigs med
Jampa Gelek	'Byams pa dge legs
Jampel Gyatso (Ch. Jiangbian Jiacuo)	'Jam dpal rgya mtsho
Jampel Gyepé Lodrö	'Jam dpal dgyes pa'i blo gros
Jamyang Drakpa	'Jam dbyangs grags pa
Jamyang Norbu	'Jam dbyangs nor bu
Jamyang Zhepa	'Jam dbyangs bzhad pa
Jangbu (Jangwu)	Ljang bu
Jangtsé Dönko	'Jang rtse don kho
Jikmé Damchö Gyatso	'Jigs med dam chos rgya mtsho
Jikmé Püntsok (Ch. Liemei Pingcuo)	'Jigs med phun tshogs

Jikmé Samten	'Jigs med bsam gtan
Jikmé Tekchok	'Jigs med theg mchog
Jokhang	Jo khang
Jonang Tāranātha Künga Nyingpo	Jo nang Tā ra nā tha Kun dga' snying po
Jowo	Jo bo
Ju Kelzang (Ju Kabzang)	'Ju Skal bzang
Ju Mipam Gyatso	'Ju Mi pham ryga mtsho
Kadampa	Bka' gdams pa
Kalzang Tenzin*	Skal bzang bstan 'dzin
Karing	Ka ring
Karmay, Samten G.*	Mkhar rme'u Bsam gtan rygal mtshan
Kelsang Namdröl*	Skal lozang rnam 'grol
Kelzang Dorjé (Ch. Geseng Duojie)	Skal bzang rdor je
Kelzang Khedrup	Skal bzang mkhas grub
Kelzang Lhamo	Skal bzang lha mo
Kham	Khams
Khardrong	Mkhar grongs
Khedrup Jé	Mkhas grub rjes
Kherkyé	Kher skyes
Khotsé	Kho tshe
Khyenrap Ösel	Mkhyen rab 'od gsal
Khyungtruk Gyel	'Khyung phrug rgyal
Khyungzang	Khyung bzang
Könlo	Dkon lo
Kumbum Monastery (Ch. Ta'er si)	Sku' bum
Künzang Gyel	Kun bzang rgyal
Kyabha	Skya bha
Kyapchen Dedröl	Skyabs chen bde grol
Labrang (Ch. Xiahe)	Bla brang
Lachung Apo	Bla chung A pho
Langdarma	Glang dar ma
Langka	Lang ka
Lewang Drölma	Las dbang sgrol ma
Lewang Village	Las dbang sde ba

PHONETIC SPELLING	TIBETAN SPELLING
Lhachap Jinpa	Lha chab sbyin pa
Lhachen	Lha chen
Lhagyel Tsering	Lha rgyal tshe ring
Lhagyel Tsering (Lharjya Tsering)	Lha rgyal tshe ring
Lhakpa Püntsok	Lhags pa phun tshogs
Lhakyi	Lha skyid
Lhalung Pelgyi Dorjé	Lha lung dpal gyi rdo rje
Lhamo Döndrup (Ch. Lamu Dongzhi)	Lha mo don 'grub
Lhasa	Lha sa
Lhazang	Lha bzang
Lhündup Namgyel	Lhun grub rnam rgyal
Lodrö Gyatso	Blo gros rgya mtsho
Luchu	Klu chu
Lugu Gyel	Lugu rgyal
Lugyel Bum	Klu rgyal 'bum
Lumokyi	Klu mo skyid
Lunyön Heruka	Klu smyon He ru ka
Lutsang Lozang Yeshé	Klu tshang Blo bzang ye shes
Lutsang Nyuktsen	Klu tshang smyug rtsen
Machen Pomra	Rma chen spom ra
Machu	Rma chu
Ma Ö	Rma 'od
Markham	Mar kham
Marnang Dorjechang	Mar nang Rdo rje chang
Martön Chökyi Gyelpo	Dmar ston chos kyi rgyal po
Medrön (Ch. Meizhuo)	Me sgrol
Mengwu (ne Dondrup Tsering)	Smreng bu
Menla Kyap	Sman bla skyabs
Milarepa	Mi la ras pa
Mipam Gelek Namgyel	Mi pham dge legs rnam rgyal
Monkey Bodhisattva	Spre'u byang chub sems dpa'
Mönlam Chenmo	Smon lam chen mo
Mugé Samten	Dmu dge bsam gtan
Nakchu	Nag chu
Nakto	Nag tho
Namdröl	Rnam 'grol

Namga	Rnam dga'
Namgyal Phuntsok*	Rnam rgyal phun tshogs
Namgyel	Rnam rgyal
Namkhai Norbu	Nam mkha'i nor bu
Namsé	Rnam sras
Nangkhok	Nang khog
Netsö Drotülchen	Ne tso'i sgro thul can
Ngaba	Rnga ba
Ngakwang Tenpé Gyatso	Ngag dbang bstan pa'i rgya mtsho
Ngangwé Bumo	Ngang ba'i bu mo
Ngawa Chödrag	Rnga ba Chos grags
Ngodup Penjor	Dngos sgrub dpal 'byor
Norbu Chophel*	Nor bu chos 'phel
Nordé	Nor sde
Nyagong Könchok Tseten	Nya gong Dkon mchog tshe tan
Nya Lodrö Gyentsen	Gnya' Blo gros rgyal mtshan
Nyenzang	Snyan bzang
Nyida	Nyi zla
Onyön	O smyon
Orgyen Dorjé	O rgyan rdo rje
Özer (Ch. Weise)	'Od zer
Pakpa Lodrö Gyentsen	'Phags pa blo gros rgyal mtshan
Palden Gyal*	Dpal ldan rgyal
Patsé (Huartse)	Dpa' rtse
Pelhamo	Dpal lhamo
Pelmo	Dpal mo
Pema Bhum*	Pad ma 'bum
Pema Tsering	Pad ma tshe ring
Pema Tseten (Wema Tseten, Ch. Wanma Caidan)	Pad ma tshe brtan
Pema Tsewang Shastri	Pad ma tshe bang shāstri
Pemakyi	Pad ma skyid
Pematso	Pad ma mtsho
Penden	Dpal ldan
Penjor Langdün	Dpal 'byor glang mdun
Penjor Tsering	Dpal 'byor tshe ring

| --- | --- |
Pomda Rapga	Spom mda' Rab dga'
Puntsok Tashi Takla★	Phun tshogs bkra shis Stag lha
Püntsok Wanggyel (Ch. Pingcuo Wangjie)	Phun tshogs dbang rgyal
Rakra Tethong Thupten Chodar ★	Rak ra Bkras thong Thub bstan chos dar
Ramtsebo	Rams tshe bho
Rangdra	Rang sgra
Rangdröl	Rang 'grol
Rapgyé Pasang (Ch. Raojie Baseng)	Rab rgyas pa sangs
Rekangling	Re rkang gling
Repgong (Ch. Tongren)	Reb gong
Repgong Dorjekhar	Reb gong rdo rje mkhar
Rikden Gyatso	Rig ldan rgya mtsho
Rikdzin Wangpo	Rig 'dzin dbang po
Rinchen Trashi	Rin chen bkra shi
Rinpoché	Rin po che
Rinpung	Rin spungs
Rongwo	Rong bo
Sakya Khenpo Sanggyé Tenzin	Sa skya mkhan po Sangs rgyas bstan 'dzin
Sakya Paṇḍita Kunga Gyentsen	Sa skya Paṇḍita Kun dga' rgyal mtshan
Samphel★	Bsam 'phel
Sangdak Dorjé	Gsang bdag rdo rje
Sanggyé	Sangs rgyas
Sangkhok	Bsang khog
Sangye Gyatso★	Sangs rgyas rgya mtsho
Senalek	Sad na legs
Seru	Bse ru
Serzangtang	Gser bzang thang
Shar Kelden Gyatso	Shar Skal ldan rgya mtsho
Shawo Gyurmé	Sha bo 'Gyur med
Shichung	Shis chung
Shidé Nyima	Zhi bde nyi ma
Shongtön Lotsāwa Dorjé Gyentsen	Shong ston lo tsā ba Rdo rje rgyal mtshan

Phonetic Spelling	Tibetan Spelling
Söbo (Ch. Suobao)	Bsod bho
Sonam, Bhuchung D.*	Bu chung bsod nams
Sonam Gyalpo*	Bsod nams rgyal po
Sönam Tenpa	Bsod nams brtan pa
Sonam Topgyal*	Bsod nams stobs rgyal
Songtsen Gampo	Srong btsan sgam po
Sumdo Mang Ba Cha	Gsum mdo Mang 'Ba' Bya
Takbum Gyel	Stag 'bum rgyal
Taktsa	Stag tsha
Taktser Rinpoché	Stag 'tsher Rinpoche
Tamdrin Gönpo (Ch. Danzhen Gongbu)	Rtam mgrin mgon po
Tamdrin Tso	Rta mgrin 'tsho
tangka	thang ka
Tashi Dawa* (Ch. Zhaxi Dawa)	Bkra shis zla ba
Tashi Tsering*	Bkra shis tshe ring
Tawu (Ch. Dawu)	Rta'u
Teling Wangdor	Bkras gling Dbang rdor
Tendzin Drakpa	Bstan 'dzin grags pa
Tendzin Gönpo	Bstan 'dzin mgon po
Tendzin Namgyel	Bstan 'dzin rnam rgyal
Tenpa Yargyé	Bstan pa yar rgyas
Tenzin Sonam*	Bstan 'dzin bsod nams
Tenzin Tsundue	Bstan 'dzin brtson grus
Tertön	gter ston
Thubten Jigme Norbu*	Thub bstan 'jigs med nor bu
Thubten Nyima*	Thub bstan nyi ma
Tise	Ti se
Topden	Stobs ldan
Topgyel	Stobs rgyal
Trabha	Bkra bha
Tragya	Bkra rgya
Trashikhyil	Bkra shis 'khyil
Trashilhunpo	Bkra shis lhun po
Trashi Penden	Bkra shis dpal ldan
Trashi Tsering (Ch. Zhaxi Cairang)	Bkra shis tshe ring

Tredrön	Bkras sgron
Trijang Rinpoché	Khri byang rin po che
Trika (Ch. Guide)	Khri ka
Tri Sempa	Khri Sems dpa'
Tromzikkhang	Khrom gzigs khang
trülku	sprul sku
Tsamchö Drölma	Mtshams chos sgrol ma
tsampa	rtsam pa
Tsangnyön Heruka	Gtsang smyon He ru ka
Tsangyang Gyatso	Tshangs dbyangs rgya mtsho
Tsatrül Ngakwang Lozang	Tsha sprul Ngag dbang blo bzang
Tsedor (Ch. Ci Duo)	Tshe rdor
Tsegyel	Tshe rgyal
Tsepak Rigzin*	Tshe dpag rig 'dzin
Tsering	Tshe ring
Tsering Döndrup	Tshe ring don grub
Tsering Kyi	Tshe ring skyid
Tsering Tar	Tshe ring thar
Tsering Wangmo	Tshe ring dbang mo
Tsering Yangkyi	Tshe ring dbyangs skyid
Tsetang	Rtse thang
Tseten Zhapdrung	Tshe tan zhabs drung
Tsewang Norbu (Ch. Caiwang Naoru)	Tshe dbang nor bu
Tseyang Gyatso*	Tshangs dbyangs rgya mtsho
Tsokye	Mtsho skyes
Tsongkha (Ch. Ping'an)	Tsong kha
Tsongkha Lhamo Tsering	Tsong kha Lha mo tshe ring
Tsongkha Lozang Drakpa	Tsong kha Blo bzang grags pa
Tsultrim	Tshul khrim
Tupten Nyima	Thub bstan nyi ma
Wandekhar	Ban de mkhar
Wangchuk	Dbang phyug
Wangchuk Chenpo	Dbang phyug chen po
Wangdor	Dbang rdor
Wanko (Ch. Banguo)	Ban ko
Wayemache Chopathar (Ch. Ma Jiaobata)	Ba ye ma khye Gcod pa thar

Phonetic Spelling	Tibetan Spelling
Yangbha	Dbyangs bha
Yangdon (Ch. Yangchen)	Dbyangs sgron
Yangdrön Dhondrup*	Dbyangs sgron don grub
Yangtsokyi	G.yang mtsho skyid
Yarlung Tsangpo	Yar klung tsang po
Yeshé Lhamo	Ye shes lha mo
Yidam Tsering (Ch. Yidan Cairang)	Yi dam tshe ring
Yumkyap Gyel	Yum skyabs rgyal
Yungdrung	G.yung drung
Yuzhün	G.yu zhun
Zhangzhung Chöwang Drakpa	Zhang zhung Chos dbang grags pa
Zhapdrung	Zhabs drung
Zhapkar (Shabkar*)	Zhabs dkar
Zhikatsé	Gzhis ka rtse
Zhokdung	Zhogs dung
Zhönnu Damé	Gzhon nu zla med
Zho-ong Kelzang Gyatso	Zho 'ong Skal bzang rgya mtsho
Zungchuk Kyi	Gzungs phyug skyid

Appendix 2:

Glossary of Chinese Terms

Aba zhou zhi	阿坝州志	guwei jinyong,	古为今用
Alai	阿来	yangwei zhongyong	洋为中用
Aliwa	阿里哇	Gyakar (Ch. Jiage)	迦格
Awa	阿瓦	Gyanak (Ch. Jiana)	迦那
bai hua	白话	hongjun	红军
Bai Ye	白烨	Hu Yaobang	胡耀邦
baogao wenxue	报告文学	Jiamu chawarong	嘉木察瓦绒
Batang	巴塘	Jiangbian Jiacuo	降边嘉措
biming	笔名	Jiangpu	江瀑
Bön	本	Jiarong	嘉绒
Chongqing	重庆	(Tib. Rgyal rong)	
Ci Duo	次多	Jiefangjun	解放军
Da Dan Zeng	大旦曾	Jin Zhiguo	金志国
Dangba	党坝	Kangding	康定
Danzhen Gongbu	丹真共布	Lanzhou	兰州
Danzhu Angben	丹珠昂奔	lao Xizang	老西藏
daohua qun fan	导化群番	Lha Shopa	拉雪巴
da zhi ruo yu	大智若愚	(Ch. La Xueba)	
Dejicuo	德吉措	Liemei Pingcuo	列美平措
Deng Xiaoping	邓小平	Li Jiajun	李佳俊
Duoji Cailang	多吉才郎	Li Tuo	李陀
Duojie Qunzeng	多杰群增	Li Zhaozheng	李肇正
fandui ziyou zhuyi	反对自由主义	Lu Xun	鲁迅
Gao Ping	高平	Ma Bufang	马步芳
Gao Xingjian	高行健	Ma Buqing	马步清
Geng Yufang	耿予方	Maichi (Ch. Maiqi)	麦其
Gesang hua	格桑花	Ma Jian	马建
Gesang Meiduo	格桑梅朵	Ma Lihua	马丽华
Geseng Duojie	格僧多杰	Mao wenti	毛文体
Gongbu Zhaxi	工布扎西	Ma Qi	马麒
Gongga shan	贡嘎山	Meizhuo	梅卓
Guangming Ribao	光明日报	menglong shi	朦胧诗
guojia	国家	minjian wenxue	民间文学

minzhu gaige	民主改革	xibei wenxue	西北文学
minzu tese	民族特色	Xibu wenxue	西部文学
Minzu Wenxue	民族文学	Xinan minzu xueyuan	西南民族学院
Mohuan xianshi zhuyi	魔幻现实主义	xuebao—*Zhexue*	学报——哲学
neibu	内部	shehui kexue ban	社会 科学版
pantu	叛徒	Xinan wenxue	西南文学
Pingcuo Zhaxi	平措扎西	Xiyu wenxue	西域文学
pinglun	评论	Xizang difang	西藏地方文学
piping xianshi zhuyi	批评现实主义	wenxue	
Qiang	羌	Xizang lüyou	西藏旅游
Qing	清	Xizang ribao	西藏日报
Qinghai qunzhong wenyi	青海群众文艺	*Xizang wenxue*	西藏文学
Qinghai wenhuabu	青海文化部	Xizang wenyi	西藏文艺
Que Dan	雀丹	Xu Mingliang	徐明亮
Raojie Baseng	饶阶巴桑	Xueyu wenxue	雪域文学
Rikaze	日喀则	xungen	寻根
Ronggong	茸贡	Yangzhen	央珍
Sebo	色波	Yan Songbo	燕松柏
shalong	沙龙	Yidan Cairang	伊丹才让
shanghen wenxue	伤痕文学	Yue Gang	乐刚
Shannan	山南	Yu Xiaodong	于小冬
Shannan wenyi	山南文艺	yuyan re	语言热
shaoshu minzu	少数民族文学	Zangqu wenxue	藏区文学
wenxue		Zangzu wenxue	藏族文学
shishi	史诗	Zangzu xiaoshuo	藏族小说专号
sige xiandai hua	四个现代化	zhuanhao	
Siru	如	Zha Haisheng	查海生 (aka
Situ	四土		Haizi 海子)
Songgang	松岗	Zhang Jun	张军
Suomo	梭磨	Zhang Niansheng	张念生
Tadu	大渡	Zhangge Nima	章戈。尼马
tai qiguai	太奇怪	Zhaxi Dawa	扎西达娃
tusi	土司	Zhaxi Dongzhu	扎西东珠
Wanma Caidan	万玛才旦	Zhongguo gongnong	中国工农红军
Wangbo	汪波	hongjun	
(Tib. Dbang po)		Zhou Shaoxi	周韶西
Wengbo Yixi	翁波意西	Zhou Yanyang	周艳炀
(Tib. Dbang po		Zhuokeji	卓克基
ye shes)		zi you shi	自由诗
Weise	唯色		
wenhua fansi	文化反思		
Xiahe	夏河		
xibei minzu xueyuan	西北民族学院		

Appendix 3: Contemporary Tibetan Literary Works in Translation

Anthologies

Action Poétique: Tibet Aujourd'hui 157 (winter 1999–2000).

Batt, Herbert J., ed. and trans. *Tales of Tibet: Sky Burials, Prayer Wheels and Wind Horses.* New York: Rowman and Littlefield, 2001.

Grünfelder, Alice. *An den lederriemen geknotete Seele: Erzäler aus Tibet.* Zurich: Unions-verlag, 1997.

Stewart, Frank, Herbert J. Batt, and Tsering Shakya, eds. *Song of the Snow Lion: New Writing from Tibet.* Mānoa 12, no. 2 (2000).

Virtanen, Riika J., ed. and comp. *A Blighted Flower and Other Stories.* Dharamsala: Library of Tibetan Works and Archives, 2000.

Works by Individual Authors

Alai. "The Grassland Sings Itself," trans. H. J. Batt. Mānoa 12, no. 2 (2000), 118.

———. "The Wolf," trans. H. J. Batt. Mānoa 12, no. 2 (2000), 119.

———. *Red Poppies* [Chen'ai luoding, lit. "The dust settles"], trans. H. Goldblatt and S. Lin. Boston: Houghton Mifflin, 2000.

———. *Les Pavots Rouges* [Chen'ai luoding]. Trans. from the English edition of *Red Poppies* by Aline Weill. Paris: Le Rocher, 2003.

———. *Rode papavers,* trans. I. Vanwalle. Amsterdam: Meulenhoff, 2002.

———. *Sources lointaines* [Yao yuan de wen quan], trans. Marie-France de Mirbeck. Paris: Bleu de Chine, 2003.

Döndrup Gyel [Don grub rgyal]. "Here Also Is a Living Heart Beating Strongly." *A Blighted Flower and Other Stories,* comp. and trans. R. J. Virtanen, 141–44. Dharamsala: Library of Tibetan Works and Archives, 2000.

———[Rang grol]. "A Threadlike Path" [Rkang lam phra mo], trans. M. Stevenson and Lama Choedak T. Yuthok. *Tibet Journal* 22, no. 3 (1997), 61–66.

———. "Waterfall of Youth" [Lang tsho'i rbab chu], trans. T. Shakya. Mānoa 12, no. 2 (2000), 9–13.

———. "A Blighted Flower" [Sad kyis bcom pa'i me tog]. *A Blighted Flower and Other Stories,* comp. and trans. R. J. Virtanen. Dharamsala: Library of Tibetan Works and Archives, 2000.

————[Thöndrupgyäl]. *La Fleur vaincue par le gel* [Sad kyis bcom pa'i me tog], trans. F. Robin. Paris: Bleu de Chine, 2006.

————[Thöndrupgyäl]. *L'Artiste tibétain* [Sha dang rus pa'i brtse dungs]. Paris: Bleu de Chine, 2007.

————[Döndrub Gyel]. "Nuoruuden Vesiputous" [Lang tsho'i rbab chu], trans. R. Virtanen. *Kirjo: Kirjallisuus-ja kulttuurilehti* 2 (2002), 10–11.

Döndrup Gyel [Don grub rgyal] and Tsering Dondrup. "A Shameless Bride" [Rgyu 'bras med pa'i mna' ma]. *A Blighted Flower and Other Stories*, comp. and trans. R. J. Virtanen. Dharamsala: Library of Tibetan Works and Archives, 2000.

Dongzhu Cairang. "Nuit, Une bouteille de vin" [Ye. Yi ping jiu], trans. Lara Maconi. *Neige d'août: Lyrisme et extrême-orient* 4 (2001), 80–81.

Drongbu Dorje Rinchen ['Brong bu Rdo rje rin chen]. "Roadside Journal" [Lam 'gram gyi nyin tho], trans. L. Hartley. *Exchanges* [Journal of the Translation Laboratory at Iowa University] 10 (spring 1998), 20–34.

Ermao. "Dans la rue" [Jietou], trans. Lara Maconi. *Neige d'août: Lyrisme et extrême-orient* 4 (2001), 78–79.

Gangzhün [Gangs zhun]. "The Essence of Saṃsāra" ['Khor ba'i snying bo], trans. F. Robin. *Latse Library Newsletter*, fall 2003, 23–25.

————[Kangshün]. "La mélodie de l'incréé originel" [Ma bcos dang po'i 'gyur 'khugs], trans. F. Robin. *Action poétique* 157, 112–13.

————[Kangshün]. "Rendez-vous" ['Du 'bral], trans. F. Robin. *Action poétique* 157, 113.

Geyang. "An Old Nun Tells Her Story," trans. H. Batt. *Mānoa* 12, no. 2 (2000), 83–94.

Jangbu [Ljang bu]. "Selections from *Poems: The Nine-Eyed Gzi*," trans. Y. Dhondup. *Inner Asia* 4, no. 2 (2002), 235–37.

————. "Conquête" [Gzung rnam], trans. Lara Maconi. *Neige d'août: Lyrisme et extrême-orient* 4 (2001), 72.

————. "L'existence et les hommes" ['Jig rten dang mi], trans. Lara Maconi. *Neige d'août: Lyrisme et extrême-orient* 4 (2001), 71.

————. "Je sais bien. Mais je n'ai pas encore posé toutes les questions" [Ngas los shes / 'On kyang dri ba rdzogs mtha' bral], trans. F. Robin. *Action poétique* 157, 104–5.

————. "Nausée" [Zhe mer mer], trans. Lara Maconi. *Neige d'août: Lyrisme et extrême-orient* 4 (2001), 74.

————. "Le Pasteur nomade—Après voir regardé la statue en argile d'un vieux nomade" ['Brog pa / 'Brog pa rgan po zhig gi 'jim brnyan la bltas rjes], trans. F. Robin. *Action poétique* 157, 105.

————. "Pratique des funérailles" [Mkha' spyod kyi nyams len], trans. F. Robin. *Action poétique* 157, 105–6.

————. "Quatre *gzi*." *Linea* 3 (fall 2004), 42–45 [transl. of Gzi 1, Gzi 2, Gzi 5, and Gzi 8, all published in *Gzi mi dgu pa*, 2001].

———. "Regard sur moi-même" [Rang la bltas pa], trans. Lara Maconi. *Neige d'août: Lyrisme et extrême-orient* 4 (2001), 73.

———. "Une Sorte d'inquiétude" [Sems khral rigs shig], trans. F. Robin. *Action poétique* 157, 104.

Ju Kelzang ['Ju Skal bzang]. "Ideal of a Tree" [Ljon pa'i phugs bsam], trans. L. Hartley. *Latse Library Newsletter*, fall 2004, 27.

———. "Tibet, Mother, Mani" [Bod a ma ma ni], trans. L. Hartley. *Lungta* 12 (summer 1999), 37; repr. in *Mānoa* 12, no. 2 (2000), 115–16.

———. "World Viewed from a Different Angle" [Gru ga gzhan zhig nas mthong ba'i 'jig rten], trans. R. Schwartz. *Mānoa* 12, no. 2 (2002), 116–17.

———[Ju Kalsang]. "Le Monde tel qu'il est vu depuis un autre angle" [Gru ga gzhan zhig nas mthong ba'i 'jig rten], trans. F. Robin. *Action poétique* 157, 102–3.

———[Ju Kalsang]. "Un Jour à la tente" [Sbra nang gi nyin zhag], trans. F. Robin. *Action poétique* 157, 103.

Khedrup [Mkhas grub]. "I Accuse You!" [Ngas khyod la ka rdung gtong], trans. H. Stoddard. *Don grub rgyal (1953–1985): Suicide of a Modern Tibetan Writer and Scholar*, 831–32.

———. "Je t'accuse" [Ngas khyod la ka rdung gtong], *Caravanes* 4 (1995).

Langdün Penjor / Langdün Päljor [Glang mdun Dpal 'byor]. *Controverse dans le jardin aux fleurs* [Me tog ldum ra'i nang gi klan ka]. Paris: Bleu de Chine, 2006.

Lhagyal Tsering [Lha rgyal tshe ring]. "Song of the Wind" [Dri bzhon bu mo'i glu dbyangs], trans. L. Hartley. *Lungta* 12 (summer 1999), 38–39; repr. in *Persimmon: Asian Literature, Arts, and Culture* 3, no. 2 (summer 2002), 48–51.

———. "Tears of Regret Flow Uncontrollably," trans. J. Upton. *Mānoa* 12, no. 2 (2002), 14–15.

Meizhuo. [Three Poems], trans. Y. Dhondup. *Mānoa* 12, no. 2 (2002), 146–49.

Orgyen Dorjé / Orgyän Dorjé [O rgyan rdo rje]. "Chant hâbleur d'un homme petit" [Mi chung gi 'gying glu], trans. F. Robin. *Action poétique* 157, 107.

———[Orgyän Dorjé]. "Esquisses de la steppe" [Rtswa thang gi mgyogs bris], trans. N. Tournadre. *Action poétique* 157, 108–9.

———[Orgyän Dorjé]. "Liberté" [Rang dbang], trans. F. Robin. *Action poétique* 157, 107.

———[Orgyän Dorjé]. "Sans titre" [Ming med], trans. F. Robin. *Action poétique* 157, 107–8.

———[Orgyän Dorjé]. "Une soirée interminable" [Gyal dka' ba'i mtshan mo zhig], trans. F. Robin. *Action poétique* 157, 108.

Padar [Dpa' dar]. "Snow Mountain Tears," trans. J. Upton. *Mānoa* 12, no. 2 (2000), 16–17.

Palden Gyal / Päldän Gyäl [Dpal ldan rgyal]. "Les actes, les ancêtres, la tombe" [Las dbang / yab mes / dur sa], trans. M. J. Lamothe. *Action poétique* 157, 114–15.

———. "Offrande" [Mchod], trans. F. Robin. *Action poétique* 157, 116.

———. "Offrande aux poètes du pays des neiges" [Gangs ri'i yul gyi snyan ngag mkhan la phul ba], trans. M. J. Lamothe. *Action poétique* 157, 115–16.

Pema Bhum [Padma 'bum]. *Six Stars with a Crooked Neck: Tibetan Memoirs of the Cultural Revolution* [Dran tho smin 'drug ske 'khyog], trans. L. Hartley. Dharamsala: Tibet Times, 2001.

———. *Memòries tibetanes de la Revolució Cultural: Sis Estels amb el coll torçat* [Dran tho smin 'drug ske 'khyog], trans. F. Mestanza. Barcelona: Ellago, 2006.

———. *Soleil cou coupé: Souvenirs tibétains de la révolution culturelle* [Dran tho smin 'drug ske 'khyog], trans. Francoise Robin. Paris: Bleu de Chine, forthcoming.

Phuntshog Trashi [Phun tshog bkra shis]. "Guests of the Or tog Bar," trans. R. Schwartz. *World Literature Today*, January–April 2004, 57–61.

Ramtsebo [Ram tshe bho]. "Conte d'avant les funérailles" [Dur sngon gyi gtam rgyud], trans. F. Robin. *Action poétique* 157, 110–11.

Sangdak Dorje / Sangda Dorje [Gsang bdag rdo rje]. *Le Chant de la séparation* [Rgyang glu], trans. N. Tournadre. *Action poétique* 157, 101; also pubd. in N. Tournadre and Sangda Dorje, *Manuel de tibétain standard* (Paris: Langues et Mondes—L'Asiathèque, 2002), 344–45. and in English in *Manual of Standard Tibetan* (Ithaca: Snow Lion, 2003), 392–93.

Sebo. "Get the Boat Here" [Zai zheli shang chuan], trans. H. Batt. *Mānoa* 12, no. 2 (2002), 42–48.

———. "Ce son de l'illusion," trans. with an introd. by L. Maconi. *Neige d'août: Lyrisme et Extrême-Orient* 6 (2002), 95–103.

———. "Flots de couleur et sons de l'illusion," trans. L. Maconi. *Neige d'août: Lyrisme et Extrême-Orient* 6 (2002), 95–103.

———. "Richiami magici," trans. L. Maconi. *Il Diario della Settimana* 37 (September 1997).

Tailing, W. *The Secret Tale of Tesur House* [Bkras zur tshang gi gsang ba'i gtam rgyud]. Beijing: China Tibetology Publishing House, 1998.

Trashi Penden [Bkra shis dpal ldan]. "The Yellow Leaves of Summer" [Dbyar kha'i lo ma ser po]. *A Blighted Flower and Other Stories*, comp. and trans. R. J. Virtanen. Dharamsala: Library of Tibetan Works and Archives, 2000.

———. "Tomorrow's Weather Will Be Better," trans. Y. Dhondup. *Mānoa* 12, no. 2 (2002), 152–61.

Tenpa Yargye [Bstan pa yar rgyas]. "A Girl with Her Face Concealed by a Scarf" [Mgo ras kyis btums pa'i bu mo]. *A Blighted Flower and Other Stories*, comp. and trans. R. J. Virtanen. Dharamsala: Library of Tibetan Works and Archives, 2000.

Tonga. "Room 218, Hurrah!" [Eryaoba wangsui!], trans. H. Batt. *Mānoa* 12, no. 2 (2002), 125–33.

Tsering Döndrup [Tshe ring don grub]. "Dashed Hope" [Re chad], trans. R. Schwartz. *Latse Library Newsletter*, fall 2003, 28–29.

———. "A Show to Delight the Masses" [Dmangs rabs tu dga' ba'i zlos gar], trans. L. Hartley. *Persimmon* 1, no. 3 (winter 2001), 61–77.

Weise. "Métisse" [Hunxue'er], trans. Lara Maconi. *Neige d'août: Lyrisme et extrême-orient* 4 (2001), 76–77.

Yang Zhen [Yangdön]. "A God without Gender" [Wu xingbie de shen], trans. H. J. Batt. *Mānoa* 12, no. 2 (2002), 134–43.

———. "Le Roman et moi," trans. L. Maconi. *Neige d'août: Lyrisme et Extrême-Orient* 5 (2001), 52.

———. "La Divinité asexuée" [Wu xingbie de shen], trans. L. Maconi. *Neige d'août: Lyrisme et Extrême-Orient* 5 (2001), 112–25.

Yangtso Kyi. "Journal of the Grassland" [Rtswa thang gi nyin tho], trans. L. Hartley. *Mānoa* 12, no. 2 (2000), 19–26; orig. pubd. in *Beacons* (ATA Journal of Literary Translation) 4 (1998), 99–111.

Yeshe Tenzin. *The Defiant Ones*, trans. D. Kwan. Bejing: China Books and Periodicals, 2000.

Yidan Cairen [Yidam Tsering]. "Crystalline Seeds: Thonmi Sambhota," trans. L. Maconi. *Lion of the Snowy Mountains: The Tibetan Poet Yidan Cairang and his Chinese Poetry: Re-constructing Tibetan National Identity in Chinese. Tibetan Studies: Proceedings of the Ninth Seminar of the IATS 2000*, 193–94. Leiden: E. J. Brill, 2002; repr. in *Latse Library Newsletter*, fall 2005, 42.

———. "The Path," trans. Y. Dhondup. *Latse Library Newsletter*, fall 2005, 44.

———. "Reply," trans. Y. Dhondup. *Latse Library Newsletter*, fall 2005, 44.

———["Two Poems"], trans. H. J. Batt. *Mānoa* 12, no. 2 (2002), 150.

———. "What Is True Cannot Be Falsified," trans. Y. Dhondup. *Latse Library Newsletter*, fall 2005, 43.

Zhaxi Dawa [Tashi Dawa]. "Chimi, the Free Man" [Ziyouren Qimi], trans. H. Batt. *Mānoa* 12, no. 2 (2002), 1–6.

———. "The Glory of the Wind Horse" [Fengma zhiyao], trans. H. Batt. *Mānoa* 12, no. 2 (2002), 96–113.

———. "Le Mutisme du Sage" [Zhizhe de chenmo], trans. B. Rouis. *Anthologie de nouvelles chinoises contémporaines*, ed. Annie Curien, 315–21. Paris: Gallimard, 1994.

———. *A Soul in Bondage: Stories from Tibet*. Beijing: Panda, 1992.

———. *La Splendeur des chevaux du vent* [Fengma zhiyao], trans. B. Rouis. Arles: Actes Sud, 1990.

———. *Tibet: Les Années cachées*, trans. E. Daubian. Paris: Bleu de Chine, 1995 [incl. the short stories "Tibet, une âme ligotée," "Tibet, les années cachées," and "Un Prince en exil"].

 Bibliography

Chinese-Language Sources

"Aba Zangzu zizhizhou gaikuang" bianxiezu, comps. *Aba Zangzu zizhizhou gaikuang* [A brief survey of the Aba Tibetan Autonomous Prefecture]. Chengdu: Sichuan minzu chubanshe, 1985.

Alai. *Chen'ai luoding* [The dust settles]. Beijing: Renmin wenxue chubanshe, 1998.

———. *Dadi de jieti* [Terraces of the earth]. Kunming: Yunnan renmin chubanshe, 2000.

Bai Ye. "Bailuyuan, Chen'ai luoding ji qita: Dangqian xiaoshuo chuangzuo dawenlu" [*White Deer Plain*, *The Dust Settles*, and others: Recent fictional writings Q&A]. *Zhong shan* [Mount Zhong] 1 (1999), 200–204.

Caiwang Naoru and Wangxiu Caidan, eds. *Zangzu dangdai shiren shixuan* [Poetic anthology of contemporary Tibetan poets]. Xining: Qinghai renmin chubanshe, 1997.

Chang Xiwu. "Guomindang zai Lasa ban xue jianjie" [A brief introduction to the establishment of a school in Lhasa by the Guomindang]. *Xizang wenshi ziliao xuanji* [Selected materials in History and Literature or Tibet] 5, 85–92. Beijing: Xizang zizhiqu zhengxie wenshi ziliao yanjiu weiyuanhui, 1985.

Chen, Kuiyuan. "Zai zhuanti yinyuehui 'Huigui song' chuangzuo zongjie biaozhang dahui de jianghua" [Speech at the meeting for summarizing and commenting on the creation of the thematic concert "Praising the return"]. *Xizang ribao* [Tibet daily], 16 July 1997.

Ci Duo. "Yuelun zangzu wenxue he wenxue fanyi" [On Tibetan literature and literary translation]. *Zangyuwen wenzuo* [Writings on Tibetan language and literature] 1 (1994).

———. "Zangwen chuangzuo ji fanyi" [Composing and translating into Tibetan]. *Xueyu wenhua* [Snow Land culture], winter 1990, 29–30.

Danzhu Angben. *Zangzu wenhua fazhan shi* [History of the development of Tibetan culture]. Lanzhou: Gansu jiaoyu chubanshe, 2001.

Dejicuo. *Gezhe wuhui* [The singer does not regret]. Beijing: Minzu chubanshe, 2000.

Duozhi Ge. *Xin ganjue / Tshor snang gsar ba* [New feelings]. Lanzhou: Gansu minzu chubanshe, 1995.

Du Yongbin. *20 shiji Xizang qiseng: renwenzhuyi xianqu Gengdun Qunpei dashi pingzhuan.*

[The legendary monk of twentieth century's Tibet: Biography of master Gendün Chömpel, pioneer of humanism]. Beijing: Zhongguo zangxue chubanse, 2000.

Feng Liang, ed. *Xizang xin xiaoshuo* [New fiction from Tibet]. Lhasa: Xizang renmin chubanshe, 1989.

Gaxue Qujie Nima and Lalu Ciwang Duojie. "Lasa yingyu xuexiao pochan ji" [Notes on the bankruptcy of the Lhasa English School]. *Xizang wenshi ziliao xuanji* 2, 27–34. Beijing: Xizang zizhiqu zhengxie wenshi ziliao yanjiu weiyuanhui, 1984.

Geng Yufang. *Zangzu dangdai wenxue* [Tibetan contemporary literature]. Beijing: Zhongguo zangxue chubanshe, 1994.

Gongbu Zhaxi. *Gongbu Zhaxi shiji* [Collected poems by Gönpo Trashi], trans. Reb gong rdo rje mkhar. Beijing: Minzu chubanshe, 1997.

Huang Pingtang and Yang Zhen, eds. *Lingting Xizang* [Listening to Tibet]. Kunming: Yunnan renmin chubanshe, 1999.

Jiangbian Jiacuo. *Ganxie shenghuo: Wo he wode changbian xiaoshuo* Gesang meiduo. [Thankful to life: Me and my novel Kelzang Metok]. Beijing: Minzu chubanshe, 2000.

Jia Pingwa. *Fei du* [The abandoned capital]. Beijing: Beijing chubanshe, 1993.

Li Shuangyan. "Yang Zhen yu ta de gaotian houtu" [Yang Zhen, her high sky and vast land]. *Xueyu dangdai xueren* [Snow Land's contemporary intellectuals], ed. Qujiang Cairang, 315–19. Beijing: Zhongguo zangxue chubanshe, 1995.

Ma Lihua. *Xueyu wenhua yu Xizang wenxue* [Snow Land culture and Tibetan literature]. Changsha: Hunan jiaoyu chubanshe, 1998.

Meizhuo. *Meizhuo, sanwen shixuan* [Anthology of prose and poems by Mëdrön]. Guiyang: Guizhou renmin chubanshe, 1998.

———. *Taiyang Buluo* [The clan of the sun]. Beijing: Zhongguo wenlian chuban gongsi, 1998.

Pingcuo Zhaxi. *Pingcuo Zhaxi xiaoping xiangshen xuan* [Selected sketches and cross talks by Püntsok Tashi]. Lhasa: Xizang renmin chubanshe, 1999.

Qinghai sheng tongji nianjian 2005 [Qinghai province statistics yearbook 2005], ed. Qinghai Sheng tongji yu. Beijung: Zhongguo tongji chubanshe, 2005.

Ran Yunfei and Alai. "Tongxiang keneng zhilu: yu zangzu zuojia Alai tanhua lu" [A path to possibilities: A dialogue with Tibetan author Alai]. *Xinan minzu xueyuan xuebao—zhexue shehui kexue ban* 20, no. 2 (September 1999), 9.

Sangs rgyas. "Zangzu wenxue chuangzuo bixu yong zangyuwen" [When writing Tibetan new literature it must be in Tibetan], abridged trans. version, unpublished; orig. in Tibetan.

Sichuan sheng Aba zangzu Qiangzu zizhizhou difangzhi bianzuan weiyuanhui eds. [Editorial committee of the gazetteer of Aba Tibetan and Qiang Autonomous prefecture, Sichuan Province]. *Aba zhou zhi* [Gazetteer of Aba prefecture]. Chengdu: Minzu chubanshe, 1994.

Wang Lixiong. "Xizang miandui de liangzhong diguo zhuyi: toushi Weise shijian" [The dual imperialism faced by Tibet: A perspective on the Weise incident]. *Zhongguo zhi chun* [China spring], 18 January 2006, http://www.zgzc.org/2005/citizen ship/00105.htm.

Weise. "Ling yige huashen" [Another embodiment]. *Xizang zai shang* [To Tibet], 80–85. Xining: Qinghai renmin chubanshe, 1999.

———. *Xizang biji* [Notes on Tibet]. Guanzhou: Huacheng chubanshe, 2003.

———. *Xizang zai shang* [To Tibet]. Xining: Qinghai renmin chubanshe, 1999.

Wu Liang et al., eds. *Mohuan xianshi zhuyi xiaoshuo* [Magical realistic novels]. Changchun: Shidai wenyi chubanshe, 1988.

Xizang tongji nianjian 2005 [TAR statistics yearbook 2005], ed. Xizang zizhiqu tongji ju. Beijing: Zhongguo tongji chubanshe, 2005.

Xue Li, ed. *Zhongguo dangdai zangzu zuojia youxiu zuopin xuan* [A selection of the best works by Tibetan contemporary writers from China]. Lanzhou: Gansu minzu chubanshe, 1991.

Yangzhen. *Wu xingbie de shen* [A god without gender]. Beijing: Zhongguo qingnian chubanshe, 1994.

Yan Songbo and Que Dan. *Aba diqu zongjiao shiyao* [A brief religious history of the Aba district]. Chengdu: Chengdu ditu chubanshe, 1993.

Yidan Cairang. "Cong shiji *Liming tiannü de zhaohuan* kan zangzu dangdai muyu shige de fazhan" [On the development of Tibetan contemporary mother-language poetry: Reading the collection of poems *The Call of the Goddess of Dawn*]. *Xibei minzu xueyuan xuebao* [Journal of the Northwest Minorities Institute] 3 (1998), 52–59.

———. *Xueyu de taiyang* [The sun of the Snow Land]. Beijing: Zuojia chubanshe, 1997.

———. *Xueyun ji* [Snow rhymes collection]. Lanzhou, 1996.

Zhang Jun. "Rumo de shijie: Lun dangdai Xizang xiaoshuo" [A magic world: Contemporary novels from Tibet]. *Xizang xin xiaoshuo*, ed. Feng Liang, 431–69. Lhasa: Xizang renmin chubanshe, 1989.

Zhaxi Dawa. "Basang he ta de dimei men" [Basang and her siblings]. *Xizang, ji zai pisheng jie shang de hun*, 256–351. Tianjin: Baihua wenyi chubanshe, 1986.

———. "Chao fo" [Buddhist pilgrimage]. *Xizang wenyi*, 1980, no. 4, 3–9.

———. "Chenmo" [Silence]. *Xizang wenyi* [Literature and art from Tibet], 1979, no. 1, 4–14.

———. "Daoyan yu Sezhen" [The director and Sezhen]. *Xizang wenyi*, 1982, no. 3, 18–21.

———. "Fengma zhi yao" [The glory of the wind horse]. *Xizang, yinmi suiyue*, 93–118. Wuhan: Changjiang wenyi chubanshe, 1993.

———. "Meiyou xingguang de ye" [A night without stars]. *Xizang, ji zai pisheng jieshang de hun*, 68–78. Tianjin: Baihua wenyi chubanshe, 1986.

———. "A Night without Stars." *China's Tibet*, 1995, no. 3, 32–35.

———. *Saodong de Xiangbala* [Turbulent Shambala]. Beijing: Zuojia chubanshe, 1993.

———. "Shiji zhi yao" [The invitation of the century]. *Xizang, yinmi suiyue*, 119–33. Wuhan: Changjiang wenyi chubanshe, 1993.

———. "Weigan dingshang de zhuiluo zhe" [Those fallen from the mast]. *Xizang wenxue* [Literature from Tibet], 1994, no. 2, 4–25.

———. "Xizang, ji zai pisheng jieshang de hun" [Tibet: The soul tied to the knots of a leather rope]. *Xizang, ji zai pisheng jieshang de hun*, 174–98. Tianjin: Baihua wenyi chubanshe, 1986.

———. "Xizang xiaoshuo = 'mohuan xianshi zhuyi?'" [Tibetan novels = "Magical realism"?]. Transcript of talk, Wenxue chuangzuo, wenhua fansi [Literary creation, cultural introspection]. Hong Kong, January 1989.

———. "Xizang, yinmi suiyue" [Tibet: The mysterious years]. *Xizang, yinmi suiyue*, 1–46. Wuhan: Changjiang wenyi chubanshe, 1993.

Zhaxi Dongzhu. "Dangdai zangzu xiaoshuo sikao" [Reflections on contemporary Tibetan novels]. *Gesang hua* [Gesang flower] 3 (1986), 68–75.

Zhongguo renkou tongji nianjian 2005/ China Population Statistics Yearbook 2005, comp. Guojia tongji ju renkou he jiu ye tongji si. Beijing: Zhongguo tongji chubanshe, 2005.

Zhongguo renkou tongji nianjian 2006/ China Population Statistics Yearbook 2006, comp. Guojia tongji ju renkou he jiu ye tongji si. Beijing: Zhongguo tongji chubanshe, 2006.

Zhongguo zuojia xiehui Xizang fenhui [Tibetan branch of the association of Chinese writers]. "Yipian chouhua, wuru Zangzu renmin de liezuo" [A poor novel that slanders and humiliates the Tibetan people]. *Wenyi bao* [Journal of literature and art], 28 March 1987, 2–3.

Zhu Jielin. *Zangzu jinxiandai jiaoyu shilue* [A brief history of modern Tibetan education]. Xining: Qinghai renmin chubanshe, 1990.

Tibetan-Language Sources

A bu (Sdo sbis chos skyong). "Don grub rgyal bsam blo ba yin min skor gleng ba" [A discussion about whether or not Döndrup Gyel is a philosopher]. *Mtsho sngon bod yig gsar 'gyur*, 20 June 2005, 4.

———. "Sgrung gtam 'Gangs' las 'phros pa'i gtam" [A discussion about the story "Snow"]. *Mtsho sngon bod yig gsar 'gyur* [Qinghai Tibetan news], 10 June 2002, 4.

A smyon Bkra shis don grub. "'Dris yun ring na re khengs mang" [A long acquaintance leads to many hopes]. *Ston gyi rang sgra*, 9–14. Xining: Mtsho sngon mi rigs dpe skrun khang, 1999.

———. *Ston gyi rang sgra* [The sound of autumn]. Xining: Mtsho sngon mi rigs dpe skrun khang, 1999.

Ban de mkhar. "Bod kyi mi rigs rang mtshan pa'i khyad chos dang deng rabs rtsom rig gnyis kyi rten 'brel gyi dgos pa syi bshad" [On the need for a connection between the Tibetan nationality's own characteristics and its modern literature]. *Nub byang mi rigs slob grwa chen mo'i rig gzhung dus deb* [The journal of Northwest Nationalities University], 1994, no. 2, 58–69.

Bdud lha rgyal. "'A khu thod pa la bcar 'drir phyin pa' zhes pa'i sgrung gtam la 'brel ba'i gtam." [A discussion about the story "Journey to interview Akhu Töpa"]. *Sbrang char*, 2002, no. 1, 135–40.

Be ri 'Jigs med dbang rgyal. *Dus rabs gsar pa'i rtsom rig pa zhig gi snying khams nas phos pa'i zhungs khrag* [Drops of blood from the heart of a writer in the new era]. Mundgod: Blo gling dpe skrun khang, 1995.

Bkra bha. "Re smon" [Hope]. *Sbrang char*, 1995, no. 2, 49–51.

———. "Sha yu mo she'u" [Fawn]. *Sbrang char*, 2000, no. 3, 29–33.

Bkras gling Dbang rdor. *Bkras zur tshang gi gsang ba'i gtam rgyud* [The secret tale of the Tesur house]. Lhasa: Bod ljongs mi dmangs dpe skrun khang, 1997.

Bkra shis dpal ldan. "Bgres song Tshe ring la go 'dzol byung ba [Old man Tsering's misunderstanding]." *Bod kyi rtsom rig sgyu rtsal* [Tibetan art and literature], 1983, no. 3, 3–12.

———. "Don grub rgyal gyi brtsams 'bras dang des Bod rigs kyi rtsom rig gsar par thebs pa'i shugs rkyen skor" [On Döndrup Gyel's literary production and its effect on Tibetan new literature]. *Bod ljongs zhib 'jug* [Tibetan studies], 1989, no. 1, 64–85.

———. *Phal pa'i khyim tshang gi skyid sdug* [The joys and sorrows of an ordinary family]. Lhasa: Bod ljongs mi dmangs dpe skrun khang, 1992.

Bkras mthong Thub bstan chos dar. *Dge 'dun chos 'phel gyi lo rgyus* [Biography of Gendün Chömpel]. Dharamsala: Library of Tibetan Works and Archives, 1980.

Bkras sgron. "A shel Bde chen mtsho mo" [Elder sister Dechen Tsomo]. *Bod kyi rtsom rig sgyu rtsal*, 1988, no. 6, 1–14.

Blo bzang chos grags and Bsod nams rtse mo, eds. *Gangs ljongs mkhas dbang rim byon gyi rtsom yig gser gyi sbram bu* [Writings by Tibetan scholars: Ingots of gold], vol. 3. Xining: Mtsho sngon mi rigs dpe skrun khang, 1988.

Blon phrug Gnam lha rgyal. "Yongs 'dzin Blo bzang dpal ldan gyi snyan rtsom las 'Pho nya gzhon grub' kyi sgyu rtsal gyi Khyad chos rags tsam gleng ba" [On the aesthetic qualities of Lazang Penden's 'Young Döndrup the Courier']. *Bod ljongs zhib 'jug*, 1991, no. 1, 43–57.

Bod ljongs deng rabs can du 'phel rgyas 'gro bzhin yod [Tibet is modernizing]. Beijing: Krung hwa mi dmangs spyi mthun rgyal khab kyi rgyal srid spyi khyab khang gi gsar thos gzhung las khang, 2001.

'Brong bu Rdo rje rin chen. "Lam gram gyi nyin tho" [Roadside journal]. *Sbrang char*, 1992, no. 3, 17–24.

Bsam gtan, ed. *Dag yig gsar bsgrigs* [A reorganized lexicon]. Dharamsala: Tibetan Cultural Printing Press, 1992.

Bse ru (Ljang bu). "Sin rga phur sger langs thob rjes kyi lo ngo bco lnga'i ring gi (1965–1980) Dbyin yig rtsom rig" [On anglophone literature in Singapore since it achieved independence, 1965–1980]. *Bod kyi rtsom rig sgyu rtsal*, 1995, no. 6, 80–84.

Bsod nams. "Rtsom rig gi mi rigs khyad chos dang Bod rigs rtsom rig skor gleng ba" [On national characteristics in literature and in Tibetan literature]. *Bod rigs pa'i ched rtsom gces bdams* [Selected Tibetological articles], ed. Ngag dbang, 192–238. Lhasa: Bod ljongs mi dmangs dpe skrun khang, 1987.

Bstan 'dzin rgan pa. "Bod kyi rtsom rig gsar pa'i skyed tshal" [The garden of new Tibetan literature]. *Bod kyi rtsom rig sgyu rtsal*, 1997, no. 2, 1–4.

Bstan pa yar rgyas. *Byang thang gi mdzes ljongs* [The scenery of the northern plain]. Lhasa: Bod ljongs mi dmangs dpe skrun khang, 1995.

———. "'Char snang" [A strange occurrence]. *Bod kyi rtsom rig sgyu rtsal*, 2003, no. 3, 43–44.

———. "Mgo ras kyi btums pa'i bu mo" [Girl swathed in a headscarf]. *Byang thang gi mdzes ljongs*, 89–115. Lhasa: Bod ljongs mi dmangs dpe skrun khang, 1995.

———. *Thag ring gi sbra nag* [A distant nomad tent]. Beijing: Mi rigs dpe skrun khang, 2005.

Chab 'gag Rta mgrin. "Krung go gsar pa dbu brnyes pa'i dus 'go'i Bod kyi rtsom pa po grags can 'ga' dang khong tsho'i brtsams chos brjod pa" [On famous Tibetan writers who helped found the new China and their writings]. *Krung go'i Bod kyi shes rig* [China's Tibetology], 1999, no. 3, 11–46.

Chu skyes sgrol ma. *Sprin bral zla ba'i 'dzum rlabs* [Smile of the cloudless moon]. Dharamsala: Tibetan Cultural Printing Press, 1999.

Dge 'dun chos 'phel. *Collected Works*. Orig. pubd in Tibetan as *Dge 'dun chos 'phel gyi gsung 'bum*, ed. Hor khang Bsod nams dpal 'bar. Lhasa: Bod ljongs Bod yig dpe rnying dpe skrun khang, 1994 [1990].

Don grub rgyal. "Bod kyi tshig rgyan rig pa'i sgo 'byed 'phrul gyi lde mig bklags pa'i myong tshor" [Impressions after reading *Magic Key Opening the Door to the Study of Tibetan Poetic Figures*]. *Sbrang char*, 1984, no. 2, 83–89.

———. "'Brong stag thang" [The plain of the wild yak and tiger]. *Dpal Don grub rgyal gyi gsung 'bum*, vol. 2, 193–217. Beijing: Mi rigs dpe skrun khang, 1997.

———. "Bstod pa bklags pa'i 'char snang" [Impressions after reading praise verse]. *Sbrang char*, 1984, no. 1, 41–43.

———. *Collected Works*. Orig. pubd in Tibetan as *Dpal Don grub rgyal gyi gsung 'bum*, ed. Ban kho and Bkra rgyal. Beijing: Mi rigs dpe skrun khang, 1997.

———. *Don grub rgyal gyi lang tsho'i rbab chu/ dang ljags rtsom bdams sgrig* [Dhondup Gyal's "Waterfall of Youth" and selected writings], ed. Padma 'bum. Dharamsala: Amnye Machen Institute, 1994.

———. "Lang tsho'i rbab chu" [Waterfall of youth]. *Sbrang char*, 1983, no. 2, 56–61.

———. *Mgur glu'i lo rgyus dang khyad chos* [History and features of song-poetry]. Beijing: Mi rigs dpe skrun khang, 1985.

———. "Pad mtsho" [Pema Tso]. *Dpal Don grub rgyal gyi gsung 'bum*, vol. 2, 289–301. Beijing: Mi rigs dpe skrun khang, 1997.

———. "Rgyal po Rā maṇa'i rtogs brjod kyi 'grel ba blo gsar ngang mo'i rol mtsho ba bzhugs so" [Pleasure-lake of swans: A novice commentary on the story of King Rāmaṇa]. *Zla zer* [Moon shine], 1990, no. 1, 68–81, 61.

———. "Rkang lam phra mo" [A narrow footpath]. *Sbrang char*, 1984, no. 3, 1–6.

———. "Sad kyis bcom pa'i me tog" [The frost-bitten flower]. *Dpal Don grub rgyal gyi gsung 'bum*, vol. 2, 218–88. Beijing: Mi rigs dpe skrun khang, 1997.

———. "Sgrung ba" [The bard]. *Dpal Don grub rgyal gyi gsung 'bum*, vol. 2, 318–28. Beijing: Mi rigs dpe skrun khang, 1997.

———. "Sprul sku" [The reincarnate lama]. *Sbrang char*, 1981, no. 3, 3–34. Repr. in *Dpal Don grub rgyal gyi gsung 'bum*, vol. 2, 119–55. Beijing: Mi rigs dpe skrun khang, 1997.

Dpal 'byor. *Gtsug g.yu* [The crown turquoise]. Lhasa: Bod ljongs mi dmangs dpe skrun khang, 1985.

Dpal mo, ed. *Bzho lung* [Zholung]. Beijing: Mi rigs dpe skrun khang, 2005.

Dung dkar Blo bzang 'phrin las. "Bod kyi dkar chag rig pa" [Tibetan bibliography studies]. *Sbrang char*, 1986, no. 3, 72–98.

———. *Collected Works*. Orig. pubd in Tibetan as *Mkhas dbang Dung dkar Blo bzang 'phrin las kyi gsung 'bum*. Beijing: Mi rigs dpe skrun khang, 2004.

———. *Snyan ngag la 'jug tshul tshig rgyan rig pa'i sgo 'byed* [Opening the door to the study of ornamentation for writing poetry]. Xining: Mtsho sngon mi rigs dpe skrun khang, 1982.

Gangs zhun. "Go dka' ba snyan ngag gi yon tan yin nam" [Is obscurity a poetic virtue?]. *Sbrang char*, 1999, no. 1, 124–28.

Gcan Rang sad. *Lang tsho'i zhabs rjes* [The footprints of youth]. Xining: Mtsho sngon mi rigs dpe skrun khang, 2002.

Gcan tsha'i Rdo rje rin chen. "Rtsom rig gi lad 'bri sgyu rtsal gyi skor ras tsam gleng ba" [On the art of literary mimesis]. *Sbrang char*, 1994, no. 1, 51–62.

Go po lin. "Dus skabs gsar pa'i Bod kyi sgrung gtam gyi brjod bya'i bstan don skor rags tsam gleng ba" [A brief discussion of content in Tibetan short stories in the New Era]. *Rtsom dpyad gtam tshogs* [Collected literary studies], 145–68. Xining: Mtsho sngon mi rigs dpe skrun khang, 1990.

Gsang bdag rdo rje. *Mig yid rna ba'i dga' ston legs bshad gter gyi bum bzang* [Feast for the eyes, mind, and ears: The excellent treasure vase of elegant writing]. Lhasa: Bod ljongs mi dmangs dpe skrun khang, 1994.

Gsar bzhad me tog tshom bu. Beijing: Mi rigs dpe skrun khang, 1983.

Gsung rab rgya mtsho. "Grong khyer Khran khrun gyi gnas tshul zhu ba'i 'phrin yig" [Letter in honor of the city Changchun]. *Sbrang char*, 1982, no. 2, 76–78.

G.yang mtsho skyid. "Rtswa thang gi nyin tho" [Diary of the grassland]. *Mtsho sngon mang tshogs sgyu rtsal* [Qinghai people's arts], 1988, no. 3, 1–9.

'Gyur med, ed. *Bod kyi deng rabs rtsom rig dpe tshogs* [Tibetan contemporary literature series]. Xining: Qinghai minzu chubanshe, 1991–94.

Gzungs phyug skyid. *Byu ru'i las dbang* [Fate of the coral]. Hong Kong: Then mā dpe skrun kung zi, 1999.

———. *'Jags mi srid pa'i rlabs rgyun* [The wave that cannot be stilled]. Dharamsala: Shes bya kun btus rtsom sgrig khang, 2004.

Hor gtsang 'Jigs med. *Gdon 'phrul lta bu'i bzi kha* [Drunk as a demon]. Dharamsala: Youtse Publishing House, 2002.

'Jam dpal rgya mtsho. *Skal bzang me tog* [Kelzang Metok]. Beijing: Mi rigs dpe skrun khang, 1982.

'Jigs med 'phel rgyas. "Nu bo sprul skur ngos bzung rjes" [After my younger brother was recognized as an incarnate lama], trans. Bsam 'phel. *Sbrang char*, 1996, no. 4, 3–49.

'Ju Skal bzang. "Deng rabs snyan ngag ngo sprod rags bsdus log rtogs mun pa sel ba'i skya rengs" [The dawn dispersing the darkness of misunderstanding: A brief introduction to contemporary poetry], *Bod kyi rtsom rig sgyu rtsal*, 1991, no. 1, 15–31.

———. "Sgyu ma'i pho nya skul ba'i snyan tshig gzhon nu'i rol rtsed" [Poetic words to encourage the illusory courier: The play of youth]. *Sbrang char*, 1984, no. 1, 35–40.

Klu tshang Blo bzang ye shes. *Tshor ba'i pha bong* [Boulder of feeling]. Dharamsala: Shes bya kun btus rtsom sgrig khang, 2004.

Ko zhul Grags pa 'byung gnas and Rgyal ba Blo bzang mkhas grub. *Gangs can mkhas grub rim byon ming mdzod* [Biographical dictionary of Tibetan scholars]. Lanzhou: Kan su'u mi rigs dpe skrun khang, 1992.

Lhag pa phun tshogs. "Bud med rtsom pa po zhig gi snying dbus kyi 'bod sgra: Bkras sgron gyi sgrung gtam *'A shel Bde chen mtsho mo'* zhes par rags tsam dpyad pa" [The call from the heart of a female author: A short analysis of "A Shel Bde chen mtsho mo," a story by Tedrön]. *Rtsom dpyad gtam tshogs* [An anthology of critical articles], ed. 'Gyur med, 335–58. Xining: Mtsho sngon mi rigs dpe skrun khang, 1993.

Lha rgyal tshe ring. *Skya rengs lha mo'i 'bod brda'* [The call of the Goddess of Dawn]. Beijing: Mi rigs dpe skrun khang, 1998.

Lhun grub rnam rgyal. *Ka bshad bung ba dga' tshal* [Acrostics: The paradise of bees]. Lhasa: Bod ljongs mi dmangs dpe skrun khang, 1995.

Ljang bu. *Ljang bu'i rtsom btus: Snyan ngag deb* [Collected works of Jangbu: Poems]. Lanzhou: Kan su'u mi vigs dpe skrun khang, 1996.

Mdo mkhar Tshe ring dbang rgyal. *Gzhon nu zla med kyi gtam rgyud* [The tale of the incomparable prince]. Lhasa: Bod ljongs mi dmangs dpe skrun khang, 1987.

Mi ro rtse sgrung [Vetala tales]. Xining: Mtsho sngon mi rigs dpe skrun khang, 1994 [1963].

Ngag dbang bstan pa'i rgya mtsho. *Rā ma ṇa'i rtogs brjod / Zhang zhung ba Chos dbang grags pas brtsoms / Ngag dbang bstan pa'i rgya mtshos 'grel bshad byas* [The Story of Rāmaṇa by Zhangzhungwa Chöwang Drakpa with commentary by Ngakwang Tenpé Gyatso]. Chengdu: Si khron mi rigs dpe skrun khang, 1983.

Pad ma 'bum. *Mi rabs gsar pa'i snying khams kyi 'phar lding* [The heartbeat of a new generation]. Dharamsala: Amnye Machen Institute, 1999.

Pad ma tshe brtan. "A khu thod pa la bcar 'drir phyin pa" [Journey to interview Akhu Thöpa]. *Sbrang char*, 2002, no. 1, 44–65.

———. "Chos sgron dang mo'i bu blo ldan" [Chödön and her son Loden]. *Sbrang char*, 2002, no. 3, 4–16.

———. "Gangs" [Snow]. *Sbrang char*, 1999, no. 2, 26–36.

———. "Grong khyer gyi 'tsho ba" [Life in town]. *Sbrang char*, 2003, no. 1, 5–42.

———. "Gza' nyi ma" [Sunday]. *Sbrang char*, 2001, no. 1, 4–14.

———. "Rtse thang la 'gro" [Let's go to Tsetang]. *Mang tshogs sgyu rtsal*, 2002, no. 3, 5–11, 80.

Pad ma tshe dbang shāstri. *Mi tshe'i bro ba mngar skyur* [The sweet and sour taste of life]. Dharamsala: Bod kyi dus bab, 2001.

———. *Nga ni Bod yin* [I am Tibet]. Dharamsala: Bod kyi dus bab, forthcoming.

———. *Nub kyi grang ngar dang shar gyi drod 'jam* [Cold west and warm east]. Dharamsala: Bod kyi dus bab, 2000.

Rang sgra. "Dre rkang to" [Limping devil]. *Sbrang char*, 1996, no. 2, 33–59.

———. "Gangs 'dabs kyi gtam rgyud" [A story at the foot of the snow mountain]. *Gangs 'dabs kyi gtam rgyud*, 57–71. Xining: Mtsho sngon mi rigs dpe skrun khang, 1999.

———. "'Pho' gyur" [Changes, 1998]. *Mtsho sngon po'i glu sgra* [Song melodies from the blue lake], ed. Gcod pa don grub, 361–408. Xining: Mtsho sngon mi rigs dpe skrun khang, 1999.

Rdo rje rgyal. *'Dzam gling rig pa'i dpa' bo rdo brag Dge 'dun chos 'phel gyi byung ba brjod pa bden gtam rna ba'i bcud len* [The history of Gendün Chömpel, a hero of world knowledge; true speech, nourishment for the ears]. Lanzhou: Kan su'u mi rigs dpe skrun khang, 1997.

Rdo rje rgyal po. *Collected Works.* Orig. pubd in Tibetan as *Rdo rje rgyal po'i gsung rtsom phyogs bsgrigs.* Beijing: Krung go'i bod kyi shes rig dpe skrun khang, 1992.

———. *Snyan ngag gi rnam bshad gsal sgron* [Exegesis on kāvya]. Beijiing: Mi rigs dpe skrun khang, 1983.

Rdo sbis rdo rje, ed. *Mtsho lho'i rtsom rig brtsams chos gces bsdus* [The essence of Hainan literary works]. Gonghe: Hainan zhou zuojia xiehui, 1999.

Reb gong Rdo rje mkhar. "Ca ne" [The bowl; 1986]. *Gtsang po'i pha rol* [Beyond the Tsangpo river], ed. 'Gyur med, 401–4. Xining: Mtsho sngon mi rigs dpe skrun khang, 1991.

Rig dpal. "Dus skabs gsar pa'i Bod yig brtsoms sgrung gi 'phel phyogs." [Directions in Tibetan stories in the new era]. *Bod kyi rtsom rig sgyu rtsal*, 1992, no. 1, 26–34.

Rig gnas lo rgyus dpyad gzhi'i rgyu cha rtsom sgrig pu'u. "Tsha sprul Ngag dbang blo bzang gi sku tshe smad cha'i mdzad rnam mdor bsdus" [On the accomplishments of Tsatrül Ngakwang Lozang in his later years]. *Bod kyi rig gnas lo rgyus dpyad gzhi'i rgyu cha bdams bsgrigs*, vol. 4, 33–43. Lhasa: Bod ljongs mi dmangs dpe skrun khang, 1981.

Rmog Don grub tshe ring. "'Ston gyi rang sgra' nas Bkra shis don grub gleng ba" [Discussing Trashi Döndrup, the author of "The Sound of Autumn"]. *Mtsho sngon Bod yig gsar 'gyur*, 28 January 2001, 3.

Rnam 'grol. "Char shul gyi nags tshal" [Forest after a storm]. *Gsar bzhad me tog tshom bu*, vol. 1. Beijing: Mi rigs dpe skrun khang, 1983.

Ro sgrung [Vetala tales]. Lhasa: Bod ljongs mi dmangs dpe skrun khang, 2000.

Sangs rgyas. "Bod rigs kyi rtsom rig gsar rtsom byed na nges par du Bod kyi skad dang yi ger brten dgos" [When writing Tibetan new literature it must be written in Tibetan]. *Mi rigs skad yig gi bya ba* [Nationality language affairs] 1 (1983), 23–29. Repr. in *Bod ljongs zhib 'jug*, 1987, no. 1, 119–26, 144.

———. "Gces su 'os pa'i pha yul" [Endearing homeland]. *Sbrang char*, 1982, no. 1, 26–28.

Sha bo tshe ring, "Mkhas dbang Dge 'dun chos 'phel dang khong gi snyan rtsom bshad pa lhag bsam 'o ma'i rdzing bu" [On Gendün Chömpel and his poetic writings: Pool of altruistic milk]. *Bod kyi shes rigs dpyad rtsom phyogs bsgrigs*, vol. 3, 57–107. Beijing: Krung go'i Bod kyi shes rig dpe skrun khang, 1992.

Shes rab rgya mtsho. *Collected Works*. Orig. pubd in Tibetan as *Rje btsun Shes rab rgya mtsho 'jam dpal dgyes pa'i blo gros kyi gsung rtsom*. Xining: Mtsho sngon mi rigs dpe skrun khang, n.d.

Skal bzang lha mo (Chos 'dzin). *Drang srong bsti gnas kyi rmi lam yun ci / Dreaming at the Sage's Abode: Biographical Sketches of Four Living Tibetan Nuns*. Dharamsala: Amnye Machen Institute, 1999.

Skal bzang ye shes. "Bod rigs kyi rtsom rig lo rgyus thog gi dus rabs gsar pa" [A new era in Tibetan literary history]. *Bod ljongs zhib 'jug*, 1983, no. 3, 62–78.

Tsha sprul Ngag dbang blo bzang. *Sum cu pa'i snying po legs bshad ljon pa'i dbang po'i slob deb* [Aphorisms regarding grammar: First textbook for youth]. Beijing: Mi rigs dpe skrun khang, 1981 [1959].

Tshe dbang rnam rgyal. "Bod kyi nye dus kyi grags can snyan ngag pa Shel gling Mi 'gyur lhun grub kyi snyan ngag rtsom las skor cung zad gleng ba" [A brief discussion of poems by the famous Tibetan classical poet Shelling Mingyur Lhundup]. *Bod kyi rtsom rig sgyu rtsal*, 1983, no. 5, 61–72.

Tshe rdor. *Skyed ma'i bka' drin* [The kindness of the mother]. Lhasa: Bod ljongs mi dmangs dpe skrun khang, 1995.

Tshe ring don grub. "Dmangs rab tu dga' ba'i zlos gar" [A show to delight the masses]. *Tshe ring don grub kyi sgrung thung bdams bsgrigs* [Selected short stories by Tsering Döndrup], 171–201. Xining: Mtsho sngon mi rigs dpe skrun khang, 1996.

———. *Gzhon nu'i rang sgra dbyar gyi rnga gsang* [The sound of a young man: The secret drum-sound of summer]. *Tshe ring don grub kyi sgrung thung bdams bsgrigs*, 1–19. Xining: Mtsho sngon mi rigs dpe skrun khang, 1996 [1983].

———. "Lha ba 'dre ston *A mes Dpal ldan dang*" [An oracle showing the Devil; 1988]. *Tshe ring don grub kyi sgrung thung bdams bsgrigs*, 20–22. Xining: Mtsho sngon mi rigs dpe skrun khang, 1996.

———. *Mes po* [Ancestors]. Hong Kong: Ling dpe skrun kung si, 2001.

———. "Rtse chus khrel dgod byed bzhin" [Ridiculed by Rtse chu river]. *Tshe ring don grub kyi sgrung thung bdams bsgrigs*, 32–43. Xining: Mtsho sngon mi rigs dpe skrun khang, 1996 [1988].

———. "Zla ba" [Dawa]. *Tshe ring don grub kyi sgrung thung bdams bsgrigs*, 43–62. Xining: Mtsho sngon mi rigs dpe skrun khang, 1996.

Tshe ring g.yang skyid. *So nam shor ba'i ljang bu* [A young sprout that missed harvest]. *Sbrang char*, 1998, no. 3, 4–30.

Tshe ring thar. "Bod kyi deng rabs brtsams sgrung las 'phros pa'i gtam chu yi zegs ma" [Waterdrops of discussion splashing from contemporary Tibetan fiction writing]. *Bod kyi shes rig zhib 'jug*, 84–93. Beijing: Mi rigs dpe skrun khang, 1998.

Tshe tan zhabs drung. *Snyan ngag me long gi spyi don sdeb legs rig pa'i 'char sgo* [Summary of the *Mirror of Poetics*]. Lanzhou: Kan su'u mi rigs dpe skrun khang, 1981.

Ye shes rdo rje et al., eds. *Gangs can mkhas dbang rim byon gyi rnam thar mdor bsdus* [Concise biographies of former Tibetan scholars]. Beijing: Mi rigs dpe skrun khang, 2000.

Zhang Yisun et al. *Bod Rgya tshig mdzod chen mo* [Great Tibetan-Chinese dictionary]. Beijing: Mi rigs dpe skrun khang, 1996 [1993].

Western-Language Sources

Achebe, Chinua. "The African Writer and the English Language." *Colonial Discourse and Post-colonial Theory: A Reader*, ed. Patrick Williams and Laura Chrisman, 428–34. New York: Columbia University Press, 1994.

Action Poétique: Tibet Aujourd'hui, numéro spécial 157 (winter 1999–2000), 3–119.

Alai. *Red Poppies*, trans. Howard Goldblatt and Sylvia Li-chun Lin. Boston: Houghton Mifflin, 2002.

Ashcroft, Bill, Gareth Williams, and Helen Tiffin, eds. *The Post-colonial Studies Reader*. New York: Routledge, 1999 [1995].

Atkinson, Michael. *The Secret Marriage of Sherlock Holmes, and Other Eccentric Readings*. Ann Arbor: University of Michigan Press, 1996.

Auerbach, Erich. *Mimesis*. Princeton: Princeton University Press, 1973 [1946].

Bailey, H. W. "Rāma." *Bulletin of the School of Oriental Studies* 10, no. 2 (1940), 365–76.

———. "Rāma II." *Bulletin of the School of Oriental Studies* 10, no. 2 (1940), 559–98.

———. "The Rāma Story in Khotanese." *Journal of the American Oriental Society* 59, no. 4 (December 1939), 460–68.

Barmé, Geremie, and John Minford, eds. *Seeds of Fire: Chinese Voices of Conscience*. New York: Hill and Wang, 1988.

Barnett, Robert, ed. *Resistance and Reform in Tibet*. Bloomington: Indiana University Press, 1994.

Bass, Catriona. *Education in Tibet: Policy and Practice since 1950*. London: Zed, 1998.

Batt, Herbert, ed. and trans. *Tales of Tibet: Sky Burials, Prayer Wheels and Wind Horses*. New York: Rowman and Littlefield, 2001.

Beckwith, Christopher I. *The Tibetan Empire in Central Asia*. Princeton: Princeton University Press, 1987.

Bertens, Hans, and Douwe Fokkema, eds. *International Postmodernism: Theory and Literary Practice*. Philadelphia: John Benjamins, 1997.

Bhabha, Homi. *The Location of Culture*. New York: Routledge, 1994.

Bhuchung D. Sonam, ed. *Muses in Exile: An Anthology of Tibetan Poetry*. New Delhi: Paljor, 2004.

Bishop, Peter. *The Myth of Shangri-La: Tibet, Travel Writing, and the Western Creation of Sacred Landscape*. Berkeley: University of California Press, 1989.

———. "Not Only Shangri-la: Images of Tibet in Western Literature." *Imagining Tibet: Perceptions, Projections, and Fantasies*, ed. Thierry Dodin and Heinz Räther, 201–21. Boston: Wisdom, 2001.

Blanchard, March Eli. *In Search of the City: Engels, Baudelaire, Rimbaud*. Saratoga: Anma Libri, 1985.

Borges, Jorge Luis. *Labyrinths: Selected Stories and Other Writings*. New York: New Directions, 1964.

Broich, Ulrich. "Intertextuality." *International Postmodernism: Theory and Literary Practice*, ed. Hans Bertens and Douwe Fokkema, 249–55. Philadelphia: John Benjamins, 1997.

Cabezón, José Ignacio. "Authorship and Literary Production in Classical Buddhist Tibet." *Changing Minds: Contributions to the Study of Buddhism and Tibet in Honor of Jeffrey Hopkins*, ed. Guy Newland, 233–63. Ithaca: Snow Lion, 2001.

Cabézon, José, and Roger R. Jackson, eds. *Tibetan Literature: Studies in Genre*. Ithaca: Snow Lion, 1996.

Calinescu, Matei. "Rewriting." *International Postmodernism: Theory and Literary Practice*, ed. Hans Bertens and Douwe Fokkema, 243–48. Philadelphia: John Benjamins, 1997.

Cao Changching. "Brainwashing the Chinese." *Tibet through Dissident Chinese Eyes: Essays on Self-Determination*, ed. Cao Changching and James D. Seymour, 25–30. Armonk: M. E. Sharpe, 1998.

Carpentier, Alejo. *Obras Completas de Alejo Carpentier*, vol. 2. Mexico City: Siglo XXI, 1983.

Chatterjee, Partha. *The Nation and Its Fragments: Colonial and Postcolonial Histories*. Princeton: Princeton University, 1993.

Chen Xiaoming. "The Mysterious Other: Postpolitics in Chinese Film." *Postmodernism and China*, ed. Arif Dirlik and Xudong Zhang, 222–38. Durham: Duke University Press, 2000 [1997].

Chhoyang, Dicki Tsomo. "Tibetan-Medium Higher Education in Qinghai." Master's thesis, Indiana University, 1999.

Chögyam Trungpa. *Timely Rain*. Boston: Shambhala, 1998.

———. *First Thought, Best Thought*. Boston: Shambhala, 2001.

Chow, Rey. "Rereading Mandarin Ducks and Butterflies: A Response to the 'Postmodern' Condition." *Postmodernism: A Reader*, ed. Thomas Docherty. New York: Columbia University Press.

Choy, Howard Y. F. "Historiographic Alternatives for China: Tibet in Contemporary Fiction by Tashi Dawa, Alai, and Ge Fei." *American Journal of Chinese Studies* 12, no. 1 (April 2005), 65–84.

Clark, Paul. "Ethnic Minorities in Chinese Films: Cinema and the Exotic." *East-West Film Journal* 1, no. 2 (1987), 15–31.

Clausen, Christopher. "Sherlock Holmes, Order, and the Late-Victorian Mind." *Critical Essays on Sir Arthur Conan Doyle*, ed. Harold Orel, 66–91. New York: G. K. Hall, 1992.

"A Conversation between Jamyang Norbu and Elliot Sperling." *Latse Library Newsletter* 2 (fall 2004), 14–17.

Cooper, Brenda. *Magical Realism in West African Fiction: Seeing with a Third Eye.* London: Routledge, 1998.

Costello, Susan. "The Economics of Cultural Production in Contemporary Amdo." *Amdo Tibetans in Transition: Society and Culture in the Post-Mao Era,* ed. Toni Huber, 221–39. Proceedings of the Ninth Seminar of the International Association for Tibetan Studies, Leiden 2000. Leiden: E. J. Brill, 2002.

Das, Sarat Chandra. *Indian Pandits in the Land of Snow,* ed. Nobin Chandra Das. New Delhi: Asian Educational Services, 1992 [1893].

———. *A Journey to Lhasa and Central Tibet.* New Delhi: Book Faith India, 1998 [1899].

Daubian, Émilienne, trans. *Tibet: Les Années cachées.* Paris: Bleu de Chine, 1995.

Davenport, John, trans. *Ordinary Wisdom: Sakya Pandita's Treasury of Good Advice.* Boston: Wisdom, 2000.

Davis, Lennard J. *Factual Fictions: The Origins of the English Novel.* Philadelphia: University of Pennsylvania Press, 1996.

de Jong, J. W. "The Story of Rama in Tibet." *A Critical Inventory of Ramayana Studies in the World,* vol. 2, ed. K. Krishnamoorthy and Satkari Mukhopadhyaya, xxxviii–xli. New Delhi: Sahitya Akademi in collaboration with Union Académique Internationale, Brussels, 1991.

———. *The Story of Rāma in Tibet: Text and Translation of the Tun-Huang Manuscripts.* Stuttgart: Steiner, 1989.

De Nebesky-Wojkowitz, Réne. *Oracles and Demons of Tibet.* Kathmandu: Tiwari's Pilgrims Book House, 1993.

D'haen, Theo. "Postmodernism: From Fantastic to Magic Realist." *International Postmodernism: Theory and Literary Practice,* ed. Hans Bertens and Douwe Fokkema, 283–93. Philadelphia: John Benjamins, 1997.

Dimmitt, Cornelia, and J. A. B. van Buitenen, eds. and trans. *Classical Hindu Mythology: A Reader in the Sanskirt Purāõas.* Philadelphia: Temple University Press, 1978.

Dirks, Nicholas B. *Colonialism and Culture.* Ann Arbor: University of Michigan Press, 1992.

Dirlik, Arif, and Xudong Zhang. "Postmodernism and China." *Postmodernism and China,* 1–17. Durham: Duke University Press, 2000.

Dodin, Thierry, and Heinz Räther, eds. *Imagining Tibet: Perceptions, Projections and Fantasies.* Boston: Wisdom, 2001.

Dondrup Wangbum. Preface. *A Soul in Bondage: Stories from Tibet,* by Tashi Dawa, 5–11. Beijing: Panda, 1992.

Doyle, Arthur Conan. *Sherlock Holmes: The Complete Novels and Stories,* vol. 1. New York: Bantam, 1986 [1887–1903].

Dreyer, June Teufel. *China's Forty Million.* Harvard East Asian Series 87. Cambridge: Harvard University Press, 1976.

Dreyfus, Georges B. J. *The Sound of Two Hands Clapping: The Education of a Tibetan Buddhist Monk.* Berkeley: University of California Press, 2003.

Dutt, Romesh C. *Ramayana: The Epic of Rama, Prince of India.* London: J. M. Dent, 1899.

Dwyer, Arienne M. "The Texture of Tongues: Languages and Power in China." *Nationalism and Ethnoregional Identities in China*, ed. William Safran, 68–85. London: Frank Cass, 1998.

Eagleton, Terry. *After Theory*. London: Penguin, 2003.

Eber, Irene. "Western Literature in Chinese Translation, 1949–1979." *Asian and African Studies* 3, no. 1 (1994), 34–54

Ekvall, Robert. "The Tibetan Self-Image." *The History of Tibet*, vol. 3, *The Modern Period: 1895–1959, The Encounter with Modernity*, ed. Alex McKay. London: Routledge Curzon, 2003.

Erhard, Franz Xaver. "Magical Realism and Tibetan Literature." *Contemporary Tibetan Literary Studies*, ed. Steven Venturino, 133–46. Proceedings of the Tenth Seminar of the International Association for Tibetan Studies, Oxford 2003. Leiden: E. J. Brill, 2007.

Flood, Gavin. *An Introduction to Hinduism*. Cambridge: Cambridge University Press, 1996.

Frye, Northrop. *Anatomy of Criticism: Four Essays*. Princeton: Princeton University Press, 1957.

Gálik, Marián. "Foreign Literature in the People's Republic of China between 1970–1979." *Asian and African Studies* 19 (1983), 55–95.

Gang Yue. "Review of *Red Poppies*." MCLC Resource Center, April 2005, http://mclc .osu.edu/rc/pubs/reviews/yue.htm.

Gates, Henry Louis, Jr. *The Signifying Monkey: A Theory of African-American Literary Criticism*. New York: Oxford University Press, 1988.

Ge Fei. "Meetings," trans. Deborah Mills. *Abandoned Wine: Chinese Writing Today*, vol. 2, ed. Henry Y. H. Zhao and John Cayley, 15–49. London: Wellsweep, 1996.

Gladney, Dru C. *Dislocating China: Muslims, Minorities and Other Subaltern Subjects*. Chicago: University of Chicago Press, 2004.

———. "Representing Nationality in China: Refiguring Majority/Minority Identities." *Journal of Asian Studies* 53, no. 1 (1994), 92–123.

Gold, Jonathan. "Intellectual Gatekeeper: Sa-skya Paṇḍita Envisions the Ideal Scholar." Ph.D. diss., University of Chicago, 2003.

Goldman, Robert P., gen. ed. and trans. *The Rāmāyaṇa of Vālmīki: An Epic of Ancient India*. Princeton: Princeton University Press, 1984–96.

Goldstein, Melvyn C. *A History of Modern Tibet, 1913–1951: The Demise of the Lamaist State*. Berkeley: University of California Press, 1989.

———, ed. *Tibetan-English Dictionary of Modern Tibetan*. Kathmandu: Ratna Pustak Bhandar, 1975.

Goldstein, Melvyn C., Dawei Sherap, and William R. Siebenschuh. *A Tibetan Revolutionary: The Political Life and Times of Bapa Phüntso Wangye*. Berkeley: University of California Press, 2004.

"Golmud-Lhasa railway to Open Earlier Than Planned." *Tibet News Digest*, 10–23 December 2005, TibetInfoNet [e-mail newsletter].

Gray, Jack. *Rebellions and Revolutions: China from the 1800s to the 1980s.* Oxford: Oxford University Press, 1990.

Griswold, Wendy. *Bearing Witness: Readers, Writers, and the Novel in Nigeria.* Princeton: Princeton University Press, 2000.

Grünfelder Alice. *An den lenderriemen geknotete Seele: Erzäler aus Tibet.* Zurich: Unionsverlag, 1997.

———. "Tashi Dawa and Modern Tibetan Literature." *Tibetan Studies: Proceedings of the Seventh Seminar of the International Association for Tibetan Studies,* ed. Helmut Krasser et al., 337–46. Beitrage zur Kultur-unid Geistesgeschichte Asiens, no. 21. Vienna: Osterreichischen Akademie der Wissenschaften, 1997.

Gyatso, Janet. *Apparitions of the Self: The Secret Autobiographies of a Tibetan Visionary.* Princeton: Princeton University Press, 1998.

———. "Autobiography in Tibetan Religious Literature: Reflections on Its Modes of Self-Presentation." *Tibetan Studies: Proceedings of the Fifth International Association of Tibetan Studies Seminar,* ed. Shoren Ihara and Zuiho Yamaguchi, vol. 2, 465–78. Narita: Naritasan Institute for Buddhist Studies, 1992.

Harrell, Steven. *Cultural Encounters on China's Ethnic Frontiers.* Seattle: University of Washington Press, 1995.

Harris, Clare. *In the Image of Tibet: Tibetan Painting after 1959.* London: Reaktion, 1999.

Hartley, Lauran R. "Ascendancy of the Term *rtsom rig* in Tibetan Literary Discourse." *Contemporary Tibetan Literary Studies,* ed. Steven Venturino, 1–16. Proceedings of the Tenth Seminar of the International Association for Tibetan Studies, Oxford 2003. Leiden: E. J. Brill, 2007.

———. "Contextually Speaking: Tibetan Literary Discourse and Social Change in the People's Republic of China (1980–2000)." Ph.D. diss., Indiana University, 2003.

———. "Inventing 'Modernity' in Amdo: Views on the Role of Traditional Tibetan Culture in a Developing Society." *Amdo Tibetans in Transition: Society and Culture in the Post-Mao Era,* ed. Toni Huber, 1–25. Proceedings of the Ninth Seminar of the International Association for Tibetan Studies, Leiden 2000. Leiden: E. J. Brill, 2002.

———. "The Role of Regional Factors in the Standardization of Spoken Tibetan." *Tibet Journal* 21, no. 4 (winter 1996), 30–57.

———. "Themes of Tradition and Change in Modern Tibetan Literature." *Lungta* 12 (1999), 29–44.

———. "Tibetan Publishing in the Early Post-Mao Period." *Cahiers d'Extrême Asie* 15 (2005), 233–55.

Henrion-Dourcy, Isabelle. "Ache lhamo: Jeux et enjeux d'une tradition théâtrale tibétaine." Ph.D. diss., Université Libre de Bruxelles and EPHE IVe section, 2004.

Hopkirk, Peter. *Quest for Kim: In Search of Kipling's Great Game.* Ann Arbor: University of Michigan Press, 1997.

Huber, Toni. "Colonial Archaeology, International Missionary Buddhism and the First Example of Modern Tibetan Literature." *Bauddhavidyasudhakarah: Studies in Honour of Heinz Becher on the Occasion of His 65th Birthday,* ed. Petra Kieffer-Pulz and Jens-Uwe Hartmann, 297–318. *Indica et Tibetica* 30 (Swisttal-Odendorf, 1997).

———. *The Guide to India: A Tibetan Account by Amdo Gendun Chöphel*. Dharamsala: Library of Tibetan Works and Archives, 2000.

———, ed. *Amdo Tibetans in Transition: Society and Culture in the Post-Mao Era*. PIATS 2000: Tibetan Studies: Proceedings of the Ninth Seminar of the International Association for Tibetan Studies, Leiden 2000. Leiden: E. J. Brill, 2002.

Hutcheon, Linda. *The Politics of Postmodernism*. New York: Routledge, 1989.

"Illiteracy and Education Levels Worsen in the TAR despite Development Drive." *TibetInfoNet Update*, 27 September 2005 [e-mail newsletter].

Jackson, David Paul. *The Entrance Gate for the Wise (Section III): Sa-skya Paṇḍita on Indian and Tibetan Traditions of Pramāṇa and Philosophical Debate*. Vienna: Arbeitskreis für tibetische und buddhistische Studien, Universität Wien, 1987.

Jamyang Norbu. *Illusion and Reality: Essays on the Tibetan and Chinese Political Scene, from 1978 to 1989*. New Delhi: Tibetan Youth Congress, 1989.

———. *The Mandala of Sherlock Holmes*. New York: Bloomsbury, 1999.

———. "Newspeak & New Tibet: Part I–V: The Myth of China's Modernization of Tibet and the Tibetan Language," http://www.tibetwrites.org/articles/jamyang_norbu/jamyang_norbu13.htm.

JanMohamed, Abdul R. 1986. "The Economy of Manichean Allegory: The Function of Racial Difference in Colonialist Literature." *"Race," Writing, and Difference*, ed. Henry Louis Gates Jr., 78–106. Chicago: University of Chicago Press, 1986.

Kapstein, Matthew T. "Dhondup Gyal: The Making of a Modern Hero." *Lungta* 12 (summer 1999), 45–48.

———. "The Indian Literary Identity in Tibet." *Literary Cultures in History: Reconstructions from South Asia*, ed. Sheldon Pollock, 747–802. Berkeley: University of California Press, 2003.

———. "The Tulku's Miserable Lot: Critical Voices from Eastern Tibet." *Amdo Tibetans in Transition: Society and Culture in the Post-Mao Era*, ed. Toni Huber, 99–111. Leiden: E. J. Brill, 2002.

Kipling, Rudyard. *Kim*. New York: Penguin, 1989 [1901].

Kolås, Åshild. "Chinese Media Discourses on Tibet: The Language of Inequality." *Tibet Journal* 23, no. 3 (1998), 69–77.

Kolås, Åshild, and Monika P. Thowsen. *On the Margins of Tibet: Cultural Survival on the Sino-Tibetan Frontier*. Seattle: University of Washington Press, 2005.

Kronfeld, Chana. *On the Margins of Modernism: Decentering Literary Dynamics*. Berkeley: University of California Press, 1996.

Landon, Perceval. *The Opening of Tibet*. New York: Doubleday, 1905.

Lazar, Edward, ed. *Tibet: The Issue Is Independence: Tibetans in Exile Address the Key Tibetan Issue the World Avoids*. Berkeley: Parallax, 1994.

Leal, Luís. "El realismo mágico en la literatura hispanoamericana." *Cuadernos americanos* 153, no. 4 (1967), 230–35.

Lerner, Laurence. *The Literary Imagination: Essays on Literature and Society*. Sussex: Harvester, 1982.

Li Huijuan. "Silent Mani Stone Wins a Prize on Pusan Film Festival." China Tibet

Information Center, 26 October, http://en.tibet.cn/news/tin/t20051026_65189
.htm, visited 28 December 2005.

Lin, Julia C. *Modern Chinese Poetry: An Introduction.* London: Allen and Unwin, 1972.

Link, Perry. *Evening Chats in Beijing: Probing China's Predicament.* New York: W. W. Norton, 1992.

———. "The Genie and the Lamp: Revolutionary Xiangsheng." *Popular Literature and Performing Arts in the People's Republic of China, 1949–1979,* ed. Bonnie MacDougall, 83–111. Berkeley: University of California Press, 1984.

———. "The Limits of Cultural Reform in Deng Xiaoing's China." *Modern China* 13, no. 2 (1987), 115–76.

———. *The Uses of Literature: Life in the Socialist Chinese Literary System.* Princeton: Princeton University Press, 2000.

Lokesh Chandra. *Materials for a History of Tibetan Literature,* vol. 1. New Delhi: International Academy of Indian Culture, 1963.

Lopez, Donald S., Jr. *Prisoners of Shangri-La: Tibetan Buddhism and the West.* Chicago: University of Chicago Press, 1998.

Lü, Tonglin. *Misogyny, Cultural Nihilism and Oppositional Politics.* Stanford: Stanford University Press, 1995.

Lutwack, Leonard. *The Role of Place in Literature.* Syracuse: Syracuse University Press, 1984.

Lycett, Andrew. *Rudyard Kipling.* London: Weidenfeld and Nicolson, 1999.

Lyotard, Jean-François. "Answering the Question: What Is Postmodernism?" *Postmodernism: A Reader,* ed. Thomas Docherty, 38–46. New York: Columbia University Press, 1993.

Maconi, Lara. "Flots de couleur et sons de l'illusion." *Neige d'août: Lyrisme et Extrême-Orient* 4 (2002), 95–103.

———. "Frontières de l'imaginaire: La Problématique de l'identité culturelle dans la littérature tibétaine d'expression chinoise en PRC." Ph.D. diss., Langues'O INALCO, 2006.

———. "Interview de Yang Zhen," "Le Roman et moi," and "La Divinité asexuée." *Neige d'août: Lyrisme et Extrême-Orient* 5 (2001).

———. "Lhasa-Pékin: L'exemple de Yang Zhen, jeune femme écrivain tibétaine, mémoire de DEA." Paris, Langues'O INALCO, 1998, unpublished.

———. "Lion of the Snowy Mountains: The Tibetan Poet Yidan Cairang and His Chinese Poetry: Re-constructing Tibetan National Identity in Chinese." *Tibet, Self, and the Tibetan Diaspora: Voices of Difference,* ed. P. Christiaan Klieger, 165–93. Leiden: E. J. Brill, 2002.

———. "Poètes tibétains." *Neige d'août: Lyrisme et Extrême-Orient* 4 (2001).

———. "Roars Echoing through the Snowy Mountains: In Memory of Yidam Tsering, Lion of the Snowy Mountains (1933–2004)." *Latse Library Newsletter* 3 (fall 2005), 38–41.

———. "Une longue marche translinguistique: Présence française dans la nouvelle littérature tibétaine: Modes de médiation et d'integration, réception, intertextu-

alité." *France-Asie: Un siècle d'échanges littéraires*, 205–36. Actes du colloque "Litté-
ratures asiatiques en France et littérature française en Asie au XXe siècle," Paris,
20–21 octobre 2000. Paris: You Feng, 2001.

———, trans. "'Richiami magici,' by Se Bo." *Il Diario della Settimana* 37, September
1997.

Ma Huiping, ed. *Catalogue of Chinese Publications in Tibetan Studies (1949–1991)*. Beijing,
Foreign Language Press, 1994.

———. *Catalogue of Chinese Publications in Tibetan Studies (1992–1995)*. Beijing: Foreign
Language Press, 1997.

———. *Catalogue of Chinese Publications in Tibetan Studies (1996–2000)*. Beijing: Foreign
Language Press, 2001.

Ma Jian. "Stick Out the Fur on Your Tongue or It's All a Void." *Tales of Tibet: Sky Burials,
Prayer Wheels and Wind Horses*, ed. and trans. Herbert Batt. New York: Rowman and
Littlefield, 2001.

Makley, Charlene. "The Power of the Drunk: Humor and Resistance in China's Tibet."
Linguistic Form and Social Action, special issue of *Michigan Discussions in Anthropology*
13 (1998), 39–79.

Mani, Lata. "Contentious Traditions: The Debate on Sati in Colonial India." *Recasting
Women*, ed. K. Sangari and S. Vaid, 86–126. New Delhi: Kali for Women, 1990.

Margolis, Eric. *War at the Top of the World: The Struggle for Afghanistan, Kashmir, and Tibet*.
New York: Routledge, 2000.

McDougall, Bonnie S., and Louie, Kam. *The Literature of China in the Twentieth Century*.
London: Hurst, 1997.

McGranahan, Carol. "Empire, Archive, Diary: A Tibetan Nationalist in India and
China, 1946–1950." Paper presented at Columbia University, 17 October 2002.

Mengele, Irmgard. *dGe-'dun-chos-'phel: A Biography of the 20th-Century Tibetan Scholar*.
Dharamsala: LTWA, 1999.

Milner, Andrew. *Literature, Culture and Society*. London: Routledge, 2005 [1996].

Min, Lin, and Maria Galikowski, eds. *The Search for Modernity: Chinese Intellectuals and
Cultural Discourse in the Post-Mao Era*. New York: St. Martin's, 1999.

Moon, Adrian. "Modern Tibetan Fiction," parts 1–3. *Tibetan Review* 27, nos. 10–12
(October–December 1991).

Muir, Lynette R. *Literature and Society in Medieval France: The Mirror and the Image, 1100–
1500*. London: Macmillan, 1985.

Newman, Beth. "The Tibetan Novel and its Sources." *Tibetan Literature: Studies in Genre*,
ed. José Ignacio Cabezón and Roger R. Jackson, 411–21. Ithaca: Snow Lion,
1996.

Ngũgĩ wa Thiong'o. *Colonial Discourse and Post-colonial Theory: A Reader*, ed. Patrick Williams and Laura Chrisman, 435–55. New York: Columbia University Press, 1994.

Orofino, Giacomella. "The Tibetan School of Khri ka'i stong che: A Report on Italian
Development Aid in Amdo." *Amdo Tibetans in Transition*, ed. Toni Huber, 291–300.
Leiden: E. J. Brill, 2002.

Padura, Leonardo. *Lo real-maravilloso: creación y realidad*. Havana: Letras Cubanas, 1989.

Pema Bhum [Padma 'bum]. *Dran tho smin drug ske 'khyog / Six Stars with a Crooked Neck: Tibetan Memoirs of the Cultural Revolution*, trans. Lauran Hartley. Dharamsala: Bod kyi dus bab [Tibet Times], 2001.

———. "The Heart-beat of a New Generation: A Discussion of the New Poetry" [Mi rabs gsar pa'i snying khams kyi 'phar lding / snyan ngag gsar pa'i skor gleng ba], trans. Ronald Schwartz. *Lungta* 12 (summer 1999), 2–16.

———. "The Life of Dhondup Gyal: A Shooting Star That Cleaved the Night Sky and Vanished" [Don grub gyal gyi mi tshe: skar mda' mtshan mo'i nam mkha' od kyis bshegs nas yal], trans. Lauran R. Hartley. *Lungta* 9 (1995), 17–29.

———. "Mao's Cuckoo." *Index on Censorship* 30, no. 1 (2001), 176–81.

Pema Tsering. "A Deceitfully Erected Stone Pillar and the Beginnings of Modern Tibetan Literature," trans. Riika Virtanen. *The Tibet Journal* 24, no. 2 (1999), 112–24.

Petech, Luciano. *Aristocracy and Government in Tibet (1728–1959)*. Serie Orientale Roma XLV. Roma: Istituto Italiano per il Medio ed Estremo Oriente, 1973.

Pitavy, François L. "Idiocy and Idealism: A Reflection on the Faulknerian Idiot." *Faulkner and Idealism: Perspectives from Paris*, ed. Michel Gresset and Patrick Samway, 97–111. Jackson: University Press of Mississippi, 1983.

Raghavan, V. *The Ramayana in Greater India*. Surat, India: South Gujarat University, 1973.

———, ed. *The Ramayana Tradition in Asia: Papers Presented at the International Seminar on the Ramayana Tradition in Asia*. New Delhi: Sahitya Akademi, 1980.

Richman, Paula. *Questioning Ramayanas: A South Asian Tradition*. Berkeley: University of California Press, 2001.

———, ed. *Many Rāmāyaṇas: The Diversity of a Narrative Tradition in South Asia*. Berkeley: University of California Press, 1991.

Robin, Françoise. *Don grub rgyal: L'Enfant terrible de la nouvelle littérature tibétaine*. Unpublished mémoire de maîtrise, Langues'O INALCO, Paris, 1998.

———. *La Poésie libre au Tibet contemporain: Ses acteurs et thèmes principaux*. Unpublished Mémoire de DEA, Langues'O INALCO, Paris, 1999.

———. "Les jeux de la sapience et de la censure: Genèse des *Contes facétieux du cadavre* au Tibet." *Journal Asiatique* 294, no. 1 (2006), 181–96.

———. "Silent Stones as Minority Discourse: Agency and Representation in Padma Tshe tan's *The Silent Holy Stones*." *Tibetan Modernities: Notes from the Field on Cultural and Social Change in Contemporary Tibet*, ed. Robert Barnett and Ron Schwartz. Proceedings of the Eleventh International Association for Tibetan Studies. Leiden: E. J. Brill, forthcoming.

———. "Stories and History: The Emergence of Historical Fiction in Contemporary Tibet." *Contemporary Tibetan Literary Studies*, ed. Steven Venturino, 23–41. Proceedings of the Tenth Seminar of the International Association for Tibetan Studies, Oxford 2003. Leiden: E. J. Brill, 2007.

———. "Tibetan Free Verse Poetry." *Religion and Secular Culture in Tibet*, ed. Toni Huber, 451–70. Proceedings of the Ninth Seminar of the International Association for Tibetan Studies, Oxford 2003. Leiden: E. J. Brill, 2007.

Roesler, Ulrike. "The Great Indian Epics in the Version of Dmar ston chos kyi rgyal po." *Religion and Secular Culture in Tibet*, ed. Henk Blezer, 442–48. Proceedings of the Ninth Seminar of the International Association for Tibetan Studies, Leiden 2000. Leiden: E. J. Brill, 2002.

———. "Not a Mere Imitation: Indian Narratives in a Tibetan Context." *Facets of Tibetan Religious Tradition and Contacts with Neighboring Cultural Areas*, ed. Alfredo Cadonna and Ester Bianchi, 153–77. Orientalia Venetiana XII. Florence: Leo S. Olschki, 2002.

Rouis, Bernadette. "Le Mutisme du Sage." *Anthologie de nouvelles chinoises contémporaines*, ed. Annie Curien, 315–21. Paris: Gallimard, 1994.

———, trans. *Les Splendeurs des chevaux du vents*. Arles: Actes Sud, 1990.

Rudelson, Justin Jon. *Oasis Identities: Uyghur Nationalism along China's Silk Road*. New York: Columbia University Press, 1997.

Safran, William, ed. *Nationalism and Ethnoregional Identities in China*. London: Frank Cass, 1998.

Said, Edward W. *Culture and Imperialism*. New York: Vintage, 1993.

Samuel, Geoffrey. "The Gesar Epic of East Tibet." *Tibetan Literature: Studies in Genre*, ed. José Ignacio Cabezón and Roger R. Jackson, 358–67. Ithaca: Snow Lion, 1996.

Schaeffer, Kurtis R. *Dreaming the Great Brahmin: Tibetan Traditions of the Buddhist Poet-Saint Saraha*. Oxford: Oxford University Press, 2005.

Schein, Louisa. "Gender and Internal Orientalism in China." *Modern China* 23, no. 1 (1997), 69–98.

Schiaffini-Vedani, Patricia. "Changing Identities: The Creation of 'Tibetan' Literary Voices in the PRC." *Contemporary Tibetan Literary Studies*, ed. Steven Venturino, 111–31. Proceedings of the Tenth Seminar of the International Association for Tibetan Studies, Oxford 2003. Leiden: E. J. Brill, 2007.

———. "The Language Divide: Identity and Literary Choices in Modern Tibet." *Journal of International Affairs*, spring 2004, 81–98.

———. "Realism, Humor and Social Commitment: An Interview with the Tibetan Writer Phuntshog Tashi." *World Literature Today*, May–August 2004, 67–69.

———. "Tashi Dawa: Magical Realism and Contested Identity in Modern Tibet." Ph.D. diss., University of Pennsylvania, 2002.

Schwartz, Ronald D. *Circle of Protest: Political Ritual in the Tibetan Uprising*. New York: Columbia University Press, 1994.

Shabkar Tsogdruk Rangdrol. *The Life of Shabkar: The Autobiography of a Tibetan Yogin*, trans. Matthieu Ricard. Albany: State University of New York Press, 1994.

Silbey, Susan S. "'Let Them Eat Cake': Globalization, Postmodern Colonialism and the Possibilities of Justice." *Law and Society Review* 31, no. 2 (1997), 207–35.

Smith, E. Gene. *Among Tibetan Texts: History and Literature of the Himalayan Plateau*. Studies in Indian and Tibetan Buddhism. Boston: Wisdom, 2001.

Smith, Warren W. *Tibetan Nation: A History of Tibetan Nationalism and Sino-Tibetan Relations*. Boulder: Westview, 1996.

Sorenson, Per K. *Divinity Secularized: An Inquiry into the Nature and Form of the Songs Ascribed to the Sixth Dalai Lama*. Vienna: Arbeitskreis für tibetetische und buddhistische Studien Universität Wien, 1990.

Spivak, Gayatri Chakravorty. *A Critique of Postcolonial Reason: Toward a History of the Vanishing Present*. Cambridge: Harvard University Press, 1999.

———. *In Other Worlds*. New York: Routledge, 1987.

Stevenson, Mark. "Paths and Progress: Some Thoughts on Don grub rgyal's 'A Threadlike Path.'" *Tibet Journal* 22, no. 3 (1997), 57–60.

Stewart, Frank, Tsering Shakya, and Herbert Batt, eds. *Song of the Snow Lion: New Writing from Tibet*. Manoa 12, no. 2 (2000) [special issue].

Stoddard, Heather. "Don grub rgyal (1953–1985): Suicide of a Modern Tibetan Writer and Scholar." *Tibetan Studies: Proceedings of the Sixth Seminar of the International Association for Tibetan Studies, Fagernes 1992*, ed. Per Kvaerne, 825–36. Oslo: Institute for Comparative Research in Human Culture, 1994.

———. "Je t'accuse." *Caravanes* 4 (Paris, 1995).

———. "Le maître spirituel, l'artiste et le saint-fou: Individu 'sans-soi' tibétain." *Singularités: Les voies d'émergence individuelle: Textes pour Eric de Dampierre*, ed. Laboratoire d'ethnologie et de sociologie comparative, 263–73. Paris: Plon, 1989.

———. *Le Mendiant de l'Amdo*. Paris: Société d'Ethnographie, 1985.

———. "Tibetan Publications and National Identity." *Resistance and Reform in Tibet*, ed. Robert Barnett, 121–56. Bloomington: Indiana University Press, 1994.

Tailing, W. *The Secret Tale of Tesur House*. Beijing: China Tibetology Publishing House, 1998.

Tang, Xiaobing. "The Function of New Theory: What Does It Mean to Talk about Postmodernism in China?" *Politics, Ideology, and Literary Discourse in Modern China: Theoretical Interventions and Cultural Critique*, ed. Liu Kang and Xiaobing Tang, 278–99. Durham: Duke University Press, 1993.

Tashi Dawa. *A Soul in Bondage: Stories from Tibet*. Beijing: Panda, 1992.

Tashi Tsering. "The Life of Rev. G. Tharchin: Missionary and Pioneer." *Lungta* 11 (winter 1998), 9–10.

———. "Tibetan Poetry down the Ages." *Lotus Fields Fresh Winds* 2 (spring 1979), 47–52.

Tibet Information Network. "Language and Tibetan Identity." *News Review: Reports from Tibet 2000*, no. 29 (2001), 53–61.

———. "Official Documents: 1) The Study, Use and Development of the Tibetan Language; 2) White Paper on Tibetan Culture; 3) Chinese Press on Culture and Education." *News Review: Reports from Tibet 2000* 29 (2001), 61–66.

Tenzin Tsundue. *Kora: Stories and Poems*. Kathmandu: TCV Alumni Association, 2002.

Tsering Shakya. *The Dragon in the Land of Snows: A History of Modern Tibet since 1947*. London: Pimlico, 1999.

———. "The Emergence of Modern Tibetan Literature: *gsar rtsom*." Ph.D. diss., School of Oriental and African Studies, 2004.

———. "Literature or Propaganda? The Development of Literature since 1950." *Lungta* 11 (1999), 57–67.

———. "Politicisation and the Tibetan Language." *Resistance and Reform in Tibet*, ed. Robert Barnett, 157–65. Bloomington: Indiana University Press, 1994.

———. "The Waterfall and Fragrant Flowers: The Development of Tibetan Literature since 1950." *Song of the Snow Lion*, *Mānoa* 12, no. 2 (2000), ed. Frank Stewart, Tsering Shakya, and Herbert Batt, 28–40.

Tsering Wangmo Dhompa. *Rules of the House*. Berkeley: Apogee, 2002.

Tshe ring dbang rgyal. *The Tale of the Incomparable Prince*, trans. Beth Newman. New York: Harper Collins, 1996.

Ude, Wayne. "Forging an American Style: The Romance-Novel and Magical Realism as Response to the Frontier and Wilderness Experiences." *The Frontier Experience and the American Dream: Essays on American Literature*, ed. David Mogen, Mark Busby, and Paul Bryant. College Station: Texas A&M University Press, 1989.

Upton, Janet. "Cascades of Change: Modern and Contemporary Literature in the PRC's Junior-Secondary Tibetan Language and Literature Curriculum." *Lungta* 12 (1999), 17–28.

van der Kuijp, Leonard W. J. Review of *Dag-yig ngag-sgron-gyi rtsa-ba dang de'i 'grel-pa*, by Dpal-khang Lo-tsā-ba/Bstan-'dzin rgyal-mtshan. *Indo-Iranian Journal* 28, no. 3 (July 1985), 214–17.

———. Review of *Snyan-ngag me-long-gi spyi-don sdeb-legs rig-pa'i 'char-sgo*, by Tshe-tan Zhab-drung 'Jigs-med rigs-pa'i blo-gros. *Indo-Iranian Journal* 28, no. 3 (July 1985), 212–14.

———. "Tibetan Belles-Lettres: The Influence of Daṇḍin and Kṣemendra." *Tibetan Literature: Studies in Genre*, ed. José Ignacio Cabezón and Roger R. Jackson, 393–410. Ithaca: Snow Lion, 1996.

———. "Tibetan Historiography." *Tibetan Literature: Studies in Genre*, ed. Jose Ignacio Cabezón and Roger R. Jackson, 39–56. Ithaca: Snow Lion, 1996.

Veivo, Harri. *The Written Space: Semiotic Analysis of the Representation of Space and Its Rhetorical Functions in Literature*. Acta Semiotica Fennica 10. Imatra: International Semiotics Institute, 2001.

Venturino, Steven J. *Critical Baggage: Traveling Theory in China, Tibet, and the Transnational Academy*. Ph. D. Diss., Loyola University of Chicago, 2000.

———. "Inquiring after Theory in China." *boundary 2* 33, no. 2 (2006), 91–113.

———. "Reading Negotiations in the Tibetan Diaspora." *Constructing Tibetan Culture: Contemporary Perspectives*, ed. Frank Korom, 98–121. Quebec: World Heritage, 98–121.

———. "Signifying on China: African-American Literary Theory and Tibetan Discourse." *Sinographies: Writing China*, ed. Eric Hayot, Steve Yao, and Haun Saussy. Minneapolis: University of Minnesota Press, 2007.

———. "Where Is Tibet in World Literature?" *World Literature Today* 78, no. 1 (January 2004), 51–56.

———, ed. *Contemporary Tibetan Literary Studies*. Proceedings of the Tenth Seminar of the International Association for Tibetan Studies, Oxford 2003. Leiden: E. J. Brill, 2007.

Virtanen, Riika J., comp. and trans. *A Blighted Flower and Other Stories*. Dharamsala: Library of Tibetan Works and Archives, 2000.

Vostrikov A. I., *Tibetan Historical Literature*, trans. Harish Chandra Gupta. Richmond: Curzon, 1994.

Waddell, L. Augustine. *Lhasa and Its Mysteries, with a Record of the British Tibetan Expedition of 1903–1904*. New York: Dover, 1988 [1905].

Walton, Kendall L. *Mimesis as Make-Believe: On the Foundations of the Representational Arts*. Cambridge: Harvard University Press, 1990.

Wang, David Der-wei. *Fictional Realism in Twentieth Century China*. New York: Columbia University Press, 1992.

Wang, Jing, *High Culture Fever: Politics, Aesthetics, and Ideology in Deng's China*. Berkeley: University of California Press, 1996.

Wang, Ning. "The Reception of Postmodernism in China: The Case of Avant-Garde Fiction." *International Postmodernism: Theory and Literary Practice*, ed. Hans Bertens and Douwe Fokkema, 499–510. Philadelphia: John Benjamins, 1997.

Wang, Yao. "Hu Yaobang's visit to Tibet, May 22–31 1980." *Resistance and Reform in Tibet*, ed. Robert Barnett and Shirin Akiner, 285–89. Bloomington: Indiana University Press, 1994.

Warder, A. K. *Indian Kāvya Literature*. Delhi: Motilal Banarsidass, 1989 [1972].

Watt, Ian. *The Rise of the Novel: Studies in Defoe, Richardson and Fielding*. London: Pimlico, 2000.

White, Hayden. *The Content of the Form: Narrative Discourse and Historical Representation*. Baltimore: Johns Hopkins University Press, 1987.

White, Lynn T. *Policies of Chaos: The Organizational Causes of Violence in China's Cultural Revolution*. Princeton: Princeton University Press, 1989.

Williams, Patrick. "Kim and Orientalism." *Colonial Discourse and Post-colonial Theory: A Reader*, ed. Patrick Williams and Laura Chrisman, 480–97. New York: Columbia University Press, 1994.

Willock, Nicole. "A Mellifluous Voice: The Life Work of Alag Tsetan Zhabdrung Jigmé Rigpé Lodrö." Paper presented at the Annual Meeting of the Association for Asian Studies, 22 March 2007, Boston.

World Tibet Network News, 15 December 1999, <http://www.tibet.ca/wtnarchive/1999/12/15_2.html>.

Yangdon Dhondup. "Writers at the Cross-roads: The Mongolian-Tibetan Authors Tsering Dondup and Jangbu." *Inner Asia* 4, no. 2 (2002), 225–40.

Zhang, Xudong. *Chinese Modernism in the Era of Reforms*. Durham: Duke University Press, 1997.

Zhang, Yingjin. "Building a National Literature in Modern China: Literary Criticism, Gender Ideology, and the Public Sphere." *Journal of Modern Literature in Chinese* 1, no. 1 (July 1997), 47–74.

———. "The Institutionalization of Modern Literary History in China, 1922–1980." *Modern China* 20, no. 3 (July 1994), 347–77.

Zheng, Yangwen. *The Social Life of Opium in China.* New York: Cambridge University Press, 2005.

About the Contributors

PEMA BHUM is the director of the Latse Contemporary Tibetan Cultural Library. He holds an M.A. in Tibetan Literature and Language from Northwest Nationalities Institute (now University) in Lanzhou, Gansu Province (PRC). He has co-founded several initiatives in exile, including the Amnye Machen Institute, the newspaper *Dmangs gtso* (Democracy), and the literary magazine *Ljang gzhon*. His memoirs of the Cultural Revolution have been translated under the title *Six Stars with a Crooked Neck* (Dharamsala: Tibet Times, 2001), with a recent sequel *Dran tho rdo ring ma* (Stone Pillar Memoirs) published by the same press.

HOWARD Y. F. CHOY is an assistant professor at Wittenberg University. He earned his Ph.D. in comparative literature at the University of Colorado in 2004 and is the assistant author of *The Illustrated Encyclopedia of Confucianism* (New York: Rosen, 2005). His recent publications also include "Historiographic Alternatives for China: Tibet in Contemporary Fiction by Tashi Dawa, Alai, and Ge Fei," *American Journal of Chinese Studies* 12, no. 1 (2005), and "'To Construct an Unknown China': Ethnoreligious Historiography in Zhang Chengzhi's Islamic Fiction," *positions* 14, no. 3 (2006).

YANGDON DHONDUP received her Ph.D. in East Asian Literature from the School of Oriental and African Studies, University of London, in 2004. Recent and forthcoming publications include translations and contributions in *Himal*, *The Drunken Boat*, *Inner Asia*, *Mānoa*, and *Tibetan Modernities: Notes from the Field on Social and Cultural Change: Proceedings of the Tenth Seminar of the International Association for Tibetan Studies* (Leiden: E. J. Brill, 2007).

LAURAN R. HARTLEY is the Tibetan studies librarian at the C. V. Starr East Asian Library of Columbia University. She earned her Ph.D. in Tibetan Studies at Indiana University in 2003 and has taught courses on Tibetan literature and religion at Columbia, Rutgers, and Indiana universities. Her articles and translations have appeared in the *Journal of Asian Studies*, *Journal of the International Association for Tibetan Studies*, *Cahiers d'Extrême-Asie*, *Tibet Journal*, *Persimmon*, *Index on Censhorship*, and *Mānoa*, and in proceedings of the ninth and tenth seminars of the IATS (Leiden: E. J. Brill, 2002, 2007).

HORTSANG JIGME studied for nearly four years at the Gansu Provincial Buddhist University in Labrang and earned the equivalent of a B.A. in 1988. He then studied for another two years in Beijing. Since 1992 he has lived in Dharamsala, India, where he opened a small bookshop and founded Youtse Publications. He has served as a lecturer at Tibetan Medical College in Dharamsala (1993–96) and director of literary research at Norbulingka (1997–99). His publications include five volumes of poetry in Tibetan and an autobiographical account in English, *Under the Blue Sky*. He is currently working on a history of Amdo.

MATTHEW T. KAPSTEIN is the director of Tibetan studies at the École Pratique des Hautes Études, Paris, and Numata Visiting Professor of Buddhist Studies at the University of Chicago. His publications include *The Tibetan Assimilation of Buddhism: Conversion, Contestation and Memory* (Oxford, 2000) and *Buddhism in Contemporary Tibet: Religious Revival and Cultural Identity* (Berkeley: University of California Press, 1998), as well as an introduction to the study of Tibetan civilization, *The Tibetans* (Oxford: Blackwell, 2006).

NANCY G. LIN is a doctoral candidate in Buddhist studies at the University of California, Berkeley. She completed an M.A. in Tibetan studies at Columbia University in 2003. She is currently researching her dissertation on Buddhist literary culture in eighteenth-century Derge through the poetic work *Dpag bsam 'khri shing*.

LARA MACONI earned her Ph.D. in Oriental languages, literatures, and societies in 2008 at the INALCO Institute (Paris), where she has been teaching Tibetan classical grammar and the history of Tibetan literature since 1998. Having graduated in Chinese studies from Ca' Foscari University in Venice, she focuses her present research on contemporary Tibetan literature, especially works written in Chinese, and questions of identity and diglossyia. Recent and forthcoming publications include translations and contributions in *Neige d'août*, *Lyrisme et Extrême-Orient*, and *Contemporary Tibetan Literary Studies: Proceedings of the Tenth Seminar of the International Association for Tibetan Studies* (Leiden: E. J. Brill, 2007).

FRANÇOISE ROBIN earned her Ph.D. in Tibetan studies in 2003 at the INALCO Institute (Paris), where she has been teaching Tibetan language, dialects, and literature since 1999. Recent and forthcoming publications include translations of Tibetan folktales, proverbs, poetry, and short stories, as well as articles in the *World Encyclopaedia of Religions*, *Revue d'Études Tibétaines*, *Cahiers d'Extrême-Asie*, and proceedings of the ninth and tenth seminars of the International Association for Tibetan Studies (Leiden: E. J. Brill, 2002, 2007). Her published translations include *Les Contes facétieux du cadavre* (Paris: Langues et Monde / L'Asiathèque, 2005); *La Controverse dans le jardin aux fleurs* by Langdün Päljor (Paris: Bleu de Chine, 2006); and *La Fleur vaincue par le gel* by Thöndrupgyäl (Paris: Bleu de Chine, 2006).

PATRICIA SCHIAFFINI-VEDANI earned her Ph.D. in Chinese literature at the University of Pennsylvania in 2002. She is currently a part-time assistant professor of Chinese language and literature at Southwestern University, and the founding director of the Tibetan Arts and Literature Initiative (TALI), a nonprofit organization dedicated to supporting Tibetan publishing. She has also taught at Pomona College, where until recently she was director of the Oldenborg Center for Modern Languages and International Relations. Her research articles, which focus on modern Tibetan literature written in Chinese language, have been published in the *Journal of International Affairs*, *World Literature Today*, and *Contemporary Tibetan Literary Studies: Proceedings of the Tenth Seminar for the International Association for Tibetan Studies* (Leiden: E. J. Brill, 2007).

RONALD D. SCHWARTZ is a professor of sociology at Memorial University in St. John's, Newfoundland. He has written extensively on contemporary Tibetan society and culture and is the author of *Circle of Protest: Political Ritual In the Tibetan Uprising* (New York: Columbia University Press, 1994) and an editor with Robert Barnett of *Tibetan Modernities: Notes from the Field on Cultural and Social Change in Contemporary Tibet* (Leiden: E. J. Brill, 2007). His translations of modern Tibetan poetry and fiction have appeared in *World Literature Today* and *Mānoa*.

TSERING SHAKYA was born in Lhasa, Tibet, and escaped the Cultural Revolution by fleeing with his family to India in 1967. In 2004 he earned his Ph.D. in South Asian studies from the School of Oriental and African Studies, University of London. His publications include *Fire under the Snow: The Testimony of a Tibetan Prisoner* (London: Harvill, 1997), which has been translated into ten languages, and *The Dragon in the Land of Snows: A History of Modern Tibet since 1947* (New York: Columbia University Press, 2000). Shakya was also a co-editor of the first anthology of modern Tibetan short stories and poems, *Song of the Snow Lion: New Writing from Tibet* (Honolulu: University of Hawaii Press, 2000). Currently Tsering Shakya holds the Canadian Research Chair of Religion and Contemporary Society in Asia at the Institute of Asian Research, University of British Columbia.

SANGYE GYATSO (also known as Gangzhün) earned his M.A. in Tibetan literature and language from the Northwest Nationalities Institute (Lanzhou, PRC) in 2001. He has published several poems and essays in major literary journals in Tibet and was a founding editor of the literary newspaper *Dus kyi pho nya* (Messenger of the Times) in Lanzhou. After working for several years to administer aid projects for the Trace Foundation, he is now working for a film production office in Beijing.

STEVEN J. VENTURINO is an adjunct professor of English at Loyola University Chicago. His recent publications include "Signifying on China: African-American Literary Theory and Tibetan Discourse" in *Sinographies: Writing China*, ed. Eric Hayot, Steve Yao, and Haun Saussy (Minneapolis: University of Minnesota Press), "Inquiring after Theory in China" in *boundary 2* 33, no. 2, and "Where Is Tibet in World Literature?," in *World Literature Today* 78, no. 1. He is also the editor of *Contemporary Tibetan Literary Studies: Proceedings of the Tenth Seminar for the International Association for Tibetan Studies* (Leiden: E. J. Brill, 2007).

RIIKA J. VIRTANEN is a Ph.D. candidate in South Asian studies at the University of Helsinki, where she received her M.A. in South Asian studies in 2003. She is currently writing her dissertation on the works of Döndrup Gyel, focusing on his use of imagery. She has been teaching Tibetan language at the University of Helsinki since 2001. Between 1996 and 2001 she was the assistant editor of the *Tibet Journal* at the Library of Tibetan Works and Archives in Dharamsala, India.

Index

LAURAN R. HARTLEY is the Tibetan studies librarian at Columbia University.

PATRICIA SCHIAFFINI-VEDANI is an assistant professor of Chinese language and literature in the Department of Modern Languages and Literatures at Southwestern University.

Library of Congress Cataloging-in-Publication Data
Modern Tibetan literature and social change / edited by Lauran R. Hartley and Patricia Schiaffini ; foreword by Matthew T. Kapstein.
p. cm.
Includes bibliographical references and index.
ISBN-13: 978-0-8223-4254-0 (cloth : alk. paper)
ISBN-13: 978-0-8223-4277-9 (pbk. : alk. paper)
1. Tibetan literature—20th century—History and criticism. I. Hartley, Lauran R., 1964– II. Schiaffini, Patricia, 1967–
PL3705.M626 2008
895′.409355—dc22 2007047887